Winning in Service Markets is a co[...]
managers to access the best of acac[...]
Jochen Wirtz has done a masterfu[...]
research in a comprehensive anc[...]
organizations. Few business scholars are able to translate rigorous academic
research to managers as well as him. This book is a shining example.

Leonard Berry
University Distinguished Professor of Marketing, Texas A&M University

Winning in Service Markets is an essential part of any service executive's library
as well as being an excellent text book for service marketing classes. It lays out
a clear and complete structure for developing an effective service strategy, and
provides great examples and tools for implementing strategies once developed. I
can't recommend it highly enough.

Richard B. Chase
Justin Dart Professor Emeritus in Operations Management
University of Southern California

The book should be read and deeply studied by anyone in a service business, and
since everyone is in a service business, I suggest you become an expert at your
most important product which is exceptional service to all. You will need quality
reliable products and top-notch service to win and keep customers in the highly
competitive world we live in today. This book will make you an expert.

Lee Cockerell
Former Vice President, Walt Disney World® Resort, and
Bestselling author of Creating Magic: 10 Common Sense Leadership Strategies
from a Life at Disney; The Customer Rules: The 39 Essential Rules for Delivering
Sensational Service; Time Management Magic: How To Get More Done Every
Day; and Creating Career Magic: How to Keep Your Career on Track.

Winning in Service Markets: Success Through People, Technology and Strategy
addresses burning issues for all organizations competing on value-creation
through service. It is a must read not only for companies in the traditional service
sector but also for manufacturing companies and businesses, in particular, firms
adopting service-based business strategies and business models. It is the first
trade book that provides a comprehensive overview and application of service
research accessible to business managers. This book is an important contribution
to the ongoing process of shifting from a goods-based to a service-based logic of
exchange, marketing and business development. It provides important lessons
for anyone involved in improving a firm's competitive advantage in a service-
driven and digital economy.

Bo Edvardsson
Professor of Business Administration and Founder of Service Research Center (CTF)
and Vice Rector Karlstad University, Sweden

If your business is to thrive and succeed in this economy, there must be an intentional focus placed on your customers and their experience. Different challenges arise, depending on the type of business you are in, manufacturing or services. Every other book written about customer experience and customer service devotes little to no time to the services sector, a rapidly-growing sector globally. Finally there's a book that takes on the challenges faced by services organizations! *Winning in Service Markets* is practical, well-organized and detailed. It will be your go-to guidebook to help you achieve service excellence.

Annette Franz
Customer experience consultant and author, CX Journey

Winning in Service Markets provides a thorough yet highly readable discussion of what matters in the most important sector of advanced and emerging economies — services. Jochen Wirtz pays close attention to the marketing, production and human resource aspects of service businesses, and provides up-to-date references to important source material. I highly recommend the book for executives and scholars in this area alike.

Dominique M. Hanssens
Distinguished Professor of Marketing, Anderson School of Management, UCLA

Jochen Wirtz brings to his writing the same combination of vitality and practicality as he does to his teaching. I am sure that *Winning in Services Marketing* will be of great value to those working in the service sector, both in marketing and more general management roles.

Gay Haskins
Associate Fellow and former Dean of Executive Education,
Saïd Business School, University of Oxford.

People, technology and strategy are three pivotal factors underlying the success of companies that are known for their seamless services. Through a myriad of important and relevant research findings and cases, this book provides services marketing professionals with an excellent framework and useful guidelines on ways to create competitive edge through effective integration of human resources management, operations and marketing, the three functional areas that drive people, technology and strategy respectively within a service firm.

Michael Hui
Pro-Vice-Chancellor of The Chinese University of Hong Kong,
and Choh-ming Li Professor of Marketing

You won't find opinion here. Rather, this book is based on rock-solid academic evidence. Jochen Wirtz does an excellent job of taking the body of academic research and translating it into best practices for service organizations with actionable insights that even the most experienced managers can learn from.

Shep Hyken
Customer service expert and New York Times Bestselling author of
The Amazement Revolution

Finally, a book that delivers the most important academic insights with engaging examples and practical action steps. Professor Wirtz's inspirational teaching style is now available in this engaging and easy-to-read new book. Highly recommended for anyone who wants to win in service markets anywhere in the world.

Ron Kaufman
New York Times bestselling author of Uplifting Service

Winning in Service Markets cuts to the heart of what it takes to be customers' first choice and reap the lion's share of their spending in the category. Jochen Wirtz is one of the real thought leaders in service marketing, and this book demonstrates why. A must read for managers serious about winning in highly competitive markets.

Timothy Keiningham, Ph.D.
New York Times bestselling author of The Wallet Allocation Rule and
J. Donald Kennedy Endowed Chair in E-Commerce at St. John's University

No matter if you are working in service or want to transform your business into a service-oriented organization, this book is a must read. It's well-written, provides a wealth of highly-relevant insights and illustrates many home-hitting examples. This book will stimulate thinking and provide ideas for your own business. So, if you want to stay ahead of your completion, you should go and get this book!

Anton Meyer
Chair of Marketing and Head of Marketing department,
Munich School of Management, Ludwig-Maximilians-University, Munich

Winning in Service Markets: Success through People, Technology and Strategy by Jochen Wirtz, is a fresh, readable and interesting up-to-date text. It has plenty of examples, illustrations, while providing meaningful information about the issues, problems and solutions for managing a successful service-oriented business. The author very clearly takes a value-oriented approach and "escapes" the goods versus services problematic dichotomy. Very importantly, the text carefully delineates the vital interaction between marketing, operations, human resources, and information management for an effective management of services. The book is beautifully laid out in multiple colors and many illustrations, including humorous cartoons that also make substantive contributions. The tables and frameworks are excellent learning tools and they support the textual material extremely well. This is a winning book on service marketing!

Kent B. Monroe
J. M. Jones Distinguished Professor of Marketing Emeritus,
University of Illinois at Urbana-Champaign

Winning in Service Markets, winning in every market... it is all about the customer experience. Marketing, communications and customer service are all interconnected, and in order to deliver an OmniChannel experience externally, you must create an OmniChannel culture internally! Always remember that the only time you have 100% of your customers' attention is when they are looking for customer service... do not miss that opportunity. Your brand or business is what you do; your reputation is what people remember and share.

Ted Rubin
Social Marketing Strategist, Keynote Speaker, Brand Evangelist
and Acting CMO Brand Innovators

Winning in Service Markets does a great job of summarizing, in easily digestible form, the traditional research and thinking in services, along with some of the latest ideas and research about service.

Roland T. Rust
Distinguished University Professor and David Bruce Smith Chair in Marketing,
Executive Director, Center for Excellence in Service, and Executive Director,
Center for Complexity in Business, University of Maryland

Winning in Service Markets provides a set of useful frameworks and prescriptions rooted in both practice and research. As such, it represents a refreshing alternative to the prevailing literature available to managers who are looking for insights rooted in sound theory. A must read for any practicing manager in the service economy.

Leonard A. Schlesinger
Baker Foundation Professor, Harvard Business School

If you think service can be a winning approach in your market and if you believe it may be worth the effort but you are not sure how to make it happen, this is the book for you. *Winning in Service Markets: Success Through People, Technology and Strategy* provides research evidence and corporate examples of the inter-related systems to which companies must attend to do service right. There are no silver bullets here; the book presents the reality that it is all of the systems — the service operations, the people, the setting and the strategy — that matter to be the best at what you do. In short, if you want to do service right, this is the book for you.

Benjamin Schneider
Professor Emeritus, University of Maryland

A top new source of trends and best practices for service innovation professionals.

Dr James "Jim" C. Spohrer
Director, IBM University Programs (IBM UP) and Cognitive Systems Institute

In today's marketplace, success is driven by service excellence. Creating this excellence is demanding and requires the implementation of a mind-set and a set of practices that great service companies have in common. By illustrating and explaining these practices, this book is the ultimate bridge between theory and practice. With vivid examples and comprehensive frameworks, it is an excellent guide for those who want to find the balance between satisfying the ever more demanding customers and producing sustainable returns for shareholders.

Kaj Storbacka
Professor, Graduate School of Management at the University of Auckland Business School

Winning in Service Markets is a highly practical book. I love the comprehensive coverage of services marketing and the rigor. Also, it is easy to read and full of interesting, best practice examples. I recommend this book to everyone working in a service organization.

Jan Swartz
President, Princess Cruises

I started studying services marketing 30 years ago. If I had this book then, I might have cut my college time in half! Reading *Winning in Service Markets* will give you the framework and language you need to effectively plan, manage and communicate your service business. The one-page summaries and case studies are priceless. My favorite was how Rolls-Royce moved from selling engines (products) to selling power by the hour (services). Applying this book's principles will help you see things differently and more clearly. Also, using the context Jochen shares will make your business design easier to understand, and guide your marketing messaging to be more on point. In short, using the information in this book will help you connect with customers and employees in ways that win their support and advocacy.

Mike Wittenstein
Founder and Managing Partner at Storyminers, www.storyminers.com

Two-thirds of the Gross World Product come from the service sector. It is high time to adapt our management methods to reflect this, putting people at the center of interest.

Dr. Joerg Wolle
Chief Executive Officer and President of DKSH and
Chairman of the Board of Directors of Kuehne + Nagel International AG

Winning
in
Service
Markets

Success through
People, Technology and Strategy

Jochen Wirtz

WS **World Scientific**

NEW JERSEY • LONDON • SINGAPORE • BEIJING • SHANGHAI • HONG KONG • TAIPEI • CHENNAI • TOKYO

Published by

WS Professional, an imprint of

World Scientific Publishing Co. Inc.

27 Warren Street, Suite 401-402, Hackensack, NJ 07601, USA

Head office: 5 Toh Tuck Link, Singapore 596224

UK office: 57 Shelton Street, Covent Garden, London WC2H 9HE

For orders of individual copies, course adoptions, and bulk purchases: sales@wspc.com
For orders of individual chapters and customized course packs: sales@wspc.com
For adaptations or translation rights and permissions to reprint; rights@wspc.com

Library of Congress Cataloging-in-Publication Data
Names: Wirtz, Jochen, author.
Title: Winning in service markets : success through people, technology and strategy /
    Jochen Wirtz, Professor, School of Business, National University of Singapore.
Description: New Jersey : World Scientific, 2016. | Includes bibliographical references and index.
Identifiers: LCCN 2016007496| ISBN 9781944659042 (hardcover) | ISBN 9781944659059 (pbk.)
Subjects: LCSH: Service industries--Marketing. | Branding (Marketing) | Customer relations.
Classification: LCC HD9980.5 .W546 2016 | DDC 658--dc23
LC record available at http://lccn.loc.gov/2016007496

British Library Cataloguing-in-Publication Data
A catalogue record for this book is available from the British Library.

Desk Editor: Karimah Samsudin

Printed in Singapore

Dedications

With gratitude and in loving memory of
Professor Christopher Lovelock,
one of the guiding lights of services marketing
and management thinking.

To my past and future EMBA and Executive Program participants.

I have been teaching EMBA and Executive Programs for over
20 years. *Winning in Service Markets* is dedicated to you, the participants
from these programs. You brought so much knowledge and experience to
the classroom, and this book synthesizes this learning for future EMBA
candidates and managers who want to know how to bring their service
organizations to the next level.

Preface

The main objective of this book is to cover the key aspects of services marketing and management, and that is based on sound academic research. Therefore, I used a globally leading text book I co-authored with Professor Christopher Lovelock (*Services Marketing: People, Technology, Strategy*, 8th edition) as a base for this book and adapted and rewrote it for managers. This is a unique approach. There are a lot of books that focus on certain aspects of service management and marketing, such as on managing customer loyalty, complaint handling and service recovery, revenue management, driving change and building a customer-focused service culture, or on the experience of individual organizations. What I wanted to achieve with this book is to provide a more comprehensive coverage of the latest academic research and its implications for best-practice service management and marketing. The book aims to bridge the all-too-frequent gap between cutting edge academic research and theory, and management practice. That is, it provides a *strongly managerial perspective*, yet is *rooted in solid academic research*, complemented by memorable frameworks.

In particular, creating and marketing value in today's increasingly service and knowledge-intensive economy requires an understanding of the powerful design and packaging of 'intangible' benefits and products, high-quality service operations and customer information management processes, a pool of motivated and competent front-line employees, building and maintaining a loyal and profitable customer base, and the development and implementation of a coherent service strategy to transform these assets into improved business performance. This book aims to provide this knowledge.

Contents

Contents

Introduction to
The World of Services

Unfortunately, consumers are not always happy with the quality and value of the services they receive. Both individual and corporate consumers complain about broken promises, poor value for money, rude or incompetent personnel, inconvenient service hours, bureaucratic procedures, wasted time, malfunctioning self-service technologies, complicated websites, a lack of understanding of their needs, and various other problems.

On the other hand, suppliers of services, who often face stiff competition, appear to have a very different set of concerns. Many owners and managers complain about how difficult it is to find skilled and motivated employees, to keep costs down and make a profit, or to satisfy customers, who, they sometimes grumble, have become unreasonably demanding.

Fortunately, there are service companies that know how to please their customers while also running a productive and profitable operation. These organizations are staffed by pleasant and competent employees, and are accessible through user-friendly, self-service technologies, websites and apps.

This book will show how service businesses can be managed to achieve customer satisfaction and profitability. In addition to studying key concepts, organizing frameworks, and tools of services marketing, there are many examples from firms across the US and around the world. From the experiences of other firms, important lessons can be drawn on how to succeed in increasingly competitive service markets. This book aims to provide the knowledge and skills necessary and relevant in tomorrow's business environment.

Below are the key contents of the five parts of this book:

PART I

Understanding Service Products, Consumers, and Markets

Part I of the book lays the building blocks for studying services and learning how to become an effective services marketer.

- Chapter 1 *defines services* and shows how to create value without transfer of ownership.

- Chapter 2 discusses *consumer behavior* in both high- and low-contact services. The three-stage model of service consumption is used to explore how customers search for and evaluate alternative services, make purchase decisions, experience and respond to service encounters, and evaluate service performance.

- Chapter 3 discusses how a service *value proposition should be positioned* in a way that creates competitive advantage for the firm. The chapter shows how firms can segment a service market, position their value proposition, and focus on attracting their target segment.

PART II

Applying the 4 'P's of Marketing to Services

Part II revisits the 4 'P's of the traditional marketing mix, expanded to take into account the characteristics of services that different from goods.

- Chapter 4 discusses about *product* that includes both the core and supplementary service elements. The supplementary elements facilitate and enhance the core service offering.

- Chapter 5 discusses *place and time elements* which refer to the delivery of the product elements to the customers.

- Chapter 6 deals with the *prices of services* that need to be set with reference to costs, competition and value, and revenue management considerations.

- Chapter 7 explains *promotion and education*, and how firms should inform customers about their services. In services marketing, much communication is educational in nature to teach customers how to effectively move through service processes.

PART III

Managing the Customer Interface

Part III of the book focuses on managing the interface between the customers and service firm. It covers the additional 3 'P's that are unique to services marketing.

- Chapter 8 describes *processes* to create and deliver the product elements. It begins with the design of effective delivery processes, specifying how the operating and delivery systems link together to deliver the value proposition. Very often, customers are involved in these processes as co-producers, and well-designed processes need to account for that.

- Chapter 9 also relates to *process management* and focuses on *balancing demand and capacity* for each step of a customer service process. Marketing strategies for managing demand involve smoothing demand fluctuations, inventorying demand through reservation systems, and formalized queuing. Managing customer waiting is also explored in this chapter.

- Chapter 10 describes the *physical environment*, also known as the *servicescape*, needs to be engineered to create the right impression and facilitate effective service process delivery. The servicescape provides tangible evidence of a firm's image and service quality.

- Chapter 11 emphasizes that *people* play a key role in services marketing when direct interaction between customers and service personnel is part of the service. The nature of these interactions strongly influences how customers perceive service quality. Hence, service firms devote a significant amount of effort to recruit, train, and motivate employees. How to get all this right is explained using the Service Talent Cycle as an integrative framework.

PART IV

Developing Customer Relationships

Part IV focuses on how to develop customer relationships and build loyalty.

- Chapter 12 shows that achieving profitability requires *creating relationships with customers* from the right segments and then finding ways to build and reinforce their loyalty. This chapter introduces the Wheel of Loyalty, which shows three systematic steps in building customer loyalty. The chapter closes with a discussion of customer relationship management (CRM) systems.

- Chapter 13 shows that loyal customer base is often built from *effective complaint handling* and *service recovery*, which are discussed in this chapter. Service guarantees are explored as a powerful way of institutionalizing service recovery and as an effective marketing tool to signal high-quality service.

PART V

Striving for Service Excellence

Part V focuses on how to develop and transform a firm to achieve service excellence.

- Chapter 14 discusses that *productivity and quality* are both necessary and are strongly related to financial success in services. This chapter focuses on service quality, diagnosing quality shortfalls using the Gaps Model, and strategies to close quality gaps. Customer feedback systems are discussed as an effective tool for systematically listening to and learning from customers. Productivity is introduced as closely related to quality, and it is emphasized that in today's competitive markets, firms need to simultaneously improve both quality and productivity — not one at the expense of the other.

- Chapter 15 is the final chapter that discusses how to move a service organization to *higher levels of performance* in each functional area.

Figure I: Organizing Framework for Winning in Service Markets

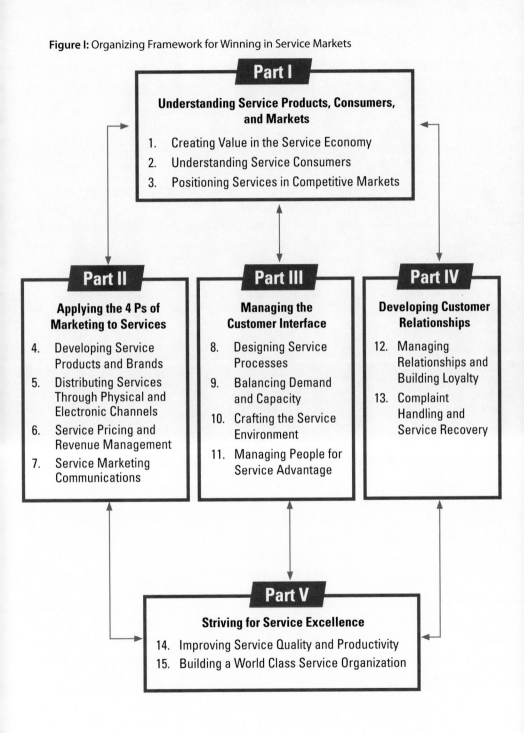

Part I

Understanding Service Products, Consumers and Markets

CHAPTER 1

Creating and Capturing Value in the Service Economy

Ours is a service economy and has been for some time.
Karl Albrecht and Ron Zemke
Thought leaders in business and service

In today's marketplace, consumers have the power to pick and choose as never before.
From the article "Crowned At Last",
published in The Economist, 31 March 2005

This chapter discusses the modern, ever-changing service economy, defines the nature of services, and highlights some challenges involved in marketing and managing services, and concludes with a framework for developing and implementing service strategies that establishes the structure of this book.

WHY STUDY SERVICES?

In the modern service-driven economy, marketing is taught from a manufacturing perspective in most of the business schools. Almost all marketing courses focus more on marketing manufactured products, especially consumer goods, rather than marketing services. However, a growing and enthusiastic group of scholars, consultants, and educators, including the authors of this book, have chosen to focus on services marketing and build on the extensive research conducted in this field over the past four decades.

Services Dominate the Global Economy

The size of the service sector is increasing in almost all countries around the world. As an economy develops, the relative share of employment between agriculture, industry (including manufacturing and mining), and services changes dramatically.[1] Even in emerging economies, the service output is growing rapidly and often represents at least half of the Gross Domestic Product (GDP). Fig. 1.1 shows how the evolution to a service-dominated economy is likely to take place over time as the per capita income rises. In developed economies, knowledge-based services — defined as having intensive users of high technology or relatively skilled workforces — have been the most dynamic component.[2] Fig. 1.2 shows that the service sector already accounts for almost two-thirds of the value

Figure 1.1: Changing structure of employment as an economy develops.

Figure 1.2: Contribution of services industries to GDP globally.

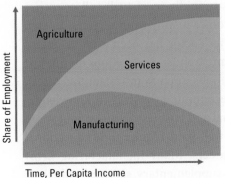

Source: International Monetary Fund, 1997

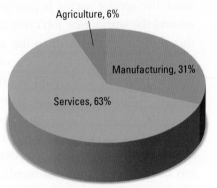

Source: The World Factbook 2015, Central Intelligence Agency, www.cia.gov, accessed 22 January, 2016.

Figure 1.3: Estimated size of service sector in selected countries as a percentage of GDP.

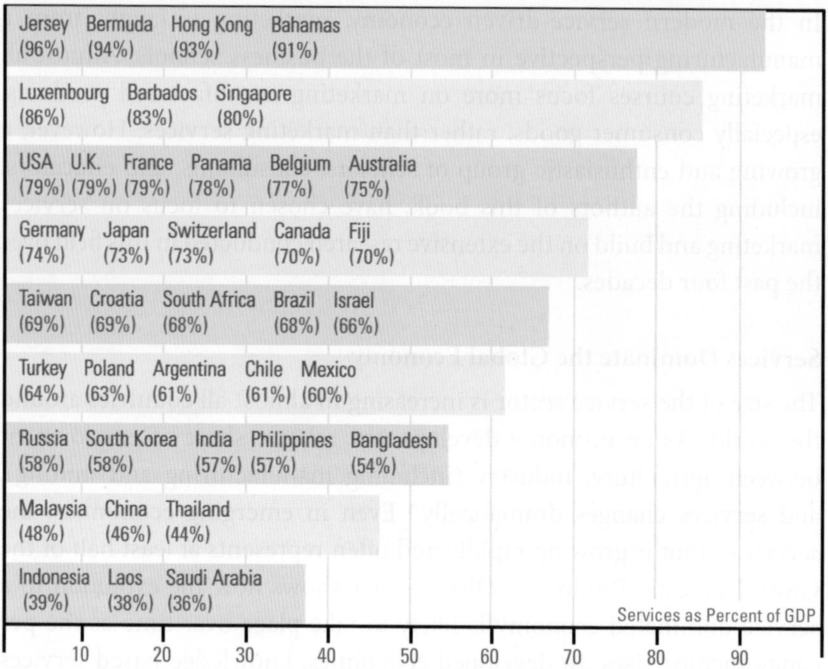

Jersey (96%)	Bermuda (94%)	Hong Kong (93%)	Bahamas (91%)
Luxembourg (86%)	Barbados (83%)	Singapore (80%)	
USA (79%) U.K. (79%) France (79%)	Panama (78%)	Belgium (77%)	Australia (75%)
Germany (74%)	Japan (73%) Switzerland (73%)	Canada (70%)	Fiji (70%)
Taiwan (69%)	Croatia (69%) South Africa (68%)	Brazil (68%)	Israel (66%)
Turkey (64%)	Poland (63%) Argentina (61%)	Chile (61%) Mexico (60%)	
Russia (58%)	South Korea (58%) India (57%)	Philippines (57%)	Bangladesh (54%)
Malaysia (48%)	China (46%) Thailand (44%)		
Indonesia (39%)	Laos (38%) Saudi Arabia (36%)		

Services as Percent of GDP

10   20   30   40   50   60   70   80   90

Source: The World Factbook 2015, Central Intelligence Agency, www.cia.gov, accessed 22 January, 2016.

of the global GDP, and Fig. 1.3 shows the size of the service sector of a few selected countries.

Most New Jobs are Generated by Services

Since the service sector is growing so rapidly in virtually all countries around the world, new job creation comes mainly from services. In fact, this shift in employment to the service sector has been seen as one of the longest and most stable of economic trends.[3] Service jobs do not just refer to relatively lowly-paid frontline jobs, such as in restaurants or call centers. Rather, some of the fastest economic growth is in knowledge-based industries — such as professional and business services, education, and healthcare.[4] These jobs tend to be well-paid, require good educational qualifications, and offer attractive careers. Many manufacturing firms too have moved from just bundling supplementary services with their physical products to marketing certain elements as standalone services.

There are number of leading research centers that focus on the integration of key disciplines to better equip future service professionals. Some of the leading centers include (in alphabetical order): the Center for Excellence in Service of Robert H. Smith School of Business at University of Maryland (see www.rhsmith.umd.edu/ces), the Center for Services Leadership at the W. P. Carey School of Business at Arizona State University (http://wpcarey.asu.edu/csl), and The Service Research Center at Karlstad University in Sweden (www.ctf.kau.se).

Understanding Services Offers Personal Competitive Advantage

This book is in response to the global transformation of our economies towards services, and gives an insight about distinctive characteristics of services and how they affect both customer behavior and marketing strategy. Apart from the family-owned manufacturing and agricultural business, majority of professions involve working in service organizations. The objective of the book is to make the reader aware of the service industry.

WHAT ARE THE PRINCIPAL INDUSTRIES OF THE SERVICE SECTOR?

To determine the type of industry that makes the service sector and the biggest players of the field, the best place to start with is the national economic statistics. The biggest players of the industry may include diverse sectors with services targeted to business customers, many of which are only known to people working in that industry.

Fig. 1.4 shows how much value each of the major service industry groups contributes to the US GDP. The real estate and rental and leasing are the largest for-profit service industry sector in the US, accounting for 13% in 2013, almost one-eighth of GDP. Over 90% of this figure comes from activities such as renting residential or commercial property; managing properties on behalf of their owners; providing realty services to facilitate purchases, sales, and rentals; and appraising property to determine its condition and value. The balance is accounted for by renting or leasing a wide variety of other manufactured products, ranging from heavy construction equipment (with or without operators) to office furniture, tents, and party supplies. Another large cluster of services provides for

Figure 1.4: Value added by Service Industry categories to US GDP.

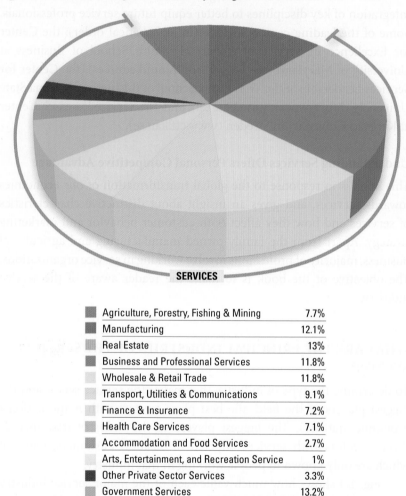

SERVICES

▪	Agriculture, Forestry, Fishing & Mining	7.7%
▪	Manufacturing	12.1%
▨	Real Estate	13%
▪	Business and Professional Services	11.8%
▫	Wholesale & Retail Trade	11.8%
▫	Transport, Utilities & Communications	9.1%
▫	Finance & Insurance	7.2%
▪	Health Care Services	7.1%
▪	Accommodation and Food Services	2.7%
▫	Arts, Entertainment, and Recreation Service	1%
▪	Other Private Sector Services	3.3%
▫	Government Services	13.2%

Source: Adapted from: U.S. Department of Commerce, Bureau of Economic Analysis, GDP by Industry Accounts for 2013, 2007, www.bea.gov; accessed 22 January, 2016.

distribution of physical products. Wholesale and retail trade accounts for about 11.8% of GDP.

Other substantial industry sectors or subsectors include professional and business services (11.8%), finance and insurance (7.2%), and healthcare (7.1%). Accommodation and food services constitute 2.7%, while the arts, entertainment, and recreation services — which include high-profile consumer services such as spectator sports, fitness centers, skiing facilities, museums and zoos, performing arts, casinos, golf courses, marinas, and theme parks — collectively represent a mere 1% of GDP. Nevertheless, in an economy with an output of over $17.1 trillion, this last group of services was still valued at an impressive $164 billion in 2013.

POWERFUL FORCES TRANSFORMING SERVICE MARKETS

Government policies, social changes, business trends, globalization, and advances in information technology and communications in particular, are among the powerful forces transforming today's service markets (Fig. 1.5). Collectively, these forces reshape demand, supply, the competitive landscape, and even the way customers buy and use services.

Of these forces, the dramatic development of IT and communications is perhaps the most important at the moment. Innovations in big data, cloud computing, user-generated content, mobile communications, networking technologies, artificial intelligence, and increasingly app-based self-service technologies bring their own service revolution. These technologies enable firms to deepen the relationships with their customers, offer multi-way information flow and more personalized services, improved analytics, and increase productivity and profitability.[5] More importantly, these new technologies also lead to a vast array of highly innovative business models, ranging from peer-to-peer services (e.g., Airbnb for short-term accommodation and Lending Club for personal loans), integrators (e.g., Uber, connects passengers with independent drivers through apps), to crowd-based services (e.g., crowdSPRING, which, is a leading provider of logo and graphic design services).

B2B Services as a Core Engine of Economic Development[6]

A key driver of successful economies is their ecosystem of advanced, competitive, and innovative business services. In order to know why would business services improve the productivity of a manufacturing firm and an economy as a whole, consider the example of a large manufacturing firm with its own canteen with 100 workers, who in the national statistics are classified as "manufacturing employees" producing "manufacturing output" (their output is captured in the added value created by their employer, i.e., the manufacturing firm). However, how good is a manufacturing firm in buying food ingredients, cooking, designing and

Figure 1.5: Factors stimulating the transformation of the service economy.

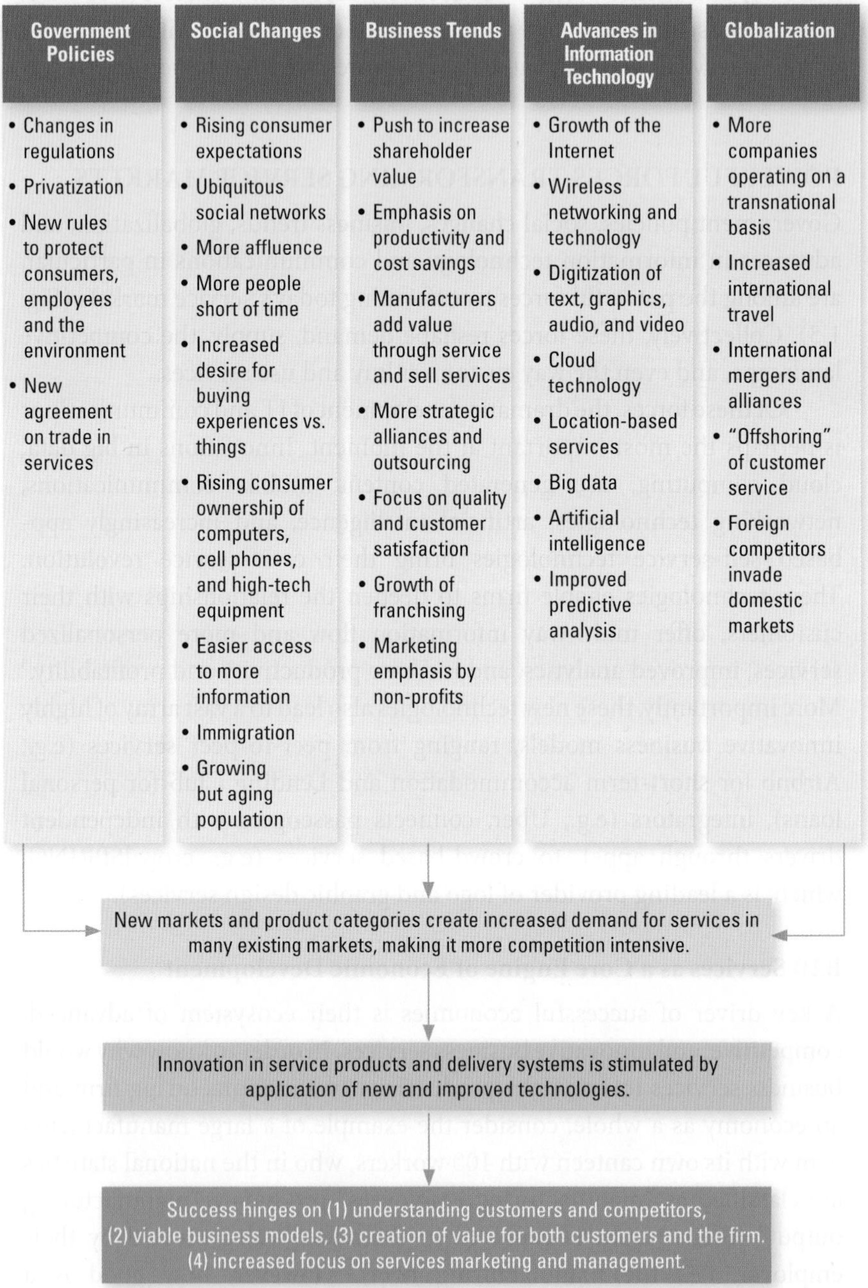

Government Policies	Social Changes	Business Trends	Advances in Information Technology	Globalization
• Changes in regulations • Privatization • New rules to protect consumers, employees and the environment • New agreement on trade in services	• Rising consumer expectations • Ubiquitous social networks • More affluence • More people short of time • Increased desire for buying experiences vs. things • Rising consumer ownership of computers, cell phones, and high-tech equipment • Easier access to more information • Immigration • Growing but aging population	• Push to increase shareholder value • Emphasis on productivity and cost savings • Manufacturers add value through service and sell services • More strategic alliances and outsourcing • Focus on quality and customer satisfaction • Growth of franchising • Marketing emphasis by non-profits	• Growth of the Internet • Wireless networking and technology • Digitization of text, graphics, audio, and video • Cloud technology • Location-based services • Big data • Artificial intelligence • Improved predictive analysis	• More companies operating on a transnational basis • Increased international travel • International mergers and alliances • "Offshoring" of customer service • Foreign competitors invade domestic markets

New markets and product categories create increased demand for services in many existing markets, making it more competition intensive.

Innovation in service products and delivery systems is stimulated by application of new and improved technologies.

Success hinges on (1) understanding customers and competitors, (2) viable business models, (3) creation of value for both customers and the firm. (4) increased focus on services marketing and management.

running kitchen processes, supervising chefs, and controlling quality and costs in a canteen? The general answer is that the firm would probably not be capable of producing fantastic food. As the operations that take place in the canteen are low-volume and of little importance to the overall business, they will neither justify greater management attention, nor significant investments in process improvements and R&D.

Many manufacturing firms have recognized this problem and outsourced their canteen operations, most likely via a tendering process with a renewal period of every few years. The winning bidder is likely to be a firm that specializes in running canteens and kitchens across many sites or branches. That company makes "operating canteens" its core competency. As such, the operation is managed with an emphasis on the quality of the services and food provided, and the efficiency of its cost structure. Branches can be benchmarked internally, and the overall operation has economies of scale, and is way down the learning curve. It also makes sense for the firm to invest in process improvements and R&D as the benefits can be reaped across multiple sites. What used to be a neglected support activity within a manufacturing firm has become a management focus and core competency of an independent service provider. The same logic applies to almost all non-core activities, assets, goods, and services a company can source more cost-effectively from third-party providers (Fig. 1.6). McKinsey estimates that such service inputs to manufacturing output are about 20–25%, offering much potential for further outsourcing.[7] This development leads to an increasing specialization of our economies with significant gains in overall productivity and living standards.

Outsourcing and Offshoring Often Work in Tandem[8]

Will service jobs be lost to low-wage countries? New communications technologies mean that some service work can be carried out far from where customers are located. Offshoring here refers to services that are *conducted* in one country and *consumed* in another (Fig. 1.7). Prior to the turn of the century, offshoring was mostly confined to the manufacturing sector. However, offshore services have since emerged as a dynamic global sector over the past two decades, driven by the rise of information and communication technologies, the international tradability of services, and the evolution of global business services models.

Figure 1.6: Outsourcing is an important driver for the growth of the service sector.

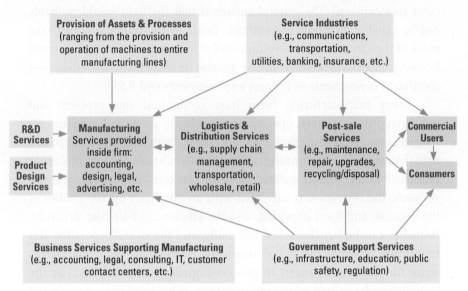

Provision of Assets & Processes (ranging from the provision and operation of machines to entire manufacturing lines)		Service Industries (e.g., communications, transportation, utilities, banking, insurance, etc.)

| R&D Services | Manufacturing Services provided inside firm: accounting, design, legal, advertising, etc. | Logistics & Distribution Services (e.g., supply chain management, transportation, wholesale, retail) | Post-sale Services (e.g., maintenance, repair, upgrades, recycling/disposal) | Commercial Users |
| Product Design Services | | | | Consumers |

| Business Services Supporting Manufacturing (e.g., accounting, legal, consulting, IT, customer contact centers, etc.) | Government Support Services (e.g., infrastructure, education, public safety, regulation) |

Source: Jochen Wirtz and Michael Ehret (2013), "Service-based Business Models: Transforming Businesses, Industries and Economies," in: Serving Customers: Global Services Marketing Perspectives, by Raymond P. Fisk, Rebekah Russell-Bennett, and Lloyd C. Harris (eds.), Tilde University Press, Melbourne, Australia, 28–46.

Figure 1.7: Many service today can be outsourced to lower cost destinations

Copyright 2005 by Randy Glasbergen.
www.glasbergen.com

"We found someone overseas who can drink coffee and talk about sports all day for a fraction of what we're paying you."

Figure 1.8: Outsourcing and offshoring are independent, but often work in tandem.

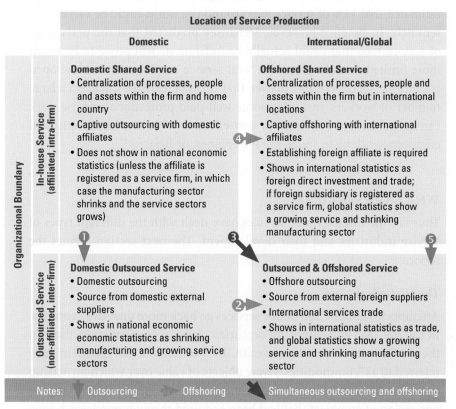

		Location of Service Production	
		Domestic	**International/Global**
Organizational Boundary	**In-house Service** (affiliated, intra-firm)	**Domestic Shared Service** • Centralization of processes, people and assets within the firm and home country • Captive outsourcing with domestic affiliates • Does not show in national economic statistics (unless the affiliate is registered as a service firm, in which case the manufacturing sector shrinks and the service sectors grows)	**Offshored Shared Service** • Centralization of processes, people and assets within the firm but in international locations • Captive offshoring with international affiliates • Establishing foreign affiliate is required • Shows in international statistics as foreign direct investment and trade; if foreign subsidiary is registered as a service firm, global statistics show a growing service and shrinking manufacturing sector
	Outsourced Service (non-affiliated, inter-firm)	**Domestic Outsourced Service** • Domestic outsourcing • Source from domestic external suppliers • Shows in national economic economic statistics as shrinking manufacturing and growing service sectors	**Outsourced & Offshored Service** • Offshore outsourcing • Source from external foreign suppliers • International services trade • Shows in international statistics as trade, and global statistics show a growing service and shrinking manufacturing sector

Notes: ▼ Outsourcing   ➤ Offshoring   ◤ Simultaneous outsourcing and offshoring

Source: Jochen Wirtz, Sven Tuzovic and Michael Ehret (2015), "Global Business Services: Increasing Specialization and Integration of the World Economy as Drivers of Economic Growth," Journal of Service Management.

Fig. 1.8 shows different business models that can develop in the outsourcing and offshoring of services.[9] The first scenario (Arrow 1) describes a firm's decision to outsource services domestically. Arrow 2 describes a situation where a firm switches from a domestic supplier to a foreign supplier. In some cases, firms make the decision to outsource and offshore to a foreign supplier simultaneously (Arrow 3). The fourth scenario is when firms source from foreign locations by establishing a subsidiary abroad (Arrow 4). This is often referred to as "captive offshoring". Finally, combining outsourcing and offshoring implies shifting the service provision from a foreign affiliate to a foreign-owned supplier (Arrow 5).

A study by the international consulting firm McKinsey & Company estimated that 11% of service jobs around the world could be carried out remotely. In practice however, McKinsey predicted that the percentage of service jobs that could actually be "offshored" will prove to be much more limited — only 1% of the total service employment in developed countries.[10] Of course, loss of even that small percentage can affect a large number of workers, including some well-paid professionals whose work can be performed much more cost-effectively by, say, highly qualified engineers working in India, the Philippines, or Belarus.[11]

WHAT ARE SERVICES?

Thus far, the discussion of services have dealt with the different types of service industries and their development. The next section defines the *service*.

The Historical View

Attempts to describe and define services go back more than two centuries. In the late 18th and early 19th centuries, classical economists focused on the creation and possession of wealth. They contended that goods (initially referred to as "commodities") were objects of value over which ownership rights could be established and exchanged. Ownership implied tangible possession of an object that had been acquired through purchase, barter, or gift from the producer or a previous owner, and was legally identifiable as the property of the current owner.

Adam Smith's famous book *The Wealth of Nations*, published in Great Britain in 1776, distinguished between the outputs of what he termed "productive" and "unproductive" labor.[12] The former, he stated, produced goods that could be stored after production and subsequently exchanged for money or other items of value. Unproductive labor, however "honorable, useful, or necessary", created services that *perished* at the time of production and therefore did not contribute to wealth. Building on this theme, the French economist Jean-Baptiste Say argued that production and consumption were inseparable in services, coining the term "immaterial products" to describe them.[13]

Today, it is established that production and consumption are indeed *separable* for many services (think of dry cleaning, lawn mowing, and weather forecasting), and that not all service performances are perishable (consider video recordings of concert performances and sports events). Very significantly, many services are designed to create *durable value* for their recipients (e.g., education and healthcare). However, the distinction between ownership and *non-ownership*, discussed in the next section, remains a valid one, emphasized by several leading service marketing scholars.

Benefits without Ownership

Services cover a huge variety of different and often very complex activities, making them difficult to define. The word *service* was originally associated with the work that servants did for their masters. In time, a broader association emerged, captured in the dictionary definition of "the action of serving, helping, or benefiting; conduct tending to the welfare or advantage of another".[14] Early marketing definitions of services contrasted them against goods and described them as "acts, deeds, performances, or efforts" and argued that they had different characteristics from goods — defined as "articles, devices, materials, objects, or things".[15] However, services need to be defined in their own right, not in relation to goods. A short and snappy definition, such as the oft-repeated "something which can be bought and sold but which cannot be dropped on your foot"[16] is amusing and memorable, but may not be particularly helpful as a guide to marketing strategy. The modern mindset has advanced and focuses on the lack of transfer of ownership when buying a service.

For example, a guest does not acquire ownership of the hotel room in which he stayed last weekend, nor does a patient have ownership over the physical therapist who helps him, and similarly attending a concert does not mean owning it. None of these purchases resulted in actual ownership. So what does a customer receive when a service is bought?

Christopher Lovelock and Evert Gummesson argue that services involve a form of *rental* through which customers can obtain benefits.[17] What customers value and are willing to pay for are desired experiences and solutions. *Rent* is used as a general term to describe payment made for the use of something or to gain access to skills and expertise, facilities, or networks (usually for a defined period of time), instead of buying it outright (which may not even be possible in many instances).

Five broad categories can be identified within the non-ownership framework that focus on (1) the use of labor, skills and expertise, (2 to 4) various degrees of the use of goods and facilities (exclusive, defined, or shared), and (5) the access and use of networks and systems:

1) *Labor, skills and expertise rentals.* People are hired to perform work that customers either cannot or choose not to do themselves. Examples include:

   - Car repair
   - Medical check-up
   - Management consulting

2) *Rented goods services.* These services allow customers to obtain the exclusive temporary right to use a physical object that they prefer not to own. Examples include:

   - Boats
   - Fancy dress costumes
   - Construction and excavation equipment

3) *Defined space and facility rentals.* Customers obtain the use of a certain portion of a larger facility such as a building, vehicle, or area. They usually share this facility with other customers. Examples include:

   - A seat in an aircraft
   - A suite in an office building
   - A storage container in a warehouse

4) *Access to shared facilities.* Customers rent the right to share the use of the facility. The facilities may be a combination of indoors, outdoors, and virtual. Examples include:

   - Theme parks
   - Golf clubs
   - Toll roads

5) *Access and use of networks and systems.* Customers rent the right to participate in a specified network. Service providers offer a variety of terms for access and use, depending on customer needs. Examples include:

- Telecommunications
- Utilities and banking
- Social online networks and games (e.g., *League of Legends*)

The difference between ownership and non-ownership affects the nature of marketing tasks and strategy. For example, the criteria for a customer's choice of service differ when something is being rented instead of owned. For a rental car to be used on vacation in Hawaii, for example, customers may focus on the ease of making reservations, the rental location and hours, the attitudes and performance of service personnel, and the cleanliness and maintenance of vehicles. If the customers are looking to own a car, then they are more likely to consider price, brand image, ease of maintenance, running costs, design, color, and upholstery.

Defining Services

Based on the non-ownership perspective of services, the following is a comprehensive definition of services:

DEFINITION OF SERVICES

Services are economic activities performed by one party for another. Often time-based, these performances bring about desired results to recipients, objects, or other assets.

In exchange for money, time, and effort, service customers expect value from access to labor, skills, expertise, goods, facilities, networks, and systems. However, they do not normally take ownership of the physical elements involved.[18]

Note that services are also defined as *economic activities* between two parties, implying an exchange of value between the seller and buyer in the marketplace, and describe them as *performances* that are most commonly *time-based*. Purchasers buy services because they are looking for *desired results*. In fact, many firms explicitly market their services as "solutions" to prospective customers' needs. Finally, while *customers expect to obtain value* from their service purchases in exchange for their money, time, and effort, this value comes from access to a variety of value-creating elements rather than transfer of ownership. (Spare parts installed during repairs, and restaurant-prepared food and beverages are among the few exceptions, but the value added by these items is usually less than that of the accompanying service elements).

Service Products versus Customer Service and After-Sales Service

With the growth of service economy, and the emphasis on adding value-enhancing services to manufactured goods, the line between services and manufacturing becomes increasingly blurred. Many manufacturing firms — from carmakers Toyota, aerospace engine producers GE and Rolls-Royce to high-tech equipment manufacturers Samsung and Siemens — are moving aggressively into service businesses. Quite a few firms have transitioned from simply bundling supplementary services with their physical products to reformulating and enhancing certain elements, so that they can be marketed as standalone services (see Fig. 1.9).[19] Another success story is Rolls-Royce featured in *Service Insights 1.1.*

The principles and tools discussed in services marketing (e.g., how to price a service, manage capacity in a call center, improve service quality, or manage service employees) are equally applicable to manufacturing firms that increase the service component of their offering. As Theodore Levitt long ago observed, "There are no such things as service industries. There are only industries whose service components are greater or less than those of other industries. Everybody is in service".[20] More recently, Roland Rust and Ming-Hui Huang suggested that "the 'product versus services' conceptualization is out-of-date and that service is everywhere, not just in the ser-

Figure 1.9: Gulfstream advertises its award-winning maintenance and support services.

vice sector".[21] An even more radical a view has been advanced by Stephen Vargo and Robert Lusch in their award-winning article on a new mindset, the *service-dominant* (S-D) *logic*. S-D logic suggests that all products are valued for the service they provide, and that the value derived from a physical good, for example, is not the good itself, but the service it provides during consumption (which they termed "value-in-use".[22])

SERVICE INSIGHTS 1.1
Rolls-Royce Sells Power by the Hour

Many manufacturing firms increase their competitive edge by providing superior value to their customers in the form of service. Rolls-Royce is one such example. Rolls-Royce, which makes world-class aircraft engines, is a successful company because it focuses on technical innovation. Rolls-Royce engines power about half of the latest wide-bodied passenger jets and a quarter of all single-aisle aircrafts in the world. A very important factor for its success has been the move from manufacturing to selling "power by the hour" — a bundle of goods and services that keeps the customers' engines running smoothly.

Imagine this — high above the Pacific, passengers doze on a long-haul flight from Tokyo to Los Angeles. Suddenly, there is a bolt of lightning. Passengers may not think much of it, but on the other side of the world in Derby, England, engineers at Rolls-Royce get busy. Lightning strikes on jets are common and usually harmless, but this one has caused some problems in one of the engines. The aircraft will still be able to land safely and could do so even with the affected engine shut down. The question is whether it will need a full engine inspection in Los Angeles, which would be normal practice but would also inconvenience hundreds of passengers waiting in the departure lounge.

A stream of data is beamed from the plane to Derby. Numbers dance across screens, graphs are drawn, and engineers scratch their heads. Before the aircraft lands, word comes that the engine is running smoothly, will not need a physical inspection, and the plane will be able to take off on time.

Industry experts estimate that manufacturers of jet engines can make about seven times the revenue from servicing and selling spare parts than they do from just selling the engines. Since it is so profitable, many independent servicing firms compete with companies like Rolls-Royce and offer spare parts for as low as one-third of the price charged by the original equipment manufacturers (OEMs). This is where Rolls-Royce has used a combination of technology and service to make it more difficult for competitors to steal its clients. Instead of selling engines first and parts and service later, Rolls-Royce has created an attractive bundle, which it branded TotalCare®. Customers are charged for every hour that an engine runs. Its website advertises it as a solution ensuring "peace of mind" for the lifetime of an engine. Rolls-Royce promises to maintain the engine and replace it if it breaks down. The operations room in Derby continuously monitors the performance of some 3,500 engines, enabling it to predict when engines are likely to fail and let airlines schedule engine changes efficiently, reduce repairs and unhappy passengers. Today, about 80% of the engines shipped to its customers are covered by such contracts! Although Rolls-Royce had engines troubles on its A380, they fixed the problem quickly and bounced back from the incident with many more orders for their engines.

Sources: *The Economist*, "Briefing Rolls-Royce. Britain's Lonely High Flyer" 10 January 2009, pp. 58–60; *The Economist*, "Per Ardua" 5 February 2011, p. 68; www.roll-royce.com, accessed 22 January 2016.

FOUR BROAD CATEGORIES OF SERVICES: A PROCESS PERSPECTIVE

The definition of services emphasizes not only value creation through rental and access, but also the desired results that can be brought about to recipients of the service, objects, and other assets. There are major differences among services depending on what is being processed. Services can "process" people, physical objects, and data, and the nature of the processing can be tangible or intangible. Tangible actions are performed on people's bodies or to their physical possessions. Intangible actions are performed on people's minds or to their intangible assets. This gives rise to the classification of services into four broad categories. They are *people-processing, possession-processing, mental stimulus-processing and information-processing* (Fig. 1.10).[23] Although the industries within each category may appear at first sight to be very different, analysis will show that they do, in fact, share important process-related characteristics. As a result, managers from different industries within the same category may obtain useful insights by studying others to generate useful innovations for their own organization. These four different types of processes often have distinctive implications for marketing, operations, and human resource management.

People Processing

From ancient times, people have sought out services directed at themselves, including transportation, food, lodging, health restoration, or beautification. To receive these types of services, customers must physically enter the service system as they are an integral part of the process and cannot obtain the desired benefits by dealing at arm's length with service suppliers. In short, they must enter the *service factory*, a physical location where people or machines (or both) create and deliver service benefits to customers. In some cases, service providers are sometimes willing to

Figure 1.10: Four broad categories of services.

	Name of the Service Act	
Name of the Service Act	**People**	**Possessions**
Tangible Actions	**People-processing** (services directed at people's bodies): • Hairstylist • Passenger Transportation • Health Care	**Possession-processing** (services directed at physical possessions): • Freight Transportation • Laundry and Dry Cleaning • Repair and Maintenance
Intangible Actions	**Mental stimulus-processing** (services directed at people's mind): • Education • Advertising & PR • Psychotherapy	**Information-processing** (services directed at intangible assets): • Accounting • Banking • Legal Services

come to customers, bringing the necessary tools of their trade to create the desired benefits at the customers' preferred location. Implications of people processing services include:

- Service production and consumption are simultaneous, which means that the customers typically must be present in the physical location (*service factory*). This requires planning about the location of the service operation, careful design of service processes and the service environment, and demand and capacity management.

- Active cooperation of the customer is needed in the service delivery process. For example, for a manicure service, the customer has to cooperate with the manicurist by specifying what she wants, sitting still, and presenting each finger for treatment when requested.

- There is a need for managers to think carefully about the location of the service operation, the design of service processes and the service environment, demand and capacity management, and output from the customer's point of view. Apart from financial costs, non-financial costs such as time, mental, and physical efforts need to be taken into account.

Possession Processing

Customers often ask a service organization to provide tangible treatment for some physical possession — a house that has been invaded by insects, a hedge that has grown too high, a malfunctioning elevator, a broken screen of a smartphone, a parcel that needs to be sent to another city, or a sick pet. The implications of such services are:

- Unlike people processing services, production and consumption are not necessarily simultaneous, giving more flexibility to the service firm in designing such services for cost-efficiency.

- Customers tend to be less involved in these services, compared to people processing services. Their involvement may be limited to just dropping off or collecting the item. In such instances, production and consumption can be described as *separable*. However, in some instances, the customer may prefer to be present during service delivery, perhaps wishing to supervise cutting of the hedge or comfort the family dog while it receives an injection at the veterinary clinic.

Mental Stimulus Processing

These services touch people's minds and have the power to shape attitudes and influence behavior. Mental stimulus processing services include education, news and information, professional advice, and some religious activities. Obtaining the full benefits of such services requires an investment of time and a degree of mental effort on the customer's part. However, recipients do not necessarily have to be physically present in a service factory, just mentally in communication with the information being presented. Here is an interesting contrast with people processing services. Passengers can sleep through a flight and still arrive at their desired destination. However, if a student falls asleep during an online lecture, he will not be any wiser at the end than at the beginning!

As the core content of services in this category is information-based (whether text, speech, music, visual images, or video), it can be digitized and made available via downloads, YouTube, and the likes. For instance, the Boston Symphony Orchestra's concerts can be attended live, viewed or heard live, pre-recorded on TV, or sold as digital recordings. Services in this category can thus be "inventoried", for consumption at a date later than their production. In fact, the same performance can be consumed repeatedly. For some students, accessing a lecture online and perhaps viewing key parts repeatedly may be a better solution than taking a physical class. Key implications that arise from these kinds of services are:

- Customers do not have to be physically present in the service factory. They only access the information remotely when they need it.

- Services in this category can be "inventoried" for consumption at a later date, or consumed repeatedly.

Information Processing

Information can be processed by information and communications technology (often referred to as ICT), and/or by professionals who use their brains to perform information processing and packaging. Information is the most intangible form of service output. However, it can be transformed into more permanent and tangible forms such as letters, reports, books, or files in any type of format. Some services that are highly dependent on the effective collection and processing of information are financial and professional services such as accounting, law, marketing research, management consulting, and medical diagnosis.

It is sometimes difficult to tell the difference between information processing and mental stimulus processing services. For example, if a stockbroker performs an analysis of a client's brokerage transactions, it seems like information processing. However, when the results of the analysis are used to make a recommendation about the most suitable type of investment strategy for the future, it would seem like mental stimulus processing. Therefore, for simplicity, the coverage of mental stimulus and information processing services in this book will be periodically combined under the umbrella term of *information-based services*.

SERVICES POSE DISTINCT MARKETING AND MANAGEMENT CHALLENGES

Can the marketing concepts and practices developed in manufacturing companies be directly transferred to service organizations without transfer of ownership? The answer is often "no". Services tend to have different features from goods, including the frequently cited four characteristics of *i*ntangibility, *h*eterogeneity (variability of quality), *i*nseparability of production and consumption, and *p*erishability of output,[24] or IHIP for short.[25] Table 1.1 explains these characteristics, and other common differences between services and goods. Together, these differences cause the marketing of services to differ from that of manufactured goods in several important respects.

It is important to recognize that these differences, while useful generalizations, *do not apply equally to all services*. Intangibility for example, ranges from tangible–dominant to intangible–dominant (see Fig. 1.11 for a scale that presents a variety of examples).[26] Large differences also exist between the four categories of services discussed in the previous section. For example, people tend to be part of the service experience only if the customer has direct contact with service employees. This is usually the case for people processing services but not for many information-processing service transactions such as online banking. These differences will be recognizable as the marketing mix for services is discussed throughout this book.

Table 1.1: Managerial Implications of Eight Common Features of Service

Difference	Implications	Marketing-related Topics
Most service products cannot be inventoried (i.e., output is perishable)	• Customers may be turned away or have to wait	• Smooth demand through promotions, dynamic pricing, and reservations • Work with operations to adjust capacity
Intangible elements usually dominate value creation (i.e., service is physically intangible)	• Customers cannot taste, smell, or touch these elements and may not be able to see or hear them • Harder to evaluate service and distinguish from competitors	• Make services tangible through emphasis on physical clues • Employ concrete metaphors and vivid images in advertising and branding
Services are often difficult to visualize and understand (i.e., service is mentally intangible)	• Customers perceive greater risk and uncertainty	• Educate customers to make good choices, explain what to look for, document performance, offer guarantees
Customers may be involved in co-production (i.e., if people processing is involved, the service is inseparable)	• Customers interact with providers' equipment, facilities, and systems • Poor task execution by customers may hurt productivity, spoil the service experience, and curtail benefits	• Educate customers to make good choices, explain what to look for, document performance, offer guarantees
People may be part of the service experience	• Appearance, attitude and behavior of service personnel and other customers can shape the experience and affect satisfaction	• Recruit, train, and reward employees to reinforce the planned service concept • Target the right customers at the right times; shape their behavior

Operational inputs and outputs tend to vary more widely (i.e., services are heterogeneous)	• Harder to maintain consistency, reliability, and service quality or to lower costs through higher productivity • Difficult to shield customers from results of service failures	• Set quality standards based on customer expectations; redesign product elements for simplicity and failure-proofing • Institute good service recovery procedures • Automate customer–provider interactions; perform work while customers are absent
The time factor often assumes great importance	• Customers see time as a scarce resource to be spent wisely, dislike wasting time waiting, want service at times that are convenient	• Find ways to compete on speed of delivery, minimize burden of waiting, offer extended service hours
Distribution may take place through non-physical channels	• Information-based services can be delivered through electronic channels such as the Internet or voice telecommunications, but core products involving physical activities or products cannot • Channel integration is a challenge; that is, to ensure consistent delivery of service through diverse channels, including branches, call centres and websites.	• Seek to create user-friendly, secure websites and free access by telephone • Ensure that all information-based service elements are delivered effectively and reliably through all key channels

THE 7 'P'S OF SERVICES MARKETING

When developing strategies to market manufactured goods, marketers usually address four basic strategic elements: *product*, *price*, *place* (or distribution), and *promotion* (or communication). As a group, these are usually referred to as the 4 'P's of the marketing mix.[27] As is evident from Table 1.1, the nature of services poses distinct marketing challenges. Hence, the 4 'P's of goods marketing are not adequate to deal with the

Figure 1.11: Relative value added by physical versus intangible elements in goods and services.

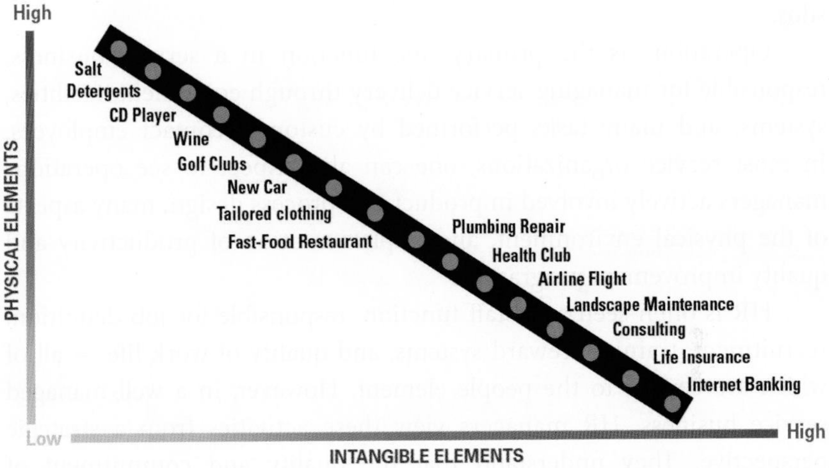

High

PHYSICAL ELEMENTS

Salt
Detergents
CD Player
Wine
Golf Clubs
New Car
Tailored clothing
Fast-Food Restaurant
Plumbing Repair
Health Club
Airline Flight
Landscape Maintenance
Consulting
Life Insurance
Internet Banking

Low ▪▪▪▪▪▪▪▪▪▪▪▪▪▪▪▪▪▪▪▪▪▪▪▪▪▪▪▪▪▪▪ High

INTANGIBLE ELEMENTS

Source: Adapted from Lynn Shostack.

issues arising from marketing services and have to be adapted and extended. This book revisits the traditional 4 'P's of marketing mix.

Furthermore, the traditional marketing mix does not cover the customer interface, and has to be extended by adding 3 'P's associated with service delivery — *process, physical environment,* and *people.*[28] Collectively, these seven elements are referred to as the 7 'P's of services marketing. These elements can be considered as the seven strategic levers of services marketing used to develop strategies for meeting customer needs profitably in competitive marketplaces.

MARKETING MUST BE INTEGRATED WITH OTHER MANAGEMENT FUNCTIONS

Previous section introduced 7 'P's as the strategic levers of services marketing. These different elements make it clear that marketers working in a service business cannot expect to operate successfully in isolation from managers in other functions. In fact, four management functions play central and interrelated roles in meeting the needs of service customers: marketing, operations, human resources (HR), and information technology (IT). Fig. 1.12 illustrates this interdependency. One of top management's responsibilities is to ensure that managers and other employees in each of these functions do not operate in departmental silos.

Operations is the primary line function in a service business, responsible for managing service delivery through equipment, facilities, systems, and many tasks performed by customer–contact employees. In most service organizations, one can also expect to see operations managers actively involved in product and process design, many aspects of the physical environment, and implementation of productivity and quality improvement programs.

HR is often seen as a staff function, responsible for job definition, recruitment, training, reward systems, and quality of work life — all of which are central to the people element. However, in a well-managed service business, HR managers view these activities from a strategic perspective. They understand that the quality and commitment of the frontline have become a major source of competitive advantage. Service organizations cannot afford to have HR specialists who do not understand customers. When employees understand and support the goals of their organization, have the skills and training needed to succeed in their jobs, and recognize the importance of creating and maintaining

Figure 1.12: Marketing, operations, human resources and IT departments must collaborate to serve the customer.

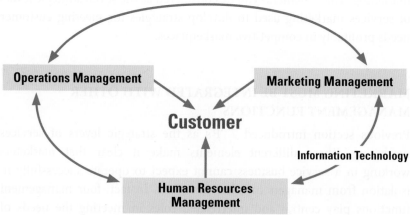

customer satisfaction, both marketing and operations activities are easier to manage and more likely to be successful.

IT is a key function as service processes are information-heavy — at almost every customer touch point, real-time information is needed (from customer data to prices and available capacity). Operations, HR, and marketing are critically dependent on IT to manage their functions and create value for the organization's customers.

For these reasons, this book does not limit itself exclusively to marketing. Many chapters refer to service operations, human resource management, and IT. Some firms deliberately rotate their managers among different job functions, especially between marketing and operations positions, precisely so that they will be able to appreciate different perspectives.

Whether as a manager of a small hotel or as the chief executive officer (CEO) of a major bank, one needs to be concerned about satisfying the customers on a daily basis, about operational systems running smoothly and efficiently, and about making sure that employees are not only working productively, but are also delivering good service. In short, integration of activities between these functions is the name of the game in services. Problems in any one of these areas can negatively affect the execution of tasks in other functions and might result in dissatisfied customers. Only a minority of people who work in a service firm are employed in formal marketing positions. However, Evert Gummesson argues that all those whose work affects the customer in some way — either through direct contact or the design of processes, IT systems, and policies that shape customers' experiences — need to think of themselves as *part-time marketers.*[29]

SERVICE–PROFIT CHAIN

A conceptual framework that shows how marketing, operations, HR, and IT are integrated in high-performance service organizations is called the Service–Profit Chain. James Heskett and his colleagues at Harvard argue that when service companies put employees and customers first, there is a big change in the way they manage and measure success. They relate profitability, customer loyalty, and customer satisfaction to the value created by satisfied, loyal, and productive employees, and supported by customer- and employee-centric operations and technology:

> Top-level executives of outstanding service organizations spend little time setting profit goals or focusing on market share... Instead they understand that in the new economics of service, frontline workers and customers need to be the center of management concern. Successful service managers pay attention to the factors that drive profitability...investment in people, technology that supports frontline workers, revamped recruiting and training practices, and compensation linked to performance for employees at every level.
>
> *The service–profit chain, developed from analyses of successful service organizations, puts "hard" values on "soft" measures. It helps managers target new investments to develop service and satisfaction levels for maximum competitive impact, widening the gap between service leaders and their merely good competitors.*[30]

The Service–Profit Chain, in Fig. 1.13, shows the links in a managerial process that are proposed to lead to success in service businesses.

Table 1.2 provides a useful summary, highlighting the behaviors required of service leaders in order to manage their organizations effectively. Working backwards, from the desired end results of revenue growth and profitability, links 1 and 2 focus on customers. These links include an emphasis on identifying and understanding customer needs, making investments to ensure customer retention, and having a commitment to adopt new performance measures that track such variables as satisfaction and loyalty among both customers and employees. Link 3 focuses on the value for customers created by the service concept and highlights the need for investments to continually improve both service quality and productivity.

Another set of service leadership behaviors (links 4 to 7) relate to employees and include organizational focus on the front line. The design of jobs should offer greater freedom for employees. Managers with potential should be developed. This category also stressed the idea that

Figure 1.13: The Service-Profit Chain.

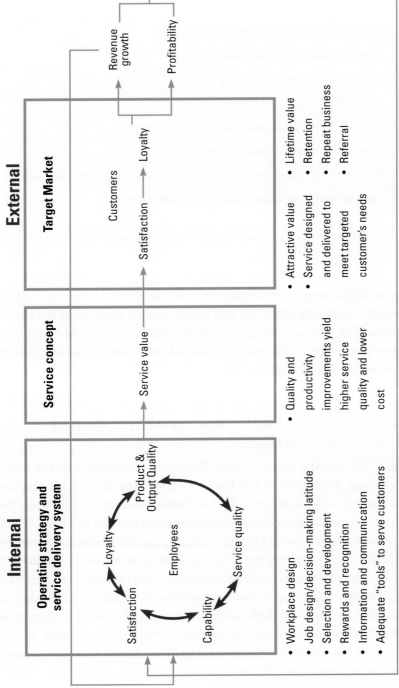

Table 1.2: Links in the Service–Profit Chain.

1. Customer loyalty drives profitability and growth
2. Customer satisfaction drives customer loyalty
3. Value drives customer satisfaction
4. Quality and productivity drive value
5. Employee loyalty drives service quality and productivity
6. Employee satisfaction drives employee loyalty
7. Internal quality as delivered by operations and IT drives employee satisfaction
8. Top management leadership underlies the chain's success.

Source: James L. Heskett et al., "Putting the Service Profit Chain to Work," *Harvard Business Review,* March April 1994; James L. Heskett, W. Earl Sasser, and Leonard L. Schlesinger, *The Service Profit Chain,* Boston: Harvard Business School Press, 1997.

paying higher wages can actually decrease labor costs because of reduced turnover, higher productivity, and higher quality. Underlying the chain's success (link 8) is top management leadership. Service–Profit Chain is an important guiding philosophy for this book, with core chapters explaining how to successfully implement it.

FRAMEWORK FOR DEVELOPING EFFECTIVE SERVICE MARKETING STRATEGIES

The 7 'P's and the Service–Profit Chain are integrated into the wider organizing framework of this book. It shows how each of the chapters fits together with the others as they address related topics and issues. The Chapter Summary presents the organizing framework for this book, which is divided into five parts: (1) understanding service products, consumers and markets; (2) applying the 4 'P's of marketing to services; (3) managing the customer interface (i.e., the additional 3 'P's of services marketing); (4) developing customer relationships; and (5) striving for service excellence. Note that the arrows link the different boxes in the model — they stress the interdependences between different parts. Decisions made in one area must be consistent with those taken in another, so that each strategic element will mutually reinforce the rest.

CONCLUSION

We study service because modern economies are driven by individual service businesses operating within a remarkable array of industries. Collectively, services are responsible for the creation of a substantial majority of all new jobs, both skilled and unskilled, around the world. Many of these industries are undergoing dramatic transformations, driven by advances in technology, globalization, changes in government policies, evolving consumer needs, and lifestyles. In such an environment, effective marketing plays a vital role in determining whether an individual organization survives and thrives — or declines and fails.

This chapter has demonstrated that services require a distinctive approach to marketing and management, because the context and the tasks often differ in important aspects from those in the manufacturing sector. Succeeding as a marketing manager in a service business requires one not only to understand key marketing concepts and tools, but also know how to use them effectively. Each of the 7 'P's — the strategic levers of services marketing and management — has a role to play, but it is also how well one ties them together that will make the difference. The winners in today's highly competitive service markets succeed by continually rethinking the way they do business, by looking for innovative ways to serve their customers better, by taking advantage of new developments in technology, and by embracing a disciplined and well-organized approach to developing and implementing services marketing strategy.

CHAPTER SUMMARY

Why Study Services
- Services dominate the global economy
- Most new jobs are generated by services
- Understanding services offers personal competitive advantage

Definition of Services
- Services provide benefits without ownership
- Services are economic activities performed by one party to another. Often time-based, these performances bring about desired results to recipients, objects, or other assets. In exchange for money, time, and effort, service customers expect value from access to labor, skills, expertise, goods, facilities, networks, and systems.

Service Sector Industries
In order of contribution to US GDP:
- Government services
- Real estate
- Business and professional services
- Wholesale & retail trade
- Transport, utilities & communications
- Finance & insurance
- Healthcare services
- Accommodation & food services
- Arts, entertainment & recreation service
- Other private sector services

Categories of Services by Type of Processing
- People-processing (e.g., passenger transport, hairstyling)
- Possession-processing (e.g., freight transport, repair services)
- Mental stimulus-processing (e.g., education)
- Information-processing (e.g., accounting)

Key Trends

General Trends
- Government policies
- Social changes
- Business trends
- Advances in IT
- Globalization

B2B Services Growth
- Outsourcing
- Offshoring
- Firms increasing focus on core competencies
- Increasing specialization of economies
- Increasing productivity through R&D

Services Pose Distinct Marketing Challenges
Services tend to have four frequently cited characteristics: *i*ntangibility, *h*eterogeneity (variability of quality), *i*nseparability of *p*roduction and consumption, and perishability of output, or **IHIP** for short. Key implications of these features include:
- Most services cannot be inventoried (i.e., output is perishable)
- Intangible elements typically dominate value creation (i.e., services are physically intangible)
- Services are often difficult to understand (i.e., services are mentally intangible)
- Customers are often involved in co-production (i.e., if people processing is involved, the service in inseparable)
- People (service employees) may be part of the service product and experience
- Operational inputs and outputs tend to vary more widely (i.e., services are heterogeneous)
- The time factor often assumes great importance (e.g., capacity management)
- Distribution may take place through non-physical channels (e.g., information processing services)

Functions
need to be tightly integrated as together they shape the customer experience, especially:
- Marketing
- Operations
- Human resources
- Information technology

Service-Profit Chain
Shows the tight links between
- Leadership
- Internal quality & IT
- Employee engagement
- Customer value, satisfaction & loyalty
- Profitability & growth

Putting Service Strategy Into Action
This book is structured around an integrated model of services marketing and management that covers:
- Understanding Service Products, Consumers & Markets
- Applying the 4 'P's of Marketing to Services
- Designing & Managing the Customer Interface using the additional 3 'P's of Services Marketing (Process, People & Physical Environment)
- Developing Customer Relationships
- Striving for Service Excellence

CHAPTER 2

Consumer Behavior in a Services Context

I can't get no satisfaction.

From the song "(I Can't Get No) Satisfaction"
Mick Jagger, lead singer of The Rolling Stones

An individual who seeks out the necessary information and chooses wisely has a better chance of getting satisfaction than Mick Jagger.

Claes Fornell
Distinguished Donald C. Cook Emeritus Professor of Business
at the University of Michigan and Founder of the American
Customer Satisfaction Index

THREE-STAGE MODEL OF SERVICE CONSUMPTION

In marketing, it is very important to understand why customers behave the way they do. How do they make decisions about buying and using a service? What determines their satisfaction with it after consumption?

Without this understanding, no firm can hope to create and deliver services that will result in satisfied customers who will buy again.

Service consumption can be divided into three main stages: prepurchase, service encounter, and post-encounter stages. Fig. 2.1 shows that each stage consists of several steps. The prepurchase stage includes need-awareness, information search, evaluation of alternatives, and making a purchase decision. During the service encounter stage, the customer initiates, experiences, and consumes the service. The post-encounter stage includes evaluation of the service performance, which determines future intentions such as wanting to buy again from the same firm, and recommending it to friends. The rest of this chapter is organized around the three stages and the related key concepts of service consumption.

PREPURCHASE STAGE

The prepurchase stage begins with *need-awareness* and continues through to information search and evaluation of alternatives to deciding whether or not to buy a particular service.

Need Awareness

When a person or organization decides to buy or use a service, it is triggered by an underlying need or *need arousal*. The awareness of a need will lead to information search and evaluation of alternatives before a decision is reached. Needs may be triggered by:

- People's unconscious minds (e.g., personal identity and aspirations).
- Physical conditions (e.g., hunger can drive one to a fast food restaurant).
- External sources (e.g., social media or a service firm's marketing activities)

When a need is recognized, people are likely to be motivated to take action to resolve it. Needs and wants are continuously developing; e.g., the need for increasingly novel and innovative service experiences in extreme sports, such as guided mountain climbing, paragliding, white-water rafting, mountain biking, and bungee jumping.

Figure 2.1: The three stage model of service consumption

Pre-purchase Stage

Stages of Service Consumption	Key Concepts

► Awareness of need
  • Information search
  • Clarify needs
  • Explore solutions
  • Identify alternative service products and suppliers
	► Need arousal
	► Evoked set
	► Consideration set
	► Multi-attribute model

► Evaluation of alternatives (solutions and suppliers)
  • Review supplier information (e.g., advertising, brochures, websites)
  • Review information from third parties (e.g., published reviews, ratings, comments on the Web, blogs, complaints to public agencies, satisfaction ratings, awards)
  • Discuss options with service personnel
  • Get advice and feedback from third-party advisors and other customers
	► Search, experience, and credence attributes
	► Perceived risk

► Make decisions on service purchase and often make reservations	► Formation of expectations: desired service level, predicted service level, adequate service level, zone of tolerance

Service Encounter Stage

Stages of Service Consumption	Key Concepts
► Request service from a chosen supplier or initiate self-service (payment may be upfront or billed later) ► Service delivery by personnel or self-service	► Moments of truth ► Service encounters ► Servuction system ► Theater as a metaphor ► Role and script theories ► Perceived control theory

Post-encounter Stage

Stages of Service Consumption	Key Concepts
► Evaluation of service performance ► Future intentions	► Confirmation/ Disconfirmation of expectations ► Dissatisfaction, satisfaction, and delight ► Service Quality ► Word-of-mouth ► Repurchase ► Loyalty

Information Search

Once a need has been recognized, customers are motivated to search for solutions to satisfy that need. Several alternatives may come to mind, and these form the *evoked set*. The evoked set can be derived from past experiences or external sources such as social media, online reviews, online searches, advertising, retail displays, news stories, and recommendations from service personnel, friends, and family. However, a consumer is unlikely to use all the alternatives in the evoked set for decision-making. The consumer is likely to narrow it down to a few alternatives to seriously consider, and these alternatives form the *consideration set*. During the search process, consumers also learn about service attributes they should consider and form expectations of how firms in the consideration set perform on those attributes.

Evaluation of Alternative Services

Once the consideration set and key attributes are understood, the consumer typically makes a purchase decision. In marketing, often multi-attribute models are used to simulate consumer decision-making.

Multi-attribute Model

This model holds that consumers use service attributes important to them to evaluate and compare alternative offerings in their consideration set. Each attribute has an importance weight. A higher weight means the attribute is more important. For example, assuming a student has three alternative dry cleaners in her consideration set. Table 2.1 shows the alternatives as well as the attributes she would use to compare them. The table shows that the quality of the dry cleaning is most important to her, followed by convenience of location, and then price (Table 2.1). The student can use these two common decision rules to decide. They are the very simple linear compensatory rule and the more complex, but also more realistic, conjunctive rule. Using the same information, the student can end up choosing different alternatives if she uses different decision rules. It is therefore important for firms to understand which rule their target customers are using through careful market research!

Using the linear compensatory rule, the student mentally computes

Table 2.1: Modeling Consumer Choice — A Student's Multi-Attribute Model for Choosing a Dry Cleaner

	Current Dry Cleaner	Campus Dry Cleaner	New Dry Cleaner	Importance Weight
Quality of Dry Cleaning	9	10	10	30%
Convenience of Location	10	8	9	25%
Price	8	10	8	20%
Opening Hours	6	10	9	10%
Reliability of On-time Delivery	2	9	9	5%
Friendliness of Staff	2	8	8	5%
Design of Shop	2	7	8	5%
Total Score	7.7	9.2	9.0	100%

a global score ranging from 1 to 10 for each dry cleaner. This is done by multiplying the score for the dry cleaner on each attribute by the importance weight. The scores are then added up. For example, the current dry cleaner would score 9 × 30% for quality of dry cleaning, plus 10 × 25% for convenience of location, plus 8 × 20% for price. Computation for all three alternatives yields a total score of 7.7 for the current dry cleaner, 9.2 for the campus dry cleaner, and 9.0 for the new dry cleaner. Therefore, the choice would be the on-campus dry cleaner.

In the conjunctive rule, the consumer will make the decision based on the total overall score in conjunction with minimum performance levels on one or several attributes. For example, the student may only consider a dry cleaner that scores a minimum of 9 on convenience of location as she does not want to carry her laundry over longer distances. In that case, the choice is between the current and new dry cleaner in her neighborhood. She will pick the new dry cleaner of the two as it has the higher overall score. If none of the brands meet all the cutoffs in a conjunctive model, then the student may delay making a choice, change the decision rule, or modify the cutoffs.

Service providers who understand the decision-making process of their target customers can then try to influence that process in a number of ways to enhance their chance of being the chosen provider:

- First, firms need to ensure that their service is in the consideration set, as without being considered, a firm cannot be chosen. This can be done through advertising or viral marketing (see Chap. 7).

- Next, firms can change and correct consumer perceptions (e.g., if a clinic has superior performance on personalized and special care offered by their doctors but customers do not see this, it can focus its communications on correcting customer perceptions).

- They can also shift importance weights (e.g., communicate messages that increase weights of attributes the firm excels in, and de-emphasize those the firm is not so strong at).

- Firms can even introduce new attributes such as what Hertz did when advertising its environmental-friendly car. Consumers who are eco-conscious would consider the environment aspect when deciding which car rental company to use (Fig. 2.6).

The objective is to shape the target customers' decision making so that they make the "right" choice, that is, choose the firm's service offering.

Service attributes

The multi-attribute model assumes that consumers can evaluate all important attributes before purchase. However, this is often not the case as some attributes are harder to evaluate than others. There are three types of attributes as follows:[1]

- *Search attributes* are tangible characteristics that customers can evaluate before purchase. For example, search attributes for a restaurant include type of food, location, type of restaurant (e.g., fine dining, casual, or family-friendly), and price. Customers can also check out a golf course before actually playing a round, or take a tour of a health club and try working out with one or two gym equipment. These tangible search attributes help customers better understand and evaluate a service, therefore reducing the sense of uncertainty or risk associated with the purchase.

Figure 2.2: Holiday-makers hiking up the mountains

- *Experience attributes* cannot be evaluated before purchase. Customers must "experience" the service before they can assess attributes such as reliability, ease-of-use, and customer support. For example, in the case of a restaurant, it is difficult to know the quality of food, service provided by the waiter, and the atmosphere in the restaurant until the services are actually used.

Vacations (Fig. 2.2), live entertainment performances, and medical procedures all have high experience attributes. Although people can scroll through websites describing a specific holiday destination, view travel films, read reviews by travel experts and past guests, or hear about the experiences from family and friends, they cannot really evaluate or feel the dramatic beauty associated with, say, hiking in the Canadian Rockies or snorkeling in the Caribbean until they experience these activities themselves.

Finally, reviews and recommendations cannot possibly account for all situation-specific circumstances. For example, the excellent chef may be on a vacation or a boisterous birthday party at the neighboring table may spoil the romantic candlelight dinner one came for to celebrate an anniversary.

- *Credence Attributes* are characteristics that customers find hard to evaluate even after consumption. Here, the customer is forced to believe or trust that certain tasks have been performed at the promised level of quality. In the restaurant example, credence attributes include the hygiene conditions in the kitchen, the nutritional quality, and the quality of ingredients used (e.g., "Do they really use the higher grade olive oil for cooking?").

It is not easy for a customer to determine the quality of repair and maintenance work performed on a car, and patients cannot usually evaluate how well their dentists have performed complex dental procedures. Consider the purchase of professional services. People seek such assistance precisely because they lack the necessary training and expertise themselves — e.g., counseling, surgery, legal advice, and consulting services. How can it be ensured that the best possible job was done? Often it comes down to a matter of having confidence in the provider's skills and professionalism.

Figure 2.3: How product characteristics affect ease of evaluation

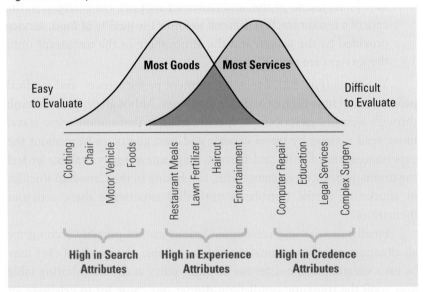

Source: Adapted from Valarie A. Zeithaml, "How Consumer Evaluation Processes Differ Between Goods and Services," in J. H. Donnelly and W. R. George, Marketing of Services (Chicago: American Marketing Association, 1981).

All products can be placed on a continuum ranging from "easy to evaluate" to "difficult to evaluate", depending on whether they are high in search, experience, or credence attributes. As shown in Fig. 2.3, most physical goods are located somewhere toward the left of the continuum because they rank high in search attributes. Most services tend to be located from the center to the right of the continuum as they tend to be high in experience and credence attributes.

The harder it is to evaluate a service, the higher is the perceived risk associated with that decision. Perceived risk is discussed in the next section.

Perceived Risk

If a physical good is unsatisfactory, it can be returned or replaced. With services, this option may not be possible. Susan Munro never tried coloring her hair before and was uncertain how it would turn out. Hence, when her hairstylist suggested she lighten her hair color, she declined. Her uncertainty increased her *perceived risk*. Perceived risk is usually greater for services that are high in experience and credence attributes, and first-time users are likely to face greater uncertainty. Every time we have to make a decision about an unfamiliar service, especially one with important consequences such as choosing a college or a health insurance plan, it is a usual phenomenon to worry about the possibility of not making the best choice, or not even a good choice. The worse the possible consequences and the higher likelihood of these negative consequences happening, the higher the perception of risk. Table 2.2 shows seven categories of perceived risks.

- Consumers usually feel uncomfortable with perceived risks and use a variety of methods to reduce them, including:
- Seeking information from trusted and respected personal sources such as family, friends, and peers.[2]
- Using the Internet to compare service offerings, to search for independent reviews and ratings, and to explore discussions on social media.
- Relying on a firm that has good reputation.
- Looking for guarantees and warranties.
- Visiting service facilities or trying aspects of the service before

Table 2.2: Perceived Risks in Purchasing and Using Services

Type of Risk	Examples of Customer Concerns
Functional (unsatisfactory performance outcomes)	• Will this training course give me the skills I need to get a better job? • Will this credit card be accepted wherever and whenever I want to make a purchase? • Will the dry cleaner be able to remove the stains from this jacket?
Financial (monetary loss, unexpected costs)	• Will I lose money if I make the investment recommended by my stockbroker? • Could my credit card details be stolen if I register with this website? • Will repairing my car cost more than the original estimate?
Temporal (wasting time, consequences of delays)	• Will I have to wait in line for a long time before I can enter the exhibition? • Will service at this restaurant be so slow that I will be late for my afternoon meeting? • Will the renovations to our bathroom be completed before our friends come to stay with us?
Physical (personal injury or damage to possessions)	• Will there be complications or scars if I go for this cosmetic surgery? • Will the contents of this package get damaged in the mail? • Will I get an upset stomach if I eat at this roadside stall?
Psychological (personal fears and emotions)	• How can I be sure that this aircraft will not crash? • Will the consultant make me feel embarrassed or stupid? • Will the doctor's diagnosis upset me?
Social (how others think and react)	• What will my friends think of me if they learned that I registered for the dating service? • Will my relatives approve of the restaurant I have chosen for the family reunion dinner? • Will my business colleagues disapprove of my selection of an unknown law firm?
Sensory (unwanted effects on any of the five senses)	• Will I get a view of the parking lot rather than the beach from my restaurant table? • Will I be kept awake by noise from the guests in the room next door? • Will my room smell of stale cigarette smoke?

purchasing, and examining tangible cues or other physical evidence such as the feel and look of the service setting or the awards won by the firm.

- Asking knowledgeable employees about competing services to learn about what to look out for when making this decision.

Customers are risk-averse and, all else being equal, will choose the service with the lower perceived risk. Therefore, firms need to proactively work on reducing customer risk perceptions. Suitable strategies vary according to the nature of the service and may include some or all of the following:

- Encourage prospective customers to preview the service through their company websites and videos.

- Encourage prospective customers to visit the service facilities before purchase.

- Offer free trials suitable for services with high experience attributes. Many caterers and restaurants allow potential wedding customers to have free food tasting sessions before making a booking for their wedding banquet.

- For services with high credence qualities and high customer involvement, advertising helps to communicate the benefits, usage, and how consumers can enjoy the best results.

- Professionals such as doctors, architects, and lawyers often display their credentials such as degrees and other certifications as they want customers to "see" they are qualified to provide expert service. Many professional firms' websites inform prospective clients about their services, highlight their expertise, and even showcase successful past engagements.

- Use evidence management, an organized approach where customers are presented with coherent evidence of company's targeted image and its value proposition. This includes the appearance of furnishings, equipment and facilities, and employees' dress and behavior.[3] For example, the bright and trendy decor at the hairdressing salon may have helped Susan Munro choose the salon on her first visit. It probably contributed to her feeling satisfied in the end, although her stylist kept her waiting for 20 minutes.

- Have visible safety procedures that build confidence and trust.

- Give customers access to online information about the status of an order or procedure. Many courier service providers use this (e.g., FedEx, DHL, and UPS).

- Offer service guarantees such as money-back guarantees and performance warranties.

When a company does a good job in managing potential customers' risk perceptions, uncertainty is reduced, thereby increasing the chances of them being the chosen service provider. Also important to consumer choice (and subsequently satisfaction) are customer expectations, which are discussed next.

Service Expectations

Expectations are formed during the search and decision-making process, through a customer's search and evaluation of information and alternatives. If the customer does not have any previous experience with the service, their prepurchase expectations can be based on online searches and reviews, word-of-mouth comments, news stories, or the firm's own marketing efforts. Expectations can even be situation-specific. For example, if it is peak period, expectations of service delivery timing will be lower than during non-peak periods.

Expectations change and can be managed, as discussed in the section on multi-attribute models. Firms try to shape expectations through their communications and introduction of new services and technologies. Increased access to information through the media and internet can also change expectations. For instance, healthcare consumers are well-informed nowadays and often seek a participative role in decisions relating to medical treatment.

What are the components of customer expectations? Expectations embrace several elements, including desired, adequate and predicted service, and a zone of tolerance that falls between desired and adequate service levels.[4] The model in Fig. 2.4 shows the factors influencing different levels of customer expectations. These factors are:

- *Desired service.* The type of service customers hope to receive is termed as desired service. It is a "wished for" level — a combination

Figure 2.4: Factors influencing customer expectations of service

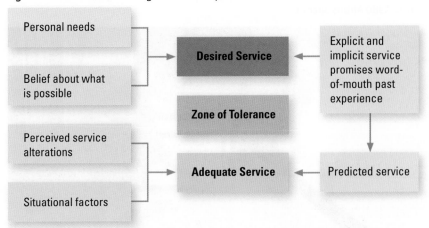

Source: Adapted from Valarie A. Zeithaml, Leonard A. Berry, and A. Parasuraman, "The Nature and Determinants of Customer Expectations of Service," Journal of the Academy of Marketing Science, 21, 1, 1993, 1–12.

of what customers believe can and should be delivered in the context of their personal needs. Desired service could also be influenced by explicit and implicit promises made by service providers, word-of-mouth, and past experiences. However, most customers are realistic. Recognizing that a firm cannot always deliver the "wished for" level of service, they also have a threshold level of expectations, termed *adequate service*, and a predicted service level.

- *Adequate service.* The minimum level of service customers will accept without being dissatisfied.
- *Predicted service.* This is the level of service that customers actually anticipate to receive. Predicted service can also be affected by service provider's promises (Fig. 2.5), word-of-mouth, and past experiences. Predicted service level directly affects how customers define "adequate service" on that occasion. If good service is predicted, the adequate level will be higher than when poorer service is predicted.

Customer predictions of service often are situation-specific. From past experience for example, customers visiting a museum on a summer's day may expect to see larger crowds if the weather is poor than if the sun is shining. A 10-minute wait to buy tickets on a cool, rainy day in summer might not fall below their level of

Figure 2.5: This advertisement creates high expectations for Singapore Airline Suites on its A380 Airbus aircraft

Courtesy of Singapore Airlines

adequate service. Another factor that may set this expectation is the level of service anticipated from alternative service providers.

- *Zone of tolerance.* It can be difficult for firms to achieve consistent service delivery at all touch points across many service delivery channels, branches, and often thousands of employees. Even the performance by the same service employee is likely to vary over the course of a day and from one day to another. The extent to which customers are willing to accept this variation is called the zone of tolerance. Performing too low causes frustration and dissatisfaction, whereas exceeding the zone of tolerance can surprise and delight customers. Another way of looking at the zone of tolerance is to think of it as the range of service within which customers do not pay explicit attention to service performance. When service falls outside this range, customers will react, either positively or negatively.[5]

The size of the zone of tolerance can be larger or smaller for individual customers, depending on factors such as competition, price, or importance of specific service attributes — each of which can influence the expectation of adequate service levels. In contrast, desired service levels tend to move up very slowly in response to accumulated customer experiences. Consider a small business owner who needs some advice from her accountant. Her ideal level of professional service may be receiving a thoughtful response by the following day. However, if she makes her request at the time of year when all accountants are busy preparing corporate and individual tax returns, she will know from experience not to expect a fast reply. Although her ideal service level probably will not change, her zone of tolerance for response time may be broader because she has a lower adequate service threshold at busy periods of the year.

The predicted service level is the most important level for the consumer choice process, which is discussed in the next section. Desired and adequate levels, and the zone of tolerance become important determinants to customer satisfaction, which we will discuss in the post-encounter purchase stage section.

Purchase Decision

After consumers have evaluated possible alternatives by, for example, comparing the performance of the important attributes of competing service offerings; assessed the perceived risk associated with each offering; and developed their desired, adequate, and predicted service level expectations, they are ready to select the option they like the best.

Many purchase decisions for frequently purchased services are quite simple and can be made quickly without too much thought — the perceived risks are low, the alternatives are clear, and, because they have been used before, their characteristics are easily understood. If the consumer already has a favorite supplier, he or she will probably choose it again in the absence of a compelling reason to do otherwise. In many instances however, purchase decisions involve trade-offs. Price is often a key factor. For example, is it worth paying more for faster service, a larger room with a better view, or a better seat in a theater performance?

For more complex decisions, trade-offs can involve multiple attributes, as seen in consumer choice based on the multi-attribute model. In choosing an airline, convenience of schedules, reliability, seating comfort, attentiveness of cabin crew, and availability and quality of meals may well vary among different carriers, even at the same rates.

Once a decision is made, the consumer is ready to move to the service encounter stage. This next step may take place immediately, as it is in deciding to enter a fast-food restaurant, or it may first involve an advance reservation, as what usually happens with taking a flight or attending a live theater performance.

SERVICE ENCOUNTER STAGE

After making a purchase decision, customers move on to the core of the service experience. The service encounter stage is when the customer interacts directly with the service firm. A number of models and frameworks will be used to better understand the consumers' behavior and experience during the service encounter. First, the "moments of truth" metaphor shows the importance of effectively managing service touch points. A second framework, the high- or low-contact service model, helps us to better understand the extent and nature of points of contact. A third concept, the servuction model, focuses on the various types of interactions that together create the customer's service experience. Finally, the theater metaphor together with the script, role, and perceived control theories communicate effectively how one can look at "staging" service performances to create the experience customers desire.

Service Encounters Are "Moments of Truth"

Jan Carlzon, former chief executive of Scandinavian Airlines System (SAS), used the "moment of truth" metaphor as a reference point for transforming SAS from an operations-driven business into a customer-driven airline. Carlzon made the following comments about his airline:

> Last year, each of our 10 million customers came into contact with approximately five SAS employees, and this contact lasted an average of 15 seconds each time. Thus, SAS is "created" 50 million times a year, 15 seconds at a time. These 50 million "moments of truth" are the moments that ultimately determine whether SAS will succeed or fail as a company. They are the moments when we must prove to our customers that SAS is their best alternative.[6]

Each service business faces similar challenges in defining and managing the "moments of truth" its customers will encounter.

Figure 2.6: The Servuction System

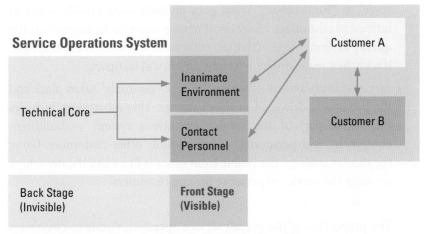

Source: Adapted and expanded from an original concept by Eric Langeard and Pierre Eiglier.

The Servuction System

French researchers Pierre Eiglier and Eric Langeard were the first to conceptualize the service business as a system that integrates marketing, operations, and customers. They coined the term *servuction system* (combining the terms "service" and "production"), which is part of the service organization's physical environment visible to and experienced by customers.[7] The servuction model in Fig. 2.6 shows all the interactions that together make up a typical customer experience in a high-contact service. Customers interact with the service environment, service employees, and even other customers present during the service encounter. Each type of interaction can create value (e.g., a pleasant environment, friendly and competent employees, or other customers who are interesting to observe) or destroy value (e.g., another customer blocking your view in a movie theater). Firms have to "engineer" all interactions to make sure their customers get the service experience they came for.

The servuction system consists of a technical core and service delivery system:

- *Technical core* — where inputs are processed and the elements of the service product are created. This technical core is typically back-stage and invisible to the customer (e.g., kitchen of a restaurant).

In theater, the invisible components can be termed "back-stage" or "back office", while the visible components can be termed "front-stage" or "front office".[8] What goes on back-stage usually is not of interest to customers. However, if what goes on back-stage affects the quality of front-stage activities, customers will notice. For example, if a kitchen reads orders wrongly, diners will be upset.

- *Service delivery system* — where the final "assembly" takes place and the product is delivered to the customer. This sub-system includes the visible part of the service operations system — buildings, equipment, and personnel — and possibly other customers. Using the theater analogy, the visible front office is like a live theater where we stage the service experience for our customers.

The proportion of the overall service operation visible to customers varies according to the level of customer contact. Because high-contact services directly involve the physical person of the customer, the visible component of the entire service operation tends to be substantial, and many interactions — or "moments of truth" — have to be managed. In contrast, low-contact services usually have most of the service operations system back-stage with front-stage elements limited to online, telephone, or mail contacts. Here, customers normally do not see the "factory" where the work is performed, making the design, and management of such facilities is much easier. For example, credit card customers may never have to visit a physical bank — they only transact online and may once in a while talk to a service employee on the phone if there is a problem, and there is very little left of the "theater" performance.

Theater as Metaphor for Service Delivery: An Integrative Perspective

As service delivery consists of a series of events that customers experience as a *performance,* the theater is a good metaphor for services and creation of service experiences through the servuction system[9]. This metaphor is a particularly useful approach for high-contact service providers, such as physicians and hotels, and for businesses that serve many people simultaneously, such as hospitals, professional sports facilities, and entertainment. The stages (i.e., service facilities) and the members of the cast (i.e., the frontline personnel) will be discussed next:

- *Service facilities.* Imagine service facilities as the *stage* on which the drama unfolds. Sometimes, the setting changes from one act to another (e.g., when airline passengers move from the entrance to the terminal, to check-in stations, and then on to the boarding gate, and finally step inside the aircraft). Some stages have minimal "props," such as a taxi for instance. In contrast, other stages have more elaborate "props", such as resort hotels with elaborate architecture, luxurious interior design, and lush landscaping.
- *Personnel.* The front-stage personnel are like the members of a crew playing roles as *actors* in a drama supported by a backstage production team. In some instances, service personnel are expected to wear special costumes when on stage (such as the fanciful uniforms often worn by hotel doormen, or the more basic brown uniforms worn by UPS drivers).

The theater metaphor also includes the roles of the players on stage and the scripts they have to follow, which is discussed next.

Role and Script Theories

The actors in a theater need to know what roles they play and familiarize themselves with the script. Similarly, in service encounters, knowledge of role and script theories can help organizations better understand, design, and manage both employee and customer behaviors during service encounters.

Role Theory

If we view service delivery from a theatrical perspective, then both employees and customers act out their parts in the performance according to predetermined roles. Stephen Grove and Ray Fisk define a role as "a set of behavior patterns learned through experience and communication, to be performed by an individual in a certain social interaction in order to attain maximum effectiveness in goal accomplishment".[10] Roles have also been defined as combinations of social cues or expectations of society that guide behavior in a specific setting or context. The satisfaction and productivity of both parties depend on role congruence, or the extent to which each person acts out his or her prescribed role during a service encounter. Employees must perform their roles in accordance to customer expectations or risk dissatisfying customers. As a customer must "play by the rules" or risk causing problems for the firm, its employees, and even other customers. If either party is uncomfortable in their roles or if they do not act accordingly, it will affect the satisfaction and productivity of both parties.

Script Theory

Much like a movie script, a service script specifies the sequences of behavior employees and customers are expected to learn and follow during service delivery. Employees receive formal training. Customers learn scripts through experience, communication with others, and through designed communications and education. The more experience a customer has with a service company, the more familiar that particular script becomes. Unwillingness to learn a new script may be a reason not to switch to a competing organization. Any deviations from this known script may frustrate both customers and employees, and can lead to dissatisfaction. If a company decides to change a service script (for example, by using technology to transform a high-contact service into a low-contact one), service personnel and customers need to be educated about the new approach and the benefits it provides.

Many service dramas are tightly scripted (e.g., the flight attendants' scripts for economy class), which reduces variability and ensures uniform quality. However, not all services involve tightly scripted performances. Scripts tend to be more flexible for providers of highly customized services — designers, educators, consultants — and may vary by situation and customer.

Fig. 2.7 shows a script for teeth cleaning and a simple dental examination, involving three players — the patient, the receptionist, and the dental hygienist. Each has a specific role to play, reflecting what he or she brings to the encounter. The role of the customer (who is probably not looking forward to this encounter) is different from that of the two service providers, and the receptionist's role differs from the hygienist's, reflecting their distinctive jobs. This script is driven partly by the need to run an efficient dental office, but even more importantly, by the need to perform a technical task proficiently and safely (note the mask and gloves). The core service of examining and cleaning teeth can only be accomplished satisfactorily if the patient cooperates during the delivery of the service.

Role and Script Theory Complement Each Other

Think of professor and student *roles* in a class. Typically, a professor's role is to deliver a well-structured lecture, focusing on the key topics assigned for that day, making them interesting, and engaging students in discussion. A student is basically supposed to come to class prepared and on time, listen attentively, participate in discussions, and not disrupt the class. By contrast, the opening portion of the *script* for a lecture describes specific actions to be taken by each party. For instance, students should arrive at the lecture hall before class starts, select a seat, sit down, and open their laptops; the professor enters, puts notes on the table, turns on the notebook and LCD projector, greets the class, makes any preliminary announcements needed, and starts the class on time.

The frameworks offered by the two theories are complementary and describe the behavior during the encounter from two different perspectives. Excellent service marketers understand both perspectives and proactively define, communicate and train their employees and customers in their roles and service scripts to achieve a performance that yields high customer satisfaction and service productivity.

The core components of the service delivery system and design of scripts and roles will be explored in detail in the later chapters of this book. Specifically, Chap. 7 focuses on educating customers to move through the service delivery process to play their part in the service performance; Chap. 8 covers how to design scripts and roles; Chap. 10 discusses the process of designing the service environment, and Chap. 11 explores how to manage service employees.

Perceived Control Theory[11]

Another underlying dimension of every service encounter is perceived control, which holds that customers have a need for control during the service encounter, and that control is a major driving force of their behavior and satisfaction.[12] The higher the level of perceived control during a service situation, the higher their level of satisfaction will be.

Figure 2.7: Script for teeth cleaning and simple dental examination

 Patient	 Receptionist	 Dental Hygienist
1. Phone for appointment		
	2. Confirms needs and sets date	
3. Arrive at dental office		
	4. Greets patient; verify purpose; direct to waiting room; notify hygienist of arrival	
		5. Review notes on patient
6. Sits in waiting room		
		7. Greets patient and leads way to treatment room
8. Enters room, sits in dental chair		
		9. Verify medical and dental history; ask about any issues since previous visit
10. Respond to hygienist's questions		
		11. Place protective cover over patient's clothes
		12. Lower dental chair, put on own protective face mask, gloves and glasses
		13. Inspect patient's teeth (option to ask questions)
		14. Place suction device in patient's mouth

		15. Use high-speed equipment and hand tools to clean teeth in sequence
		16. Remove suction device; complete cleaning process
		17. Raise chair to sitting position; ask patient to rinse
18. Rinse mouth		
		19. Remove and dispose of mask and gloves; remove glasses
		20. Complete notes on treatment; return patient file to receptionist
		21. Remove cover for patient
		22. Give patient free toothbrush; offer advice on personal dental care for future
23. Rise from chair		
		24. Thank patient and say goodbye
25. Leave treatment room		
	26. Greet patient; confirm treatment received; present bill	
27. Pay bill		
	28. Give receipt; agree on date for next appointment; document agreed-upon date	
29. Take appointment card		
	30. Thank patient and say good-bye	
31. Leave dental office		

The perception of control can be managed via different types, including behavioral, decisional, and cognitive control.

Behavioral control means that the customer can change the situation and ask for customization beyond what the firm typically offers (e.g., by asking frontline employees to accommodate a special arrangement for a romantic candle light dinner). Decisional control means that the customer can choose between two or more standardized options, but without changing either option (e.g., choose between two tables in a restaurant). Cognitive control refers to the customer understanding why something happens (e.g., a flight delay due to a technical problem with the aircraft), and knowing what will happen next (also called predictive control, e.g., know how long the flight will be delayed). We are often mollified when someone keeps us informed about the situation.[13]

If you imagine yourself in these situations, you can quickly understand how having these types of control immediately makes one feel better. In contrast, imagine that you do not have control and how it would make you feel — for instance, you do not know why the flight is delayed or how long it will be. The same applies also to online services — users want to know where they are on a website, whether their transaction is being processed or whether the site "died" on them (that is why websites usually have a moving icon or processing bar to show that it is still processing). Even self-service machines like ATMs are designed to make the user feel in control. They make noises to indicate that they are processing and have not simply swallowed the user's card. These sounds are often generated by a chip, as the machine alone would be silent for much of the process.

In short, it is important to design perceived control into service encounters. However, if processes, scripts, and roles are tightly defined (as is the case for self-service technologies and highly scripted services such as fast-food and consumer banking), the scope for customization is limited. This means, firms cannot give much behavioral control as carefully designed processes would simply collapse, and productivity and quality would suffer. In those cases, firms can focus on giving customers decisional control (e.g., offer two or more fixed options), cognitive control (e.g., hospitals often go through great lengths to explain what is being done and why), and predictive control (e.g., never let the customer wait without giving an indication how long the wait will be). The good news is that perceived control is largely a compensatory additive, which means

Figure 2.8: The expectancy-disconfirmation model of satisfaction

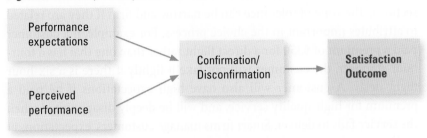

Source: Adapted from Richard L. Oliver, Satisfaction: A Behavioral Perspective on the Consumer, 1997, New York: McGraw-Hill, p. 110.

that a reduction in behavioral control can be compensated through higher decisional and cognitive control.

POST-ENCOUNTER STAGE[14]

The last stage of service consumption is the post-encounter stage which involves consumers' attitudinal and behavioral responses to the service experience. Important consumer responses are customer satisfaction, service quality perceptions, repeat purchase, and customer loyalty. Each concept is discussed in detail in the following sections.

Customer Satisfaction

In the post-encounter stage, customers evaluate the service performance they have experienced and compare it with their prior expectations. Service expectations is closely related to customer satisfaction and delight.

The Expectancy-Disconfirmation Model of Satisfaction

Satisfaction is a judgment following a series of consumer product interactions. Most customer satisfaction studies are based on the expectancy-disconfirmation model of satisfaction (Fig. 2.8).[15] In the model, confirmation, or disconfirmation of pre-consumption expectations is the essential determinant of satisfaction.

Where do service expectations in our satisfaction model come from? During the decision-making process, customers assess the attributes and risks related to a service offering. In the process, they develop expectations about how the service they choose will perform (i.e., predicted, desired, and adequate service levels discussed in the consumer decision making section). The zone of tolerance can be narrow and firm if they are related to attributes important in the choice process. For example, if a customer paid a premium of $350 for a direct flight rather than one that has a four-hour stopover, the customer will not take it lightly if there is a six-hour flight delay. A customer will also have high expectations if he paid a premium for high-quality service, and will be deeply disappointed when the service fails to deliver. Smart firms manage customers' expectations at each step in the service encounter so that customers expect what the firm can deliver.[16]

During and after consumption, consumers experience the service performance and compare it to their expectations. Satisfaction judgments are then formed based on this comparison. If performance perceptions are worse than expected, it is called *negative disconfirmation*. If performance is better than expected, it is called *positive disconfirmation*, and if it is as expected, then it is simply called *confirmation of expectations*.[17]

Customers will be reasonably satisfied as long as perceived performance falls within the zone of tolerance, that is, above the adequate service level. If performance perceptions approach or exceed desired levels, customers will be very pleased. Satisfied customers are more likely to make repeat purchases, remain loyal, and spread positive word-of-mouth.[18] However, if the service experience does not meet their expectations, customers may suffer in silence, complain about poor service quality, or switch providers in the future.[19]

The same attributes used in the choice process are also used in satisfaction evaluation, whereby the individual satisfaction judgments are aggregated for each consumer to evaluate the overall customer satisfaction. Satisfaction with service attributes thus results from the experience of attribute — specific performance strongly influences consumers' overall satisfaction.

Multi-attribute models help to better understand the formation process of customer satisfaction. Especially, they help managers identify specific attributes with strong impacts on overall satisfaction, which is especially important if customers are satisfied with some attributes but dissatisfied with others.[20] Understanding this helps managers to cement the strengths of the firm's services and focus improvement efforts on where it matters the most.

Service Quality

Since services are intangible, it is hard to evaluate the quality of a service compared to goods. In addition, customers often experience the servuction process, so a distinction needs to be drawn between the process of service delivery and the actual output (or outcome) of the service.[21] We define excellent service quality as a high standard of performance that *consistently* meets or exceeds customer expectations. Service quality can be difficult to manage, even when failures are tangible in nature. Nevertheless, it is critical to improve service quality and keep it at high levels, as it is a key driver of important customer behaviors, including word-of-mouth recommendations, repurchasing, and loyalty.

Customer Satisfaction versus Service Quality[22]

Both customer satisfaction and service quality are defined as contrasting customers' expectations with their performance perceptions. Yet, satisfaction and service quality are very different constructs. Specifically, satisfaction is an evaluation of a single consumption experience, a fleeting judgment, and a direct and immediate response to that experience. In contrast, service quality refers to relatively stable attitudes and beliefs about a firm, which can differ significantly from satisfaction. To illustrate, a customer can be dissatisfied with a particular visit to a favorite Starbucks outlet, but still thinks the café is fantastic with great service. Of course, satisfaction and quality are linked. While the perceptions of a firm's overall service quality is relatively stable, it will change over time in the same direction as transaction-specific satisfaction ratings.[23] And it is service quality that in turn influences behavioral intentions (e.g., positive word-of-mouth and repurchase intentions).

Sometimes people also refer to the transaction quality (e.g., the quality of food, the friendliness of the server, and the ambiance of a restaurant), which then relates to attribute satisfaction (e.g., satisfaction with food and service in a restaurant). Both are transaction-specific and determine overall customer satisfaction, which in turn drives service quality beliefs (whether at the attribute or overall level). It is the interchangeable use of these terms that confuses people. When you distinguish between transaction-specific judgments and more stable beliefs and attitudes, the difference in meaning can be clearly seen. That is, attribute-specific transaction quality and satisfaction precedes overall

Figure 2.9: From attribute satisfaction to repeat purchase

consumer satisfaction, which in turn influences the formation of beliefs regarding a firm's service quality for specific attributes and overall.

Note that consumers' repurchase intentions are influenced by their general beliefs about the service quality of the firm at the time of their next purchase decision, and less so by individual, transaction-specific satisfaction judgments formed during and after consumption. That is, consumers try to predict how good the next service transaction will be, as was discussed in context of the multi-attribute choice model. For example, consumers might return to a hairstylist if they think the stylist is generally fantastic, even if they were unhappy at their last visit. They may view the poor experience as an exception. However, a second or even third dissatisfaction evaluation will reduce the overall perception of the firm's service quality more dramatically and jeopardize repeat visits (Fig. 2.9).

Dimensions of Service Quality

Valarie Zeithaml, Leonard Berry, and A. Parasuraman have conducted intensive research on service quality and identified 10 dimensions used by consumers in evaluating service quality (Table 2.3). In subsequent research, they found a high degree of correlation between several of these variables and consolidated them into five broad dimensions:

- *Tangibles* (appearance of physical elements)
- *Reliability* (dependable and accurate performance)
- *Responsiveness* (promptness and helpfulness)
- *Assurance* (credibility, security, competence, and courtesy)
- *Empathy* (easy access, good communications, and customer understanding)[24]

Table 2.3: Generic Dimensions used by Customers to Evaluate Service Quality

Dimensions of Service Quality	Definition	Sample Illustrations
Tangibles	Appearance of physical facilities, equipment, personnel, and communication materials	Are the hotel's facilities attractive? Is my accountant dressed appropriately? Is my bank statement easy to understand?
Reliability	Ability to perform the promised service dependably and accurately	Does my lawyer call me back when promised? Is my telephone bill free of errors? Is my TV repaired right the first time?
Responsiveness	Willingness to help customers and provide prompt service	When there is a problem, does the firm resolve it quickly? Is my stockbroker willing to answer my questions? Is the cable TV company willing to give me a specific time when the installer will show up?
Assurance • Credibility	Trustworthiness, believability, honesty of the service provider	Does the hospital have a good reputation? Does my stockbroker refrain from pressuring me to trade? Does the repair firm guarantee its work?
• Security	Freedom from danger, risk, or doubt	Is it safe for me to use the bank's ATMs at night? Is my credit card protected against unauthorized use? Can I be sure that my insurance policy provides complete coverage?
• Competence	Possession of the skills and knowledge required to perform the service	Can the bank teller process my transaction without fumbling around? Is my health insurance able to obtain the information I need when I call? Does the dentist appear to be competent?
• Courtesy	Politeness, respect, consideration, and friendliness of contact personnel	Does the flight attendant have a pleasant demeanor? Are the telephone operators consistently polite when answering my calls? Does the plumber take off muddy shoes before stepping on my carpet?

Empathy		
• Access	Approachability and ease of contact	How easy is it for me to talk to a supervisor when I have a problem? Does the airline have a 24-hour, toll-free phone number? Is the hotel conveniently located?
• Communication	Listening to customers and keeping them informed in the language they can understand	When I have a complaint, is the manager willing to listen to me? Does my doctor avoid using technical jargon? Does the electrician call when he or she is unable to keep a scheduled appointment?
• Understanding the customer	Making the effort to know customers and their needs	Does someone in the hotel recognize me as a regular guest? Does my stockbroker try to determine my specific financial objectives? Is the moving company willing to accommodate my schedule?

Measuring Service Quality

To measure service quality, Valarie Zeithaml and her colleagues developed a survey instrument called SERVQUAL.[25] It is based on the premise that customers evaluate a firm's service quality by comparing their perceptions of its service with their own expectations. SERVQUAL is seen as a generic measurement tool that can be applied across a broad spectrum of service industries. In its basic form, respondents answer 21 questions measuring their expectations of companies in a particular industry on a wide array of specific service characteristics (Table 2.4). Subsequently, they are asked a matching set of questions on their perceptions of a specific company whose services quality they assess. When perceived performance ratings are lower than expectations, service quality is poor, while the reverse indicates good quality.

Customizing SERVQUAL

SERVQUAL has been widely used in its generic form as shown in Table 2.4. However, many managers found that the measure provides more insights if it is adapted to their specific industry and context. Therefore, the majority of researchers omits from, adds to, or changes the list of

Table 2.4: The SERVQUAL Scale

The SERVQUAL scale includes five dimensions: tangibles, reliability, responsiveness, assurance and empathy. Within each dimension, several items are measured. There are many different formats in use, and we show the most basic 21 items for ideal perceptions below. The statements are accompanied by a seven-point scale, ranging from "strongly disagree = 1" to "strongly agree = 7".

The firm's performance is measured by rewording the same items (e.g., for item 1 in the table below: "XYZ firm has modern-looking equipment"). The difference between the scores for each item, dimension and for overall service quality is the computed and used as an indicator of a firm's level of service quality.

If measuring both ideal (or expected) and actual performance perceptions is not possible due to time constraints during the interview, both measures can also be combined by using the same 21 items (e.g., "modern looking equipment") and scale anchors "Lower than my desired service level", "The same as my desired service level", and "Higher than my desired service level".

Tangibles
- Excellent banks (refer to cable TV companies, hospitals, or the appropriate service business throughout the questionnaire) will have modern-looking equipment.
- The physical facilities at excellent banks will be visually appealing.
- Employees at excellent banks will be neat in appearance.
- Materials (e.g., brochures or statements) associated with the service will be visually appealing in an excellent bank.

Reliability
- When excellent banks promise to do something by a certain time, they will do so.
- Excellent banks will perform the service right the first time.
- Excellent banks will provide their services at the time they promise to do so.
- Excellent banks will insist on error-free records.

Responsiveness
- Employees of excellent banks will tell customers exactly when service will be performed.
- Employees of excellent banks will give prompt service to customers.
- Employees of excellent banks will always be willing to help customers.
- Employees of excellent banks will never be too busy to respond to customer requests.

Assurance
- The behavior of employees of excellent banks will instill confidence in customers.
- Customers of excellent banks will feel safe in their transactions.
- Employees of excellent banks will be consistently courteous with customers.
- Employees of excellent banks will have the knowledge to answer customer questions.

Empathy
- Excellent banks will give customers individual attention.
- Excellent banks will have operating hours convenient to all their customers.
- Excellent banks will have employees who give customers personal attention.
- The employees of excellent banks will understand the specific needs of their customers.
- Excellent banks have your best interest at heart.

Source: Adapted from Parasuraman, A., Zeithaml, V. A., and Berry, L. "SERVQUAL: A Multiple Item Scale for Measuring Consumer Perceptions of Service Quality," *Journal of Retailing* 64, (1988): 12–40.

statements used to measure service quality.[26] Other research suggests that SERVQUAL mainly measures two factors: intrinsic service quality (resembling what Grönroos termed functional quality) and extrinsic service quality (which refers to the tangible aspects of service delivery and resembles what Grönroos referred to as technical quality").[27]

These findings highlight the difficulty of measuring customer perceptions of service quality and the need to adapt dimensions and measures to specific research contexts. In any case, it is important for firms to understand how the dimensions of service quality apply to their business context so that they can measure service quality, diagnose shortfalls and then take actions to improve (this will be discussed in Chap. 14).

Customer Loyalty

Loyalty is a customer's willingness to continue patronizing a firm over the long-term, preferably on an exclusive basis, and recommending the firm's products to friends and associates. Customer loyalty extends beyond behavior and includes preference, liking, and future intentions.

The opposite of loyalty is defection, which is used to describe customers who drop off a company's radar screen and transfer their loyalty to another supplier. Not only does a rising defection rate indicate that something is wrong with quality (or that competitors offer better value), it may also be a leading indicator signaling a fall in profits. Big customers do not necessarily disappear overnight; they often may signal their mounting dissatisfaction by steadily reducing their purchases and shifting part of their business elsewhere.

Loyalty is an important outcome of satisfied customers who believe that the firm delivers great service. Customers are not inherently loyal to any one firm. Rather, they need a reason to consolidate their buying and then stay with a particular supplier. Delivering great service experiences that satisfy your customers and build positive service quality perceptions is the first and probably the most important step toward building a loyal customer base. Later in this book, we discuss in-depth a number of strategies and tools that are key for driving loyalty, such as the Wheel of Loyalty in Chap. 12, and complaint management and service recovery in Chap. 13.

CONCLUSION

The three-stage model of service consumption — prepurchase, service encounter, and post-encounter — helps us to understand how individuals recognize their needs; search for alternative solutions; address perceived risks; choose, use, and experience a particular service; and finally, evaluate their service experience resulting in a customer satisfaction outcome. The various models explored for each of the stages are complementary and together provide a rich and deep understanding of consumer behavior in a services context. In all types of services, managing customer behavior in the three stages of service consumption effectively is central to creating satisfied customers who will be willing to enter into long-term relationships with the service provider. As such, gaining a better understanding of customer behavior should lie at the heart of all services marketing strategies, as discussed in the remainder of this book.

CHAPTER SUMMARY

Pre-purchase Stage

Stages of Service Consumption

- ► Awareness of need
  - Information search
  - Clarify needs
  - Explore solutions
  - Identify alternative service products and suppliers

- ► Evaluation of alternatives (solutions and suppliers)
  - Review supplier information (e.g., advertising, brochures, websites)
  - Review information from third parties (e.g., published reviews, ratings, comments on the Web, blogs, complaints to public agencies, satisfaction ratings, awards)
  - Discuss options with service personnel
  - Get advice and feedback from third-party advisors and other customers

- ► Make decisions on service purchase and often make reservations

Key Concepts

- ► Need arousal
- ► Evoked set
- ► Consideration set
- ► Multi-attribute model

- ► Search, experience, and credence attributes
- ► Perceived risk

- ► Formation of expectations: desired service level, predicted service level, adequate service level, zone of tolerance

Service Encounter Stage

Stages of Service Consumption

- ► Request service from a chosen supplier or initiate self-service (payment may be upfront or billed later)
- ► Service delivery by personnel or self-service

Key Concepts

- ► Moments of truth
- ► Service encounters
- ► Servuction system
- ► Theater as a metaphor
- ► Role and script theories
- ► Perceived control theory

Post-encounter Stage

Stages of Service Consumption

- ► Evaluation of service performance
- ► Future intentions

Key Concepts

- ► Confirmation/ Disconfirmation of expectations
- ► Dissatisfaction, satisfaction, and delight
- ► Service Quality
- ► Word-of-mouth
- ► Repurchase
- ► Loyalty

CHAPTER 3

Positioning Services in Competitive Markets

To succeed in our over-communicated society, a company must create a position in the prospect's mind, a position that takes into consideration not only a company's own strengths and weaknesses, but those of its competitors as well.

Al Reis and Jack Trout
Thought leaders who coined the term "positioning"
as related to marketing

The essence of strategy is choosing to perform activities differently than rivals do.

Michael Porter
Professor at Harvard Business School and
leading authority on competitive strategy

CUSTOMER-DRIVEN SERVICES MARKETING STRATEGY

As competition intensifies in the service sector, it is becoming more important for service organizations to differentiate their products in ways meaningful to customers. This is especially true for many mature service industries (e.g., banking, insurance, hospitality, and education), where for a firm to grow, it has to take market share from its competitors or expand into new markets. However, ask a group of managers from different service businesses on how they compete, and chances are many will say simply, "on service". Press them a little further, and they may add words and phrases such as "value for money," "service quality," "our people," or "convenience." None of this is very helpful to a marketing specialist who is trying to develop a meaningful value proposition and a viable business model for a service product that will enable it to compete profitably in the marketplace.

What makes consumers or institutional buyers select — and remain loyal to — one supplier over another? Terms such as "service" typically subsume a variety of specific characteristics, ranging from the speed with which a service is delivered to the quality of interactions between customers and service personnel; and from avoiding errors to providing desirable "extras" to supplement the core service. Likewise, "convenience" could refer to a service that is delivered at a convenient location, available at convenient times, or easy to use. Without knowing which product features are of specific interest to customers, it is hard for managers to develop an appropriate strategy. In a highly competitive environment, there is a risk that customers will perceive little real difference between competing alternatives and therefore make their choices based on who offers the lowest price.

Managers thus need to think systematically about all aspects of the service offering and to emphasize competitive advantage on attributes that will be valued by customers in their target segment(s). A systematic way to do this typically starts with an analysis of Customers, Competitors and Company, collectively often referred to as the 3 'C's. This analysis then helps a firm to determine the key elements of its services positioning strategy, which are Segmentation, targeting and positioning, frequently called **STP** by marketing experts. The basic steps involved in identifying a suitable market position are shown in Fig. 3.1. The desired positioning has wide-reaching implications on firm's services marketing strategy,

Figure 3.1: Developing a services marketing positioning strategy

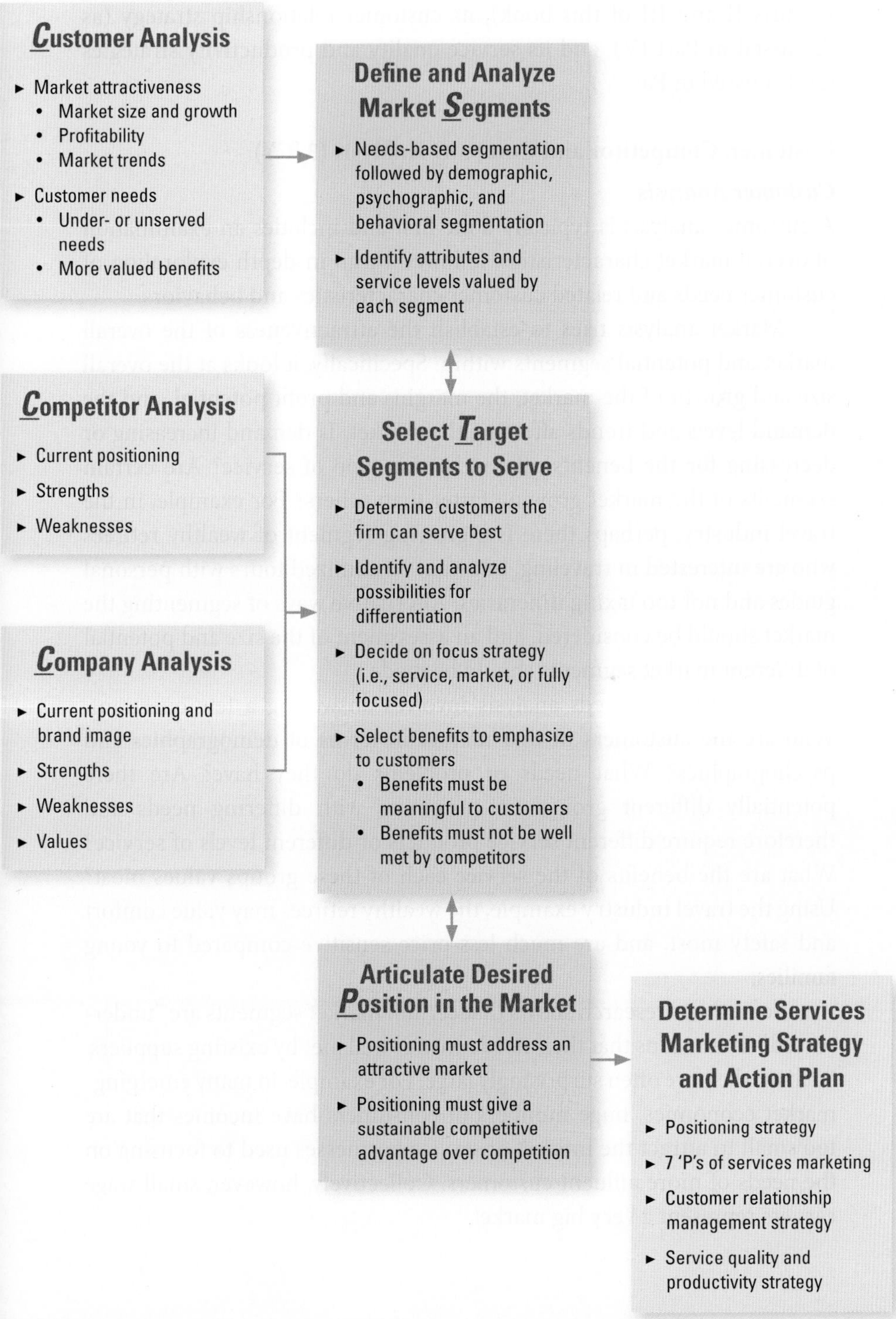

Customer Analysis

► Market attractiveness
  • Market size and growth
  • Profitability
  • Market trends
► Customer needs
  • Under- or unserved needs
  • More valued benefits

Define and Analyze Market Segments

► Needs-based segmentation followed by demographic, psychographic, and behavioral segmentation
► Identify attributes and service levels valued by each segment

Competitor Analysis

► Current positioning
► Strengths
► Weaknesses

Select Target Segments to Serve

► Determine customers the firm can serve best
► Identify and analyze possibilities for differentiation
► Decide on focus strategy (i.e., service, market, or fully focused)
► Select benefits to emphasize to customers
  • Benefits must be meaningful to customers
  • Benefits must not be well met by competitors

Company Analysis

► Current positioning and brand image
► Strengths
► Weaknesses
► Values

Articulate Desired Position in the Market

► Positioning must address an attractive market
► Positioning must give a sustainable competitive advantage over competition

Determine Services Marketing Strategy and Action Plan

► Positioning strategy
► 7 'P's of services marketing
► Customer relationship management strategy
► Service quality and productivity strategy

including the development of its 7 'P's of Services Marketing (as discussed in Parts II and III of this book), its customer relationship strategy (as discussed in Part IV), and its service quality and productivity strategies (as discussed in Part V).

Customer, Competitor and Company Analysis (3 'C's)

Customer Analysis

A customer analysis is typically done first and includes an examination of overall market characteristics, followed by an in-depth exploration of customer needs and related customer characteristics and behaviors.

Market analysis tries to establish the attractiveness of the overall market and potential segments within. Specifically, it looks at the overall size and growth of the market, the margins and profit potential, and the demand levels and trends affecting the market. Is demand increasing or decreasing for the benefits offered by this type of service? Are certain segments of the market growing faster than others? For example, in the travel industry, perhaps there is a growing segment of wealthy retirees who are interested in traveling, but want customized tours with personal guides and not too taxing itineraries. Alternative ways of segmenting the market should be considered, and an assessment of the size and potential of different market segments should be made.

The customer-needs analysis involves answering a few questions. Who are the customers in that market in terms of demographics and psychographics? What needs or problems do they have? Are there potentially different groups of customers with differing needs and therefore require different service products or different levels of service? What are the benefits of the service each of these groups values most? Using the travel industry example, the wealthy retirees may value comfort and safety most, and are much less price sensitive compared to young families.

Sometimes research shows that certain market segments are "underserved." This means that their needs are not well met by existing suppliers. Such markets are often surprisingly large. For example, in many emerging-market economies, huge numbers of consumers have incomes that are too small to attract the interest of service businesses used to focusing on the needs of more affluent customers. Collectively, however, small wage earners represent a very big market.

Competitor Analysis

Identification and analysis of competitors can provide a marketing strategist with a sense of competitors' strengths and weaknesses. Relating these to the company analysis in the next section should suggest what the opportunities for differentiation and competitive advantage might be, thereby enabling managers to decide which benefits could be emphasized to which target segments.

Company Analysis

In an internal corporate analysis, the objective is to identify the organization's strengths in terms of its current brand positioning and image, and the resources the organization has (financial, human labor and know-how, and physical assets). It also examines the organization's limitations or constraints, and how its values shape the way it does business. Using insights from this analysis, management should be able to select a limited number of target market segments that can be served with either existing or new services. The core question is how well can a company and its services address the needs and problems faced by each customer segment?

Segmentation, Targeting and Positioning (STP)

Linking customer and competitor analysis to company analysis allows the service organization to develop an effective positioning strategy. Here, the basic steps involved in identifying a suitable market position and developing a strategy to reach it are:

- *Segmentation* refers to the dividing of the population of possible customers into groups. A market segment is composed of a group of buyers who share common characteristics, needs, purchasing behavior, and/or consumption patterns. Effective segmentation groups buyers into segments in ways that result in as much similarity as possible on the relevant characteristics within each segment. Once customers with similar needs are grouped together, demographic, geographic, psychographic, and behavioral variables can be used to describe them. Customers in the same segment should have as similar needs as possible, but between segments, their needs should be as different as possible.

Table 3.1: Elements and Key Concepts of a Services Positioning Strategy

Elements of a Positioning Strategy	Key Concepts

Segmentation	• Segmenting service markets
	• Service attributes and service levels relevant for segmentation
	  – Important versus determinant attributes
	  – Establishing service levels

Targeting	• Targeting service markets through four focus strategies:
	  – Fully focused
	  – Market focused
	  – Service focused
	  – Unfocused

Positioning	• Positioning services in competitive markets • Using positioning maps to plot competitive strategy • Developing an effective positioning strategy

- *Targeting* refers to when a firm decides which segment(s) would most likely be interested in its service after segmenting and assessing the attractiveness of each segment, and focusing on how to serve them well.

- *Positioning* refers to the unique place that the firm and/or its service offerings occupy in the minds of its consumers. Before a firm can create a unique position for its service, it must first differentiate the service from that of their competitors. Hence, differentiation is the first step towards creating a unique positioning for a service.

Table 3.1 shows the key elements of services positioning strategy on the left-hand side and related concepts on the right-hand side. We will discuss each concept in the remainder of this chapter.

SEGMENTING SERVICE MARKETS

Segmentation is one of the most important concepts in marketing. Service firms vary widely in their abilities to serve different types of customers. Hence, rather than trying to compete in an entire market, perhaps against superior competitors, each firm should adopt a strategy of market segmentation, identifying those parts, or segments, of the market that it can serve best.

There are many ways to segment a market, and marketing experts typically combine and integrate several approaches. Traditionally, demographic segmentation (e.g., based on age, gender, and income) has frequently been used. However, this often does not result in meaningful segmentation as two people in the exact same demographics can exhibit very different buying behaviors (e.g., not all 20-year-old middle-class males feel and behave the same way). As a result, *psychographic segmentation* has become more popular as it reflects people's lifestyles, attitudes, and aspirations. Psychographic segmentation can be very useful in strengthening brand identity and creating an emotional connection with the brand, but may not necessarily map to behaviors and sales. *Behavioral segmentation* addresses this shortcoming as it focuses on observable behaviors, such as people being non-users, light users, or heavy users. *Needs-based segmentation* focuses on what customers truly want in a service and maps closely to the multi-attribute decision models discussed in Chap. 2 (e.g., a time and quality sensitive segment versus a price-sensitive segment). In addition, people often have different needs and their decision-making criteria vary according to:

- Purpose of using the service,
- Who makes the decision,
- Timing of use (time of day/week/season),
- Whether the individual is using the service alone or with a group, and if the latter, the composition of that group.

Consider the criteria that you might use when choosing a restaurant for lunch when you are (1) on vacation with friends or family, (2) meeting with a prospective business client, or (3) going for a quick meal with a co-worker. Given a reasonable selection of alternatives, it is unlikely that you would choose the same type of restaurant in each instance, let alone the same one. It is possible too, that if you left the decision to another person in the party, he or she would make a different choice. It is therefore important to be quite specific about the occasion and context a service is purchased for, and explicitly include that in the segmentation analysis.

Figure 3.2: Contiki targets young and fun-loving travelers

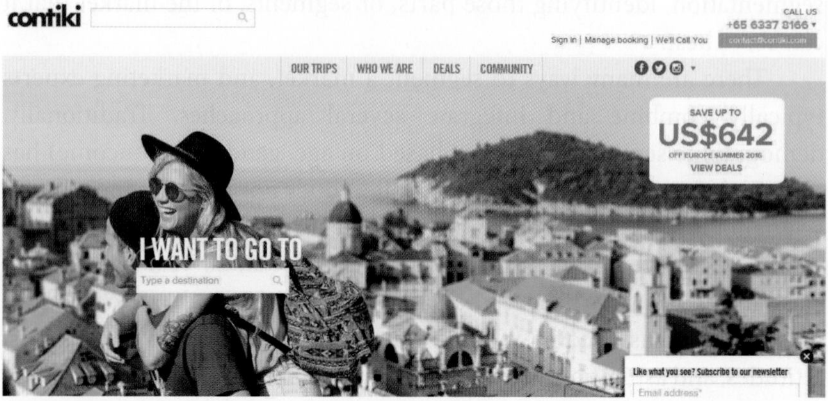

For companies to effectively segment a market, it is often best to start with a deep understanding of customers' needs. The availability of *big data* and marketing analytics on the cloud enables marketers to collect accurate and detailed information at the individual consumer level, allowing for very narrow and specific segmentation analyses.[1] Marketers can then overlay this understanding with demographic, psychographic, behavioral, and consumption context variables to further define and describe key segments in a market.[2]

Contiki Holiday is an example of a company that uses needs-based segmentation as a foundation, and then fine-tunes it with other types of segmentation. It found that some singles do not want to join tours where there are families. They prefer holidays where they can meet others with similar preferences (*needs-based segmentation*). Contiki serves this special group of people. In fact, it is a worldwide leader in holidays for the 18–35 age group (*demographic segmentation*) (Fig. 3.2). Some of its holiday packages are aimed at fun-loving youths. Contiki further segments its packages by catering to different lifestyles and budgets (*psychographic segmentation*). For example, those going to Europe can choose "High Energy" (for people who are outgoing and want event-packed day and night itineraries), "Camping" (for the budget-conscious exploring the same Europe for less), or "Discovery Plus" (with lots of sightseeing, extra excursions and more choices of accommodation and destinations).

Important versus Determinant Service Attributes

It is important to select the right needs and their corresponding service attributes for segmentation. Consumers usually make their choices among alternative service offerings on the basis of perceived differences between them. However, the attributes that distinguish competing services from one another may not always be the most important ones. For instance, many travelers rank "safety" as a very important attribute in their choice of an airline and avoid traveling in airlines with a poor safety reputation. However, after eliminating such alternatives from consideration, a traveler flying on major routes is still likely to have several choices of carriers available that are perceived as equally safe. Hence, safety is not usually an attribute that influences the customer's choice at this point.

Determinant attributes (i.e., those that actually determine buyers' choices among competing alternatives) are often lower on the list of service characteristics important to purchasers. However, they are the attributes where customers see significant differences among competing alternatives. For example, convenience of departure and arrival times, availability of frequent flyer miles and related loyalty privileges, quality of in-flight service, or the ease of making reservations might be determinant characteristics for business travelers when selecting an airline. For budget-conscious vacation travelers on the other hand, price might assume primary importance.

As discussed in Chap. 2, consumers may use different decision rules and therefore arrive at different decisions even though the important attributes are all the same. For example, in Table 2.1, the most important attribute is the quality of dry cleaning. However, if the consumer uses the conjunctive rule, depending on what the cut-offs are, the determinant attribute may actually be price, which is the third most important variable. Identifying determinant attributes is therefore crucial for effective positioning to make a firm's service stand out in the minds of its target customers.

Segmentation Based on Service Levels

Apart from identifying attributes to be used for segmentation, decisions must also be made on the service levels to offer on each attribute.[3] Some service attributes are easily quantified, while others are qualitative. For instance, price is a quantitative attribute. Punctuality of transport services can be expressed in terms of the percentage of trains, buses, or flights arriving within a specified number of minutes from the scheduled time. Both of these attributes are easy to understand and are therefore quantifiable. However, characteristics such as the quality of personal service or a hotel's degree of luxury are subject to individual interpretation. To facilitate both service design and performance measurement, each attribute needs to be operationalized and standards established. For instance, if customers say they value physical comfort, what does that mean for a hotel or an airline, beyond the size of the room or the seat? In a hotel context, does it refer to ambient conditions, such as absence of noise? Or to more visible, tangible elements such as the bed (e.g., Westin Hotels & Resorts use their "Heavenly Bed" to tangibalize their superior beds). In practice, hotel managers need to address both the ambient conditions and tangible elements.

Customers can often be segmented according to their willingness to give up some level of service for a lower price. Price-insensitive customers are willing to pay a relatively high price to obtain higher levels of service on each of the attributes important to them. In contrast, price-sensitive customers will look for an inexpensive service that offers a relatively low level of performance on many key attributes.

Segmentation helps to identify potential attributes and service levels that have different degrees of relevance for key market segments. Once the segment structure of a market is understood, the firm can then move on to determine which of those segments should be targeted.

TARGETING SERVICE MARKETS

Service firms vary widely in their abilities to serve different types of customers well. Hence, achieving competitive advantage usually requires a firm to be more focused, which will be discussed in the next section.

Achieving Competitive Advantage through Focus

It is usually not realistic for a firm to try to appeal to all potential buyers in a market, because customers are varied in their needs, purchasing behavior, and consumption patterns, and are often too numerous and

Figure 3.3: Basic focus strategies for services

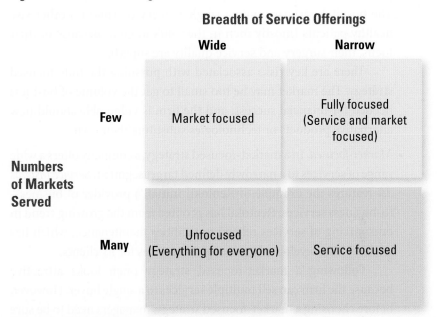

geographically widespread. Service firms also vary widely in their abilities to serve different types of customers well. Hence, a company needs to focus its efforts on customers it can serve best.

In marketing terms, *focus* means providing a relatively narrow product mix for a particular target segment. Nearly all successful service firms apply this concept. They identify the strategically important elements in their service operations and concentrate their resources on them. The extent of a company's focus can be described along two dimensions: market focus and service focus.[4] Market focus is the extent to which a firm serves few or many markets, while service focus describes the extent to which a firm offers few or many services. These two dimensions define the four basic focus strategies (Fig. 3.3)

- *Fully focused.* A fully focused organization provides limited range of services (perhaps just a single core product) to a narrow and specific market segment. For example, private jet charter services may focus on the high net-worth individuals or corporations. Developing recognized expertise in a well-defined niche may provide protection against would-be competitors and allows a firm to charge premium prices. An example of a fully focused firm is Shouldice Hospital. The hospital performs only a single surgery (hernia) on otherwise healthy patients (mostly men in their 40's to 60's). Because of their focus, their surgery and service quality are superb.

There are key risks associated with pursuing the fully focused strategy. The market may be too small to get the volume of business needed for financial success, and the firm is vulnerable should new alternative products or technologies substitute their own.

- *Market-focused.* In a market-focused strategy, a company offers a wide range of services to a narrowly defined target segment. *Service Insights 3.1* features the example of Rentokil Initial, a provider of business-to-business services. Rentokil has profited from the growing trend in outsourcing of services related to facilities maintenance, which has enabled it to develop a large range of services for its clients.

  Following a market-focused strategy often looks attractive because the firm can sell multiple services to a single buyer. However, before choosing a market-focused strategy, managers need to be sure their firms are capable of doing an excellent job of delivering each of the different services selected.

- *Service-focused.* Service-focused firms offer a narrow range of services to a fairly broad market. Lasik eye surgery clinics and Starbucks coffee shops follow this strategy, serving a broad customer base with a largely standardized product. However, as new segments are added, the firm needs to develop expertise in serving each segment. Furthermore, this strategy is likely to require a broader sales effort and greater investment in marketing communication, particularly in B2B markets.

- *Unfocused.* Many service providers fall into the unfocused category, because they try to serve broad markets and provide a wide range of services. The danger with this strategy is that unfocused firms often are "jacks of all trades and masters of none". In general, it is not a good idea, although public utilities and government agencies may be obliged to do so. A few departmental stores followed this strategy, and as a result, have been struggling against more focused competitors (e.g., hypermarkets and specialty stores).

It is recommended that firms have some sort of focus, whether on market segments and/or on services. How then should a firm select which of the three "focused" strategies to pursue? This decision relates back to the 3 'C's, segmentation, and targeting analyses. For example, a market-focused strategy may be appropriate if (a) customers value the convenience of one-stop-shopping, (b) the firm has the capabilities of delivering these multiple services better than competition, and/or (c) there are significant synergies in selling multiple services to the same customer (as is often the case in B2B services, see Rentokil Initial in *Service Insights 3.1*), which then enables the firm to either lower its price or provide better service.

A service-focused strategy can work best if the firm has a unique set of capabilities and resources to deliver a particular service exceptionally well or cost effectively. The firm may then want to ride on its advantage to deliver the service to a broad market (i.e., many customer segments at the same time).

Finally, a fully focused strategy may work well if a particular segment has very specific needs and requires unique design of the service environment, service processes, and interaction with the firm's frontline employees. Here, a fully focused strategy can deliver superb quality and at low costs because of its focus and experience. The Shouldice Hospital is a good example. The entire hospital is designed around the needs of hernia patients, making it the perfect hospital for people who are otherwise well and do not have to stay in bed. Patients get their perfect hospital experience and outstanding surgery quality all at a low price. However, this hospital cannot deal with any other types of patients.

The decision on focus is very important for service firms as they have distributed operations (i.e., each Starbuck's café is like a mini-factory), and any additional service offered increases the complexity of processes and the costs of the operation significantly. Likewise, even if a firm wants to sell the same basic service to different segments, it will find often that each additional segment may require some changes to the facility and processes to cater to their different needs and requirements. They also need to understand customer purchasing practices and preferences. In a B2B context, when trying to cross-sell additional services to the same client, many firms have been disappointed to find that decisions on purchasing the new service are made by an entirely different group within the client company.[5]

Inherent in focus and excellence are trade-offs. According to Frances Frei and Anne Morriss, there are a lot of heroic people in service organizations who feel compelled to be the best at everything. However, trying to do that will almost inevitably lead to mediocrity. The authors argue that excellence requires sacrifice (another way of looking at focus), and service firms should excel where it matters. For example, the Mayo Clinic decided to focus on reducing the time it takes for patients from scheduling an examination, to being examined by a doctor, and receiving a diagnosis in 24 hours or less. That is important for anxious patients who want to know fast what is wrong with them. However, focusing on speed does not allow patients to select a specific physician. Therefore, it is important to decide on areas where the firm does not have to perform as well (i.e., where their customers care less about) with the knowledge that it gives it the resources to excel where it matters most to their target customers.[6]

SERVICE INSIGHTS 3.1
Market-Focused Brand Across Multiple Services at Rentokil Initial

With revenue for 2015 at over £2.3 billion, Rentokil Initial is one of the world's largest business support service companies. The company has about 27,000 employees in over 50 countries where the "Rentokil" and "Initial" brands have come to represent innovation, deep expertise, and consistent quality of service. The UK-based firm has grown and developed from its origins as a manufacturer of rat poison and pesticide for killing wood-destroying beetles. When the firm realized it could make more money by providing a service to kill rodents than by selling products customers would use, it shifted to pest control and extermination services.

Through organic growth and acquisitions, Rentokil Initial has developed an extensive product range that includes testing and safety services, security, package delivery, interior plants landscaping (including sale or rental of tropical plants), specialized cleaning services, pest control, uniform rental and cleaning, clinical waste collection and disposal, personnel services, and a

washroom solutions service that supplies and maintains a full array of equipment, dispensers, and consumables. The firm sees its core competence as "the ability to carry out high-quality services on other people's premises through well-recruited, well-trained, and motivated staff".

Promoting use of additional services to existing customers is an important aspect of the firm's strategy. Initial Integrated Services offers clients the opportunity to move beyond the established concept of "bundling" services — bringing together several free-standing support services contracts from one provider — to full integration of services. Clients purchase sector-specific solutions that deliver multiple services, but feature just "one invoice, one account manager, one help desk, one contract, and one motivated service team".

According to former chief executive, Sir Clive Thomson: "Our objective has been to create a virtuous circle. We provide a quality service in industrial and commercial activities under the same brand-name, so that a customer satisfied with one Rentokil Initial Service is potentially a satisfied customer for another.

Although it was considered somewhat odd at the time, one of the reasons we moved into [providing and maintaining] tropical plants [for building interiors] was in fact to put the brand in front of decision makers. Our service people maintaining the plants go in through the front door and are visible to the customer. This contrasts with pest control where no one really notices unless we fail... The brand stands for honesty, reliability, consistency, integrity and technical leadership.

Investment in research and development (R&D) ensures constant improvement in its many service lines. For example, the company has built the RADAR intelligent rodent trap. RADAR attracts rats and mice into a sealable chamber and kills them humanely by injecting carbon dioxide. Using Rentokil's unique "PestConnect" technology, the trap causes emails to be sent to the customer and the local branch when a rodent is caught, and a Rentokil technician receives a text message identifying which unit has been activated at which customer's premises, and its precise location. PestConnect checks each individual RADAR unit every 10 minutes, 24/7. Getting information in real time enables technicians to remove dead rodents promptly and to control future infestation better.

Rentokil Initial's success lies in its ability to position each of its many business services in terms of the company's core brand values, which include providing superior standards of customer care and using the most technologically advanced services and products. The brand image is strengthened through physical evidence in terms of distinctive uniforms, vehicle color schemes, and use of the corporate logo.

Sources: Clive Thompson, "Rentokil Initial: Building a Strong Corporate Brand for Growth and Diversity," in F. Gilmore (ed.) *Brand Warriors* (London: HarperCollinsBusiness, 1997), pp. 123–124; http://www.rentokil-initial.com/, accessed 3 February 2016.

PRINCIPLES OF POSITIONING SERVICES

Positioning strategy is concerned with creating, communicating, and maintaining distinctive differences that will be noticed and valued by customers the firm would most like to develop a long-term relationship with. Successful positioning requires managers to understand their target customers' preferences, their conception of value, and the characteristics of their competitors' offerings. Price and product attributes are the two of the 4 'P's of marketing most commonly associated with positioning strategy. For services, however, positioning often relates also to other 'P's of the services marketing mix, including service processes (e.g., their convenience, ease of use), distribution systems, service schedules, locations, services environment, and service personnel. Competitive strategy can take many different routes. George Day observes:

> *The diversity of ways a business can achieve a competitive advantage quickly defeats any generalizations or facile prescriptions... First and foremost, a business must set itself apart from its competition. To be successful, it must identify and promote itself as the best provider of attributes that are important to target customers.*[7]

Jack Trout distilled the essence of positioning into the following four principles:[8]

Figure 3.4: Visa has one simple message globally

Reprinted with permission from Visa

Figure 3.5: For powerful positioning, a firm needs to set itself apart from its competitors

"In hindsight, I'd say my first mistake was letting my competitors advertise on my website."

1. A company must establish a position in the minds of its targeted customers.

2. The position should be singular, providing one simple and consistent message (Fig. 3.4).

3. The position must set a company apart from its competitors (Fig. 3.5).

4. A company cannot be all things to all people — it must focus its efforts.

These principles apply to any type of organization that competes for customers. Firms must understand the principles of positioning in order to develop an effective competitive position. The concept of positioning offers valuable insights by forcing service managers to analyze their firm's existing offerings and provide specific answers to the following six questions:

1. What does our firm currently stand for in the minds of current and potential customers?

2. What customers do we serve now, and which ones would we like to target in the future?

3. What is the value proposition for each of our current service offerings, and what market segments is each one targeted at?

4. How does each of our service products differ from those of our competitors?

5. How well do customers in the chosen target segments perceive our service offerings as meeting their needs?

6. What changes do we need to make to our service offerings in order to strengthen our competitive position within our target segment(s)?

One of the challenges in developing a viable positioning strategy is to avoid the trap of investing too much in points of difference that can easily be copied. As researchers Kevin Keller, Brian Sternthal, and Alice Tybout note: "Positioning needs to keep competitors out, not draw them in".[9] When Roger Brown and Linda Mason, founders of the Bright Horizons chain of childcare centers were developing their service concept and business model, they took a long, hard look at the industry.[10] Discovering that for-profit childcare companies had adopted low-cost strategies, Brown and Mason selected a different approach that competitors would find very difficult to copy. In an industry with low barriers of entry and a lot of competition, Bright Horizons managed to find a niche position and differentiate itself from the competition. They linked up with employers instead of individual parents, emphasized service quality, and used accreditation as a selling point (see *Service Insights 3.2*)

SERVICE INSIGHTS 3.2
Positioning a Chain of Child Care Centers
Away from the Competition

Roger Brown and Linda Mason met at business school, following previous experience as management consultants. After graduation, they operated programs for refugee children in Cambodia and then ran a "Save the Children" relief program in East Africa. When they returned to the US, they saw a need for childcare centers that would provide caring, educational environments, and give parents confidence in their children's well-being.

Through research, they discovered an industry that had many weaknesses. There were no barriers to entry, profit margins were low, the industry was labor intensive, there were low economies of scale, there was no clear brand differentiation, and there was a lack of regulation in the industry. Brown and Mason developed a service concept that would allow them to turn these industry weaknesses into strengths for their own company, Bright Horizons. Instead of marketing their services directly to parents — a one-customer-at-a-time sale — Bright Horizons formed partnerships with companies seeking to offer an on-site day-care center for employees with small children. The advantages included:

- A powerful, low-cost marketing channel.
- A partner/customer who supplied the funds to build and equip the center and would therefore want to help Bright Horizons to achieve its goal of delivering high-quality care.
- Benefits for parents who would be attracted to a Bright Horizons center (rather than competing alternatives) as a result of its nearness to their own workplace, thus decreasing traveling time and offering a greater peace of mind.

Bright Horizons offered a high pay and benefits package to attract the best staff so that they could provide quality service, one aspect that was lacking in many of the other providers. Since traditional approaches to childcare either did not have a proper teaching plan, or had strict, cookie-cutter lesson plans, Bright Horizons developed a flexible teaching plan. It was called "World at Their Fingertips" and had a course outline, but it also gave teachers control over daily lesson plans.

The company sought accreditation for its centers from the National Association for the Education of Young Children (NAEYC) and actively promoted this. Bright Horizons' emphasis on quality meant that it could meet or exceed the highest local and state government licensing standards. As a result, the lack of regulation became an opportunity, not a threat, for Bright Horizons and gave it a competitive edge.

With the support and help from its clients, which included many high-tech firms, Bright Horizons developed innovative technologies such as streaming video of its classrooms to the parents' desktop computers; digitally scanned or photographed artwork; electronic posting of menus, calendars, and student assessments; as well as online student assessment capabilities. All of these served to differentiate Bright Horizons and helped it to stay ahead of the competition.

Bright Horizons sees labor as a competitive advantage. It seeks to recruit and retain the best people. In 2014, it had been listed for the 14th time as one of the "100 Best Companies to Work for in America" by FORTUNE magazine. By then, Bright Horizons had some 20,000 employees globally, and was operating for more than 700 clients organizations in the US, Canada, and Europe. These clients are the world's leading employers, which included corporations, hospitals, universities, and government offices. Clients want to hire Bright Horizons as a partner because they know they can trust the staff.

Source: Roger Brown, "How We Built a Strong Company in a Weak Industry", *Harvard Business Review*, February 2001, pp. 51–57; www.brighthorizons.com, accessed 3 February 2016.

USING POSITIONING MAPS TO PLOT COMPETITIVE STRATEGY

Positioning maps are great tools to visualize competitive positioning along key aspects of its services marketing strategy, to map developments over time, and to develop scenarios of potential competitor responses. Developing a positioning map — a task sometimes referred to as perceptual mapping — is a useful way of representing consumers' perceptions of alternative products graphically. A map usually has two attributes, although three-dimensional models can be used to show three of these attributes. When more than three dimensions are needed to describe product performance in a given market, a series of separate charts needs to be drawn.

Information about a product (or company's position relative to any one attribute) can be inferred from market data, derived from ratings by representative consumers, or both. If consumer perceptions of service characteristics differ sharply from "reality" as defined by management, then communications efforts may be needed to change these perceptions, which we will discuss in Chap. 7.

An Example of Applying Positioning Maps to the Hotel Industry

The hotel business is highly competitive, especially during seasons when the supply of rooms exceeds demand. Within each class of hotels, customers visiting a large city find that they have many alternatives to choose from. The degree of luxury and comfort in physical amenities will be one choice criterion; others may include attributes such as location, safety, availability of meeting rooms, business center, restaurants, swimming pool and gym, and loyalty programs for frequent guests.

The following is a real-world situation of how to apply the use of positioning maps. Managers of The Palace, a successful four-star hotel, developed a positioning map showing their own and competing hotels, to get a better understanding of future threats to their established market position in a large city that we will call Belleville.

Located on the edge of the booming financial district, The Palace was an elegant old hotel that had been renovated to a great extent and modernized a few years earlier. Its competitors included eight four-star establishments, and one of the city's oldest hotels The Grand, which had a five-star rating. The Palace had been very profitable in recent years and has had an above average occupancy rate. For many months of the year, it was sold out on weekdays, reflecting its strong appeal to business travelers, who were very attracted to the hotel because of their willingness to pay a higher room rate than tourists or conference delegates. However, the general manager and his staff saw problems on the horizon. Planning permissions had recently been granted for four large new hotels in the city, and The Grand had just started a major renovation and expansion project, which included the construction of a new wing. There was a risk that customers might see The Palace as falling behind.

To better understand the nature of the competitive threat, the hotel's management team worked with a consultant to prepare charts that displayed The Palace's position in the business traveler market both before and after the entrance of new competition. Four key attributes were selected for study: room price, level of personal service, level of physical luxury, and location.

Data Sources

In this instance, management did not conduct new consumer research. Instead, they got their customer perceptions data from various sources such as:

- published information,
- data from past surveys done by the hotel, and
- reports from travel agents and knowledgeable hotel staff members who frequently interacted with guests.

Information on competing hotels was not difficult to obtain, because the locations were known. Information was obtained through:

- Visiting and evaluating the physical structures.
- Sales staff who kept themselves informed on pricing policies and discounts.
- To evaluate service level, they used the ratio of rooms per employee. It is easily calculated from the published number of rooms and employment data provided to the city authorities.
- Data from surveys of travel agents conducted by The Palace provided additional insights on the quality of personal service at each competitor.

Scales and Hotel Ratings

Scales were then created for each attribute, and each hotel was rated on each of the attributes so the positioning maps could be drawn:

- Price was simple because the average price charged to business travelers for a standard single room at each hotel was already quantified.
- The rooms-per-employee ratio formed the basis for a service level scale, with low ratios equated to high service. This rating was then fine-tuned because of what was known about the quality of service actually delivered by each major competitor.

- Level of physical luxury was more subjective. The management team identified the hotel that the members agreed was as the most luxurious (The Grand) and then the four-star hotel they viewed as having the least luxurious physical facilities (the Airport Plaza). All other four-star hotels were then rated on this attribute relative to these two benchmarks.

- Location was defined using the stock exchange building in the heart of the financial district as a reference point. Past research had shown that a majority of The Palace's business guests were visiting destinations in this area. The location scale plotted each hotel in terms of its distance from the stock exchange. The competitive set of 10 hotels lay within a four-mile, fan-shaped radius, extending from the exchange through the city's principal retail area (where the convention center was also located) to the inner suburbs and the nearby airport.

Two positioning maps were created to portray the existing competitive situation. The first (Fig. 3.6) showed the 10 hotels on the dimensions of price and service level; the second (Fig. 3.7) displayed them on the location and the degree of physical luxury.

Findings

Some findings were intuitive, but others provided valuable insights:

- A quick glance at Fig. 3.6 shows a clear correlation between the attributes of price and service: Hotels that offer higher levels of service are relatively more expensive. The shaded bar running from upper-left to lower-right highlights this relationship, which is not a surprising one (and can be expected to continue diagonally downward for three-star and lesser-rated establishments).

- Further analysis shows there appears to be three groups of hotels within what is already an upscale market category. At the top end, the four-star Regency is close to the five-star The Grand. In the middle, The Palace is clustered with four other hotels, and at the lower end, there is another group of three hotels. One surprising insight from this map is that The Palace appears to be charging a lot more (on a relative basis) than its service level would seem to justify. However,

Figure 3.6: Positioning map of Belleville's principal business hotels: Service Level versus Price Level

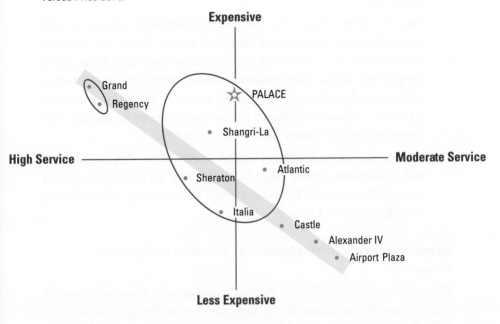

Figure 3.7: Positioning map of Belleville's principal business hotels: Location versus Physical Luxury

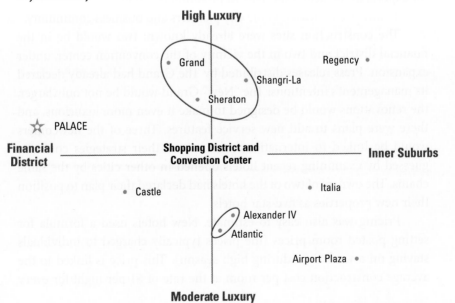

since its occupancy rate is very high, guests seem willing to pay the going rate.

- Fig. 3.7 shows how The Palace is positioned relative to the competition on location and degree of luxury. These two variables are not expected to be related, and they do not appear to be so. A key insight here is that The Palace occupies a relatively empty portion of the map. It is the only hotel in the financial district — a fact that probably explains its ability to charge more than its service level (or degree of physical luxury) seems to justify.

- There are two groups of hotels in the vicinity of the shopping district and convention center (Fig. 3.7). There is a relatively luxurious group of three, led by The Grand, and a second group of two offering a moderate level of luxury.

Mapping Future Scenarios to Identify Potential Competitive Responses

What about the future? The Palace's management team next sought to anticipate the positions of the four new hotels being constructed in Belleville as well as the probable repositioning of The Grand (see Figs. 3.8 and 3.9). Predicting the positions of the four new hotels was not difficult for experts in the field, especially as preliminary details of the new hotels had already been released to the city planners and business community.

The construction sites were already known; two would be in the financial district and two in the vicinity of the convention center, under expansion. Press releases distributed by The Grand had already declared its management's intentions: The "New" Grand would be not only larger, the renovations would be designed to make it even more luxurious, and there were plans to add new service features. Three of the newcomers would be linked to international chains and their strategies could be guessed by examining recent hotels opened in other cities by the same chains. The owners of two of the hotels had declared their plan to position their new properties as five-star hotels.

Pricing was also easy to estimate. New hotels used a formula for setting posted room prices (the prices typically charged to individuals staying on a weeknight during high season). This price is linked to the average construction cost per room at the rate of $1 per night for every

Figure 3.8: Future positioning map of Belleville's business hotels: Service Level versus Price Level

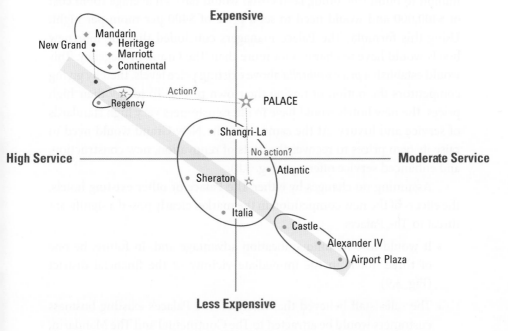

Figure 3.9: Future positioning map of Belleville's business hotels: Location versus Physical Luxury

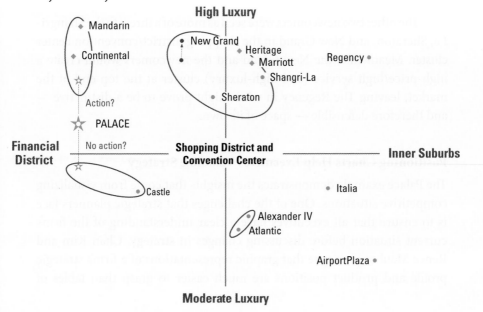

$1,000 of construction costs. Thus, a 200-room hotel that costs $80 million to build (including land costs) would have an average room cost of $400,000 and would need to set a price of $400 per room per night. Using this formula, The Palace managers concluded that the four new hotels would have to charge a lot more than The Grand or Regency. This would establish a *price umbrella* above existing price levels, thereby giving competitors the option of raising their own prices. To justify their high prices, the new hotels would have to offer customers very high standards of service and luxury. At the same time, the New Grand would need to raise its own prices to recover the costs of renovation, new construction, and enhanced service offerings (Fig. 3.8).

Assuming no changes by either The Palace or other existing hotels, the effects of the new competition in the market clearly posed a significant threat to The Palace:

- It would lose its unique location advantage and, in future, be one of three hotels in the immediate vicinity of the financial district (Fig. 3.9).
- The sales staff believed that many of The Palace's existing business customers would be attracted to The Continental and The Mandarin, and would be willing to pay the higher rates to obtain the superior benefits offered.

The other two newcomers were seen as more of a threat to the Shangri-La, Sheraton, and New Grand in the shopping district/convention center cluster. Meanwhile, the New Grand and the newcomers would create a high-price/high-service (and high-luxury) cluster at the top end of the market, leaving The Regency in what might prove to be a distinctive — and therefore defensible — space of its own.

Positioning Charts Help Executives Visualize Strategy

The Palace example demonstrates the insights that come from visualizing competitive situations. One of the challenges that strategic planners face is to ensure that all executives have a clear understanding of the firm's current situation before discussing changes in strategy. Chan Kim and Renée Mauborgne argue that graphic representations of a firm's strategic profile and product positions are much easier to grasp than tables of quantitative data or paragraphs of text. Charts and maps can help achieve "visual awakening". By allowing senior managers to compare their business with that of competitors and understand the nature of competitive threats and opportunities, visual presentations can highlight gaps between how customers (or prospective customers) see the organization and how management sees it, and thus help confirm or dispel beliefs that a service or a firm occupies a unique niche in the marketplace.[11]

By examining how anticipated changes in the competitive environment would literally redraw the current positioning map, the management team at The Palace could see that the hotel could not hope to remain in its current market position once it lost its location advantage. Unless they moved proactively to enhance their level of service and physical luxury, and raising prices to pay for such improvements, the hotel was likely to find itself being pushed into a lower price bracket that might even make it difficult to maintain current standards of service and physical upkeep.

DEVELOPING AN EFFECTIVE POSITIONING STRATEGY

After understanding the importance of focus, the principles of positioning, and having used positioning maps to visualize competitive positioning, developing an effective positioning strategy can be discussed. As shown in Fig. 3.1 at the beginning of this chapter, *STP* links the 3 'C's (i.e., customer, competitor, and company) analyses to services marketing strategy and action plan. From what is found, a position statement can be developed that enables the service organization to answer the questions: "What is our service product? Who are our customers? What do we want it to become? What actions must we take to get there?"

For example, LinkedIn has worked hard to focus on the professional networking space and to position itself away from other social networks such as Facebook. LinkedIn focuses on building a user's work experience profile, rather than a repository of holiday and party snapshots (Fig. 3.10). It also has steered clear of games and inane updates that seem to plague its social network brethren. Instead, LinkedIn has opted for a cleaner layout that resembles an online curriculum vitae. This focus on professionals as its primary customers is closely tied to its revenue generation model, which charges recruiters for access to its member base, and advertisers for

Figure 3.10: LinkedIn positioned itself away from social networks by focusing exclusively on professional networking and career development

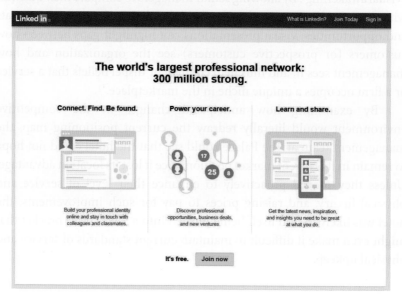

highly targeted placement ads to a senior and professional target audience that is difficult to reach via other channels.[12] This strategy clearly worked. As of 2015, LinkedIn had more than 300 million members in over 200 countries and territories, significantly ahead of its competitors Viadeo from France and XING from Germany which had 70 million and 10 million members, respectively.

There are four basic elements to writing a good positioning statement,[13] and this is illustrated in the LinkedIn example:

- *Target audience* — the specific group(s) of people that the brand wants to sell to and serve (e.g., professionals as primary target customers, and employers and advertisers as secondary target audiences).
- *Frame of reference* — the category that the brand is competing in (e.g., in the social networking space).
- *Point of difference* — the most compelling benefit offered by the brand that stands out from its competition (e.g., largest network of professionals and recruiters to help advance your career, develop your business acumen, industry knowledge, and personal development).

- *Reason to believe* — proof that the brand can deliver the promised benefits (e.g., our network is many times bigger than that of our nearest competitor).

Developing a positioning strategy can take place at several different levels, depending on the nature of the business in question. Among other multi-site, multi-product service businesses, a position can be established for the entire organization, for a given service outlet or for a specific service offered at that outlet. There must be consistency between the positioning of different services offered at the same location, because the image of one may spill over the others, especially if it is perceived to be related. For instance, if a hospital has an excellent reputation for warm and competent obstetrical services, it may enhance perceptions of its services in gynecology and pediatrics. By contrast, it would be detrimental to all three services, if their positioning was conflicting.

The outcome of integrating the 3 'C's and the **STP** analyses is the positioning statement that defines the desired position of the organization in the marketplace. With this understanding, marketers can now develop a specific plan of action that includes its positioning strategy along the 7 'P's of services marketing, its customer relationship management and loyalty strategies, and its service quality and productivity strategies. The remaining chapters in this book will discuss this in more detail.

CONCLUSION

Most service businesses face active competition. Marketers need to find ways of creating meaningful value propositions for their products that stake a distinctive and defensible *position* in the market against competing alternatives. The nature of services introduces a number of distinctive possibilities for competitive differentiation, going beyond price and physical product features to include: location and scheduling, performance levels such as speed of service delivery and the caliber of service personnel, and a range of options for customer involvement in the production process.

Nearly all successful service firms pursue a focus strategy. They identify the strategically important elements in their service operations and concentrate their resources on them. They target segments which they can serve better than other providers, offering and promoting a higher level of performance on those attributes particularly valued by their target customers.

CHAPTER SUMMARY

*C*ustomer Analysis

- ▶ Market attractiveness
  - Market size and growth
  - Profitability
  - Market trends
- ▶ Customer needs
  - Under- or unserved needs
  - More valued benefits

Define and Analyze Market *S*egments

- ▶ Needs-based segmentation followed by demographic, psychographic, and behavioral segmentation
- ▶ Identify attributes and service levels valued by each segment

*C*ompetitor Analysis

- ▶ Current positioning
- ▶ Strengths
- ▶ Weaknesses

*C*ompany Analysis

- ▶ Current positioning and brand image
- ▶ Strengths
- ▶ Weaknesses
- ▶ Values

Select *T*arget Segments to Serve

- ▶ Determine customers the firm can serve best
- ▶ Identify and analyze possibilities for differentiation
- ▶ Decide on focus strategy (i.e., service, market, or fully focused)
- ▶ Select benefits to emphasize to customers
  - Benefits must be meaningful to customers
  - Benefits must not be well met by competitors

Articulate Desired *P*osition in the Market

- ▶ Positioning must address an attractive market
- ▶ Positioning must give a sustainable competitive advantage over competition

Determine Services Marketing Strategy and Action Plan

- ▶ Positioning strategy
- ▶ 7 'P's of services marketing
- ▶ Customer relationship management strategy
- ▶ Service quality and productivity strategy

Part II

Applying the 4 Ps of Marketing to Services

CHAPTER 4

Developing Service Products and Brands

Each and every one of you will make or break the promise that our brand makes to customers.

An American Express manager speaking to his employees

CREATING SERVICE PRODUCTS

In recent years, more and more service firms have started talking about their *products* — a term previously largely associated with manufactured goods. What is the distinction between these two terms in today's business environment? A product implies a defined and consistent "bundle of output" as well as the ability to differentiate one bundle of output from another. In a manufacturing context, the concept is easy to understand and visualize. Service firms can also differentiate their products in a similar fashion using the various "models" offered by manufacturers. For example, fast-food restaurants display a menu of their products, which are, of course, highly tangible. If you are a burger connoisseur, you can easily distinguish Burger King's Whopper from its Whopper with Cheese, or from McDonald's Big Mac.

Providers of more intangible services, also offer various "models" of products, representing an assembly of carefully prescribed value-added supplementary services built around a core product. For instance, credit card companies develop different cards each with a distinct bundle of benefits and fees; insurance companies offer different types of policies; and universities offer different degree programs, each composed of a mix of required and elective courses. The objective of product development is to design bundles of output that are distinct and can be easily differentiated from another.

All service organizations face choices concerning the types of products to offer and how to deliver them to customers. To better understand the nature of services, it is useful to distinguish between the core product and supplementary elements that facilitate its use and enhance its value for customers. Designing a service product is a complex task that requires an understanding of how the core and supplementary services should be combined, sequenced, and delivered to create a value proposition that meets the needs of target segments.

What are the Components of a Service Product?

What does a service "product" mean? Service performances are experienced rather than owned. Even when there are physical elements to which the customer takes a title of ownership — such as a meal (which is promptly consumed), a surgically implanted pacemaker, or a replacement part for a car — a significant portion of the price paid by customers is for the value added by the service elements, including expert labor, and the use of specialized equipment. A service product comprises all the elements of service performance, both physical and intangible that creates value for customers.

How should a service product be designed? Experienced service marketers recognize the need to take a holistic view of the entire performance that they want customers to experience. The value proposition must address and integrate three components: (1) *core product*, (2) *supplementary services*, and (3) *delivery processes*.

Core Product

The core product is "what" the customer is fundamentally buying. When buying a one-night stay in a hotel, the core service is accommodation and security. When paying to have a package delivered, the core service is that the package arrives at the correct address, on time, and undamaged. In short, a core product is the central component supplying the principal benefits and solutions that customers seek. The core product is the main component that supplies the desired experience (e.g., a rejuvenating spa treatment or an exhilarating roller coaster ride) or the problem-solving benefit (e.g., a management consultant provides advice on how to develop a growth strategy, or a repair service restores a piece of equipment to proper working condition) that customers are looking for.

Some core products are highly intangible. For example, credit card and travel insurance products and their innovative design of features, benefits and pricing (note that many fees are hidden transaction costs, especially if used abroad). Equally, if not more intangible, are exchange traded funds (ETFs) which revolutionized the mutual fund industry. An ETF is essentially a low-cost mutual fund that usually tracks an index (e.g., the Dow Jones or Nikkei 225) and is listed on a stock exchange so that investors can trade in and out as they like. These funds are cheap, tax-efficient, and allow retail investors to buy a diversified portfolio. The development of ETF products has been an exciting journey with major product innovation involved.[1]

Supplementary Services

Delivery of the core product is usually accompanied by a variety of other service-related activities collectively referred to as supplementary services, which augment the core product, both facilitating its use and enhancing its value. Core products tend to become commoditized as an industry matures and competition increases. So the search for competitive advantage often emphasizes supplementary services, which can play an important role in differentiating and positioning the core product against competing services.

Delivery Processes

The third component in designing a service concept concerns the processes used to deliver both the core product and each of the supplementary

Figure 4.1: Depicting the service offering for an overnight hotel stay

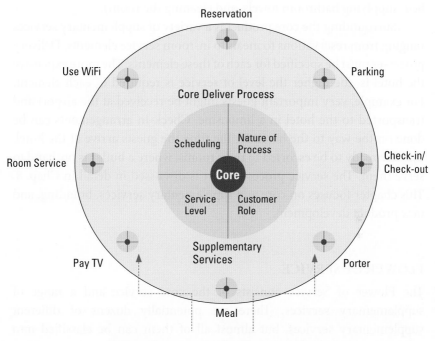

Delivery Processes for Supplementary Services

services. The design of the service offering must address the following issues:

- How the different service components are delivered to the customer.
- Nature of the customer's role in those processes.
- How long delivery lasts.
- Prescribed level and style of service to be offered.

The integration of the core product, supplementary services, and delivery processes is captured in Fig. 4.1, which illustrates the components of the service offering for an overnight stay at a luxury hotel. The core product — overnight rental of a bedroom — dimensioned by service level, scheduling (how long the room may be used before another payment becomes due), nature of the process (in this instance, people processing), and the role of customers (in terms of what they are expected to do themselves and what the hotel will do for them, such as making the bed, supplying bathroom towels, and cleaning the room).

Surrounding the core product is a variety of supplementary services ranging from reservations to meals to in-room service elements. Delivery processes must be specified for each of these elements. The more expensive the hotel is, the higher the level of service is required of each element. For example, very important guests might be received at the airport and transported to the hotel in a limousine. Check-in arrangements can be done on the way to the hotel. By the time the guests arrive at the hotel, they are ready to be escorted to their rooms, where a butler is on-hand to serve them. The service process aspect is discussed in detail in Chap. 8. This chapter focuses on core and supplementary services, branding, and new product development.

FLOWER OF SERVICE

The Flower of Service consists of the core service and a range of supplementary services. There are potentially dozens of different supplementary services, but almost all of them can be classified into one of the following eight clusters shown in Fig. 4.2, identified as either facilitating or enhancing: (1) facilitating supplementary services are required for either service delivery (e.g., making a reservation) or aiding in the use of the core product (e.g., information), and (2) enhancing supplementary services add extra value and appeal for customers (Fig. 4.1) — for example, consultation and hospitality can be very important supplementary services in a health care context.

Fig. 4.3 shows eight clusters displayed as petals surrounding the center of a flower. The petals are arranged in a clockwise sequence starting with "information," following the order they are likely to be encountered

Figure 4.2: Facilitating and enhancing services provide value to the core product

Facilitating Services	Enhancing Services
• Information	• Consultation
• Order taking	• Hospitality
• Billing	• Safekeeping
• Payment	• Exceptions

Figure 4.3: The Flower of Service: Core product surrounded by cluster of supplementary services

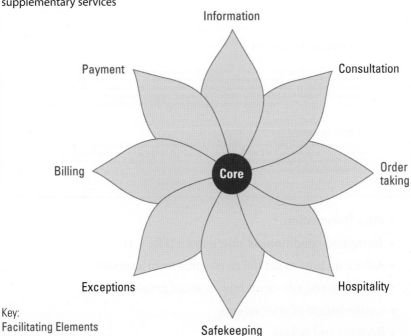

by customers. In a well-designed and well-managed service product, the petals and core are fresh and well-formed. A badly designed or poorly delivered service is a like a flower with missing, wilted, or discolored petals. Even if the core is perfect, the flower looks unattractive. Think about your own experiences as a customer (or when buying on behalf of an organization). When you were dissatisfied with a particular purchase, was it the core that was at fault, or was it a problem with one or more of the petals?

Facilitating Supplementary Services

Information

To obtain full value from any good or service, customers need relevant information, which includes the following:

- Direction to service site
- Schedules/service hours

Figure 4.4: Twitter.com provides conditions of service to users

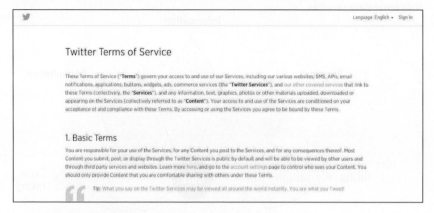

- Price information
- Terms and conditions of sale/service (Fig. 4.4)
- Advice on how to get the most value from a service
- Warnings and advice on how to avoid problems
- Confirmation of reservations
- Receipts and tickets
- Notification of changes
- Summaries of account activities

New customers are especially information-hungry. Companies should make sure the information they provide is both timely and accurate. If not, it is likely to cause customers inconvenience, make them feel irritated, and perceive a lack of control.

Traditional ways of providing information include using company websites, mobile apps, front-line employees, signs, printed notices, and brochures. Information can also be provided through videos or software-driven tutorials, touch-screen video displays on tablets and self-service machines.

Order-Taking

Once customers are ready to buy, a key supplementary element comes into play — order-taking. Order-taking includes:

- Order entry

Figure 4.5: Websites like OpenTable take dining reservations to a whole new level by allowing diners to bypass the traditional call-and-book experience, with a mere click

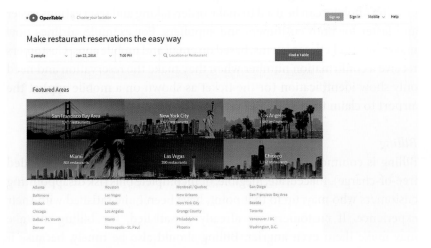

- – On-site order entry
- – Mail/telephone/e-mail/online/mobile app order
- Reservations or check-ins
  - – Seats/tables/rooms
  - – Vehicles or equipment rental
  - – Professional appointment
- Applications
  - – Memberships in club/programs
  - – Subscription services (e.g., utilities)
  - – Enrolment-based services (e.g., financial credit, college enrolment)

Order entry can be received through a variety of sources such as through sales personnel, phone and email, or online. The process of order-taking should be polite, fast, and accurate so that customers do not waste time and endure unnecessary mental or physical effort (Fig. 4.5).

Reservations (including appointments and check-ins) represent a special type of order-taking that entitles customers to a specified unit of service. These can be an airline seat, a restaurant table, a hotel room, time with a qualified professional, or admission to a facility such as a theater or sports arena with designated seating.

Technology can be used to make order-taking and reservations easier and faster for both customers and suppliers. For example, airlines now make use of ticketless systems, based on email and mobile apps. Customers receive a confirmation number when they make the reservation and need only show identification (or the ticket as shown on a mobile app) at the airport to claim their seats and receive a boarding pass.

Billing

Billing is common to almost all services (unless the service is provided free-of-charge). Inaccurate, illegible, or incomplete bills risk disappointing customers who may, up to that point, have been quite satisfied with their experience. If customers are already dissatisfied, the billing mistake may make them even angrier. Billing should also be timely, because it encourages people to make faster payment. Billing can be:

- Periodic statements of account activity
- Invoices for individual transactions
- Verbal statements of amount due
- Online or machine display of amount due for self-payment transactions

Perhaps the simplest approach is self-billing, by which the customer tallies up the amount of an order and authorizes a card payment. In such instances, billing and payment are combined into a single act, although the seller may still need to check for accuracy.

Customers usually expect bills to be clear and informative, and itemized in ways that make it clear how the total was computed. Unexplained, arcane symbols that have all the meaning of hieroglyphics on an Egyptian monument (and are decipherable only by the high priests of accounting and data processing) do not create a favorable impression of the service firm; but unfortunately, are all too common (think of a cell phone service or a hospital bill). Online or emailed statements, and laser printers with their ability to switch fonts and typefaces, to box and to highlight, can produce statements that are not only more legible but also organize information in useful ways. Marketing research can help here, by asking customers what information they want and how they would like it to be organized and presented.

Busy customers hate to be kept waiting for a bill to be prepared in a hotel, restaurant, or rental car lot. Many hotels and car rental firms have created express check-out options, taking customers' credit card details in advance and documenting charges later by email. However, accuracy is essential. Even though customers use the express check-outs to save time, they certainly would not want to waste time later with corrections and refunds.

Payment

In most cases, a bill requires the customer to take action on payment (and such action may be very slow in coming!) Exceptions include bank statements and other direct debit payment services, which show the charges to be deducted from a customer's account.

A variety of payment options exist, but customers expect them to be easy to use and convenient. These include:

- Self-service
  - Inserting card, cash, or token into machine
  - Electronic funds transfer
  - Mailing a check
  - Entering credit card information online
  - Online payment systems such as PayPal, Google Wallet, or Bitcoins
- Direct to payee or intermediary
  - Cash handling or change giving
  - Check handling
  - Credit/charge/debit card handling
  - Coupon redemption
- Automatic deduction from financial deposits
  - Automated systems (e.g., machine-readable tickets that operate entry gate)
  - Pre-arranged automatic deduction for bill payment through direct debit (e.g., for bank loans and post-paid cell phone subscription plans)

Enhancing Supplementary Services

Consultation

This section deals with enhancing supplementary services led by consultation. In contrast to information, which suggests a simple response to customers' questions (or printed information that anticipates their needs), consultation involves a dialog to probe for customer requirements, and then develop a tailored solution. At its simplest, consultation consists of advice from a knowledgeable service person in response to the request: "What do you suggest"? For example, asking a hairstylist for advice on different hairstyles and products. Effective consultation requires an understanding of each customer's current situation, before suggesting a suitable course of action. Examples of consultation include:

- Customized advice
- Personal counseling
- Tutoring/training in service use
- Management or technical consulting

More formalized efforts to provide management and technical consulting for corporate customers include "solution selling" for expensive industrial equipment and services. The sales engineer studies a customer's situation and then offers advice about what particular package of equipment and systems will yield the best results. Some consulting services are offered free of charge in the hopes of making a sale. In other instances however, the service is "unbundled" and customers are expected to pay for it (e.g., for diagnostic tests before a surgery, or a feasibility study before a solution is being proposed). Advice can also be offered through tutorials, group training programs, and public demonstrations.

Hospitality

Hospitality related services should ideally reflect pleasure at meeting new customers and greeting old ones when they return. Well-managed businesses try, at least in small ways, to ensure that their employees treat customers as guests. Courtesy and consideration for customers' needs apply to both face-to-face encounters and telephone interactions. Hospitality elements include:

Figure 4.6: Abercrombie & Fitch provides hospitality with a smile

- Greeting
- Food and beverages
- Toilets and washrooms
- Waiting facilities and amenities
  - Lounges, waiting areas, seating
  - Weather protection
  - Magazines, entertainment, newspapers
- Transport

Hospitality finds its fullest expression in face-to-face encounters. In some cases, it starts (and ends) with an offer of transport to and from the service site on courtesy shuttle buses. If customers must wait outdoors before the service can be delivered, then a thoughtful service provider will offer weather protection. If customers have to wait indoors, a waiting area with seating and even entertainment (TV, newspapers, or magazines) may be provided to pass the time. Recruiting customer-contact employees who are naturally warm, welcoming, and considerate helps create a hospitable atmosphere. Shoppers at retailers such as Abercrombie & Fitch, a global clothing retailer, are given a welcoming "hello" and "thank you" when they enter and leave the store, even if they did not buy anything (Fig. 4.6).

Safekeeping

When customers are visiting a service site, they often want assistance with their personal possessions. In fact, some customers may not visit at all unless certain safekeeping services are provided (such as safe and convenient parking for their cars). Safekeeping includes caring for:

- Child care, pet care
- Parking for vehicles, valet parking
- Coat rooms
- Baggage handling
- Storage space
- Safe deposit boxes
- Security personnel

Responsible businesses pay close attention to safety and security issues for customers who are visiting the firm's premises. Wells Fargo Bank mails a brochure with its bank statements containing information about using its ATM machines safely, educating its customers about how to protect both their ATM cards and themselves from theft and personal injury. The bank also makes sure that its machines are in brightly lit, highly visible locations, and are equipped with CCTV. It takes a similarly careful approach to customer privacy and security for their online services. For more details, check https://www.wellsfargo.com for "online security".

Additional safekeeping services may involve physical products that customers buy or rent. They may include packaging, pick-up and delivery, assembly, installation, cleaning, and inspection.

Exceptions

Exceptions involve supplementary services that fall outside the routine of normal service delivery. Astute businesses anticipate such exceptions and develop contingency plans and guidelines in advance. That way, employees will not appear helpless and unprepared when customers ask for special assistance. Well-defined procedures make it easier for employees to respond promptly and effectively. There are several types of exceptions:

- *Special requests.* A customer may request service that requires a departure from normal operating procedures. Common requests relate to personal needs, including the care of children, dietary requirements, medical needs, religious observance, and personal disabilities. Such requests are particularly common in travel and hospitality sectors.

- *Problem solving.* Sometimes normal service delivery (or product performance) fails to run smoothly as a result of accident, delay, equipment failure, or a customer having difficulty in using a product.

- *Handling of complaints/suggestions/compliments.* This activity requires well-defined procedures. It should be easy for customers to express dissatisfaction, offer suggestions for improvement, or pass on compliments, and service providers should be able to make an appropriate response quickly (see Chap. 13 on complaint handling and service recovery).

- *Restitution.* Many customers expect to be compensated for serious performance failures. Compensation may take the form of repairs under warranty, legal settlements, refunds, an offer of free service, or other form of payment-in-kind.

Managers need to keep an eye on the level of exception requests. Too many requests may indicate that standard procedures need revamping. For instance, frequent requests for special vegetarian meals as there are none on the menu, could mean it's time to revise the menu to include at least one or two such dishes. A flexible approach to exceptions is generally a good idea, because it reflects responsiveness to customer needs. On the other hand, too many exceptions may compromise safety, negatively impact other customers, and overburden employees.

Managerial Implications

The eight categories of supplementary services that form the Flower of Service collectively provide many options for enhancing core products. Most supplementary services do (or should) represent responses to customer needs. As noted earlier, some are facilitating services — such as information and reservations — that enable customers to use the core product more effectively. Others are "extras" that enhance the core or even reduce its non-financial costs (e.g., meals, magazines, and entertainment are hospitality elements that help pass the waiting time). Some elements — notably billing and payment — are, in effect, imposed by the service provider. Even if they are not actively desired by the customer, they still are a part of the overall service experience.

Not every core product is surrounded by supplementary elements from all eight petals of the Flower of Service. Each of the four categories of processes introduced in Chap. 2 — people, possession, mental stimulus, and information processing — has different implications on operational procedures, the degree of customer contact with service personnel and facilities, and requirements for supplementary services. As anticipated, people-processing services tend to be the most demanding in terms of supplementary elements, as they involve close and often extended interactions with customers, especially in the hospitality industry. When customers don't visit the service factory, the need for hospitality may be limited to simple courtesies in communications. Possession-processing services sometimes place heavy demands on safekeeping elements, but there may be less need for this particular "petal" when providing information-processing services in which customers and suppliers deal entirely at arm's length. However, many services deal with sensitive information (e.g., healthcare providers and financial services) — these companies must ensure that their customers' intangible financial assets and privacy are carefully safeguarded in transactions that occur via phone or the Internet.[2]

A company's market positioning strategy helps to determine which supplementary services should be included. A strategy of adding benefits to increase customers' perceptions of quality will require more supplementary services, as well as a higher level of performance on all such elements, than what a strategy of price-competitiveness requires. Furthermore, offering progressively higher levels of supplementary services around a common core may offer the basis for a product line of differentiated offerings, similar to various classes of travel offered by airlines.

B2B service firms were found to simply add layer upon layer of services to their core offerings without knowing what customers really valued.[3] Managers surveyed in the study indicated that they did not understand which services should be offered to customers as a standard package accompanying the core, and which options could be offered for an extra charge. Without this knowledge, developing effective pricing policies can be tricky. There are no simple rules governing pricing decisions for core products and supplementary services, but managers should continually review their own policies and those of their competitors to make sure they are in line with both market practice and customer needs. We'll discuss these and other pricing issues in more detail in Chap. 6.

In summary, the Flower of Service and its petals discussed here can serve as a checklist in the continuing search for new ways to augment existing core products and to design new offerings. Regardless of which supplementary services a firm decides to offer, all of the elements in each petal should receive the care and attention needed to consistently meet defined service standards. That way the resulting "flower" will always have a fresh and appealing appearance.

BRANDING SERVICE FIRMS, PRODUCTS, AND EXPERIENCES

Branding plays an important role in services, as explained by Leonard Berry:

> *Strong brands enable customers to better visualize and understand intangible products. They reduce customers' perceived monetary, social, or safety risk in busying services, which are difficult to evaluate prior to purchase. Strong brands are surrogates when the company offers no fabric to touch, no trousers to try on, no watermelons or apples to scrutinize, no automobile to test drive.[4]*

Branding can be employed at both the corporate and product levels by almost any service business. In a well-managed firm, the corporate brand is not only easily recognized but also has meaning for customers, representing a particular way of doing business. Applying distinctive brand names to individual products enables the firm to communicate

Figure 4.7: The spectrum of branding alternatives

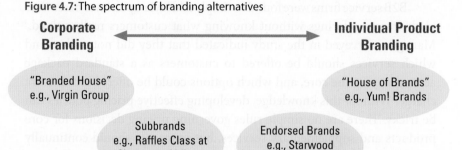

Source: Adapted from James Devlin "Brand Architecture in Services: The Examples of Retail Financial Services." *Journal of Marketing Management*, No. 19, 2003, 1046.

the distinctive experiences and benefits associated with a specific service concept to the target market. In short, it helps marketers to establish a mental picture of the service in customers' minds and clarify the nature of the value proposition.

Branding individual service products helps to differentiate one bundle of output from another. One example is prepackaged solutions offered by hotels, which carefully crafted specified products for various target segments branded as Heavenly Honeymoon, Spa Indulgence, or Intimate Moments, etc. The latter was a product specially created for couples who may celebrate their wedding anniversary. It is presented as a surprise to the partner or spouse when guests return to find their villas decorated with lit candles, incense burning, flower petals spread throughout the room, satin sheets on the decorated bed, chilled champagne or wine, and a private outdoor pool decorated with a variety of aromatic massage oils to further inspire those intimate moments. Having "packaged" and "branded" this product allows Banyan Tree to sell it via its website, distributors, and reservations centers, and train it at the individual hotels. Without specifying exactly what this product means, giving it a name, marketing, selling, and delivery would not be effective. Next section describes alternative branding strategies for services.

Branding Strategies for Services

Most service organizations offer a line of products rather than just a single product. As a result, they must choose from four broad branding alternatives: branded house (i.e., using a single brand to cover all products and services), house of brands (i.e., using a separate stand-alone brand for each offering), or sub-brands and endorsed brands which are both combination of these two extremes.[5] These alternatives are represented as a spectrum in Fig. 4.7 and are discussed in the following sections.

Branded House

The term *branded house* is used to describe a company, such as the Virgin Group, that applies its brand name to multiple offerings in often unrelated fields.[6] Virgin's core business areas are travel, entertainment, and lifestyle, but it also offers financial services, healthcare, media, and telecommunications services. The danger of such a branding strategy is that the brand gets overstretched and weakened.

Sub-brands

Next on the spectrum are sub-brands, for which the corporate or the master brand is the main reference point but the product itself has a distinctive name, too. Examples are the Singapore Airlines Raffles Class, denoting the company's business class, and the Singapore Airlines Suits, its "beyond first class" service on the A380.

FedEx has been successfully using a sub-branding strategy. When the company decided to rebrand a ground delivery service it had purchased, it chose the name FedEx Ground and developed an alternative color for the standard logo (purple and green rather than purple and orange). Its goal was to transfer the positive image of reliable, on-time service associated with its air services to its less expensive, small-package ground service. The well-known air service was then rebranded as FedEx Express. Its other sub-brands, what the firm refers to as "the FedEx family of companies", include FedEx Home Delivery (which delivers to US residential addresses), FedEx Freight (regional, less-than-truckload transportation for heavyweight freight), FedEx Custom Critical (nonstop, door-to-door delivery of time-critical shipments), FedEx Trade Networks (customs brokerage, international freight forwarding, and trade facilitation), Fedex Supply Chain (comprehensive suite of solutions that synchronize the movement of goods), and Fedex Office (office and printing services, technology services, shipping supplies, and packing services located at both city and suburban retail stores).[7]

Figure 4.8: KFC, Pizza Hut and Taco Bell are just some of the few popular fast-food brands under Yum! Brands.

Photo Courtesy of Yum! Brands, Inc.

Endorsed Brands

For *endorsed brands*, the product brand dominates but the corporate name is still featured. Many hotel companies use this approach. They offer a family of sub-brands and/or endorsed brands. For instance, Intercontinental Hotel Group in itself is well known. However, its product brands are dominant. They include the Intercontinental Hotels & Resorts, Crowne Plaza Hotels & Resorts, Hotel Indigo, Holiday Inn, Holiday Inn Club Vacations, Holiday Inn Resort, Holiday Inn Express, Staybridge Suites, Candlewood Suites, Even Hotels, and Hualuxe, and its loyalty program IHG Rewards Club.[8]

For a multi-brand strategy to succeed, each brand must promise a distinctive value proposition, targeted at a different customer segment. It is important to note that in some instances, segmentation is situation-based: The same individual may have different needs (and willingness to pay) under differing circumstances, such as when traveling with family or traveling on business. A multi-brand strategy is aimed at encouraging customers to continue buying from within the brand family. Loyalty programs are often used to encourage this, whereby loyalty points are collected in one sub-brand when on business travel, but are then redeemed through another brand on leisure trips.

House of Brands

At the far end of the spectrum is the *house of brands* strategy. A good service example is Yum! Brands Inc., which owns more than 40,000 restaurants in 125 countries with a sales of US$13 billion. While many may not have heard of Yum! Brands, people certainly are familiar with their restaurant brands — Taco Bell, KFC, Pizza Hut, and WingStreet. Prior to 2011, Yum! also owned Long John Silver's and A&W Restaurants (Fig. 4.8).

Tiering Service Products with Branding

In a number of service industries, branding is not only used to differentiate core services, but also to clearly differentiate service levels. This is known

Table 4.1: Examples of Service Tiering

Industry	Tiers	Key Service Attributes and Physical Elements Used in Tiering
Lodging	Star or diamond rating (5 to 1)	Architecture; landscaping; room size; furnishings, and décor; restaurant facilities and menus, room service hours; array of services and physical amenities; staffing levels' caliber and attitudes of employees
Airline	Classes (Intercontinental); first, business, premium economy, economy[a]	Seat pitch (distance between rows), seat width, and reclining capability; meal and beverage service, staffing ratios; check-in speed; departure and arrival lounges; baggage retrieval speed
Car rental	Class of vehicle[b]	Based on vehicle size (from subcompact to full size), degree of luxury, plus special vehicle types (minivan, SUV, convertible)
Hardware and software support	Support levels	Hours and days of service; speed of response; speed of delivering replacement parts; technician-delivered service versus advice on self-service; availability of additional services

a Only a few airlines offer as many as four classes of intercontinental service; domestic services usually feature one or two classes.
b Avis and Hertz offer seven classes based on size and luxury, plus several special vehicle types

as *service tiering*. It is common in industries such as hotels, airlines, car rentals, and computer hardware and software support. Table 4.1 shows examples of the key tiers within each of these industries. Other examples of tiering include healthcare insurance, cable television, and credit cards.

In the airline industry, individual carriers decide what level of performance should be included with each class of service. Innovative carriers, such as British Airways and Virgin Atlantic are continually trying to add new service features such as business class seats that unfold into flat beds for overnight travel. In other industries, tiering often reflects an individual firm's strategy of bundling service elements into a limited number of packages, each priced separately. In other industries, tiering often reflects an individual firm's strategy of bundling service elements into a limited number of packages, rather than offering a broad *a la carte* menu of options, each priced separately. A few examples are given as follows.

- *Avis Car Rental*. Avis focuses on two kinds of customers — consumer customers and business customers. For consumer customers, they tier their service based on different car classes (e.g., subcompact, compact, intermediate, standard, full size, specialty, signature, premium, luxury, standard elite SUV, intermediate SUV, full size SUV, premium SUV, convertible, minivan and passenger van) and also service. For example, if a customer does not want to drive, they can opt for Avis Chauffeur Drive. The chauffeur not only drives, but also acts as a mobile concierge. Business customers have four programs that cater to different types of business customers (small- and mid-sized business, entertainment and productions, meeting and group services, and government and military) to choose from.[9]

- *British Airways*. A comprehensive example of strong sub-branding of service tiers in the airline industry comes from British Airways (BA), which offers a number of distinct air travel products: First (deluxe service), Club Europe (business class for flights within Europe), Club World (business class for longer international flights), Club World London City (business class for flights between London City and JFK, New York), World Traveller Plus (premium economy class), World Traveller (economy class on longer international flights); Euro Traveller (economy class on flights within Europe) and UK Domestic (economy class on flights within the UK). Each BA sub-brand represents a specific service concept and a set of clearly stated product specifications for pre-flight, in-flight, and on-arrival service elements. To provide additional focus on product, pricing, and marketing communications, the responsibility for managing and developing each service is assigned to separate management teams. Through internal training and external communications, staff and passengers alike are kept informed of the characteristics of each service. Except for the UK Domestic, most aircrafts in BA's fleet are configured in several classes. For instance, the airline's intercontinental fleet of Boeing 777-300s is equipped to serve First, Club World, World Traveller Plus, and World Traveller passengers.

On any given route, all passengers traveling on a particular flight receive the same core product — say, a 10-hour journey from Los Angeles to London — but the nature and extent of most of the supplementary elements both on the ground and in the air can differ widely. Passengers in Club World, for instance, not only benefit from better tangible elements, they also receive more personalized service from airline employees and benefit from faster service on the ground at check-in, passport control in London (special lines), and baggage retrieval (priority handling).[10]

- *Sun's Hardware and Software Support.* Sun, a brand of Oracle, is an example of branding different tiers in a high-tech, B2B product line. The company offers full range of hardware and software support in a program branded as "SunSpectrum Support".[11] Four different levels of support are available, sub-branded from platinum to bronze. The objective is to give buyers the flexibility to choose a level of support consistent with their own organization's needs (and willingness to pay), ranging from expensive, mission-critical support at the enterprise level (Platinum Service Plan) to relatively inexpensive assistance with self-service maintenance support (Bronze Service Plan):

  - Platinum: Mission-critical support with onsite service 24/7 and a two-hour response time.
  - Gold: Business critical support with onsite service from Monday to Friday, 8 a.m. to 8 p.m., telephone service 24/7, and a four-hour response time.

Figure 4.9: A Service-Branding Model

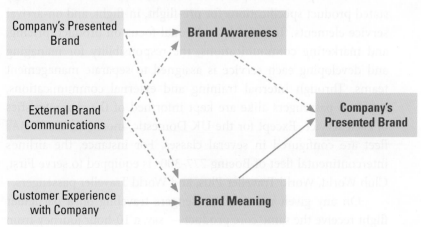

- Silver: Basic support with on-site service from Monday to Friday, 8 a.m. to 5 p.m., telephone service from Monday to Friday, 8 a.m. to 8 p.m., and a four-hour response time.
- Bronze: Self-support with phone service 8 a.m. to 5p.m.

Building Brand Equity

To build a strong brand, we need to understand what contributes to brand equity. Brand equity is the value premium that comes with a brand. It is what customers are willing to pay for the service, beyond what they are willing to pay for a similar service that has no brand. Fig. 4.9 shows the following six key components:

- *Company's presented brand* — mainly through advertising, service facilities, and personnel.
- *External brand communications* — from word of mouth and publicity. These are outside of firm's control.
- *Customer experience with the company* — what the customer has gone through when they patronized the company.
- *Brand awareness* — the ability to recognize and recall a brand when provided with a cue.
- *Brand meaning* — what comes to the customer's mind when a brand is mentioned.

• *Brand equity* — the degree of marketing advantage that a brand has over its competitors.

Fig. 4.9 shows that a company's marketing and external communications help to build brand awareness. However, it is the customer's actual experience with the brand, or the "moments of truth", which are more powerful in building brand equity. Firms need to focus on customers, deliver great experiences, and create an emotional connection with their customers. Next section describes how this can be achieved.

Delivering Branded Service Experiences

Around the world, many financial service firms continue to create and register brand names to distinguish different accounts and service packages that they offer. Their objective is to transform a series of service elements and processes into a consistent and recognizable service experience, offering a definable and predictable output at a specified price. Unfortunately, there is often little discernible difference — other than the name — between two banks' branded offerings, and their value proposition may be unclear. Don Shultz emphasizes: "The brand promise or value proposition is not a tagline, an icon, or a color or a graphic element, although all of these may contribute. It is, instead, the heart and soul of the brand…"[12]

An important role for service marketers is to become brand champions, familiar with and responsible for shaping every aspect of the customer's experience. We can relate the notion of a branded service experience to the Flower of Service metaphor by emphasizing the need for consistency in the color and texture of each petal. Unfortunately, many service experiences remain very haphazard and create the impression of a flower stitched together with petals drawn from many different plants. See Chap. 7 for more discussion on branding in the context of marketing communications strategy.

Besides designing great service products and giving them a brand name, how else can a branded service experiences be delivered?[13] It starts with aligning the service product and brand with its delivery process, servicescape, and people with the brand proposition. To start off, we need to have great processes in place (see Chap. 8). Next, creating the emotional experience can be done effectively through the servicescape (see Chap. 10). The hardest part of crafting the emotional experience is the building of interpersonal relationships, where trust is established between the consumers and the firm's employees.[14] In order for this to happen, we need to invest in our employees for they will be the ones who can deliver the brand experience that creates customer loyalty (see Chap. 11).

NEW SERVICE DEVELOPMENT

Intense competition and rising consumer expectations have an impact on nearly all service industries. Thus, great brands not only provide existing services well, but also continuously improve through innovation and by creating new approaches to service.[15]

A Hierarchy of New Service Categories

There are many ways for a service provider to innovate. Below, we identify seven categories of new services, ranging from simple style changes to major innovations.

1. *Style changes* represent the simplest type of innovation, typically involving no changes in either processes or performance. However, they are often highly visible, create excitement, and may serve to motivate employees. Examples include redesigning retail branches, websites, or new uniforms for service employees.

2. *Service improvements* are the most common type of innovation. They involve small changes in the performance of current products, including improvements to either the core product or to existing supplementary services. Often, it is the little things that matter and customers appreciate it. For example, Lydmar hotel in Stockholm has a series of buttons where passengers can choose their music from a choice of garage, funk, and rhythm and blues. This is just a simple improvement that can add to a customer's experience as it is unique and surprising.[16]

3. *Supplementary service innovations* take the form of adding new facilitating or enhancing service elements to an existing core service or significantly improving an existing supplementary service. Low-tech innovations for an existing service can be as simple as adding parking at a retail site or agreeing to accept

payment via smartphone for payment.

4. *Process line extensions* often represent distinctive new ways of delivering existing products. The intention is to offer more convenience and a different experience for existing customers, or attract new customers who find the traditional approach unappealing. They often involve adding a lower-contact distribution channel to an existing high-contact one, such as having self-service to complement delivery by service employees, or creating online or app-based service delivery.

5. *Product line extensions* are additions to a company's current product lines. The first company in a market to offer such a product may be seen as an innovator. The others are merely followers, often to defend themselves. These new services may be targeted at existing customers to serve a broader variety of needs or are designed to attract new customers with different needs, or both. For example, a restaurant may extend the product line to offer dog lovers a menu as well, so both the owners and their dogs are able to dine in the same restaurant.

6. *Major process innovations* consist of using new processes to deliver existing core products in new ways with additional benefits. For example, online courses are transforming higher education by using cutting-edge technology, internet and smart devices. Sebastian Thrun, while still a tenured professor at Stanford University, launched for-profit educational organization Udacity in 2012, while Andrew Ng and Daphne Koller, also from Stanford, launched Coursera, a non-profit competitor using massive open online courses (MOOCS) to completely redesign education.

Major redesign was required to make online courses effective and successful, and today, these courses take full advantage of online interactivity, video, short assessment tasks, simulations, and discussion forums. Students can watch and do any part of a course as often as they want until they internalize the content. According to Salman Khan, founder of Khan Academy and former hedge fund analyst, "If people are meeting, they don't need a lecture; if you don't need them

SERVICE INSIGHTS 4.1

Major Service Innovation Enables by Technology

Digital startups are bubbling up in an astonishing variety of services, penetrating every nook and cranny of our economies. They are reshaping entire industries and according to Marc Andreessen, a Silicon Valley venture capitalist, "Software is eating the world". Just think of recent successes such as Uber's taxi, private car and rideshare service (www.uber.com), or Airbnb's platform that lets people rent out their homes for holidays and short-term stays (www.airbnb.com). This digital frenzy has given rise to a global movement, with most big cities, from London to Berlin and Singapore to Shanghai, having sizeable startup ecosystems. Among them, they have hundreds of startup schools (i.e., "accelerators") and thousands of co-working spaces where caffeinated folks in their 20s and 30s toil hunched over their laptops. All these ecosystems are highly interconnected, making them a global crowd. They travel from city to city, and a few of them spend a semester with "Unreasonable at Sea", an accelerator on a ship which cruises the world while its passengers work on their business models and write code. "Anyone who writes code can become an entrepreneur — anywhere in the world", says Simon Levene, a venture capitalist in London.

Today's entrepreneurial boom is based on solid foundations which makes it likely to continue for the foreseeable future. The basic building blocks for digital services or, in the words of Josh Lerner of Harvard Business School, "the technologies for startup production" have become so evolved, cheap, and ubiquitous that they can be easily combined, build upon, and reconfigured. These building blocks include snippets of code that can be copied free from the internet, easy-to-learn programming frameworks (e.g., Ruby on Rails), services for finding developers (eLance, oDesk), sharing code (GitHub) and testing usability (UserTesting.com), and application programming interfaces (APIs). Others include services that can be used as inputs such as voice calls (Twilio), maps (Google), and payments (PayPal). Probably the most important are

Figure 4.10: Robots serve guests at Henn-na Hotel, Japan

platform services that can host startup's services (e.g., Amazon's cloud computing), distribute them (app stores by Apple, Samsung or Google), and market them (Facebook, Twitter and LinkedIn).

Thanks to the Internet, even information on how to do a startup has become easily accessible. Global standards are emerging for all things related to startups, from term sheets for investments to business plans.

Innovation does not stop at the virtual world. Hardware, from processors to cameras to sensors, is getting better, smaller and cheaper. Technologies such as robots, drones, wearable computers and sensors, self-driving cars, virtual reality, speech recognition, biometrics, artificial intelligence, and the Internet of things will bring opportunities for a wide range of service innovations that will dramatically improve the customer experience, service quality, and productivity.

For example, Henn-na Hotel in Nagasaki, Japan is run by robots. It aims to have 90% of hotel services provided by robots (Fig. 4.10), including porter service, room cleaning, front desk, and other services to reduce costs and ensure comfort. Many other processes were also redesigned such as using facial recognition to give access to the hotel, rooms, and other facilities, effectively replacing cumbersome room card systems.

Never before has technological development been so fast and far-reaching! It will need highly skilled managers with a deep knowledge of the service consumer and services marketing to translate these opportunities into well-designed service products.

Sources: The Economist, "A Cambrian Moment", 18 January 2014, p 4; The Economist, "The Third Great Wave", 4 October 2014, p. 3. Mail Online, "Japan Opens Hotel Run by Robots that Will Welcome Guests, Carry Bags and Even Clean Your Room," http://www.dailymail.co.uk/sciencetech/article-2946103/FAULTY-towers-Japan-opens-hotel-multi-lingual-ROBOTS-welcome-guests-carry-bags-clean-room.html ; accessed on 17 February 2016.

to interact, information should just be in a video or a memo".[17] Sebastian Thrun also predicts that in 50 years, there will be only ten universities left in the world. If not quite on that scale, online education will clearly mean upheaval for universities around the world, and for students, education will be transformed.[18]

7. *Major service innovations* are new core products for markets that have not been previously defined. They usually include both new service characteristics and radical new processes. For example, Amazon diversified into providing on-demand computing power and became a leader in cloud computing services. Other examples are Virgin Galactic and XCOR Aerospace, hoping to create demand for suborbital space tourism. Space Adventures, a leading company in the spaceflight industry, flew the first space tourist on the Russian Soyuz spacecraft to the International Space Station in 2001. Today, they provide different space experiences, including lunar missions, orbital space flights, suborbital space flights and a spacewalk program. These experiences do not come cheap. Suborbital space flights for example, start from over $100,000 and the lunar mission costs $100 million per seat.[19]

Major service innovations are relatively rare. More common is the use of new technologies to deliver existing services in new ways, enhancing or creating new supplementary services, and greatly improving performance on existing ones through process redesign. However, technology is improving so fast that we will see major service innovations as discussed in *Service Insights 4.1*.

Achieving Success in New Service Development

Consumer goods have high failure rates, with more than 90% of the 30,000 new products introduced each year ending in failure[20]. Services are not immune to the high failure rates either. For example, Delta Airlines was one of several major carriers attempting to launch a separate low-cost carrier designed to compete with discount airlines such as Jet Blue and Southwest Airlines. However, none of these operations were successful. In banking, many banks have tried to sell insurance products in the hopes of increasing the number of profitable relationships with existing customers, but many of these product extensions also failed.

There are various reasons for failure, including not meeting a consumer need, inability to cover costs from revenues, and poor execution. For example, a study in the restaurant business found a failure rate of about 26% during the first year rising to close to 60% within three years.[21] How then can we successfully develop new services? A number of studies have found that the following three factors contribute most to success[22]:

1. *Market synergy* — The new product fits well with the existing image of the firm, its expertise and resources; it is better than competing products in terms of meeting customers' needs, as the firm has a good understanding of its customers' purchase behavior and receives strong support during and after the launch from the firm and its branches.

2. *Organizational factors* — These are strong inter-functional cooperation and coordination. Development personnel need to be fully aware of why they are involved and the importance of new products to the company. Before the launch, staff must understand the new product and its underlying processes, as well as details about direct competitors.

3. *Market research factors* — Detailed and scientifically designed market research studies are conducted early in the development process with a clear idea of the type of information to be obtained. A good definition of the product concept is developed before undertaking field surveys.

This research supports the notion that a highly structured development process increases the chances of success for a complex service innovation. However, it is worth noting that there are limits to the degree of structure that can and should be imposed. Swedish researchers Bo Edwardsson, Lars Haglund, and Jan Mattson reviewed new service development in telecommunications, transport, and financial services and concluded that:

> [C]omplex processes like the development of new services cannot be formally planned altogether. Creativity and innovation cannot only rely on planning and control. There must be some elements of improvisation, anarchy, and internal competition in the development of new services... We believe that a contingency approach is needed and that creativity on the one hand and formal planning and control on the other can be balanced, with successful new services as the outcome.[23]

An important conclusion from subsequent research in Sweden concerns the role of customers in service innovation. Researchers found that in the idea-generation stage, the nature of submitted ideas differed significantly depending on whether they were created by professional service developers or by the users themselves. Users' ideas were judged to be more original and had a higher perceived value for customers. However, on an average, these ideas were harder to convert into commercial services.[24] The emergence of crowds as innovation partners provides additional exciting opportunities for cost-effective innovation that can lead to breakthroughs in new service development.[25] Chap. 8 and 14 discuss the role of customer feedback on improving service quality and productivity.

CONCLUSION

A service product comprises all the elements of the service performance that create value for the customer, and it consists of a core product bundled with a variety of supplementary service elements and their delivery processes. In mature industries where the core service tends to become commoditized, the search for competitive advantage often centers on creating new supplementary services or significantly improving the performance on existing ones. Another important differentiator can be the way the product is delivered, that is, the service delivery processes. It is not the outcome of a service delivery but the way this outcome is achieved that often differentiates one service provider from another.

Designing a service product is a complex task that requires an understanding of how the core and supplementary services should be combined, sequenced, delivered, and branded to create a value proposition that meets the needs of target market segments. Flower of Service, branding strategies, and new service development are considered as key tools for product development.

CHAPTER SUMMARY

Branding Service Firms, Products and Experiences

Branding Strategies
- Branded house
- Subbrands
- Endorsed brands
- House of brands

Tiering Services Through Branding
- Use branding to define and differentiate bundles of services and service levels

Building Brand Equity
- Company's presented brand
- External brand communications
- Customer experience with company
- Brand awareness
- Brand meaning

Branded Service Experiences
- Alignment of product and brand with the delivery process, servicescape and service employees
- Create an emotional connection

Components of a Service Product

▸ **Core Product**

▸ **Supplementary Services**

Facilitating Supplementary Services
- Information
- Order-taking
- Billing
- Payment

Enhancing Supplementary Services
- Consultation
- Hospitality
- Safekeeping
- Exceptions

▸ **Delivery Process**

New Service Development (NSD)

Hierarchy of NSD
- Style changes
- Service improvements
- Supplementary service innovations
- Process line extensions
- Product line extensions
- Major process innovations
- Major service innovation

Achieving Success in NSD

Key success factors are:
- Market synergy
- Organizational factors (alignment and support)
- Market research factors
- Involvement of customers early in the process, ideally at idea generation

CHAPTER 5

Distributing Services

Think globally, act locally.

John Naisbitt
American author of best-seller "Megatrends"

One thing we're not trying to drive is the proliferation of more and more apps… customers don't want that. We want to create that single platform that's device agnostic.

Simon Pomeroy
Chief Digital Officer, Westpac New Zealand Limited

DISTRIBUTION IN A SERVICES CONTEXT

What? How? Where? When? Responses to these four questions form the foundation of any service distribution strategy. They determine the customer's service experience, which is a function of how the different elements of the Flower of Service (Chap. 4) are distributed and delivered through physical and electronic channels. These questions are summarized in the Flow Model of Service Distribution in Fig. 5.1. The "what" determines what exactly will flow through the distribution channel (i.e., information, negotiation, and the core and other supplementary services), and a distribution strategy needs to cover for each of these flows the remaining three questions of how, where, and when. This model is the organizing framework for this chapter, and the following sections describe various components of this model.

WHAT IS BEING DISTRIBUTED?

For majority of people, distribution literally means moving boxes through physical channels to distributors and retailers for sale to end-users. In services though, often there is nothing to move. Experiences, performances, and solutions cannot be physically shipped and stored. Meanwhile, informational transactions are increasingly conducted via electronic channels. How then does distribution work in context of service? In a typical service sales cycle, distribution embraces three interrelated flows which partially address the question of *what* is being distributed:

- *Information and promotion flow* — distribution of information and promotion materials relating to the service offer. The objective is to get the customer interested in buying the service.
- *Negotiation flow* — reaching an agreement on the service features and configuration, and the terms of the offer, so that a purchase contract can be closed. The objective is often to sell the *right* to use a service (e.g., sell a reservation or a ticket).
- *Product flow* — many services, especially those involving people processing or possession processing, require physical facilities for delivery. Here, distribution strategy requires development of a network of local sites. For information-processing services, such as Internet banking and distance learning, the product flow can be via electronic channels, employing one or more centralized sites.

The flow perspective on what is being distributed can relate to the core service as well as to supplementary services of the Flower of Service. Distinguishing between core and supplementary services is important,

Figure 5.1: The flow model of service distribution

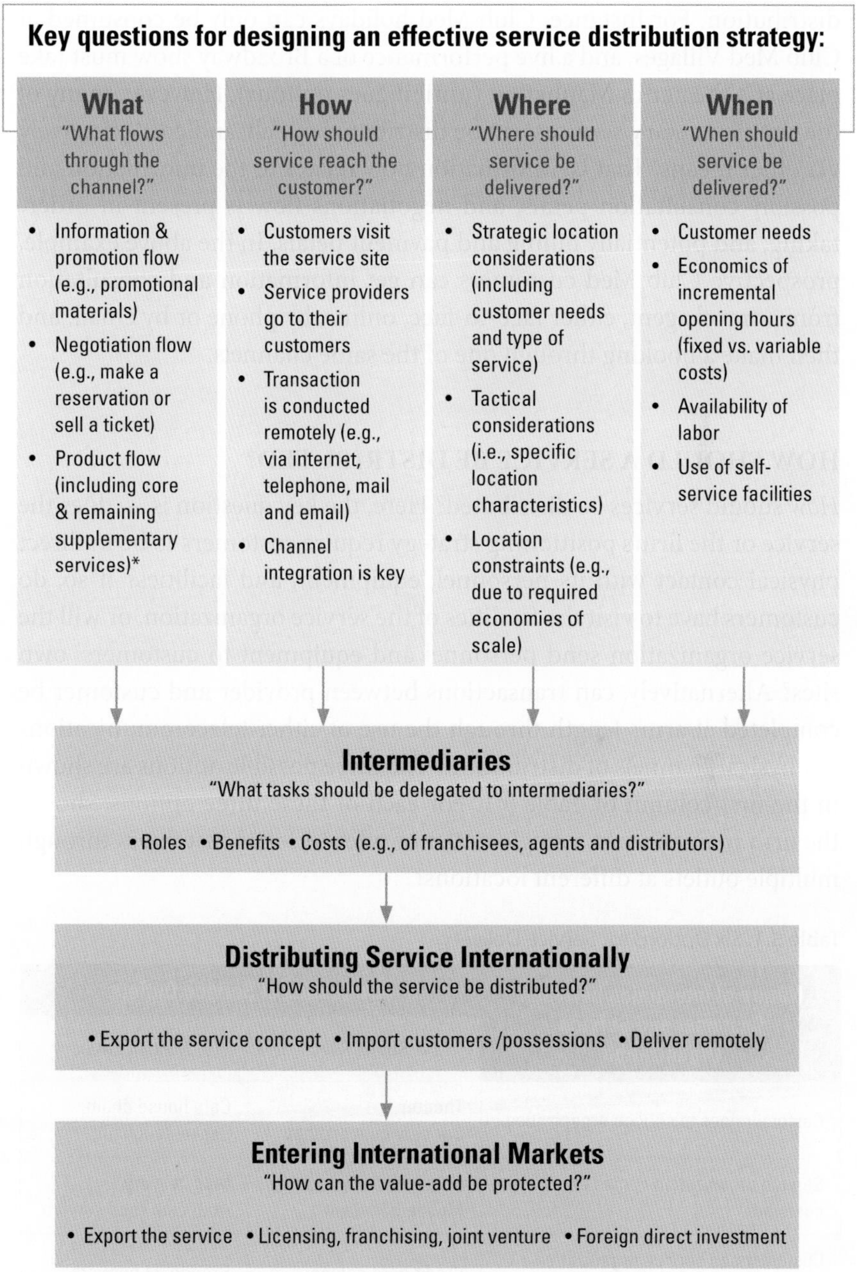

Key questions for designing an effective service distribution strategy:

What	How	Where	When
"What flows through the channel?"	"How should service reach the customer?"	"Where should service be delivered?"	"When should service be delivered?"
• Information & promotion flow (e.g., promotional materials) • Negotiation flow (e.g., make a reservation or sell a ticket) • Product flow (including core & remaining supplementary services)*	• Customers visit the service site • Service providers go to their customers • Transaction is conducted remotely (e.g., via internet, telephone, mail and email) • Channel integration is key	• Strategic location considerations (including customer needs and type of service) • Tactical considerations (i.e., specific location characteristics) • Location constraints (e.g., due to required economies of scale)	• Customer needs • Economics of incremental opening hours (fixed vs. variable costs) • Availability of labor • Use of self-service facilities

Intermediaries
"What tasks should be delegated to intermediaries?"

• Roles • Benefits • Costs (e.g., of franchisees, agents and distributors)

Distributing Service Internationally
"How should the service be distributed?"

• Export the service concept • Import customers /possessions • Deliver remotely

Entering International Markets
"How can the value-add be protected?"

• Export the service • Licensing, franchising, joint venture • Foreign direct investment

*Note that information and negotiations are types of supplementary services, but were listed separately here to emphasize their importance in any service distribution strategy.

as many core services require a physical location, which severely restricts distribution. For instance, Club Med holidays can only be consumed at Club Med Villages, and a live performance of a Broadway show must take place at a theater in Manhattan (until it goes on tour). However, many of the supplementary services can be distributed widely and cost-effectively via other means. That is, information flow relates to the information and possibly consultation petals, and negotiations flow is present in order-taking, and potentially billing and payment petals. In the above example, prospective Club Med customers can get information and consultation from a travel agent, either face-to-face, online, by phone or by email, and then make a booking through one of the same channels.

HOW SHOULD A SERVICE BE DISTRIBUTED?

How should services be distributed? Here, the key question is — does the service or the firm's positioning strategy require customers to be in direct physical contact with its personnel, equipment, and facilities? If so, do customers have to visit the facilities of the service organization, or will the service organization send personnel and equipment to customers' own sites? Alternatively, can transactions between provider and customer be completed at arm's length through the use of either telecommunications or physical channels of distribution? The three possible options are shown in the first column of Table 5.1. For each of these three options, should the firm maintain just a single outlet or offer to serve customers through multiple outlets at different locations?

Table 5.1: Six Options for Service Delivery

Nature of Interaction between Customer and Service Organization	Availability of Service Outlets	
	Single Site	Multiple Sites
Customer goes to service organization	Theater Car service workshop	Café house chain Car rental chain
Service organization comes to customer	House painting Mobile car wash	Mail delivery Auto club road service
Customer and service organization transact remotely (mail or electronic communication)	Credit card company Local TV station	Broadcast network Telephone company

Customers Visit the Service Site

When customers have to visit the service site, key factors that need to be considered include costs (e.g., rental), customer catchment areas, and the convenience of service outlet locations for customer. Elaborate statistical analysis including retail gravity models are used to help firms make decisions on where to locate supermarkets or similar large stores, relative to homes and workplaces of future customers.

Service Providers Go to Their Customers

For some types of services, the service provider visits the customer. Compass Group, the largest food service organization in the United Kingdom and Ireland, provides catering and support services to over 8,500 locations in 50 countries with over 500,000 employees. They must visit the customer's site, because the need is location-specific. When else should service providers go to their customers?

- Going to the customer's site is unavoidable whenever the object of the service is some immovable physical item, such as a tree to be pruned, installed machinery to be repaired, or a house that requires pest control treatment.

- There may be a profitable niche in serving individuals who are willing to pay a premium for the convenience of receiving personal visits or home delivery. Think of Domino's Pizza's delivery service, or Starbucks which only started to offer delivery to office buildings in 2015. The service was launched in Manhattan and Seattle, with workers in the Empire State building being the first who were able to enjoy the convenience of having their favorite Espresso Frappuccino blended coffee and other energy boosters delivered directly to their desks.

Another example is a young veterinary doctor who has built her business around house calls to care for sick pets. She found that customers are happy to pay extra for service that not only saves them time, but is less stressful for their pets, compared to waiting in a crowded veterinary clinic, full of other animals and their worried owners. Other consumer services of this kind include mobile car-washing, office and in-home catering, and made-to-measure tailoring services for business people.

A growing service activity involves the rental of both equipment and labor at the customer's site for special occasions or in response to customers who need to expand their capacity during busy periods.

The Service Transaction is Conducted Remotely

Developments in telecommunications, online technology and sophisticated logistics solutions have spurred many new approaches to service delivery. A customer may never see the service facilities or meet service personnel face-to-face when dealing with a service firm through remote transactions. Service encounters with service personnel are more likely via a customer contact center, mail, email, chat or Twitter, and should physical products, documents, or other tangibles (e.g., credit cards or membership cards) need to reach a customer, logistics providers offer integrated, reliable, and cost-effective solutions to service firms. Examples of service transactions at arm's length are:

- Repair services for small pieces of equipment sometimes require customers to ship the product to a maintenance facility, where it is serviced and then returned by mail (with the option of paying extra for express shipment). Many service providers offer solutions with the help of integrated logistics firms such as FedEx, TNT, or UPS. These solutions range from the storage and express delivery of spare parts for aircraft (B2B delivery), to the pickup of defective cell phones from customers' homes and return of the repaired phones (B2C pickup and delivery, also called "reverse logistics").

- Any information-based product can be delivered almost instantly through the Internet from almost any point on the globe to any smart device, phone, tablet and their apps connected via high-speed Internet technology.

Looking at the eight petals of the Flower of Service, you can see that there is no lesser than five supplementary services are information based (Fig. 5.2). Information, consultation, order-taking, billing, and payment (e.g., via credit card) can all be transmitted using online channels. Even service businesses that involve physical core products, such as retailing and repair, are shifting delivery of many supplementary services to the Internet, closing physical branches, and relying on speedy business

Figure 5.2: Information and physical processes of the Flower of Service

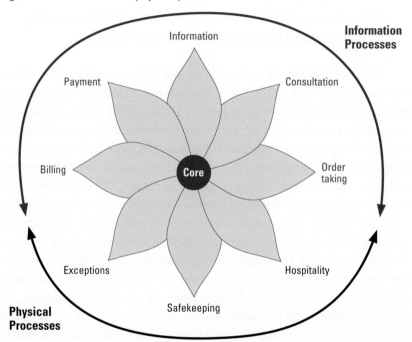

logistics to enable a strategy of arm's-length transactions with their customers.

Web and app-delivered services are becoming increasingly sophisticated, but also more user-friendly. They often simulate the services of a well-informed sales assistant in steering customers toward items that are likely to be of interest. Some even provide the opportunity for "live" email or chat dialog with helpful customer service personnel. Facilitating searches is another useful service on many sites, ranging from browsing available books by a particular author, to finding flight schedules between two cities on a specific date. Important factors that attract customers to use online services are:

- Convenience.
- Ease of search (obtaining information and searching for desired items or services).
- Broader selection.

- Potential for better prices.
- 24/7 service with prompt delivery. This is particularly appealing to customers whose busy lives leave them short of time.

The distribution of information, consultation, and order-taking (or reservations and ticket sales) has reached extremely sophisticated levels in some global service industries (think of the hotel, airline, and car rental services), requiring a number of carefully integrated channels targeted at key customer segments. For example, large hotel management companies have global sales offices (GSOs) around the world to manage customer relationships with key global accounts, offering a one-stop solution to corporate travel planners, wholesalers, meeting planners, incentive houses, and major travel organizations.[1] They also operate customer contact centers strategically located around the globe to cover all time zones and key language requirements. This helps to provide one-stop customer service for its guests, encompassing worldwide hotel reservations, enrolment, and redemption of its loyalty program, in addition to its general customer service. The customer just needs to call a toll-free number to book any of a chain's hotels. Alternatively, rooms can also be reserved through electronic channels, including their websites and apps.

Channel Preferences Vary among Customers

The use of different channels to deliver the same service not only has vastly different cost implications for a service organization, it also drastically affects the nature of the service experience for the customer. Although electronic self-service channels tend to be the most cost-effective, not all customers like to use them. This means that if we want to migrate customers to new electronic channels, we may require different strategies for different segments.[2] We also need to recognize that some proportion of customers will never voluntarily change from their preferred high-contact delivery environments. Recent research has explored how customers choose among personal, impersonal, and self-service channels, and has identified the following key drivers[3]:

- For complex and perceived high-risk services, people tend to rely on personal channels. For example, customers are happy to apply

Figure 5.3: Frequent travelers are often willing to use self-check-ins so as to avoid queues

for credit cards using remote channels, but prefer a face-to-face transaction when obtaining a mortgage.

- Individuals with higher confidence and knowledge about a service and/or the channel are more likely to use impersonal and self-service channels (Fig. 5.3).

- Customers who look for the functional aspects of a transaction prefer more convenience. This often means the use of impersonal and self-service channels. Customers with social motives tend to use personal channels.

- Convenience is a key driver of channel choice for the majority of consumers. Service convenience means saving time and effort rather than saving money. A customer's search for convenience is not just confined to the purchase of core products but also extends to convenient times and places. People want easy access to supplementary services too — especially information, reservations, and problem solving.

Channel Integration is Key

Individually or in combination, electronic channels offer a complement or alternative to traditional physical channels for delivering information-based services. However, channel integration is key for successfully delivering through multiple channels.[4] As consumers are using more devices while still using traditional channels (e.g., ATMs, branches, and call centers), it is important for service organizations to deliver a seamless and consistent user experience across channels. New delivery channels have created an inconsistent and frequently disjointed experience for many customers.

Finally, service providers have to be careful when channels are priced differently. Increasingly, customers are taking advantage of price variation among channels and markets, a strategy known as channel arbitrage.[5] For example, customers can ask the expensive full-service broker for advice (and perhaps place a small order), and then conduct the bulk of their trades via the much lower-priced discount broker. Service providers need to develop effective pricing strategies that will enable them to deliver value and capture it through the appropriate channel.

WHERE SHOULD A SERVICE FACILITY BE LOCATED?[6]

Unless a service is delivered remotely, location decisions for physical sites have to be made carefully. A physical site location requires a sizable investment and a long-term commitment. Due to its fixed nature as a result of long leases and high investments into a site, a firm cannot easily move to another site or convert to another format. Even if sunk costs are written off, moving to another location causes the problem of a portion of loyal customers and employees being lost; the farther the distance between the new and old location, the bigger the loss.

How then should service managers make decisions on the places *where* service is delivered? Frequently, a two-step approach is used; first, strategic location considerations are developed to help identify the general types of location a service firm should aim for. Second, tactical considerations are used to choose between specific sites of a similar type that fit the overall location strategy.

Strategic Location Considerations

The site location is an integral part of the overall service strategy; it must be at a location consistent with its marketing strategy and target segments for an extended period of time. To develop a location strategy, start by

Figure 5.4: Millions of people from around the world are willing to travel to Munich to experience the Oktoberfest

understanding customer needs and expectations, competitive activity, and the nature of the service operation. As we noted earlier, the distribution strategies used for some of the supplementary service elements may differ from those used to deliver the core product itself. For instance, as a customer, you're probably willing to go to a particular location at a specific time to attend a sporting or entertainment event. But you probably want greater flexibility and convenience when reserving a seat in advance, so you may expect the reservations service to be open for extended hours, to offer booking and credit card payment by phone or the Internet, and to deliver tickets through postal or electronic channels.

Likewise, firms should make it easy for people to access frequently purchased services, especially those that face active competition.[7] Examples include retail banks and fast-food restaurants. However, customers may be willing to travel further from their homes or workplaces to reach specialty services (Fig. 5.4).

In general, firms have to trade-off between ease of access and convenience for their customers versus the cost of providing that access and convenience. Markets can often be segmented by accessibility preferences and price sensitivity. There will always be segments that are willing to pay premium for ease of access and convenience (even if that applies only to certain consumption situations such as the occasional pizza TV dinner at home for home delivery services), and segments that are willing to travel and spend time for a lower price.

Tactical Location Considerations

In the second step for selecting a specific site, key factors that need to be considered include:

- Population size and characteristics (i.e., to assess the density and number of target customers that could be served with this site)
- Pedestrian and vehicular traffic and its characteristics (i.e., to assess the number of target customers passing a site that could be served with this outlet)
- Convenience of access for customers (e.g., public transportation, availability of parking)
- Competitors in this area
- Nature of nearby businesses and stores
- Availability of labor
- Availability of site locations, rental costs and contractual conditions (e.g., length of lease, legal restrictions), and regulations (e.g., on zoning and opening hours)

Elaborate statistical analyses and models are used to help firms make decisions on where to locate supermarkets or similar large stores, relative to the homes and workplaces of future customers. Geographic information system (GIS) tools combine maps with key location data, including population demographics, purchase data, and listing of current and proposed competitor locations. Mapping software can be accessed or leased for as little as $100 to several thousands of dollars, such as Autodesk (http://usa.autodesk.com) or Nielsen site reports (www.claritas.com/sitereports/default.jsp). These tools help firms to find locations with the most desirable attributes and derive the sales potential of these sites. For example, Starbucks uses GIS software as part of its site selection. Patrick O'Hagan, Starbucks' manager of global market planning, said:

> *My team provides analytics, decision support, business intelligence, and geospatial intelligence to our real-estate partners… We need tools that provide decision support to answer critical questions — what's going on in this trade area; what are general retail trends in this area; where are competitors; who are those competitors; where is business generated; where's the highest traffic volume; where are people living; where are they working; and how are they travelling to work?*[28]

Locational Constraints

Although customer convenience is important, the need for economies of scale and operational requirements may restrict choice of locations.

- Major hospitals offer many different healthcare services at a single location, requiring a very large facility. Customers requiring complex, in-patient treatment must go to the service facility rather than be treated at home. However, an ambulance — or even a helicopter — can be sent to pick them up. Medical specialists, as opposed to general practitioners, often find it convenient to locate their offices close to a hospital because it saves them time when they need to treat their patients.

- Airports, for instance, are often inconveniently located relative to travelers' homes, offices, or destinations. Because of noise and environmental factors, finding suitable sites for construction of new airports or expansion of existing ones is a very difficult task. A governor of Massachusetts was once asked what would be an acceptable location for a second airport to serve Boston; he thought for a moment and then responded, "Nebraska!" One way to make airport access more convenient is to install fast rail links, such as San Francisco's BART service (Fig. 5.5) or London's Heathrow Express.

Figure 5.5: San Francisco's BART service helps passengers get to the city from the airport more conveniently

SFO BART station photo courtesy of Bay Area Rapid Transit District.

Innovative Location Strategies

Innovative distribution strategies can be at the core of powerful new service models. We highlight mini-stores and related location strategies, and locating in multi-purpose facilities in the following sections. What these strategies have in common is that accessibility is a key component of these services' value propositions.

Mini-stores: An interesting innovation among multisite service businesses involves creating numerous small service factories to maximize geographic coverage. Examples include:

- Automated kiosks are one example. Automated teller machines (ATMs) offer many of the functions of a bank branch within a self-service machine that can be located within stores, hospitals, colleges, airports, and office buildings. Automated vending machines for stamps purchase and payment of bills is another example.

- Another approach results from separating the front and back stages of the operation. Taco Bell's innovative K-Minus strategy involves restaurants without kitchens. Food preparation takes place in a central location. The meals are then shipped to restaurants (which can now devote more of their expensive floor area to customer use) and to other "points of access" (such as mobile food carts), where the food can be reheated before serving.

- Increasingly, firms offering one type of service business are purchasing space from another provider in a complementary field. Perhaps you've noticed small bank branches inside supermarkets, and food outlets such as Dunkin Donuts and Subway sharing space with a fast-food restaurant such as Burger King.

Locating in Multi-purpose Facilities: The most obvious locations for consumer services are close to where customers live or work. Modern buildings are often designed to be multi-purpose, featuring not only office or production space but also services such as a bank (or at least an ATM), a restaurant, a hair salon, several stores, and maybe a health club. Some companies even include a children's day-care facility to make life easier for busy working parents.

Entire new business models are based on co-location strategies. For example, Walgreens, a US-pharmacy chain, is locating clinics increasingly in shopping malls vying to offer convenient and low(er) cost health services. Its clinics look like a doctor's office, but do not operate like one. Patients can check waiting times online before coming to the store, see a nurse for a diagnosis in a private room, and at kiosks, they use touch screens to pull up prescriptions and pay for them. The pharmacists devote their time to patients' questions, whereas pharmacy clerical work is done centrally elsewhere. Some doctors and their lobbyists huff that such clinics are doomed to provide substandard healthcare. However, there is little evidence of this — a study by RAND Corporation found that retail clinics were less expensive for treating common health conditions, without any apparent loss in quality.[9]

Interest is growing in locating retail and other services on transportation routes and in bus, rail, and air terminals. Most major oil companies have developed chains of small retail stores to complement the fuel pumps at their service stations, thus offering customers the convenience of one-stop shopping for fuel, vehicle supplies, food, and a selection of basic household products. Truck stops on major highways often include laundry centers, restrooms, ATMs, Internet access, restaurants, and inexpensive accommodation in addition to a variety of vehicle maintenance and repair services. Airport terminals — designed as part of infrastructure for air transportation services — have been transformed into vibrant shopping malls.

WHEN SHOULD SERVICE BE DELIVERED?

In the past, most retail and professional services in industrialized countries followed a traditional schedule of being available about 40 or 50 hours a week. In large measure, this routine reflected social norms (and even legal requirements or union agreements) as to what were appropriate hours for people to work and for enterprises to sell things. Historically, Sunday opening was strongly discouraged in most Christian cultures and was often prohibited by law, reflecting a long tradition based on religious practice. The situation inconvenienced working people who had to shop either during their lunch break or on Saturdays. Today, the situation has changed. For some highly responsive service operations, the standard has become 24/7 service — 24 hours a day, 7 days a week, around the world.

Key factors determining the opening hours of a service facility include customer needs and wants, and the economics of opening hours whereby the fixed costs of the facility and the variable costs of extending opening hours (including labor and energy costs) are weighted against the expected contribution generated from incremental sales and potential operational benefits (e.g., shifting demand from peak periods to extended opening hours). For a more detailed overview of the factors behind the move to more extended hours, see *Service Insights 5.2.*

Some firms, however, have resisted the trend to seven-day operations. Atlanta-based Chick-fil-A, a highly successful restaurant chain, declares that "being closed on Sunday is part of our value proposition" and claims that giving managers and crew a day off is a factor in the firm's extremely low attrition rate.

SERVICE INSIGHTS 5.2
Factors That Encourage Extended Operating Hours

There are at least five factors driving the move toward extended operating hours and seven-day operations. The trend that originated in the United States and Canada has since spread to many other countries around the world.

- **Pressure from consumers:** The growing number of two-income families and single wage-earners who live alone need time outside normal working hours to shop and use other services. Other customers like to enjoy the convenience to go shopping and do their service transactions at any time of the day and the week. Once one store or firm in any given area extends its hours to meet the needs of these market segments, competitors often feel the need to follow. Chain stores have frequently led the way.

- **Changes in legislation:** Support has declined for the traditional religious view that a specific day (Sunday in predominantly Christian cultures) should be legalized as a day of rest for one and all, regardless of religious affiliation. In a multicultural society, of course, it's a moot point which day should be designated as special for observant Jews and Seventh Day Adventists, Saturday is the Sabbath; for Muslims, Friday is the holy day; and agnostics or atheists are presumably indifferent. There has been a gradual erosion of such legislation in Western nations in recent years.

- **Economic incentives to improve asset utilization:** A great deal of capital is often tied up in service facilities. The incremental cost of extending hours tends to be relatively modest, and if it reduces crowding and increases revenues, then it is economically attractive. There are costs involved in shutting down and reopening a facility such as a supermarket, yet climate control and some lighting must be left running all night, and security personnel must be paid 24/7. So, even if the number of extra customers served is minimal, there are both operational and marketing advantages to remaining open 24 hours.

- **Availability of employees to work during "unsocial" hours:** Changing lifestyles and a desire for part-time employment have created a growing labor pool of people who are willing to work evenings and nights. They include students looking for part-  time work outside classroom hours, people working second jobs, parents juggling childcare responsibilities, and others who simply prefer to work at night and relax or sleep in the day.

- **Automated self-service facilities:** Self-service equipment has become increasingly reliable and user-friendly. Many machines now accept card- and cellphone-based payments, in addition to coins and banknotes. Therefore, installing unattended machines may be economically feasible alternative for locations that cannot support a staffed facility. Unless a machine requires frequent servicing or is particularly vulnerable to vandalism, the incremental cost of going from limited hours to 24-h operation is minimal. In fact, it may be simpler to leave machines running continuously than to turn them on and off.

THE ROLE OF INTERMEDIARIES

The previous sections discussed *what* is being distributed and *how*, and this section discusses *who* should be involved in delivering which parts of the service (i.e., information, negotiation, and the core and remaining supplementary services) to the customer. Should a service organization deliver all aspects of its service itself, or should it involve intermediaries to take on certain parts of service delivery? In practice, many service organizations find it cost-effective to outsource certain aspects of distribution. Most frequently, this delegation concerns supplementary service elements. For instance, despite their increased use of telephone call centers and the Internet, cruise lines and resort hotels still rely on travel agents to handle a significant portion of their customer interactions such as giving out information, taking reservations, accepting payment, and ticketing.

Benefits and Costs of Alternative Distribution Channels

How should a service provider work in partnership with one or more intermediaries to deliver a complete service package to customers? In Fig. 5.6, the Flower of Service framework shows an example in which the core product and certain supplementary elements such as information, consultation, and exception are delivered by the original supplier. The delivery of other supplementary services is delegated to an intermediary to

Figure 5.6: Splitting responsibilities for service delivery

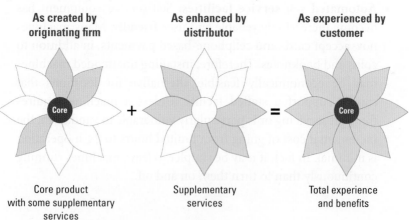

| As created by originating firm | As enhanced by distributor | As experienced by customer |

Core product with some supplementary services

Supplementary services

Total experience and benefits

complete the offering as experienced by the customer. In other instances, several specialist outsourcers might be involved as intermediaries for specific elements. The challenge for the original supplier is to act as a guardian of the overall process, ensuring that each element offered by the intermediaries fits the overall service concept in order to create a consistent and seamless branded service experience.

In addition to "outsourcing" certain tasks to intermediaries, they are frequently used to achieve reach and generate business. For example, various sales and reservation channels that are used in the travel industry (Fig. 5.7) offer different benefits and also have vastly different costs. The lowest cost distribution channel would be the service firm's own website (incremental costs are typically less than $1 per sales transaction), followed

Figure 5.7: Alternative sales channels in the hospitality industry

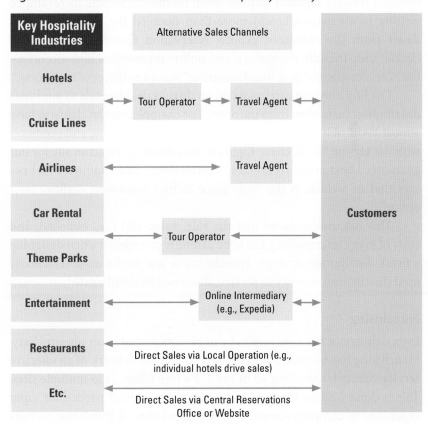

by its call-center-based central reservation systems (typically between $5 and $25 per sales transaction — note that one sales transaction can involve more than one call). Retail travel agents usually charge 10% commission, and tour operators typically mark-up to 20–30% of the transaction value. The most expensive channels are often online distributors such as Expedia and Priceline, which can charge up to 30% of the transaction value. Therefore, many service firms who have achieved brand equity aim to migrate their customers and sales to lower cost channels to circumvent or remove intermediaries, a process also called disintermediation. The profit implications will be high if a firm can save up to 30% by distributing to end customers directly.

An example of an early campaign to switch transactions to direct distribution channels, Swissôtel Hotels & Resorts executed an entire campaign to increase online bookings, especially among the important business traveler segment. Within seven months of launch, its revamped website (www.swissotel.com) more than doubled the online revenues. Apart from the enhanced express reservation functions (with fewer clicks), user-friendly navigation, and online promotions and incentives, the hotel company's "Best Rate Guarantee" was a key driver of its success.[10]

Leading low-cost carriers relied on direct sales channels to minimize distribution costs often from the onset. For example, easyJet claims to have almost 100% of its customers bookings through its website and promotes with the tagline "Book cheap flights at the official easyJet.com site for our guaranteed best prices to over 140 destinations", and Southwest Airlines says that its website is the "only place to find Southwest Airlines fares online".[11]

This discussion shows that the role, value-add (i.e., benefits), and costs of every intermediary has to be carefully considered when designing a firm's distribution strategy. Franchising is one of the most commonly used distribution strategy in service, discussed in detail next.

Franchising

Even delivery of the core product can be outsourced to an intermediary. Franchising has become a popular way to expand delivery of an effective service concept, spreading all of the 7 'P's (see Chap. 1) to multiple sites. This is done without the level of monetary investment needed for rapid expansion of company-owned and -managed sites. A franchisor recruits entrepreneurs who are willing to invest their time, effort, and equity in managing a previously developed service concept. In return, the franchisor provides training on how to operate and market the business, sells necessary supplies, and provides promotional support at a national or regional level. Local marketing activities are typically paid for by the franchisee, but they must adhere to copy and media guidelines prescribed by the franchisor.[12]

The International Franchise Association, the world's oldest and largest organization representing franchising worldwide, has defined franchising as follows:

> A franchise is the agreement or license between two legally independent parties which gives: (a) a person or group of people (franchisee) the right to market a product or service using the trademark or trade name of another business (franchisor); (b) the franchisee the right to market a product or service using the operating methods of the franchisor; (c) the franchisee the obligation to pay the franchisor fees for these rights, and (d) the franchisor the obligation to provide rights and support to franchisees.[13]

Franchising is a particularly attractive strategy for service firms when:

- The firm has limited resources and fast growth is necessary to pre-empt competition. Service firms often have little protection beyond their brand as almost everything else they do can be copied by others. The firm that first managed to become top of mind in their target segments for a particular category (e.g., coffee chain) tends to become the market leader in the long run. Franchisees often invest significant funds into their franchise and thereby facilitate fast growth of the overall chain.
- The long-term commitment of the store manager is crucial. Franchisees tend to be highly motivated to ensure high customer satisfaction, build customer loyalty, and run high-quality service operations.[14]
- Local knowledge is important. Franchisees tend to be from the

Figure 5.8: Subway is a popular American fast food franchise

local community and therefore can be highly effective in dealing with local authorities (e.g., during the construction and renovation of facilities), labor markets, media, and customers.

The US is the global leader in franchising, a position it has held since the 1930s when it first used the approach for fast-food restaurants, inns and, slightly later, for motels. Although franchising is still most commonly associated with fast-food restaurants (Fig. 5.8), the concept has been applied to a wide variety of both consumer and B2B services, and now spans some 300 different product categories. New concepts are created and commercialized all the time in most countries around the world. The fastest-growing categories of concepts are related to health and fitness, publications, security, and consumer services. The franchise industry

Table 5.2: The Top 10 Franchises in the US in 2015 and Their Start-up Costs

Rank	Franchise Name	Type	Startup Costs (US$ in thousands)
1	Hampton Hotels	Hotel	$4,000 – $14,000
2	Anytime Fitness	Fitness	$79 – $371
3	Subway	Fast-food	$117 – 263
4	Jack in the Box	Fast-food	$1,000 – $2,000
5	Supercuts	Hair-salon	$114 – $234
6	Jimmy John's Gourmet Sandwiches	Restaurant	$331 – $520
7	Servpro	Fire and water cleanup and restoration	$139 – $187
8	Denny's Inc.	Restaurant	$1,000 – $3,000
9	Pizza Hut Inc.	Restaurant	$297 – $2,000
10	7-Eleven Inc.	Convenience store	$37 – $2,000

Source: http://www.entrepreneur.com/franchise500/index.html, accessed February 18, 2016

accounts for approximately 50% of all retail sales and services in the United States. One out of every 12 businesses is a franchised business. Some 900,000 franchise businesses in the US provide jobs for more than 18 million people and create over $2.1 trillion in economic activity.[15] Among the cases featured in this book is "Aussie Pooch Mobile", which describes a successful Australian-based franchised dog washing service. In your own role as a consumer, you probably patronize more franchises than you realize (Table 5.2).

From a franchisee perspective, a longitudinal study in the restaurant industry has shown that buying a franchise is, on average, more profitable than starting an independent restaurant.[16] Nevertheless, there is a high drop-out rate among franchisors in the initial years of a new franchise system, with one-third of all systems failing within the first four years and no less than three-quarters of all franchisors ceasing to exist after 12 years.[17] Success factors for franchisors include:

- The ability to achieve a larger size with a more recognizable brand name.
- Offering fewer supporting services but longer-term contracts to franchisees.
- Having lower overhead per outlet.
- Providing accurate and realistic information about expected characteristics of franchise operations, and support given.
- Building a cooperative rather than controlling relationship.[18]

Because growth is very important to achieve an efficient scale, some franchisors adopt a strategy known as "master franchising", which involves delegating the responsibility for recruiting, training, and supporting franchisees within a given geographic area. Master franchisees often are individuals who have already succeeded as operators of one or several individual franchise outlets. They have the responsibility for recruiting, training, and supporting franchisees within a given geographic area.

While franchising has many success stories, it also has some disadvantages.

- It entails some loss of control over the delivery system and, consequently, over how customers experience the actual service.
- Ensuring that an intermediary adopts exactly the same priorities and

procedures as prescribed by the franchisor is difficult, yet it's vital for effective quality control. Franchisors usually seek to exercise control over all the aspects of the service performance through a contract that specifies adherence to tightly defined service standards, procedures, scripts, and physical presentation. Franchisors frequently control not only output specifications, but also the appearance of the servicescape, employee performance, and elements such as service timetables.

- An ongoing problem is that as franchisees gain experience, they may start to resent the various fees paid to the franchisor and instead, begin to believe they can operate the business better without the constraints imposed by the agreement, often resulting in legal disputes between the two parties.

Other Intermediaries

Service intermediaries take on many forms in terms of their role, structure, legal status and relationship with the service firm (often referred to as "principle"). Franchising is one of the most common distribution strategies used, but a range of alternative distribution intermediaries are also available. One is licensing another supplier to act on the original supplier's behalf to deliver the core product. Trucking companies regularly make use of independent agents, instead of locating company-owned branches in each of the different cities they serve. They may also choose to contract with independent "owner-operators" who drive their own trucks.[19]

Other service distribution agreements can be contractual such as those used in financial services. Banks seeking to move into investment services will often act as the distributor for mutual fund products created by an investment firm lacking extensive distribution channels of its own. Many banks also sell insurance products underwritten by an insurance company. They collect a commission on the sale, but are normally not involved in handling claims.

DISTRIBUTING SERVICES INTERNATIONALLY

Many firms distribute their services internationally, including CNN,

Figure 5.9: How to go international?

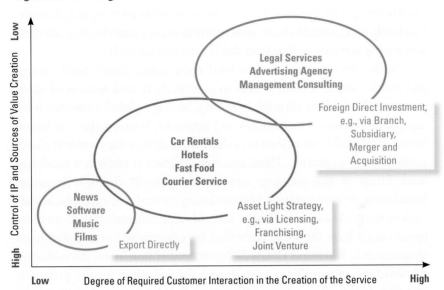

Reuters, Google, AMEX, Starbucks, Hertz, Citibank, and McKinsey. When service companies plan to go international, how should they enter new markets?[20]

How to Enter International Markets?

The strategy most suitable for entering a new international market depends on (1) how a firm can protect its intellectual property (IP) and control its key sources of value creation, and (2) whether the level of desired interaction with the customer is high or low (Fig. 5.9).

In case where a firm's IP and value creation sources can be protected through copyright or other legal means, and if only low customer contact is required (i.e., the service is distributed at arm's length via the Internet or telephone), then a company can simply export the service. In these cases, there is little risk of losing the business to local competitors, distributors or other local partners. Examples include database services (e.g., Thomson Reuters' Web of Science and Social Sciences Citation Index-related services), online news (e.g., those offered by CNN or the Financial Times), online advertising (e.g., sold globally by Google or Facebook), and the downloading of music, films, e-books, and software.

If these firms do establish a local presence in international markets, it is usually to organize their local corporate sales and marketing (e.g., Google, Facebook, and LinkedIn have sales teams in many countries that sell their advertising services) rather than deliver the service itself.[21]

Some services such as fast-food restaurants, global hotel chains, and courier services allow a firm to control its IP and sources of value creation. This is done through branding, having a global customer base, and global resources, capabilities and networks. Without these, it would become impossible, or at least very difficult, to deliver the service at a level customers are expecting. Here, customer contact is often at a moderate level. Firms in this category can expand globally through licensing, franchising, or joint ventures without losing control. For example, brands such as Starbucks and Hard Rock Café add value, and outlets without these brands don't have the same attraction for customers. Large global hotel chains such as Starwood Hotels & Resorts and Hilton "own" the customer relationships with millions of customer through their loyalty programs and global sales offices. These offices then feed business to locally owned and operated properties. These properties need the customer traffic from the global chain.

To cite another example, unlike the global courier service firm with global resources, capabilities and an extensive network, a local courier service provider is not able to source for inbound shipments from around the world. They also cannot deliver outbound shipments on a global level. Thus, the global courier service firm can safely appoint a local agent without having to fear that the agent will, at some point, become a competitor.

Finally, there are services where the value-add comes mainly from the skills and knowledge of the service provider, and where a high degree of customer contact is needed to deliver value. These are often knowledge-based, professional services. Examples include creative design of advertising campaigns and management consulting projects. For such services, value is typically created by the firm's employees through their knowledge and relationship built with their clients. It is difficult to control the sources of value creation for such services. For example, if a firm worked through a licensee or joint-venture partner, it would face the risk that once skill transfer to that partner has happened after a few years of operation, the partner would be able to deliver the service without the support of the firm. When this happens, the partner is likely to show increasing resistance to paying licensing fees or sharing profits. They are then likely to renegotiate the terms of the venture, and could even threaten to go 'independent' and cut out the original service firm. Hence, it is necessary for firms in this category to have tight control over its local resources. This usually includes having the local staff on its own payroll, with carefully written contracts that protect the firm's IP and customer base. Here, the most effective ways to enter a new market are typically through foreign direct investment by setting up a branch office, a subsidiary, or through mergers and acquisitions.[22]

CONCLUSION

What? How? Where? When? Responses to these four questions form the foundation of any service distribution strategy. The customer's service experience is a function of how the different elements of Flower of Service are distributed and delivered through selective physical and electronic channels. In addition to "what" and "how", service marketing strategy must address issues of place and time, paying as much attention to speed, scheduling, and electronic access as to the more traditional notion of physical location. Here, the rapid growth of the Internet and broadband mobile communications is especially exciting for service firms, and many elements of service are informational in nature. Furthermore, in the heat of globalization, important questions are raised concerning the design and implementation of franchising and international service distribution strategies.

CHAPTER SUMMARY

Key questions for designing an effective service distribution strategy:

What	How	Where	When
"What flows through the channel?"	"How should service reach the customer?"	"Where should service be delivered?"	"When should service be delivered?"

What	How	Where	When
• Information & promotion flow (e.g., promotional materials) • Negotiation flow (e.g., make a reservation or sell a ticket) • Product flow (including core & remaining supplementary services)*	• Customers visit the service site • Service providers go to their customers • Transaction is conducted remotely (e.g., via internet, telephone, mail and email) • Channel integration is key	• Strategic location considerations (including customer needs and type of service) • Tactical considerations (i.e., specific location characteristics) • Location constraints (e.g., due to required economies of scale)	• Customer needs • Economics of incremental opening hours (fixed vs. variable costs) • Availability of labor • Use of self-service facilities

Intermediaries
"What tasks should be delegated to intermediaries?"

• Roles • Benefits • Costs (e.g., of franchisees, agents and distributors)

Distributing Service Internationally
"How should the service be distributed?"

• Export the service concept • Import customers /possessions • Deliver remotely

Entering International Markets
"How can the value-add be protected?"

• Export the service • Licensing, franchising, joint venture • Foreign direct investment

*Note that information and negotiations are types of supplementary services, but were listed separately here to emphasize their importance in any service distribution strategy.

CHAPTER 6

Pricing Services and Revenue Management

What is a cynic? A man who knows the price of everything and the value of nothing.

Oscar Wilde
Irish author, playwright and poet, (1854–1900)

There are two fools in any market: One does not charge enough. The other charges too much.

Russian Proverb

EFFECTIVE PRICING IS CENTRAL TO FINANCIAL SUCCESS

Importantly, marketing is the only function that brings operating revenues into the organization. All other management functions incur costs. A *business model* is the mechanism whereby, through effective pricing, sales are transformed into revenues, costs are recovered, and value is created for owners of the business. As noted by Joan Magretta:

> A good business model answer [American management consultant] Peter Drucker's age-old questions: Who is the customer? And what does the customer value? It also answers the fundamental questions that every manager must ask: How do we make money in this business? What is the underlying economic logic that explains how we can deliver value to customers at an appropriate cost?[1]

Creating a viable service requires a business model that allows for the costs of creating and delivering the service, in addition to a margin for profits, to be recovered through realistic pricing and revenue management strategies.

However, the pricing of services is complicated. Consider the bewildering fee schedules of many consumer banks or cellphone service providers, or the fluctuating fare structure of a full-service airline. Service organizations even use different terms to describe the prices they set. Universities talk about tuition fees, professional firms collect fees, banks impose interest and service charges, brokers charge commissions, some expressways impose tolls, utilities set tariffs, and insurance companies determine premiums; the list goes on. Consumers often find service pricing difficult to understand (e.g., insurance products or hospital bills), risky (when enquiring about an intercontinental flight on three different days, three different prices may be offered), and sometimes even unethical (e.g., many bank and credit card users complain about a variety of fees and charges they consider to be unfair).

This chapter explains how to set an effective pricing and revenue management strategy that fulfills the promise of the value proposition so that a value exchange takes place (i.e., the consumer decides to buy the service).

Objectives for Establishing Prices

Any pricing strategy must be based on a clear understanding of a company's pricing objectives. The most common high-level pricing objectives are summarized in Table 6.1.

Table 6.1: Objectives for pricing of services

Revenue and Profit Objectives

Gain Profit

- Make the largest possible long-term contribution or profit.
- Achieve a specific target level, but do not seek to maximize profits.
- Maximize revenue from a fixed capacity by varying prices and target segments over time. This is done typically using revenue management systems.

Cover Costs

- Cover fully allocated costs, including corporate overhead.
- Cover costs of providing one particular service, excluding overhead.
- Cover incremental costs of selling one extra unit or to serve one extra customer.

Patronage and User Base-Related Objectives

Build Demand

- Maximize demand (when capacity is not a restriction), provided a certain minimum level of revenue is achieved (e.g., many non-profit organizations are focused on encouraging usage rather than revenue, but they still have to cover costs).
- Achieve full capacity utilization, especially when high capacity utilization adds to the value created for all customers (e.g., a "full house" adds excitement to a theater play or basketball game).

Develop a User Base

- Encourage trial and adoption of a service. This is especially important for new services with high infrastructure costs, and for membership-type services that generate a large amount of revenues from their continued usage after adoption (e.g., cell phone service subscriptions, or life insurance plans).
- Build market share and/or a large user base, especially if there are large economies of scale that can lead to a competitive cost advantage (e.g., if development or fixed costs are high), or network effects where additional users enhance the value of the service to the existing user base (e.g., Facebook and LinkedIn).

Strategy-Related Objectives

Support Positioning Strategy

- Help and support the firm's overall positioning and differentiation strategy (e.g., as a price leader, or portrait a premium image with premium pricing).
- Promote a "We-will-not-be-undersold" positioning, whereby a firm promises the best possible service at the best possible price. That is, the firm wants to communicate that the offered quality of service products cannot be bought at a lower cost elsewhere.

Support Competitive Strategy

- Discourage existing competitors to expand capacity.
- Discourage potential new competitors to enter the market.

PRICING STRATEGY STANDS ON THREE FOUNDATIONS

The foundations of pricing strategy can be described as a tripod, with costs to the provider, competitors' pricing, and value to the customer as the three legs (Fig. 6.1). In many service industries, pricing used to be viewed from a financial and accounting standpoint, and therefore cost-plus pricing was used. Today, however, most service firms have a good understanding of value-based and competitive pricing. In the pricing tripod, the costs a firm needs to recover usually set a minimum price, or price floor, for a specific service offering, and the customer's perceived value of the offering sets a maximum price, or price ceiling.

Figure 6.1: The pricing tripod

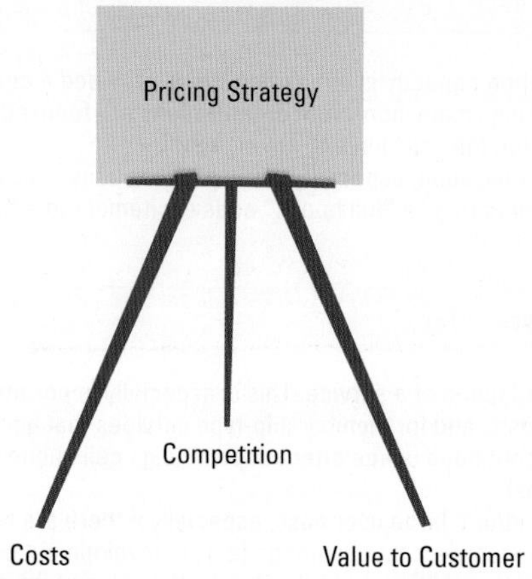

The price charged by competing services typically determines where the price can be set within the floor-to-ceiling range. The pricing objectives of the organization then determine where actual prices should be set, given the possible range provided by the pricing tripod analysis. Each leg of the pricing tripod will be examined in detail later.

Cost-Based Pricing

Pricing is typically more complex in services than it is in manufacturing. As there is no ownership of services, it is usually harder to determine the financial costs of creating a process or intangible real-time performance for a customer than it is to identify the labor, materials, machine time, storage, and shipping costs associated with producing and distributing a physical good. In addition, due to the labor and infrastructure needed to create performances, many service organizations have a much higher ratio of fixed costs to variable costs than is typically found in manufacturing firms. Service businesses with high fixed costs include those with expensive physical facilities (such as hospitals or colleges), or a fleet of vehicles (such as airlines or trucking companies), or a network (such as railroad, telecommunications, and gas pipeline companies).

Establishing the Costs of Providing Service. It is helpful to review how service costs can be estimated, using fixed, semi-variable, and variable costs, as well as how the notions of contribution and breakeven analysis can help in pricing decisions (see *Marketing Review 6.1*). These traditional cost-accounting approaches work well for service firms with a large proportion of variable and/or semi-variable costs (e.g., many professional services).

MARKETING REVIEW 6.1
Understanding Costs, Contribution, and Break-Even Analysis

Fixed costs are economic costs a supplier would continue to incur (at least in the short run) even if no services were sold. These costs typically include rent, depreciation, utilities, taxes, insurance, salaries and wages for managers and long-term employees, security, and interest payments.

Variable costs refer to the economic costs associated with serving an additional customer, such as making an additional bank transaction, or selling an additional seat on a flight. In many services, such costs are very low. For instance, very little labor or fuel cost is involved in transporting an extra passenger on a flight. In a theater, the cost of seating an extra patron is close to zero. More significant variable costs are associated with activities such as serving food and beverages or installing new parts when undertaking repairs, as they often include providing costly physical products in addition to labor. Just because a firm has sold a service at a price that exceeds its variable cost does not mean the firm is now profitable, since there are still fixed and semi-variable costs to be recouped.

Semi-variable costs fall in between fixed and variable costs. They represent expenses that rise or fall in a stepwise fashion as the volume of business increases or decreases. Examples include adding an extra flight to meet increased demand on a specific route, or hiring a part-time employee to work in a restaurant on busy weekends.

Contribution is the difference between the variable cost of selling an extra unit of service and the money received from the buyer of that service. It goes to cover fixed and semi-variable costs before creating profits.

Determining and allocating economic costs can be a challenging task in some service operations due to the difficulty of deciding how to assign fixed costs in a multi-service facility such as a hospital. For instance, certain fixed costs are associated with running the emergency department in a hospital. Beyond that, there are fixed costs of running the hospital. So, how much of the hospital's fixed costs should be allocated to the emergency department? A hospital manager might use one of several approaches to calculate the emergency department's share of overhead costs. These could include (1) the percentage of total floor space it occupies, (2) the percentage of employee hours or payroll it accounts for, or (3) the percentage of total patient contact hours involved. Each method is likely to yield a different fixed-cost allocation. One method might show the emergency department to be very profitable, while the other might flag it as a loss-making operation.

Breakeven analysis allows managers to know at what sales volume a service will become profitable. This is called the breakeven point. The necessary analysis involves dividing the total fixed and semi-variable costs by the contribution obtained on each unit of service. For example, if a 100-room hotel needs to cover fixed and semi-variable costs of $2 million a year, and the average contribution per room-night is $100, then the hotel will need to sell 20,000 room-nights per year out of a total annual capacity of

36,500. If prices are cut by an average of $20 per room-night (or if variable costs rise by $20), then the contribution will drop to $80, and the hotel's breakeven volume will rise to 25,000 room-nights.

Activity-based Costing.[2] For service firms with high fixed costs and complex product lines with shared infrastructure such as in retail banking, it may be worthwhile considering the more complex activity-based costing (also called ABC) approach. For such firms, the activity-based costing is a more accurate way to allocate indirect costs (i.e., overheads).

Activity-based costing links resources needed to perform an activity. A set of activities that comprises the processes needed to create and deliver a particular service is then combined. When determining the indirect cost of a service, a firm looks at the resources needed to perform each activity, and then allocates the indirect cost to a service based on the quantities and types of activities required to perform the service. Thus, resource expenses (or indirect costs) are linked to the variety and complexity of services produced and not just on physical volume.

If implemented well, firms will be in a better position to estimate the costs of its various services, activities, and processes — and about the costs of creating specific types of services, delivering services in different locations (even different countries), or serving specific customers. The net result is a management tool that can help companies to pinpoint the profitability of different services, channels, market segments, and even individual customers.

Pricing Implications of Cost Analysis. To make a profit, a firm must set its price high enough to recover the full costs of producing and marketing the service, and add a sufficient margin to yield the desired profit at the predicted sales volume.

Managers in businesses with high fixed and marginal variable costs may feel that they have tremendous pricing flexibility and be tempted to set low prices in order to boost sales. Some firms promote *loss leaders*, which are services sold at less than full cost to attract customers, who (it is hoped) will then be tempted to buy profitable service offerings from the same organization in the future. However, there will be no profit at the end of the year unless all relevant costs have been recovered. Many service businesses have gone bankrupt because they ignored this fact. Hence, firms that compete on low prices need to have a very good understanding of their cost structure and the sales volumes needed to breakeven.

Value-Based Pricing

Another leg of the pricing tripod is value to the customer. No customer will pay more for a service than he or she thinks it is worth. Marketers need to understand how customers perceive service value in order to set an appropriate price.[3]

Understanding Net Value. When customers purchase a service, they are weighing the perceived benefits of the service against the perceived costs they will incur. This book uses the term *net value* — the sum of all perceived benefits (gross value) minus the sum of all the perceived costs of the service. The greater the positive difference between the two, the greater the net value.

Economists use the term *consumer surplus* to define the difference between the price customers pay and the amount they would have been willing to pay to obtain the desired benefits (or "utility") offered by a specific product. If the perceived costs of a service are greater than its perceived benefits, the service in question will possess negative net value, and the consumer will not buy it. Calculations that customers make in their minds are similar to weighing with a pair of old-fashioned scales, with product benefits in one tray and the costs associated with obtaining those benefits in the other tray (Fig. 6.2). When customers evaluate competing services, they are comparing the relative net values (see also multi-attribute models in Chap. 2). As discussed in Chap. 4, a marketer can increase the value of a service by adding benefits to the core product and by improving supplementary services, which typically entails enhancing the benefits while reducing the burdens for customers.

Managing the Perception of Value.[4] Since value is subjective, not all customers have the skills or knowledge to judge the quality and value they receive. This is true especially for credence services (discussed in Chap. 2), for which customers cannot assess the quality of a service even after consumption.[5] Marketers of services such as strategy consulting must find ways to communicate the time, research, professional expertise, and attention to detail that go into, for example, completing a best practice consulting project. The invisibility of back-stage facilities and labor

Figure 6.2: Net value equals perceived benefits minus perceived costs

makes it hard for customers to see what they are getting for their money. Therefore, the firm will have to manage the perception of value.

Consider a homeowner who calls an electrician to repair a defective circuit. The electrician arrives, carrying a small bag of tools. He disappears into the closet where the circuit board is located, locates the problem, replaces a defective circuit breaker, and presto! Everything works. A mere 20 minutes has lapsed. A few days later, the homeowner is horrified to receive a bill for $150, most of it for labor charges. Not surprisingly, customers are often left feeling they have been taken advantage of, as is illustrated in Blondie's reaction to the plumber in Fig. 6.3.

To manage the perception of value, effective communications and even personal explanations are needed to help customers understand the value they receive. What customers often fail to recognize are the fixed costs business owners need to recoup. The electrician in the earlier example has to cover the costs for his office, telephone, insurance, vehicles, tools, fuel, and office support staff. The variable costs of a home visit are also higher than they appear. To the 20 minutes spent at the house, 15 minutes of driving each way might be added, an additional five minutes each spent to unload and reload needed tools and supplies from the van,

Figure 6.3: Blondie seeks her money's worth from the plumber

thus effectively tripling the labor time to a total of 60 minutes devoted to this call. The firm still has to add a margin in order to make a profit.

Reducing-Related Monetary and Non-monetary Costs

When considering customer net value, it is important to understand the customers' perceived costs. From a customer's point of view, the price charged by a supplier is only part of the costs involved in buying and using a service. There are other costs of service, which are made up of the related monetary and non-monetary costs.

Related Monetary Costs. Customers often incur significant financial costs in searching for, purchasing, and using the service, above and beyond the purchase price paid to the supplier. For instance, the cost of an evening at the theater for a couple with young children usually far exceeds the price of the two tickets, because it can include expenses such as hiring a babysitter, travel, parking, food and beverages.

Non-monetary Costs. Non-monetary costs reflect the time, effort, and discomfort associated with the search, purchase, and use of a service and can be collectively referred to as "effort" or "hassle". Non-monetary costs tend to be higher when customers are involved in production (which is particularly important in people-processing services and self-service) and must travel to the service site. Services high on experience and credence attributes may also create psychological costs such as anxiety. There are four distinct categories of non-monetary costs: time, physical, psychological, and sensory costs.

- *Time costs* are part of the service delivery. Today's customers often complain that they do not have enough time and are therefore reluctant to waste time on unenjoyable and non-value adding activities such as travelling to a government office and waiting in a queue. Customers may even use similar terms to define time usage as they do for money; for instance, consumers talk about budgeting, spending, investing, wasting, losing, and saving time. Time spent on one activity represents an opportunity cost because it could be spent more pleasurably or profitably in other ways. Internet users are often frustrated by the amount of time spent looking for information on a website. Many people loath visiting government offices to obtain passports, driving licenses, or permits, not because of the fees involved, but because of the time "wasted".[6]

- *Physical costs* (e.g., effort, fatigue, discomfort) may be part of the costs of obtaining services, especially if customers must go to the service factory, if waiting and long queues are involved, if body treatments are involved such as for medical treatments, piercing or waxing, and if delivery is through self-service.

- *Psychological costs* such as mental effort (e.g., filling in account opening forms requesting for detailed information), perceived risk and anxiety ("Is this the best treatment?" or "Is this be best mortgage for me?", Fig. 6.4), cognitive dissonance ("Was it good to sign up for this life insurance, this annual gym membership?"), feelings of inadequacy and fear ("Will I be smart enough to succeed in this MBA program?") are sometimes attached to buying and using a particular service.

Figure 6.4: Does adding options always create value or will it confuse the customer?

Copyright 2005 by Randy Glasbergen.
www.glasbergen.com

GLASBERGEN

"As an alternative to the traditional 30-year mortgage, we also offer an interest-only mortgage, balloon mortgage, reverse mortgage, upside down mortgage, inside out mortgage, loop-de-loop mortgage, and the spinning double axel mortgage with a triple lutz."

Figure 6.5: Defining total user costs

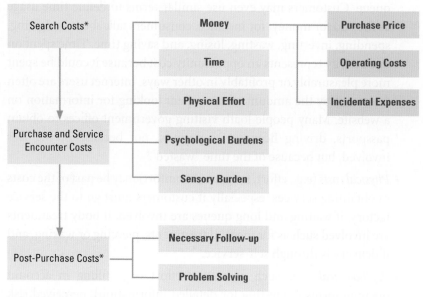

* Includes all five cost categories

- *Sensory costs* relate to unpleasant sensations affecting any of the five senses. In a service environment, these costs may include putting up with crowding, noise, unpleasant smells, drafts, excessive heat or cold, uncomfortable seating, and visually unappealing environments.

As shown in Fig. 6.5, service users can incur costs during any of the three stages of the service consumption model as introduced in Chap. 2. Consequently, firms have to consider (1) search costs, (2) purchase and service encounter costs, and (3) post-purchase or after costs. Consider how much money, time, and effort is spent when deciding which college or university a potential student can apply to; or how much time and effort is put into selecting a new cellphone service provider or a bank, or when planning a vacation.

A firm can create competitive advantage by minimizing those non-monetary and related monetary costs, and thereby increase consumer value. Possible approaches include:

- Working with operations experts to reduce time required to complete service purchase, delivery, and consumption; become "easy-to-do-business-with"
- Minimizing unwanted psychological costs of service at each stage by eliminating or redesigning unpleasant or inconvenient procedures, educating customers on what to expect, and retraining staff to be friendlier and more helpful
- Eliminating or minimizing unwanted physical effort during search and delivery processes; improving signage and "road mapping" in facilities and on webpages can help customers to find their way and prevent them from getting lost and frustrated
- Decreasing unpleasant sensory costs of service by creating more attractive visual environments, reducing noise, installing more comfortable furniture and equipment, and curtailing offensive smells
- Suggesting ways in which customers can reduce associated monetary costs, including discounts with partner suppliers (e.g., parking) or offering mail or online delivery of activities that previously required a personal visit

Perceptions of net value may vary widely among customers and from one situation to another for the same customer. Most services have at least two segments; one that spends time to save money, and another that spends money to save time. Therefore, many service markets can be segmented according to the sensitivity to time savings and convenience versus price sensitivity.[7] Consider Fig. 6.6, which identifies a choice of three clinics available to an individual who needs to obtain a routine chest x-ray. In addition to varying dollar prices for the service, different time and effort costs are associated with using each service. Depending on the customer's priorities, non-monetary costs may be as important, or even more, than the price charged by the service provider.

Competition-Based Pricing

The last leg of the pricing tripod is competition. Firms with relatively undifferentiated services need to monitor what competitors are charging and should to try to price accordingly.[8] When customers see little or no

Figure 6.6: Trading off monetary and non-monetary costs

Which clinic would you patronize if you needed a chest x-ray (assuming that all three clinics offer good technical quality)?		
Clinic A	**Clinic B**	**Clinic C**
• Price: $85	• Price: $145	• Price: $225
• Located 1 hour away by car or transit	• Located 15 minutes away by car or transit	• Located next to your office or college building
• Next available appointment is in 3 weeks	• Next available appointment is in 1 week	• Next available appointment is in 1 day
• Hours: Monday to Friday, 9 am to 5 pm	• Hours: Monday to Friday, 8 am to 10 pm	• Hours: Monday to Saturday, 8 am to 10 pm
• Estimated waiting time is about 2 hours	• Estimated waiting is about 30 to 45 minutes	• By appointment; estimated waiting time is 0 to 15 minutes

difference between competing offerings, they may just choose what they perceive to be the cheapest. In such a situation, the firm with the lowest cost per unit of service enjoys an enviable market advantage and often assumes *price leadership*. Here, one firm acts as the price leader, with others take their cue from this company, e.g., when several gas stations compete within a short distance of one another, as soon as one station raises or lowers its prices, others follow suit.

Price Competition Intensifiers. Price competition intensifies with:

- Increasing number of competitors
- Increasing number of substituting offers
- Wider distribution of competitor and/or substitution offers
- Increasing surplus capacity in the industry

Price Competition Inhibitors. Although some service industries can be fiercely competitive (e.g., airlines and online banking), not all are, especially when one or more of the following circumstances reduce price competition:

- *Non-price-related costs of using competing alternatives are high.* When saving time and effort are of equal or greater importance to customers than price in selecting a supplier, the intensity of price competition is reduced. Competitor services have their own set of related monetary and non-monetary costs. In such cases, the actual prices charged sometimes become secondary for competitive comparisons (see Fig. 6.11).

- *Personal relationships matter.* For highly personalized and customized services such as hairstyling or family medical care, relationships with individual providers are often very important to customers, thus discouraging them from responding to competitive offers. For example, many global banks prefer to focus on wealthy customers in order to form long-term personal relationships with them.

- *Switching costs are high.* When it takes effort, time, and money to switch providers, customers are less likely to take advantage of competing offers.[9] Cellphone service providers often require one- or two-year contracts from their subscribers and charge significant financial penalties for early cancellation of service. Likewise, life insurance firms charge administrative fees or cancellation charges when policy holders want to cancel their policy within a certain time period.

- *Services are often time and location specific.* When people want to use a service at a specific location or at a particular time or perhaps both simultaneously, they usually find they have fewer options, which reduces price competition.[10]

Firms that always react to competitors' price changes run the risk of pricing *lower* than what might be necessary. Managers should be aware of falling into the trap of comparing competitors' prices dollar-for-dollar, and then seeking to match them. A better strategy is to take into account the entire cost to customers of each competitive offering, including all related monetary and non-monetary costs, plus potential switching costs. Managers should also assess the impact of distribution, time, and location factors, as well as estimating competitors' available capacity before deciding what response is appropriate.

REVENUE MANAGEMENT: WHAT IT IS AND HOW IT WORKS[11]

Many service businesses now focus on strategies to maximize the revenue (or contribution) that can be obtained from available capacity at any given point in time. Revenue management is important in value creation as it ensures better capacity utilization and reserves capacity for higher-paying segments. It is a sophisticated approach to manage supply and demand under varying degrees of constraint.

Airlines, hotels, and car rental firms in particular have become adept at varying their prices in response to the price sensitivity and needs of different market segments at different times of the day, week or season. More recently, hospitals, restaurants, golf courses, on-demand IT services, data-processing centers, concert organizers, and even nonprofit organizations increasingly use revenue management.[12] It is most effective when applied to service businesses characterized by:

- High fixed-cost structure and relatively fixed capacity resulting in perishable inventory
- Variable and uncertain demand
- Varying customer price sensitivity

Reserving Capacity for High-Yield Customers

In practice, revenue management (also known as yield management) involves setting prices according to predicted demand levels among different market segments. The least price sensitive segment is the first to be provided capacity, paying the highest price; other segments follow at increasingly lower prices. As higher-paying segments often book closer to the time of actual consumption, firms need a disciplined approach to save capacity for them instead of simply selling on a first-come, first-served basis. For example, business travelers often reserve airline seats, hotel rooms, and rental cars at short notice, but vacationers may book leisure travel months in advance, and convention organizers often block hotel space years in advance for big events.

Fig. 6.7 illustrates the capacity allocation in a hotel setting, where demand from different types of customers varies not only by day of the week but also by season. These allocation decisions by segment, captured in reservation databases accessible worldwide, tell reservations personnel when to stop accepting reservations at certain prices, even though many

Figure 6.7: Setting capacity allocation targets by segment for a hotel

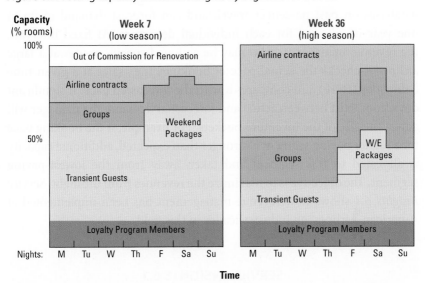

rooms may still remain available. Loyalty program members, who are mainly business travelers paying high corporate rates, are obviously a very desirable segment, followed by transient guests, and weekend packages. Airline contracts typically offer the lowest rates per room, as airlines book large volumes far in advance and can therefore negotiate attractive rates.

Similar charts can be constructed for most capacity-constrained businesses. In some instances, capacity is measured in terms of seats for a given performance, seat-miles, or rooms-nights; in others, it may be in terms of machine time, labor time, billable professional hours, vehicle miles, or storage volume, whichever is the scarce resource.

A well-designed revenue management system can predict with reasonable accuracy how many customers will use a given service at a specific time at each of several different price levels and then block the relevant amount of capacity at each level (known as a *price bucket*). Sophisticated firms use complex mathematical models for this purpose and employ revenue managers to make decisions about inventory allocation. This information can also be used to predict periods of excess capacity with the aim to increase usage through promotions and incentives. The objective is to maximize revenues on a day-to-day basis.

In the case of airlines, these models integrate massive historical databases on past passenger travel, and can forecast demand of up to one year in advance for each individual departure. At fixed intervals, the revenue manager — who may be assigned specific routes at a large airline — checks the actual pace of bookings (i.e., sales at a given time before departure) and compares it with the forecasted pace. If significant deviations exist between actual and forecasted demand, the manager will adjust the size of the inventory buckets. For example, if the booking pace for a higher paying segment is stronger than expected, additional capacity is allocated to this segment and taken away from the lowest-paying segment. The objective is to maximize the revenues from the flight. *Service Insights 6.1* shows how revenue management has been implemented at American Airlines, an industry leader in this field.

SERVICE INSIGHTS 6.1
Pricing Seats on Flight AA 333

Revenue management departments use sophisticated revenue management software and powerful computers to forecast, track and manage each flight on a given date separately. Look at American Airlines (AA) Flight 333, a popular flight from Chicago to Phoenix, Arizona, which departs daily at 4.50 p.m. on the 1,440 mile (2,317 kilometer) journey.

The 124 seats in coach (economy class) are divided into different fare categories, referred to by revenue management specialists as "buckets". There is enormous variation in ticket prices among these seats: round-trip fares range from $298 for a bargain excursion ticket (with various restrictions and a cancellation penalty attached) all the way up to an unrestricted fare of $1,065. Seats are also available at an even higher price in the small first-class section at $1,530. Scott McCartney tells how ongoing analysis by the computer program changes the allocation of seats between each of the seven buckets in economy class.

In the weeks before each Chicago–Phoenix flight, AA's revenue management system constantly adjusts the number of seats in each bucket, taking into account tickets sold, historical ridership patterns, and connecting passengers likely to use the route as one leg of a longer trip.

If advance bookings are slim, AA adds seats to low-fare buckets. If business customers buy unrestricted fares earlier than expected, the revenue management system takes seats out of the discount buckets and preserves them for last-minute bookings that the system predicts will still show up.

With 69 of 124 coach seats already sold four weeks before one recent departure of Flight AA333, American's revenue management system begins to limit the number of seats in lower-priced buckets. A week later, it totally shut off sales for the bottom three buckets, priced $300 or less. To a Chicago customer looking for a cheap seat, the flight was 'sold out'.

One day before departure, with 130 passengers booked for the 124-seat flight, AA still offered four seats at full fare because its revenue management system indicated that 10 passengers were likely to not show up or take other flights. Flight AA333 departed full and no one was bumped.

Although Flight AA333 for that date is now history, it has not been forgotten. The booking experience for this flight was saved in the memory of the revenue management system to help the airline do an even better job of forecasting in the future.

Source: Scott McCartney, "Ticket Shock: Business Fares Increase Even as Leisure Travel Keeps Getting Cheaper", *The Wall Street Journal*, 3 November 1997, pp. A1, A10. http://www.aa.com, accessed 2 March 2016. Note that flight details and prices are illustrative only.

How Can We Measure the Effectiveness of a Firm's Revenue Management?

Many capacity-constrained service organizations use percentage of capacity sold as a basic indicator of success. For instance, airlines talk of 'load factor' achieved, hotels of 'occupancy rate' and hospitals of 'census'. Similarly, professional firms monitor the proportion of their partners' and associates' time that is 'billable hours'. However, these percentages by themselves tell little of the relative profitability of the business attracted, since high usage rates may simply be a reflection of heavy discounting.

Therefore, success in revenue management is generally defined as maximizing the revenue per available capacity for a given space and time unit (RevPAST). For example, airlines seek to maximize revenue per available seat kilometer (RevPASK); hotels try to maximize their revenue per available room night (RevPAR); and performing arts centers try to maximize their revenue per available seat performance. These indices show the interplay between capacity utilization and average rate or price achieved, and can be tracked over time and benchmarked across operating units within a service firm (e.g., across hotel properties in a larger chain) and across firms. Success in revenue management means increasing RevPAST.

How Does Competitors' Pricing Affect Revenue Management?

As revenue management systems monitor booking pace, they indirectly pick up the effects of competitors' pricing. For example, if an airline prices a flight too low, it will experience a higher booking pace, and its cheaper seats fill up quickly. That is generally not desirable, as it means a higher share of late-booking as well as high fare-paying customers are not able to get their seats confirmed, and therefore will choose to fly on competing airlines. If the initial pricing is too high, the firm will get too low a share of early booking segments (although this still tends to offer a reasonable yield) and may later have to offer deeply discounted "last-minute" tickets to sell excess capacity. Some of the sales of distressed inventory, as it is called in industry, may take place through reverse auctions, using intermediaries such as Priceline.com.

Price Elasticity

For revenue management to work effectively, there needs to be two or more segments that attach different values to the service and have different price elasticities. The concept of elasticity describes how sensitive demand is to changes in price and is computed as follows:

$$\text{Price elasticity} = \frac{\text{Percentage change in demand}}{\text{Percentage change in price}}$$

When price elasticity is at unity, sales of a service rise (or fall) by the same percentage that price falls (or rises). If a small change in price has a big impact on sales, demand for that product is said to be price elastic. If a change in price has little effect on sales, demand is described as price inelastic. The concept is illustrated in the simple chart presented in Fig. 6.8, which shows the price elasticity for two segments, one with a highly elastic demand (a small change in price results in a big change in the amount demanded), and the other with a highly inelastic demand (even big changes in price have little impact on the amount demanded). To allocate the price capacity effectively, revenue manager needs to find out how sensitive demand is to price and what net revenues will be generated at different price points for each target segment.

Figure 6.8: Illustration of price elasticity

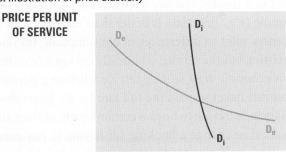

PRICE PER UNIT OF SERVICE

QUANTITY OF UNITS DEMANDED

D_e: Demand is *price elastic*. Small changes in price lead to big changes in demand.
D_i: Demand for service is *price inelastic*. Big changes in price have little impact on demand.

$$\textbf{Price elasticity} = \frac{\text{Percentage change in demand}}{\text{Percentage change in price}}$$

Designing Rate Fences

Inherent in revenue management is the concept of *price customization;* that is, charging different customers different prices for what is actually the same product. As noted by Hermann Simon and Robert Dolan,

> The basic idea of price customization is simple: Have people pay prices based on the value they put on the product. Obviously you can't just hang out a sign saying "Pay me what it's worth to you", or "It's $80 if you value it that much but only $40 if you don't". You have to find a way to segment customers by their valuations. In a sense, you have to "build a fence" between high-value customers and low-value customers so the "high" buyers can't take advantage of the low price.[13]

How can a firm make sure that customers who are willing to pay higher prices are unable to take advantage of lower price buckets? Properly designed rate fences allow customers to self-segment on the basis of service characteristics and willingness to pay. Rate fences help companies to restrict lower prices to customers willing to accept certain restrictions on their purchase and consumption experiences.

Fences can be either physical or non-physical. Physical fences refer to tangible product differences related to the different prices, such as the seat location in a theater, the size and furnishing of a hotel room, or the product bundle (e.g., first class is better than economy). In contrast, non-physical fences refer to differences in consumption, transaction, or buyer characteristics, but the service is basically the same (e.g., there is no difference in an economy class seat or service whether a person bought a heavily discounted ticket or paid the full fare for it). Examples of non-physical fences include having to book a certain length of time ahead, not being able to cancel or change a booking (or having to pay cancellation or change penalties), or having to stay over a weekend night. Examples of common rate fences are shown in Table 6.2.

In summary, based on a detailed understanding of customer needs, preferences, and willingness to pay, product and revenue managers can design effective products comprising the core service, physical product features (physical fences), and non-physical product features (non-physical fences). In addition, a good understanding of the demand curve

Table 6.2: Key Categories of Rate Fences

Rate Fences	Examples
Physical (product-related) Fences	
Basic product	• Class of travel (business/economy class) • Size of rental car • Size and furnishing of a hotel room • Seat location in a theater or stadium
Amenities	• Free breakfast at a hotel, airport pick up, etc. • Free golf cart at a golf course • Valet parking
Service level	• Priority wait-listing, separate check-in counters with no or only short queues • Improved food and beverage selection • Dedicated service hotlines • Personal butler • Dedicated account management team
Other physical characteristics	• Table location pricing (e.g., restaurant table with view in a high rise building), seat location pricing (e.g., a window or aisle seat in an aircraft cabin) • Extra legroom on an airline
Non-Physical Fences	
Transaction Characteristics	
Time of booking or reservation	• Discounts for advance purchase
Location of booking or reservation	• Passengers booking air tickets for an identical route in different countries are charged different prices (e.g., prices tend to be higher at an airline's hub because of higher frequency flights and more direct flights) • Customers making reservations online are charged a lower price than those making reservations by phone
Flexibility of ticket usage	• Fees/penalties for canceling or changing a reservation (up to loss of entire ticket price) • Non-refundable reservation fees
Consumption Characteristics	
Time or duration of use	• Happy hour offer in a bar, early-bird special in a restaurant before 6 pm, and minimum required spending during peak periods • Must stay over a Saturday night for a hotel booking • Must stay at least for five nights
Location of consumption	• Price depends on departure location, especially in international travel • Prices vary by location (between cities, city center versus edges of the city)

Buyer Characteristics	
Frequency or volume of consumption	• Members of certain loyalty tier with the firm (e.g., platinum member) get priority pricing, discounts or loyalty benefits • Season tickets
Group membership	• Child, student, senior citizen discounts • Affiliation with certain groups (e.g., alumni) • Membership with the firm's loyalty program • Corporate rates
Size of customer group	• Group discounts based on size of group
Geographic location	• Local customers are charged lower rates than tourists • Customers from certain countries are charged higher prices

is needed so that "buckets" of inventory can be assigned to the various products and price categories. An example from the airline industry is shown in Fig. 6.9, and an interview with a senior executive with a career in revenue management is featured in *Service Insights 6.2*.

Figure 6.9: Relating price buckets to the demand curve

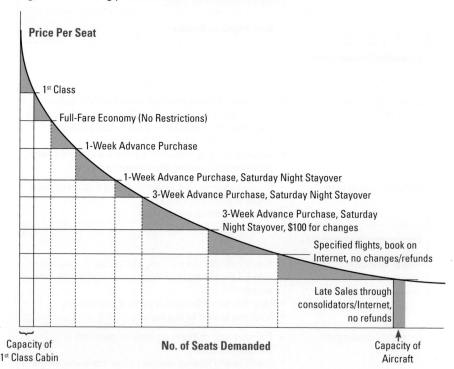

Price Per Seat

1st Class

Full-Fare Economy (No Restrictions)

1-Week Advance Purchase

1-Week Advance Purchase, Saturday Night Stayover

3-Week Advance Purchase, Saturday Night Stayover

3-Week Advance Purchase, Saturday Night Stayover, $100 for changes

Specified flights, book on Internet, no changes/refunds

Late Sales through consolidators/Internet, no refunds

Capacity of 1st Class Cabin   **No. of Seats Demanded**   Capacity of Aircraft

*Dark areas denote amount of consumer surplus (goal of segmented pricing is to reduce this).

SERVICE INSIGHTS 6.2.
Interview with a Vice President
of Revenue Management and Analytics

Q: What is the role of a revenue manager?
A: When I started my career, the primary focus was on forecasting, inventory control, pricing, market segment and geographic mix, and allotment control. The Internet changed the scene significantly and several global giants, like Expedia and Travelocity, emerged after 9/11 when travel bookings plummeted and the industry realized the power of the Internet to help them sell distressed inventory. But airlines and hotels want to control their own inventory and pricing to cut costs and reduce reliance on intermediaries, so there's increasing focus on driving bookings via direct channels such as their own branded websites, building online brands, and implementing CRM programs to build loyalty and encourage repeat purchase. Responsibilities have also broadened beyond mainstream hotel rooms to include revenue management of secondary income sources such as function space, restaurants, golf courses and spa.

Q: What differences do you see between revenue management for airlines and hotels?
A: Fundamentally, the techniques of forecasting and optimizing pricing and inventory controls are the same. However, some key differences exist. Airlines have a larger ability to use pricing to expand travel demand from their key markets. By contrast, pricing practices in hotels can shift market share within a location but, as a rule, not overall market size. Consumers are also more likely to view many pricing practices, such as advance purchase restrictions and discounts, as fair practice for the airline industry, but less so when applied by the hotel industry.

Organizational structure also tends to be different. The airlines adopt central revenue management control for all flights, and revenue managers have little interaction with the reservations and sales teams in the field. A precise and statistical application of pricing and inventory control is thus the focus. In the hotel industry, revenue management is still often decentralized to every hotel, requiring daily interaction with reservations and sales. The human element is key for successful implementation in hotels, requiring a more cohesive culture of revenue management across multiple hotel departments such as reservations, sales, catering and even front office, to gain the biggest impact on hotel performance.

Q: What skills do you need to succeed as a revenue manager?
A: Strong statistical and analytical skills are essential, but to be really successful, revenue managers need to have equally strong interpersonal and influencing skills for their decisions and analyses to be embraced by other departments. Traditional ways of segmenting customers via their transactional characteristics such as booking lead time, channel of reservation and type of promotion are insufficient. Both behavioral characteristics (such as motive for travel, products sought, spending pattern and degree of autonomy) and emotional characteristics (such as self-image, conspicuous consumer or reluctant traveler, impulse or planned) need to be incorporated into revenue management considerations.

Q: How are revenue management practices perceived by customers?
A: The art of implementation is not to let the customers feel that your pricing and inventory control practices are unfair and meant primarily to increase the top and bottom line of the company. Intelligent and meaningful rate fences and product packaging have to be used to allow customers to self-segment so that they retain a feeling of choice. Now with the importance of Big Data application, intelligent integration of individual customer needs and wants to create personalized pricing and product offer is key to not only maximizing the revenue for a given period, but maximizing the share of wallet from a loyal customer over their lifecycle.

Q: What is the daily nature of the job?

A: The market presents a lot of demand changes and you need to monitor your competitors' price as it fluctuates daily across the various distribution changes. The customer needs and willingness to pay are also changing over time. It's definitely a pre-requisite to be quick in analysis and decisive. One needs to feel comfortable taking calculated risks and choose from a plethora of revenue management and pricing tools to decide on the best fit for the situation.

We thank Jeannette Ho, who was Vice President Revenue Management and Distribution at Fairmont Raffles Hotels International when this interview was conducted on 25 June 2013. Jeannette was responsible for spearheading and implementing the revenue management initiatives for the Group. Her team drove the company's global distribution strategy, oversaw its E-commerce channels and Central Reservations System, and developed its performance intelligence capabilities. Prior to her current role, Jeannette has been working in revenue management, distribution and CRM with various international companies such as Singapore Airlines, Banyan Tree, and Starwood Hotels & Resorts.

FAIRNESS AND ETHICAL CONCERNS IN SERVICE PRICING

Do you sometimes have difficulty understanding how much it is going to cost you to use a service? Do you believe that many prices are unfair? If so, you are not alone.[14] Service users cannot always be sure in advance what they will receive in return for their money. There is an implicit assumption among many customers that a higher priced service should offer more benefits and greater quality than a lower priced one. For example, a professional lawyer who charges very high fees is assumed to be more skilled than one who is relatively inexpensive. Although price can serve as an indication of quality, it is difficult to be sure if the extra value is really there.

Service Pricing Is Complex

Pricing for services tend to be complex and hard to understand. Comparison across providers may even require complex spreadsheets or even mathematical formulas. Consumer advocates sometimes charge that this complexity represents a deliberate choice on the part of service suppliers who do not want customers to be able to determine who offers the best value for money, and therefore reduce price competition. In fact, complexity makes it easy (and perhaps more tempting) for firms to engage in unethical behavior. The quoted prices typically used by consumers for price comparisons may be only the first of several charges that can be billed.

For example, cellphone companies have a confusing variety of plans to meet the distinct needs and usage patterns of different market segments. Plans can be national, regional, or purely local in scope. Monthly fees vary according to the number of minutes and mobile data capacity selected in advance. There can be separate allowances for peak and off-peak minutes. Overtime minutes and "roaming minutes" on other carriers are charged at higher rates. Some plans allow unlimited off-peak calling, others have free incoming calls. Some providers charge calls per second, per six-second block or even per-minute block, resulting in vastly different costs per month. Data plans (including features such as being allowed to roll over unused mobile data to the next month), handset subsidies for new phones, roaming fees, family and bundled plans that can include several cellphones and other mobile devices, landline, and Internet services add to this complexity. On top of complex pricing plans, many find it difficult to forecast their own usage, which makes it even harder to compute comparative prices when evaluating competing suppliers whose fees are based on a variety of usage-related factors.

In addition, puzzling new fees have started to appear on bills. Phone bills of course include real taxes (e.g., sales tax), but on many bills, the majority of surcharges, which users often misread as taxes, go directly to the phone company. For instance, the "property tax allotment" is nothing more than a factor for the property taxes the carrier pays, the "single bill fee" charges for consolidated billing of the mobile and landline service, and the "carrier cost recovery fee" is a catch-all for all sorts of operating expenses. In an editorial entitled "Cell Hell," Jim Guest, Consumer Union's president, observed:

> *In the 10 years since Consumer Reports started rating cell phones and calling plans, we've never found an easy way to compare actual costs. From what our readers tell us, they haven't either. Each carrier presents*

its rates, extra charges, and calling areas differently. Deciphering one company's plan is hard enough, but comparing plans from various carries is nearly impossible.[15]

It seems no coincidence that humorist Scott Adams (the creator of Dilbert) used exclusively service examples when he "branded" the future of pricing as "confusopoly". Noting that firms such as telecommunication companies, banks, insurance firms, and other financial service providers, offer nearly identical services, Adams remarks:

> *You would think this would create a price war and drive prices down to the cost of providing it (that's what I learned between naps in my economics classes), but it isn't happening. The companies are forming efficient confusopolies so customers can't tell who has the lowest prices. Companies have learned to use the complexities of life as an economic tool.*[16]

One of the roles of effective government regulation, says Adams, should be to discourage this tendency for certain service industries to develop into "confusopolies".

Piling on the Fees

Not all business models are based on generating income from sales. There is a growing trend today to impose fees that sometimes have little to do with usage. In the US, the car rental industry has attracted some notoriety for advertising bargain rental prices and then telling customers on arrival that other fees such as collision insurance and personal insurance are compulsory. Also, staff sometimes fail to clarify certain "small print" contract terms such as a high mileage charge that is added once the car exceeds a very low limit of free miles. The "hidden extras" for car rentals in some Florida resort towns got so bad at one point that people were joking: "The car is free, the keys are extra!"[17]

There has also been a trend to adding (or increasing) fines and penalties. Banks have been heavily criticized for using penalties as an important revenue-generating tool as opposed to using them merely to educate customers and achieve compliance with payment deadlines.

Chris Keeley, a New York University student, used his debit card to buy $230 worth of Christmas gifts. His holiday mood soured when he received a notice from his bank that he had overdrawn his checking account. Although his bank authorized each of his seven transactions, it charged him a fee of $31 per payment, totaling $217 for only $230 in purchases. Keeley maintained that he had never requested the so-called overdraft protection on his account and wished his bank had rejected the transactions, because he would then simply have paid by credit card. He fumed, "I can't help but think they wanted me to keep spending money so that they could collect these fees".[18] In fact, for some banks, such fees and penalties now exceed earnings from mortgages, credit cards, and all other lending combined.

The Consumer Financial Protection Bureau (CFPB) has repeatedly raised concerns about overdraft protections and its study found that the majority of debit card overdraft fees are incurred on transactions of $24 or less and the majority of overdrafts are repaid within three days.[19] Put in lending terms, if a consumer borrowed $24 for three days and paid the median overdraft fee of $34, such a loan would carry a 17,000% annual percentage rate (APR). Richard Cordray, CFPB Director, said "Consumers who opt in to overdraft coverage put themselves at serious risk when they use their debit card... Despite recent regulatory and industry changes, overdrafts continue to impose heavy costs on consumers who have low account balances and no cushion for error. Overdraft fees should not be 'gotchas' when people use their debit cards".

Some banks do not charge for overdraft protection. Said Dennis DiFlorio, President for Retail Banking at Commerce Bancorp Inc. in Cherry Hill, New Jersey: "It's outrageous. It's not about customer convenience. Its just a way for banks to make money off customers". Some banks now offer services that cover overdrafts automatically from savings accounts, other accounts, or even the customer's credit card, and do not charge fees for doing so.[20]

It is possible to design fees and even penalties that do not seem unfair to customers. *Service Insights 6.3* describes what drives customers' fairness perceptions with service fees and penalties.[21]

SERVICE INSIGHTS 6.3
Crime and Punishment:
How Customers Respond to Fines and Penalties

Various types of "penalties" are part and parcel of many pricing schedules to discourage undesirable consumer behaviors, ranging from late fees for DVD rentals to cancellation charges for hotel bookings, and charges for late credit card payments. Customer responses to penalties can be highly negative, and can lead to switching providers and poor word-of-mouth. Young Kim and Amy Smith conducted an online survey using the Critical Incident Technique (CIT) in which the 201 respondents were asked to recall a recent penalty incident, describe the situation, and then complete a set of structured questions based on how the respondents felt and how they responded to that incident. Their findings showed that negative consumer responses can be reduced significantly by following these three guidelines:

1. **Make Penalties Relative to the Crime Committed.** The survey showed that customers' negative reaction to a penalty increased greatly when they perceived that the penalty was out of proportion to the 'crime' committed. Customers' negative feelings were further aggravated if they were "surprised" by the penalty being charged to them suddenly and they had not been aware of the fee or the magnitude of it. These findings suggest that firms can reduce negative customer responses significantly by exploring which amounts are seen as reasonable or fair for a given "customer lapse", and the fines/fees are communicated effectively even before a chargeable incident happens (e.g., in a banking context through a clearly explained fee schedule, and through frontline staff that explain at the point of opening an account or selling additional services the potential fines or fees associated with various "violations", such as overdrawing beyond the authorized limits, bounced checks, or late payments).

2. **Consider Causal Factors and Customize Penalties.** The study showed that customers' perceptions of fairness were lower and negative responses were higher when they perceived the causes that led to the penalty to be out of their control ("I mailed the check on time — there must have been a delay in the postal system"), rather than when they felt it was within their control and really their fault (e.g., "I forgot to mail the check"). To increase the perception of fairness, firms may want to identify common penalty cases that typically are out of the customer's control and allow the frontline to waive or reduce such fees.

   In addition, it was found that customers who generally observe all the rules, and therefore have not paid fines in the past, react particularly negatively, if they are fined. One respondent said, "I have always made timely payments and have never been late with a payment — they should have considered this fact and waived the fee". Service firms can improve fairness perceptions by taking into account customers' penalties history in dealing with penalties, and offer different treatments based on past behavior; perhaps waiving the fine for the first incident, while at the same time communicating that the fee will be charged for future incidents.

3. **Focus on Fairness and Manage Emotions during Penalty Situations.** Consumers' responses are heavily driven by their fairness perceptions. Customers are likely to perceive penalties as excessive and respond negatively, if they find that a penalty is out of proportion compared to the damage or extra work caused by the penalized incident to the service firm. One consumer complained, "I thought this particular penalty (credit card late payment) was excessive. You are already paying high interest; the penalty should have been more in line with the payment. The penalty was more than the payment!" Considering customers' perceptions of fairness might mean, for example, that the late fee for keeping a DVD or library book should not exceed the potentially lost rental fees during that period.

Service companies can also make penalties seem fairer by providing adequate explanations and justifications for the penalty. Ideally, penalties should be imposed for the good of other customers (e.g., "We kept the room for you which we could have given to another guest on our wait list") or community (e.g., "others are already waiting for this book to be returned"), but not as a means for generating significant profit. Finally, frontline employees should be trained to handle customers who are angry or distressed and complain about penalties (see Chap. 13 for recommendations on how to deal with such situations).

Source: Young "Sally" K. Kim and Amy K. Smith, "Crime and Punishment: Examining Customers' Responses to Service Organizations' Penalties", *Journal of Service Research*, 8, No. 2, 2005, pp. 162–180.

Designing Fairness into Revenue Management

Similar to pricing plans and fees, revenue management practices can be perceived as highly unfair, and customer perceptions have to be carefully managed. Therefore, a well-implemented revenue management strategy cannot mean a blind pursuit of short-term yield maximization. Rather, the following approaches can help firms to reconcile revenue management practices with customers' fairness perceptions, satisfaction, trust, and goodwill[22]:

- *Design price schedules and fences that are clear, logical, and fair.* Firms should proactively spell out all fees and expenses (e.g., no-show or cancellation charges) clearly in advance so that there are no surprises. A related approach is to develop a simple fee structure so customers can more easily understand the financial implications of a specific usage situation. For a rate fence to be perceived as fair, customers must understand them easily (i.e., fences have to be transparent and upfront) and see the logic in them.

- *Use high published prices and frame fences as discounts.* Rate fences framed as customer gains (i.e., discounts) are generally perceived as fairer than those framed as customer losses (i.e., surcharges), even if the situations are economically equivalent. For example, a customer who patronizes her hair salon on Saturdays may perceive the salon as profiteering if she finds herself facing a weekend surcharge. However, she is likely to find the higher weekend price more acceptable if the hair salon advertises its peak weekend price as the published price and offers a $5 discount for weekday haircuts. Furthermore, having a high published price helps to increase the reference price and related quality perceptions in addition to the feeling of being rewarded for the weekday patronage.

- *Communicate consumer benefits of revenue management.* Marketing communications should position revenue management as a win-win practice. Providing different price and value enables a broader spectrum of customers to self-segment and enjoy the service. It allows each customer to find the price and benefits (value) that best satisfies his or her needs. For example, charging a higher price for the best seats in the theater recognizes that some people are willing and able to pay more for a better location and makes it possible to sell other seats at a lower price. Furthermore, perceived fairness is affected by what customers perceive as normal. Hence, when communication makes customers more familiar with particular revenue management practices, unfairness perceptions are likely to decrease over time.[23]

- *"Hide" discounts through bundling, product design, and targeting.* Bundling a service into a package effectively obscures the discounted price. When a cruise line includes the price of air travel or ground transportation in the cruise package, the customer knows only the total price, not the cost of the individual components. Bundling usually makes price comparisons between the bundles and its components impossible, and thereby sidesteps potential unfairness perceptions and reductions in reference prices. This reduces unfairness perceptions.[24]

  Service products can be designed to hide discounts. Instead of varying the prices of food, which makes it difficult to increase once it has been lowered, restaurants can vary the product. For example, restaurants can offer smaller portions for lower cost set-lunches, and they can impose a minimum spending level during peak periods. Diners having a set-lunch feel they are getting a good deal. When demand is high, a minimum spending per diner can be set at a high level. That is, menu prices will not be changed and price perceptions of diners are unaffected. These two tactics give restaurants flexibility in adjusting effective revenue per seat according to demand levels.[25]

Finally, instead of widely advertising low prices and thereby reducing the reference price and potential quality perceptions, special deals can be offered only to members of a firm's loyalty program and be positioned as a benefit of the program. Members are likely to feel appreciated and the firm can generate incremental demand without reducing its published prices.

- *Take care of loyal customers.* Firms should build in strategies for retaining valued customers, even to the extent of not charging the maximum feasible amount on a given transaction. After all, customer perceptions of price gouging do not build trust. Revenue management systems can be programmed to incorporate "loyalty multipliers" for regular customers, so that reservations systems can give them "special treatment" status at peak times, even when they are not paying premium rates.

- *Use service recovery to compensate for overbooking.* Many service firms overbook to compensate for anticipated cancellations and no-shows. Profits increase but so does the incidence of being unable to honor reservations. Being "bumped" by an airline or "walked" by a hotel can lead to a loss of customer loyalty and adversely affect a firm's reputation.[26] It is important to back up overbooking programs with well-designed service recovery procedures, such as:

1. Giving customers a choice between retaining their reservation or receiving compensation (e.g., many airlines practice voluntary offloading at check-in against cash compensation and a later flight).

2. Providing sufficient advance notice for customers to make alternative arrangements (e.g., pre-emptive offloading and rescheduling to another flight the day before departure, often in combination with cash compensation).

3. Offering a substitute service that delights customers if possible (e.g., upgrading a passenger to business or first class on the next available flight, often in combination with options 1 and 2 above).

A Westin beach resort found that it can free up capacity by offering guests who are departing the next day the choice of spending their last night in a luxury hotel near the airport or in the city at no cost. Guest feedback on the free room, upgraded service, and a night in the city after a beach holiday has been very positive. From the hotel's perspective, this practice trades the cost of getting a one-night stay in another hotel against that of turning away a multiple-night guest arriving that same day.

PUTTING SERVICE PRICING INTO PRACTICE

The first thing a manager has to realize is that service pricing is multifaceted. It is not just about "How much do I charge?" There are other important decisions to be made that can have a major impact on the behavior and value perceptions of customers. Table 6.3 summarizes the questions service marketers need to ask themselves to develop a well-thought out pricing strategy.

How Much to Charge?

Realistic decisions on pricing are critical for financial solvency. The pricing tripod model discussed earlier (Fig. 6.3) provides a useful starting point. First, all the relevant economic costs need to be recovered at different sales volumes and these set the relevant floor price. Next, the elasticity of demand of the service from both the providers' and customers' perspectives will help to set a "ceiling" price for any given market segment. Finally, firms need to analyze the intensity of price competition among the providers, before they come to a final price.

A specific figure must be set for the price itself. This task involves several considerations, including the need to consider the pros and cons of setting a rounded price, and the ethical issues involved in setting a price exclusive of taxes, service charges, and other extras.

More recently, auctions and dynamic pricing have become increasingly popular as a way to price according to demand and the value perceptions of customers, as seen in the examples of dynamic pricing in the Internet environment in *Service Insights 6.4.*

Table 6.3: Issues to Consider When Developing a Service Pricing Schedule

1.	**How much should be charged for this service?**
	• What costs is the organization attempting to recover? Is the organization trying to achieve a specific profit margin or return on investment by selling this service?
	• How sensitive are customers to various prices?
	• What prices are charged by competitors?
	• What discount(s) should be offered from basic prices?
	• Are psychological pricing points (e.g., $4.95 versus $5.00) customarily used?
	• Should auctions and dynamic pricing be used?
2.	**What should be the basis of pricing?**
	• Execution of a specific task
	• Admission to a service facility
	• Units of time (hour, week, month, year)
	• Percentage commission on the value of the transaction
	• Physical resources consumed
	• Geographic distance covered, weight or size of object serviced
	• Outcome of service or cost-saving generated for the client
	• Should each service element be billed independently?
	• Should a single price be charged for a bundled package?
	• Should discounting be used for selective segments?
	• Is a freemium pricing strategy beneficial?
3.	**Who should collect payment and where?**
	• The organization that provides the service collects payment at the location of service delivery or at arm's length (e.g., by mail, phone or online).
	• A specialist intermediary (travel or ticket agent, bank, retail, etc.) with a convenient retail outlet location.
	• How should the intermediary be compensated for this work — flat fee or percentage commission?
4.	**When should payment be made?**
	• In advance or after service delivery?
	• In a lump sum or by installments over time?
5.	**How should payment be made?**
	• Cash (exact change or not?)
	• Token (where can these be purchase?)
	• Stored value card
	• Check (how to verify?)
	• Electronic funds transfer
	• Charge card (credit or debit)
	• Credit account with service provider
	• Vouchers
	• Third-party payment (e.g., insurance company or government agency)?
6.	**How should prices be communicated to the target market?**
	• Through what communication medium? (advertising, signage, electronic display, salespeople, customer service personnel)
	• What message content (how much emphasis should be placed on price?)
	• Can the psychology of pricing presentation and communications be used?

SERVICE INSIGHTS 6.4
Dynamic Pricing on the Internet

Dynamic pricing, also known as customized or personalized pricing, is a version of the age-old practice of price discrimination. It is popular with service providers because of its potential to increase profits and at the same time provides customers with what they value. E-tailing, or retailing over the Internet, lends itself well to this strategy because changing prices electronically is a simple procedure. Dynamic pricing enables service firms to charge different customers different prices for the same product based on information collected about their purchase history, preferences, price sensitivity, and so on. However, customers may not be happy.

E-tailers are often uncomfortable about admitting the use of dynamic pricing due to ethical and legal issues associated with price discrimination. Customers of Amazon.com were upset when they learned the online megastore, in its early days of e-commerce, was not charging everyone the same price for DVDs of the same movie. A study of online consumers by the University of Pennsylvania's Annenberg Public Policy Center found that 87% of respondents did not think dynamic pricing was acceptable.

Reverse Auctions

Travel e-tailers such as Priceline.com and Hotwire.com follow a customer-driven pricing strategy known as a reverse auction. Each firm acts as an intermediary between potential buyers who ask for quotations for a product or service, and multiple suppliers who quote the best price they're willing to offer. Buyers can then compare the offers and choose the supplier that best meets their needs. For example, if a buyer is looking for a flight and accommodation package, search results often show a variety of combinations of packages one can choose from. All the different airlines and hotels are listed by brand, and the price of each package is listed clearly.

Different business models underlie these services. Although some are provided free to end users, most e-tailers either receive a commission from the supplier or do not pass on the whole savings to their customers. Others charge customers either a fixed fee or a percentage of the savings.

Traditional Auctions
Other e-tailers, such as eBay, uBid or OnlineAuction, follow the traditional online auction model in which bidders place bids for an item and compete with each other to determine who buys it. Marketers of both consumer and industrial products use such auctions to sell obsolete or overstocked items, collectibles, rare items, and secondhand merchandise. This form of retailing has become very successful since eBay first launched it in 1995.

Shopbots and Metasearch Engines Help Consumers to Benefit from Dynamic Pricing
Consumers now have tools of their own to prevent them from being taken advantage of by practices of dynamic pricing. One approach involves using shopbots and metasearch engines to do a comparison of prices and find the cheapest prices available. Shopbots, or shopping robots, basically are intelligent agents that automatically collect price and product information from multiple vendors. A customer has only to visit a shopbot site, such as Dealtime.com, and run a search for what they are looking for. In the travel industry, Kayak is a leading metasearch engine. These shopbots instantly query all the associated service providers to check availability, features, and price, and then present the results in a comparison table. Different shopbots have links to different retailers. There is even a shopbot site called MegaShopBot.com, which searches for deals within the best shopbots!

There's little doubt that dynamic pricing is here to stay. With further advances in technology and wider application, its reach will extend to more and more service categories.

Sources: Laura Sydell, "New Pricing Plan Soon to Be at Play For Online Music", 27 July 2009, http://www.npr.org/templates/story/story.php?storyId=111046679&ft=1&f=1006, accessed 2 March 2016; Jean-Michel Sahut, "The Impact of Internet on Pricing Strategies in the Tourism Industry" *Journal of Internet Banking and Finance*, 14, No. 1, 2009, pp. 1-8; Promotional Pricing: Dynamic Pricing (2015). From Setting Price: Part 2 Tutorial. KnowThis.com. http://www.knowthis.com/setting-price-part-2/promotional-pricing-dynamic-pricing, accessed 2 March 2016; Thad Rueter (2014), "The Price is Right — Then it's Not", *https://www.internetretailer.com/2014/08/04/price-rightthen-its-not-2?p=1*, accessed 2 March 2016; Max Starkov and Tara Dyer (2013), "Meta Search Marketing: The New Revenue Frontier in Hospitality", http://blog.hebsdigital.com/meta-search-marketing-the-new-revenue-frontier-in-hospitality, accessed 12 March 2016.

What Should Be the Specified Basis for Pricing?

It is not always easy to define a unit of service as the specified basis for pricing as there may be many options. For instance, should price be based on completing a promised service task, such as repairing a piece of equipment or cleaning a jacket? Should it be based on admission to a service performance, such as an educational program, a concert, or a sports event? Should it be time-based, for instance, using an hour of a lawyer's time? Alternatively, should it be related to a monetary value linked to the service delivery, such as when an insurance company scales its premiums to reflect the amount of coverage provided, or a real estate company takes a commission that is a percentage of the selling price of a house?

Some service prices are tied to the consumption of physical resources such as food, drinks, water, or natural gas. Transport firms have traditionally charged by distance, with freight companies using a combination of weight or cubic volume and distance to set their rates. For some services, prices may include separate charges for access and for usage. Recent research suggests that access or subscription fees are an important driver of adoption and customer retention, whereas usage fees are much more important drivers of actual usage.[27] Consumers of hedonic services such as amusement parks tend to prefer flat rates for access rather than by individual usage as they do not like to be reminded of the pain of paying while enjoying the service. This is also called the taximeter effect, as customers do not want to "hear" the price ticking upward; it lowers their consumption of enjoyment![28]

In B2B markets in particular, innovative business models charge based on outcomes rather than services provided. For example, Rolls-Royce's 'Power-by-the-Hour' service does not charge for services such as maintenance, repairs, and materials, but based on the outcome of these activities, that is, the number of flying hours.[29] Some supply chain service providers, such as DHL Supply Chain, charge a base price and then add a variable component that depends on the cost-saving generated for the client. In effect, generated cost savings are shared between the provider and their client.

Price Bundling. An important question for service marketers is whether to charge an inclusive price for all elements (referred to as a "bundle") or to price each element separately. If customers prefer to avoid making many small payments, then bundled pricing may be preferable. However, if they dislike being charged for product elements they do not use, itemized pricing is preferable. Bundled prices offer firms a certain level of guaranteed revenue from each customer, while providing customers a clear idea in advance of how much they can expect to pay. Unbundled pricing provides customers with the freedom to choose what to buy and pay for.[30] For instance, many US airlines now charge economy class passengers for meals, drinks, check-in baggage, seat selection, and surcharges for credit card payment on their domestic flights. However, customers may be angered if they discover that the actual price of what they consume, inflated by all the "extras", is substantially higher than the advertised base price that attracted them in the first place.[31]

Discounting. Selective price discounting targeted at specific market segments can offer important opportunities to attract new customers and fill the capacity that would otherwise go unused. However, unless it is used with effective rate fences that allow specific segments to be targeted cleanly, a strategy of discounting should be approached with caution. It reduces the average price and contribution received, and may attract customers whose only loyalty is to the firm that can offer the lowest price on the next transaction. Volume discounts are sometimes used to cement the loyalty of large corporate customers who might otherwise spread their purchases among several different suppliers.

Freemium. Over the past decade, "freemium", a combination of "free" and "premium", has become a popular pricing strategy for online and mobile services. Users get the basic service at no cost (typically funded by advertising) and can upgrade to a richer functionality for a subscription fee. If you have shared files on Dropbox, networked on LinkedIn or streamed music from Spotify, you have experienced this business model first-hand. As marginal costs for technology and bandwidth are dropping, "freemium" models are likely to become more attractive.[32]

Who Should Collect Payment and Where Should Payment be Made?

As discussed in Chap. 4, supplementary services include information, order taking, billing, and payment. However, service delivery sites are not always conveniently located. Airports, theaters, and stadiums, for instance, are often situated some distance from where potential customers may live or work. When consumers need such services and/or have to purchase a service before using it, and there is no convenient online channel available, there are benefits to using intermediaries that are more conveniently located. Therefore, firms sometimes delegate these services to intermediaries, such as travel agents who make hotel and transport bookings, and collect payment from customers, or ticket agents who sell seats for theaters, concert halls, and sports stadiums.

Although the original supplier pays a commission, the intermediary is usually able to offer customers greater convenience in terms of where, when, and how payment can be made. Using intermediaries may also result in savings in administrative costs. However, many service firms nowadays are promoting their websites and apps with best rate guarantees as direct channels for customer self-service, thus bypassing the traditional intermediaries and avoiding the payment of commissions. Tickets are then simply delivered to an email account or a smart phone.

When Should Payment be Made?

Two basic ways are to ask customers to pay in advance (as with an admission charge, airline ticket, or postage stamps), or to bill them once service delivery has been completed (as with restaurant bills and repair charges). Occasionally, a service provider may ask for an initial payment

Figure 6.10: Some firms do not leave their customers with much flexibility in dealing with late payment

© 1999 Randy Glasbergen.
www.glasbergen.com

GLASBERGEN

"Unless we receive the outstanding balance within ten days, we will have no choice but to destroy your credit rating, ruin your reputation, and make you wish you were never born. If you have already sent the seven cents, please disregard this notice."

in advance of service delivery, with the balance due later (Fig. 6.10). This approach is quite common for expensive repair and maintenance jobs, when the firm — often a small business with limited working capital — must buy and pay for materials.

Asking customers to pay in advance means the buyer is paying before the benefits are received. However, prepayments may offer advantages to the customer and the provider. Sometimes it is inconvenient to pay each time a regularly patronized service — such as the postal service or public transport — is used. To save time and effort, customers may prefer the convenience of buying a book of stamps or a monthly travel pass. Performing arts organizations with heavy upfront financing requirements can also offer discounted subscription tickets in order to bring in money before the season begins.

Finally, the timing of payment can determine usage patterns. From an analysis of the payment and attendance records of a Colorado-based health club, John Gourville and Dilip Soman found that its members' usage patterns were closely related to their payment schedules. When members made payments, their use of the club was highest during the months immediately following payment and then slowed down steadily until the next payment; members with monthly payment plans used the health club much more consistently and were more likely to renew, perhaps because each month's payment encouraged them to use what they were paying for.[33]

Gourville and Soman concluded that the timing of payment can be used more strategically to manage capacity utilization. For instance, if a golf club wants to reduce the demand during its busiest time, it can bill its fees long before the season begins (e.g., in January rather than in May or June), as the member's pain of payment will have faded by the time the peak summer months come, thereby reducing the need to get his or her "money's worth". A reduction in peak demand during the peak period would then allow the club to increase its overall membership.

Conversely, the timing of payment can also be used to boost consumption. Consider the Boston Red Sox (i.e., the famous American professional baseball team) season ticket holders, who are billed five months before the season starts. To build attendance and strong fan support throughout the season, Red Sox could spread out this large annual payment to four installments that coincide with their games. The team would garner a high game attendance and fan support, and their fans might prefer the lower and financially more manageable installments.

How Should Payment be Made?

There are many different forms of payment. Cash may appear to be the simplest method, but it raises security problems and is inconvenient when exact change is required to operate machines. Credit and debit cards can be used around the world as their acceptance has become almost universal. Other payment procedures include tokens or vouchers as supplements to, or instead of, cash. Vouchers are sometimes provided by social service agencies to the elderly or individuals in the low-income bracket. Such a policy achieves the same benefits as discounting, but avoids the need to publicize different prices, and to require cashiers to check eligibility.

Service marketers should remember that the simplicity and speed with which payment is made may influence the customer's perception of overall service quality. Coming into broader usage are prepayment systems based on cards that store value on a magnetic strip or in a microchip embedded within the card. Contactless payments systems based on credit and debit cards with radio-frequency identification (RFID) technology are increasingly used. Starbucks launched a smartphone app-based payment system integrated with its "My Starbucks Reward Program", which allows its customers to earn special discounts and freebies. Soon, order-taking will be integrated to cut wait time at the counter. Apple users can pay by holding their device to the point of sale system and authenticating the transaction by holding their fingerprint to the phone's Touch ID sensor. Suppliers of these systems claim transactions can be up to twice as fast as conventional cash, credit, or debit card purchases.

Interestingly, a recent study found that the payment mechanism has an effect on the total spending of customers, especially for discretionary consumption items such as spending in cafes.[34] The less tangible or immediate the payment mechanism, the more consumers tend to spend. Cash is the most tangible (i.e., consumers will be more careful and spend less), followed by credit cards, prepayment cards, and finally more sophisticated and even less tangible and immediate mechanisms such as payment via one's cell phone service bill.

How Should Prices be Communicated to the Target Markets?

The final task, once each of the other issues has been addressed, is to decide how the organization's pricing policies can best be communicated to its target market(s). Consumers need to know the price they are expected to pay before purchase. They may also need to know how, where, and when that price is payable. This information must be presented in intelligible and unambiguous ways so that customers will not be misled and question the ethical standards of the firm. Managers must decide whether or not to include information on pricing in advertising for the service. It may be suitable to relate the price to the costs of competing products. Salespeople and customer service representatives should be able to give immediate, accurate responses to customer queries about pricing, payment, and credit. Good signage at retail points of sale will save staff members from having to answer basic questions on prices.

How to communicate prices is important and shapes buying behavior. For example, in a restaurant context, menu psychology looks at how diners respond to pricing information on a menu (*Service Insights 6.5*).

Finally, when the price is presented in the form of an itemized bill, marketers should make sure that it is both accurate and easy to understand. Hospital bills, which may run up to several pages and contain dozens or even hundreds of items, have been much criticized for inaccuracy. Hotel bills, despite containing fewer entries, are also notoriously inaccurate. One study estimated that business travelers in the US may be overpaying for their hotel rooms by half-a-billion dollars a year, with 11.6% of all bills incorrect, resulting in an average overpayment of $11.36.[35]

SERVICE INSIGHTS 6.5
The Psychology of Menu Pricing in Restaurants

Have you ever wondered why you choose certain dishes on the menu and not others? It could be due to the way the dish is displayed. Menu psychology is a growing field of research. Menu engineers and consultants research on the most effective ways to design a menu, including layout and pricing information, in the hope that the diner will spend more money. What can we do to get people to spend more money, and to order items with high profit margins?

When showing prices on the menu, avoid using a dollar sign. Prices that come with dollar signs will result in customers spending less, compared to when there are no dollar signs on the menu.

Prices that end with "9", e.g., $9.99, make diners feel that they are getting value for money. This is good for a low price and for good value positioning, but should not be used by high-end restaurants.

The best position to place prices should be at the end of the description of an item and it should not be highlighted in any way.

In terms of the order of items, place the most expensive item at the top of the menu so the price of the other items looks lower in comparison.

For layout, the most profitable item on the menu should be placed at the top right hand corner of the page because people tend to look there first.

A longer description of a dish tends to encourage people to order it. Therefore, menus can be designed to have more detailed and more appetizing descriptions of dishes that are more profitable, and have less description for the less profitable dishes.

What kind of names should be given to dishes? Using names of mothers, grandmothers and other relatives (e.g., Aunty May's beef stew) has been shown to encourage people to order that item.

The next time you have selected a dish from the menu, you may want to stop and see how it was displayed, and whether that potentially swayed you towards a dish the restaurant wanted you to order.

Sources: Sarah Kershaw, "In Search of a Formula to Entice Mind, Stomach and Wallet", *The New York Times*, 23 December 2009.

CHAPTER SUMMARY

Objectives of Service Pricing
- Gain profit & cover costs
- Build demand & develop a user base
- Support positioning strategy

Components of the Pricing Tripod

Value to Customer (Price Ceiling)
- Net value & price
- Value perception
- Related monetary & non-monetary costs

Competitor Pricing (Competitive Benchmark)
- Price competition intensifiers
- Price competition inhibitors

Viable Price Range

Unit Cost to Firm (Price Floor)
- Fixed & variable costs
- Contribution
- Break-even analysis
- Activity-based costing

Revenue Management (RM)

When Should RM be Used?
- Fixed capacity & high fixed costs
- Variable & uncertain demand
- Varying customer price sensitivity

How to Apply RM?
- Predict demand by segment
- Reserve capacity for high-yield customers
- Maximise revenue per available space and time unit (RevPAST)
- "Pick up" competitor pricing through booking pace in the RM system
- Implement price segmentation through "rate fences"

Rate Fences
- Physical fences
  - Basic product
  - Amenities
  - Service level
- Non-physical fences
  - Transaction characteristics
  - Consumption characteristics
  - Buyer characteristics

Fairness & Ethical Concerns in Service Pricing

Ethical Concerns
- Service pricing is complex
- Confusopoly
- Fees: Crime & punishment

Design Fairness into RM
- Clear, logical & fair prices and rate fences
- Frame rate fences as discounts
- Communicate benefits of RM
- 'Hide' discounts
- Take care of loyal customers
- Use service recovery to deal with overbooking

Putting Service Pricing into Practice
- How much should be charged?
- What should be the basis of pricing?
- Who should collect payment & where?
- When should payment be made?
- How should payment be made?
- How should prices be communicated?

CHAPTER 7

Service Marketing Communications

Life is for one generation; a good name is forever.

Japanese proverb

Education costs money, but then so does ignorance.

Sir Claus Moser
British statistician

We don't have a choice on whether we do social media; the question is how well we do it.

Erik Qualman
Author of Socialnomics

INTEGRATED SERVICE MARKETING COMMUNICATIONS[1]

Although communication is the most visible or audible form of marketing activities, its value is limited unless used intelligently in conjunction with other marketing efforts. According to an old marketing axiom, the fastest way to kill a poor product is to advertise it heavily. By the same token, an otherwise well-researched and well-planned marketing strategy is likely to fail if prospects are not aware of a service firm's existence, what it has to offer, the value proposition of each of its products, and how to use them to their best advantage. Customers can be easily lured away by competitive offerings, if there is no proactive management and control on the firm's identity. Marketing communications, in one form or another, are essential to a company's success. This chapter focuses on how to plan and design an effective marketing communication strategy for the services offered. Through communications, marketers explain and promote the value proposition their firm is offering.

Communications must be viewed more broadly than just as media advertising, public relations, social media, and professional salespeople. There are many other ways for a service business to communicate with current and prospective customers. Location and atmosphere of a service delivery facility, corporate design features, such as consistent use of colors and graphic elements, appearance and behavior of employees, design of a website, all these make a profound impression on customer's mind that reinforces or contradicts the specific content of formal communication messages.

In the past few years, Internet and mobile apps have emerged as new and exciting opportunities for reaching prospects with previously unimaginable targeting and message specificity. All these media have to be effectively synchronized to attract new customers and to affirm the choice of existing customers, while educating them on how to proceed through a service process.

Developing an effective service marketing communications strategy starts with a good understanding of the service product and its prospective buyers. It is essential to understand target market segments and their exposure to different media, consumers' awareness of the service product, their attitudes toward it, and how they can easily evaluate the products characteristics prior to purchase, and during and after consumption. Decisions include determining the content, structure and style of the message to be communicated, its manner of presentation, and the media most suited to reach the intended audience.

To integrate all these considerations, the Integrated Service Communications Model was developed as shown in Fig. 7.1, which serves as the organizing framework for this chapter. It starts with the 5 'W's model, which offers a useful checklist for marketing communications planning:

- *Who* is the target audience?
- *What* do we need to communicate and achieve?
- *How* should we communicate this?
- *Where* should we communicate this?
- *When* do the communications need to take place?

The following section discusses the issues of defining the target audience ("who") and specifying communication objectives ("what"), which are the key strategic communications decisions to be made. Further sections deal with the tactical decisions of service communications plan required to implement the communications strategy, which include the wide array of communication channels available to service marketers ("*where*"), how service-specific challenges of communications can be overcome ("*how*"), and when scheduling of communication activities should take place ("*when*"). Additional considerations included in this model are discussed in the subsequent sections — the budget available for execution and methods of measuring and evaluating a communications program performance; ethics and consumer privacy, and corporate design. The final section then discusses how communications across channels should be aligned using integrated marketing communications.

DEFINING TARGET AUDIENCE

Prospects, users, and employees are the three broad target audiences for any service communications strategy:

- *Prospects*: As marketers of consumer services do not usually know the prospects in advance, they typically need to employ a traditional communications mix, comprising elements such as media advertising, online advertising, public relations, and use of purchased lists for direct mail or telemarketing.

- *Users*: In contrast to prospects, more cost-effective channels are often available to reach existing users, including cross- or up-selling

Figure 7.1: Integrated Service Communications Model

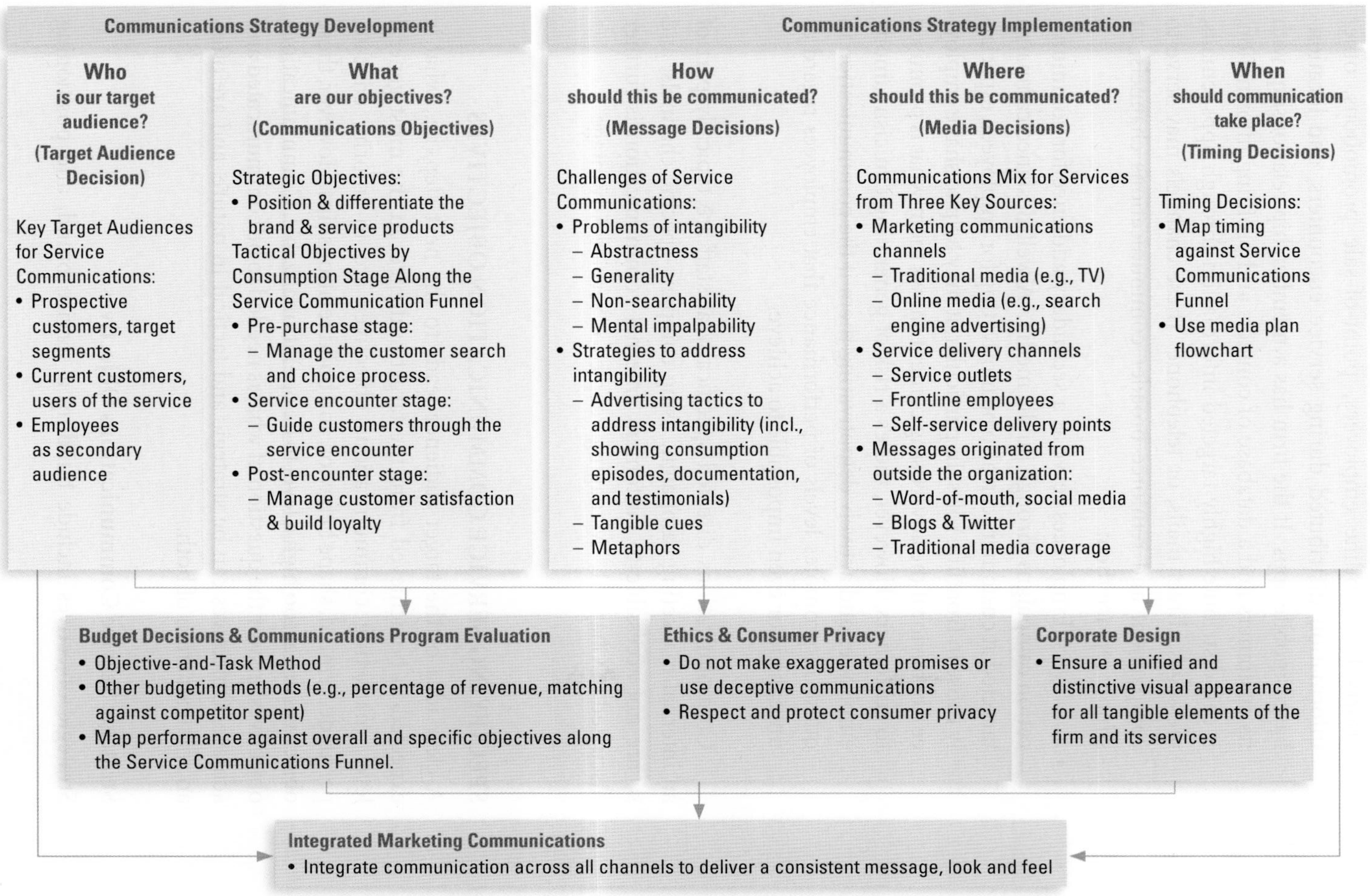

Communications Strategy Development

Who is our target audience?
(Target Audience Decision)

Key Target Audiences for Service Communications:
• Prospective customers, target segments
• Current customers, users of the service
• Employees as secondary audience

What are our objectives?
(Communications Objectives)

Strategic Objectives:
• Position & differentiate the brand & service products
Tactical Objectives by Consumption Stage Along the Service Communication Funnel
• Pre-purchase stage:
  – Manage the customer search and choice process.
• Service encounter stage:
  – Guide customers through the service encounter
• Post-encounter stage:
  – Manage customer satisfaction & build loyalty

Communications Strategy Implementation

How should this be communicated?
(Message Decisions)

Challenges of Service Communications:
• Problems of intangibility
  – Abstractness
  – Generality
  – Non-searchability
  – Mental impalpability
• Strategies to address intangibility
  – Advertising tactics to address intangibility (incl., showing consumption episodes, documentation, and testimonials)
  – Tangible cues
  – Metaphors

Where should this be communicated?
(Media Decisions)

Communications Mix for Services from Three Key Sources:
• Marketing communications channels
  – Traditional media (e.g., TV)
  – Online media (e.g., search engine advertising)
• Service delivery channels
  – Service outlets
  – Frontline employees
  – Self-service delivery points
• Messages originated from outside the organization:
  – Word-of-mouth, social media
  – Blogs & Twitter
  – Traditional media coverage

When should communication take place?
(Timing Decisions)

Timing Decisions:
• Map timing against Service Communications Funnel
• Use media plan flowchart

Budget Decisions & Communications Program Evaluation
• Objective-and-Task Method
• Other budgeting methods (e.g., percentage of revenue, matching against competitor spent)
• Map performance against overall and specific objectives along the Service Communications Funnel.

Ethics & Consumer Privacy
• Do not make exaggerated promises or use deceptive communications
• Respect and protect consumer privacy

Corporate Design
• Ensure a unified and distinctive visual appearance for all tangible elements of the firm and its services

Integrated Marketing Communications
• Integrate communication across all channels to deliver a consistent message, look and feel

efforts by frontline employees, point-of-sale promotions, other information distributed during service encounters, and location-based mobile apps. If the firm has a membership relationship with its customers and a database of contacts and profiling information, it can distribute highly targeted information through apps, emails, messages, direct mails, or telephone. These channels may serve to complement and reinforce broader communications channels, or simply replace them.

• *Employees*: Employees serve as a secondary audience for communication campaigns through public media.[2] A well-designed campaign targeted at customers can also be motivating for employees, especially those in frontline roles. In particular, it may help to shape employees' behavior if the advertising content shows them what is promised to customers. However, there's a risk of generating cynicism among employees and actively demotivating them if the communication in question promotes levels of performance that employees regard as unrealistic or even impossible to achieve.

Communications directed specifically at staff are typically part of an internal marketing campaign, using company-specific channels, and so are not accessible to customers. Internal communication is further discussed in Chap. 11, "Managing People for Service Advantage".

SPECIFYING SERVICE COMMUNICATION OBJECTIVES

A clear idea of the target audience leads to the next step, i.e., what is expected to be achieved from the target audience. At the most general level, marketing communications objectives are to inform, educate, persuade, remind, shape behavior, and build relationships. However, these objectives are at too high a level to be operationalizable. Communications objectives answer the question of what is needed to be communicated and achieve. Objectives can be strategic and tactical in nature, and are often an amalgamation of both.

Strategic Service Communications Objectives

Strategic objectives include building a service brand, and positioning it and its service products against competition. That is, companies use marketing communications to persuade target customers that their service product offers the best solution to meet those customers' needs, compared to the offerings of competing firms. Communication efforts serve not only to attract new users but also to maintain contact with an organization's existing customers and nurture relationships with them. That is, marketing communications is used to convince potential and current customers about the firm's overall superior performance.

To document the superior quality and reliability of its small package delivery services, a FedEx advertisement showcased the awards it received for being rated as highest in customer satisfaction for air, ground, and international delivery from J.D. Power and Associates, widely known and respected for its customer satisfaction research in numerous industries.[3] To reposition a service relative to competitive offerings is also a common strategic objective of communications.

Tactical Service Communications Objectives

Tactical objectives relate to shaping and managing customer's perceptions, beliefs, attitudes and behavior in any of the three stages of the service consumption process discussed in Chap. 2 (i.e., the prepurchase, service encounter, and post-encounter stages). The *Service Marketing Communications Funnel* in Fig. 7.2 shows how common tactical communications objective map against the three stages of the service consumption (left column in Fig. 7.3) and related key consumer behavior concepts and theories (right column in Fig. 7.3).

There are a few study models that deal with the prepurchase phase, generally referred to as sales funnel (or purchase funnel from the customer's perspective) and those that depict the stages a consumer typically passes through from not being aware of a product to all the way of actually buying it. Probably the oldest model, "AIDA", standing for Awareness, Interest, Desire, and Action, developed almost a century ago, holds that persuasion to buy a product occurs over time, and explains how customers move from cognitive (awareness), to affective (interest and desire), to behavioral (action) responses.[4] As with many basic models, it has stood the test of time and is still being used. Currently, the *hierarchy of effects* model is probably the most widely used framework to describe this process by extending the steps described in the AIDA model as follows:

Figure 7.2: Common communications objectives along the Service Marketing Communications Funnel

Three–Stage Model of Service Consumption	Common Communication Objectives Along the Services Marketing Communications Funnel	Key Consumer Behavior Concepts and Theories
Pre-purchase Stage **Awareness of need** • Information search • Clarify needs • Explore solutions • Identify alternative service products **Evaluation of alternatives** • Review supplier information (e.g., advertising, website) • Review information from third parties (e.g., published reviews, ratings, blogs) • Discuss options with service personnel • Get advice from third-parties • Make purchase decision	**Customer Acquisition** • Move customers along the key stages of the sales funnel • Build awareness, knowledge, and interest in the service or brand – Encourage to explore the firm's website or social media sites – Register for your online newsletter, service updates, or YouTube channel • Develop liking, preference, and conviction for the service or brand – Compare a service favorably with competitors' offerings – Convince potential customers about the firm's superior performance on determinant attributes • Encourage potential customers to purchase – Reduce perceived risk by providing information and service guarantees – Encourage trial by offering promotional incentives • Create memorable images of brands and services • Stimulate and shift demand to match capacity	**Pre-purchase Stage** • Need arousal • Evoked set • Consideration set **Multi-attribute choice model** • Search, experience, and credence attributes • Perceived risk • Formation of expectations • Purchase decision
Service Encounter Stage • Request service from the chosen supplier or initiate self-service • Experience the service encounter	**Service Encounter Management** • Familiarize customers with service processes in advance of use (e.g., what to prepare & expect) • Guide customers through the service process • Manage customer behavior and perceptions during the service encounter (e.g., teach roles, script for queuing, inject perceived control) • Manage quality perceptions • Cross-sell & upsell services	**Service Encounter Stage** • Moments of truth • Service encounters • Servuction system • Theatre as metaphor • Role and script theories • Perceived control theory
Post-encounter Stage • Evaluation of service performance • Future intentions • Future behaviors	**Customer Engagement** • Manage customer satisfaction • Manage service quality perceptions • Build loyalty • Encourage WOM (offline and online) • Encourage referrals • Build a brand community	**Post-encounter Stage** • Confirmation/ disconfirmation of expectations • Dissatisfaction, satisfaction, and delight • Service quality • WOM and referrals • Online reviews • Repurchase • Customer loyalty

Figure 7.3: This Chicago School advert creates awareness and interest

The hierarchy of effects model starts with a cognitive stage of awareness and knowledge, followed by an affective stage that leads to liking, preference and conviction, and finally, a behavioral stage of buying.[5] Along each of those stages and the individual steps within, marketing communications assumes different roles to guide consumers toward the purchase decision (Fig. 7.4).

The Service Marketing Communications Funnel is aligned to the AIDA and hierarchy of effects models in the prepurchase stage, and extends them by incorporating a wider range of service-specific objectives. Furthermore, as neither of the two models covers the service encounter and post-encounter stages, service communications objectives relating to the service encounter itself (which can include the full gamut of customer behaviors that needs to be managed, ranging from queuing behaviors to performance perceptions), and to the post-encounter stage (e.g., many services are membership-type or contractual in nature, which therefore includes a host of post-encounter behaviors that can be shaped by communications) were added.

The Service Marketing Communications Funnel starts with a broad target audience at the top (i.e., all prospects in the firm's target segments), narrows down to customers who actually buy and consume the service, and finally — even for loyalty initiatives, firms typically do not target all their customers with the same intensity — the focus tends to be on their "platinum" or premium customers with high purchase volumes (see Chap. 12). Marketing communications plays specific roles during all three stages of the service consumption process and not just the prepurchase stage.

A key takeaway from Fig. 7.3 is that the communications objectives can be highly specific and can address any aspect of service consumer behavior. Chap. 2 describes the consumer behavior in a service context and how communications can be used to shape consumer behavior in the firm-desired direction at any stage. For example, in the prepurchase stage, how communications can be used to trigger a need, get a service evoked and then into the consideration set, reduce perceived risk, and shape multi-attribute model-type processing (e.g., shifting attribute performance perceptions, attribute weightings, and decision rules in the favor of the firm's services). During the service encounter stage, how can communications be employed to shape performance perceptions, to help customers move effectively through the service encounter, to shape quality perceptions, teach service roles and scripts, and to inject perceived control into the service encounter? Finally, how can communications be used in the post-encounter stage to shape customer satisfaction and service quality evaluations, and encourage word-of-mouth, referrals, repurchase, and loyalty?

To discuss all possible objectives that can be derived from the Services Marketing Communications Funnel is beyond the scope of this chapter. However, a few important communications objectives are highlighted in the following sections.

Promote Tangible Cues To Communicate Quality. Companies should use concrete cues to communicate service performance by highlighting the quality of equipment and facilities, and by emphasizing employee characteristics such as qualifications, experience, commitment, and professionalism, because even if customers understand what a service is supposed to do, they may find it hard to tell the difference between offerings from different suppliers. Some performance attributes are easier or more appropriate to communicate than others. Airlines and hospitals do not advertise safety because even the slightest suggestion that things might go wrong will make many people nervous. Instead, they approach this ongoing customer concern indirectly by communicating the overall high quality of their people, facilities, equipment, and processes.

Add Value through Communication Content. Information and consultation represent important ways to add value to a product. Prospective customers may need information and advice about what service options are available to them (Fig. 7.4); where and when these services are available; how much they cost; and what specific features, functions, and service benefits there are. (For more details, see the Flower

Figure 7.4: Itau stresses its global reach, but also its intimate knowledge of Latin America.

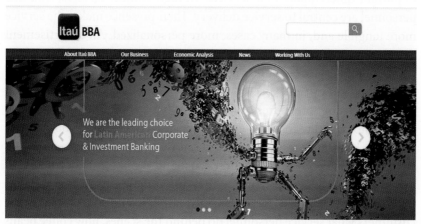

of Service Framework in Chap. 4.)

Facilitate Customer Involvement in Service Production. When customers are actively involved in service production, they need training to help them perform well — just as employees do. Improving productivity often involves making innovations in service delivery. However, the desired benefits will not be achieved if customers resist new, technologically-based systems or avoid self-service alternatives.

Marketers often use sales promotions as incentives to encourage customers to make the necessary changes in their behavior. For example, giving price discounts or running lucky draws are a few ways to encourage customers to try and switch to self-service, and if necessary, well-trained service personnel can provide one-to-one tutoring to help customers adapt to new procedures.

One way to train customers, as recommended by advertising experts, is to show service delivery in action. Television and videos are effective because of their ability to engage the viewer and display a seamless sequence of events in visual form. Some dentists show their patients videos of surgical procedures before the surgery takes place so that the customers know what to expect. This educational technique helps patients prepare mentally for the experience, and shows them what role they need to play in service delivery to ensure a successful surgery and speedy recovery.

Promote the Contribution of Service Personnel and Backstage

Operations. High quality, frontline staff and backstage operations can be important differentiators for services. In high-contact services, frontline personnel are central to service delivery. Their presence makes the service more tangible and, in many cases, more personalized. An advertisement that shows employees at work helps prospective customers understand the nature of the service encounter and implies a promise of the personalized attention that they can expect to receive.

Advertising, brochures, websites, and videos on YouTube can also show customers the work that goes on "backstage" to ensure good service delivery. Highlighting the expertise and commitment of employees whom customers normally never encounter may enhance trust in the organization's competence and commitment to service quality. For example, Starbucks has publicity materials and videos that show customers what service personnel do behind the scenes, how coffee beans are cultivated, harvested, and produced — highlighting its use of the finest and freshest.[6]

Advertising messages set customer expectations high, so advertisers must be reasonably realistic in their depiction of service personnel. They should also inform employees about the content of new campaigns that promise specific attitudes and behaviors so that employees know what is expected of them.

Stimulate and Shift Demand to Match Capacity. Low demand outside peak periods is a serious problem for service industries with high fixed costs, such as hotels. One strategy is to run promotions that offer extra value — such as room upgrades or free breakfasts — to encourage demand without decreasing price. When demand increases, the number of promotions can be reduced or eliminated (see Chap. 6 and 9).

Advertising and sales promotions can also help to shift usage from peak to low-demand periods and thus help to match demand with the available capacity at a given time.

CRAFTING EFFECTIVE SERVICE COMMUNICATION MESSAGES

This section deals with the communication challenges service firms face when developing their communications messages. For goods and services alike, messages have to break through the clutter as communications can only succeed if it gains the attention of its target group. Marketers have to make decisions on what they want to say (i.e., the message content) and how to say that (i.e., the message structure and format).[7] While any good marketing and communications book deals with these questions, traditional marketing communication strategies were shaped largely by the needs and practices associated with marketing manufactured goods. However, several of the differences that distinguish services from goods also have a significant effect on the ways we approach the design of message and creative strategy of service marketing communication programs. This is especially true for intangibility discussed next.

Problems of Intangibility

The benefits of services can be difficult to communicate to customers as they are "performances" rather than objects, especially when the service in question does not involve tangible actions to customers or their possessions.[8] Intangibility creates four problems for marketers seeking to promote its attributes or benefits: abstractness, generality, non-searchability, and mental impalpability.[9] Each problem has implications for service communications[10] as follows:

- *Abstractness* refers to concepts such as financial security or investment-related matters, expert advice, or safe transportation and do not have one-to-one correspondence with physical objects. It can be challenging for marketers to connect their services to those intangible concepts.

- *Generality* refers to items that comprise a class of objects, persons, or events such as airline seats, flight attendants, and cabin service. There may be physical objects that can show these services, so abstractness is not a problem. However, it is general and not specific enough, so even though most consumers know what they are, it is difficult for marketers to create a unique value proposition to communicate what makes a specific offering distinctly different from — and superior to — competing offerings.

- *Non-searchability* refers to the fact that many of the service attributes cannot be searched or inspected before they are purchased. Physical service attributes, such as the appearance of a health club and types of equipment installed, can be checked in advance, but the experience of working with the trainers can only be determined through extended personal involvement. As noted in Chap. 2, services usually have more experience and credence attributes than search attributes. Experience attributes are those that need consumers to go through the service to understand it. Services high in credence attributes, such as surgeon expertise, must be taken on faith.

- *Mental impalpability.* Many services are sufficiently complex, multi-dimensional, or novel that it is difficult for consumers — especially new prospects — to understand what the experience of using them will be like and what benefits will result.

Overcoming the Problems of Intangibility

The next step is to communicate the service messages. Here, the intangibility of service presents problems for advertising that need to be overcome. Table 7.1 suggests specific communications strategies marketers can follow to create messages that help to overcome each of the four problems created by the intangibility of services.

In addition to using the strategies presented in Table 7.1, tangible cues and metaphors are two other methods firms can use to overcome the four challenges of intangibility. Both of these methods help to clearly communicate intangible service attributes and benefits to potential customers.

Tangible Cues. Commonly used strategies in advertising include the use of tangible cues whenever possible, especially for services that involve few tangible elements. It is also helpful to include "vivid information" that catches the audience's attention and produces a strong, clear impression on the senses, especially for services that are complex and highly intangible.[11] For example, many business schools feature successful alumni to make the benefits of their education tangible and communicate what their programs could do for prospective students in terms of career advancement, salary increases, and lifestyle.

Use Metaphors. Some companies have created metaphors that are tangible in nature to help communicate the benefits of their service offerings and to emphasize key points of differentiation. Insurance companies often use this approach to market their highly intangible products. Allstate advertises that "You're in Good Hands", and Prudential uses the Rock of Gibraltar as a symbol of corporate strength. The Merrill Lynch bull

Table 7.1: Advertising strategies for overcoming intangibility

Intangibility Problem	Advertising Strategy	Description
Abstractness	Service consumption episode	Capture and show typical customers benefiting from the service, e.g., by smiling in satisfaction at a staff going out of his way to help
Generality • For objective claim	System documentation	Document facts and statistics about the service delivery system. For example, in the UPS website, they state that they have 227 aircraft in operation
• For subjective claim	Performance documentation	Document and cite past service performance statistics, such as the number of packages that have been delivered on time
	Service performance episode	Present actual service delivery being performed by the service personnel. The video mode is best for showing this
Non-searchability	Consumption documentation	Obtain and present testimonials from customers who have experienced the service
	Reputation documentation	If the service is high in credence attributes, then document the awards received, or the qualifications of the service provider
Mental impalpability	Service process episode	Present a clear step-by-step documentation of what exactly will happen during the service experience
	Case history episode	Present an actual case history of what the firm did for a specific client and how it solved the client's problem
	Service consumption episode	A story or depiction of a customer's experience with a service

has been a symbol for the wealth manager's business philosophy, which suggests both a bullish market and a strong commitment to financial performance of its clients (Fig. 7.5).

Figure 7.5: Merrill Lynch bull showing a strong commitment to the financial performance of its clients.

Where possible, advertising metaphors should highlight *how* service benefits are actually provided.[12] Consulting firm AT Kearney emphasizes that it includes all management levels in seeking solutions, not just higher-level management. Its clever advertisement, showing bear traps across the office floor, draws attention to the way in which the company differentiates its service through careful work with all levels in its client organizations, thus avoiding the problems left behind by other consulting firms who work mostly with senior management (Fig. 7.6).

Figure 7.6: AT Kearney using bear traps as a metaphor for problems.

THE SERVICES MARKETING COMMUNICATIONS MIX

Most service marketers have access to numerous forms of communication, referred to collectively as the *service marketing communications mix*. Different communication elements have distinctive capabilities for the types of messages they can convey and the market segments most likely to be exposed to them, and the mix needs to be optimized to achieve the best possible results for a given budget.[13]

Fig. 7.8 provides an overview of the wide range of communications channels available to service firms. Note that these media can be categorized in several ways. For example, service employees providing service are, at the same time, part of the service delivery point and a type of personal communications. Each communications mix element can be categorized according to the most suitable category for the purpose of discussing the overall media strategy of service organizations.

There are a few other ways to categorize these channels — often, they are split into non-personal (e.g., advertising) and personal (e.g., direct marketing and personal communications), or traditional media (e.g., TV, print, and outdoor) versus online media (e.g., online advertising, social media and mobile communications). Each type of media has its own strengths and weaknesses, and can be used for different objectives. For example, non-personal mass media tend to be effective for creating awareness and positioning the service, whereas personal communications can be highly effective for explaining complex service information, reducing risk perceptions and persuading to buy. Communications in the servicescape (e.g., signs and posters) can be used to manage consumer behavior during service encounter such as queuing, following the service script, and trying new services (i.e., cross-selling). Direct marketing is highly cost-effective in the post-encounter stage, such as to encourage customers to come back and recommend the service to their friends and family.

Communications Originate from Different Sources

As shown in Fig. 7.9, the services marketing communications mix featured in Fig. 7.10 can also be categorized into three broad categories of sources of communications: (1) marketing communications channels, which include traditional media and online channels, (2) service delivery channels, and (3) messages that originate from outside the organization.[14]

Figure 7.8: The marketing communications mix for services

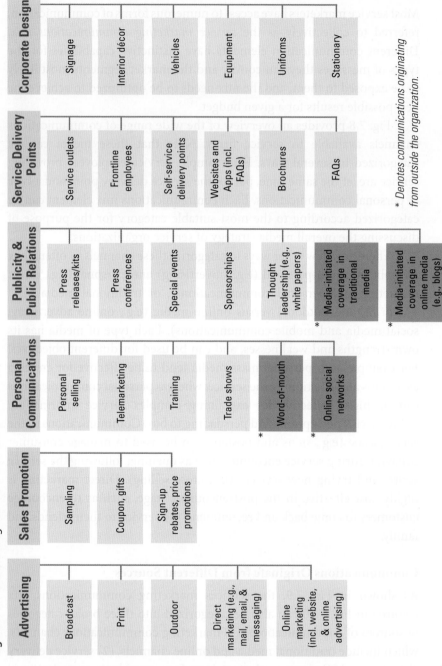

* Denotes communications originating from outside the organization.

Figure 7.9: Three key sources of messages received by the target audience.

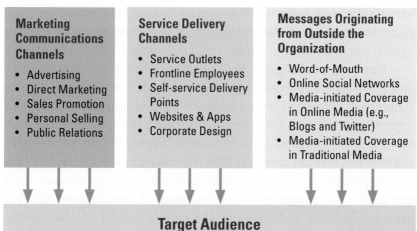

Marketing Communications Channels	Service Delivery Channels	Messages Originating from Outside the Organization
• Advertising • Direct Marketing • Sales Promotion • Personal Selling • Public Relations	• Service Outlets • Frontline Employees • Self-service Delivery Points • Websites & Apps • Corporate Design	• Word-of-Mouth • Online Social Networks • Media-initiated Coverage in Online Media (e.g., Blogs and Twitter) • Media-initiated Coverage in Traditional Media

Target Audience

Each of these three originating sources has key tools, however, traditional and online media have vastly different characteristics and applications and are discussed separately.

Messages Transmitted through Traditional Marketing Channels

As shown in Fig. 7.10, service marketers have a wide array of communication tools at their disposal. Following are the principle elements:

Advertising. A wide array of paid advertising media is available, including broadcast (TV and radio), print (magazines and newspapers), movie theaters, and many types of outdoor media (posters, billboards, electronic message boards, and the exteriors of buses or bicycles). Some media are more focused than others, targeting specific geographic areas or audiences with a particular interest. Advertising messages delivered through mass media are often reinforced by direct marketing tools such as mailings, telemarketing, or email.

As the most dominant form of communication in consumer marketing, advertising is often the first point of contact between service marketers and their customers, serving to build awareness, inform, persuade, and remind. It plays a vital role in providing factual information about services and educating customers about product features and capabilities. For instance, a review of 11,543 television and

30,940 newspaper advertisements found that advertisements for services were significantly more likely to contain factual information on price, guarantees/warranties, documentation of performance, and availability (where, when, and how to acquire products) compared to ads for goods.[15]

One of the challenges facing advertisers is how to get their messages noticed. In general, people are getting tired of ads in all forms. A study by Yankelovich Partner, a US marketing services consulting firm, found that consumer resistance to advertising has reached an all-time high. The study found that 65% of people feel "constantly bombarded" by ad messages, and 59% feel that ads have very little relevance to them.[16] Television and radio broadcasts, websites, and online games are cluttered with ads, while newspapers and magazines sometimes seem to contain more ads than news and features. Robert Shaw of Cranfield School of Management runs a forum in which large companies try to monitor the "marketing payback" from advertising. According to Shaw, the results were "never terribly good", with less than half of the ads generating a positive return on their investment.[17]

How can a firm hope to stand out from the crowd? Longer, louder commercials and larger-format ads are not the answer. Marketers are trying to be more creative with their advertising to allow their messages to be more effective. For example, when customers have low involvement

Figure 7.10: Virtual video game worlds such as Second Life leading the wave of in-game advertising.

with a service, firms should focus on more emotional appeals and the service experience itself.[18] Some advertisers stand out by using striking designs or a distinctively different format. Others, such as Comcast, seek to catch the audience's attention through use of humor as it seeks to show how slow competing services are, compared to its own high-speed Internet. Some firms are now placing advertisements in video games and multiplayer online role-playing games, which can be dynamic advertisements if the games are connected to the Internet (Fig. 7.10).[19] Furthermore, mobile apps are becoming increasingly important avenues for communication with potential and current customers.

Direct Marketing. This category embraces tools such as mailings, email, and text messaging. These channels offer the potential to send personalized messages to highly-targeted microsegments. Direct strategies will most likely succeed when marketers possess a detailed database of information about prospects and customers.

Commercial services that combine company-collected data with rich, third-party online and offline data sources are available. Experian, one of the globally leading providers in this market, stated on its website: "We can help you to build a richer picture of your customers' behavior so you can predict and engineer how they behave in the future. Using internal and external data sources, our proven customer management tools allow you to tailor strategies to an individual...powered by up to 6,000 variables...uses lifestyle, demographic, transaction, permissible credit and consumer classification data".[20]

Advances in on-demand technologies such as email spam filters, TiVo, podcasting, and pop-up blockers allow consumers to decide how and when they like to be reached and by whom. As a 30-second television spot interrupts a viewer's favorite program and a telemarketing call interrupts a meal, customers increasingly use such technologies to protect their time, thereby reducing the effectiveness of mass media. These developments gave rise to *permission marketing,* where customers are encouraged to "raise their hands" and agree to learn more about a company and its products in anticipation of receiving useful marketing information or something else of value. Instead of annoying prospects by interrupting their personal time, permission marketing allows customers to self-select into the target segments.

In the permission marketing model, the goal is to persuade consumers to volunteer their attention. By reaching out only to individuals who have expressed prior interest in receiving a certain type of message, permission marketing enables service firms to build stronger relationships with their customers. In particular, email and messaging, in combination with websites and mobile apps, can be merged into a one-to-one permission-based medium. For instance, people can be invited to register at the firm's website or download an app and state what type of information they would like to receive.[21]

These messages can be designed at the start of a more interactive, multilayered communication process in which customers can request regular information about topics of their interest. In addition, if they are particularly excited about a new service or piece of information, they can click through a link embedded in the message to access more in-depth information and video materials. Finally, they can subscribe for additional services, communicate with other customers, recommend the service to their friends, and like it on Facebook or LinkedIn.

Many service firms increased their focus on permission-based marketing because of its high effectiveness combined with the falling prices and improving quality of customer relationship management (CRM) systems, big data, social media and communications technology, which together empower permission-based marketing. To see how some firms have implemented excellent permission-based marketing strategies, check Amazon.com or Hallmark.com, and register at these websites or download their apps.

Sales Promotion. A useful way of looking at sales promotions is as a communication with an incentive. Sales promotions usually are specific to a time period, price or customer group — sometimes all three as in direct marketing. Typically, it is employed for short-term objectives such as to accelerate the purchasing decision or motivate customers to use a specific service sooner, in greater volume with each purchase, or more frequently.[22] Sales promotions for service firms may take forms such as samples, coupons and other discounts, gifts, and competitions with prizes. Used in these forms, sales promotions increase sales during periods when demand would otherwise be weak, speed up the introduction and acceptance of new services, and generally get customers to act faster than they would in the absence of any promotional incentive.[23] However, sales promotions need to be used with care because research shows that customers acquired through sales promotions may have lower repurchase rates and lower lifetime values.[24]

Some years ago, SAS International Hotels devised an interesting sales promotion targeted at older customers. If a hotel had vacant rooms, guests over 65 years of age could get a discount equivalent to their years (e.g., a 75-year-old could save 75% of the normal room price). All went well until a Swedish guest checked into one of the SAS chain's hotels in Vienna, announced his age as 102, and asked to be paid 2% of the room rate in return for staying the night. This request was granted, whereupon the spry centenarian challenged the general manager to a game of tennis — and got that, too. (However, the results of the game were not disclosed!) Events like these are the stuff of dreams for public relations people. In this case, a clever promotion led to a humorous, widely reported story that placed the hotel chain in a favorable light.

Personal Selling. Interpersonal encounters in which efforts are made to educate customers and promote a particular brand or product are referred to as personal selling. Many firms, especially those marketing business-to-business (B2B) services, maintain a sales team or employ agents and distributors to undertake personal selling efforts on their behalf. For services that are bought less often such as property, insurance, and funeral services, the firm's representative may act as a consultant to help buyers make their selections. For industrial and professional firms that sell relatively complex services, customers may have an account manager they can turn to for advice, education, and consultation.

However, face-to-face selling to new prospects is expensive. A lower-cost alternative is *telemarketing*, involving use of the telephone to reach prospective customers. At the consumer level, there is growing frustration with the intrusive nature of telemarketing, which is often timed to reach people when they are home in the evening or on weekends (Fig. 7.11). Today, many people in the US subscribe to a "Do Not Call Registry", which has dramatically reduced the number of solicitor calls that reach their prospects.[25]

Figure 7.11: Telemarketers call in the evenings.

© 1999 Randy Glasbergen.

GLASBERGEN

**"Before you hang up, Mrs. Johnson, are you aware
that you can lose up to 50 pounds a year by listening
to telemarketers instead of eating your dinner?"**

Public Relations. Public relations (PR) involves efforts to stimulate positive interest in an organization and its products by sending out news releases, holding press conferences, staging special events, and sponsoring newsworthy activities put on by third parties. A basic element in PR strategy is the preparation and distribution of press releases (including photos and/or videos) that feature stories about the company, its products, and its employees.

Other widely used PR techniques include recognition and reward programs, obtaining testimonials from public figures, community involvement and fund raising, and obtaining favorable publicity for the organization through special events and *pro bono* work. These tools can help a service organization build its reputation and credibility, form strong relationships with its employees, customers and the community, and secure an image conducive to business success.

Firms can also gain wide exposure through sponsorship of sporting events and other high-profile activities such as the Olympics and World Cup where banners, decals, and other visual displays provide continuing repetition of the corporate name and symbol. Furthermore, unusual activities can present an opportunity to promote a company's expertise. For example, the "Oscar" campaign shown in *Service Insights 7.1* was successful in creating a following on its Facebook pages as a result of the hotels employees who were quick and innovative.

SERVICE INSIGHTS 7.1
Oscar Is Having The Time Of His Life

Employees of the Kilronan Castle Hotel in Ireland found a bright orange and yellow monkey soft toy in a linen bin, which clearly would be missed by its owner. Rather than putting it into the lost property shelf, the employees had the great idea of starting a social media campaign to reunite Oscar, the name the employees gave to the toy, with his rightful owner, and they had a lot of fun in the process as seen in the photos!

They took photos showing Oscar living the high life, and uploaded them to Facebook. The message was that Oscar is looking for his owner, and although he is lost, he has the time of his life at this luxury castle hotel. The photos show him enjoying afternoon tea, having beauty treatments, and having a buffet prepared for him by the executive chef. It almost seemed as if Oscar didn't mind not being found for a little while longer...

Have a look online whether he was eventually reunited with his owner.

While the employees hoped that Oscar's owner would come forward, there is no doubt about the significant social media publicity generated for the Kilronan Castle Hotel. Speed, creativity

Figure 7.12: Oscar is having the time of his life

Notice put up by staff of Kilronan Castle on its Facebook Page

LOST CUDDLY TOY ALERT
Kilronan Castle are launching an appeal to find the owner of a very cute and cuddly monkey found here at the castle...

Little Oscar (named by the staff at Kilronan) was found in a linen bin and we are now asking any guests who stayed here over the weekend if they have any information on Oscars owner.

Please help us find Oscar's owner... in the meantime he is being well looked after and experiencing the exceptional customer experience here at Kilronan Castle.

and fun are some of the attributes that can make a social media campaign go viral.

Sources: https://www.facebook.com/media/set/?set=a.913675381980829.1073741840.125951937419848&type=3; http://www.evoke.ie/news/oscar-the-lost-teddy-is-having-the-time-of-his-life-and-lapping-up-the-luxury-at-this-irish-castle-waiting-on-his-owners, Google search for "Kilronan Castle and Oscar", March 12, 2015; MavSocial, "Fun + Engagement – Superb Social Media Campaigns, http://mavsocial.com/fun-engagement-superb-social-media-campaigns, accessed on 12 March, 2016.

Messages Transmitted Online[26]

Online and mobile advertising using the Internet, social media, and apps allow companies to complement, and sometimes even substitute traditional communications channels at a reasonable cost. However, like any of the elements of the marketing communications mix, online and mobile advertising should be part of an integrated, well-designed communications strategy.[27]

Company's Website. Marketers use their own website for a variety of communications tasks:

- Creating consumer awareness and interest.
- Providing information and consultation.
- Allowing two-way communications with customers through email and chat rooms.
- Encouraging product trial.
- Enabling customers to place orders.
- Measuring the effectiveness of specific advertising or promotional campaigns.

Innovative companies continue to constantly look for ways to improve the appeal and usefulness of their websites. Suitable communication content varies widely from one type of service to another. A B2B site may offer visitors access to a library of technical information (e.g., Oracle or SAP both provide substantial information on their customer relationship management solutions at their respective websites). By contrast, a B2C website for an MBA program might include attractive photographs and videos featuring the university, its professors and facilities, student testimonials, information on alumni, location, and even a graduation ceremony.

Marketers must also address other factors such as downloading speed that affect website "stickiness" (i.e., whether visitors are willing to spend time on the site and will revisit it in the future). A sticky site is:

- *High in quality content.* Relevant and useful content is king. A site needs to contain what visitors are looking for.

- *Easy to use.* Easy to use means it is easy to find their way around the site with good navigation, and a site structure that is well signposted, neither overcomplicated nor too big. Customers do not get lost in good sites!

- *Quick to download.* Viewers do not want to wait, and will often give up if it takes too long for pages to download from a site. Good sites download quickly, and bad sites are slow; which means that the content has to be "light".

- *Updated frequently.* Good sites look fresh and up-to-date. They include recently posted information that visitors find relevant and timely.[28]

A memorable web address helps to attract visitors to a site. Ideally, they are based on the company's name (e.g., www.citibank.com or www.aol.com). Ensuring that people are aware of the address requires displaying it prominently on business cards, letterhead stationery, email templates, brochures, advertising, promotional materials, and even vehicles.

Online Advertising. There are two main types of online advertising, namely banner advertising and search engine advertising.

- *Banner Advertising:* Many firms pay to place advertising banners and buttons on portals such as Yahoo or CNN, social media websites such as Facebook and LinkedIn, and apps, online games and advertising-funded content websites. The usual goal is to draw online traffic to the advertiser's own site. In many instances, websites include advertising messages from other marketers with services that are related but not competing. For example, Yahoo's stock quotes page has a sequence of advertisements for various financial service providers.

Simply getting a large number of exposures ("eyeballs") to a banner (a thin horizontal ad running across all or part of a web page), or a skyscraper (a long skinny ad running vertically down one side of a website) doesn't necessarily lead to an increase in awareness, preference, or sales for the advertiser. Even when visitors click through to the advertiser's site, this act doesn't necessarily result in sales. Consequently, there is now more emphasis on advertising contracts that link fees to marketing-relevant behavior by these visitors, such as providing the advertiser with some information about themselves or when making a purchase. Most of the Internet advertisers pay only if a visitor to the host site clicks through to the link onto the advertisers' site. This is similar to paying for the delivery of junk mail only to households that read it.[29]

- *Search Engine Advertising*: Search engines are a form of a reverse broadcast network. Instead of advertisers broadcasting their messages to consumers, search engines let advertisers know exactly what consumers want through their keyword search, and advertisers can then target relevant marketing communications directly at these consumers. Search engine advertising is currently the most popular online advertising instrument,[30] and Google is the leader in this space (*Service Insights 7.2*), with firms like Bling and Yahoo! seeking to increase their market share.

  A key advantage of online advertising is that it provides a very clear and measurable return on investment, especially when compared to other forms of advertising. Particularly in performance-priced online advertising (e.g., pay-per-click), the link between advertising costs and the customers who were attracted to a company's website or offer is traceable.[31] Compare this to traditional media advertising on TV or in magazines, where it is notoriously difficult to assess the success and return of investment of an advertisement. Advertisers have several options where they can:

  - Buy top rankings in the display of search results through "pay-for-placement". Since users expect the rankings to reflect the best fit with the keywords used in the search, Google's policy is to shade paid listings that appear at the top of the rankings column and identify them as "sponsored links". Pricing for these ads and placements can be based on either the number of impressions (i.e., eyeballs) or clickthroughs.

As sponsored links aim to connect to customers just before they make a purchase decision, some firms buy keywords that are closely related to their competitor's offering. This allows them to "poach" customers and free ride on the market created by other firms.[32]

– Pay for the targeted placement of ads to keyword searches related to their offer.

– Sponsor a short text message with a clickthrough link, located next to the search results.

– Pay for performance online advertising. The advertiser is charged on the basis of pre-agreed results of their communication campaign, which could include actions such as registration on a website, downloading of a brochure, and even sales.

– Regularly conduct search engine optimization (SEO) of the firm's website. SEO improves the ranking of a website in organic (i.e., unsponsored) search lists. Doing this should be a "no-brainer" as firms do not have to spend to get the attention of potential customers. But do note that SEO only works well if the website is well-designed, contains relevant information and is aligned with target customers' interests.[33]

SERVICE INSIGHTS 7.2
Google: The Online Marketing Powerhouse

Larry Page and Sergey Brin, who were both fascinated by mathematics, computers and programming from an early age, founded Google in 1998 while they were Ph.D. students at Stanford University. Seven years later, following Google's successful public offering, they had become multi-billionaires and Google itself had become one of the world's most valuable companies.

The company has the grand vision "to organize the world's information and make it universally accessible and useful". The utility and ease of its search engine has made it immensely successful, almost entirely through word-of-mouth from satisfied users. Few company names have become verbs, but "to Google" is now a common use in English.

Its popularity has enabled Google to become a highly targeted advertising medium, allowing advertisers two important ways to reach their customers — through sponsored links and through content ads.

Sponsored links appear at the top of search results on Google's website and are identified as "sponsored links". Google prices its sponsored links service as "cost per click", using a sealed-bid auction (i.e., where advertisers submit bids for a search term without knowing the bids of other advertisers for the same term). This means prices depend on the popularity of the search terms with which the advertiser wants to be associated. Heavily used terms such as "MBA" are more expensive than less popular terms such as "MSc in Business". Advertisers can easily keep track of their ad performance using the reports in Google's online account control center.

Google allows content ads to be highly targeted through a number of ways via its Google AdWords service. Ads can be placed next to search results on Google.com (i.e., they are displayed as banner ads). These ads allow businesses to connect with potential customers at the precise moment when they are looking at related topics or even specific product categories. Here, firms buy the opportunity to be associated with particular search categories or terms. To explore this part of Google's advertising business model, just "Google" a few words and observe what appears on your screen in addition to the search results.

AdWords also allows advertisers to display their ads at websites that are part of the Google content network rather than only on Google.com. This means these ads are not initiated by a search, but are simply displayed when a user browses a website. Such ads are called "placement-targeted ads". Advertisers can specify either individual websites or website content (e.g., about travel or baseball). Placement targeting allows advertisers to handpick their target audiences, which can be really large (e.g., all baseball fans in the US or even in the world) or small and focused (e.g., people interested in fine dining in the Boston area). Google places the ads alongside relevant content of a Google partner's websites. For example, if you read an article on a partner website, you will see an ad block at the foot of the article. These ads have been dynamically targeted to the content of that article by Google. They can be the same ads that appear on Google.com alongside searches, but they are distributed in a different way here and appear on websites of publishers of all size of ads in the Google partner network.

AdWords is complemented by a second service, called AdSense, which represents the other side of Google's advertising model. AdSense is used by website owners who wish to make money by displaying ads on their websites. In return for allowing Google to display relevant ads on their content pages, these website owners receive a share of the advertising revenue generated. An important side effect of AdSense has been that it has created advertising income streams for thousands of small and medium online publishers and blogs, making those businesses sustainable. Although big media companies like *The New York Times* and CNN also use AdSense, it generates a smaller portion of their total online advertising revenue compared to the typical niche website or blogs.

Google's ability to deliver an advertising medium that is highly targeted, contextual, and results-based has been very attractive to advertisers leading to rapid revenue growth and profits. It's no surprise that Google's success frightens other advertising media.

Sources: https://www.google.com.sg/intl/en/about/ and http://en.wikipedia.org/wiki/AdWords, accessed on 21 March 2016.

Moving from Impersonal to Personal Communications. Communication experts divide communications as impersonal — where messages move only in one direction and are generally targeted at a large group of customers and prospects rather than at a single individual — and personal communications such as personal selling, telemarketing, and word-of-mouth. However, technology has created a gray area between personal and impersonal communications. Think about the email messages you may have received, containing a personal salutation and perhaps some reference to your specific situation or past use of a particular product. Similarly, interactive software can simulate a two-way conversation. For example, a few firms are beginning to experiment with web-based agents — on-screen simulations that move, speak, and even change expression.

Through the widespread use of smart mobile devices coupled with social networking platforms, firms have unprecedented opportunities to communicate with their customers and to facilitate firm-relevant communications between customers. Based on the analysis of customer data, highly targeted and personalized services and messages can be generated for each customer. These messages supplement, or in some cases replace, traditional marketing communications.[34] For a brief description of important new media and their implications, see *Service Insights 7.3*.

SERVICE INSIGHTS 7.3
New Media and Their Implications for Marketing Communications

Technology has created exciting new communication channels that offer important opportunities for targeting. Among the key developments are mobile advertising, mobile apps, Web 2.0, social media and social networks, and podcasting.

Mobile Advertising[35]

Mobile advertising through cell phones and other mobile wireless devices is one of the fastest-growing forms of advertising, and is expected to exceed US$62.8 billion by 2017. Mobile advertising is quite complex as it can include the Internet, video, text, gaming, music, and much more. For example, advertisements can come in the form of SMS, advertisements in mobile games, and videos. Through mobile advertising and use of a global positioning system, customers can walk into shopping malls and receive targeted advertisements with discounts when they visit a particular store within the mall. The most prevalent type is still mobile display

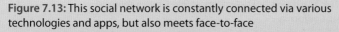

Figure 7.13: This social network is constantly connected via various technologies and apps, but also meets face-to-face

advertising (MDA), which takes the form of banners on mobile web pages and in mobile applications. What will such messages mean for the consumer? It might be greater convenience and more relevant advertising — or it might mean the invasion of privacy.

2D codes, better known as QR (for "quick response") codes appear on many ads, allowing those interested to learn more to take a photo of the code with their smart phone and get connected to an in-store promotion, coupons or a real world treasure hunt. For firms, QR codes bridge its offline and online communication channels and help to funnel potential customers from other media to the firm's online channels and richer content.

Mobile Apps

Apps have become an increasingly popular tool to help customers navigate extended service encounters, get the most out of the experience, while at the same time pursuing the firm's objectives such as cross-sell, up-sell, manage demand, and queuing. For example, major cruise lines such as Disney, Norwegian, and Royal Caribbean all have their own apps to help passengers navigate their large ships and explore their onboard entertainment options, spa services, and ports of call.[36]

Figure 7.14: YouTube's headquarters at 901 Cherry Avenue, San Bruno, California.

YouTube HQ photo: https://commons.wikimedia.org/wiki/File:901cherryave.jpg

Web 2.0, Social Media and Social Networking[37]

Web 2.0 technology helps the rise of user-generated content and combines it with the power of peer-to-peer communications. It is an umbrella term for various media including Facebook (the grandpa of social networks), Google+, LinkedIn, YouTube, Vine, Twitter, Instagram, Snapchat, Pinterest, Wikipedia, Flickr, and other social networks. In Web 2.0, content is generated, updated, and shared by multiple users. Social networking is the fastest growing media behavior online.

Service firms use social media for various purposes, which include learning from the market, targeting potential customers, creating buzz, and shaping customer behavior. They do this by advertising on social media, listening to what is being discussed, and selectively also participating in conversations. Given the importance of social media, marketers need to understand and carefully integrate them into their communications mix.

Podcasting

Podcasting comes from the words "iPod" and "broadcasting". It refers to a group of technologies for distributing audio or video programs over the Internet using a publisher/subscriber model. Podcasting gives broadcast radio or television programs a method of distribution. Once someone has subscribed to a certain feed, they will automatically receive new "episodes" that become available.

Podcasting has several forms. These include video podcasting for delivery of video clips, mobilecast for downloads onto a cell phone, and blogcast for attachment of an audio or video file to a blog. It is beneficial to include podcasting as part of a firm's marketing communications program because once a listener has subscribed to a specific show, it means the listener is interested in the topic. Hence, podcasts can reach a wide audience of listeners that have a narrow focus, more like "narrowcasting" than broadcasting. When the advertising message is more targeted, this leads to a higher return on investment for the advertising dollars spent.

Integrating online and traditional media. To show the complexity for integration of mostly online channels, see the potential integration of various media in a budget carrier context. The largest budget carriers in the US (Southwest Airlines), Europe (Ryanair) and Asia (AirAsia) each has a different strategy, but their common goal is to have travelers book directly at their own websites. Southwest Airlines integrates heavy TV advertising in its communications mix. Ryanair focuses heavily on search engine optimization and buys strategic keywords for its online ad campaigns. AirAsia has been highly active on various social media platforms such as Twitter and Facebook to update its followers on a regular basis, push promotions, and collect customer feedback. Although each airline has a different emphasis of its communications campaigns, most use all of the channels shown in Fig. 7.15 to drive online traffic to its website to generate ticket sales.

Messages Transmitted through Service Delivery Channels

Unlike most goods marketers, service firms typically control the point-of-

Figure 7.15: Budget carriers are excellent at integrating a vast array of mostly online channels to drive ticket sales on their websites.

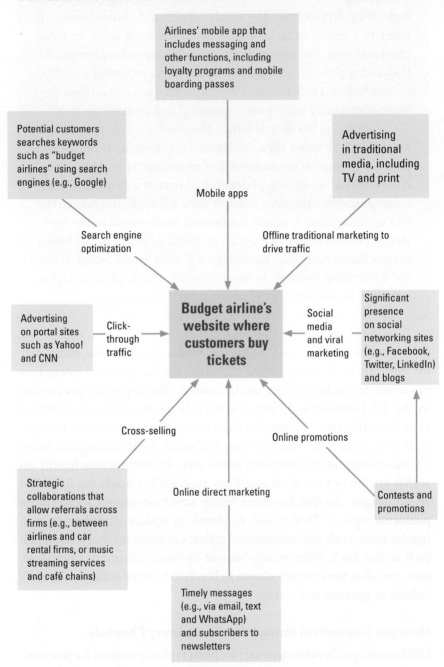

Figure 7.16: The Salentein Winery in Argentine has a very unique servicescape.

Bodegas Salentein – Uco Valley – Argentina

sale and service delivery channels, which offer them particularly powerful and cost-effective communications opportunities. Specifically, messages can be transmitted through service outlets, frontline employees, self-service delivery points, and location-enabled apps.

Service outlets. Both planned and unintended messages reach customers through the medium of the service delivery environment itself. Impersonal messages can be distributed in the form of banners, posters, signage, brochures, video screens, and audio. "Crafting the Service Environment", the physical design of the service outlet — what we call the servicescape — sends important messages to customers (see Chap. 10). Interior architects and corporate design consultants can help to design the servicescape to coordinate the visual elements of both interiors and exteriors so that they communicate and strengthen the positioning of the firm and shape the nature of the customers' service experiences in positive ways (Fig. 7.16).

Frontline Employees. Employees in frontline positions may serve customers face to face, by telephone, or via e-mail. Communication from frontline staff takes the form of the core service and a variety of supplementary services, including providing information, giving advice,[38] taking reservations, receiving payments, and solving problems. New customers, in particular, often rely on customer service personnel for help in learning to use a service effectively and to solve problems.

Frontline employees have a very important part to play. Brand equity is created largely through a customer's personal experience with the service firm rather than through mass communications, which is more suitable for creating awareness and interest (see Chap. 4). Furthermore, many service firms encourage their customer service staff to cross-sell additional services, or to up-sell to higher value services. Tony Hsieh has an interesting perspective on how to use customer contact centers for brand building, see *Service Insights 7.4*.

SERVICE INSIGHTS 7.4
Using the Call Centre for Building Brand Equity

Have you ever tried to call Google, or EBay or even Amazon.com, the company that owns Zappos? More likely than not, the phone number is buried many links deep, if it can be found at all! Zappos takes the exact opposite approach and puts its customer service hotline at the top of every single page of its website.

Tony Hsieh, the founding CEO of the highly successful multi-billion dollar revenue e-tailer Zappos, thinks it is funny that when he attends marketing conferences and hears companies talking about customers being bombarded with thousands of advertising messages every day, and that there is a lot of buzz about social media. He feels that "as unsexy and low-tech as it may sound, the telephone is one of the best branding devices out there. You have the customers' undivided attention for five to 10 minutes, and if you get the interaction right, what we've found is that the customer remembers this experience for a very long time". He explains that "a lot of people may think it's strange that an Internet company would be so focused on the telephone, when only 5% of our sales happen by phone. But we've found that on average, our customers telephone us at least once at some point, and if we handle the call well, we have an opportunity to create an emotional impact and a lasting memory. We receive thousands of phone calls and e-mails every day, and we view each one of them as an opportunity to build the Zappos brand... Our philosophy has been that most of the money we might ordinarily have spent of advertising should be invested in customer service, so that our customers will do the marketing for us through word-of-mouth".

In contrast, many service firms view their call centers through an expense-minimizing lens and focus on managing carefully average handling times and how many calls an agent can handle a day, which makes customer service representatives worry about how quickly they can get a customer off the phone, which in the eyes of Zappos is not delivering great service. Zappos' longest phone call from a customer, till this day, took almost six hours to help go through what seemed like thousands of pairs of shoes. Zappos representatives also don't use scripts or upsell, and handling customer calls is viewed as an investment in marketing and branding, and not an expense. Hsieh's view is that call centers are "a huge untapped opportunity for most companies, not only because it can result in word-of-mouth marketing, but because of its potential to increase the lifetime value of the customer".

Zappos CEO Tony Hsieh

Sources: Tony Hsieh (2010), "How I Did It: Zappos's CEO on Going to Extremes for Customers", Harvard Business Review, Vol. 88, No. 7/8, pp. 41-45; Tony Hsieh (2010), Delivering Happiness: A Path to Profits, Passion, and Purpose. Grand Central Publishing.

Self-Service Delivery Points. ATMs, vending machines, websites and service apps are all examples of self-service delivery points. Promoting self-service delivery requires clear signage, step-by-step instructions (perhaps through diagrams or animated videos) on how to operate the equipment, and user-friendly design. Self-service delivery points can often be used effectively in communications with current and potential customers, and to cross-sell services and promote new services. Similarly, location-enabled apps can guide customers through complex servicescapes such as cruise ships, airports, hospitals, and shopping malls, while also selling to and informing customers.

Messages Originating from Outside the Organization

Some of the most powerful messages about a company and its products come from outside the organization and are not controlled by the marketer. They include word-of-mouth (both in person and in electronic form on social media), online reviews on third-party websites, blogs, twitter, and media coverage.

Word-of-Mouth (WOM). Recommendations from other customers are generally viewed as more credible than firm-initiated promotional activities and can have a powerful influence on people's decisions to use (or avoid using) a service. In fact, the greater the risk customers perceive in purchasing a service, the more actively they will seek and rely on WOM to guide their decision-making,[39] and customers who are less knowledgeable about a service rely more on WOM than expert consumers do.[40] WOM even takes place during service encounters. When customers talk to each other about some aspect of service, this information can influence both their behavior and satisfaction with the service,[41] and this has been found to be an important predictor of top-line growth.[42] There are now ways to measure WOM and allow firms to test the effect of WOM on sales and market share for brands, individual promotions campaign and also for the company as a whole.[43]

Research shows that the extent and content of word-of-mouth is related to satisfaction levels. Customers who hold strong views are likely to tell more people about their experiences than those with milder views, and extremely dissatisfied customers tell more people than those who are highly satisfied.[44] Interestingly, even customers who were initially dissatisfied with a service can end up spreading positive WOM if they are delighted with the way the firm handled service recovery[45] (see Chap. 13 "Complaint Handling and Service Recovery").

Positive WOM is particularly important for service firms, as services tend to have a high proportion of experience and credence attributes, and are therefore associated with high perceived risk by potential buyers. In fact, many successful service firms such as Starbucks and Mayo Clinic have built powerful brands largely by relying on WOM of their satisfied customers. As Ron Kaufman, bestselling author, and founder of UP Your Service! College says: "Delighted customers are the only advertisement everyone believes".[46] Because WOM can act as such a powerful and highly credible selling agent, marketers use a variety of strategies to stimulate positive and persuasive comments from existing customers.[47] These include:

- Creating exciting stories, promotions and competitions that get people talking about the great service the firm provides. Richard Branson of Virgin Atlantic Airways has repeatedly generated global news that got people talking about his airline. For example, Branson abseiled off a 407-feet Las Vegas hotel dressed like James Bond in a tuxedo to promote his, then new, Virgin America airline. More and more firms are running creative promotions on social media that can get global attention in a few days.

- Offering promotions that encourage customers to persuade others to join them in using the service (for instance "bring two friends, and one of you eats for free" or offering a household with several family members to "subscribe to three cell phone service plans or more, and we'll extend a 35% discount off the monthly bill").

- Developing referral reward programs that incentivize existing customers to make referrals with units of free service, a voucher, or even cash for introducing new customers to the firm. Such programs can be highly effective and profitable, so much that they have become ubiquitous — just type "recommend a friend program" into your browser you will get hundreds of millions of hits.[48] Such programs work offline (e.g., clubs, credit card companies and even diving schools use it), online (think of Dropbox's highly effective viral incentive scheme, see Fig. 7.17), and on mobile apps (e.g., Uber's incentive program which encourages users to "send friends a free ride and you'll get worth $10").

  Referral reward programs work well for close friends and family because they trust that you will recommend the service not for the incentive but because you have the best interest of your friends and family at heart. However, firms have to be more careful using referral reward programs when targeting acquaintances and colleagues of current customers as the latter may worry what the people they recommend the service to will think of them and about the impression they create.[49] Think about a finance professor who gets an incentive for recommending a discount broker to her students or colleagues — probably, she would rather not recommend the broker than being

Figure 7.17: Dropbox's online referral reward program.

How do I earn bonus space for referring friends to Dropbox?

You can get extra space by inviting your friends to try out Dropbox. Both you and your referral will receive bonus space if your referral completes these steps:

1. Accepts your invitation to sign up for an account.
2. Installs the Dropbox desktop app.
3. Signs in from the desktop app.
4. Verifies their email address.

Bonus space by account type

- Basic accounts get 500 MB per referral and can earn up to 16 GB.
- Pro accounts get 1 GB per referral and can earn up to 32 GB.

Note: Services Marketing: People, Technology, Strategy is not affiliated with or otherwise sponsored by Dropbox, Inc.

seen as receiving an incentive! Creative program design can change these programs so that the person who is being referred receives the reward and not the recommendation giver. In our example, the finance professor's students would get the reward, not her, and the professor would look good by recommending a great service firm and facilitating her students to get this great deal. Sometimes, it is more important for customers to look good and knowledgeable, and receiving an incentive may only achieve the opposite!

- Referencing other purchasers and knowledgeable individuals, for instance: "We have done a great job for ABC Corp., and if you wish, feel free to talk to Mr Cabral, their MIS manager, who oversaw the implementation of our project".

- Presenting and publicizing testimonials. Advertising and websites sometimes feature comments from satisfied customers.

- Provide opportunities for online reviews, and support and respond to them frequently. As online reviews become ubiquitous, positive postings help and negative ones damage a firm's brand equity and sales. For example, a study set in the London metropolitan area showed that while all hotels benefit, luxury hotels were particularly strongly influenced by the valence of reviews (and not so much by the volume; that is, a few highly positive or negative reviews had a strong impact and potential discerning guests seem to read those reviews carefully), whereas those of lower-end hotels were more driven by the volume of reviews (a hotel needed a lot of positive or negative reviews before those reviews had impact; potential guests seemed to scan the reviews to see whether the hotel is of acceptable quality and they trust volume for that).[50]

In either case, the firm's communications strategy should be to encourage satisfied customers to post positive reviews, while ideally dissatisfied customers complain to the firm and get a service recovery (see Chap. 13, "Complaint Handling and Service Recovery") instead of going online to vent their frustration.[51] A small hair stylist shop was trying to precisely achieve this by posting the following sign at the exit: "If you like our service, please tell a friend; if you don't like it, please tell us".

- Support brand communities, which can be done with relatively low costs online.[52] See, for example, the successful online brand communities supported by Google and LinkedIn in Fig. 7.18.

In addition to WOM, we also have "word-of-mouse" or viral marketing. Internet has accelerated the spread of personal influence, causing it to evolve into a viral marketing phenomenon that businesses cannot afford to ignore.[53] One of the very early success stories of viral marketing was the Hotmail free email service, which grew from zero to 12 million users in just 18 months while on a miniscule advertising budget, mostly thanks to the inclusion of a promotional message that included the Hotmail's URL in every email sent by its users.[54] Today, virtually every online startup relies on viral marketing in one way or another. Similarly, eBay and other electronic auction firms rely on users to rate sellers and buyers in order to build trust in the items offered on their websites and thereby facilitate transactions between strangers who, without access to such peer ratings, might be reluctant to transact on these sites.

Besides e-mail, "word of mouse" is spread by service reviews on third-party websites, chat, social media, and online communities that have potential for global reach in a matter of days! Companies are taking advantage of this. Swipely is a company that allows users to conveniently

Figure 7.18: Online brand communities as seen on the Google and LinkedIn websites.

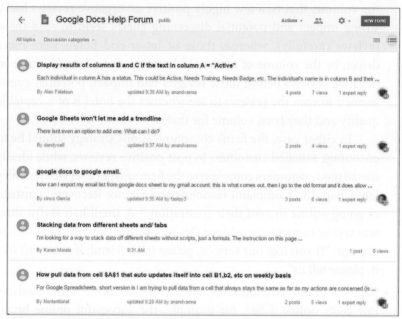

Google and the Google logo are registered trademarks of Google Inc., used with permission.

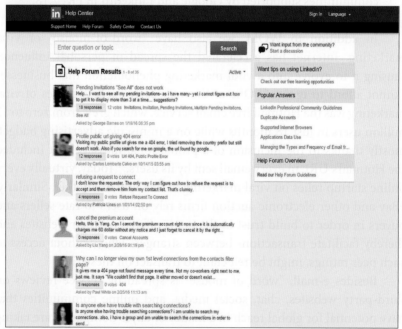

upload their purchases whenever they swipe their credit or debit cards, and their friends can then immediately see these transactions and discuss the purchase.[55] It is one way users can update their friends on what they are buying. There are constantly new types of social networks emerging which all feed into the online ecosystem where consumers share their experiences.

Blogs, Twitter, and Other Social Media as a Type of Online WOM. Web logs, usually referred to as blogs, have also become ubiquitous. Blogs are web pages best described as online journals, diaries, or news listings where people can post anything about whatever they like. Their authors, known as bloggers, usually focus on narrow topics, and quite a few have become self-proclaimed experts in certain fields. Blogs can be about anything, ranging from baseball and sex, to karate and financial engineering. There are a growing number of travel-oriented sites, ranging from Hotelchatter.com (focused on boutique hotels), CruiseDiva.com (reporting on the cruise industry), and pestiside.hu ("the daily dish of cosmopolitan Budapest"). Some sites, such as the travel-focused tripadvisor.com, allow users to post their own reviews or ask questions that more experienced travelers may be able to answer.

Marketers are interested in the way blogs have developed into a new form of social interaction on the Internet; a massively distributed but completely connected conversation covering every imaginable topic, including consumers' experiences with service firms and their recommendations on avoiding or patronizing certain firms. A byproduct of this online communication is a set of hyperlinks between blogs created in the exchange of dialog. These links allows customers to share information with others and influence opinions of a brand or product — just Google for the terms "Citibank and blog" or "Charles Schwab and blog", and you will see an entire list of blogs or blog entries relating to these service firms. Increasingly, service firms monitor blogs and view them as a form of immediate market research and feedback. Some service companies have even started their own blogs; for example, you can take a look at Google's blog at http://googleblog.blogspot.com (Fig. 7.19).

Blogs and other online media such as Twitter, can be seen as in-between WOM (there are millions of bloggers with not many followers, more akin to traditional WOM), and online media (some bloggers have a large following, similar to popular media). Marketers therefore can treat

Figure 7.19: Google has its own blog.

Google and the Google logo are registered trademarks of Google Inc., used with permission.

the WOM part of the spectrum through their standard referral programs and WOM initiatives, but will have to deal with bloggers with a large following similar as to how they would with a publisher of traditional media.[56] These bloggers are important industry players and they need to be treated with respect and engaged at eye level.

Twitter is a social networking and microblogging service that allows its users to send updates or read other users' updates. These updates are up to 140 characters in length and can be sent and received through the Twitter website, SMS, or external applications. Created in 2006 by Jack Dorsey, Twitter has become a highly popular global social networking service.[57] Service firms use Twitter in various ways. Comcast, the U.S. cable service provider, has set up @comcastcares to answer customer queries in real time. Zappos's CEO interacts with his customers as if they were friends, celebrity Ashton Kutcher interacts with his fans while on the move, and airline branding firm SimpliFlying used Twitter to help establish itself as a thought leader in its niche by holding special trivia quizzes and competitions for its followers around the world.

Media Coverage. Although the online world is rapidly increasing in importance, coverage on traditional media cannot be neglected, especially as newsworthy events are often first discussed in the online world, and are then picked up and reported in the traditional media that reach the masses. Media coverage of firms and their services is often through a firm's PR activity, but broadcasters and publishers also often initiate their own coverage.

In addition to news stories about a company and its services, editorial coverage can take several other forms. For example, journalists responsible for consumer affairs often contrast and compare service offerings from competing organizations, identifying their strong and weak points, and offering advice on "best buys". In a more specialized context, *Consumer Reports,* the monthly publication of Consumers' Union, periodically evaluates services that are offered on a national basis, including financial services and telecommunications, and commenting on the strengths and weaknesses of different service providers and seeking to determine the true cost of their often confusing fee schedules and pricing plans.

Furthermore, investigative reporters may conduct an in-depth study of a company, especially if they believe it is putting customers at risk, cheating them, employing deceptive advertising, damaging the environment, or taking advantage of poor workers in developing countries. Some columnists specialize in helping customers who have been unable to get complaints resolved.

TIMING DECISIONS OF SERVICES MARKETING COMMUNICATIONS

Goods such as champagne, jewelry and Christmas pudding are heavily promoted in the three months leading up to Christmas, as often half of their annual sales will happen then. Service firms, in contrast, are capacity constrained and therefore generally do not promote during heavy usage periods. Rather, timing is closely matched to the various perceptions and behaviors the firm wants to manage in the service communications funnel. Often, different communications channels are used to move a customer along from awareness, preference all the way to the post-consumption stage.

Timing of communications is typically managed in a media plan flowchart which looks like a large Excel spreadsheet. It gives a bird's eye view of the media where and when communications is planned. Typically, software is used to assist with tedious tasks to crunch numbers to get toward an optimal media mix and media plan, and it computes key numbers such as reach of the target audience and cost per thousand contacts of the target segment. Professional firms such as Telmar (http://www.telmar.com) help companies with their planning.

BUDGET DECISIONS AND PROGRAM EVALUATION[58]

Most service firms will allocate more budgets to services marketing communications as long as they believe it will increase sales and profits. However, the optimal point of communications expenditure is difficult to predict, and setting a budget is one of the hardest decisions to make. In practice, service firms use a number of methods to determine their communications budget, including allocating a percentage of sales or profit, matching competitors' spent, and using last year's budget and adding to or subtracting from it, depending on the success of last year's communications and the firm's future plans.

The most logical method, however, is the objective-and-task method, which is also known as the budget buildup method. This method entails three steps: (1) defining the communications objectives along the services marketing communications funnel, (2) determining the tasks needed to achieve these objectives, and (3) estimating the costs of the program. The estimated costs become the basis for the proposed promotions budget. Of course, a firm's financial position and estimated returns on these investments always need to be integrated as well. If costs are too high or expected returns too low, the budget needs to be scaled back. The key challenge though remains that it is difficult to determine in advance the intensity of communications required to achieve a certain goal.

Finally, the empirical research method can be used alone or in combination with the objective-and-task method. The empirical research method runs a series of tests or field experiments with different communications budgets to determine the optimum level of communications spent. Online, of course, such experiments can be done easily and fast, and are regularly used in professional campaign management.

Once the budget is spent, next is the evaluation of the success of the communications program. For specific objectives, it is easy to measure. For example, if specific communications programs were targeted at changing customer behavior (e.g., shifting usage away from peaks, teaching customers how to keep their PINs safe, shifting customers from paper-based statements to e-statements and upselling to a higher-level service) the results are directly measurable. The same applies to direct response marketing, such as email campaigns or online marketing where clickthroughs, newsletter signups, followers, registrations, lead generation, and sales can be matched directly to specific marketing communications.

Similarly, advertising and research agencies have become experts at measuring whether wider communications objectives (e.g., awareness, knowledge, and preference) have been achieved. However, the effect of market communications on sales and profit is notoriously hard to measure. A key reason is that marketing communications affects sales, but it is only one of the many drivers of sales which range from service features and quality to price and competitor activities.

ETHICAL AND CONSUMER PRIVACY ISSUES IN COMMUNICATIONS

In addition to how to reach, persuade and manage the behavior of prospects and customers, firms also need to consider the ethical and privacy issues associated with communications, especially as few aspects of marketing are so easily misused (and even abused), such as advertising, selling, and sales promotion. The fact that customers often find it hard to evaluate services makes them more dependent on marketing communication for information and advice. Communication messages frequently include promises about the benefits that customers will receive and the quality of service delivery. When promises are made and then broken, customers will be disappointed.

Some unrealistic service promises result from poor internal communications between operations and marketing personnel concerning the level of service performance that customers can reasonably expect. In other instances, unethical advertisers and salespeople deliberately make exaggerated promises to secure sales. Finally, there are deceptive promotions that lead people to think that they have a much higher chance of winning prizes or awards than is really the case. Fortunately, many consumer watchdog groups are on the lookout for these deceptive marketing practices. They include consumer protection agencies, trade associations within specific industries, and journalists seeking to expose cheating schemes and misrepresentations.

A different type of ethical issue concerns unwanted intrusion by aggressive marketers into people's personal lives. The increase in telemarketing, direct mail, email and messaging is frustrating for those who receive unwanted sales communications. How do you feel when your dinner at home is interrupted by a telephone call from a stranger trying to get you to buy services in which you have no interest? Even if you are interested, you may feel, as many do, that your privacy has been violated (*Service Insights 7.5*). See also the earlier section on direct marketing where the concept of permission marketing as one way to address consumer concerns is discussed.

To address growing hostility toward these practices, both government agencies and trade associations have acted to protect consumers. In the United States, the Federal Trade Commission's National "Do Not Call" Registry enables consumers to remove their home and mobile numbers from telemarketing lists for a five-year period. People who continue to receive unauthorized calls from commercial telemarketers can file a complaint, and the telemarketing firm can be subjected to heavy fines for such violations.[59] Similarly, the Direct Marketing Association helps consumers remove their names from mailing, telemarketing, and e-mail lists.[60]

SERVICE INSIGHTS 7.5
Consumer Concerns about Online Privacy

Technological advances have made Internet a threat to consumer privacy. Information is collected on not only people who register, shop or use email, but also on those who just surf the Internet, participate in social networks, or contribute to blogs! Individuals are increasingly fearful of databases and concerned about their online privacy. Hence, they use several ways to protect themselves, including:

- Providing false information about themselves (e.g., disguising their identity).
- Using technology such as Microsoft's InPrivate Browsing, anti-spam filters, e-mail shredders, and cookie-busters to hide the identity of their computers from websites.
- Refusing to provide information and avoiding websites that require personal information to be disclosed.

Such consumer responses will make information used in CRM systems inaccurate and incomplete, thereby reducing the effectiveness of a firm's customer relationship marketing and its efforts to provide more customized, personalized, and convenient service. Firms can take several steps to reduce consumer privacy concerns, including:

- Customers' fairness perceptions are key — marketers need to be careful about how they use the information they collect and whether consumers see their treatment and outcomes as fair. In particular, marketers should continually provide the customer with enhanced value such as customization, convenience, and improved offers and promotions to increase fairness perceptions of the information exchange.
- The information asked for should be perceived to be related to the transaction, especially if it is highly sensitive. Therefore, firms should clearly communicate why the information is needed, and how information disclosure will benefit the consumer.
- Firms should have a good privacy policy in place, one that can be readily found on its websites, is easily understood and comprehensive enough to be effective. Ideally, websites should give customers control over how their information can be used.
- Fair information practices need to be embedded in the work practices of all service employees to prevent any situation whereby an employee may allow personal customer information to be misused.
- Firms should have high ethical standards of data protection. They can use third party endorsements such as TRUSTe or the

Better Business Bureau and have recognizable privacy seals displayed clearly on their website.

Sources: M. Lwin, J. Wirtz, and J. D. Williams, "Consumer Online Privacy Concerns and Responses: A Power-Responsibility Equilibrium Perspective", *Journal of the Academy of Marketing Science*, Vol. 35, No. 2, 2007, 572–585; Jochen Wirtz and May O. Lwin, "Regulatory Focus Theory, Trust, and Privacy Concern", *Journal of Service Research*, Vol. 12, No. 2, 2009, 199–207; Catherine E. Tucker (2014), "Social Networks, Personalized Advertising, and Privacy Controls", *Journal of Marketing Research*, Vol. 51 (October), pp. 546-562.

THE ROLE OF CORPORATE DESIGN

Corporate design is key to ensure a consistent style and message is communicated through all of firm's communications mix channels. Corporate design is particularly important for companies operating in competitive markets where it's necessary to stand out from the crowd to be instantly recognizable in different locations. Many companies stand out in the crowd because of the colors they use, the widespread application of their logos, the uniforms worn by their employees, or the design of their physical facilities?

Many service firms employ a unified and distinctive visual appearance for all tangible elements to facilitate recognition and reinforce a desired brand image. Corporate design strategies are usually created by external consulting firms, and include stationery and promotional materials, retail signage, uniforms, and color schemes for painting vehicles, equipment, and building interiors. The objective is to provide a unifying and recognizable theme that links all the firm's operations in a branded service experience through the strategic use of physical evidence. Companies can do that by using the following approaches either individually or in combination:

- Companies in the highly competitive express delivery industry tend to use their name as a central element in their corporate design. When Federal Express changed its trading name to the more modern "FedEx", it featured the new name in a distinctive, new logo.
- Many companies use a trademarked symbol, rather than a name, as their primary logo. Shell makes a pun of its name by displaying a yellow scalloped shell on a red background, which has the advantage of making its vehicles and service stations instantly recognizable. McDonald's "Golden Arches" (Fig. 7.20) is said to be the most widely recognized corporate symbol in the world and is featured

Figure 7.20: The Golden Arches at the Times Square McDonald's restaurant in New York.

at all touchpoints, including its restaurants, employee uniforms, packaging, and in all the company's communications materials (see Table 7.2).

- Some companies have succeeded in creating tangible, recognizable symbols to associate with their corporate brand names. Animal motifs are common physical symbols for services. Examples include the eagles of the U.S. Postal Service and AeroMexico, the lions of ING Bank and the Royal Bank of Canada, and the ram of the investment firm T. Rowe Price, and the Chinese dragon of Hong Kong's Dragonair.

- Many companies use colors in their corporate designs. If we look at gasoline retailing, we see BP's immediately recognizable bright green and yellow service stations; Texaco's red, black and white; and Sunoco's blue, maroon, and yellow.

INTEGRATED MARKETING COMMUNICATIONS

Have you ever seen a new, exciting service promotion being touted at a firm's website, only to find that the counter staff was not aware of the promotion and couldn't sell it to you when you visited a branch office?

What went wrong? In many service firms, different departments look after different aspects of a firm's market communications. For example, the marketing department is in charge of advertising, the PR department of public relations, functional specialists look after a company's website and its direct marketing and promotions activities, operations of customer service, and human resource of training. The service failure described above is a consequence of these various departments not coordinating their efforts effectively.

With so many channels delivering messages to customers and prospects, it becomes more and more important for firms to adopt the concept of integrated marketing communications (IMC). IMC ties together and reinforces all communications to deliver a strong brand identity. It means that a firm's various media deliver the same messages and have the same look and feel, and the communications from the different media and communications approaches all become part of a single, overall message about the service firm and its products. Firms can

Table 7.2: Corporate Design Strategies

Examples of Corporate Design Strategies			
Name as central element	Trademarked symbol	Tangible recognizable symbol	Distinctive color used in corporate design
FedEx	McDonald's "Golden Arches"	ING Bank's lion	DHL's yellow (Pantone 116) and red (Pantone 200) colors of its logo.
FedEx Corporation	M	**ING** 🦁	*DHL* EXPRESS
DHL	Shell's yellow scalloped shell	Hong Kong's Dragon Air's Chinese dragon	BP's bright green and yellow service stations
DHL EXPRESS	(shell logo)	**DRAGONAIR**	bp

achieve this by giving the ownership of IMC to a single department (e.g., marketing), or by appointing a marketing communications director who has overall responsibility for all of the firm's market communications.

CONCLUSION

The *promotion* and *education* element of the 7 'P's requires a somewhat different emphasis from the communication strategy used to market goods. The communication tasks facing service marketers include emphasizing tangible clues for services that are difficult to evaluate, clarifying the nature and sequence of the service performance, highlighting the performance of customer contact personnel, and educating the customer about how to effectively participate in service delivery. A key takeaway point is that effective service marketers are good educators who can use a variety of communication media in cost-efficient ways, not only to promote their firm's value propositions but also to teach both prospects and customers what they need to know about selecting and using the firm's services.

CHAPTER SUMMARY

Communications Strategy Development

Who is our target audience? (Target Audience Decision)

Key Target Audiences for Service Communications:
- Prospective customers, target segments
- Current customers, users of the service
- Employees as secondary audience

What are our objectives? (Communications Objectives)

Strategic Objectives:
- Position & differentiate the brand & service products

Tactical Objectives by Consumption Stage Along the Service Communication Funnel
- Pre-purchase stage:
  – Manage the customer search and choice process.
- Service encounter stage:
  – Guide customers through the service encounter
- Post-encounter stage:
  – Manage customer satisfaction & build loyalty

Communications Strategy Implementation

How should this be communicated? (Message Decisions)

Challenges of Service Communications:
- Problems of intangibility
  – Abstractness
  – Generality
  – Non-searchability
  – Mental impalpability
- Strategies to address intangibility
  – Advertising tactics to address intangibility (incl., showing consumption episodes, documentation, and testimonials)
  – Tangible cues
  – Metaphors

Where should this be communicated? (Media Decisions)

Communications Mix for Services from Three Key Sources:
- Marketing communications channels
  – Traditional media (e.g., TV)
  – Online media (e.g., search engine advertising)
- Service delivery channels
  – Service outlets
  – Frontline employees
  – Self-service delivery points
- Messages originated from outside the organization:
  – Word-of-mouth, social media
  – Blogs & Twitter
  – Traditional media coverage

When should communication take place? (Timing Decisions)

Timing Decisions:
- Map timing against Service Communications Funnel
- Use media plan flowchart

Corporate Design
- Ensure a unified and distinctive visual appearance for all tangible elements of the firm and its services

Ethics & Consumer Privacy
- Don't make exaggerated promises or use deceptive communications
- Respect and protect consumer privacy

Budget Decisions & Communications Program Evaluation
- Objective-and-Task Method
- Other budgeting methods (e.g., percentage of revenue, matching against competitor spent)
- Map performance against overall and specific objectives along the Service Communications Funnel.

Integrated Marketing Communications
- Integrate communication across all channels to deliver a consistent message, look and feel

Part III

Managing the Customer Interface

CHAPTER 8

Designing Service Processes

Well done is better than well said.

Benjamin Franklin
one of the Founding Fathers of the US, 1706–1790

The new frontier of competitive advantage is the customer interface. Making yours a winner will require the right people and, increasingly, the right machines — on the front lines.

Jeffrey Rayport and Bernard Jaworski
Professor at Harvard Business School, founder and
chairman of Marketspace LLC; and Professor at
Claremont Graduate University, respectively

Ultimately, only one thing really matters in service encounters — the customer's perceptions of what occurred.

Richard B. Chase and Sriram Dasu
Professors at University of Southern California

WHAT IS A SERVICE PROCESS?

From a customer's perspective, services are experiences. From the organization's perspective, services are processes that have to be designed and managed to create the desired customer experience. This makes processes the architecture of services. Processes describe the method and sequence in which service operating systems work, and specify how they are linked together to create the value proposition promised to the customers. Badly designed processes are likely to annoy customers because they often result in slow, frustrating, and poor quality service delivery. Similarly, poor processes make it difficult for front-line employees to do their jobs well, thus resulting in low productivity and increasing the risk of service failures. This chapter will discuss how service processes can be designed and improved to deliver the promised value proposition.

DESIGNING AND DOCUMENTING SERVICE PROCESSES

The first step to design or analyze a process is to document or describe it. Flowcharting and blueprinting are two key tools used for documenting

Figure 8.1: Simple flowchart for delivery of motel service and health insurance service.

People Processing — Stay at Motel

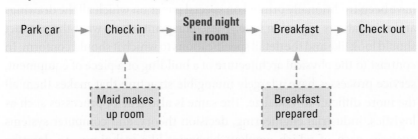

Information Processing — Health Insurance

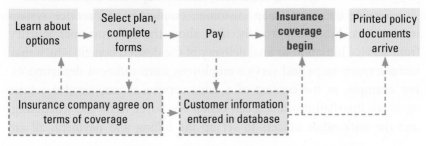

and redesigning existing service processes, and for designing new ones. To distinguish flowcharting and blueprinting from each other in a service context, a flowchart can be described as an existing process, often in a fairly simple form, while flowcharting is a technique for displaying the nature and sequence of different steps involved when a customer "flows" through the service process. It is an easy way to quickly understand the total customer service experience. Flowcharting the sequence of encounters customers have with a service organization yields valuable insights into the nature of an existing service. Fig. 8.1 displays two simple flowcharts that demonstrate what is involved in each of the featured services.

Blueprinting is a more complex form of flowcharting that specifies in detail how a service process is constructed, including what is visible to the customer, and all that goes on in the back-office. It is not an easy task to create a service, especially one that must be delivered in real time with customers present in the service factory. To design services that are both satisfying for customers and operationally efficient, marketers and operations specialists need to work together, and a blueprint can provide a common perspective and language for the various departments involved.

The term blueprinting originated from the ship designing and construction industry who used to capture the architectural drawings for a new building or a ship called blueprints, the reproductions of which have been traditionally printed on special paper on which all the drawings and annotations appear in blue. These blueprints show what the product should look like and the detail specifications to which it should conform. In contrast to the physical architecture of a building or a piece of equipment, service processes have a largely intangible structure that makes them all the more difficult to visualize. The same is also true of processes such as logistics, industrial engineering, decision theory, and computer systems analysis, each of which employs blueprint-like techniques to describe processes involving flows, sequences, relationships, and dependencies.

Service blueprints map customer, employee, and service system interactions. More importantly, they show the full customer journey from service initiation to final delivery of the desired benefit, which may include many steps and service employees from different departments. For example, in the context of a cable service, it may involve a sales agent, an installation team, a call-center employee to do the scheduling, and the back-office officers to set up the billing and payment; all are equally responsible for a trouble-free installation.[1] Blueprints show the key customer actions, how customers and employees from different departments interact (called the line of interaction), the front-stage actions by those service employees, and how these are supported by backstage activities and systems. By showing inter-relationships among employee roles, operational processes, supplies, information technology, and customer interactions, blueprints can help bring together marketing, operations, and human resource management within a firm. Together, they can then develop better service processes, including defining service scripts and roles to guide interactions between staff and customers (as discussed in Chap. 2); designing fail points and excessive customer waits out of processes; and finally, setting the service standards and targets for service delivery teams.

Developing a Service Blueprint

In order to develop a service blueprint, all the key activities involved in creating and delivering the service in question have to be identified in the first step, and then the linkages between these activities are specified. Initially, it is best to keep the activities relatively aggregated in order to define the "big picture". This can be done by first developing a simple flowchart documenting the process from the customer's perspective and then refine any given activity by drilling down to obtain a higher level of detail. In an airline context for instance, the passenger activity of "boards aircraft" actually represents a series of actions and can be broken down into steps such as "wait for seat rows to be announced, give agent boarding pass for verification, walk down the jet way, enter aircraft, let flight attendant verify boarding pass, find a seat, stow carry-on bag, and sit down".

More details can be added next. Typical service blueprints have the following design characteristics that help to see how a blueprint should be developed[2]:

- *Front-stage activities* map the overall customer experience, the desired inputs and outputs, and the sequence in which delivery of that output should take place.

- *Physical evidence of front-stage activities* is what the customer can see and use to assess service quality.

- *Line of visibility* is a key characteristic of service blueprinting that distinguishes between what customers experience "front-stage", and the activities of employees and support processes "backstage" where customers cannot see them, between the two lines of what is called the line of visibility. When a firm clearly understands the line of visibility, it is able to better manage physical and other evidence for front-stage activities to give customers the desired experience and quality signals. Some firms are too focused on operations and neglect the customer's purely front-stage perspective. For instance, accounting firms often have detailed documented procedures and standards on how to conduct an audit, but may lack clear standards for hosting a meeting with clients, or for how staff members should answer the telephone.

- *Backstage activities* that must be performed to support a particular front-stage step.

- *Support processes and supplies* involve a lot of information. The information needed at each step in the blueprint is usually provided by information systems. For example, without the right information at the front-line staff's fingertips, processes such as banking, online broking, or even borrowing a book from your university library could not be completed, and the service process could break down. Supplies required to be made available for both front and backstage steps are also necessary for many services. For example, restaurants need to have the supplies of the right fresh produce and wines; and car rental firms of vehicles, global positioning systems (GPSs) and child seats. Supplies are essential to deliver high quality core services.

- *Potential fail points* can be identified by managers when they develop a blueprint of the service process. Fail points are where there is a risk of things going wrong, resulting in diminished service quality. When managers are aware of these fail points, they are better able to design them out of a process (such as by using *poka-yokes*, as discussed later in this chapter) and have backup plans (such as for service recovery, as discussed in Chap. 13) for unavoidable failures (e.g., departure delays due to bad weather).

Figure 8.2: Long waiting lines indicate operational problems that need to be addressed.

- *Identifying customer waits* — Blueprints can also pinpoint stages in the process at which customers commonly have to wait (Fig. 8.2), and where there are points of potentially excessive waits. These can then either be designed out of the process, or if not always possible, firms can implement strategies to make waits less unpleasant for customers (see Chap. 9).

- *Service standards and targets* should be established for each activity to reflect customer expectations. They include specific times set for the completion of each task and the acceptable wait between each customer activity. Developing service blueprints gives marketing and operational personnel detailed process knowledge that can then be used to develop standards. The final service blueprint should contain key service standards for each front-stage activity, including the estimated time for the completion of a task and maximum customer wait times in between tasks. Standards should then be used to set targets for service delivery teams to ensure that service processes perform well against customer expectations.

Blueprinting the Restaurant Experience: A Three-Act Performance

To illustrate how the blueprinting of a high-contact, people-processing service can be done, we examine the dinner experience for two at Chez Jean, an upscale restaurant that enhances its core food service with a variety of other supplementary services (Fig. 8.3). A rule of thumb in full-service restaurants is that the cost of purchasing the food ingredients represents about 20% to 30% of the price of the meal. The balance can be seen as the fees that customers are willing to pay for a great dining experience that includes "renting" tables and chairs in a pleasant setting,

Figure 8.3: Blueprinting a full-service restaurant experience.

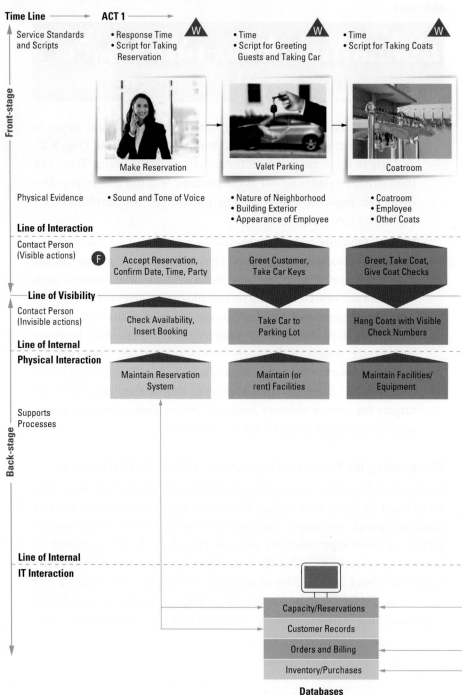

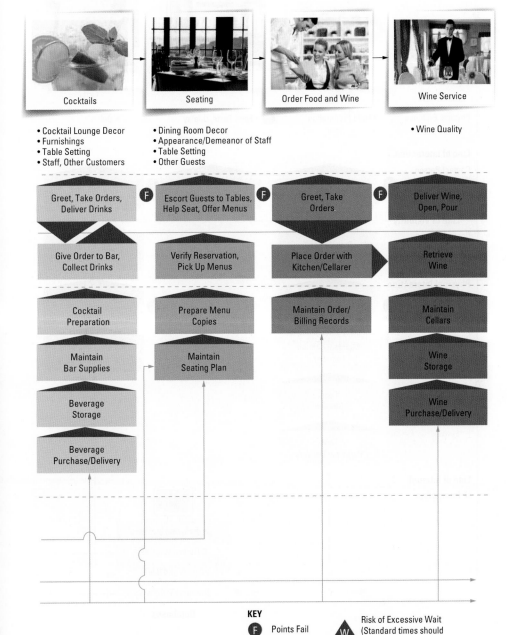

ACT II ——→

- Time
- Order Accuracy
- Script for Serving Drinks

- Punctuality vs. Reservation
- Script for Seating

- Time
- Script for Greeting Guests, Taking Order

- Time
- Script for Wine Service

Cocktails → **Seating** → **Order Food and Wine** → **Wine Service**

- Cocktail Lounge Decor
- Furnishings
- Table Setting
- Staff, Other Customers

- Dining Room Decor
- Appearance/Demeanor of Staff
- Table Setting
- Other Guests

- Wine Quality

Greet, Take Orders, Deliver Drinks **F**

Escort Guests to Tables, Help Seat, Offer Menus **F**

Greet, Take Orders **F**

Deliver Wine, Open, Pour

Give Order to Bar, Collect Drinks

Verify Reservation, Pick Up Menus

Place Order with Kitchen/Cellarer

Retrieve Wine

Cocktail Preparation

Prepare Menu Copies

Maintain Order/ Billing Records

Maintain Cellars

Maintain Bar Supplies

Maintain Seating Plan

Wine Storage

Beverage Storage

Wine Purchase/Delivery

Beverage Purchase/Delivery

KEY

F Points Fail

W Risk of Excessive Wait (Standard times should specify limits.)

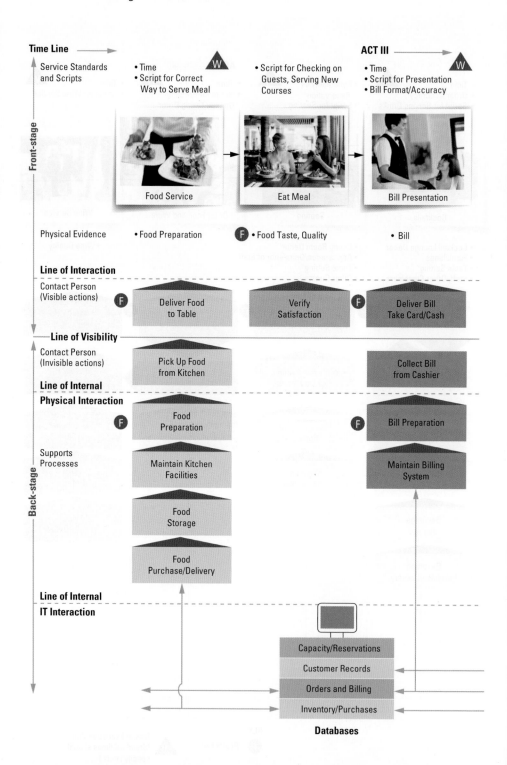

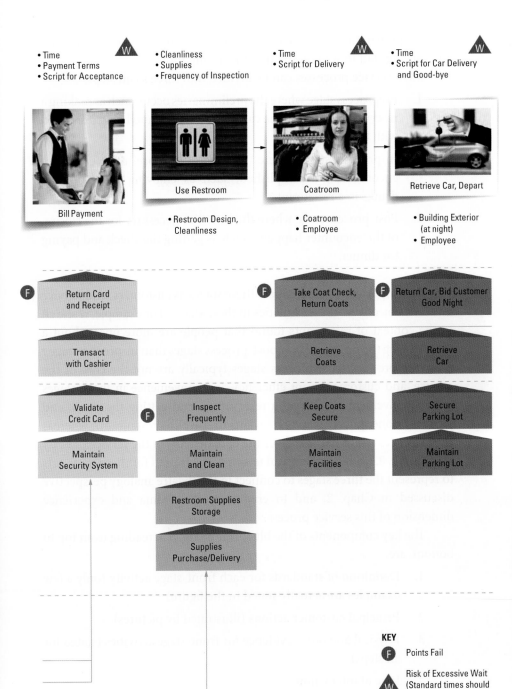

the food preparation services of expert chefs and their kitchen equipment, and serving staff to wait on them in the dining room.

Most service processes can be divided into three main steps:

1. Preprocess stage where the preliminaries occur, such as making a reservation, parking the car, getting seated, and being presented with the menu.

2. In-process stage where the main purpose of the service encounter is accomplished, such as enjoying the food and drinks in a restaurant.

3. Post-process stage where the activities necessary for the closing of the encounter happens, such as getting the check and paying for dinner.

It is important to differentiate these stages as customers tend to have different objectives and sensitivities in these stages. For example, research in the context of restaurants found that people are more upset about a delay during the pre-process or post-process stages than in-process stage.[3] Also, the pre- and post-process stages typically are not the core of the service, and customers want efficiency and convenience in those stages (e.g., a convenient way to get a reservation, and getting the check and payment done quickly when one wants to leave the restaurant), whereas the in-process stage has to deliver the core benefits of the service.

In Fig. 8.3, a more theatrical terminology is used for these three acts to represent the three stages to connect to the theatre analogy perspective discussed in Chap. 2, and to emphasize the drama and experience dimension of this service process.

The key components of the blueprint in Fig. 8.3, reading from top to bottom, are:

1. Definition of standards for each front-stage activity (only a few examples are actually stated in the figure)

2. Principal customer actions (illustrated by pictures)

3. Physical and other evidence for front-stage activities (stated for all steps)

4. Line of interaction

5. Front-stage actions by customer-contact personnel

6. Line of visibility

7. Back-stage actions by customer-contact personnel

8. Support processes involving other service personnel

9. Support processes involving information technology

Reading from left to right, the blueprint prescribes the sequence of actions over time. In Chap. 2, we compared service performances to theater. To emphasize the involvement of human actors in service delivery, we followed the practices adopted by some service organizations by using pictures to illustrate each of the 14 principal steps involving our two customers, beginning with making a reservation, and concluding with their departure from the restaurant after the meal. Like many high-contact services involving discrete transactions — as opposed to the continuous delivery found in utility or insurance services — the "restaurant drama" can be divided into three "acts", representing activities that take place before the core product is encountered, the delivery of the core product (in this case, the meal), and the subsequent activities still involved with the service provider.

The "stage" or servicescape includes both the exterior and interior of the restaurant. Front-stage actions take place in a very visual environment; restaurants are often quite theatrical in their use of physical evidence (such as furnishings, décor, uniforms, lighting, and table settings) and often employ background music in their efforts to create a themed environment that matches their market positioning (Fig. 8.4).

Figure 8.4 Two hosts welcome diners in a servicescape that clearly communicates the restaurant's positioning.

Act I — Prologue and Introductory Scenes. In this particular drama, Act I begins with a customer making a reservation by telephone. This action could take place hours or even days in advance of visiting the restaurant. In theatrical terms, the telephone conversation can be matched with a radio drama, with impressions being created by the nature of the respondent's voice, speed of response, and style of the conversation. When our customers arrive at the restaurant, a valet parks their car, they leave their coats in the coatroom, and enjoy a drink in the bar area while waiting for their table. The act concludes with them being escorted to a table and seated.

These five steps constitute the couple's initial experience of the restaurant performance, each involving an interaction with an employee

— by phone or face-to-face. By the time the two of them reach their table in the dining room, they have been exposed to several supplementary services, and have also encountered a sizeable cast of characters, including five or more contact personnel, as well as many other customers.

Standards can be set for each service activity, but these should be based on a good understanding of guest expectations (as discussed in Chap. 2). Below the line of visibility, the blueprint identifies key actions to ensure that each front-stage step is performed in a manner that meets or exceeds customer expectations. These actions include recording reservations, handling customers' coats, delivery and preparation of food, maintenance of facilities and equipment, training and assignment of staff for each task, and the use of information technology to access, input, store, and transfer relevant data.

Act II — Delivery of the Core Product. As the curtain rises on Act II, our customers are finally about to experience the core service they came for. For simplicity, the meal scenario is condensed into four scenes. In practice, reviewing the menu and placing the order are two separate activities; whereas meal service proceeds on a course-by-course basis. If you were actually running a restaurant yourself, you would need to go into greater detail to identify each of the many steps involved in what is often a tightly-scripted drama. Assuming all goes well, the two guests will have an excellent meal, well-served in a pleasant atmosphere, and perhaps a fine wine to enhance it. However, if the restaurant fails to satisfy their expectations (and those of its many other guests) during Act II, it is going to be in serious trouble. There are numerous potential fail points. Is the menu information accurate? Is everything listed on the menu available this evening? Will explanations and advice be given in a friendly and non-condescending manner for guests who have questions about specific menu items, or are unsure about which wine to order?

After our customers decide on their meals, they place their orders with the server, who must then pass on the details to personnel in the kitchen, bar, and billing desk. Mistakes in transmitting information are a frequent cause of quality failures in many organizations. Bad handwriting, unclear verbal requests, or a wrong entry into a handheld wireless ordering device can lead to incorrect preparation or delivery of the wrong items altogether.

In the subsequent scenes of Act II, our customers may evaluate not only the quality of food and drink — the most important dimension of all — but also how promptly it is served (not too quickly, for guests do not want to feel rushed), and the style of service. Even if the server can perform the job correctly, the experience of the customer can still be spoiled if the server is disinterested, unfriendly, or has an overly casual behavior.

Act III — The Drama Concludes. The meal may be over, but much is still taking place both front-stage and backstage as the drama moves to its close. The core service has now been delivered, and our customers are happily digesting. Act III should be short. The action in each of the remaining scenes should move smoothly, quickly and pleasantly, with no shocking surprises at the end. Most customers' expectations would probably include the following:

- An accurate, intelligible bill is presented promptly as soon as the customer requests it.
- Payment is handled politely and expeditiously (with all major credit cards accepted).
- The guests are thanked for their patronage and invited to come again.
- Customers visiting the restrooms find them clean and properly supplied.
- The right coats are promptly retrieved from the coatroom.
- The customer's car is brought to the door without much of a wait, in the same condition as when it was left. The attendant thanks them again and bids them a good evening.

Identifying Fail Points

Running a restaurant is a complex business and much can go wrong. A good blueprint should draw attention to the points in service delivery where things are particularly at risk of going wrong. From a customer's perspective, the most serious fail points, marked in our blueprint by *an F in a circle*, are those that will result in the failure to access or enjoy the core product. They involve items such as the reservation ("Could the customer get through by phone?", "Was a table available at the desired time and date?", or "Was the reservation recorded accurately?") and seating ("Was a table available when promised?").

Since service delivery takes place over time, there is also the possibility of delays between specific actions that require the customers to wait. Common locations for such waits are identified on the blueprint by *a W within a triangle*. Excessive waits will annoy customers. In practice, every step in the process — both front- and backstage — has some potential for failures and delays. In fact, failures often lead directly to delays (e.g., orders that were never passed on) or time spent correcting mistakes.

David Maister coined the acronym OTSU (opportunity to screw up) to stress the importance of thinking through all the things that might go wrong in the delivery of a particular service.[4] It is only by identifying all the possible OTSUs associated with a particular process that service managers can put together a delivery system that is designed to avoid such problems.

Fail-Proofing to Design Fail Points Out of Service Processes

Once fail points have been identified, careful analysis of the reasons for failure in service processes is necessary. This analysis often reveals opportunities for fail-proofing certain activities in order to reduce or even eliminate the risk of errors.[5]

One of the most useful Total Quality Management (TQM) methods in manufacturing is the application of *poka-yokes* or fail-safe methods to prevent errors in the manufacturing processes. The term *poka-yoke* is derived from the Japanese words *poka* (inadvertent errors) and *yokeru* (to prevent). Richard Chase and Douglas Steward introduced this concept to fail-safe service processes.[6] Server *poka-yokes* ensure that service employees do things correctly, as asked, in the right order and at the right speed. Examples include surgeons whose surgical instrument trays have individual indentations for each instrument. For a given operation, all of the instruments are nested in the tray so that it is clear if the surgeon has not removed all the instruments from the patient before closing the incision (Fig. 8.5).

Some service firms use *poka-yokes* to design frequently occurring service failures out of the service processes, and to ensure that certain steps or standards in the customer-staff interaction are followed. A bank ensures eye contact by requiring tellers to record the customer's eye color on a checklist at the start of a transaction. Some firms place mirrors at the exits of staff areas, and front-line staff can then automatically check their

Figure 8.5: The practice of poka-yoke is observed in the operating room.

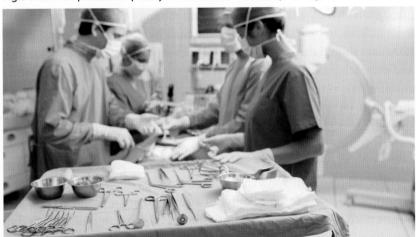

appearance before greeting a customer. At one restaurant, servers place round coasters in front of those diners who have ordered a decaffeinated coffee and square coasters in front of the others, and Starbucks barristers are trained to repeat their customers' orders to ensure that the correct coffee is served.

Designing *poka-yokes* is part art and part science as most of the procedures seem trivial, but this is actually a key advantage of this method. A three-step approach for effectively using *poka-yokes* includes systematically collecting data on problem occurrence, analyzing the root causes, and establishing preventive solutions. This process is described in the context of preventing failures caused by customers in *Service Insights 8.3* later in this chapter.

Setting Service Standards and Targets

The service blueprint, combined with discussions with customers and front-line employees, helps firms to see which service and process attributes are important to customers at each touch point. Through both formal research and on-the-job experience, service managers can learn the nature of customer expectations at each step in the process. As outlined in Chap. 2, customers' expectations range across a spectrum — referred to as the zone of tolerance — from desired service (an ideal) to a threshold level of merely adequate service.

Those aspects of the service process that require the attention of management (i.e., attributes that are most important to customers and most difficult to manage) should be the basis for setting standards. Service providers should design standards for each step sufficiently high to satisfy and even delight customers; if that is not possible, they will need to modify customer expectations. These standards might include time parameters, the script for a technically correct performance, and prescriptions for appropriate style and demeanor. Our restaurant blueprint shows key standards for each touch point.

As the axiom "What is not measured is not managed" goes, standards must be expressed in ways that permit objective measurement. Process performance needs to be monitored against standards, and compliance targets need to be determined. Importantly, even soft and intangible (but important) service attributes need to be made measurable. This is often achieved through using service process indicators that try to capture the essence of, or at least approximate, these important attributes.

For example, in a retail banking context, the attribute "responsiveness" can be operationalized as "processing time to approve a loan application". Service standards are then ideally based on customer expectations and policy decisions which, in turn, are based on how these expectations can be met cost effectively. In cases where standards do not meet customer needs, expectations need to be managed (e.g., when dealing with exceptional cases, expected application approval times can be communicated by service employees verbally).

Finally, performance targets define specific process and/or team performance targets (e.g., 80% of all applications within 24 hours) for which team leaders will be held accountable for. Fig. 8.6 shows the relationship between indicators, standards, and targets.

The distinction between standards and performance targets is important. As they are subsequently used for evaluating staff, branch, and/or team performance, it makes the setting of standards and targets highly sensitive and political. By separating standards and targets, the firm can be 'hard' about reflecting customer expectations in the performance standards, but 'realistic' about what the teams can actually deliver.

In practice, management can stand firm on setting the right standards (i.e., according to customer needs and expectations), and go easy on negotiating performance targets that reflect operational reality

Figure 8.6: Setting standards and targets for customer service processes.

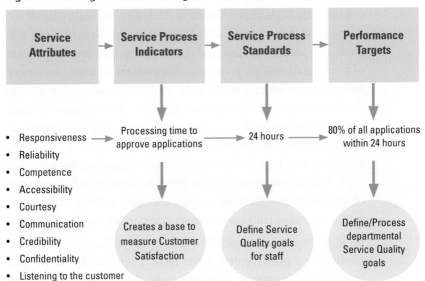

(i.e., it may not be possible to consistently achieve the standards). This separation of standards and targets can be important for three reasons. First, the correct (i.e., customer-driven) standards get communicated to and are internalized by the organization. Second, when implemented well, process owners, and department or branch managers will, over time, raise their performance levels through continuous and incremental improvements to bring them more in line with customer expectations. Third, it facilitates buy-in and support for the (tough) service standards as it also provides latitude to management and staff.[7]

Consumer Perceptions and Emotions in Service Process Design[8]

As Jason Barger, author and consultant, said: "People will forget what you said, people will forget what you do, but people will never forget how you made them feel". Therefore, service processes also need to be designed with emotional intelligence.

Sriram Dasu and Richard Chase highlighted key principles about sequencing service encounters based on their in-depth research in designing emotionally smart processes[9]:

1. *Start strong.* Ideally, service firms should try to provide consistently high performance at each step. In reality however, many service performances are inconsistent. Nevertheless, it is always important to start and finish strong. The opening scenes of a service drama are particularly important because customers' first impressions can affect their evaluations of quality during the later stages of the service delivery. Perceptions of their service experiences tend to be cumulative. If a few things go badly at the outset, customers may simply walk out. Even if they stay, they may now be looking for other things that are not quite right. On the other hand, if the first few steps go well, their zone of tolerance may increase so they are more willing to overlook minor mistakes later on in the service performance.

2. *Build an improving trend.* People in general like things to keep moving in a positive direction. Thus, a service encounter that is perceived to start at an adequate level and then builds up in quality is generally rated better than one that starts well but declines at the end.[10]

3. *Create a peak.* To improve the perception of your service, you are better off making one step sensational and the other steps merely adequate. Customers tend to remember the peak! For example, the Sea World in Orlando could spend more money on various attractions, but the thing that counts — the signature Shamu the Whale show — must be done to perfection.

4. *Get bad experiences over with early.* Unpleasant news (e.g., about delays), discomfort (e.g., as part of medical treatments), unpleasant tasks (e.g., completing registration forms), and unavoidable long waits should be early in the experience, not at the end. This way, customers avoid the dread of pain or aggravation, and these negative aspects of the experience are less likely to dominate the memory of the entire service encounter.

5. *Segment pleasure, combine pain.* Since an event is perceived as longer when it is segmented or broken up into separate steps, service processes should extend the feeling of pleasurable experiences by dividing them, and combining unpleasant experiences into a single event as far as possible.

6. *Finish strong.* Performance standards should not be allowed to fall off toward the end of service delivery. Rather, the finish should be strong — think of rock concerts which always conclude with big hits, comedians who save their best jokes for the end, and fireworks close with an amazing array of colors lighting the sky and a deafening finale. Ending on a high note is an important aspect of every service encounter, even if it is just a cheerful and affirmative: "Have a nice day!"

Emotionprints. In order to manage the customer experience well and implement the principles for sequencing service processes, firms can also map the expected associated emotions at each stage of the service processes. Flowcharts that describe how customers feel are called emotionprints. For example, it can be anticipated that expectant mothers will feel happy and excited when they first see the ultrasound photo of their baby. On the other hand, they may also be anxious during a test for abnormalities in a fetus. Hence, hospitals can anticipate common customer emotions at each step in a process and train their staff to react accordingly. An attitude of celebration would include cheering and applauding. On the other hand, faced with an emotionally negative situation in the service process, staff could show compassion, listen attentively and speak softly.[11]

Finally, the restaurant example was deliberately chosen to illustrate a familiar high-contact, people-processing service. However, many possession-processing services (such as repair or maintenance) and information-processing services (such as insurance or accounting) involve far less contact with customers, because much of the action takes place backstage. In these situations, a failure committed at the front-stage is likely to be viewed even more seriously by customers as it represents a higher proportion of the customer's service encounters with a company. Furthermore, the firm has fewer subsequent opportunities to create a favorable impression.

SERVICE PROCESS REDESIGN

Service processes become outdated over time as changes in technology, customer needs, added service features, new service offerings, and even changes in legislation make existing processes inefficient or irrelevant.

Mitchell T. Rabkin MD, former president of Boston's Beth Israel Hospital (now Beth Israel-Deaconess Medical Center, a teaching hospital of Harvard Medical School), characterized the problem as "institutional rust" and declared: "Institutions are like steel beams — they tend to rust. What was once smooth, shiny and nice tends to become rusty".[12] He suggested two main reasons for this deterioration of processes. The first involves changes in the external environment that make existing practices obsolete, and thus, require the redesign of underlying processes — or even the creation of brand-new processes — in order for the organization to remain relevant and responsive. In healthcare, such changes may reflect new forms of competition, legislation, technology, health insurance policies, and evolving customer needs.

The second reason for institutional rusting occurs internally. Often, it reflects a natural weakening of internal processes, creeping bureaucracy, or the development of unofficial standards (*Service Insights 8.1*). There are many symptoms that indicate the processes are not working well and need to be redesigned. They include:

- A lot of information exchange is needed with the customer and between different service units as the data available is not useful.

- A high ratio of checking or control activities to value-adding activities.

- Increased processing of exceptions.

- Growing number of customer complaints about inconvenient and unnecessary procedures.

SERVICE INSIGHTS 8.1
Rooting Out Unofficial Standards in a Hospital[13]

One of the distinctive characteristics of Mitchell T. Rabkin's 30-year tenure as president of Boston's Beth Israel Hospital was his policy of routinely visiting all areas of the hospital. He usually did so unannounced and in a low-key fashion. No one working at the hospital was surprised to see Dr. Rabkin drop by at almost any time of the day or night. His natural curiosity gave him unparalleled insights into how effectively service procedures were working and the subtle ways in which things could go wrong. As the following story reveals, he discovered that there is often a natural deterioration of messages over time.

One day, I was in the EU (emergency unit), chatting with a house officer (physician) who was treating a patient with asthma. He was giving her medication through an intravenous drip. I looked at the formula for the medication and asked him, "Why are you using this particular cocktail?" "Oh," he replied, "that's hospital policy." Since I was certain that there was no such policy, I decided to investigate.

What had happened went something like this. A few months earlier, Resident (physician) A says to Intern B, who is observing her treat a patient: "This is what I use for asthma." On the next month's rotation, Intern B says to new Resident C: "This is what Dr. A uses for asthma." The following month, Resident C says to Intern D, "This is what we use for asthma." And finally, within another month, Intern D is telling Resident E, "It's hospital policy to use this medication."

As a result of conversations like these, well-intentioned but unofficial standards keep cropping up. It is a particular problem in a place like this, which is not burdened by an inhuman policy manual where you must look up the policy for everything you do. We prefer to rely on people's intelligence and judgment and limit written policies to overall, more general issues. One always has to be aware of the growth of institutional rust and to be clear about what is being done and why it is being done.

Service Process Redesign Should Improve Both Quality and Productivity

Managers in charge of service process redesign projects should look for opportunities to achieve a quantum leap in both productivity and service quality at the same time.[14] *Service Insights 8.2* shows how a small hospital practice did just that.

SERVICE INSIGHTS 8.2

Redesigning Customer Service in a Small Hospital Practice[15]

Things were not going smoothly at Family Medicine Faculty Practice (FMFP), a small practice within a hospital system. Its patients were often placed on hold for long times when they called; there was a lack of available and convenient appointment slots; the waiting room was frequently crowded with lengthy delays before patients could see their doctors.

Dr Schwartz, the medical director, and Dr Bryan, the assistant medical director, decided to change this situation and engaged Coleman Associates, a consulting firm that specializes in redesigning processes. Over the course of four days, a Coleman Associates team worked closely with the clinic's staff on-site, shoulder-to-shoulder, and radically redesigned work processes. It was an amazing transformation; the redesign started on a Monday afternoon, and by Friday morning the Faculty Practice was operating in a whole new way!

The Redesigned Service Model

FMFP had altogether 12 staff, of which nine were support staff and three were physicians. The clinic was considered lean with only three support staff per physician, which is much lower than the national average of 4.8. As a central part of the redesign, staff were reorganized into three Patient Care Teams. Each Patient Care Team consisted of a clinician, a medical assistant, and a receptionist who acted like a one-stop shop for all the patients in their care. The Patient Care Teams took care of all tasks related to their patients, including walk-ins, collection of co-payments, filing of medical charts, confirming the next day's appointments, checking insurance eligibility, and any other patient transactions.

The three Patient Care Teams shared three 'back office' staff which had the following redesigned roles: a medical records staffer, a phone attendant, and a flowmaster not specifically assigned to any of the three teams. The medical records staff was in charge of getting medical charts 24-hours in advance of clinic sessions and filing lab results in charts on a real-time basis so that no work was left to accumulate. If a patient called FMFP for an appointment, the call would be answered by the phone attendant. The flowmaster was in-charge of moving patients from the front waiting room into the exam rooms and out as smoothly and as fast as possible. The flowmaster communicated with each Patient Care Team's medical assistant to get an accurate estimate of the wait time for each patient. Basically, the flowmaster solved any flow problems occurring in the clinic to keep the visit cycle time within 45 minutes for 90% of all visits.

After the redesign, the phone attendant picked up calls and passed it to the relevant Patient Care Team receptionist. In future, they had further plans for direct lines to each Patient Care Team to eliminate the traffic to the phone attendant. The receptionists would be given wireless phones so that patient calls could still be picked up even as they filed medical charts from visits already completed. Patient Care Team receptionists filed charts immediately after visits, thus reducing the incidence of lost charts.

During the booking of appointments, if a patient had a question the receptionist could not answer, she would communicate directly, via walkie-talkie, with the Patient Care Team's medical assistant to get an immediate answer so that work was handled on a real-time basis and not stacked up to be dealt with later.

New tools and equipment helped to stretch FMFP's available resources. For example, digital floor scales were placed in every exam room to weigh adult patients quickly and privately, so there was no need for an extra stop at vitals station. In fact, all work was done in the exam room reflecting the redesign principle: "Organize our work around the patient, not the patient around our work."

As staff gained more experience working together every day in their Patient Care Teams, they also became stronger and more adept in handling variations in patient flow. Stacks of paper seemingly melted during the week when work was redesigned.

FMFP's staff worked harder than ever, but they were also thrilled with the results and all the compliments they received from delighted patients about the new service processes.

Examining service blueprints is an important step in identifying such opportunities and then redesigning the ways in which tasks are performed. Redesign efforts typically focus on achieving the following four key objectives, and ideally, redesign efforts should achieve all four simultaneously:

1. Reduced number of service failures
2. Reduced cycle time from customer initiation of a service process to its completion
3. Enhanced productivity
4. Increased customer satisfaction

Service process redesign often involves reconstruction, rearrangement, and substitution of service processes. These efforts typically include[16]:

- *Examining the service blueprint with key stakeholders.* By closely examining blueprints of existing services, managers can identify problems in a service process, and discover ways to improve it. Each of the stakeholders in a process (i.e., customers, front-line employees, support staff, and IT teams) should be invited to review the blueprint with the purpose of brainstorming for ideas on how to improve the process. This involves identification of missing or unnecessary steps and changes in sequence. Stakeholders also highlight ways in which developments in information technology, equipment and new methods offer advantages.

  For example, Avis does research each year on what factors car renters care about the most. The company breaks down the car rental process into more than 100 incremental steps, including making reservations, finding the pickup counter, getting to the car, driving it, returning it, paying the bill, and so forth. Because Avis knows customers' key concerns, it claims it can quickly identify ways to improve their satisfaction while also driving the firm's productivity. What travelers desire most is to get their rental car quickly and drive away, so the firm has designed its processes to achieve that goal. "We're constantly making little enhancements around the edges," says Scott Deaver, company's then-Executive Vice President for Marketing. Obviously, Avis is living up to its tagline, "We Try

Harder", which the company has employed for some 40 years. "It's not a slogan," says Deaver, "it's in the DNA of the place."

- *Eliminating non-value adding steps.* Often, activities at the front- and back-end processes of services can be streamlined with the goal of focusing on the benefit-producing part of the service encounter. The outcomes of such process redesigns typically include increased productivity and customer satisfaction at the same time.

  For example, a customer wanting to rent a car is not interested in filling out forms, processing payment, or waiting for the returned car to be checked. Service redesign tries to eliminate such steps that customers do not view as value adding. Now, some car rental companies allow customers to rent a car online and pick it up from a designated car park, where a large electronic board lists the name of the customer, the car, and the parking lot numbers. The key is in the car, and the only interaction with a car rental employee is at the exit when driving the car out of the carpark where the customer's driving license is checked and the contract is signed (including the customer confirming the condition of the car). When returning the car, it is simply parked at an allocated area at the rental company's carpark, the key is dropped into a safe deposit box, the final bill is deducted from a predetermined customer credit card and emailed to the billing address, and the customer does not have to come into contact with service personnel.

- *Addressing bottlenecks in the process.*[17] Bottlenecks and resulting customer waits are a feature of many service processes. It is the step in the service process with the lowest throughput rate that determines the effective capacity of the entire process. For an efficient process, ideally all the steps should have the same capacity so that none of the stations form a bottleneck or stays idle. The objective is to design a balanced process in which the processing times of all the steps are approximately the same, and consumers "flow" smoothly through the process without having to wait at any one step.

  Determining the processing time and capacity for each step in the blueprint allows one to see the actual capacity available in each step. One way to identify bottlenecks is to simply observe where customers have to wait. Once bottlenecks are identified, management can address them by devoting more and better resources, and/or redesigning the process and its tasks to increase capacity (see also Chap. 9 for other ways to manage service capacity).

- *Shifting to self-service.* Significant productivity and sometimes even service quality gains can be achieved by increasing self-service (Fig. 8.7). For example, decades ago, FedEx already aimed and succeeded in shifting more and more of its transactions from its call centers to its website, thus reducing the number of employees in its call centers by tens of thousands of people.[18] Businesses are also taking advantage of smartphones and tablets to shift to self-service. One example is Fish & Co., an innovative seafood restaurant chain in Southeast Asia and the Middle East which replaced its menu with an iPad so that customers can perform self-service ordering. An app shows all the delicious food available with lots of drilldown information if desired, and allows diners to send their orders directly to the kitchen. At the back-end, the app links to the restaurant's point-of-sale system to complete the order. Customers can have fun by connecting to social media websites like Facebook to share their meal orders and comments with their friends. The app also has features that upsell menu items and combine dishes with recommended side orders.[19]

Figure 8.7: Here is a look at Nao, the 58-centimeter-tall humanoid robot that can analyze customers' facial expressions and behaviors, and answer the most basic questions related to customer-service.

© HUIS TEN BOSCH/J-17116

Although not self-service in the traditional sense, robots will increasingly be deployed to serve customers, and customers need to feel comfortable interacting with robots in the same way they learned to interact with ATMs and websites. For example, the Bank of Tokyo Mitsubishi UFJ in Tokyo will use robots to greet their customers, answer basic questions, and guide them to the correct service counter. Nao, a 58-centimeter tall robot model, can analyze customers' facial expressions and behaviors, and answer the most basic questions related to customer service (Fig. 8.7). Bank spokesman Kazunobu Takahara said: "We can ramp up communication with our customers by adding a tool like this." The robot costs around $8,000, a fraction of the costs of having front-line employees performing these tasks, and it can speak up to 19 languages in preparation for the Tokyo 2020 Olympics![20]

CUSTOMER PARTICIPATION IN SERVICE PROCESSES

Service process redesign for productivity and efficiency often calls for customers to become more involved in the delivery of the service. Blueprinting helps to specify the role of customers, and to identify the extent of contact between them and service providers.

Customers as Service Co-Creators

Customer participation refers to the actions and resources supplied by customers during service production, including mental, physical, and even emotional inputs.[21] Some degree of customer participation in service delivery is unavoidable in many services that involve real-time contact between customers and providers. However, the extent of such participation varies widely.[22]

Customers can be thought of as service co-creators. Value is created when the customer and service providers interact during production, consumption, and delivery of the service. This means that customers are actively participating in the process, and that their performance affects the quality and productivity of output. Therefore, service firms need to look at how customers themselves can contribute effectively to value creation, and firms need to educate and train customers to have the skills and motivation needed to perform their tasks well.[23]

Reducing Service Failures Caused by Customers

In addition to educating customers, *poka-yokes* can be used to develop systems that make customers perform their roles effectively in service processes. Stephen Tax, Mark Colgate, and David Bowen found that customers cause about one-third of all service problems.[24] Therefore, firms should focus on preventing customer failures as is described in *Service Insights 8.3*.

SERVICE INSIGHTS 8.3
A Three-Step Approach to Preventing Customer Failures

Fail-safe methods (or *poka-yokes*) need to be designed not only for employees but also for customers, especially when customers participate actively in the creation and delivery processes. Customer *poka-yokes* focus on preparing the customer for the encounter (including getting them to bring the right materials for the transaction and to arrive on time, if applicable), understanding and anticipating their role in the service transaction, and selecting the correct service or transaction.

A good way is to use the following three-step approach to prevent customer-generated failures:

(1) Systematically collect information on the most common failure points.

(2) Identify their root causes. It is important to note that an employee's explanation may not be the true cause. Instead, the cause must be investigated from the customer's point of view. Human causes of customer failure include lack of needed skills, failure to understand their role, and insufficient preparation. Some processes are complex and unclear. Other causes may include weaknesses in the design of the servicescape or self-service technology (e.g., "unfriendly" user machines and websites).

(3) Create strategies to prevent the failures that have been identified. The five strategies listed below may need to be combined for maximum effectiveness.

(i) Redesign the customer involvement in the process (e.g., redesign customers' role as well as processes). For example, aircraft lavatory doors must be locked in order for the lights to be switched on. ATMs use beepers so that customers do not forget to retrieve their cards at the end of their transaction. In future, customer identification with cards and PINs at ATMs are likely to be replaced by biometric identification (e.g., retina reading combined with voice recognition), thereby designing lost cards or forgotten PIN problems out of the process, and increasing customer convenience.

(ii) Use technology. For example, some hospitals use automated systems that send short text messages or emails to patients to confirm and remind them of their appointments, and inform them on how to reschedule an appointment, if required.

(iii) Manage customer behavior. For example, one may print dress code requests on invitations, send reminders of dental appointments, or print user guidelines on customer cards (e.g., "Please have your account and PIN number ready before calling our service representatives").

(iv) Encourage "customer citizenship" (e.g., customers help one another to prevent failure, e.g., in weight-loss programs).

(v) Improve the servicescape. For example, many firms forget that customers need user-friendly directional signs to help them find their way around; failing which, they might become frustrated.

Helping customers to avoid failure can become a source of competitive advantage, especially when companies increasingly use self-service technologies.

Source: Stephen S. Tax, Mark Colgate, and David E. Bowen, "How to Prevent Customers from Failing," *MIT Sloan Management Review*, 47, Spring 2006, pp. 30–38.

SELF-SERVICE TECHNOLOGIES

The ultimate form of involvement in service production is for customers to undertake a specific activity on their own, using facilities or systems provided by the service supplier. In effect, customer's time and effort replaces that of a service employee. In the case of Internet- and app-based services, customers even provide their own terminals.

Consumers are faced with an array of self-service technologies (SSTs) that allow them to produce a service without direct service employee involvement.[25] SSTs include automated banking terminals, self-service scanning at supermarket checkouts, self-service gasoline pumps, and automated telephone systems such as phone banking, automated hotel checkout, self-service train ticketing machines (Fig. 8.8), and numerous Internet- and app-based services.

Information-based services lend themselves particularly well to the use of SSTs, and include not only supplementary services such as getting information, placing orders and reservations, and making payments, but also the delivery of core products in fields such as banking, research, entertainment, and self-paced education. Even consultation and sales processes, traditionally carried out face-to-face, have been transformed into self-service processes with the use of electronic recommendation agents (*Service Insights 8.4*).[26]

Figure 8.8: Tourists appreciate easy-to-understand instructions when traveling abroad and making payment for train tickets.

Many companies have developed strategies designed to encourage customers to serve themselves through apps and the Internet. They hope to divert customers from using more expensive alternatives such as face-to-face contact with employees, use of intermediaries such as brokers and travel agents, or voice-to-voice telephony. Using service blueprints (Fig. 8.9) helps to visualize and design self-service processes.

Increasingly, customers also help each other in peer-to-peer problem solving, facilitated by online brand communities and firm-hosted platforms. Research has

Figure 8.9: Blueprint for a self-service internet-delivered banking process.

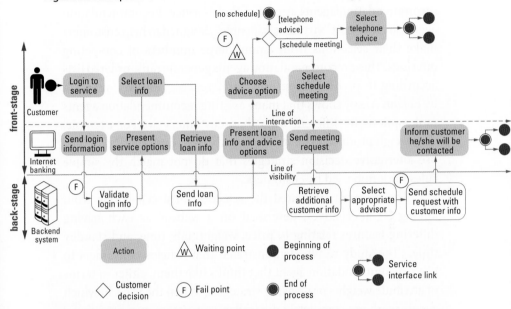

Source: Lia Patrício, Raymond P. Fisk, João Falcão e Cunha, and Larry Constantine (2011), "Multilevel Service Design: From Customer Value Constellation to Service Experience Blueprinting," *Journal of Service Research*, Vol. 14, No. 2, pp. 180–200; Reprinted by Permission of SAGE Publications, Inc.

shown that encouraging customers to help themselves by posting their questions, and to help others by responding to peer questions reduces the resources a firm has to expand on traditional customer support services. Promoting peer-to-peer customer interactions is a strategic lever to increase the efficiency and effectiveness of a firm's support service.[27]

Nevertheless, not all customers take advantage of SSTs. Matthew Meuter and his colleagues observe: "For many firms, often the challenge is not managing the technology but rather getting consumers to try the technology".[28]

SERVICE INSIGHTS 8.4
Making Electronic Recommendation Agents More Effective

Consumers often face a bewildering array of choices when purchasing goods and services from online vendors. One way in which these "e-tailers" try to assist consumers is to offer electronic recommendation agents as part of their service. Recommendation agents are low-cost "virtual salespeople" designed to help customers make their selections from among large numbers of competing offerings. These recommendation agents generate rank-ordered lists according to predicted consumer preferences. However, research by Lerzan Aksoy shows that many existing recommendation agents rank options in different ways than customers do. For example, they weigh product attributes differently from customers, and they use alternative decision strategies that do not match the simple rules of thumb used by customers.

The research simulated the selection of a cell phone from among 32 alternatives, described on a website as each having differing features relating to price, weight, talk time, and standby time. The study results demonstrated that it helps consumers to use a recommendation agent that thinks like them, either in terms of attribute weights or decision strategies. When the ways in which agents work are completely dissimilar, consumers may actually be worse off than if they had simply used a randomly ordered list of options. Even though the subjects in this research tended to listen to the agent's recommendations, those who felt it had a dissimilar decision strategy and dissimilar attribute weights from their own, were less likely to come back to the website, recommend it to friends, or believe that the site had met their expectations well.

In conclusion, to make recommendation agents add value to the customer and enhance sales and repeat business, firms need to closely understand their customers' decision making strategies, attributes, and attribute weightings (refer to Chap. 2 and 3).

Source: Lerzan Aksoy, Paul N. Bloom, Nicholas H. Lurie, and Bruce Cooil, "Should Recommendation Agents Think Like People?" *Journal of Service Research*, 8, May 2006, pp. 297–315.

Customer Benefits and Adoption of Self-Service Technology

Given the significant investment in time and money required for firms to design, implement and manage SSTs, it is critical for service marketers to understand how consumers decide between using an SST option and relying on a human provider. Multiple attitudes drive customer intentions to use a specific SST, including overall attitudes toward related service technologies, toward the specific service firm and its employees, and importantly, the overall perceived benefits, convenience, costs and ease of use customers see in using an SST.[29] Firms need to recognize that SSTs present both advantages and disadvantages for their customers. Key advantages of using SSTs include[30]:

- Greater convenience, including time savings, faster service, flexibility of timing (e.g., through 24/7 availability) and flexibility of location (e.g., many ATMs). Customers love SSTs when they bail them out of difficult situations, often because SST machines are conveniently located and accessible 24/7. A website is as close as the nearest computer or smartphone, making this option much more accessible than the company's physical sites.
- Greater control over service delivery, more information, and higher perceived level of customization.
- Lower prices and fees.

Success at the customer interface requires an understanding of what target customers want from an interaction. Sometimes a well-designed SST can deliver better service than a human being. Said one customer about the experience of purchasing convenience store items from a new model of automated vending machine, "A guy in the store can make a mistake or give you a hard time, but not the machine. I definitely prefer the machine".[31] Many SSTs enable users to get detailed information and complete transactions faster than they could through face-to-face or telephone contact. Experienced travelers rely on SSTs to save time and effort at airports, rental car facilities, and hotels. A Wall Street Journal article summarized the trend — "Have a Pleasant Trip: Eliminate Human Contact".[32] In short, many customers like SSTs when they work well and especially when customers have to use them frequently.

Customers may derive fun, enjoyment, and even spontaneous delight from SST usage. For example, children take a lot of delight in doing self-scanning at supermarket checkouts or making orders on tablets in restaurants as they find this activity enjoyable.

However, there are always some consumers who feel uncomfortable with SSTs, feel anxious and stressed, or may view service encounters as social experiences, and prefer to deal with people. Even after an initial trial, not all customers will continue using an SST. It is important that the first trial is satisfying, and customers feel confident that they can use the SST effectively in the future. If this is not the case, customers are likely to go back to using traditional, front-line employee-provided services. Some retail banks, for example, use "greeters" in their branches to assist customers in migrating to in-branch SSTs. This not only helps customers to overcome technology anxiety and ensures a successful first trial, but also builds confidence in their ability to use the SST again.[33]

In sum, customers love SSTs when they are easy to use, perform better, and cheaper than the alternative of being served by a service employee. However, not all customers are comfortable with using SSTs.

Customer Disadvantages and Barriers of Adoption of Self-Service Technology

Customers hate SSTs when they fail. Users get angry when they find that self-service machines are out of service, their PIN numbers are rejected, websites are down, or tracking numbers do not work. Even when SSTs do work, customers get frustrated by poorly designed technologies that make service processes difficult to understand and use. A common complaint is the difficulty in navigating one's way around a website or completing online registrations and forms that keep rejecting their entries.

Users also get frustrated when they themselves mess up, due to errors such as forgetting their passwords, failing to provide information as requested, or simply hitting the wrong button. Self-service logically implies that customers can cause their own dissatisfaction. However, even when it is the customers' own fault, they may still blame the service provider for not providing a simpler and more user-friendly system, and on the next occasion, revert to the traditional human-based system.[34]

A key problem with SSTs is that so few of them include effective service recovery systems. In many instances, when the process fails, there is no simple way to solve the problem on the spot. Typically, customers are forced to telephone, email, or make a personal visit to the service company to solve the problem, which may be exactly what they were trying to avoid in the first place!

Thus, the challenge for the service firm is to design SSTs to be as "idiot-proof" as possible, mitigate common customer errors, use customer *poka-yokes*, and even design service recovery processes for customers so that they can help themselves should things go wrong.[35]

Assessing and Improving SSTs

Mary Jo Bitner suggests that managers should put their firms' SSTs to the test by asking the following basic questions[36]:

- *Does the SST work reliably?* Firms must make sure that SSTs work as promised and the design is user-friendly. Southwest Airlines' online ticketing system has set a high standard for simplicity and reliability. It boasts the highest percentage of online ticket sales of any airline — a clear evidence of customer acceptance!

- *Is the SST better than the interpersonal alternative?* If it does not save time or provide ease of access, cost savings or some other benefit, then customers will continue to use the familiar interpersonal choice. Amazon.com's success reflects its efforts to create a highly personalized yet efficient alternative to visiting a retail store,[37] which has become the most preferred way of browsing and buying books today. The fast growth of e-books will only accelerate this trend.

Figure 8.10: As a fail-safe measure, departmental stores normally have employees on standby near self-checkout lanes to assist if there are problems.

- *If the SST fails, are systems in place to recover the service?* It is critical for firms to provide systems, structures, and recovery technologies that will enable prompt service recovery when things go wrong (Fig. 8.10). Most banks display a phone number at their ATMs, giving customers direct access to a 24-hour customer service center where they can talk to a "real person" if they have questions or run into difficulties. Supermarkets that have installed self-service checkout lanes usually assign one employee to monitor the lanes; this practice combines security with customer assistance. In telephone-based service systems, well-designed voicemail menus include an option for customers to reach a customer-service representative.

Designing a website to be easy to use and virtually failure-proof is no easy task and can be very expensive, but it is through such investments that companies can encourage self-service and create loyal users.

Managing Customers' Reluctance to Change

Increasing the customers' participation level in a service process, or shifting the process entirely to self-service using SSTs, require the firm to change customer behavior. This is often a difficult task as customers resent being forced to use SSTs.[38] *Service Insights 8.6* identifies ways of addressing customer resistance to change, particularly when the innovation is a radical one.

Once the nature of the changes has been decided, marketing communications can help prepare customers for the change, explaining the rationale, the benefits, and what customers will need to do differently in the future.

SERVICE INSIGHTS 8.6
Managing Customers' Reluctance to Change

Customer resistance to changes in familiar processes and long-established behavior patterns can thwart attempts to improve productivity and even quality. The following six steps can help smoothen the path of change.

(1) *Develop customer trust.* It is more difficult to introduce productivity-related changes when people are distrustful of the initiator, as they often are in the case of large, seemingly impersonal institutions. Customers' willingness to accept change may be closely related to the degree of goodwill they bear towards the firm.

(2) *Understand customers' habits and expectations.* People often get into a routine of using a particular service, with certain steps being taken in a specific sequence. In effect, they have their own individual service script or flowchart in mind. Innovations that disrupt deeply-rooted routines are more likely to face resistance. Aligning new processes more closely with customers' habits and expectations enhances the chances of success.

(3) *Pre-test new procedures and equipment.* To determine probable customer response to new procedures and equipment, marketing researchers can employ concept and laboratory testing, and/or field testing. If service personnel are going to be replaced by automatic equipment, it is essential to create designs that customers of almost all types and backgrounds will find easy to use. Even the phrasing of instructions needs careful thought. Unclear or complex instructions may discourage customers with poor reading skills.

(4) *Publicize the benefits.* Introduction of self-service equipment or procedures requires consumers to perform part of the task themselves. Although this additional "work" may be associated with such benefits as extended service hours, time savings, and (in some instances) monetary savings, these benefits are not necessarily obvious — they have to be promoted. Customers have to be informed about the innovation to arouse their interest, and specific benefits to customers should be clarified of using a new delivery system.

(5) *Teach customers to use innovations and promote trial.* Assigning service personnel to demonstrate new equipment and answer

questions — providing reassurance as well as educational assistance — is a key element in gaining acceptance of new procedures and technology. The costs of such demonstration programs can be spread across multiple outlets by moving staff members from one site to another if the innovation is rolled out sequentially across the various locations. For web-based innovations, firms can consider to provide access to e-mail, chat or even telephone-based assistance. Promotional incentives such as price discounts, loyalty points, or lucky draws may also help to stimulate trial. Once customers have tried a self-service option (particularly an electronically-based one) and find that it works well, they will be more likely to use it regularly in the future.

(6) *Monitor performance and continue to seek improvements.* Introducing quality and productivity improvements is an ongoing process, especially for SSTs. It is important to monitor utilization, frequency of transaction failures (and their fail points), and customer complaints over time. Service managers have to work hard to continuously improve SSTs and keep up the momentum so that SSTs can achieve their full potential and not left to become white elephants.

CONCLUSION

In this chapter, we emphasized the importance of designing and managing service processes central in creating the service product and significantly shaping the customer experience is emphasized. Blueprinting is covered in detail as a powerful tool to understand, document, analyze, and improve service processes as it helps to identify and reduce service fail points, and provides important insights for service process redesign.

An important part of process design is to define the roles customers should play in the production of services. Their level of desired participation needs to be determined, and customers need to be motivated and taught to play their part in the service delivery to ensure customer satisfaction and firm productivity. The increasing importance of SSTs and strategies to increase their adoption were also discussed.

CHAPTER SUMMARY

Service Processes
- Are the service experience from the customer's perspective
- Are the architecture of service from the firm's perspective

Mapping & Designing Service Processes

Flowcharting of Service Processes
- Maps a service process
- Shows the nature and sequence of steps involved
- Is an easy way to visualize the customer experience

Blueprinting of Service Processes
- A more complex form of flowcharting
- Shows how a service process is constructed
- Maps the customer, employee, and service system interactions
- Design elements:
  - Front-stage activities
  - Physical evidence
  - Line of visibility
  - Backstage activities
  - Support processes & supplies
  - Potential fail points
  - Common customer waits
  - Service standards & targets
  - Details preprocess, in-process, and post-process stages of service delivery

Process Design Considerations
- Use poka-yokes to design fail points out of processes
- Set service standards and targets to manage processes
- Design customer emotions into the process:
  - Start strong
  - Build an improving trend
  - Create a peak
  - Get bad experiences over with early
  - Segment pleasure, combine pain
  - Finish strong

Redesigning Service Processes

Indicators for Redesign Need
- Excessive information exchange
- High degree of control activities
- Increased processing of exceptions
- Growing number of customer complaints about inconvenient and unnecessary procedures

Objectives of Redesign
- Reduced number of service failures
- Reduced cycle time
- Enhanced productivity
- Increased customer satisfaction

How to Redesign Service Processes?
- Examine the blueprint with key stakeholders (i.e., customers, frontline and back office employees and IT) and see how to reconstruct, rearrange and substitute tasks
- Eliminate non-value adding steps
- Address bottlenecks, balance process
- Shift to self-service

Manage Customer Participation in Service Processes

Customers as Co-creators
- Educate, train and motivate customers to do their part well
- Use customer poka-yokes to reduce failures caused by customers
- Consider peer-to-peer problem solving as part of online brand communities

Self-Service Technologies (SSTs)
- Customer benefits
  - Convenience & speed
  - Control, information & customization
  - Cost savings
- Disadvantages & barriers
  - Poorly designed SSTs
  - Unreliable SSTs
  - Poor service recovery procedures
  - Inadequate customer education
- Assessing & improving SSTs
  - Does the SST work reliably?
  - Is the SST better than the interpersonal alternative?
  - If it fails, are systems in place to recover the service?

Managing Customers' Reluctance to Change
- Develop customers' trust
- Understand customers' habits & expectations
- Pretest new procedures & equipment
- Publicize the benefits
- Teach customers to use innovations & promote trial
- Monitor performance & improve the SST

CHAPTER 9

Balancing Demand and Capacity

Balancing the supply and demand sides of a service industry is not easy, and whether a manager does it well or not makes all the difference.

W. Earl Sasser
Professor at Harvard Business School

They also serve who only stand and wait.

John Milton
English poet, 1608–1674

FLUCTUATIONS IN DEMAND THREATEN PROFITABILITY

Many services with limited capacity face wide swings in demand that can be caused by the change in seasons. This is a problem as service capacity usually cannot be kept aside for sale at a later date. The effective use of expensive productive capacity is one of the secrets of success in such businesses. The goal should be to utilize staff, labor, equipment and facilities as productively as possible. By working with managers in operations and human resources, service marketers may be able to develop strategies to bring demand and capacity into balance, in ways that create benefits for customers as well as to improve profitability for the business.

From Excess Demand to Excess Capacity

For fixed capacity firms, the problem is a familiar one. "It's either feast or famine for us!" sighs the manager. "In peak periods, we're disappointing prospective customers by turning them away. And in low periods when our facilities are idle, our employees are standing around looking bored, and we're losing money." In other words, demand and supply are not in balance.

At any given moment, a fixed-capacity service may face one of the four following conditions (Fig. 9.1):

- *Excess demand.* The level of demand exceeds the maximum available capacity, resulting in some customers being denied service and loss of business.

- *Demand exceeds optimum capacity.* No one is turned away, but conditions are crowded and customers are likely to perceive a deterioration in service quality and may feel dissatisfied.

Figure 9.1: Implications of variations in demand relative to capacity.

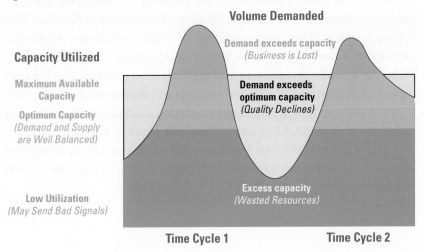

- *Demand and supply are well balanced* at the level of optimum capacity. Staff and facilities are busy without being overworked, and customers receive good service without delays.

- *Excess capacity.* Demand is below optimum capacity and productive resources are under-utilized, resulting in low productivity. Low usage also poses a risk that customers may find the experience disappointing or have doubts about the viability of the service.

Sometimes optimum and maximum capacities are one and the same. At a live theater performance or sports event, a full-house looks grand and is exciting for the performers or players and audience. It creates a more satisfying experience for all. With most other services however, a customer might feel that they will get better service if the facility is not operating at full capacity. For instance, the quality of restaurant service often deteriorates when every table is occupied, because the staff is rushed and there is a greater likelihood of errors or delays. When traveling alone in an aircraft with high density seating, a passenger tends to feel more comfortable if the seat next to them is empty. When repair and maintenance shops are fully scheduled, delays may result if there is no slack in the system to allow for unexpected problems in completing particular jobs.

Building Blocks of Managing Capacity and Demand

There are two basic approaches to the problem of fluctuating demand. One is to adjust the level of capacity to meet variations in demand. This approach requires an understanding of what constitutes productive capacity and how it may be increased or decreased on an incremental basis. The second approach is to manage the level of demand. This requires a good understanding of demand patterns and drivers on a segment-by-segment basis, so that firms can use marketing strategies to smoothen out variations in demand. Most service firms use a mix of both approaches.[1]

Fig. 9.2 shows the four building blocks that provide an integrative approach to balancing capacity and demand. The remainder of this chapter is organized along these four building blocks.

Figure 9.2: Building blocks of effective capacity and demand management.

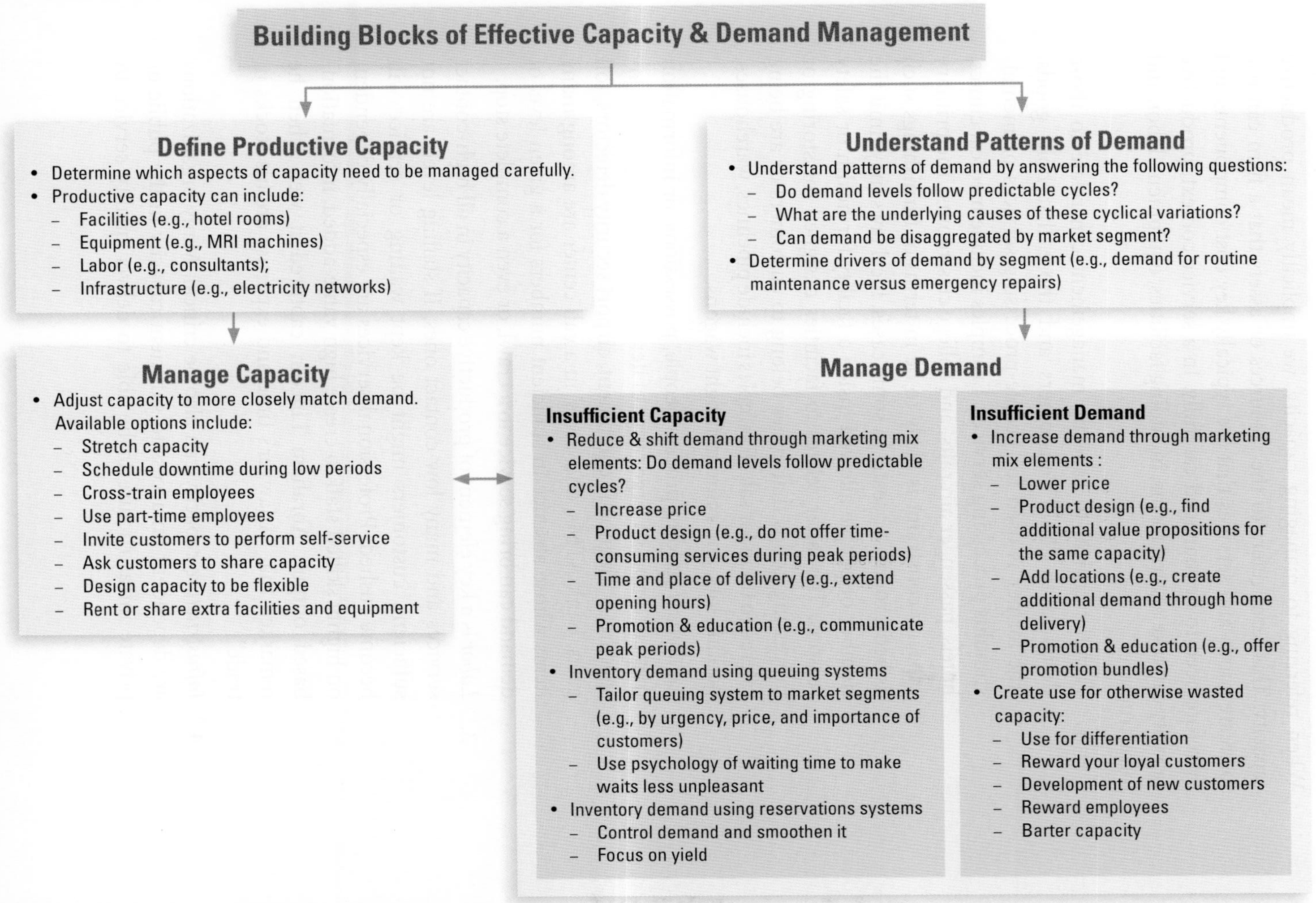

Building Blocks of Effective Capacity & Demand Management

Understand Patterns of Demand
- Understand patterns of demand by answering the following questions:
  - Do demand levels follow predictable cycles?
  - What are the underlying causes of these cyclical variations?
  - Can demand be disaggregated by market segment?
- Determine drivers of demand by segment (e.g., demand for routine maintenance versus emergency repairs)

Define Productive Capacity
- Determine which aspects of capacity need to be managed carefully.
- Productive capacity can include:
  - Facilities (e.g., hotel rooms)
  - Equipment (e.g., MRI machines)
  - Labor (e.g., consultants);
  - Infrastructure (e.g., electricity networks)

Manage Capacity
- Adjust capacity to more closely match demand. Available options include:
  - Stretch capacity
  - Schedule downtime during low periods
  - Cross-train employees
  - Use part-time employees
  - Invite customers to perform self-service
  - Ask customers to share capacity
  - Design capacity to be flexible
  - Rent or share extra facilities and equipment

Manage Demand

Insufficient Capacity
- Reduce & shift demand through marketing mix elements: Do demand levels follow predictable cycles?
  - Increase price
  - Product design (e.g., do not offer time-consuming services during peak periods)
  - Time and place of delivery (e.g., extend opening hours)
  - Promotion & education (e.g., communicate peak periods)
- Inventory demand using queuing systems
  - Tailor queuing system to market segments (e.g., by urgency, price, and importance of customers)
  - Use psychology of waiting time to make waits less unpleasant
- Inventory demand using reservations systems
  - Control demand and smoothen it
  - Focus on yield

Insufficient Demand
- Increase demand through marketing mix elements :
  - Lower price
  - Product design (e.g., find additional value propositions for the same capacity)
  - Add locations (e.g., create additional demand through home delivery)
  - Promotion & education (e.g., offer promotion bundles)
- Create use for otherwise wasted capacity:
  - Use for differentiation
  - Reward your loyal customers
  - Development of new customers
  - Reward employees
  - Barter capacity

DEFINING PRODUCTIVE SERVICE CAPACITY

When referring to managing capacity, we implicitly mean productive capacity. This term refers to the resources or assets that a firm can use to create goods and services that are typically key cost components and therefore need to be managed carefully. In a service context, productive capacity can take several forms, including facilities, equipment, labor, and infrastructure.

1. *Facilities* critical to capacity management can relate to those designed to "hold" customers and those that hold goods. The former is used for people-processing services or mental-stimulus processing services. Examples include medical clinics, hotels, passenger aircrafts, and college classrooms. The primary capacity constraint is likely to be in terms of furnishings such as beds, rooms or seats. In some cases, local laws may limit the number of people allowed inside a facility for health or safety reasons. The latter relates to facilities designed for storing or processing goods that either belong to customers or are being offered to them for sale. Examples include pipelines, warehouses, parking lots, and railroad freight wagons.

2. *Equipment* used to process people, possessions, or information may encompass a large range of items and can be very situation-specific — diagnostic equipment, airport security detectors, toll gates, bank ATMs, and 'seats' in a call center are among many items whose absence in sufficient numbers for a given level of demand can bring service to a crawl, or even a complete stop.

3. *Labor* is a key element of productive capacity in all high-contact services and many low-contact ones. If staffing levels are not sufficient, customers might be kept waiting or service will become rushed. Professional services are especially dependent on highly skilled staff to create high value-added, information-based output. Abraham Lincoln captured it well when he remarked that "A lawyer's time and expertise are his stocks in trade".

4. *Infrastructure* capacity can also be critical. Many organizations are dependent on access to sufficient capacity in the public or private infrastructure to be able to deliver quality service to

their customers. Capacity problems of this nature may include congested airways that lead to air traffic restrictions on flights, traffic jams on major highways, and power failures (or "brown outs" caused by reduced voltage).

Financial success in capacity-constrained businesses is, in large measure, a function of the management's ability to use productive capacity — labor, equipment, facilities, and infrastructure — as efficiently and as profitably as possible. In practice, however, it is difficult to achieve this all the time. Not only do demand levels vary, often randomly, but the time and effort required to process each person or thing may vary widely at any point in the process. In general, processing times for people are more varied than for objects or things, reflecting the varying levels of preparedness ("I lost my credit card"), argumentative versus cooperative personalities ("If you will not give me a table with a view, I will have to ask for your supervisor"), and so forth. Furthermore, service tasks are not necessarily homogeneous. In both professional services and repair jobs, diagnosis and treatment times vary according to the nature of the customers' problems.

MANAGING CAPACITY

Although service firms may encounter capacity limitations due to varying demand, there are a number of ways in which capacity can be adjusted to reduce the problem. Capacity can be stretched or shrunk, and the overall capacity can be adjusted to match demand.

Stretching Capacity Levels

Some capacity is elastic in its ability to absorb extra demand. Here, the actual level of capacity remains unchanged, and more people are being served with the same level of capacity. For example, normal capacity for a subway car may offer 40 seats and allow standing room for another 60 passengers with enough handrail and floor space for all. At rush hour however, up to 200 people could squeeze into a subway car, although under sardine-like conditions (Fig. 9.3). Similarly, the capacity of service personnel can be stretched, and staff may be able to work at high levels of efficiency for short periods of time. However, staff would quickly tire and

Figure 9.3: Rush hour crowd stretches the capacity of train services.

begin to provide poor service if they had to work that fast for a prolonged period of time.

Another way to stretch capacity is to utilize the facilities for longer periods. For example, some banks extend their opening hours during weekdays and even open on weekends. Universities may offer evening classes, and weekend and summer programs.

Lastly, the average amount of time customers (or their possessions) spend in process may be reduced. Sometimes, this is achieved by minimizing slack time. For example, a restaurant can buzz tables, seat arriving diners, present menus fast, and the bill can be presented promptly to a group of diners relaxing at the table after a meal.[2] In other instances, it may be achieved by cutting back the level of service — by offering a simpler menu at busy times of the day.

Adjusting Capacity to Match Demand

Unlike stretching capacity, adjusting capacity involves tailoring the overall level of capacity to match variations in demand — a strategy also known as *chasing demand*. There are several actions that managers can take to adjust capacity as needed.[3] These actions range from the easiest to implement to the more difficult:

- *Schedule downtime during periods of low demand.* To ensure 100% capacity during peak periods, maintenance, repair, and renovations should be conducted when demand is expected to be low. Employees should make use of these periods by taking leaves, etc.

- *Cross-train employees.* Even when the service delivery system operates at full capacity, some physical elements — and their attendant employees — may be under-utilized. If employees can be cross-trained to perform a variety of tasks, they can be shifted to bottleneck points whenever needed, thereby increasing total capacity. In supermarkets, for instance, the manager may call on stockers to operate cash registers when crowded. Likewise, during slow periods, the cashiers may be asked to help stock shelves.

- *Use part-time employees.* Many organizations hire extra workers during their peak periods, e.g., postal workers and retail store associates hired during festival seasons, extra staff hired in tax preparation service firms at the end of the financial year, and additional hotel employees hired during holiday periods and for major conventions.

- *Invite customers to perform self-service.* If the number of employees is limited, capacity can be increased by involving customers in the co-production of certain tasks. One way to do this is by adding self-service technologies such as electronic kiosks at the airport for airline ticketing and check-in, or automated check-out stations at supermarkets.

- *Ask customers to share.* Capacity can be stretched by asking customers to share a unit of capacity normally meant for one individual. For instance, at busy airports and train stations, where the supply of taxis is sometimes insufficient to meet demand, travelers going in the same direction may be given the option of sharing a ride at a reduced rate.

- *Create flexible capacity.*[4] Sometimes, the problem is not the overall capacity but in the mix available to serve the needs of different market segments. One solution lies in designing physical facilities to be flexible. For example, tables in a restaurant can be all two-seaters. When necessary, two tables can be combined to seat four, or three tables combined to seat six. An airline may have too few seats in the economy class even though there are empty seats in the business class cabin on any given flight. Facing tough competition from Airbus, Boeing received what it described in jest as "outrageous demands" from potential customers when it was designing its 777 airliner. The airlines wanted an aircraft where galleys as well as the lavatories with their plumbing could be relocated almost anywhere in the cabin within a matter of hours. Boeing gulped at the demands but managed to come up with solutions. Airlines can now rearrange the passenger cabin of the "Triple Seven" within hours and reconfigure it with varying number of seats allocated to the different classes.

- *Rent or share extra facilities and equipment.* To reduce spending on fixed assets, a service business may be able to rent extra space or machines during peak times. Two firms with complementary demand patterns may enter into formal sharing agreements. For example, some universities rent out student accommodation to visitors during the peak holiday season when their own students are on summer breaks and the first-year students have not moved into the campus yet.

UNDERSTAND PATTERNS OF DEMAND

In order to effectively manage demand for a particular service, managers need to understand that demand often differs by market segment.

Random fluctuations are usually caused by factors beyond management's control. However, analysis will sometimes reveal that a predictable demand cycle for one segment is concealed within a broader, seemingly random pattern. This fact illustrates the importance of breaking down demand on a segment-by-segment basis. For instance, a repair and maintenance shop that services industrial electrical equipment may already know that a certain proportion of its work consists of regularly scheduled contracts to perform preventive maintenance. The balance may come from "walk-ins" and emergency repairs. Although it might seem hard to predict or control the timing and volume of such work, further analysis might show that walk-in business is more prevalent on some days of the week than others, and that emergency repairs are frequently requested, following damage sustained during thunderstorms, which

Table 9.1: Questions about Demand Patterns and their Underlying Causes.

1. **Do demand levels follow a predictable cycle?**
   If so, is the duration of the demand cycle:
   - One day (varies by hour)
   - One week (varies by day)
   - One month (varies by day or by week)
   - One year (varies by month or by season or reflects annual public holidays)
   - Another period

2. **What are the underlying causes of these cyclical variations?**
   - Employment schedules
   - Billing and tax payment/refund cycles
   - Wage and salary payment dates
   - School hours and vacation
   - Seasonal changes in climate
   - Occurrence of public or religious holidays
   - Natural cycles, such as coastal tides

3. **Do demand levels seem to change randomly?**
   If so, could the underlying causes be:
   - Day-to-day changes in the weather
   - Health events whose occurrence cannot be pinpointed exactly
   - Accidents, fires, and certain criminal activities
   - Natural disasters (e.g., earthquakes, storms, mudslides, and volcanic eruptions)

4. **Can demand for a particular service over time be disaggregated by market segment to reflect such components as follows?**
   - Use patterns by a particular type of customer or for a particular purpose
   - Variations in the net profitability of each completed transaction

tend to be seasonal in nature and can often be forecast a day or two in advance. Understanding demand patterns allows the firm to schedule less preventive maintenance work on the days with high anticipated demand of typically more profitable emergency repairs.

To understand the patterns of demand by segment, research should begin by getting some answers to a series of important questions about the patterns of demand and their underlying causes (Table 9.1).

Most cycles influencing demand for a particular service vary in length from one day to 12 months. In many instances, multiple cycles operate simultaneously. For example, demand levels for public transport may vary according to the time of the day (highest during commute hours), day of week (less traveling to work on the weekends but more leisure travel), and season of year (more traveling by tourists in the

Figure 9.4: In summer, many tourists flock to Cologne, Germany to take in its rich heritage.

summer, as seen in Fig. 9.4). The demand for service during the peak period on a Monday in summer is likely to be very different from the demand during the peak period on a Saturday in winter, reflecting day-of-week and seasonal variations jointly.

No strategy for smoothening the demand is likely to succeed unless it is based on an understanding of why customers from a specific market segment choose to use the service when they do. For example, it is difficult for hotels to convince business travelers to remain on Saturday nights since few executives do business over the weekend. Instead, hotel managers may do better to promote weekend use of their facilities for conferences or leisure travel. Attempts to get commuters to shift their travel to off-peak periods will probably fail, since such travel is determined by people's employment hours. Instead, efforts should be directed at employers to persuade them to adopt flexi-time or staggered working hours.

Keeping good records of each transaction helps enormously when it comes to analyzing demand patterns based on past experiences. Best practice queuing systems supported by sophisticated software can automatically track customer consumption patterns by the type of customer, service requested, and date and time of day. Where relevant, it is also useful to record weather conditions and other special factors such as a strike, an accident, a big convention in town, a price change, or the launch of a competing service that might have influenced demand.

MANAGING DEMAND

Once the demand patterns of the different market segments are understood, we can proceed to manage demand. There are five basic approaches:

- Take no action and leave demand to find its own levels.
- Reduce demand during peak periods.
- Increase demand during low periods.
- Inventory demand using a queuing system.
- Inventory demand using a reservations system.

The first approach, *take no action*, has the virtue of simplicity but little else. Eventually customers learn from experience or word-of-mouth when they can expect to stand in line to use a service and when it will be available without delay. The trouble is that they may also learn to find out about a competitor who is more responsive, and low off-peak utilization cannot be improved unless action is taken. The other four proactive approaches are therefore far superior and profitable strategies.

Table 9.2 links these five approaches to the two problematic situations of excess demand and excess capacity. Many service businesses face both situations at different points in the cycle of demand, and should consider use of the interventionist strategies described. Next, how marketing mix elements can help to shape demand levels will be discussed, as well as how to inventory demand first through waiting lines and queuing systems, and second through reservation systems.

Marketing Mix Elements Can be Used to Shape Demand Patterns

Several marketing mix variables can be used to stimulate demand during periods of excess capacity, and decrease or shift around demand during periods of insufficient capacity. Price is often the first variable to be proposed for bringing demand and supply into balance. However, changes in product, distribution strategy, and communication efforts can also be

Table 9.2: Alternate demand management strategies for different capacity situations.

Approaches in Managing Demand	Capacity Situation	
	Insufficient Capacity (Excess Demand)	**Insufficient Demand (Excess Capacity)**
Take no action	• Results in unorganized queuing (may irritate customers and discourage future use).	• Capacity is wasted (customers may have a disappointing experience for services such as theater).
Manage demand through marketing mix elements	Reduce demand in peak periods: • Higher prices will increase profits. • Change product elements (e.g., do not offer time-consuming services during peak times). • Modify time and place of delivery (e.g., extend opening hours). • Communication can encourage use in other time slots. (Can this effort be focused on less profitable and less desirable segments?) • Note that demand from highly profitable segments should still be stimulated, and priority to capacity should be given to those segments. Demand reduction and shifting should primarily be focused on lower yield segments.	Increase demand in low periods: • Lower prices selectively (try to avoid cannibalizing existing business; ensure that all relevant costs are covered). • Change product elements (find alternative value propositions for service during low seasons). • Use communications and variation in products and distribution (but recognize extra costs, if any, and make sure that appropriate trade-offs are made between profitability and use levels).
Inventory demand using a queuing system	• Match appropriate queue configuration to service process. • Consider priority system for most desirable segments and make other customer shift to off-peak period. • Consider separate queues based on urgency, duration and premium pricing of service. • Shorten customer's perceptions of waiting time and make their waits more comfortable.	• Not applicable, but the queuing system can still collect data on number and type of transactions and customers served. The same applied to reservations systems below.
Inventory demand using a reservations system	• Focus on yield and reserve capacity for less price sensitive customers. • Consider a priority system for important segments. • Make other customers shift to off-peak periods.	• Clarify that capacity is available and let customers make reservations at their preferred time slots.

used to reshape demand patterns. Although each element is discussed separately, effective demand management efforts often require changes in several elements concurrently.

Use Price and Non-monetary Costs to Manage Demand. One of the most direct ways to balance supply and demand is through the use of pricing. The lure of lower prices may encourage at least some people to change the timing of their behavior, whether for shopping, travel, or sending in equipment for repair. Non-monetary costs may have a similar effect too. For instance, customers who dislike spending time waiting in crowded and unpleasant conditions will try to come during less busy periods.

For the monetary price of a service to be effective as a demand management tool, managers must have some sense of the shape and slope of a product demand curve. They must understand how the demanded quantity of the service responds to the increases or decreases in the price per unit at a particular point in time. It is important to determine whether the demand curve for a specific service varies sharply from one time period to another. For instance, will the same person be willing to pay more for a weekend stay in a hotel on Cape Cod in summer than in winter when the weather can be freezing cold? The answer is probably yes. If so, very different pricing schemes may be needed to fill capacity in each time period.

Complicating matters further, there are typically separate demand curves for different segments within each time period (e.g., business travelers are usually less price sensitive than tourists, as discussed in Chap. 6 on service pricing).

One of the most difficult tasks facing service marketers is to determine the nature of all these different demand curves. Historical data (often from revenue management systems), research, trial and error, and analysis of parallel situations in other locations or in comparable services, are all ways of understanding the situation. Many service businesses explicitly recognize the existence of different demand curves by designing distinct products with physical and non-physical design elements (or rate fences) for their key segments, each priced at levels appropriate to the demand curve of a particular segment. In essence, each segment receives a variation of the basic product, with value being added to the core service through supplementary services to appeal to higher paying segments. For instance, in computer and printing service firms, product enhancement takes the form of faster turnaround time and more specialized services. In each case, the objective is to maximize the revenues received from each segment.

However, when capacity is limited, the goal in a profit-seeking business should be to ensure that as much capacity as possible is utilized by the most profitable segments available at any given time. For instance, airlines hold a certain number of seats for business passengers paying full fare, and place restrictive conditions on excursion fares for tourists (using non-physical rate fences such as requiring advance purchase and a Saturday night stay) in order to prevent business travelers from taking advantage of cheap fares designed to attract tourists who can help fill the aircraft. Pricing strategies of this nature are known as revenue management and are discussed in Chap. 6.

Change Product Elements. Sometimes, pricing alone will be ineffective in managing demand. The opening vignette is a good case in point — in the absence of skiing opportunities, no skiers would buy lift tickets on a midsummer's day at any price. It is the same for a variety of other seasonal businesses. Thus, educational institutions offer weekend and summer programs for adults and senior citizens, small pleasure boats offer cruises in the summer and a dockside venue for private functions in winter months. These firms recognize that no amount of price discounting is likely to develop business when it is out of season, and that a new service product targeted at different segments is instead needed to encourage demand.

There can even be variations in the product offering during the course of a 24-hour period. Some restaurants provide a good example of this, marking the passage of the hours with the changing of menus and levels of service, variations in lighting and decor, opening and closing of the bar, and the presence or absence of entertainment. The goal is to appeal to different needs within the same group of customers, to reach out to different customer segments, or do both, according to the time of day. Product elements can also be changed to increase capacity during peak periods — for example, the lunch menu is designed to contain only dishes that can be prepared quickly during the busy lunch period.

Modify Place and Time of Delivery. Rather than seeking to modify the demand for a service that continues to be offered at the same time in the same place, firms can also respond to market needs by modifying the time and place of delivery. The following basic options are available:

- *Vary the times when the service is available.* This strategy reflects changing customer preference by day of week, by season, and so forth. Theaters and cinema complexes often offer matinees on weekends when people have more leisure time throughout the day. During the summer, cafes and restaurants may stay open later as people are generally inclined to enjoy the longer balmier evenings outdoors. Shops may extend their opening hours in the weeks leading up to Christmas or during school holidays.

- *Offer the service to customers at a new location.* One approach is to operate mobile units that take the service to customers, rather than requiring them to visit fixed-site service locations. Mobile car wash services, in-office tailoring services, home-delivered meals and catering services, and vans equipped with primary care medical facilities are examples of this. A cleaning and repair firm that wishes to generate business during low demand periods might offer free pickup and delivery of movable items that need servicing.

Promotion and Education. Even if other variables of the marketing mix remain unchanged, communication efforts alone may be able to help facilitate smooth demand. Signage, advertising, publicity, and sales messages can be used to educate customers about peak periods and encourage them to make use of the service at off-peak times when there will be fewer delays.[5] Examples include the US Postal Service requests to "Mail Early for Christmas", public transport messages urging non-commuters — such as shoppers or tourists — to avoid the cramped conditions of commuting hours during peak periods, and communications from sales representatives for industrial maintenance firms advising customers of periods when preventive maintenance work can be done quickly. In addition, management can ask service personnel (or intermediaries such as travel agents) to encourage customers with flexible schedules to consider off-peak travel periods.

Changes in pricing, product characteristics, and distribution must be communicated clearly. If a firm wants to obtain a particular response to the variations in the marketing mix elements, it must fully inform customers about their options. As discussed in Chap. 7, short-term promotions that combine both pricing and communication elements as well as other incentives may provide customers with attractive incentives to shift the timing of service usage.

Not all demand is desirable. In fact, some requests for service are inappropriate and make it difficult for the organization to respond to the legitimate needs of its target customers. For example, many calls to emergency numbers such as 911 are not cases that the fire department, the police, or ambulance services should be dispatched to. Such calls make it difficult for the organization to respond to the actual emergency cases. *Service Insights 9.1* shows how a marketing campaign was used to reduce undesirable demand and free up the capacity. Discouraging undesirable demand through marketing campaigns or screening procedures will not eliminate random fluctuations in the remaining demand. However, it may help to keep peak demand levels within the service capacity of the organization.

SERVICE INSIGHTS 9.1
Discouraging Demand for Non-emergency Calls

Have you ever wondered what it is like to be a dispatcher for an emergency telephone service such as 911? People differ widely in what they consider to be an emergency.

Imagine yourself in the huge communications room at Police Headquarters in New York. A gray-haired sergeant is talking patiently by phone to a woman who has dialed 911 because her cat has run up a tree and she was afraid it will get stuck there. "Ma'am, have you ever seen a cat skeleton in a tree?" the sergeant asks her. "All those cats get down somehow, don't they?" After the woman has hung up, the sergeant turns to a visitor and shrugs. "These kinds of calls keep pouring in," he says. "What can you do?"

The trouble is, when people call the emergency number with complaints about noisy parties next door, pleas to rescue cats, or requests to turn off leaking fire hydrants, they may be slowing the response times to cases that actually involve fires, heart attacks, or violent crimes.

At one point, the situation in New York City became so bad that officials were forced to develop a marketing campaign to discourage the public from making inappropriate requests for emergency assistance through the 911 number. What seemed like an emergency to the caller — a beloved cat stuck up a tree, a noisy party preventing a tired person from getting much needed sleep — was not a life (or property) threatening situation that the city's emergency services were poised to resolve. A communications campaign using a variety of media, was developed to urge the public not to call 911 unless they were reporting a *dangerous* emergency. For help in resolving other matters, they were asked to call their local police station or other city agencies. The ad shown below appeared on New York buses and subways.

INVENTORY DEMAND THROUGH WAITING LINES AND QUEUING SYSTEMS

As seen in the previous section, there are a variety of tactics for balancing demand and supply. But what is a manager supposed to do when the possibilities for shaping demand and adjusting capacity have been exhausted, and yet supply and demand are still out of balance? Not taking any action and leaving customers to sort things out on their own is no recipe for customer satisfaction. Rather than allowing matters to degenerate, customer-oriented firms must try to develop strategies to ensure order, predictability, and fairness. Therefore, for services which regularly face demand that exceeds capacity, managers often need to take steps to inventory demand.

Demands can be inventoried in two ways: (1) by asking customers to wait in line, usually on a first-come, first-served basis, or by offering customers more advanced queuing systems (e.g., systems that take into account urgency, price, or importance of the customer), and (2) by offering customers the opportunity of reserving or booking service capacity in advance. We will discuss the wait-line and queuing systems in this section, and reservation systems in the next.

Waiting Is a Universal Phenomenon

Waiting is something that occurs everywhere. Waiting lines — known to operations researchers (and the British) as "queues" — occur whenever the number of arrivals at a facility exceeds the capacity of the system to process them. In a very real sense, queues are basically a symptom of unresolved capacity management problems. Analysis and modeling of queues is a well-established branch of operations management. Queuing theory has been traced back to 1917, when a Danish telephone engineer was charged with determining how large the switching unit in a telephone system had to be to keep the number of busy signals within reason.[6]

Nobody likes to wait or to be kept waiting. It is boring, time-wasting, and sometimes physically uncomfortable, especially if there is nowhere to sit or if you are outdoors. Almost every organization faces the problem of waiting lines somewhere in its operation. People are kept waiting on the phone, listening to recorded messages such as "your call is important to us", they line up with their supermarket carts to check out their grocery purchases, and they wait for their bills after a restaurant meal. They sit in their cars waiting to enter drive-in car washes and to pay at toll booths. Some physical queues are geographically dispersed. Travelers wait at many different locations for the taxis they have ordered by phone to arrive and pick them up.

A survey in the US revealed that the waiting lines most dreaded by Americans are those in doctors' offices (cited by 27%) and in government departments that issue motor vehicle registrations and drivers' licenses (26%), followed by grocery stores (18%) and airports (14%).[7] Situations that make it even worse at retail check-outs include slow or inefficient cashiers, a shopper who changes her mind about an item that has already been rung up, or one who leaves the line to run back for an item. It does not take long before people start to lose their cool; one-third of Americans say they get frustrated after waiting in line for 10 minutes or less, although women report more patience than men and are more likely to chat with others to pass the time while waiting.

Physical and inanimate objects wait for processing too. Customers' emails sit in customer service staff's inboxes, appliances wait to be repaired, and checks wait to be cleared at a bank. In each instance, a customer may be waiting for the outcome of that work — an answer to an email, an appliance that is working again, and a check credited to a customer's balance.

Managing Waiting Lines

The problem of reducing customer waiting time often requires a multi-pronged approach, as seen by the approach taken by Disney, described in *Service Insights 9.2*. Increasing capacity by simply adding more space or staff is not always the best solution in situations where customer satisfaction must be balanced against cost considerations. Like Disney, managers should consider a variety of ways, including:

1. Rethinking the design of the queuing system (i.e., queue configuration and virtual waits).

2. Tailoring the queuing system to different market segments (e.g., by urgency, price, or importance of the customer).

3. Managing customers' behavior and their perceptions of the wait (i.e., use the psychology of waiting to make waits less unpleasant).

4. Installing a reservations system (e.g., use reservations, booking or appointments to distribute demand).

4. Redesigning processes to shorten the time of each transaction (e.g., by installing self-service machines).

Points 1 to 4 are discussed in the next few sections of this chapter. Point 5 is discussed in Chap. 8 on customer service process redesign.

SERVICE INSIGHTS 9.2
Disney Turns Queue Management into a Science

Have you ever been in a queue at Disneyland? Very often, we may not realize how long we have been waiting as they are many sights to see while queuing. We may be watching a video, playing with interactive technology and touch screens stationed along the way, looking at other customers enjoying themselves, or reading the various posters on the wall, and enjoying comfort in the form of fans and shade that help us cool off. As our waits are occupied and comfortable, we may not realize that a long time has passed. Disney's theme park line management is an extension of their entertainment philosophy!

At Disney World's 'Dumbo the Flying Elephant' ride, children and their parents can play in an interactive room resembling a circus tent. While playing, these children are also waiting for a buzzer to signal their turn to go onto the outdoor line for the ride. These children playing in the tent do not have the perception of waiting in line, but that is exactly what they are doing!

Disney has taken the management of waiting lines to another level. At Walt Disney World, there is a Disney Operational Command Center, where the technicians are monitoring the queues to make sure that they are not too long and people are moving along. To them, patience is not a virtue in the theme park business. Inside the Command Center, they have computer programs, video cameras, digital maps of the park, and other tools to help them spot where there might be queues that are too long. Once there is a wait problem, they will send a staff to fix the problem immediately. The problem may be dealt with in several ways. For example, they could send a Disney character to entertain the waiting customers. Alternatively, they could deploy more capacity. For example, if there is a long queue for the boat ride, then they will deploy more boats so that the queue moves faster. Disney World is divided into different lands. If there is less crowd in one land compared to another, they may re-route a mini-parade towards that area, so that the crowds will follow and the crowd distribution becomes more even. They have also added video games to waiting areas.

With the Command Center in place, they have managed to increase the average number of rides a visitor to Magic Kingdom normally takes, from nine rides to 10 rides. Disney will continue to experiment with different types of technology to help them manage customer waiting time. They are experimenting with smartphone technology and the Walt Disney World® app to see how it can be used to help manage waiting lines. Disney does all this in the hopes that customers will not be frustrated by the waits, and thus return more often.

Sources: Brooks Barnes, "Disney Tackles Major Theme Park Problem: Lines," *The New York Times*, December 27, 2010, http://www.nytimes.com/2010/12/28/business/media/28disney.html; Eamon McNiff, Sarah Lang, and Kimberly Launier, "Disney Theme Parks Reimagining the Wait in Line", *ABC News*, April 23, 2014; and https://itunes.apple.com/en/app/my-disney-experience-walt/id547436543?mt=8 ; all accessed on 6 April, 2016.

Different Queue Configurations

There are different types of queues, and the challenge for managers is to select the most appropriate type. Fig. 9.5 shows diagrams of several types you may have experienced yourself.

Figure 9.5: Alternative queue configurations

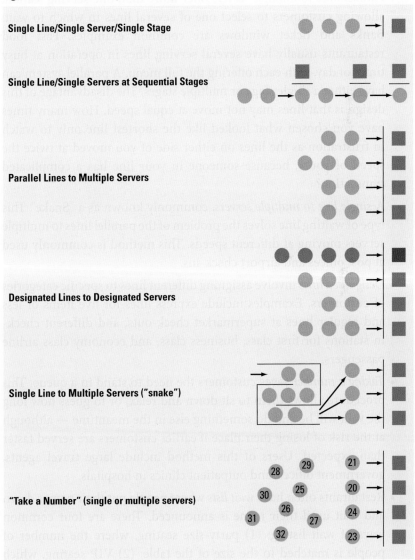

- In *single line sequential stages,* customers proceed through several serving operations, as in a cafeteria. Bottlenecks may occur at any stage where the process takes longer to execute than at previous stages. Many cafeterias have lines at the cash register because the cashier takes longer to calculate how much you owe and to return the change, than the servers take to slap food on your plate.

- *Parallel lines to multiple servers* offer more than one serving station, allowing customers to select one of several lines in which to wait. Banks and ticket windows are common examples. Fast food restaurants usually have several serving lines in operation at busy times of day, with each offering the full menu. A parallel system can have either a single stage or multiple stages. The disadvantage of this design is that lines may not move at equal speed. How many times have you chosen what looked like the shortest line only to watch in frustration as the lines on either side of you moved at twice the speed of yours, because someone in your line has a complicated transaction?

- A *single line to multiple servers*, commonly known as a "Snake". This type of waiting line solves the problem of the parallel lines to multiple servers moving at different speeds. This method is commonly used at post offices and airport check-ins.

- *Designated lines* involve assigning different lines to specific categories of customers. Examples include express lines for five items or less and regular lines at supermarket check-outs, and different check-in stations for first class, business class, and economy class airline passengers.

- *Taking a number* saves customers the need to stand in a queue. This procedure allows them to sit down and relax, or to guess how long the wait will be and do something else in the meantime — although at the risk of losing their place if earlier customers are served faster than expected. Users of this method include large travel agents, government offices, and outpatient clinics in hospitals.

- Restaurants often have *wait lists* where people put their names down and wait until their name is announced. There are four common ways of wait listing: (1) party-size seating, where the number of people is matched to the size of the table; (2) VIP seating, which involves giving special rights to favored customers; (3) call-ahead seating, which allows people to phone before arriving on-site to hold a place on the wait list; and (4) large-party reservations. If customers are familiar with wait listing techniques, they are likely to view them to be fair. If not, VIP seating is viewed as especially unfair by guests who do not enjoy the priority treatment.[8]

Queues can also be a combination of different approaches. For instance, a cafeteria with a single serving line might offer two cash register stations at the final stage. Similarly, patients at a small medical clinic might visit a single receptionist for registration, proceed sequentially through multiple channels for testing, diagnosis, and treatment, and conclude by returning to a single line for payment at the receptionist's desk.

Research suggests that selecting the most suitable type of queue is important to customer satisfaction. Anat Rafaeli and her colleagues found that the way queues in a waiting area are laid out can produce feelings of injustice and unfairness in customers. Customers who waited in parallel lines to multiple servers reported significantly higher agitation and dissatisfaction with the fairness of the service delivery process than customers who waited in a single line ("snake") to access multiple servers. This result was despite the fact that both groups of customers waited the same amount of time and were involved in completely fair service processes.[9] The issue of perceived fairness arises as waiting customers are often very conscious of their own progress towards getting served. Perhaps you have watched resentfully as other diners who arrived at a busy restaurant later than you were given priority and leapfrogged the line. It does not seem fair, especially when you are hungry!

Virtual Waits

One of the problems associated with waiting in line is the waste of time this involves for customers. The "virtual queue" strategy is a creative way of taking the physical waiting out of the wait altogether. Instead, customers register their place in line on a terminal, which estimates the time at which they will reach the front of the virtual line and should return to claim their place.[10] Sushi Tei, a restaurant chain, implemented a self-service touch screen terminal where guests can simply select the party size, which allows the restaurant to match table sizes, enter their cell phone number

Figure 9.6 An innovating queuing system allows customers to enter a virtual queue for a table.

and then go shopping (Fig. 9.6). Diners will receive a text message confirming their booking, and the message contains a link where they can view in real time how many parties are still ahead of them in the queue. They will be called by an automated system five minutes before their table is available, and diners can confirm their booking (by pressing '1'), ask for an additional 15 minutes until they will reach back to the restaurant (by pressing '2'), or they can cancel their booking if they have made alternative plans (by pressing '3'). The restaurant has a long queue on weekend evenings, but this system helps them keep customers loyal and extends the time it operates at full capacity on busy days.

Service Insights 9.3 describes the virtual queuing systems used in two very different industries; a theme park and a call center.

The concept of virtual queues has many potential applications. Cruise ships, all-inclusive resorts, and restaurants can use this strategy if customers are willing to provide their cell phone numbers or remain within buzzing range of a firm-operated pager system.

SERVICE INSIGHTS 9.3
Waiting in a Virtual Queue

Disney is well-known for its efforts to give its theme park visitors information on how long they may have to wait to ride a particular attraction, and for entertaining guests while they are waiting in line. However, the company found that the long waits at its most popular attractions were still a major source of dissatisfaction and thus created an innovative solution.

The virtual-queue concept was first tested at Disney World. At the most popular attractions, guests were able to register their place in line with a computer and were then free to use the wait time visiting other places in the park. Surveys showed that guests who used the new system spent more money, saw more attractions, and had significantly higher satisfaction. After further refinement, the system, now named Fastpass, was introduced at the five most popular attractions at Disney World, and was subsequently extended to all Disney parks worldwide. It is now used by more than 50 million guests a year.

Fastpass is easy to use. When guests approach a Fastpass attraction, they are given two clear choices — obtain a Fastpass ticket there and return at a designated time, or wait in a standby line. Signs indicate how long the wait is in each instance. The wait time for each line tends to be self-regulating, because a large difference between the two will lead to increasing numbers of people choosing the shorter line. In practice, the virtual wait tends to be slightly longer than the physical one. To use the Fastpass option, guests insert their park admission ticket into a special turnstile and receive a Fastpass ticket stating a return time. Guests have some flexibility because the system allows them a 60-minute window beyond the printed return time.

Just like the Fastpass system, call centers also use virtual queues. There are different types of virtual queuing systems for call centers. The first-in, first-out queuing system is very common. When callers call in, they will hear a message that informs them of the estimated wait time for the call to be taken by an agent. The caller can (1) wait in the queue and get connected to an agent when his turn arrives, or (2) choose to receive a call back. When the caller chooses the latter option, he has to enter his telephone number and tell his name. He then hangs up the phone and his virtual place in the queue is kept. When he is nearly at the head of the queue, the system calls the customer back and puts him at the head of the queue where an agent will attend to him next. In both situations, the customer is unlikely to complain. In the first situation, it is the customer's choice to wait in the queue, and he can still do something else as he already knows the estimated wait time. In the second situation, the person does not have to wait for very long on the phone after the call back, before reaching an agent. The call center also benefits as fewer frustrated customers will take up the valuable time of the agents by complaining about how long they had to wait. In addition, firms also reduce aborted or missed calls from customers.

Source: Duncan Dickson, Robert C. Ford, and Bruce Laval, "Managing Real and Virtual Waits in Hospitality and Service Organizations," *Cornell Hotel and Restaurant Administration Quarterly* 46, February 2005, 52–68; "Virtual Queue," Wikipedia, www.en.wikipeidao.org/wiki/virtual_queuing; and A FASTPASS Guide for Disneyland and California Adventure, http://dlrprepschool.com/a-fastpass-guide-for-disneyland-and-california-adventure ; accessed on 25 March, 2016.

Queuing Systems Can Be Tailored to Market Segments

Although the basic rule in most queuing systems is 'first come, first served', not all queuing systems are organized in that way. Market segmentation is sometimes used to design queuing strategies that set different priorities for different types of customers. Allocation to separate queuing areas may be based on any of the following:

- *Urgency of the job.* At many hospital emergency units, a nurse is assigned to greet incoming patients, and decide which patients require priority medical treatment and which patients can be safely asked to register, sit down and wait for their turn.

- *Duration of service transaction.* Banks, supermarkets, and other retail services often have "express lanes" for shorter, less complicated tasks.

- *Payment of a premium price.* Airlines usually offer separate check-in lines for first-, business- and economy-class passengers, with a higher ratio of personnel to passengers in the first- and business-class lines, resulting in reduced waits for those who paid more for their tickets. At some airports, premium passengers may also enjoy faster lanes for the security check.

- *Importance of the customer.* Members of frequent-flyer clubs frequently get priority wait-listing. For example, the next available seat is given to a platinum card holder of the airline's loyalty program, and these members can also jump the queue with priority access to call centers, and even when travelling economy class, members of frequent-flyer clubs can use the shorter business class check-in lines.

CUSTOMER PERCEPTIONS OF WAITING TIME

People do not like wasting their time on unproductive activities any more than they like wasting money. Customer dissatisfaction with delays in receiving service often can stimulate strong emotions, even anger.[11] In fact, it has been found that if customers are dissatisfied with the wait, they must be more satisfied with the service to have the same level of loyalty as customers who were satisfied with the wait.[12]

The Psychology of Waiting Time

Research shows people often think they waited longer for a service than they actually did. For instance, studies of public transportation use have shown that travelers perceive the time spent waiting for a bus or train as passing 1.5 to 7 times more slowly than the time actually spent traveling in the vehicle.[13]

Savvy service marketers recognize that customers experience waiting time in different ways, depending on the circumstances. Why are some willing to wait for 50% of their time at an amusement park, but complain when they have to wait for 20 minutes for a taxi? David Maister and other researchers have the following suggestions on how to use the psychology of waiting to make waits less stressful and unpleasant[14]:

- *Unoccupied time feels longer than occupied time.* The noted philosopher William James observed, "Boredom results from being attentive to the passage of time itself". When you are sitting around with nothing to do, time seems to crawl. The challenge for service organizations is to give customers something to do or to distract them while waiting. For example, BMW car owners can wait in comfort in BMW service centers where waiting areas are furnished with designer furniture, large-screen TVs, Wi-Fi, magazines, and freshly brewed cappuccinos. Many customers even bring their own entertainment in the form of a smart phone or tablet.

Some restaurants manage the waiting problem by inviting dinner guests to have a drink in the bar until their table is ready (that approach makes money for the house as well as keeps the customer occupied). In similar fashion, guests waiting in line for a show at a casino may find themselves queuing in a corridor lined with slot-machines.

- *Solo waits feel longer than group waits.* It is nice to wait with people you know, and talking to them is one way of helping to pass the time while waiting. However, not everyone is comfortable talking to a stranger.

- *Physically uncomfortable waits feel longer than comfortable waits.* "My feet are killing me!" is one of the most often heard comments when people are forced to stand in line for a long time. Whether they are seated or standing, waiting seems more burdensome if the temperature is too hot or too cold, if it is drafty or windy, or if there is no protection from rain or snow.

- *Pre- and post-process waits feel longer than in-process waits.* Waiting to buy a ticket to enter a theme park is different from waiting to ride on a roller coaster once you're in the park.

- *Unfair waits are longer than equitable waits.* Perceptions about what is fair or unfair sometimes vary from one culture or country to another. In the United States, Canada, or Britain, people may expect everybody to wait their turn in line and are likely to get irritated if they see others jumping ahead or being given priority for no apparent reason. When people perceive the wait as fair, it reduces the negative effect of waiting.

- *Unfamiliar waits seem longer than familiar ones.* Frequent users of a service know what to expect and are less likely to worry while waiting. New or occasional users, in contrast, are often nervous, wondering not only about the probable length of the wait but also about what happens next.

- *Uncertain waits are longer than known, finite waits.* Although any wait can be frustrating, we tend to mentally prepare ourselves to a wait of a known length. It is the unknown that keeps us on edge. Imagine waiting for a delayed flight and not being told how long the delay will be. You do not know whether you have the time to get up and walk about in the terminal, whether to stay at the gate in case the flight is called any minute, and whether you will make your connecting flight on the other end.

- *Unexplained waits are longer than explained waits.* Have you ever been in a subway or an elevator that has stopped for no apparent reason, without any announcements telling you why? In addition to uncertainty about the length of the wait, there is added worry about what is going to happen. Has there been an accident on the line? Will you be stuck there for hours?

- *Anxiety makes waits seem longer.* Can you remember waiting for someone to show up at the arranged meeting time or rendezvous, and worrying about whether you had gotten the time or location correct? While waiting in unfamiliar locations, especially outdoors and at night, people often worry about their personal safety.

- *The more valuable or important the service, the longer people will wait.* People will queue up overnight under uncomfortable conditions to get good seats to a major concert or sports event expected to sell out fast.

INVENTORY DEMAND THROUGH RESERVATIONS SYSTEMS

As an alternative, or in addition, to waiting lines, reservations systems can be used to inventory demand. Ask someone what services come to mind when you talk about reservations and they will most likely cite airlines, hotels, restaurants, car rentals, and theaters. Use synonyms like "bookings" or "appointments" and they may add haircuts, visits to professionals such as doctors and consultants, vacation rentals, and service calls to fix anything from a broken refrigerator to a temperamental laptop. There are many benefits in having a reservations system:

- Customer dissatisfaction due to excessive waits can be avoided. One aim of reservations is to guarantee that service will be available when customers want it. Customers who hold reservations should be able to count on avoiding a queue, because they have been guaranteed service at a specific time.

- Reservations allow demand to be controlled and smoothed out in a more manageable way. A well-organized reservations system allows the organization to deflect demand for service from a first-choice time to earlier or later times, from one class of service to another ("upgrades" and "downgrades"), and even from first-choice locations to alternative ones, and thereby overall contributing to higher capacity utilization.

- Reservations systems enable the implementation of revenue management and serve to pre-sell a service to different customer segments (see Chap. 6 on revenue management). For example, requiring reservations for normal repair and maintenance allows management to make sure that some capacity will be kept free for handling emergency jobs. Since these are unpredictable, higher prices can be charged, which bring higher margins with them.

- Data from reservation systems also help organizations to prepare operational and financial projections for future periods. Systems vary from a simple appointments book using handwritten entries for a doctor's office to a central, computerized data bank for an airline's global operations.

The challenge in designing reservation systems is to make them fast and user-friendly for both staff and customers. Many firms now allow customers to make their own reservations on a self-service basis via their websites and smartphones. Whether they are talking to a reservations agent or making their own bookings, customers want quick answers about whether a service is available at a preferred time and at what price. They also appreciate it if the system can provide further information about the type of service they are reserving. For instance, can a hotel assign a specific room on request, or at least assign a room with a view of the lake rather than one with a view of the parking lot? Some businesses now even charge a fee for making a reservation (see *Service Insights 9.4*).

Of course, problems arise when customers fail to show up or when service firms overbook. Marketing strategies for dealing with these operational problems include requiring a deposit, canceling non-paid reservations after a certain time, and providing compensation to victims of overbooking were discussed in Chap. 6 on revenue management.

SERVICE INSIGHTS 9.4
Pay to Get That Hard-To-Get Table Reservation!

Today's Epicure is an exclusive online company that helps customers get table reservations at the most popular dining spots in New York, such as Carbone, Lafayette or The NoMad, where only people who are 'somebody' or have the right connections can secure a table. Even then, it can take several months of patient planning. The company is able to get a table on a specific day, and on short notice. Currently, the company focuses on areas where it is difficult to get reservations, namely New York City, Philadelphia, and the Hamptons. Individuals pay a membership fee of $1,000 to join and $125 per month for access to the service.

Pascal Riffaud, the entrepreneur behind this idea, was president of Personal Concierge International, a leading company providing exclusive concierge services in the United States. During his work experience as president of Personal Concierge, Riffaud built a large network of contacts with exclusive restaurants, allowing him to obtain those hard-to-get reservations.

His clients were delighted with his service and kept flooding him with requests for reservations. However, similar to earlier start-ups, there have been protests from restaurant owners who felt these types of services were upsetting their reservation systems and also selling their tables for a price. Even though these services cancel unsold reservations, restaurant owners feel these could have been sold to other customers who really wanted a table. As more start-ups offer similar service (see www.Table8.com and www.resy.com in Los Angeles), restaurants may have to rethink the way they handle reservations!

Sources: "Would you pay $1,000 for a dinner reservation? Meet the scalper selling table spots at New York's hottest restaurants", by Daily Mail Reporter, www.dailymail.co.uk/femail/article-2384867/Meet-Pascal-Riffaud-Today-s-Epicures-scalper-selling-table-spots-New-Yorks-hottest-restaurants.html#ixzz3VOp1ZIDb, https://www.todaysepicure.com, http://resy.com, all accessed on 25 March, 2016.

Reservations Strategies Should Focus on Yield

Increasingly, service firms are looking at their "yield" — the average revenue received per unit of capacity. Yield analysis forces managers to recognize the opportunity cost of selling capacity for a given date to a customer from one market segment when another might subsequently yield a higher rate. Think about the following problems facing sales managers for different types of service organizations with capacity limitations:

- Should a hotel accept an advance booking from a tour group of 200 room nights at $140 each, when some of these same room nights might possibly be sold later at short notice to business travelers at the full posted rate of $300?

- Should a railroad with 30 empty freight cars accept an immediate request for a shipment worth $1,400 per car or hold the cars for a few more days in the hopes of getting a priority shipment that would be twice as valuable?

- Should a print shop process all jobs on a first-come, first-served basis, with a guaranteed delivery time for each job, or should it charge a premium rate for "rush" work, and tell customers with "standard" jobs to expect some variability in completion dates?

Decisions on such problems deserve to be handled with a little more sophistication than just resorting to "the bird in the hand is worth two in the bush" formula. Good information based on detailed record-keeping of past usage supported by current market intelligence is the key to allocating the inventory of capacity among different segments. The decision to accept or reject business should be based on realistic estimates of the probabilities of obtaining higher rated business and on the awareness of the need to maintain established (and desirable) customer relationships. The more sophisticated approach of revenue management systems for allocating capacity to different "rate buckets" and setting prices was discussed in Chap. 6.

CREATE ALTERNATIVE USE FOR OTHERWISE WASTED CAPACITY

Even after professional management of capacity and demand, most service firms will still experience periods of excess capacity. However, not all unsold productive capacity has to be wasted, as alternative "demand" can be created by innovative firms. Many firms take a strategic approach to the disposition of anticipated surplus capacity, allocating it in advance to build relationships with customers, suppliers, employees, and intermediaries.[15] Possible uses for otherwise wasted capacity include:

- *Use capacity for service differentiation.* When capacity utilization is low, service employees can go all the way to truly 'wow' their customers. A firm that wants to build customer loyalty and market share should use a slack in operations to focus on outstanding customer service. This can include extra attention paid to the customer, allocation of preferred seating, and the likes.

- *Reward your best customers and build loyalty.* This can be done through special promotions as part of a loyalty program, while ensuring that existing revenues are not cannibalized.

- *Customer and channel development.* Provide free or heavily discounted trials for prospective customers and for intermediaries who sell to end customers.

- *Reward employees.* In certain industries such as restaurants, beach resorts, or cruise lines, capacity can be used to reward employees and their families to build loyalty. This can improve employee satisfaction and provide employees an understanding of the service as experienced from the customer's perspective and thereby raising performance.

- *Barter free capacity.* Service firms often can save costs and increase capacity utilization by bartering capacity with their own suppliers. Among the most widely bartered services are advertising space or airtime, airline seats, and hotel rooms.

CONCLUSION

As many capacity-constrained service organizations have heavy fixed costs, even modest improvements in capacity utilization tend to have a significant effect on the bottom line. This chapter has shown how managers can manage productive capacity and demand, and improve customers' waiting and queuing experiences. Managing capacity and demand for a service at a particular place and time closely links back to what is covered in past chapters, including decisions on product elements and tiering of service seen in Chap. 4, place and time of service delivery seen in Chap. 5, revenue management as discussed in Chap. 6, promotion and education as discussed in Chap. 7, and designing and balancing the capacity of service processes as discussed in Chap. 8.

CHAPTER SUMMARY

Building Blocks of Effective Capacity & Demand Management

Understand Patterns of Demand

- Understand patterns of demand by answering the following questions:
  - Do demand levels follow predictable cycles?
  - What are the underlying causes of these cyclical variations?
  - Can demand be disaggregated by market segment?
- Determine drivers of demand by segment (e.g., demand for routine maintenance versus emergency repairs)

Define Productive Capacity

- Determine which aspects of capacity need to be managed carefully.
- Productive capacity can include:
  - Facilities (e.g., hotel rooms)
  - Equipment (e.g., MRI machines)
  - Labor (e.g., consultants);
  - Infrastructure (e.g., electricity networks)

Manage Capacity

- Adjust capacity to more closely match demand.
  Available options include:
  - Stretch capacity
  - Schedule downtime during low periods
  - Cross-train employees
  - Use part-time employees
  - Invite customers to perform self-service
  - Ask customers to share capacity
  - Design capacity to be flexible
  - Rent or share extra facilities and equipment

Manage Demand

Insufficient Capacity

- Reduce & shift demand through marketing mix elements: Do demand levels follow predictable cycles?
  - Increase price
  - Product design (e.g., don't offer time-consuming services during peak periods)
  - Time and place of delivery (e.g., extend opening hours)
  - Promotion & education (e.g., communicate peak periods)
- Inventory demand using queuing systems
  - Tailor queuing system to market segments (e.g., by urgency, price, and importance of customers)
  - Use psychology of waiting time to make waits less unpleasant
- Inventory demand using reservations systems
  - Control demand and smoothen it
  - Focus on yield

Insufficient Demand

- Increase demand through marketing mix elements :
  - Lower price
  - Product design (e.g., find additional value propositions for the same capacity)
  - Add locations (e.g., create additional demand through home delivery)
  - Promotion & education (e.g., offer promotion bundles)
- Create use for otherwise wasted capacity:
  - Use for differentiation
  - Reward your loyal customers
  - Development of new customers
  - Reward employees
  - Barter capacity

CHAPTER 10

Crafting The Service Environment

Managers…need to develop a better understanding of the interface between the resources they manipulate in atmospherics and the experience they want to create for the customer.

Jean-Charles Chebat and *Laurette Dubé*
Professors of Marketing at HEC Montréal Business School
and McGill University, Montréal respectively

Restaurant design has become as compelling an element as menu, food and wine…in determining a restaurant's success.

Danny Meyer
New York City restaurateur and CEO
of Union Square Hospitality Group

SERVICE ENVIRONMENTS — AN IMPORTANT ELEMENT OF THE SERVICE MARKETING MIX

The physical service environment customers experience plays a key role in shaping the service experience and enhancing (or undermining) customer satisfaction, especially in high-contact, people-processing services.[1] Disney theme parks are often cited as vivid examples of service environments that make customers feel comfortable and highly satisfied, and leave a long-lasting impression. In fact, organizations such as hospitals, hotels, restaurants, and offices of professional service firms have come to recognize that the service environment is an important element of their services marketing mix and overall value proposition.

Designing the service environment is an art that involves a lot of time and effort, and can be expensive to implement. Service environments, also called *servicescapes*, relate to the style and appearance of the physical surroundings and other experiential elements encountered by customers at service delivery sites.[2] Once designed and built, service environments are not easy to change. The focus of this chapter is on the key dimensions of service environments in the servicescape model and not much on its other aspects.

WHAT IS THE PURPOSE OF SERVICE ENVIRONMENTS?

The reason why many service firms take so much trouble to shape the environment in which their customers and service personnel will interact will need to be examined. For many service firms, there are four main purposes of servicescapes: (1) shape customers' experiences and behaviors; (2) signal quality and position, differentiate and strengthen the brand; (3) be a core component of the value proposition; and (4) facilitate the service encounter and enhance both service quality and productivity. Each of these four purposes are discussed in the following sections.

Shape Customers' Service Experiences and Behaviors

For organizations that deliver high-contact services, the design of the physical environment and the way in which tasks are performed by customer–contact personnel play a vital role in shaping the nature of customers' experiences. Physical surroundings help to "engineer" appropriate feelings and reactions in customers and employees, which in turn can help to build loyalty to the firm.[3] The environment and its accompanying atmosphere can affect buyer behavior in important ways, and this chapter describes how the design elements of the service environment can make customers feel excited or relaxed, help them find their way in complex servicescapes such as hospitals or airports, and shape their quality perceptions and important outcomes such as buying behavior, satisfaction and repeat purchase.

Signal Quality, and Position, Differentiate and Strengthen the Brand

Services are often intangible and customers cannot assess their quality well, so customers use the service environment as an important quality proxy, and firms go to great lengths to signal quality and portray the desired image.[4] For example, the reception area of successful professional service firms such as investment banks or management consulting firms, where the decor and furnishings tend to be elegant and are designed to impress.

Most people infer higher merchandise quality if the goods are displayed in an environment with a prestigious image rather than in one that feels cheap.[5] Consider Fig. 10.1, which shows the lobbies of two hotels. These are two different types of hotels catering to two very different target segments. One caters to younger guests who love fun and have low budgets, and the other caters to a more mature, affluent and prestigious clientele including business travelers. Each of these two servicescapes clearly communicates and reinforces each hotel's respective positioning and sets service expectations as guests arrive.

Figure 10.1: Compare the two hotel lobbies; different types of hotels have very different target segments.

Servicescapes often play an important part in building a service firm's brand, such as the role outlet design played in building Starbucks' brand! Likewise, Apple is famous for its sleek design, and their shops are no exception. With their airy and minimalist interiors, white lighting, silver steel, and beige timber, Apple Stores create a bright, open and futuristic servicescape that provides a carefree and casual atmosphere. Apple's flagship stores feature dramatic locations such as inside the Louvre in Paris, or a 40-foot-high glass cylinder in Shanghai. Apple's retail operations are an important part of its business — it has 453 retail stores in 16 countries; of its 43,000 employees in the US, 30,000 work at Apple Stores, and its sales per square foot of $4,551 per annum in 2014 were the highest of any retailer in the US![6] The Apple Stores' ability to deliver a consistent, differentiated, and high quality service experience reinforces Apple's brand image, and is consistent with the upmarket and high quality positioning of its products.

Core Component of the Value Proposition

The servicescape can even be a core component of a firm's value proposition. Consider how effectively many amusement parks use the servicescape concept to engineer their visitors' service experiences as

Figure 10.2: In LEGOLAND®, the servicescape is part of the value proposition.

Figure 10.3: At the Mirage Hotel and Casino in Las Vegas, an erupting volcano is part of the servicescape.

they come to these parks to enjoy the environment and rides. The clean environment of Disneyland or Denmark's LEGOLAND® (Fig. 10.2), in addition to employees in colorful costumes all contribute to the sense of fun and excitement that visitors encounter upon arrival and throughout their visit.

Resort hotels illustrate how servicescapes can become a core part of the value proposition. Club Med's villages, designed to create a totally carefree atmosphere, may have provided the original inspiration for "getaway" holiday environments. However, new destination resorts are not only far more luxurious than Club Med, but also draw inspiration from theme parks to create fantasy environments both indoors and outdoors. Perhaps the most extreme examples can be found in Las Vegas. Facing competition from numerous casinos in other locations, Las Vegas has repositioned itself away from being a purely adult destination, to a somewhat more wholesome entertainment destination where families too can have fun. The gambling is still there, but many of the large, recently built hotels (or rebuilt) have been transformed by adding visually attractive features, e.g., erupting "volcanoes", (Fig. 10.3) mock sea battles, striking reproductions of Paris, pyramids of Egypt, and Venice and its canals.

Figure 10.4: Bangalore Express City, a restaurant in the city of London, is designed to optimize expensive rental space.

Facilitate the Service Encounter and Enhance Productivity

Service environments are often designed to facilitate the service encounter and increase productivity. For example, childcare centers use toy outlines on walls and floors to show where toys should be returned after use. In fast food restaurants and school cafeterias, strategically located tray-return stands and notices on walls remind customers to return their trays. As shown in the Bangalore Express Restaurant (Fig. 10.4), environments can be designed to optimize the use of expensive rental space. Finally, *Service Insights 10.1* shows how the design of hospitals helps patients recover and employees perform better.

SERVICE INSIGHTS 10.1
The Hospital Servicescape and
Its Effects on Patients and Employees[7]

Thankfully, most of us do not have to stay in hospitals. If it should happen, we hope our stay will allow us to recover in a suitable environment. However, what is considered suitable in a hospital?

Patients may contract infections while in hospital, feel stressed due to the contact with many strangers, and yet become bored without much to do, dislike the food, or are unable to rest well. All these 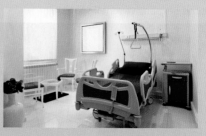 factors may delay a patient's recovery. Medical workers usually work under demanding conditions and may contract infectious diseases, be stressed by the emotional labor of dealing with difficult patients, or be at risk of injury when exposed to various types of medical equipment. Research has shown that greater care in designing the hospital servicescape reduces these risks and contributes to patient well-being and recovery, as well as staff welfare and productivity. The recommendations include:

- *Provide single-bed rooms.* These can lower the number of infections caught in the hospital, improve rest and sleep quality by lessening disturbance caused by other patients sharing the room, increase patient privacy, facilitate social support by families, and even improve communication between staff and patients.

- *Reduce noise levels.* This leads to decreased stress levels for staff, and improved sleep for patients.

- *Provide distractions for patients,* including areas of greenery and nature for them to visit or see from their beds, personalized televisions with headphones to avoid disturbing others, internet access for tablets and smart phones, and perhaps a reading room with a library with newspapers, magazines, and books. These can all aid to patient recovery.

- *Improve lighting,* especially access to natural light. A lighted environment increases cheerfulness in the building. Natural lighting can lead to a reduced length of stay for patients. Hospital staff can work better under proper lighting and make fewer errors.

- *Improve ventilation* and air filtration to reduce the transmission of airborne viruses and improve the overall air quality in the building.
- *Develop user-friendly "wayfinding" systems.* Hospitals are complex buildings, and it can be frustrating for many first-time and infrequent visitors when they cannot find their way around, especially when rushing to see a hospitalized loved one.
- *Design the layout* of patient care units and location of nurse stations to reduce unnecessary walking within the building, and the fatigue and time wastage it can cause. This way the quality of patient care can be improved. Well-designed layouts also enhance staff communication and activities.

A well-designed service environment makes customers feel good, boosts their satisfaction and allows the firm to influence their behavior (e.g., adhering to the service script and prompting impulse purchases). As service quality is often difficult to assess, customers frequently use the service environment as an important quality signal; therefore, the service environment can play a major part in shaping customers' perception of a firm's image and positioning, and can even be a core part of the firm's value proposition. Finally, a well-designed service environment will enhance the productivity of the service operation.

THE THEORY BEHIND CONSUMER RESPONSES TO SERVICE ENVIRONMENTS

It is evident why service firms take so much effort to design the service environment, but why does the service environment has such important effects on people and their behaviors? The field of environmental psychology studies how people respond to particular environments, and its theories can be applied to better understand and manage how customers behave in different service settings.

Feelings Are a Key Driver of Customer Responses to Service Environments

Two important models help to better understand consumer responses to service environments. The first, the Mehrabian–Russell Stimulus-Response Model holds that our feelings are central to how we respond to different elements in the environment. The second, Russell's Model of Affect, focuses on how we can better understand those feelings and their implications on response behaviors.

The Mehrabian–Russell Stimulus-Response Model. Fig. 10.5 displays a simple yet fundamental model of how people respond to environments. The model holds that the conscious and unconscious perception and interpretation of the environment influences how people feel in that setting.[8] People's feelings in turn drive their responses to that environment. Feelings are central to the model, which posits that feelings, rather than perceptions or thoughts, drive behavior. Similar environments can lead to very different feelings and subsequent responses.

Figure 10.5: The Mehrabian–Russell Stimulus-Response Model: a model of environmental responses.

Figure 10.6: The Russell Model of Affect

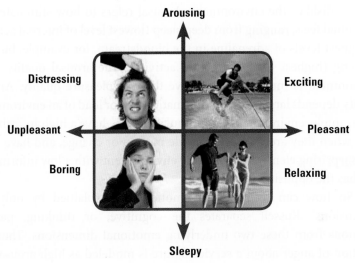

For example, we may dislike being in a crowded department store with lots of other customers, find ourselves unable to get what we want as quickly as we wish, and thus seek to avoid that environment. We do not simply avoid an environment because of the presence of many people around us; rather we are deterred by the unpleasant feelings of crowding, people being in our way, lacking perceived control, and not being able to get what we want at our pace. However, if we were not in a rush and felt excited about being part of the crowd during seasonal festivities in the very same environment, then we might derive feelings of pleasure and excitement that would make us want to stay and enjoy the experience.

In environmental psychology research, the typical outcome variable studied is the "approach" or "avoidance" of an environment. In services marketing, there is a long list of additional outcomes that a firm might want to manage, including how much time and money people spend, and how satisfied they are with the service experience after they have left the firm's premises.

Russell's Model of Affect. Given that affect or feelings are central to how people respond to an environment, Russell's Model of Affect (Fig. 10.6) is widely used to understand those feelings better. It suggests that emotional responses to environment can be described along two main dimensions of pleasure and arousal.[9] Pleasure is a direct, subjective response to the environment, depending on how much an individual likes or dislikes the environment. Arousal refers to how stimulated the individual feels, ranging from deep sleep (lowest level of internal activity) to highest levels of adrenaline in the bloodstream, for example, bungee-jumping (highest level of internal activity). The arousal quality of an environment is much less subjective than its pleasure quality. Arousal quality depends largely on the information rate or load of an environment. For example, environments are stimulating (i.e., have a high information rate) when they are complex, include motion or change, and have novel and surprising elements. A relaxing environment with a low information rate has the opposite characteristics.

So how can feelings and emotions be explained by only two dimensions? Russell separates the cognitive, or thinking, part of emotions from these two underlying emotional dimensions. Thus, the emotion of anger about a service failure is modeled as high arousal and high displeasure. This positions itself in the distressing region in our model, combined with a cognitive attribution process. When a customer attributes a service failure to the firm — he thinks it is the firm's fault this happened, it was under their control, and they did not do much to prevent it from happening — then this powerful cognitive attribution process feeds directly into high arousal and displeasure. Similarly, most other emotions can be dissected into their cognitive and affective components.

The strength of Russell's Model of Affect is its simplicity as it allows a direct assessment of how customers feel while they are in the service environment. Therefore, firms can set targets for the affective states they want their customers to be in. For example, a roller coaster operator wants its customers to feel excited (which is a relatively high arousal environment combined with pleasure), a spa may want customers to feel relaxed, a bank pleasant, and so on. How service environments can be designed to deliver the types of service experiences desired by customers will be discussed later in this chapter.

Affective and Cognitive Processes. Affect can be caused by sensing, perceptions, and other cognitive processes of any degree of complexity. However, the more complex a cognitive process becomes, the more powerful its potential impact on affect is. For example, a customer's disappointment with service level and food quality in a restaurant (a complex cognitive process, in which perceived quality is compared to previously held service expectations) cannot be compensated by a simple cognitive process such as subconscious perception of pleasant background music. Yet, this does not mean that simple cognitive processes, such as subconscious perception of scents or music, are unimportant. In practice, the large majority of people's service encounters are routine, with little high-level cognitive processing. We tend to function on "autopilot" and follow our service scripts when doing routine transactions such as using a bus or subway, or entering a fast food restaurant or bank. Most of the time, it is the simple cognitive processes that determine how people feel in the service setting. These include the conscious and even subconscious perceptions of space, colors, scents, and so on. However, should higher levels of cognitive processes be triggered — for instance, through something surprising in the service environment — then it is the interpretation of this surprise that determines people's feelings.[10]

Behavioral Consequences of Affect. At the most basic level, pleasant environments result in "approach" behaviors and unpleasant ones result in "avoidance" behaviors. Arousal acts as an amplifier of the basic effect of pleasure on behavior. If the environment is pleasant, increasing arousal can generate excitement, leading to a stronger positive response. Conversely, if a service environment is inherently unpleasant, increased arousal levels would move customers into the "distressed" region. For example, loud and fast-paced music would increase the stress levels of shoppers trying to make their way through crowded aisles on a pre-Christmas Friday evening. In such situations, retailers should try to lower the information load of the environment.

Finally, customers have strong affective expectations of some services. Think of experiences such as a romantic candlelight dinner in a restaurant, a relaxing spa visit, or an exciting time at the stadium. When customers have strong affective expectations, it is important that the environment be designed to match those expectations.[11]

The Servicescape Model — An Integrative Framework

Building on the basic models in environmental psychology, Mary Jo Bitner developed a comprehensive model named the "servicescape".[12] Fig. 10.7 shows the main dimensions identified in service environments: (1) ambient conditions, (2) space/functionality, and (3) signs, symbols, and artifacts. As individuals tend to perceive these dimensions holistically,

Figure 10.7: The servicescape model

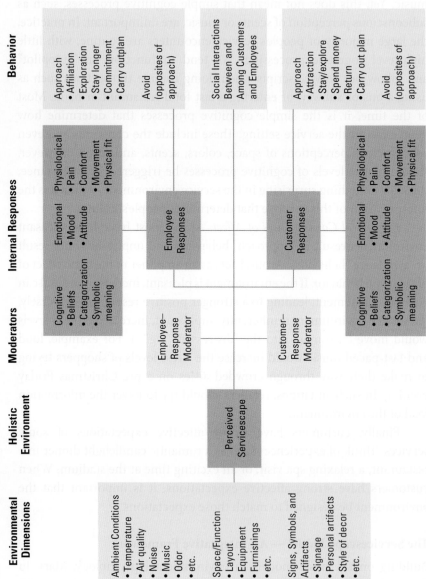

Source: Reprinted with permission from *Journal of Marketing*, published by the American Marketing Association, Mary Jo Bitner, Servicescapes: The Impact of Physical Surroundings on Customers and Employees, 56 (April).

the key to effective design is how well each individual dimension fits together with everything else.

Bitner's model shows that there are customer and employee-response moderators. This means that the same service environment can have different effects on different customers, depending on who they are and what they like — after all, beauty lies in the eyes of the beholder, and is subjective. For example, rap music or an opera may be sheer pleasure to some customer segments, but torture to others.

An important contribution of Bitner's model is the inclusion of employee responses to the service environment. After all, employees spend much more time there than customers, and it is important that designers are aware of how a particular environment enhances (or at least, does not reduce) the productivity of the frontline personnel and the quality of service they deliver.[13]

Internal customer and employee responses can be grouped into cognitive responses (e.g., quality perceptions and beliefs), emotional responses (e.g., feelings and moods), and physiological responses (e.g., pain and comfort). These internal responses lead to overt behavioral responses such as avoiding a crowded supermarket, or responding positively to a relaxing environment by staying longer and spending extra money on impulse purchases. It is important to understand that the behavioral responses of customers and employees must be shaped in ways that aid the production and purchase of high quality services. Consider how the outcomes of service transactions may differ in situations where both customers and frontline staff feel stressed rather than relaxed and happy.

DIMENSIONS OF THE SERVICE ENVIRONMENT

Service environments are complex and have many design elements. Table 10.1 gives an overview of the design elements that might be encountered in a retail outlet. This section will focus on the main dimensions of the service environment in the servicescape model, namely the ambient conditions, space and functionality, signs, symbols, and artifacts.[14]

Table 10.1: Design Elements of A Retail Store Environment

Dimensions	Design Elements	
Exterior facilities	• Architectural style • Size of building • Color of building • Exterior walls and exterior signs • Store front • Marquee • Lawns and gardens	• Window displays • Entrances • Visibility • Uniqueness • Surrounding stores • Surrounding areas • Congestion • Parking and accessibility
General interior	• Flooring and carpeting • Color schemes • Lighting • Scents • Odors (e.g., tobacco smoke) • Sounds and music • Fixtures • Wall composition • Wall textures (paint, wallpaper) • Ceiling composition	• Temperature • Cleanliness • Width of aisles • Dressing facilities • Vertical transportation • Dead areas • Merchandise layout and displays • Price levels and displays • Cash register placement • Technology, modernization
Store layout	• Allocation of floor space for selling, merchandise, personnel, and customers • Placement of merchandise • Grouping of merchandise • Workstation placement • Placement of equipment • Placement of cash register	• Waiting areas • Traffic flow • Waiting queues • Furniture • Dead areas • Department locations • Arrangements within departments
Interior displays	• Point-of-purchase displays • Posters, signs, and cards • Pictures and artwork • Wall decorations • Theme setting • Ensemble	• Racks and cases • Product display • Price display • Cut cases and dump bins • Mobiles
Social dimensions	• Personnel characteristics • Employee uniforms • Crowding	• Customer characteristics • Privacy • Self-service

Source: Adapted from: Barry Berman and Joel R. Evans, *Retail Management — A Strategic Approach*, 8th edition, Upper Saddle River, NJL Prentice Hall, 2001, p. 604; L.W. Turley and Ronald E. Milliman (2000), "Atmospheric Effects on Shopping Behavior: A Review of the Experimental Literature," *Journal of Business Research*, Vol. 49, pp. 193–211.

The Effect of Ambient Conditions

Ambient conditions refer to characteristics of the environment that pertain to our five senses. Even when they are not noted consciously, they may still affect a person's emotional well-being, perceptions, and even attitudes and behaviors. They are composed of literally hundreds of design elements and details that must work together if they are to create the desired service environment.[15] The resulting atmosphere creates a mood that is perceived and interpreted by the customer. Ambient conditions are perceived both separately and holistically, and include music, sounds and noise, scents and smells, color schemes and lighting, and temperature and air movement. Clever design of these conditions can elicit desired behavioral responses among consumers. These important ambient dimensions are discussed next, beginning with music.

Music can have powerful effects on perceptions and behaviors in service settings, even if played at barely audible volumes. The various structural characteristics of music such as tempo, volume, and harmony are perceived holistically, and their effect on internal and behavioral responses is moderated by respondent characteristics (e.g., younger people tend to like different music and therefore respond differently from older people to the same piece of music).[16] Numerous research studies have found that fast tempo and high volume music increases arousal levels, which can then lead to customers increasing the pace of various behaviors.[17] People tend to adjust their pace, either voluntarily or involuntarily, to match the tempo of music. This means that restaurants can speed up table turnover by increasing the tempo and volume of the music and serve more diners during the course of the busy lunch hour, or slow diners down with slow beat music and softer volume to keep evening diners longer in the restaurant, and increase beverage revenues. A restaurant study conducted over eight weeks showed that the customers who dined in a slow-music environment spent longer in the restaurant than the individuals in a fast-music condition. As a result, beverage revenue increased substantially when slow-beat music was played.[18]

Likewise, studies have shown that shoppers walked less rapidly and increased their level of impulse purchases when slow music was played. Playing familiar music in a store was shown to stimulate shoppers, thereby reduce their browsing time, whereas playing unfamiliar music induced shoppers to spend more time there.[19] In situations that require waiting for service, effective use of music may shorten the perceived waiting time and increase customer satisfaction. Relaxing music proved effective in lowering stress levels in a hospital's surgery waiting room. Pleasant music has even been shown to enhance customers' perceptions of service personnel.[20]

Providing the right mix of music to restaurants, retail stores, and even call centers has become an industry in its own right. Mood Media, the market leader in this space, provides music to over 300,000 commercial locations in the US. It tailors its playlists to outlets such as Christian bookstores, black barbershops, and bilingual malls where Anglo and Hispanic customers mingle, and uses "day parting" to target music to their clients' segments such as daytime mothers or after-school teens.[21]

It is not surprising to know that music can also be used to deter the wrong type of customer. Many service environments, including subway systems, supermarkets, and other publicly accessible locations, attract individuals who are not bona fide customers. Some are jaycustomers (see Chap. 13) whose behavior causes problems for management and target customers alike. In the United Kingdom, an increasingly popular strategy for driving such individuals away is to play classical music, which is apparently unpleasant to vandals' and loiterers' ears. Co-op, a UK grocery chain, has been experimenting with playing music outside its outlets to stop teenagers from hanging around and intimidating customers. Its staff are equipped with a remote control and, as reported by Steve Broughton of Co-op, "can turn the music on if there's a situation developing and they need to disperse people".[22]

The London Underground (subway) system has probably made the most extensive use of classical music as a deterrent. Thirty stations pump out Mozart and Haydn to discourage loitering and vandalism. A London Underground spokesperson reports that the most effective deterrents are anything written by Mozart or those sung by Pavarotti. According to Adrian North, a psychologist researching the link between music and behavior at Leicester University, unfamiliarity is a key factor in driving people away. When the target individuals are unused to strings and woodwind, Mozart will do. However, for the more musically literate loiterer, an atonal barrage is likely to work better. For instance, North tormented Leicester's students in the union bar who tended to linger long beyond closing time with what he describes as "computer-game music". It cleared the place![23]

Scent is the next important ambient dimension. Ambient scent or smell pervading an environment may or may not be consciously perceived by customers and is not related to any particular product. The presence of scent can have a strong impact on mood, feelings, and evaluations, and even purchase intentions and in-store behaviors.[24] We experience the power of smell when we are hungry and get a whiff of freshly baked croissants long before we pass a local bakery. This smell makes us aware of our hunger and points us to the solution (i.e., walk into the bakery and get some food). Other examples include the smell of freshly baked cookies on Main Street in Disney's Magic Kingdom to relax customers and provide a feeling of warmth, or the smell of potpourri in Victoria's Secret stores creating the ambiance of a lingerie closet.

Olfaction researcher Alan R. Hirsch, managing director of the Smell & Taste Treatment and Research Foundation based in Chicago, is convinced that at some point in the future we will understand scents so well that we will be able to use them to manage people's behaviors.[25] Service marketers are interested in how to make you hungry and thirsty in the restaurant, relax you in a dentist's waiting room, and energize you to work out harder in a gym. In aromatherapy, it is generally accepted that scents have special characteristics and can be used to solicit certain emotional, physiological, and behavioral responses. Table 10.2 shows the

Table 10.2: Aromatherapy: The Effects of Selected Fragrances on People

Fragrance	Aroma Type	Aromatherapy Class	Traditional Use	Potential Psychological Effect on People
Eucalyptus	Camphoraceous	Toning, stimulating	Deodorant, antiseptic, soothing agent	Stimulating and energizing
Lavender	Herbaceous	Calming, balancing, soothing	Muscle relaxant, soothing agent, astringent	Relaxing and calming
Lemon	Citrus	Energizing, uplifting	Antiseptic, soothing agent	Soothing energy levels
Black pepper	Spicy	Balancing, soothing	Muscle relaxant, aphrodisiac	Balancing people's emotions

Sources: http://www.aromatherapy.com/, accessed 25 April 2016; Dana Butcher, "Aromatherapy — Its Past & Future." *Drug and Cosmetic Industry*, 16, no. 3 (1998): 22–24; Shirley Price and Len Price (2011), *Aromatherapy for Health Professionals*, 4th ed.; Mattila, A. S., & Wirtz, J. (2001). Congruency of scent and music as a driver of in-store evaluations and behavior. *Journal of Retailing*, 77, pp. 273–289.

generally assumed effects of specific scents on people. In service settings, research has shown that scents can have significant impact on customers' perceptions, attitudes, and behaviors. For example:

- Gamblers plunked 45% more quarters into slot machines when a Las Vegas casino was scented with a pleasant artificial smell. When the intensity of the scent was increased, spending jumped by 53%.[26]

- People were more willing to buy Nike sneakers and pay more for them — an average of $10.33 more per pair — when they tried on the shoes in a floral-scented room. The same effect was found even when the scent was so faint that people could not detect it, i.e., the scent was perceived unconsciously.[27]

Service firms have recognized the power of scent and increasingly made it a part of their brand experience. For example, Westin Hotels uses a white tea fragrance throughout its lobbies, and Sheraton scents its lobbies with a combination of fig, clove and jasmine. As a response to the trend of scenting servicescapes, professional service firms have entered the scent marketing space. For example, Ambius, a Rentokil Initial company, offers scent-related services such as "sensory branding", "ambient scenting" and "odor remediation" for retail, hospitality, healthcare, financial, and other services. Firms can outsource their servicescape scenting to Ambius, which offers one-stop solutions ranging from consulting, designing exclusive signature scents for a service firm, to managing the ongoing scenting of all the outlets of a chain.[28] Clients of Mood Media, a leading provider of music, scents, and signage for commercial establishments, can choose their ideal ambient scent from a library of 1,500 scents![29]

Although there is an overwhelming evidence for the potentially powerful effects scent can have on customers' experiences and behaviors, it has to be implemented with caution. The ambient scent has to fit the service context and the target audience (very much as discussed for music). Furthermore, a recent study suggests that simple scents whereby the researchers used a simple orange scent in a retail environment can have an excellent impact on sales per customer, whereas more complex scents such as basil-orange with green tea used as a complex scent in this study, did not do better than unscented environments. In this study, both scents were perceived as equally pleasant, but the simple scent helped in consumer decision making (consumers spent less time deciding which items to buy), whereas the complex scent did not (consumers spent as much time deciding as in the no scent condition). The researchers concluded that complex scents cannot be fluently processed by consumers and require too much cognitive effort, which subsequently has a negative effect on consumer decision making and perceptions.[30]

While these findings are derived only from a few research projects, they suggest that managers need to carefully match their scents to their context, and probably should favor simpler rather than more complex scents. In any case, using field experiments, monitoring sales, and shopper behaviors and perceptions would be an excellent way to optimize the ambient scent in any particular servicescape.

In addition to music and scent, researchers have found that *colors* have a strong impact on people's feelings.[31] Color is "stimulating, calming, expressive, disturbing, impressionable, cultural, exuberant, symbolic. It pervades every aspect of our lives, embellishes the ordinary, and gives beauty and drama to everyday objects".[32]

The de facto system used in psychological research is the Munsell System, which defines colors in the three dimensions of hue, value, and chroma.[33] *Hue* is the pigment of the color (i.e., the name of the color: red, orange, yellow, green, blue, or violet). *Value* is the degree of lightness or

Table 10.3: Common Associations and Human Responses to Colors

Color	Degree of Warmth	Nature Symbol	Common Association and Human Responses to Color
Red	Warm	Earth	High energy and passion; can excite and stimulate emotions, expressions, and warmth
Orange	Warmest	Sunset	Emotions, expressions, and warmth
Yellow	Warm	Sun	Optimism, clarity, intellect, and mood enchancing
Green	Cool	Growth, grass, and trees	Nurturing, healing, and unconditional love
Blue	Coolest	Sky and ocean	Relaxation, serenity, and loyalty
Indigo	Cool	Sunset	Meditation and spirituality
Violet	Cool	Violet flower	Spirituality, reduces stress, can create an inner feeling of calm

Sources: Sara O. Marberry and Laurie Zagon, *The Power of Color—Creating Healthy Interior Spaces.* New York: John Wiley, 1995, p. 18; Sarah Lynch, *Bold Colors for Modern Rooms: Bright Ideas for People Who Love Color.* Gloucester, MA: Rockport Publishers, 2001, pp. 24–29

darkness of the color, relative to a scale that extends from pure black to pure white. *Chroma* refers to hue intensity, saturation, or brilliance; high chroma colors have a high intensity of pigmentation in them and are perceived as rich and vivid, whereas low chroma colors are perceived as dull.

Hues are classified into warm colors (red, orange and yellow hues) and cold colors (blue and green), with orange (a mix of red and yellow) being the warmest, and blue being the coldest of the colors. These colors can be used to manage the warmth of an environment. For example, if a violet is too warm, you can cool it off by reducing the amount of red. Or if a red is too cool, warm it up by adding a shot of orange.[34] Warm colors are associated with elated mood states and arousal, but also heightened anxiety, whereas cool colors reduce arousal levels and can elicit emotions such as peacefulness, calmness, love, and happiness.[35] Table 10.3 summarizes common associations and responses to colors.

Research in a service environment context has shown that despite differing color preferences, people are generally drawn to warm color environments. Warm colors encourage fast decision making and are best suited for low-involvement service purchase decisions or impulse buying. Cool colors are favored when consumers need time to make high-involvement purchase decisions.[36]

An early example of using color schemes to enhance the service experience was the HealthPark Medical Center in Fort Meyers, Florida, which combined full-spectrum color in its lobby with unusual lighting to achieve a dreamlike setting. The lobby walls were washed with rainbow colors by using an arrangement of high intensity blue, green, violet, red, orange, and yellow lamps. Craig Roeder, the lighting designer for the hospital, explained, "It's a hospital. People walk into it worried and sick. I tried to design an entrance space that provides them with light and energy — to 'beam them up' a little bit before they get to the patient rooms".[37]

A recent example of effective color and lighting are the new cabin designs in the Boeing 787 Dreamliner and Airbus A350 and models. In the past, cabin lights were either on or off, but with the new light-emitting diode (LED) technology a wide range of lighting palette is available. Designers start to experiment to illuminate the cabin in all kinds of hues, and ask questions such as: "Does a pinkish-purple glow soothe and calm passengers when boarding better than an amber warmth?" or "Can lighting be used to prevent jet lag as much as possible?" The Finnair A350 cabin has two dozen light settings aligned with the different stages of a long-haul flight such as featuring a 20-minute 'sunset'. It also aligns colors with the destination by featuring warmer, amber colors when flying into Asia, and cooler 'Nordic blue' hues when arriving in Finland. Similarly, Virgin Atlantic has a few main settings on its 787 flights, including rose-champagne for boarding, purple-pink for drinks, amber for dinner, a silver glow for overnight sleep, and a waking color. According to Nik Lusardi, the design manager at Virgin Atlantic: "We've always wanted to create a different kind of atmosphere aboard our aircraft, and light plays exactly into our hands. …You can get people energized or you can relax people very, very quickly".[38]

Although we have an understanding of the general effects of colors, their use in any specific context needs to be approached with caution. For example, a transportation company in Israel decided to paint its buses green as part of an environmentalism public relations campaign. Reactions to this seemingly simple act from multiple groups of people were unexpectedly negative. Some customers found the green color as hampering service performance because the green buses blended in with the environment and were more difficult to see; some felt that the green was aesthetically unappealing and inappropriate as it represented undesirable notions such as terrorism or opposing sports teams.[39]

Spatial Layout and Functionality

In addition to ambient conditions, spatial layout and functionality are other key dimensions of the service environment. As a service environment generally has to fulfill specific purposes and customer needs, spatial layout and functionality are particularly important.

Spatial layout refers to the floor plan, size and shape of furnishings, counters, and potential machinery and equipment, and the ways in which they are arranged. *Functionality* refers to the ability of those items to facilitate the performance of service transactions. Both dimensions affect the user-friendliness and the ability of the facility to service customers well. Tables that are too close in a café, counters in a bank that lack privacy, uncomfortable chairs in a lecture theatre, and lack of parking space can all leave negative impressions on customers, affect the service experience and buying behavior, and consequently, the business performance of the service facility.

Signs, Symbols, and Artifacts

Many things in the service environment act as explicit or implicit signals to communicate the firm's image, help customers find their way (e.g., to certain service counters, departments, or the exit), and to convey the service script (e.g., for a queuing system). In particular, first time customers will automatically try to draw meaning from the environment to guide them through the service processes.[40]

Examples of explicit signals include signs, which can be used (1) as labels (e.g., to indicate the name of the department or counter), (2) for giving directions (e.g., to certain service counters, entrance, exit, way to lifts and toilets), (3) for communicating the service script (e.g., take a queue number and wait for it to be called, or clear the tray after your meal), and (4) for reminders about behavioral rules (e.g., switch off or turn your mobile devices to silent mode during a performance, or smoking/non-smoking areas). Signs are often used to teach behavioral rules in service settings. Singapore, which strictly enforces rules in many service settings, especially in public buildings and on public transport, is sometimes ironically referred to as a 'fine' city (Fig. 10.8). Contrast these signs to the more creative and perhaps equally effective signed used by Singapore's Changi Airport at the entrance of its butterfly garden (Fig. 10.9). Some signs are quite interesting and may be obvious, but other signs need the person to think a little before understanding the meaning.

Table 10.4: provides an overview of the benefits well-designed signage can provide to customers and service organizations.

The challenge for servicescape designers is to use signs, symbols, and artifacts to guide customers clearly through the process of service delivery, and to teach the service script in as intuitive a manner as possible. This task assumes particular importance in situations in which there is a high proportion of new or infrequent customers (e.g., airports and hospitals), and/or a high degree of self-service with no or only a few service employees available to guide customers through the process (e.g., a self-service bank branch).

Customers become disoriented when they cannot derive clear signals from a servicescape, leading to anxiety and uncertainty about how to proceed and how to obtain the desired service. Customers can easily feel lost in a confusing environment and experience anger and frustration as a result. Think about the last time you were in a hurry and

Figure 10.8: Singapore is a 'fine' city.

Figure 10.9: Changi Airport uses a creative sign to manage visitor behavior in its butterfly garden.

Table 10.4: Benefits Well-Designed Signage for Customers and Service Organizations.

Potential Benefits of Well-developed Signage

For Customers

- Be informed, up-to-date, oriented, free to move about, guided along prepared paths, emotionally stimulated
- Creates familiarity with the servicescape
- Helps to participate with greater ease in the service process
- Increases confidence and reassurance while following signage; provides higher levels of perceived control during the service encounter
- Reduces tension, confusion, feeling lost, wrong turns and requests for information
- Reduces time to reach the desired goal as efficiently as possible

For the Service Organization

- Direct, inform, and manage the flow and the behavior of customers
- Improve the quality of service provided and increase customer satisfaction
- Reduce information-giving by frontline employees
- Help frontline employees to work with fewer interruptions
- Attract and excite curiosity, help to strengthen the corporate image
- Differentiate the firm from the competition

Adapted from: Angelo Bonfani (2013), "Towards an Approach to Signage Management Quality (SMQ)", *Journal of Services Marketing*, Vol. 27, No. 4, pp. 312-321.

tried to find your way through an unfamiliar hospital, shopping center, or a large government office where the signs and other directional cues were not intuitive to you. At many service facilities, customers' first point of contact is likely to be the car park. As emphasized in *Service Insights 10.4*, the principles of effective environment design apply even in such a very mundane environment.

SERVICE INSIGHTS 10.4
Guidelines for Parking Design[41]

Car parks play an important role at many service facilities. Effective use of signs, symbols, and artifacts in a parking lot or garage helps customers find their way, manages their behavior, and portrays a positive image for the sponsoring organization.

- *Friendly warnings* — all warning signs should communicate a customer benefit. For instance, "Fire lane — for everyone's safety we ask you not to park in the fire lane."

- *Safety lighting* — good lighting that penetrates all areas makes life easier for customers and enhances safety. Firms may want to draw attention to this feature with notices stating that "Parking lots have been specially lit for your safety."

- *Help customers remember where they left their vehicle* — forgetting where one left the family car in a large parking structure can be a nightmare. Many car parks have adopted color-coded floors to help customers remember which level they parked on. In addition, many car parks also mark sections with special symbols, such as different kinds of animals. This helps customers to not only remember the level, but also the section where the car is parked. Boston's Logan Airport goes two steps further. Each level has been assigned a theme associated with Massachusetts, such as Paul Revere's Ride, Cape Cod, or the Boston Marathon. An image is attached to each theme — a male figure on horseback, a lighthouse, or a female runner. While waiting for the elevator, travelers hear music that is tied to the theme for that level; in the case of the Boston Marathon floor, it is the theme song from

Chariots of Fire, an Oscar-winning movie about an Olympic runner.

- *Maternity parking* — disabled-friendly spaces are often required by law with special stickers displayed on the vehicle. A few thoughtful organizations have special expectant mother parking spaces, painted with a blue/pink stork. This strategy demonstrates a sense of caring and understanding of customer needs.

- *Fresh paint* — curbs, cross walks, and lot lines should be repainted regularly before any cracking, peeling, or disrepair become evident. Pro-active and frequent repainting give positive cleanliness cues and projects a positive image.

People are Part of the Service Environment Too

The appearance and behavior of both service personnel and customers can strengthen or weaken the impression created by a service environment, and some academics argue that these social dimensions should be explicitly considered when assessing the quality of servicescapes.[42] Dennis Nickson and his colleagues use the term "aesthetic labor" to capture the importance of the physical image of service personnel who serve customers directly.[43] Employees at Disney theme parks are called

Figure 10.10: Distinctive servicescapes — from table settings, furniture and room design to other customers present in the servicescape — create different customer expectations of these two restaurants.

cast members. Whether the staff are acting as Cinderella, one of the seven dwarfs, or as the park cleaner, or the person managing Buzz Lightyear's Tomorrowland booth, all of these cast members must dress up and look the part. Once dressed up, they must "perform" for the guests.

Likewise, marketing communications may seek to attract customers who will not only appreciate the ambience created by the service provider but will actively enhance it by their own appearance and behavior. In hospitality and retail settings, newcomers often survey the array of existing customers before deciding whether to patronize the establishment. Consider Fig. 10.10 which shows the interior of two restaurants. Imagine entering each of these two dining rooms. How does each restaurant position itself within the restaurant industry? What sort of dining experience can you expect, and what are the clues you use to make your judgments? In particular, what assumptions do you make from looking at the customers who are already seated in each restaurant?

PUTTING IT ALL TOGETHER

Although individuals often perceive particular aspects or individual design features of an environment, it is the total configuration of all those design features that determines consumer responses. That is, consumers perceive service environments holistically.

Design with a Holistic View

Whether a dark, glossy, wooden floor is the perfect flooring depends on everything else in that service environment, including the type, color scheme and materials of the furniture, the lighting, the promotional materials, the overall brand perception and positioning of the firm. Servicescapes have to be seen holistically, which means no dimension of the design can be optimized in isolation, because everything depends on everything else.

As the design of the environment needs to be planned as a whole, it is more like an art. Therefore, professional designers tend to focus on specific types of servicescapes. For example, a handful of famous interior designers do no other projects but create hotel lobbies around the world.

Similarly, there are design experts who focus exclusively on restaurants, bars, clubs, cafes and bistros, or retail outlets, or healthcare facilities and so forth.[44]

Design from a Customer's Perspective

Many service environments are built with an emphasis on aesthetic values, and designers sometimes forget the most important factor to consider when designing service environments — the customers who will be using them. Ron Kaufman, founder of Up Your Service! College, experienced the following design flaws in two new high-profile service environments:

A new Sheraton Hotel just had opened in Jordan without clear signage that would guide guests from the ballrooms to the restrooms. The signs that did exist were etched in muted gold on dark marble pillars. More 'obvious' signs were apparently inappropriate amidst such elegant décor. Very swish, very chic, but who were they designing it for?

At a new airport lounge in a major Asian city, a partition of colorful glass hung from the ceiling. My luggage lightly brushed against it as I walked inside. The entire partition shook and several panels came undone. A staff member hurried over and began carefully reassembling the panels. (Thank goodness nothing broke.) I apologized profusely. 'Don't worry,' she replied, 'This happens all the time.' An airport lounge is a heavy traffic area. People are always moving in and out. Kaufman keeps asking "What were the interior designers thinking? Who were they designing it for?"

"I am regularly amazed," declared Kaufman, "by brand new facilities that are obviously 'user unfriendly'!" He draws the following key learning point: "It's easy to get caught up in designing new things that are 'cool', 'elegant' or 'hot'. But if you don't keep your customer in mind throughout, you could end up with an investment that's not."[45]

Along a similar vein, Alain d'Astous explored environmental aspects that irritate shoppers. His findings highlighted the following problems:

1. *Ambient conditions* (ordered by level of irritation):
   - Store is not clean
   - Too hot inside the store or the shopping center
   - Music inside the store is too loud
   - Bad smells in the store

2. *Environmental design variables*:
   - No mirror in the dressing room
   - Unable to find what one needs
   - Directions within the store are inadequate
   - Arrangement of store items has been changed in a way that confuses customers
   - Store is too small
   - Losing one's way in a large shopping center[46]

To design servicescapes from the customer's perspective, managers have to understand how their customers use it. An in-depth study in the context of a highly functional and utilitarian service, a public transport systems, showed that consumers use servicescapes in three main ways, namely[47]: (1) identifying the resources in the environment and trying to understand the objects and persons in the service environment as resources and how they can be used (e.g., searching for a bus stop, timetable, map, or bus; approaching staff or other customers); (2) sense-making, which is the process of giving meaning to and comprehending the resources previously identified (e.g., trying to understand maps and timetables); and (3) using the resources to attain their consumption goals (e.g., finding ones way in the subway system). The implications of these findings are clear: servicescapes should be designed to support customers to attain their consumption goals by making the designs intuitive (i.e., easy to sense), meaningful (i.e., easy to understand), and easy to use.[48]

For hedonic services, customers use the service environment for additional objectives; they want to experience what they came for when they entered the servicescape (e.g., have fun, relax, or socialize). In this context, contrasting Kaufman's experiences and d'Astou's findings with the Disney example in *Service Insights 10.5* leads to interesting conclusions.

SERVICE INSIGHTS 10.5
Design of Disney's Magic Kingdom

Walt Disney was one of the undisputed champions of designing service environments. His tradition of amazingly careful and detailed planning has become one of his company's hallmarks, and is visible everywhere in its theme parks. For example, Main Street is angled to make it seem longer upon entry into the Magic Kingdom than it actually is. With a myriad of facilities and attractions strategically located at each side of the street, this makes people look forward to the relatively long journey to the Castle. However, looking down the slope from the Castle back towards the entrance makes Main Street appear shorter than it really is, relieving exhaustion and rejuvenating guests. It encourages strolling, which minimizes the number of people who take the buses and so eliminates the threatening problem of traffic congestion.

Meandering sidewalks with multiple attractions keep guests feeling entertained by both the planned activities and also by watching other guests; trash bins are aplenty and always in sight to convey the message that littering is prohibited; and the repainting of facilities is a routine procedure that signals a high level of maintenance and cleanliness;

Disney's servicescape design and upkeep help to script customer experiences, and create pleasure and satisfaction for guests, not only in its theme parks but also in its cruise ships and hotels.

Source: Lewis P. Carbone and Stephen H. Haeckel, "Engineering Customer Experiences," *Marketing Management* 3, no. 3 (Winter 1994): 10-11; Kathy Merlock Jackson, *Walt Disney, A Bio-Bibliography.* (Westport, Greenwood Press, 1993), pp. 36-39, Andrew Lainsbury, *Once Upon An American Dream: The Story of Euro Disneyland* (Lawrence, Kan, University Press of Kansas, 2000), pp. 64-72. See also: Disney Institute, *Be Our Guest: Perfecting the Art of Customer Service.* Disney Enterprises (2011).

Tools to Guide Servicescape Design

Among the tools a manager uses to determine how customers use the servicescape, and which of its aspects irritate them and which they like are:

Table 10.5: A Visit to The Movies: The Service Environment as Perceived by The Customer.

Steps in the Service Encounter	Design of the Service Environment	
	Exceeds Expectations	**Fails Expectations**
Locate a parking lot	Ample room in a bright place near the entrance, with a security officer protecting your valuables	Insufficient parking spaces, so patrons have to park in another lot
Queue up to obtain tickets	Strategic placement of mirrors, posters of upcoming movies, and entertainment news to ease perception of long wait, if any; movies and time slots easily seen; ticket availability clearly communicated	A long queue and having to wait for a long while; difficult to see quickly what movies are being shown at what time slots and whether tickets are still available
Check tickets to enter the theater	A very well-maintained lobby with clear directions to the theater and posters of the movie to enhance patrons' experience	A dirty lobby with rubbish strewn, and unclear or misleading directions to the movie theater
Go to the restroom before the movie starts	Sparkling clean, spacious, brightly lit, dry floors, well-stocked, nice décor, clear mirrors wiped regularly	Dirty, with an unbearable odor; broken toilets; no hand towels, soap, or toilet paper; overcrowded; dusty and dirty mirrors
Enter the theater and locate your seat	Spotless theater; well designed with no bad seats; sufficient lighting to locate your seat; spacious, comfortable chairs, with drink and popcorn holders on each seat; and a suitable temperature	Rubbish on the floor, broken seats, sticky floor, gloomy and insufficient lighting, burned-out exit signs
Watch the movie	Excellent sound system and film quality, nice audience, an enjoyable and memorable entertainment experience overall	Substandard sound and movie equipment, uncooperative audience that talks and smokes because of lack of "No Smoking" and other signs; a disturbing and unenjoyable entertainment experience overall
Leave the theater and return to the car	Friendly service staff greet patrons as they leave; an easy exit through brightly lit and safe parking area, back to the car with the help of clear lot signs	A difficult trip, as patrons squeeze through a narrow exit, unable to find the car because of no or insufficient lighting

Source: Adapted from Albrecht, S. (1996). "See Things from the Customer's Point of View — How to Use the 'Cycles of Service' to Understand What the Customer Goes Through to Do Business with You." *World's Executive Digest*, December, pp. 53–58.

For a manager to determine how customers use the servicescape, and which of its aspects irritate them and which do they like, following are the tools that can be used:

- *Keen observation* of customers' behavior and responses to the service environment by management, supervisors, branch managers, and frontline staff.

- *Feedback and ideas from frontline staff and customers* using a variety of research tools such as scanning social media, using suggestion boxes, focus groups and surveys. The latter are often called environmental surveys if the focus is on the design of the service environment.[49]

- *Photo audit* is a method of asking customers (or mystery shoppers) to take photographs of their service experience. These photographs can be used later as a basis for further interviews of their experience, or included as part of a survey about the service experience.[50]

- *Field experiments* can be used to manipulate specific dimensions in an environment to observe the effects. For instance, researchers can experiment with various types of music and scents, and then measure the time and money customers spend in the environment. Laboratory experiments using pictures or videos, or other ways to simulate real-world service environments (such as virtual tours via computers) can be effectively used to examine the impact of changes in design elements that cannot be easily manipulated in a field experiment, for examples testing of different color schemes, spatial layouts, or styles of furnishing.

- *Blueprinting* or flowcharting (as described in Chap. 8) can be extended to include the physical evidence in the environment. Design elements and tangible cues can be documented as the customer moves through each step of the service delivery process. Photos can supplement the map to make it more vivid.

Table 10.5 shows an examination of a customer's visit to a movie theater, identifying how different environmental elements at each step exceeded or failed to meet expectations. The service process was divided into steps, decisions, duties, and activities, all designed to take the customer through the entire service encounter. The more a service company can observe, understand, and experience from the customer's point of view, the better equipped it will be to realize errors in the design of its environment and to further improve what is already functioning well.

CONCLUSION

The service environment plays a major role in shaping customers' perception of a firm's image and positioning. As service quality often is difficult to assess, customers frequently use the service environment as an important quality signal. A well-designed service environment makes customers feel good and boosts their satisfaction, and allows the firm to influence their behavior (e.g., adhering to the service script and impulse purchasing) while enhancing the productivity of the service operation.

CHAPTER SUMMARY

Main Purposes of Service Environments
- Shape customers' service experience and behaviors
- Signal quality and position, differentiate and strengthen the brand
- Core component of the value proposition
- Facilitate the service encounter and enhance productivity

Theories from Environmental Psychology that Explain Consumer Responses to Service Environments

The Mehrabian–Russell Stimulus–Response Model
- Perceptions and interpretation of servicescapes influences how consumers feel
- These feelings then drive consumer responses to those environments

Russell's Model of Affect
- Customers' feelings (or emotions) can be modeled with two dimensions: pleasure and arousal
- Pleasure is subjective
- Arousal largely depends on the information rate of an environment
- Pleasure and arousal interact on response behaviors, whereby arousal generally amplifies the effects of pleasure (or displeasure)

Bitner's Servicescape Model

Key Dimensions of Service Environments
- Ambient conditions (e.g., music, scents, and colors)
- Spatial layout and functionality (e.g., floor plan, size and shape of furnishing, counters, equipment)
- Signs, symbols, and artifacts
- Appearance of service employees and other customers

Response Moderators
- Employees (e.g., liking of servicescape, personal tolerance for stimulation through music, noise, and crowding)
- Customers

Internal Responses
- Cognitive (e.g., beliefs, perceptions)
- Emotional (e.g., moods, attitudes)
- Physiological (e.g., comfort, pain)

Behavioral Responses
- Approach (e.g., explore, spend time, spend money in the environment)
- Avoidance (e.g., leave the environment)
- Interaction between service employees and customers

Design of Effective Services Environments
- Design with a holistic view
- Design from the customers' perspective
- Use design tools (ranging from keen observation and customer feedback to photo audits and field experiments)

CHAPTER 11

Managing People for Service Advantage

Quintessentially we are a people-based company. You couldn't find another consumer brand as dependent on human behavior.

Howard Schultz
CEO of Starbucks

The old adage 'People are your most important asset' is wrong. The right people are your most important asset.

Jim Collins
Consultant, teacher and author of best-selling book "Good to Great"

Customer satisfaction results from the realization of high levels of value compared to competitors... Value is created by satisfied, committed, loyal, and productive employees.

James I. Heskett, W. Earl Sasser, Jr., and Leonard L. Schlesinger
Current and former professors at Harvard Business School

SERVICE EMPLOYEES ARE EXTREMELY IMPORTANT

The quality of a service firm's staff — especially those working in customer-facing positions — plays a crucial role in determining market success and financial performance. Frontline employees are a key asset for delivering service excellence and competitive advantage. Market and financial results of managing people effectively for service advantage can be phenomenal. That is why the *People* element of the 7 'P's is so important.

Among the most demanding jobs in service businesses are the frontline jobs. Employees working in these customer-facing jobs span the boundary between inside and outside of the organization. They are expected to be fast and efficient in executing operational tasks, as well as courteous and helpful when dealing with customers.

Behind most of today's successful service organizations stands a firm commitment to effective management of human resources (HR), including recruitment, selection, training, motivation, and retention of employees. Organizations that display this commitment understand the economic payoff from investing in their people. These firms are also characterized by a distinctive culture of service leadership and role modeling by its top management. Good HR strategies allied with strong management leadership at all levels often lead to a sustainable competitive advantage. It is probably harder for competitors to duplicate high-performance human assets compared to any other corporate resource.

Highly capable and motivated people are at the center of service excellence and productivity. Cora Griffith in *Service Insights 11.1* is a powerful demonstration of a frontline employee delivering service excellence and productivity, and at the same time having high job satisfaction. Many of the pointers in Cora Griffith's "nine rules of success" are the result of good HR strategies for service firms. This chapter will give an insight on how to get HR right in service firms, and how to get satisfied, loyal, motivated and productive service employees.

SERVICE INSIGHTS 11.1
Cora Griffith — The Outstanding Waitress[1]

Cora Griffith, a waitress for the Orchard Café at the Paper Valley Hotel in Appleton, Wisconsin, is superb in her role, appreciated by first-time customers, famous with her regular customers, and revered by her co-workers. Cora loves her work — and it shows. Comfortable in a role that she believes is the right one for her, Cora follows nine rules of success:

1. *Treat Customers Like Family.* First-time customers are not allowed to feel like strangers. Cheerful and proactive, Cora smiles, chats, and includes everyone at the table in the conversation. She is as respectful to children as she is to adults, and makes it a point to learn and use everyone's name. "I want people to feel like they're sitting down to dinner right at my house. I want them to feel they're welcome, that they can get comfortable, and that they can relax. I don't just serve people, I pamper them".

2. *Listen First.* Cora has developed her listening skills to the point that she rarely writes down customers' orders. She listens carefully and provides a customized service: "Are they in a hurry? Or do they have a special diet or like their selection cooked in a certain way?"

3. *Anticipate Customers' Wants.* She refills beverages and brings extra bread and butter in a timely manner. One regular customer, for example, who likes honey with her coffee, gets it without having to ask. "I don't want my customers to have to ask for anything, so I always try to anticipate what they might need".

4. *Simple Things Make the Difference.* She manages the details of her service, monitoring the cleanliness of the utensils and their correct placement. The fold for napkins must be just right. She inspects each plate in the kitchen before taking it to the table. She provides crayons for small children to draw pictures while waiting for the meal. "It's the little things that please the customer", she says.

5. *Work Smart.* Cora scans all her tables at once, looking for opportunities to combine tasks. "Never do just one thing at a time", she advises. "And never go from the kitchen to the dining

room empty-handed. Take coffee or iced tea or water with you". When she refills one glass of water, she refills others. When clearing one plate, she clears others. "You have to be organized, and you have to keep in touch with the big picture".

6.   *Keep Learning.* Cora makes it an ongoing effort to improve existing skills and learn new ones.

7.   *Success Is Where You Find It.* Cora is content with her work. She finds satisfaction in pleasing her customers, and she enjoys helping other people enjoy. Her positive attitude is a positive force in the restaurant. She is hard to ignore. "If customers come to the restaurant in a bad mood, I'll try to cheer them up before they leave". Her definition of success: "To be happy in life".

8.   *All for One, One for All.* Cora has been working with many of the same co-workers for more than eight years. The team supports one another on the crazy days when 300 conventioneers come to the restaurant for breakfast at the same time. Everyone pitches in and helps. The wait staff cover for one another, the managers bus the tables, and the chefs garnish the plates. "We are like a little family", Cora says. "We know each other very well and we help each other out. If we have a crazy day, I'll go in the kitchen towards the end of the shift and say, 'Man, I'm just proud of us. We really worked hard today.'"

9.   *Take Pride in Your Work.* Cora believes in the importance of her work and in the need to do it well. "I don't think of myself as 'just a waitress'…I've chosen to be a waitress. I'm doing this to my full potential, and I give it my best. I tell anyone who's starting out: 'Take pride in what you do'. You're never just an 'anything', no matter what you do. You give it your all…and you do it with pride".

Cora Griffith is a success story. She is loyal to her employer and dedicated to her customers and co-workers. A perfectionist who seeks continuous improvement, Cora's enthusiasm for her work and unflagging spirit creates an energy that radiates through the restaurant. She is proud of being a waitress, proud of 'touching lives'. Says Cora: "I have always wanted to do my best. However, the owners really are the ones who taught me how important it is to take care of the customer and gave me the freedom to do it. The company always has listened to my concerns and followed up. Had I not worked for the Orchard Café, I would have been a good waitress, but I would not have been the same waitress".

Service Personnel as a Source of Customer Loyalty and Competitive Advantage

Almost everybody can recount a dreadful experience they had with a service business. If pressed, many of these same people can also recount a really good service experience. Service personnel usually feature prominently in such dramas. They either feature in roles as uncaring, incompetent, mean-spirited villains, or in roles as heroes who went out of their way to help customers by anticipating their needs and resolving problems in a helpful and empathetic manner. Everybody has their own set of favorite stories, featuring both villains and heroes — and most people talk more about the former than the latter.

From a customer's perspective, the encounter with service staff is probably the most important aspect of a service. From the firm's perspective, the service levels and the way service is delivered by frontline personnel can be an important source of differentiation as well as competitive advantage. Among the reasons why service employees are so important to customers and the firm's competitive positioning are that the frontline:

- *Is a core part of the product.* Often, the service employees are the most visible element of the service. They deliver the service, and greatly affect service quality.
- *Is the service firm.* Frontline employees represent the service firm, and from a customer's perspective, they are the firm.
- *Is the brand.* Frontline employees and the service they provide are often a core part of the brand. It is the employees who determine whether the brand promise is delivered.[2]

- *Affects sales.* Service personnel are often critically important for generating sales, cross-sales, and up-sales.
- *Is a key driver of customer loyalty.* Frontline employees play a key role in anticipating customers' needs, customizing the service delivery, and building personalized relationships with customers.[3] An effective performance of these activities should ultimately lead to increased customer loyalty.
- *Determines productivity.* Frontline employees have heavy influence on the productivity of frontline operations.

The story of Cora Griffith and many other success stories of employees showing discretionary effort have reinforced the truism that highly motivated people are at the core of service excellence.[4] Increasingly, they are a key factor in creating and maintaining competitive positioning and advantage.

The intuitive importance of the effect of service employees on customer loyalty was integrated and formalized by James Heskett and his colleagues in their pioneering research on what they call the *service-profit chain* (see Chap. 1 for more detail). It demonstrates the chain of relationships among (1) employee satisfaction, retention, and productivity; (2) service value; (3) customer satisfaction and loyalty; and (4) revenue growth and profitability for the firm.[5] Unlike manufacturing, "shop-floor workers" in services (i.e., frontline staff) are in constant contact with customers, and there is solid evidence showing that employee satisfaction and customer satisfaction are highly correlated.[6] Therefore, this chapter focuses on how to have satisfied, loyal and, productive service employees who care.

The Frontline in Low-Contact Services

Much research in service management relates to high-contact services. However, many services are moving towards using low-contact delivery channels such as call centers, where contact is voice-to-voice rather than face-to-face. A growing number of self-service transactions no longer involve frontline staff. As a result, a large and increasing number of customer contact employees work by telephone or e-mail, never meeting customers face-to-face. In the light of these trends, are frontline employees really all that important for such services?

Figure 11.1: The pleasant personality of call center staff can result in a positive "moment of truth", where a firm's service quality will be viewed positively

Most people do not call the service hotline or visit the service center of their cell phone service operator or credit card companies more than once or twice a year. However, these occasional service encounters are absolutely critical — they are the "moments of truth" that drive a customer's perceptions of the service firm (Fig. 11.1). Also, it is likely that these interactions are not about routine transactions, but about service problems and special requests. These very few instances of contact determine whether a customer thinks, "Your customer service is excellent! When I need help, I can call you, and this is one important reason why I bank with you!", or "Your service stinks. I don't like interacting with you, and I am going to switch away from your bank when I get the chance"!

Given that technology is relatively commoditized, the service delivered by the frontline, whether it is face to face, ear to ear, via e-mail, Twitter, or chat, is highly visible and important to customers, and therefore a critical component of a service firm's marketing strategy.

FRONTLINE WORK IS DIFFICULT AND STRESSFUL

The service-profit chain needs high-performing, satisfied employees to achieve service excellence and customer loyalty (see Chap. 1 for a detailed discussion). However, these customer-facing employees work in some of the most demanding jobs in service firms. Perhaps you have worked in one or more of such jobs, which are common in the healthcare, hospitality, retail, and travel industries. There is a story that became viral about a JetBlue flight attendant who abruptly quit his job after 28 years of service as a flight attendant. Apparently, he was fed up with a difficult passenger with a bag problem, who had sworn at him. He scolded the passenger publicly over the airplane intercom, announced that he had had enough, and opened the emergency slide to get off the plane [7]. This is an example of how stress can affect a person at work. The main reasons why these jobs are so demanding will be discussed next.

Service Jobs are Boundary Spanning Positions

The organizational behavior literature refers to service employees as *boundary spanners*. They link the inside of an organization to the outside world, operating at the boundary of the company. Due to the position they occupy, boundary spanners often have conflicting roles. In particular, customer contact personnel must attend to both operational and marketing goals. This multiplicity of roles in service jobs leading to role conflict and role stress will be discussed next.[8]

Sources of Role Conflict

There are three main causes of role conflict and role stress in frontline positions: organization/client, person/role, and inter-client conflicts.

Organization/Client Conflict. Customer contact personnel must attend to both operational and marketing goals. They are expected to delight customers, which takes time, and yet they have to be fast and efficient at operational tasks.[9] In addition, they are often expected to do selling, cross-selling, and upselling. For instance, it is common to hear customer contact personnel suggest: "Now would be a good time to open a separate account to save for your children's education"; or "For only $35 more per night, you can upgrade to the executive floor".

Finally, customer contact personnel can even be responsible for enforcing rate integrity and pricing schedules that might be in direct conflict with customer satisfaction (e.g., "I am sorry, but we don't serve ice water in this restaurant, although we do have an excellent selection of still and carbonated mineral waters", or "I am sorry, but we cannot waive the fee for the bounced check for the third time this quarter".) This type of conflict is also called the two-bosses-dilemma, where service employees have the unpleasant choice between enforcing the company's rules and satisfying customer demands. The problem is especially acute in organizations that are not customer-oriented.

Person/Role Conflict. Service staff may have conflicts between what their job requires and their own personalities, self-perception, and beliefs. For example, the job may require staff to smile and be friendly even to rude customers (see also the section on jaycustomers in Chap. 12). V. S. Mahesh and Anand Kasturi note from their consulting work with service organizations around the world that thousands of frontline staff, when asked, consistently tend to describe customers with a pronounced negative flavor — frequently using phrases such as "over-demanding", "unreasonable", "refuse to listen", "always want everything their way, immediately", and also "arrogant".[10]

Providing quality service requires an independent, warm, and friendly personality. These traits are more likely to be found in people with higher self-esteem. However, many frontline jobs are also seen as low-level jobs which require little education, offer low pay with very little career advancement. If an organization is not able to "professionalize" their frontline jobs and move away from this image, these jobs may be inconsistent with staff's self-perception and lead to person/role conflicts.

Inter-client Conflict. Conflicts between customers are not uncommon (e.g., smoking in non-smoking sections, jumping queues, talking on a cell phone in a movie theater, or being excessively noisy in a restaurant), and it is usually the service staff summoned to call the offending customer to order. This is a stressful and unpleasant task, as it is difficult and often impossible to satisfy both sides.

In conclusion, frontline employees may perform triple roles, satisfying customers, delivering productivity, and generating sales. Although employees may experience conflict and stress, they are still expected to smile and be friendly towards the customer. This is called emotional labor, which in itself is an important cause of stress.

Emotional Labor

The term *emotional labor* was first used by Arlie Hochschild in her book *The Managed Heart*.[11] Emotional labor arises when a discrepancy exists between how frontline staff feel inside and the emotions that management requires them to show in front of customers. Frontline staff are expected to have a cheerful disposition, be genial, compassionate, sincere or even self-

Figure 11.2: Emotional labor and forced smiles can be difficult for service employees.

effacing — emotions that can be conveyed through facial expressions, gestures, tone of voice, and choice of words. To make matters worse, it is the authentic display of positive emotions rather than surface acting (e.g., "faking" emotions) that affects customer satisfaction.[12] Although some service firms make an effort to recruit employees with such characteristics, there will inevitably be situations when employees do not feel such positive emotions, yet are required to suppress their true feelings in order to conform to customer expectations (Fig. 11.2). As Pannikkos Constanti and Paul Gibbs point out, "the power axis for emotional labor tends to favor both the management and the customer, with the front line employee...being subordinate", thus creating a potentially exploitative situation.[13]

The stress of emotional labor is nicely illustrated in the following, probably apocryphal story: A flight attendant was approached by a passenger with "Let's have a smile". She replied with "Okay. I'll tell you what, first you smile and then I'll smile, okay?" He smiled. "Good", she said. "Now hold that for 15 hours", and walked away.[14] Fig. 11.3 captures emotional labor with humor.

Figure 11.3: Dilbert encounters emotional labor at the bank.

Dilbert by Scott Adams. © Universal Uclick All Rights Reserved.

Firms need to be aware of ongoing emotional stress among their employees and make sure that their employees are trained to deal with emotional stress and cope with pressure from customers, as well as get support from their team leaders. If not, employees will use a variety of ways to resist the stress of emotional labor.[15] For example, because of Singapore Airlines' reputation for service excellence, its customers tend to have high expectations and can be very demanding. This puts considerable pressure on its frontline employees. The commercial training manager of Singapore Airlines (SIA) explained:

> We have recently undertaken an external survey and it appears that more of the 'demanding customers' choose to fly with SIA. So the staff are really under a lot of pressure. We have a motto: 'If SIA can't do it for you, no other airline can'. So we encourage staff to try to sort things out, and to do as much as they can for the customer. Although they are very proud, and indeed, protective of the company, we need to help them deal with the emotional turmoil of having to handle their customers well, and at the same time, feel they're not being taken advantage of. The challenge is to help our staff deal with difficult situations and take the brickbats.[16]

Service Sweat Shops?

Rapid developments in information technology are permitting service businesses to make radical improvements in business processes and even completely reengineer their operations. These developments sometimes result in wrenching changes in the nature of work for existing employees.

In some instances, deployment of new technology and methods can dramatically change the nature of the work environment (*Service Insights 11.2*). In other instances, face-to-face contact is replaced by use of the Internet or call center-provided services, and firms have redefined and relocated jobs, created new employee profiles for recruiting purposes, and sought to hire employees with a different set of qualifications.

As a result of the growing shift from high-contact to low-contact services, a large and increasing number of customer contact employees work by telephone or email, never meeting customers face to face. For example, a remarkable 3% of the total US workforce is now employed in call centers as customer service representatives (CSRs).

At best, when well-designed, such jobs can be rewarding, and often offer parents and students flexible working hours and part-time jobs (some 50% of call-center workers are single mothers or students). In fact, it has been shown that part-time workers are more satisfied with their work as CSRs than full-time staff, and perform just as well.[17] At worst, these jobs place employees in an electronic equivalent of the old-fashioned sweatshop. Even in the best-managed call centers (also called "customer contact centers") the work is intense, with CSRs expected to deal with up to two calls a minute (including trips to the toilet and breaks) and under a high level of monitoring. There is also significant stress from customers themselves, because many are irate at the time of contact.

Research on call centers found that intrinsically motivated agents suffered less customer stress.[18] As discussed in this chapter, some of the keys to success in this area involve screening applicants to make sure they already know how to present themselves well on the telephone and have the potential to learn additional skills, training them carefully, and giving them a well-designed working environment.

SERVICE INSIGHTS 11.2
Counting the Seconds — Performance Measurement of Frontline Employees

Retailers have come under tremendous pressure to cut costs, and labor is their biggest controllable expense. It is no wonder then that business is booming for the Operations Workforce Optimization

(OWO) unit, which was recently acquired by Accenture, the global consulting firm. The consulting and software company adapted time-motion concepts developed for manufacturing operations to service businesses, where it breaks down tasks such as working a cash register in a supermarket into quantifiable units and develops standard times to complete each unit or task. The firm then implements software to help its clients to monitor employee performance.

A spokesperson of a large retailer explained that they "expect employees to be at 100% performance to the standards, but we do not begin any formal counseling process until the performance falls below 95%". If a staff falls below 95% of the baseline score too many times, he or she is likely to be bounced to a lower-paying job or be fired. Employee responses to this approach can be negative. Interviews with cashiers of that large retailer suggest that the system has spurred many to hurry up and experience increased stress levels. Hanning, 25 years old, took a cashier job in one of the chain's stores in Michigan for $7.15 per hour in July 2007. She said she was "written up" three or four times for scores below 95%, and was told that she had to move to another department at a lower pay if her performance did not improve. She recalled being told, "Make sure you're just scanning, grabbing, bagging". She resigned after almost one year on the job.

The customers' experience can also be negatively affected. Gunter, 22 years old, says he recently told a longtime customer that he could not chat with her anymore as he was being timed. He said, "I was told to get people in and out". Other cashiers said that they avoided eye contact with shoppers and hurried along those customers who may take longer to unload carts or make payment. A customer reported, "Everybody is under stress. They are not as friendly. I know elderly people have a hard time making change because you lose your ability to feel. They're so rushed at checkout that they don't want to come here".

OWO recommends that retailers adjust time standards to account for customer service and other variables that can affect how long a particular task should take, but the interviews seem to suggest that quite a number of firms focus on productivity first. One clothing and footwear chain calculated that they could save $15,000 per annum for every second cut from the checkout process, and another installed fingerprint readers at the cash registers so that cashiers can sign in directly at their individual workplaces and not at a central time clock, which saves minutes of wasted time according to a former director of a major retailer. OWO says that its methods can cut labor costs by 5 to 15%.

Source: Vanessa O'Connell, "Seconds Counts as Stores Trim Costs", The Wall Street Journal, November 17, 2008.

CYCLES OF FAILURE, MEDIOCRITY, AND SUCCESS

The ways that poor, mediocre, and excellent firms set up their frontline employees for failure, mediocrity or success will be discussed next. All too often, poor working environments translate into dreadful service, with employees treating customers the way their managers treat them. Businesses with high employee turnover are often stuck in what has been termed the *Cycle of Failure*. Others, which offer job security but little scope for personal initiative and are heavily rule- and procedure-based, may suffer from an equally undesirable *Cycle of Mediocrity*. However, if managed well, there is potential for a virtuous cycle in service employment, called the *Cycle of Success*.[19]

The Cycle of Failure

In many service industries, the search for productivity is carried out with a vengeance and frequently leads to simplifying work routines and hiring workers as cheaply as possible to perform repetitive work tasks that require little or no training. Among consumer services, departmental stores, fast food restaurants, and call-center operations are often cited as examples in which this problem abounds (although there are notable exceptions). The cycle of failure captures the implications of such a strategy, with its two concentric but interactive cycles: one involving failures with employees; the second, with customers (Fig. 11.4).

The *employee cycle of failure* begins with a narrow design of jobs

Figure 11.4: The Cycle of Failure

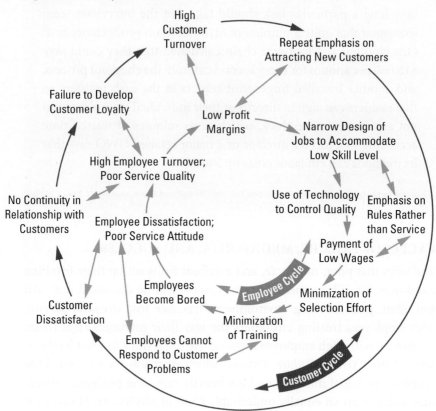

to accommodate low skill levels, an emphasis on rules rather than service, and the use of technology to control quality. Low wages are paid, accompanied by little investment in employee selection and training. Consequences include bored employees who lack the ability to respond to customer problems, who become dissatisfied, and who develop a poor service attitude. The results for the firm are low service quality and high employee turnover. Due to weak profit margins, the cycle repeats itself with the hiring of more low-paid employees to work in this unrewarding atmosphere. Some service firms can reach such low levels of employee morale that frontline staff become hostile towards customers and may even engage in "service sabotage" as described in *Service Insights 11.3*.

Figure 11.5: Examples of Service Sabotage

Openness of Service Sabotage Behaviors

Covert ←——————————————————————→ Overt

(Vertical axis, top) Routinized

(Vertical axis label) "Normality" of Service Sabotage Behaviors

(Vertical axis, bottom) Intermittent

Customary-Private Service Sabotage Many customers are rude or difficult, not even polite like you or I. Getting your own back evens the score. There are lots of things that you do that no one but you will ever know – smaller portions, doggy wine, a bad beer – all that and you serve with a smile! Sweet revenge! *Waiter* It's perfectly normal to file against some of the s**t that happens. Managers have always asked for more than fair and customers have always wanted something for nothing. Getting back at them is natural – it's always happened, nothing new in that. *Front of House Operative*	**Customer-Public Service Sabotage** You can put on a real old show. You know – if the guest is in a hurry, you slow it right down and drag it right out and if they want to chat, you can do the monosyllabic stuff. And all the time, you know that your mates are round the corner laughing their heads off! *Front of House Operative* The trick is to do it in a way that they can't complain about. I mean, you can't push it too far but some of them are so stupid that you can talk to them like a four-year-old and they would not notice. I mean, really putting them down is really patronizing. It's great fun to watch! *Waiter*
Sporadic-Private Service Sabotage I don't often work with them but the night shift here really gets to me. They are always complaining. So, to get back at them, just occasionally, I put a spanner in the works – accidentally-on-purpose misread their food orders, slow the service down, stop the glass washer so that they run out – nothing heavy. *Senior Chef* I don't know why I do it. Sometimes it's simply a bad day, a lousy week, I dunno – but kicking someone's bags down the back stairs is not that unusual – not every day – I guess a couple of times a month. *Front of House Supervisor*	**Sporadic-Public Service Sabotage** The trick is to get them and then straight away launch into the apologies. I've seen it done thousands of times – burning hot plates into someone's hands, gravy dripped on sleeves, drink spilt on backs, wigs knocked off – that was funny, soups spilt in laps, you get the idea! *Long Serving General Attendant* Listen, there's this rule that we are supposed to greet all customers and smile at them if they pass within 5 meters. Well, this ain't done 'cos we think it's silly but this guy we decided to do it to. It started off with the waiters – we'd all go up to him and grin at him and say "hello." But it spread. Before you know it, managers and all have cottoned on and this poor chap is being met and greeted every two steps! He doesn't know what the hell is going on! It was so funny – the guy spent the last three nights in his room – he didn't dare go in the restaurant. *Housekeeping Supervisor*

Source: Lloyd C. Harris and Emmanuel Ogbonna (2002), "Exploring Service Sabotage: The Antecedents, Types, and Consequences of Frontline, Deviant, Antiservice Behaviors," *Journal of Service Research*, Vol. 4, No. 3, pp. 163–183; Ramana Kumar Madupalli and Amit Poddar (2014), "Problematic Customers and Customer Service Employee Retaliation," *Journal of Service Marketing*, Vol. 28, No. 3, pp. 244–255.

SERVICE INSIGHTS 11.3
Service Sabotage by the Frontline

The next time you are dissatisfied with the service provided by a service employee — in a restaurant, for example — it is worth pausing for a moment to think about the consequences of complaining about the service. You might just become the unknowing victim of a malicious case of service sabotage, such as having something unhygienic added to one's food.

There is a fairly high incidence of service sabotage by frontline employees. Lloyd Harris and Emmanuel Ogbonna found that 90% of their interviewees accepted that frontline behavior with malicious intent to reduce or spoil the service — service sabotage — is an everyday occurrence in their organizations.

Harris and Ogbonna classify service sabotage along two dimensions: covert–overt and routinized–intermittent behaviors. Covert behaviors are concealed from customers, whereas overt actions are purposefully displayed often to co-workers and sometimes also to customers. Routinized behaviors are ingrained into the culture, whereas intermittent actions are sporadic, and less common. Some true examples of service sabotage classified along these two dimensions appear in Fig. 11.5. Another study showed that if customers are abusive in any way, some employees will retaliate!

Sources: Lloyd C. Harris and Emmanuel Ogbonna, "Exploring Service Sabotage: The Antecedents, Types, and Consequences of Frontline, Deviant, Antiservice Behaviors", *Journal of Service Research*, Vol.4, No.3, 2002, pp. 163–183; Ramana Kumar Madupalli and Amit Poddar (2014), "Problematic Customers and Customer Service Employee Retaliation", *Journal of Service Marketing*, Vol. 28, No. 3, pp. 244-255.

The *customer cycle of failure* begins with heavy organizational emphasis on attracting new customers, who become dissatisfied with employee performance and the lack of continuity implicit in continually changing faces due to high staff turnover. As these customers fail to become loyal to the supplier, they turn over as quickly as the staff, requiring an ongoing search for new customers to maintain sales volume. The departure of discontented customers is especially worrying in the light of what we know about the greater profitability of a loyal customer base (see Chap. 12).

Managers' excuses and justifications for perpetuating the cycle of failure tend to focus on employees:

- "You just cannot get good people nowadays".
- "People today just do not want to work".
- "To get good people would cost too much and you cannot pass on these cost increases to customers".
- "It is not worth training our frontline people when they leave you so quickly".
- "High turnover is simply an inevitable part of our business. You have got to learn to live with it".[20]

Too many managers ignore the long-term financial effects of low-pay/high turnover human resource strategies. Part of the problem is the failure to measure all relevant costs. In particular, three key cost variables are often omitted: (1) the cost of constant recruiting, hiring, and training (which is as much a time cost for managers as it is a financial cost); (2) the lower productivity of inexperienced new workers; and (3) the costs of constantly attracting new customers (which requires extensive advertising and promotional discounts). Also frequently ignored are two revenue variables: (1) future revenue streams that might have continued for years, but are lost when unhappy customers take their business elsewhere; and (2) the potential income lost from prospective customers who are turned off by negative word of mouth. Finally, there are less easily quantifiable costs of disruptions to service while a job remains unfilled, and the loss of the departing employee's knowledge of the business (and potentially his/her customers as well).

The Cycle of Mediocrity

The *Cycle of Mediocrity* is another potentially vicious employment cycle (Fig. 11.6), and this is most likely found in in large, bureaucratic organizations. These are often typified by state monopolies, industrial cartels, or regulated oligopolies in which there is little market pressure from more agile competitors to improve performance, and in which fear

Figure 11.6: The Cycle of Mediocrity

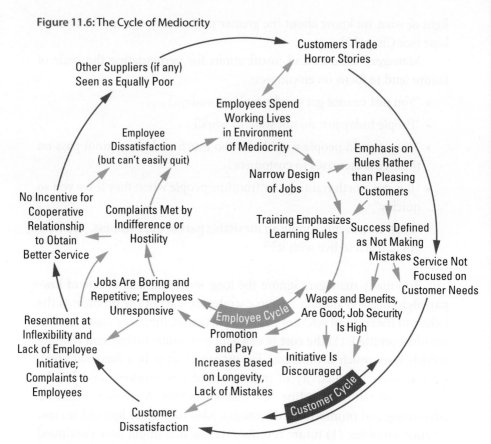

Source: Christopher Lovelock, "Managing Services: The Human Factor" in W. J. Glynn and J. G. Barnes, eds., *Understanding Service Management* (Chichester, UK: John Wiley & Sons), 228.

of entrenched unions may discourage management from adopting more innovative labor practices.

In such environments, service delivery standards tend to be prescribed by rigid rulebooks, oriented towards standardized service and operational efficiencies, and prevention of both employee fraud and favoritism toward specific customers. Job responsibilities tend to be narrowly and unimaginatively defined, tightly categorized by grade and scope of responsibilities, and further rigidified by union work rules. Salary increases and promotions are largely based on how long the person has been working in the organization. Successful performance in a job is often measured by absence of mistakes, rather than by high productivity or outstanding customer service. Employee training focuses on learning the rules and the technical aspects of the job, not on improving human interactions with customers and co-workers. Since employees are given very little freedom to do their work in the way they think is necessary or suitable, jobs tend to be boring and repetitive. However, unlike the Cycle of Failure, most positions provide adequate pay and often good benefits, combined with high job security. Thus, employees are reluctant to leave. This lack of mobility is compounded by an absence of marketable skills that would be valued by organizations in other fields.

Customers find such organizations frustrating to deal with. Faced with bureaucratic hassles, lack of service flexibility, and unwillingness of employees to make an effort to serve them well, customers can become resentful. There is little incentive for customers to cooperate with the organization to achieve better service. When they complain to employees who are already unhappy, the poor service attitude becomes worse. Employees may then protect themselves through mechanisms such as withdrawal into indifference, overtly playing by the book, or countering rudeness with rudeness.

It is not surprising that dissatisfied customers sometimes display hostility towards service employees who feel trapped in their jobs and who are powerless to improve the situation. However, customers often remain with the organization as there is nowhere else for them to go, either because the service provider holds a monopoly, or because all other available players are perceived as equally bad or worse. The net result is a vicious cycle of mediocrity in which unhappy customers continually complain to sullen employees (and also to other customers) about poor service and bad attitudes, generating greater defensiveness and lack of caring on the part of the staff.

The Cycle of Success

Some firms reject the assumptions underlying the cycles of failure or mediocrity. Instead, they take a long-term view of financial performance, seeking to prosper by investing in their people in order to create a *Cycle of Success* (Fig. 11.7).

As with failure or mediocrity, success applies to both employees and customers. Better pay and benefits attract good quality staff. Broadened job designs are accompanied by training and empowerment practices that allow frontline staff to control quality. With more focused recruitment,

Figure 11.7: The Cycle of Success

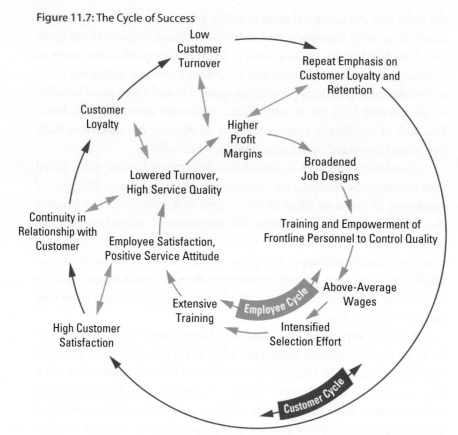

intensive training, and better wages, employees are likely to be happier in their work and provide higher quality service. Lower turnover means that regular customers appreciate the continuity in service relationships and are more likely to remain loyal. With greater customer loyalty, profit margins tend to be higher, and the organization is free to focus its marketing efforts on reinforcing customer loyalty through customer retention strategies. These strategies are usually much more profitable than strategies for attracting new customers.

A powerful demonstration of a frontline employee working in the Cycle of Success is waitress Cora Griffith (featured in the opening vignette of this chapter). Even public service organizations in many countries are increasingly working towards creating their own cycles of success, and offer their users good quality service at a lower cost to the public.[21]

When looking at the three cycles, it is undeniably ideal for firms to be operating under the conditions in the Cycle of Success. However, firms operating under the other two cycles can still survive if some element of their offering meets customer expectations. For example, in a restaurant context, customers may be dissatisfied with the service provided by the staff, but if they are willing to accept it because they like the restaurant's quality of food and location, then that element has met their expectations. Nevertheless, for long-run profitability and success, firms should ideally move towards the Cycle of Success.

HUMAN RESOURCE MANAGEMENT — HOW TO GET IT RIGHT?

Any rational manager would like to operate in the Cycle of Success. This section will discuss HR strategies that can help service firms to move towards that goal, specifically how firms can hire, motivate, and retain engaged service employees who are willing and able to deliver service excellence, productivity, and sales. Fig. 11.8 shows the Service Talent Cycle which is our guiding framework for successful HR practices in service firms. The recommended practices will be discussed in detail in this section.

Hire the Right People

It is naïve to think that it is sufficient to satisfy employees. Employee satisfaction should be seen as necessary but not sufficient for having high performing staff. For instance, a recent study showed that employee effort is a strong driver of customer satisfaction over and above employee satisfaction.[22] As Jim Collins said, "The old adage "People are the most important asset" is wrong. The *right* people are your most important asset". We would like to add: "…and the wrong people are a liability that is often difficult to get rid of". Getting it right starts with hiring the right people. Hiring the right people includes competing for applications from the best employees in the labor market, then selecting from this pool the best candidates for the specific jobs to be filled.

Be the Preferred Employer. To be able to select and hire the best people, they first have to apply for a job with you and then accept your

Figure 11.8: The Service Talent Cycle — getting HR right in service firms

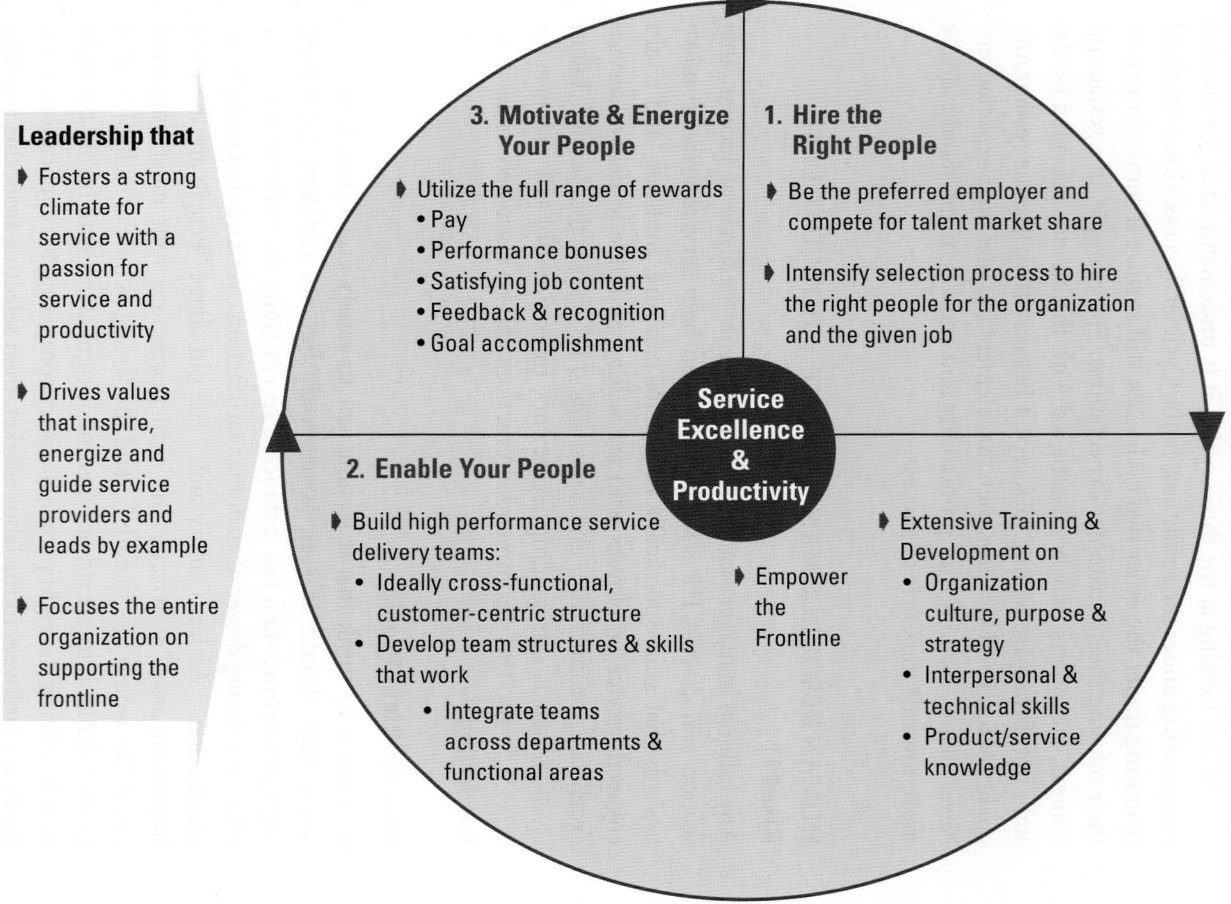

Leadership that

➤ Fosters a strong climate for service with a passion for service and productivity

➤ Drives values that inspire, energize and guide service providers and leads by example

➤ Focuses the entire organization on supporting the frontline

Service Excellence & Productivity

1. Hire the Right People

➤ Be the preferred employer and compete for talent market share

➤ Intensify selection process to hire the right people for the organization and the given job

Extensive Training & Development on

➤ Extensive Training & Development on
  • Organization culture, purpose & strategy
  • Interpersonal & technical skills
  • Product/service knowledge

➤ Empower the Frontline

2. Enable Your People

➤ Build high performance service delivery teams:
  • Ideally cross-functional, customer-centric structure
  • Develop team structures & skills that work
    • Integrate teams across departments & functional areas

3. Motivate & Energize Your People

➤ Utilize the full range of rewards
  • Pay
  • Performance bonuses
  • Satisfying job content
  • Feedback & recognition
  • Goal accomplishment

job offer in preference over others (the best people tend to be selected by several firms). Service firms have a brand in the labor market too, and potential candidates tend to seek companies that are good to work for and have an image that is congruent with their own values and beliefs.[23] Job seekers regularly approach current and former employees for information and can easily learn about salaries, benefits, working climate, and even interview questions.[24] A lot of internal company information can also be found online. For example, Glassdoor.com had over 500,000 company and job reviews in 2014, providing potential employees good insights into what it would be like to work for a particular firm.[25] A firm has to first compete for talent market share, or as global consulting firm McKinsey & Company calls it, "the war for talent".[26]

To effectively compete in the labor market means having an attractive value proposition for prospective employees. This typically includes a good image in the community as a place to work, being seen as delivering high quality products and services, and being a good corporate citizen and engaging in relevant corporate social responsibility (CSR),[27] which together make employees feel proud to be part of the team. Furthermore, the compensation package cannot be below average — top people expect above average packages. From experience, it takes a salary in the range of the 60th to 80th percentile of the market to attract top performers to top companies (Fig. 11.9). However, a firm does not have to be a top paymaster, if other important aspects of the value proposition are

Figure 11.9: A firm does not need to pay top dollars to attract top performers.

© Randy Glasbergen.
www.glasbergen.com

GLASBERGEN

**"I'm offering you a six-figure salary.
Three figures on the 15th of the month
and three figures on the 30th."**

attractive. In short, understand the needs of your target-employees and get your value proposition right. See *Service Insights 11.4* on how Google has managed to remain one of the best companies in the world to work for in the last few years. As Netflix describes the most basic element of its talent management philosophy: "The best thing you can do for employees — a perk better than football or free sushi — is hire only 'A' players to work alongside them. Excellent colleagues trump everything else". That is, just having a reputation for having the best people working in the firm is itself a powerful value proposition to prospective candidates.[28]

SERVICE INSIGHTS 11.3
Google, the Preferred Employer

Google was voted number 1 in *Fortune's* 100 Best Companies to work for in 2015 for the sixth year. The immediate question on people's minds will be: Why so? What makes it one of the best? What kind of culture does the company have? What kind of benefits do the employees enjoy? What are its employees like?

Employees of Google are called Googlers. They are widely perceived as fun-loving and interesting people. At the same time, when it comes to work, they are achievement-oriented and driven. Google has a culture of being innovative, unconventional, different, and fun, and in line with this, its employees are given the freedom to work independently. Google's experience thus far suggests that pampering employees actually results in increased productivity and profitability. Certainly, Googlers seem willing to work long hours for the company.

What kind of benefits do Googlers enjoy? The list is long, but top on the list is gourmet food for free, and this is just the appetizer! At the company's headquarters in Mountain View, California, the "campus" offers many free amenities, including Wi-Fi enabled shuttle buses, motorized scooters to get around, car washes, and oil changes. If Googlers are interested in buying hybrid cars, they get a $5,000 subsidy for that. Googlers have five free on-site doctors, unlimited sick days, free flu shots, a gym to work out at, and a pool to do laps in with lifeguards on duty. For more domestic activities, there are free on-site laundry services or one can drop off their laundry at the dry cleaners. There are also childcare services, and new parents (including dads, domestic partners, adoptive parents, and surrogate parents) can get fully-paid baby bonding time for up to 12 weeks. For leisure and sports, one can play a game of pool, do some rock climbing on the wall, or play a game of volleyball at the beach volleyball pit. The list goes on. As a result, Googlers can spend long and productive hours at work. However, it must be noted that the benefits offered to employees working at other Google offices tend to be less significant.

Google has an engineering headquarters in Zurich, Switzerland. This building was partly designed by the engineers who work there. Life there is just as fun. There are meeting places that are designed to look like Swiss chalets and igloos. People can get from one floor to another using fireman poles, and there is a slide that allows them to reach the cafeteria very quickly. There are other areas like games room, library in the style of an English country house, and an aquarium where staff can lie in a bath of red foam and look at the fishes if they feel stressed out.

"The slide gets people to the cafeteria quickly".

Because the firm is seen as such a desirable place to work, it can be extremely selective in its recruiting, hiring only the best and the brightest. This may work particularly well for its engineers, who tend to get the most kudos. However, despite the company's stellar reputation as an employer, some observers question whether this very positive environment can be maintained as the company grows and its workforce matures.

Sources: http://fortune.com/best-companies, accessed 11 May 2016; www.google.com.sg/about/careers/lifeatgoogle/benefits, accessed 11 May 2016; Jane Wakefield, "Google Your Way to a Wacky Office", *BBC News Website*, 13 March 2008, http://news.bbc.co.uk/2/hi/7290322.stm, accessed 11 May 2016.

Select the Right People. There is no such thing as the perfect employee (Fig. 11.10). Different positions are often best filled by people with different skill sets, styles and personalities. Different brands have different personalities, and it is important that there is a good employee–brand fit

Figure 11.10: There's no such thing as a perfect employee.

"Allen is an incredible, wonderful, fun, generous, exciting, kind, loving, brilliant, very special human being. This personal reference from your dog is quite impressive."

so that it is natural for employees to deliver service that supports the firm's espoused image, and that their behavior is perceived as authentic by their customers.[29] The recruitment and selection processes should be explicitly designed to encourage a good employee–brand fit.[30] This includes the recruitment advertising to explicitly display key brand attributes and firm positioning, and to encourage potential candidates to reflect on their fit with the firm; to design selection methods to convey brand values to allow employees to make a self-assessment of their fit; and to ensure recruiters are proactively looking out for brand-fit and potential misfit.

For example, The Walt Disney Company assesses prospective employees in terms of their potential brand fit ("Is magic, fun and happiness your world?") and then for on-stage or backstage work. On-stage workers, known as cast members, are given to those people with the looks, personalities and skills to match the job.

Often it is the things that *cannot* be taught that makes outstanding service performers so special. It is the qualities that are intrinsic to the people, and qualities they would bring with them to any employer. As one study of high performers observed:

> *Energy...cannot be taught, it has to be hired. The same is true for charm, for detail orientation, for work ethic, for neatness. Some of these things can be enhanced with on-the-job training... or incentives... But by and large, such qualities are instilled early on.*[31]

HR managers have also discovered that while good manners and the need to smile and make eye contact can be taught, warmth itself cannot be learnt. The only realistic solution is to ensure that the organization's recruitment criteria favors candidates with naturally warm personalities. Jim Collins emphasizes that "the right people are those who would exhibit the desired behaviors anyway, as a natural extension of their character and attitude, regardless of any control and incentive system".[32]

The logical conclusion is that service firms should devote great care to attract and hire the right candidates. Increasingly, the top companies are using employee analytics to improve their ability to attract and retain the best talent. Employee analytics are similar to customer analytics; for example, it is able to predict who would be a better performer. They can also use analytics to place the right employees in the right job.[33] Apart from the use of data analysis, some tools to help identify the right candidates for a given firm and job, and more importantly, reject candidates that are not a good fit, will be reviewed next.

Tools to Identify the Best Candidates[34]

Excellent service firms use a number of approaches to identifying the candidates with the best fit in their applicant pool. These approaches include interviewing applicants, observing behavior, conducting personality tests, and providing applicants with a realistic job preview.

Use Multiple, Structured Interviews. To improve hiring decisions, successful recruiters like to employ structured interviews built around job requirements, and to use more than one interviewer. People tend to be more careful in their judgments when they know that another individual is also judging the same applicant. Another advantage of using two or more interviewers is that it reduces the risk of a "similar to me" bias — we all tend to like people who are similar to ourselves.

Observe Candidate Behavior. The hiring decision should be based on the behavior that recruiters observe, not just the words they hear. As John Wooden said: "Show me what you can do, don't tell me what you can do. Too often, the big talkers are the little doers".[35] Behavior can be directly or indirectly observed by using behavioral simulations or assessment center tests that use standardized situations in which applicants can be observed to see whether they display the kind of behaviors the firms' clients would expect. In addition, past behavior is the best predictor of future behavior. Hire the person who has won service excellence awards, received many compliment letters, and has great references from past employers.

Conduct Personality Tests. Many managers hire employees based on personality. Personality tests help to identify traits related to a particular job. For example, willingness to treat customers and colleagues with courtesy, consideration and tact; perceptiveness of customer needs; and ability to communicate accurately and pleasantly are traits that can be measured. It is better to hire upbeat and happy people as customers report higher satisfaction when being served by more satisfied staff.[36] Research has also shown that certain traits such as being hardworking, and the belief in one's capabilities to manage situations result in strong employee performance and service quality.[37] Hiring decisions based on such tests tend to be accurate, especially in identifying, and rejecting unsuitable candidates.

For example, the Ritz-Carlton Hotels Group uses personality profiles on all job applicants. Employees are selected for their natural predisposition for working in a service context. Inherent traits such as a ready smile, a willingness to help others, and an affinity for multi-tasking enables them to go beyond learned skills. An applicant to Ritz-Carlton shared her experience of going through the personality test for a job as a junior-level concierge at the Ritz-Carlton Millenia, Singapore. Her best advice: "Tell the truth. These are experts; they will know if you are lying", and then she added:

> On the big day, they asked if I liked helping people, if I was an organized person and if I liked to smile a lot. "Yes, yes and yes", I said. But I had to support it with real life examples. This, at times, felt rather intrusive. To answer the first question for instance, I had to say a bit about the person I had helped — why she needed help, for example. The test forced me to recall even insignificant things I had done, like learning how to say hello in different languages, which helped to get a fix on my character.[38]

Apart from intensive interview-based psychological tests, cost-effective Internet-based testing kits are available. Here, applicants enter their test responses to a web-based questionnaire, and the prospective employer receives the analysis, the suitability of the candidate, and a hiring recommendation. Developing and administering such tests has become a significant service industry in its own right. A leading global supplier of such assessment products, SHL Talent Measurement (a unit of CEB), serves over 20,000 organizations in 30 languages in over 110 countries. Its website shows the available tests.

Give Applicants a Realistic Preview of the Job.[39] During the recruitment process, service companies should let candidates know the reality of the job, thereby giving them a chance to "try on the job" and assess whether it is a good fit or not. At the same time, recruiters can observe how candidates respond to the job's realities. Some candidates may withdraw if they realize the job is not a good match for them. At the same time, the company can manage new employees' expectations of their job. Many service companies adopt this approach. For example, Au Bon Pain, a chain of French bakery cafes, lets applicants work for two paid days in one of its cafés prior to the final selection interview. Here, managers can observe candidates in action, and candidates can assess whether they like the job and the work environment.[40] In the ultimate recruitment and interview process, Donald Trump worked with the NBC network to produce the reality TV series, *The Apprentice*, where the winner received the chance to join the Trump organization and manage a project selected by Trump himself.

See *Service Insights 11.5* on how Southwest Airlines uses a combination of interviews and other selection tools to identify the right candidates with the right attitude and a personality that fits the Southwest culture from its vast pool of applicants.

SERVICE INSIGHTS 11.5
Hiring at Southwest Airlines

Southwest hires people with the right attitude and with personality that matches its corporate personality. Humor is the key. Herb Kelleher, Southwest's legendary former CEO and now chairman said, "I want flying to be a helluva of fun!" "We look for attitudes; people with a sense of humor who don't take themselves too seriously. We'll train you on whatever it is you have to do, but the one thing Southwest cannot change in people is inherent attitudes". Southwest has one fundamental, consistent principle — hire people with the right spirit. Southwest looks for people with other-oriented, outgoing personalities, individuals who become part of an extended family of people who work hard and have fun at the same time.

Southwest's painstaking approach to interviewing continues to evolve in the light of experience. It is perhaps at its most innovative in the selection of flight attendants. A day-long visit to the company usually begins with applicants being gathered in a group. Recruiters watch how well they interact with each other (another chance for such observation will come at lunchtime).

Then comes a series of personal interviews. Each candidate has three one-on-one "behavioral-type" interviews during the course of the day. Based on input from supervisors and peers in a given job category, interviewers target 8 to 10 dimensions for each position. For a flight attendant, these might include a willingness to take initiative, compassion, flexibility, sensitivity, sincerity, a customer-service orientation, and a predisposition to be a team player. Even humor is "tested". Prospective employees are typically asked, "Tell me how you recently used your sense of humor in a work environment. Tell me how you have used humor to defuse a difficult situation".

Southwest describes the ideal interview as "a conversation", in which the goal is to make candidates comfortable. "The first interview of the day tends to be a bit stiff, the second is more comfortable, and by the third they tell us a whole lot more. It's really hard to fake it under those circumstances". The three interviewers do not discuss candidates during the day but compare notes afterwards, so that it reduces the risk of bias.

To help select people with the right attitude, Southwest invites supervisors and peers (with whom future candidates will be working) to participate in the in-depth interviewing and selection process. In this way, existing employees buy into the recruitment process and feel a sense of responsibility for mentoring new recruits and helping them to become successful in the job (rather than wondering, as an interviewer put it, "who hired this turkey?"). More unusually, it invites its own frequent flyers to participate in the initial interviews for flight attendants and to tell the candidates what they, the passengers, value.

The interviewing team asks a group of potential employees to prepare a five-minute presentation about themselves, and gives them plenty of time to prepare. As the presentations are delivered, the interviewers don't watch just the speakers. They watch the audience to see which applicants are using their time to work on their own presentations and which are enthusiastically cheering on and supporting their potential coworkers. Unselfish people who will support their teammates are the ones who catch Southwest's eyes, not the applicants who are tempted to polish their own presentations while others are speaking.

By hiring the right attitude, the company is able to foster the so-called Southwest spirit — an intangible quality in people that causes them to want to do whatever it takes and to want to go that extra mile whenever they need to. Southwest itself goes the extra mile for its employees and has never laid anyone off, even after it decided to close reservations centers in three cities in 2004 to cut costs. Management knows that the airline's culture is a key competitive advantage.

Sources: Kevin and Jackie Freiberg, *Nuts! Southwest Airlines' Crazy Recipe for Business and Personal Success.* New York: Broadway Books, 1997, pp. 64-69; Christopher Lovelock, *Product Plus.* New York: McGraw-Hill 1994, 323-326; Barney Gimbel, "Southwest's New Flight Plan," *Fortune,* 16 May 2005, 93-98.

Train Service Employees Actively

If a firm has good people, investments in training and development can yield outstanding results. Having a good career development program for employees helps them to feel they are valued and taken care of, and in turn, they will work to meet customers' needs, resulting in customer satisfaction, loyalty, and ultimately, profitability for the firm.[41] Service champions show a strong commitment to training in words, dollars, and action. Employees of Apple retail stores, for example, are given intensive training on how to interact with customers, phrase words in a positive rather than negative way, and what to say when customers are emotional. Employees are supposed to help customers solve problems rather than sell.[42] As Benjamin Schneider and David Bowen put it, "The combination of attracting a diverse and competent applicant pool, utilizing effective techniques for hiring the most appropriate people from that pool, and then training the heck out of them would be gangbusters in any market".[43]

Training Contents. There are many aspects in a firm that service employees need to be trained on. Service employees need to learn:

- *Organizational Culture, Purpose, and Strategy.* Start strong with new hires, and focus on getting emotional commitment to the firm's core strategy, and promote core values such as commitment to service excellence, responsiveness, team spirit, mutual respect, honesty and integrity. Use managers to teach, and focus on "what", "why", and "how", rather than the specifics of the job.[44] For example, new recruits at Disneyland attend the "Disney University Orientation". It starts with a detailed discussion of the company history and philosophy, the service standards expected of cast members, and a comprehensive tour of Disneyland's operations.[45]

- *Interpersonal and Technical Skills.* Interpersonal skills tend to be generic across service jobs, and include visual communications skills such as making eye contact, attentive listening, understanding body language, and even facial expressions, and reading customers' needs. Technical skills include all the required knowledge related to processes (e.g., how to handle a merchandized return), machines (e.g., how to operate the terminal, or cash machine), and rules and regulations related to customer service processes. Creativity in designing solutions and solving problems is also required in non-routine encounters and service recovery. Both technical and interpersonal skills are *necessary* but neither is enough for optimal job performance on its own.[46]

- *Product/Service Knowledge.* Knowledgeable staff are a key aspect of service quality. They must be able to explain product features effectively and also position the product correctly. For example, all the products are openly displayed for customers to try out at an Apple retail store. Staff members need to be able to answer questions about any of the product's features, usage, and any other aspects of service like maintenance, service bundles, and so on. See also *Service Insights 11.6* on how Jennifer Grassano coached individual staff members in a call center on how to paint pictures in the customer's mind.

SERVICE INSIGHTS 11.6
Coaching in a Call Center

Coaching is a common method employed by services leaders to train and develop staff. Dial-A-Mattress' Jennifer Grassano was a bedding consultant (BC) for three days a week, and a coach to other BCs for one day a week. She focused on staff whose productivity and sales performance were slumping.

Her first step was to listen in on the BCs' telephone calls with customers. She would listen for about an hour and take detailed notes on each call. The BCs understood that their calls may be monitored, but they received no advance notice, as that would defeat the purpose.

Grassano conducted a coaching session with the staff member, in which strengths and areas for improvements were reviewed. She knew how difficult it is to maintain a high energy level and convey enthusiasm when handling some 60 calls per shift. She liked to suggest new tactics and phrasings "to spark up their presentation". One BC was not responding effectively when customers asked why one mattress was more expensive than another. Here, she stressed the need to paint a picture in the customer's mind:

> *Customers are at our mercy when buying bedding. They don't know the difference between one coil system and another. It is just like buying a carburetor for my car. I don't even know what a carburetor looks like. We have to use very descriptive words to help bedding customers make the decision that is right for them. Tell the customer that the more costly mattress has richer, finer padding with a blend of silk and wool. Don't just say the mattress has more layers of padding.*

About two months after the initial coaching session, Grassano conducted a follow-up monitoring session with that BC. She then compared the BC's performance before and after the coaching session to assess the effectiveness of the training.

Grassano's experience and productivity as a BC gave her credibility as a coach. "If I am not doing well as a BC, then who am I to be a coach? I have to lead by example. I would be much less effective if I was a full-time trainer". She clearly relishes the opportunity to share her knowledge and pass on her craft.

Source: Leonard L. Berry, Discovering the Soul of Service – The Nine Drivers of Sustainable Business Success. New York: The Free Press, 1999, p. 171-172. Dial-a-Mattress merged with two other companies and today is called: 1800Mattress.com; see http://en.wikipedia.org/wiki/1800Mattress.com, accessed 11 May, 2016.

Reinforce Training to Shape Behaviors. Undeniably, training has to result in observable changes in behavior. If staff do not apply what they have learnt, the investment is wasted. Learning is not only about becoming smarter, but about changing behaviors and improving decision making. To achieve this, practice and reinforcement are needed. Supervisors play a crucial role by following up regularly on learning objectives, for instance, meeting with staff to reinforce key lessons from recent complaints and compliments.

Another example of constant reinforcement is Ritz-Carlton's approach. It translated the key product and service requirements of its customers into the Ritz-Carlton Gold Standards, which include a credo, motto, three steps of service and 12 service values (*Service Insights 11.7*) Ritz–Carlton's service values are split into different levels.

Service values 10, 11 and 12 represent functional values such as safety, security, and cleanliness. Ritz-Carlton refers to the next level of excellence as emotional engagement, which covers values 4 through 9. They relate to learning and professional growth of its employees, teamwork, service, problem solving and service recovery, innovation, and continuous improvement. Beyond the guests' functional needs and emotional engagement is the third level, which relates to values 1, 2 and 3, and is called "the Ritz-Carlton Mystique". This level aims to create unique, memorable, and personal guest experiences, which Ritz-Carlton believes can only occur when employees deliver on the guests' expressed and unexpressed wishes and needs, and when they strive to build lifetime relationships between Ritz-Carlton and its guests. The three levels are reflected in the Sixth Diamond in Ritz-Carlton Gold Standards as a new benchmark in the hospitality industry, and the three levels for achieving both employee and customer engagement.[47]

Tim Kirkpatrick, Director of Training and Development of Ritz-Carlton's Boston Common Hotel said, "The Gold Standards are part of our uniform, just like your name tag. But remember, it's just a laminated card until you put it into action".[48] To reinforce these standards, every morning briefing includes a discussion directly related to the standards. The aim of these discussions is to keep the Ritz-Carlton philosophy at the center of its employees' minds.

Internal Communications to Shape the Service Culture and Behaviors

In addition to having a strong training platform, it takes a significant communications effort to shape the culture and get the message to the troops. Service leaders use multiple tools to build their service culture, ranging from internal marketing and training, to core principles, and company events and celebrations. Internal communications to employees (often also referred to as *internal marketing*) play a vital role in maintaining and nurturing a corporate culture founded on specific service values.

Well-planned internal marketing efforts are especially necessary in large service businesses that operate in widely dispersed sites, sometimes around the world. Even when employees work far from the head office, they still need to be kept informed of new policies, changes in service features, and new quality initiatives. Communications may also be needed to nurture team spirit and support common corporate goals across national frontiers. Consider the challenge of maintaining a unified sense of purpose at the overseas offices of companies such as Citibank, Air Canada, Marriott or Starbucks, where people from different cultures who speak different languages must work together to create consistent levels of service.

Effective internal communications are an excellent complimentary tool to training that can help ensure efficient and satisfactory service delivery, achieve productive and harmonious working relationships, and build employee trust, respect and loyalty. Commonly used media include internal newsletters and magazines, videos, Intranets, email, face-to-face briefings, and promotional campaigns using displays, prizes, and recognition programs.

Professionalizing the Frontline. Training and learning professionalizes the frontline, and moves these individuals away from the common (self)-

image of being in low-end jobs that have no significance. Well-trained employees feel and act like professionals. A waiter who knows about food, cooking, wines, dining etiquette, and how to effectively interact with customers (even complaining ones), feels professional, has a higher self-esteem, and is respected by his customers. Training and internal communications are therefore extremely effective in reducing person/role stress, and in enabling and energizing front line employees.

Empower the Frontline [49]

After being the preferred employer, selecting the right candidates, and training them well, the next step is to empower the frontline and encourage them to show proactive customer service performance that can go beyond the call of duty.[50] Nearly all breakthrough service firms have legendary stories of employees who recovered failed service transactions, or walked the extra mile to make a customer's day, or avoid some kind of disaster for that client (see *Service Insights 11.8*). To allow this to happen, employees have to be empowered. Nordstrom trains and trusts its employees to do the right thing and empowers them to do so. Its employee handbook has only one rule: "Use good judgment in all situations".

Good judgment is important as it is a fine line between going the extra mile for a customer and service sweethearting, whereby employees unnecessarily and potentially, illicitly waive bills or give freebies to boost their unit's satisfaction rating or avoid confrontation with a customer who is wrong (see also Chap. 13).[51] It is therefore important that employee are self-directed, especially in service firms because frontline staff frequently operate on their own, face-to-face with their customers, and it tends to be difficult for managers to closely monitor their behavior.[52]

For many services, providing employees with greater discretion (and training in how to use their judgment) enables them to provide superior service on the spot, rather than taking time to get permission from supervisors. Empowerment looks to frontline staff to find solutions to service problems, and to make appropriate decisions about customizing service delivery. It is therefore not surprising that research has linked high empowerment to higher customer satisfaction.[53]

SERVICE INSIGHTS 11.8
Empowerment at Nordstrom

Van Mensah, a men's clothes sales associate at Nordstrom, received a disturbing letter from one of his loyal customers. The gentleman had purchased some $2,000 worth of shirts and ties from Mensah, and mistakenly washed the shirts in hot water. They all shrank. He was writing to ask Mensah's professional advice on how he should deal with his predicament (the gentleman did not complain and readily conceded the mistake was his).

Mensah immediately called the customer and offered to replace those shirts with new ones at no charge. He asked the customer to mail the other shirts back to Nordstrom — at Nordstrom's expense. "I didn't have to ask for anyone's permission to do what I did for that customer", said Mensah. "Nordstrom would rather leave it up to me to decide what's best".

Middlemas, a Nordstrom's veteran said to employees, "You will never be criticized for doing too much for a customer, you will only be criticized for doing too little. If you're ever in doubt as to what to do in a situation, always make a decision that favors the customer before the company". Nordtrom's Employee Handbook confirms this. It reads:

Welcome to Nordstrom
We're glad to have you with our Company.
Our number one goal is to provide outstanding customer service.
Set both your personal and professional goals high.
We have great confidence in your ability to achieve them.
Nordstrom Rules:
Rule#1: Use your good judgment in all situations.
There will be no additional rules.
Please feel free to ask your department manager, store manager, or division general manager any question at any time.

Source: Robert Spector and Patrick D. McCarthy (2012), *The Nordstrom Way to Customer Service Excellence: The Handbook For Becoming the "Nordstrom" of Your Industry.* 2nd ed., New York: John Wiley & Sons.

When are High Levels of Empowerment Appropriate? Advocates claim that the empowerment approach is more likely to yield motivated employees and satisfied customers than the "production-line" alternative, in which management designs a relatively standardized system and expects workers to execute tasks within narrow guidelines. However, David Bowen and Edward Lawler suggest that different situations may require different solutions, declaring that "both the empowerment and production-line approaches have their advantages... and... each fits certain situations. The key is to choose the management approach that best meets the needs of both employees and customers". Not all employees are necessarily eager to be empowered, and many employees do not seek personal growth within their jobs, and would prefer to work to specific directions rather than to use their own initiative. Research has shown that a strategy of empowerment is most likely to be appropriate when most of the following factors are present within the organization and its environment:

- The firm offers personalized, customized service and is based on competitive differentiation.
- The firm has extended relationships with customers rather than short-term transactions.
- The organization uses technologies that are complex and non-routine in nature.
- Service failures often are non-routine and cannot be designed out of the system. Frontline employees have to respond quickly to recover the service.
- The business environment is unpredictable and surprises are to be expected.
- Existing managers are comfortable with letting employees decide independently for the benefit of both the organization and its customers.
- Employees have a strong need to grow and deepen their skills in the work environment, are interested in working with others, and have good interpersonal and group process skills.[54]

Requirements for Empowering the Frontline. The production-line approach to managing people is based on the well-established *control* model of organization design and management. There are clearly defined roles, top-down control systems, hierarchical pyramid structures, and an assumption that the management knows best. In contrast, empowerment is based on the *involvement* (or *commitment*) model, which assumes that employees can make good decisions, and produce good ideas for operating the business, if they are properly socialized, trained and informed. This model also assumes that employees can be internally motivated to perform effectively, and that they are capable of self-control and self-direction.

Schneider and Bowen emphasize that "empowerment isn't just "setting the frontline free" or "throwing away the policy manuals". It requires systematically redistributing four key ingredients throughout the organization, from the top downwards".[55] The four features are:

- *Information* about organizational, team, and individual performance (e.g., operating results and measures of competitive performance).

- *Knowledge* that enables employees to understand and contribute to organizational, team, and individual performance (e.g., problem-solving skills).

- *Power* to make decisions that influence work procedures and organizational direction (e.g., through quality circles and self-managing teams) at the higher level, and transaction-specific decisions (e.g., decisions regarding customization for a customer and service recovery) at the micro level.

- *Rewards* based on organizational, team and individual performance, such as bonuses, profit sharing, and stock options.

In the control model, the four features are concentrated at the top of the organization, while in the involvement model, these features are pushed down through the organization. In restaurants, for example, management often schedules servers for shifts they would rather not take, and worse, the least-productive servers can be scheduled on the most profitable shifts. To solve both issues, the Boston-based restaurant chain Not Your Average Joe's pushed all four features of empowerment to the frontline. The restaurant developed a performance rating system that tracks and communicates sales and customer satisfaction (measured by tips or directly) data for each server (giving them information and knowledge). Based on their ranking, employees can now self-select their preferred shifts and restaurant sections through a self-service online system (providing them with decision making power and rewards). This system empowers and rewards high performers, fosters a culture of performance, saves each restaurant manager around three to five hours of scheduling work per week, and makes restaurants more profitable.[56]

Levels of Employee Involvement. The empowerment and production-line approaches are at opposite ends of a spectrum that reflects increasing levels of employee involvement as additional information, knowledge, power, and rewards are pushed down to the frontline. Management needs to determine the appropriate level of empowerment for its business model and customers' needs. Empowerment can take place at several levels:

- *Suggestion Involvement* empowers employees to make recommendations through formalized programs. McDonald's, often portrayed as an archetype of the production-line approach, listens closely to its frontline. Did you know that innovations ranging from Egg McMuffin, to methods of wrapping burgers without leaving a thumbprint on the bun, were invented by employees?

- *Job Involvement* represents a dramatic opening up of job content. Jobs are redesigned to allow employees to use a wider array of skills. In complex service organizations such as airlines and hospitals where individual employees cannot offer all facets of a service, job involvement is often accomplished through the use of teams. To cope with the added demands accompanying this form of empowerment, employees require training, and supervisors need to be reoriented from directing the group to facilitating its performance in supportive ways.

- *High Involvement* gives even the lowest-level employees a sense of involvement in the company's overall performance. Information is shared. Employees develop skills in teamwork, problem solving, and business operations, they participate in work-unit management decisions, and are a source of learning and innovation for the organization.[57] Frontline employees are involved in designing and implementing new services, and rewards are performance-based.[58]

Southwest Airlines illustrates a high-involvement company, promoting common sense and flexibility. It trusts its employees and gives them the latitude, discretion, and authority they need to do their jobs. The airline has eliminated inflexible work rules and rigid job descriptions so its people can assume ownership for getting the job done and enabling flights to leave on time, regardless of whose "official" responsibility it is. This gives employees the flexibility to help each other when needed. As a result, they adopt a "whatever it takes" mentality. Southwest mechanics and pilots feel free to help ramp agents load bags. When a flight is running late, it is not uncommon to see pilots helping passengers in wheelchairs to board the aircraft, assisting operations agents by taking boarding passes, or helping flight attendants clean the cabin between flights. All of these actions are their way of adapting to the situation and taking ownership for getting customers on board more quickly. In addition, Southwest employees apply common sense, not rules, when it's in the best interests for the customer.

Rod Jones, assistant chief pilot, recalls a captain who left the gate with a senior citizen who had boarded the wrong plane. The customer was confused and very upset. Southwest asks pilots not to go back to the gate with an incorrectly boarded customer. In this case, the captain was concerned about this individual's well-being. "So, he adapted to the situation", says Jones. "He came back to the gate, deplaned the customer, pushed back out, and gave us an irregularity report. Even though he broke the rules, he used his judgment and did what he thought was best. And we said, 'Attaboy!'"[59]

Build High-Performance Service-Delivery Teams

A team is defined as "a small number of people with complementary skills who are committed to a common purpose, set of performance goals, and approach for which they hold themselves mutually accountable".[60] The nature of many services requires people to work in teams, often across functions, in order to offer seamless customer service.

Traditionally, many firms were organized by functional structures — for example, one department is in charge of consulting and selling (e.g., selling a subscription contract with a cell phone), another is in charge of customer service (e.g., activation of value-added services and change of subscription plans), and yet another is in charge of billing. This structure prevents internal service teams from viewing end customers as their own, and it can also mean poorer teamwork across functions, slower service,

Figure 11.11: Lack of cooperation within a team will lead to problems in the company.

Copyright 2003 by Randy Glasbergen.
www.glasbergen.com

"We're a Limited Partnership.
We're limited by Allen's pessimism,
Elizabeth's abrasive personality, and
Dave's refusal to work weekends."

and more errors between functions. When customers have service problems, they easily fall between the cracks.

Empirical research has confirmed that frontline employees themselves regard the lack of interdepartmental support as an important factor in hindering them from satisfying their customers (Fig. 11.11).[61] As a result of these problems, service organizations in many industries need to create cross-functional teams with the authority and responsibility to serve customers from beginning of the service encounter to the end. Such teams are also called self-managed teams.[62]

The Power of Teamwork in Services. Teams, training, and empowerment go hand-in-hand. Effective teams and their leaders facilitate communication among team members, sharing of knowledge, and alignment.[63] By operating like a small, independent unit, service teams take on more responsibility and require less supervision than the more traditional functionally organized customer service units. Furthermore, teams often set higher performance targets for themselves than supervisors would. Within a good team, the pressure to perform is high.[64]

Some academics even feel that too much emphasis is placed on hiring 'individual stars', and too little attention is paid to hiring staff with

Figure 11.12: Surgical teams work under particularly demanding conditions.

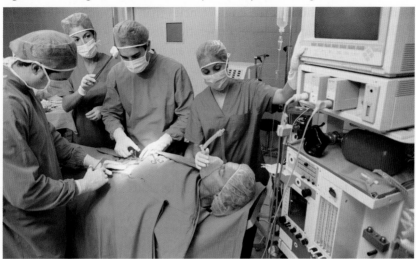

good team abilities and the motivation to work cooperatively. Stanford professors Charles O'Reilly and Jeffrey Pfeffer emphasize that how well people work in teams is often as important as how good people are, and that stars can be outperformed by others through superior teamwork.[65]

At Customer Research Inc. (CRI), a progressive and successful marketing research firm, team members' feelings are illustrated in the following quotes:

- "I like being on the team. You feel like you belong. Everyone knows what's going on".
- "We take ownership. Everyone accepts responsibility and jumps in to help".
- "When a client needs something in an hour, we work together to solve the problem".
- "There are no slugs. Everyone pulls their weight".[66]

Team ability and motivation are crucial for the effective delivery of many types of services, especially those involving individuals who each play specialist roles. For example, healthcare services heavily depend on effective teamwork of many specialists (Fig. 11.12).

Structure Service-Delivery Teams for Success. It is not easy to make teams function well. If people are not prepared for team work and the team structure is not set up right, a firm risks having initially enthusiastic team members who lack the competencies that teamwork requires. The skills needed include not only cooperation, listening to others, coaching and encouraging one another, but also an understanding of how to air their differences professionally, tell one another the hard truths, and ask the tough questions. All these require training.[67] Management also needs to set up a structure that will move the teams towards success, which includes the following:[68]

- Identify what the team will achieve. Goals need to be defined and shared with the team members.
- Select team members with care. All the skills needed to achieve the goal must be found within the team.
- Monitor the team and its team members, and provide feedback. This aligns individual and team goals with those of the organization.
- Keep team members informed of goal achievement, update them, and reward them for their efforts and performance.
- Coordinate and integrate with other teams, departments, and functions to achieve the overall company objectives (see next section for details).

Integrate Teams across Departments and Functional Areas

Even if service delivery teams work well, there exists many firms in which individuals and teams from different departments and functional areas have conflicts with each other. Marketers may see their role as one of continually adding value to the product offering, enhancing its appeal to customers, and stimulating sales. However, operations managers may see their job as cutting down on "extras" to reflect the reality of service constraints — such as staff and equipment — and the need to control cost. HR wants to control headcount and payroll, and IT is struggling with many changing demands as it often controls the information backbone of many services processes.

Part of the challenge of service management is to ensure that the different departments and functions cooperate with the other. The potential ways to reduce conflict and break down the barriers between departments include:

1. Transferring individuals internally to other departments and functional areas, allowing them to develop a more holistic perspective, and being able to view issues from the different perspectives of the various departments.

2. Establishing cross-departmental and cross-functional project teams (e.g., for new service development or customer service process redesign).

3. Having cross-departmental/functional service delivery teams.

4. Appointing individuals whose job it is to integrate specific objectives, activities, and processes between departments. For example, Robert Kwortnik and Gary Thompson suggest forming a department in charge of "service experience management" that integrates marketing and operations.[69]

5. Carrying out internal marketing and training, and integration programs (see the Southwest Airlines example in the paragraphs below).

6. Having top management's commitment to ensure that the overarching objectives of all departments are integrated.

A great example of a firm with a strong culture and strong integration across functions is Southwest Airlines, which continuously uses new and creative ways to strengthen its culture. Southwest's Culture Committee members are zealots when it comes to the continuation of Southwest's family feel. The committee represents everyone from flight attendants and reservationists to top executives, as one participant observed: "The Culture Committee is not made up of Big Shots; it is a committee of Big Hearts". The Culture Committee members are not out to gain power. They use the power of the Southwest spirit to better connect people to the cultural foundations of the company. The committee works behind the scenes to foster Southwest's commitment to its core values. The following are examples of events held to reinforce Southwest's cultures.

• *Walk a Mile in My Shoes.* This program helped Southwest employees gain an appreciation for other people's jobs. Employees were asked to visit a different department on their day off and to spend a minimum of six hours on the "walk". These participants were rewarded not only with transferable roundtrip passes, but also with goodwill and increased morale.

- *A Day in the Field.* This activity is practiced throughout the company all year long. For example, Barri Tucker, then a senior communications representative in the executive office, once joined three flight attendants working a three-day trip. Tucker gained by experiencing the company from a new angle and by hearing directly from customers. She was able to see how important it is for corporate headquarters to support Southwest's frontline employees.

- *Helping Hands.* Southwest sent out volunteers from around the system to lighten the load of employees in the cities where Southwest was in direct competition with United's Shuttle. This not only built momentum and strengthened the troops for the battle with United, it also helped rekindle the fighting spirit of Southwest employees.[70]

Motivate and Energize People[71]

Once a firm has hired the right people, trained them well, empowered them, and organized them into effective service delivery teams, how can it ensure that they are engaged and will deliver? Staff performance is a function of ability and motivation. Effective hiring, training, empowerment, and teams give a firm able people; and performance appraisal and reward systems are key to motivating them. Service staff must get the message that providing quality service efficiently holds the key for them to be rewarded. Motivating and rewarding strong service performers are some of the most effective ways of retaining them. Staff quickly pick up that those who get promoted are the truly outstanding service providers, and that those who get fired are those who do not deliver at the customer level.

However, a major reason why service businesses fail is that they do not utilize the full range of available rewards effectively. Many firms think in terms of money as reward, but it does not pass the test of an effective motivator. Receiving a fair salary is a hygiene factor rather than a motivating factor. Paying more than what is seen as fair only has short-term motivating effects, and wears off quickly. On the other hand, bonuses that are contingent on performance have to be earned again and again, and therefore they tend to be more lasting in their effectiveness. Other, more lasting rewards are the job content itself, recognition and feedback, and goal accomplishment.

Job content. People are motivated and satisfied simply by knowing they are doing a good job. They feel good about themselves, and like to reinforce that feeling. This is true especially if the job:

- has a variety of different activities;
- requires the completion of "whole" and identifiable pieces of work;
- is seen as significant in the sense that it has an impact on the lives of others;
- comes with autonomy and flexibility; and
- provides direct and clear feedback about how well employees did their work (e.g., grateful customers and sales performance).

Feedback and recognition. Humans are social beings, and they derive a sense of identity and belonging to an organization from the recognition and feedback they receive from the people around them — their customers, colleagues, and superiors. If employees are recognized and thanked for service excellence beyond what happens during formal performance appraisal meetings, they will want to continue achieving it. If done well, the star employee-of-the month type of awards recognize excellent performances, and can be highly motivating.

Positive emotions are contagious. Employees are highly satisfied and motivated when they work in jobs where they can make a positive impact on others. Hence, putting employees in touch with end-users and letting them hear positive feedback from customers can be very motivating.[72] Positive effects were observed even if frontline employees just saw pictures of customers or read stories of the "wow" experiences customers had.[73]

Goal achievement. Goals focus people's energy. Achieving important goals is a reward in itself. Goals that are specific, difficult but attainable, and accepted by the staff are strong motivators. They result in higher performance as compared to no goals, or vague goals ("do your best"), or goals that are impossible to achieve.[74] In short, well-communicated and mutually accepted goals are effective motivators.

The following are important points to note for effective goal setting:

- When goals are seen as important, achieving the goals is a reward in itself.

- Goal accomplishment can be used as a basis for giving rewards, including bonuses, feedback, and recognition as part of formal performance appraisals. Feedback and recognition from peers can be given faster, more cheaply and effectively than pay, and have the additional benefit of gratifying an employee's self-esteem.

- Service employee goals that are specific and difficult must be set publicly to be accepted. Although goals must be specific, they can be something intangible like improved employee courtesy ratings.

- Progress reports about goal accomplishment (feedback), and goal accomplishment itself must be public events (recognition), if they are to gratify employees' esteem needs.

- It is mostly unnecessary to specify the means to achieve goals. Feedback on progress while pursuing the goal serves as a corrective function. As long as the goal is specific, difficult but achievable, and accepted, goal pursuit will result in goal accomplishment, even in the absence of other rewards.

Charles O'Reilly and Jeffrey Pfeffer conducted in-depth research on why some companies can succeed over long periods of time in highly competitive industries without having the usual sources of competitive advantage such as barriers of entry or proprietary technology. They concluded that these firms did not succeed by winning the war for talent (although these firms were hiring extremely carefully for fit), "but by fully using the talent and unlocking the motivation of the people" they already had in their organizations.[75]

The Role of Labor Unions

Labor unions and service excellence do not seem to gel. The power of organized labor is widely cited as an excuse for not adopting new approaches in both service and manufacturing businesses. "We'd never get it past the unions", managers say, wringing their hands, and muttering darkly about restrictive work practices. Unions are often portrayed as villains in the press, especially when high profile strikes inconvenience millions. Many managers seem to be rather antagonistic towards unions.

Contrary to the negative view presented above, many of the world's most successful service businesses are in fact highly unionized; Southwest

Airlines is one example. The presence of unions in a service company is not an automatic barrier to high performance and innovation, unless there is a long history of mistrust, acrimonious relationships, and confrontation.

Jeffrey Pfeffer has observed wryly that "the subject of unions and collective bargaining is... one that causes otherwise sensible people to lose their objectivity".[76] He urges a pragmatic approach to this issue, emphasizing that "the effects of unions depend very much on what *management* does". The higher wages, lower turnover, clearly established grievance procedures, and improved working conditions often found in highly unionized organizations can yield positive benefits in a well-managed service organization. Furthermore, management consultation and negotiation with union representatives are essential if employees are to accept new ideas (conditions that are equally valid in non-unionized firms). The challenge is to jointly work with unions, to reduce conflict, and to create a climate for service.[77]

SERVICE CULTURE, CLIMATE AND LEADERSHIP

After the discussion on the nuts and bolts of HR in service firms, the leader's role in nurturing an effective service culture within the organization will now be covered, particularly with regards to defining the culture and climate for service.

Building a Service-Oriented Culture[78]

Service firms that strive to deliver service excellence need a strong service culture that is continuously reinforced and developed by management to achieve alignment with the firm's strategy.[79] *Organizational culture* concerns the basic assumptions and values that guide organization action; it includes:

- Shared perceptions or themes regarding what is important in the organization.
- Shared values about what is right and wrong.
- Shared understanding about what works and what does not.
- Shared beliefs and assumptions about *why* these beliefs are important.
- Shared styles of working and relating to others.

Transforming an organization to develop and nurture a new culture along each of these five dimensions is no easy task for even the most gifted leader. It is doubly difficult when the organization is part of an industry that prides itself on deeply-rooted traditions, with many different departments run by independent-minded professionals in different fields who are attuned to how they are perceived by fellow professionals in the same field at other institutions. This situation is often found in the nonprofit world, such as colleges and universities, major hospitals, and large museums.

Leonard Berry advocates a value-driven leadership that inspires and guides service providers.[80] Leadership should bring out the passion for serving. It should also tap the creativity of service providers, nourish their energy and commitment, and give them a fulfilled working life. An essential feature of a strong service culture is a strong belief in the importance of delivering superior customer value and service excellence. Some of the core values Berry found in excellent service firms included excellence, innovation, joy, teamwork, respect, integrity, and social profit (see *Service Insights 11.9* for an example of a value statement). These values are part of the firm's culture. Berry further boils down the definition of *service culture* to two points:

- shared perceptions of *what* is important in an organization, and
- shared values and beliefs of *why* those things are important.

It is the responsibility of the leaders to create a service culture with values that inspire, energize and guide service providers.

SERVICE INSIGHTS 11.9
Zappos' Value Statement

As Zappos, the legendary US online retailer, had grown, its leaders felt it was important to explicitly define the core values that determined its service culture, brand, and business strategy. These are the ten core values that Zappos lives by:

1. Deliver WOW Through Service
2. Embrace and Drive Change

3. Create Fun and A Little Weirdness

4. Be Adventurous, Creative, and Open-Minded

5. Pursue Growth and Learning

6. Build Open and Honest Relationships With Communication

7. Build a Positive Team and Family Spirit

8. Do More With Less

9. Be Passionate and Determined

10. Be Humble

Tony Hsieh, CEO and founder of Zappos, describes in his book "Delivering Happiness: A Path to Profits, Passion and Purpose" in detail each of these 10 values and why they are important. He attributes most of Zappos' success to the fact that they invested heavily into the three key areas of customer service, company culture, and employee training and development.

Sources: http://www.zappos.com/d/about-zappos-culture; accessed 12 May, 2016; Tony Hsieh (2010), Delivering Happiness: A Path to Profits, Passion and Purpose. NY: New York, Business Plus; Tony Hsieh (2010), "How I Did It: Zappos's CEO on Going to Extremes for Customers", *Harvard Business Review*, Vol. 88, No. 7/8, pp. 41-45.

A Climate for Service[81]

While culture is more overarching and values-focused, *organizational climate* is the part of the organization's culture that can be felt and seen. Employees rely heavily on their perceptions of what is important by noting what the company and their leaders do, not so much what they say.

Employees gain their understanding of what is important through their daily experiences with the firm's human resource, operations, marketing and IT policies, practices, and procedures. Its culture is translated into more concrete aspects that can be experienced by the employees, which then in turn drives employee behavior and customer outcomes.[82] In short, climate represents the shared perceptions of employees about the practices, procedures, and types of behaviors that get supported and rewarded in a particular setting.

As a climate must relate to something specific — for instance, to service, support, innovation, or safety — multiple climates often coexist within a single organization. Essential features of a climate for service include clear marketing goals, and a strong drive and support to be the best in delivering superior customer value or service quality.[83]

Qualities of Effective Leaders in Service Organizations

Leaders are responsible for creating a culture and climate for service. Why are some leaders more effective than others in bringing about a desired change in culture and climate?

Many commentators have written on the topic of leadership. It has even been described as a service in its own right. The late Sam Walton, founder of the Wal-Mart retail chain, highlighted the role of managers as "servant leaders".[84] The following are some qualities that effective leaders in a service organization should have:

- Love for the business. Excitement about the business will encourage individuals to teach the business to others and to pass on to them the art and secrets of operating it.

- Many outstanding leaders are driven by a set of core values that are related to service excellence and performance they pass on in the organization.[85] Service quality is seen as a key foundation for success.

- Recognizing the key part played by employees in delivering service, service leaders need to believe in the people who work for them and pay special attention to communicating with employees.

- Effective leaders are able to ask great questions and get answers from the team, rather than just relying on themselves to dominate the decision-making process.[86]

- Role model the behaviors they expect of their teams.

- Effective leaders have a talent for communicating with others in a way that is easy to understand. They know their audiences and are able to communicate even complicated ideas in simple terms accessible to all.[87] Effective communication is a key skill to inspire an organization to create success.

Rakesh Karma warns against excessive emphasis on charisma in selecting CEOs, arguing that it leads to unrealistic expectations.[88] He notes that unethical behavior may occur when charismatic but unprincipled leaders induce blind obedience in their followers, and cites the illegal activities stimulated by the leadership of Enron, which eventually led to the company's collapse. There is also the risk of prominent leaders becoming too externally focused at the risk of their internal effectiveness. A CEO who enjoys an enormous income (often through the exercise of huge stock options), maintains a princely lifestyle, and basks in widespread publicity may even turn off low-paid service workers at the bottom of the organization. Jim Collins concludes that a leader does not require a larger-than-life personality. Leaders who aspire to take a company to greatness, he says, need to have personal humility blended with intensive professional will, ferocious resolve, and a willingness to give credit to others while taking the blame to themselves.[89]

In hierarchical organizations, it is often assumed that leadership at the top is sufficient. However, as Sandra Vandermerwe points out, forward-looking service businesses need to be more flexible. Today's greater emphasis on using teams within service businesses means that:

[L]eaders are everywhere, disseminated throughout the teams. They are found especially in the customer facing and interfacing jobs in order that decision-making will lead to long-lasting relationships with customers...leaders are customer and project champions who energize the group by virtue of their enthusiasm, interest, and know-how.[90]

Leadership Styles, Focus on the Basics, and Role Modeling

Service climate research has contrasted two leadership styles: a management of the "basics" as compared to transformational leadership that sets strategy and drives change.[91] Research has shown that the persistent management of the basics and endless details create a strong climate for service. Leaders who demonstrate a commitment to service quality, set high standards, recognize and remove obstacles, and ensure the availability of resources required to do it — create a strong climate for service. This basic leadership style seems mundane compared to transformational leadership, yet according to James Heskett and his colleagues, both are needed; a recognition of the "importance of the mundane" and providing a strong service vision that inspires and motivates the troops.[92]

One of the traits of successful leaders is their ability to role model the behavior they expect of managers and other employees, and thereby focus the organization on the basics. Often, this requires the approach known as "management by walking around", popularized by Thomas Peters and Robert Waterman in their book *In Search of Excellence.*[93] When Herb Kelleher was CEO of Southwest Airlines, no one was surprised to see him turn up at a Southwest maintenance hangar at two in the morning, or even to encounter him working an occasional stint as a flight attendant. Walking around involves regular visits, sometimes unannounced, to various areas of the company's operation. This approach provides insights into both backstage and front-stage operations, the ability to observe and meet both employees and customers, and an opportunity to see how corporate strategy is implemented at the frontline.

Periodically, this approach may lead to a recognition that changes in a firm's strategy are needed. Encountering the CEO on such a visit can also be motivating for service personnel. It also provides an opportunity for role modeling good service. *Service Insights 11.10* describes how the CEO of a major hospital learned the power of role modeling early in his tenure.

SERVICE INSIGHTS 11.10
A Hospital President Learns the Power of Role Modeling

During his 30-year tenure as president of Boston's Beth Israel Hospital (now Beth Israel-Deaconess Medical Center), Mitchell T. Rabkin, MD, was known for regularly spending time making informal visits to all parts of the hospital. "You learn a lot from 'management by walking around'", he said. "And you're also seen. When I visit another hospital and am given a tour by its CEO, I watch how that CEO interacts with other people, and what the body language is in each instance. It's very revealing. Even more, it's very important for role modeling". To reinforce that point, Dr. Rabkin told the following story:

People learn to *do* as a result of the way they see you and others *behave*. An example from the Beth Israel that's now almost apocryphal — but *is* true — is the story of the bits of litter on the floor.

One of our trustees, the late Max Feldberg, head of the Zayre Corporation, asked me one time to take a walk around the hospital with him and inquired, "Why do you think there are so many pieces of paper scattered on the floor of this patient care unit?"

"Well, it's because people don't pick them up", I replied.

He said, "Look, you're a scientist. We'll do an experiment. We'll walk down this floor and we'll pick up every other piece of paper. And then we'll go upstairs, there's another unit, same geography, statistically the same amount of paper, but we won't pick up anything".

So this 72-year old man and I went picking up alternate bits of the litter on one floor and nothing on the other. When we came back 10 minutes later, virtually all the rest of the litter on the first floor had been removed and nothing, of course, had changed on the second.

And "Mr. Max" said to me, "You see, it's not because *people* don't pick them up, it's because *you* don't pick them up. If you're so fancy that you can't bend down and pick up a piece of paper, why should anybody else?"

Source: Christopher Lovelock, *Product Plus: How Product + Service = Competitive Advantage.* New York: McGraw-Hill, 1994

Empirical research in the hotel industry demonstrates why it is important for management to walk the talk. Judi McLean Park and Tony Simons conducted a study of 6,500 employees at 76 Holiday Inn hotels to determine whether workers perceived that their hotel managers showed behavioral integrity using measures such as "My manager delivers on promises", and "My manager practices what he preached". These statements were correlated with employee responses to questions such as "I am proud to tell others I am part of this hotel", and "My co-workers go out of the way to accommodate guests' special requests", and then to revenues and profitability.

The results were stunning. They showed that behavioral integrity of a hotel's manager was highly correlated to employees' trust, commitment, and willingness to go the extra mile. Furthermore, of all manager behaviors measured, it was the single most important factor driving profitability. In fact, a mere 1/8 point increase in a hotel's overall behavioral integrity score on a five-point scale was associated with a 2.5% increase in revenue, and a $250,000 increase in profits per hotel per year.[94]

Focusing the Entire Organization on the Frontline

A strong service culture is one where the entire organization focuses on the frontline, understanding that it is the lifeline of the business. The organization understands that today's, as well as tomorrow's, revenues are largely driven by what happens at the service encounter. In firms with a passion for service, top management shows through their actions that what happens at the frontline is crucially important to them, by being informed and actively involved. They achieve this by regularly talking to and working with frontline staff and customers. Mark Frissora, CEO of car rental company Hertz, expressed this as follows:

> *I often hear people say, 'As a CEO, you can't get too involved in the day-to-day operations of your business. That's micromanaging.' My response is, 'I have to get 'too involved' in the business because I'm setting the strategy. If I don't understand the business, then I'm a poor manager and I've failed as a leader.' It's critical that leaders spend a lot of time where the work actually gets done.*[95]

Many actually spend significant amounts of time at the frontline serving customers. For example, Disney World's management spends two weeks every year in frontline staff job such as sweeping the streets, selling ice-cream, or working as a ride attendant, in order to gain a better appreciation and understanding of what really happens on the ground.[96] Service leaders are not only interested in the big picture, but they focus on the details of the service, they see opportunities in nuances which competitors might consider trivial, and they believe the way the firm handles little things sets the tone for how it handles everything else.

Zappos focuses all new recruits on the frontline by ensuring that everyone who is hired in its headquarters goes through the same training

Figure 11.23: The inverted organizational pyramid.

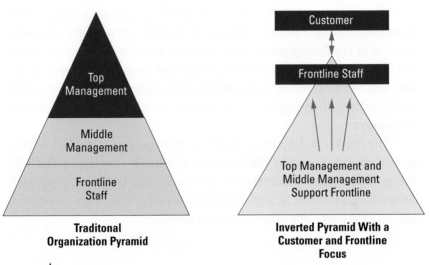

Legend: = Service encounters, or "moments of truth"

their call center employees (called "Customer Loyalty Team") go through. Whether they hire an accountant, lawyer or software developer, regardless of seniority, they go through exactly the same training program. It takes four weeks and covers the company history, the importance of customer service, the long-term vision of the company, and Zappos' philosophy about company culture. Following this training, all new hires work for two weeks in the call center taking customer calls. According to its CEO Tony Hsieh: "This goes back to our belief that customer service shouldn't just be a department, it should be the entire company".[97]

Figure 11.23 shows the inverted pyramid, which highlights the importance of the frontline. It shows that the role of top management and middle management is to support the frontline in their task of delivering service excellence to their customers.

CONCLUSION

The quality of a service firm's people — especially those working in customer-facing positions — plays a crucial role in determining market success and financial performance. That is why the *people* element of the

7 'P's is so important. Successful service organizations are committed to the effective management of human resources, and work closely with marketing and operations managers to balance what might otherwise prove to be conflicting goals. They recognize the value of investing in HR and understand the costs resulting from high levels of turnover. In the long run, offering better wages and benefits may be a more financially viable strategy than paying less to employees who have no loyalty and soon defect.

The market and financial results of managing people effectively for service advantage can be phenomenal. Good HR strategies allied with strong management leadership at all levels often lead to a sustainable competitive advantage. It is probably harder to duplicate high-performing human assets than any other corporate resource.

CHAPTER SUMMARY

Frontline Employees Are Important

- Are a core part of the service product
- Are the service firm in the eyes of the customer
- Are a core part of the brand, deliver the brand promise
- Sell, cross-sell and up-sell
- Are a key driver of customer loyalty
- Determine productivity

HR in Service Firms Is Challenging

Frontline Work Is Difficult & Stressful

- Boundary-spanning positions
- Link the inside of the organization to the outside world
- Have conflicting roles that cause role stress:
  - Organization/client conflict
  - Person/role conflict
  - Inter-client conflict
- Require emotional labor

Basic Models of HR in Service Firms

- Cycle of Failure
  - Low pay, low investment in people, high staff turnover
  - Result in customer dissatisfaction, defection, and low margins
- Cycle of Mediocrity
  - Large bureaucracies; offer job security but little scope in the job itself
  - No incentives to serve customers well
- Cycle of Success
  - Heavy investment in recruitment, development, and motivation of frontline employees
  - Employees are engaged and productive
  - Customers are satisfied and loyal, margins are improved
  - Pleasure (or displeasure)

How to Get HR Right — The Service Talent Cycle

Hire the Right People

- Be the preferred employer and compete for talent market share
- Intensify the selection process to identify the right people for the organization and given job
  - Conduct multiple structured interviews
  - Use personality tests
  - Observe candidate behavior
  - Give applicants a realistic preview of the job

Enable the Frontline

Training & Development
- Conduct extensive training on:
  - Organizational culture, purpose, & strategy
  - Interpersonal and technical skills
  - Product/service knowledge
- Reinforce training to shape behaviors
- Use internal communications/marketing to shape the service culture and behaviors
- Professionalize the frontline

Empower the Frontline
- Provide discretion to find solutions to service problems and customization of service delivery
- Set appropriate levels of empowerment depending on the business model and customer needs
- Empowerment requires: (1) information about performance, (2) knowledge that enables contribution to performance, (3) power to make decisions, and (4) performance-based rewards.

Organize Frontline Employees into Effective Service Delivery Teams
- Use cross-functional teams that can service customers from end-to-end
- Structure teams for success (e.g., set goals, carefully select members with the right skills)
- Integrate teams across departments and functional area (e.g., cross-postings, and internal campaigns such as "walk a mile in my shoes" and "a day in the field")

Motivate the Frontline

- Energize and motivate employees with a full set of rewards
- Rewards should include pay, performance bonuses, satisfying job content, feedback and recognition, and goal accomplishment

Service Culture, Climate, & Leadership

Service Culture
- Shared perceptions of what is important in an organization
- Shared values and beliefs of why those things are important

Climate for Service
- Climate is culture translated into policies, practices, and procedures
- Shared perception of practices and behaviors that get rewarded

Leadership
- Qualities of effective leaders
- Leadership styles that focus on basics versus transformation
- Strong focus on frontline

Part IV

Developing Customer
Relationships

CHAPTER 12

Managing Relationships and Building Loyalty

The first step in managing a loyalty-based business system is finding and acquiring the right customers.

Frederick F. Reichheld
Author, strategist, and fellow of Bain & Company

Strategy first, then CRM.

Steven S. Ramsey
Former senior partner with Accenture,
current executive vice president with IRi

THE SEARCH FOR CUSTOMER LOYALTY

Targeting, acquiring, and retaining the "right" customers is at the core of many successful service firms. Segmentation and positioning were discussed in Chap. 3, while this chapter emphasizes the importance of desirable, loyal customers within the chosen segments, and the painstaking process to build and maintain their loyalty through well-conceived relationship marketing strategies. The objective is to build the relationships and develop loyal customers who will contribute to a growing volume of business with the firm in the future.

Loyalty is an old-fashioned word traditionally used to describe fidelity and enthusiastic devotion to a country, a cause, or an individual. However, in a business context, loyalty describes a customer's willingness to continue patronizing a firm over a long period of time, preferably on an exclusive basis, and recommending the firm's products to friends and associates. Customer loyalty extends beyond purchasing behavior, and includes preference, liking, and future intentions.

"Defector" was a nasty word during wartime. It describes disloyal people who sell out, betray their own side, and join the enemy. Even when they defected toward "our" side, rather than away from it, they were still a suspect. In a marketing context, the term defection is used to describe customers who drop off a company's radar and transfer their purchases to another supplier. Not only does a rising defection rate indicates that something is wrong with quality (or that competitors offer better value), it may also be signaling a fall in profits. Big customers do not necessarily disappear overnight; they often may signal their mounting dissatisfaction by steadily reducing their purchases and shifting part of their business elsewhere.

Why is Customer Loyalty so Important to a Firm's Profitability?

"Few companies think of customers as annuities", says Frederick Reichheld, author of *The Loyalty Effect*, and a major researcher in this field,[1] and that is what a loyal customer can mean to a firm — a consistent source of revenue over a period of many years. How much is a loyal customer then worth in terms of profits? In a classic study, Reichheld and Sasser analyzed the profit per customer in different service businesses categorized by the number of years that a customer had been with the firm. They found that the longer customers remained with a firm in each of these industries, the more profitable they became. Annual profits increases per customer, indexed over a five-year period for easier comparison, are summarized in Fig. 12.1 for a few sample industries. The industries studied (with average profits from a first-year customer shown in parentheses) were: credit cards ($30), industrial laundry ($144), industrial distribution ($45), and automobile servicing ($25).

Figure 12.1: How much profit a customer generates over time.

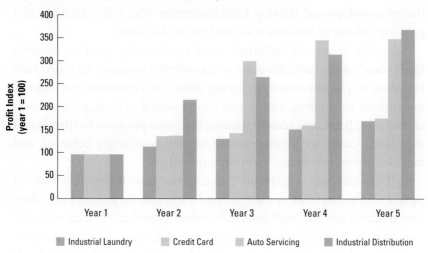

Source: Adapted from Frederick J. Reichheld and W. Earl Sasser Jr. (1990), "Zero Defections: Quality Comes to Services," *Harvard Business Review*, Vol. 73, Sept–Oct, p. 108.

Underlying this profit growth are a number of factors that work to supplier's advantage to create incremental profits. In the order of magnitude at the end of seven years, these factors are:[2]

1. *Profit derived from increased purchases (or, in a credit card and banking environment, higher account balances).* Over time, business customers often grow larger and thus, need to purchase in greater quantities. Individual customers may also purchase more as their families grow, or as they become more affluent. Both types of customers may be willing to consolidate their purchases with a single supplier who provides high quality service, resulting in what we call a high share-of-wallet.

2. *Profit from reduced customer service costs.* As customers become more experienced, they make fewer demands on the supplier (for instance, they have less need for information and assistance, and make use of self-service options more). They may also make fewer mistakes when involved in operational processes, thus contributing to greater productivity.

3. *Profit from referrals to other customers.* Positive word-of-mouth recommendations are like free sales and advertising, saving the firm from having to invest much in these areas.

4. *Profit from lower price sensitivity that allow a price premium.* New customers often benefit from introductory promotional discounts, whereas long-term customers are more likely to pay regular prices, and when they are highly satisfied they tend to be less price sensitive.[3] Moreover, customers who trust a supplier may be more willing to pay higher prices at peak periods or for express work.

5. *Acquisition costs can be amortized over a longer period.* The upfront costs of attracting new buyers can be amortized over many years. These costs can be substantial and can include sales commissions, advertising and promotions costs, administrative costs of setting up an account, and sending out welcome packages and sign-up gifts.

Fig. 12.2 shows the relative contribution of each of these different factors over a seven-year period, based on an analysis of 19 different product categories (both goods and services). Reichheld argues that the economic benefits of customer loyalty noted above often explain why one firm is more profitable than a competitor. As a response, Reichheld and Sasser popularized the term *zero defections*, which they describe as keeping every customer the company can serve profitably.[4]

Figure 12.2: Why customers are more profitable over time.

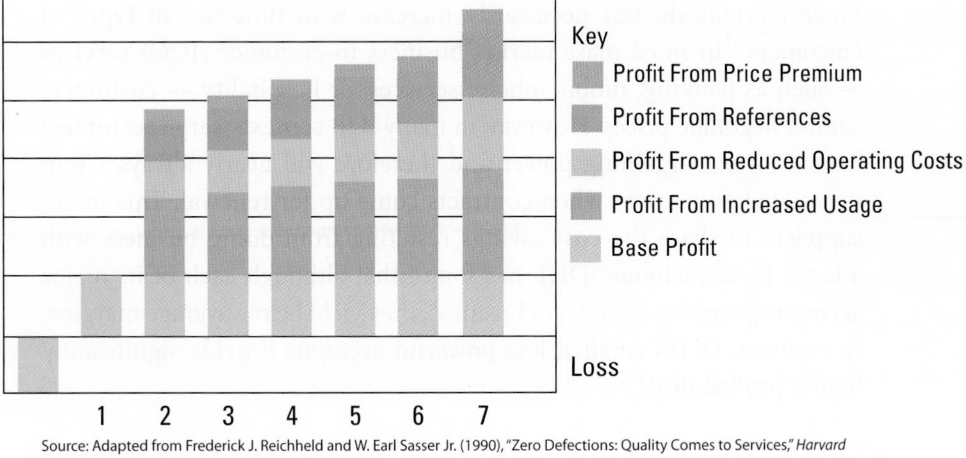

Key

Profit From Price Premium

Profit From References

Profit From Reduced Operating Costs

Profit From Increased Usage

Base Profit

Loss

1 2 3 4 5 6 7

Source: Adapted from Frederick J. Reichheld and W. Earl Sasser Jr. (1990), "Zero Defections: Quality Comes to Services," *Harvard Business Review*, Vol. 73, September–October, p. 108.

Assessing the Value of a Loyal Customer

One of the challenges faced by professionals is to determine the costs and revenues associated with serving customers to different market segments at different points in their customer lifecycles, and to predict future profitability. For insights on how to calculate customer value, see "Worksheet for Calculating Customer Lifetime Value".[5]

Recent studies have shown that the profit impact of a customer may vary dramatically depending on the stage of the service product lifecycle. For instance, referrals by satisfied customers and negative word-of-mouth from "defected" customers have a much greater effect on profit in the early stages of a service product's lifecycle — when the name of the game is acquisition of new customers — than in later stages, where the focus is more on generating cash flow from the existing customer base.[6]

Finally, it is erroneous to assume that loyal customers are always more profitable than those who make one-time transactions.[7] On the cost side, not all types of services incur heavy promotional expenditures to attract a new customer. Sometimes, it is more important to invest in a good retail location that will attract walk-in traffic. Unlike banks, insurance companies, and other "membership" organizations that incur costs for review of applications and account setup, many service firms face no such costs when a new customer seeks to make a purchase for the first time.

On the revenue side, loyal customers may not spend more than one-time buyers, and in some instances, they may even expect price discounts. Finally, profits do not necessarily increase with time for all types of customers.[8] In most mass market business-to-customer (B2C) services — such as banking, mobile phone services, or hospitality — customers cannot negotiate prices. However, in many B2B contexts, large customers have a lot of bargaining power and therefore will nearly always try to negotiate lower prices when contracts come up for renewal. This forces suppliers to share the cost savings resulting from doing business with a large, loyal customer. DHL has found that although each of its major accounts generates significant business, they yield below average margins. In contrast, DHL's smaller, less powerful accounts provide significantly higher profitability.[9]

Worksheet for Calculating Customer Lifetime Value

Calculating customer value is an inexact science that is subject to a variety of assumptions. You may want to try varying these assumptions to see how it affects the final figures. Generally speaking, revenues per customer are easier to track on an individualized basis than are the associated costs of serving a customer, unless (1) no individual records are kept and/or (2) the accounts served are very large and all account-related costs are individually documented and assigned.

Acquisition Revenues Less Costs

If individual account records are kept, the initial application fee paid and initial purchase (if relevant) should be found in these records. Costs, by contrast, may have to be based on average data. For instance, the marketing cost of acquiring a new client can be calculated by dividing the total marketing costs (advertising, promotions, selling, etc.) devoted toward acquiring new customers by the total number of new customers acquired during the same period. If each acquisition takes place over an extended period of time, you may want to build in a lagged effect between when marketing expenditures are incurred and when new customers come on board. The cost of credit checks—where relevant—must be divided by the number of new customers, not the total number of applicants, because some applicants will probably fail this hurdle. Account set-up costs will also be an average figure in most organizations.

Annual Revenues and Costs

If annual sales, account fees, and service fees are documented on an individual-account basis, account revenue streams (except referrals) can be easily identified. The first priority is to segment your customer base by the length of its relationship with your firm. Depending on the sophistication and precision of your firm's records, annual costs in each category may be directly assigned to an individual account holder or averaged for all account holders in that age category.

Value of Referrals

Computing the value of referrals requires a variety of assumptions. To get started, you may need to conduct surveys to determine (1) what percentage of new customers claim that they were influenced by a recommendation from another customer and (2) what other marketing activities also drew the firm to that individual's attention. From these two items, estimates can be made of what percentage of the credit for all new customers should be assigned to referrals.

Net Present Value

Calculating net present value (NPV) from a future profit stream will require choice of an appropriate annual discount figure. (This could reflect estimates of future inflation rates.) It also requires assessment of how long the average relationship lasts. The NPV of a customer, then, is the sum of the anticipated annual profit on each customer for the projected relationship lifetime, suitably discounted each year into the future.

Acquisition			Year 1	Year 2	Year 3	Year *n*
Initial Revenue	*Annual Revenues*					
Application fee[a]	Annual account fee[a]					
Initial purchase[a]	Sales					
	Service fees[a]					
	Value of referrals[b]					
Total Revenues						
Initial Costs	*Annual Costs*					
Marketing	Account management					
Credit check[a]	Cost of sales					
Account setup[a]	Write-offs (e.g., bad debts)					
Less total costs						
Net Profit (Loss)						

a If applicable.
b Anticipated profits from each new customer referred (could be limited to the first year or expressed as the net present value of the estimated future stream of profits through year *n*); this value could be negative if an unhappy customer starts to spread negative word-of-mouth that causes existing customers to defect.

The Gap between Actual and Potential Customer Value

For profit-seeking firms, the potential profitability of a customer should be a key driver in marketing strategy. As Alan Grant and Leonard Schlesinger said, "Achieving the full profit potential of each customer relationship should be the fundamental goal of every business... Even using conservative estimates, the gap between most companies' current and full potential performance is enormous".[10] They suggest an analysis of the following gaps between the actual and potential value of customers:

- What is the current purchasing behavior of customers in each target segment? What would be the impact on sales and profits if they exhibited the ideal behavior profile of (1) buying all services offered by the firm, (2) using these to the exclusion of any purchases from competitors, and (3) paying full price?

- On an average, how long do customers remain with the firm? What impact would it have if the association is life long?

As discussed earlier, the profitability of a customer often increases over time. Management's task is to design and implement marketing programs that increase loyalty — including share-of-wallet, upselling and cross-selling — and identify the reasons why customers defect and take corrective action. The active management of the customer-base and customer loyalty is also referred to as customer *asset* management.[11]

Why Are Customers Loyal?

Customers are not automatically loyal to any one firm. We rather need to give our customers a reason to consolidate their buying with us and then stay with us. We need to create value for them to become and remain loyal.

Relationships can create value for individual consumers through factors such as inspiring greater confidence, offering social benefits, and providing special treatment (*Service Insights 12.1*). The next section discusses how to systematically think about creating value propositions for the customers to become loyal using the Wheel of Loyalty.

SERVICE INSIGHTS 12.1
How Customers See Relational Benefits
in Service Industries

What benefits do customers see themselves receiving from an extended relationship with a service firm? Researchers seeking answers to this question conducted two studies. The first consisted of in-depth interviews with 21 respondents from a broad cross-section of backgrounds. Respondents were asked to identify service providers that they used on a regular basis, and then were invited to identify and discuss any benefits they received as a result of being a regular customer. Among the comments were:

- "I like him [hair stylist]… He's really funny and always has lots of good jokes. He's kind of like a friend now".

- "I know what I'm getting — I know that if I go to a restaurant that I regularly go to, rather than taking a chance on all of the new restaurants, the food will be good".

- "I often get price breaks. The little bakery that I go to in the morning, every once in a while, they'll give me a free muffin and say, 'You're a good customer, it's on us today.'"

- "You can get better service than drop-in customers… We continue to go to the same automobile repair shop because we have gotten to know the owner on a kind of personal basis, and he…can always work us in."

- "Once people feel comfortable, they don't want to switch to another dentist. They don't want to train or break a new dentist in".

After evaluating and grouping the comments, the researchers designed a second study in which they collected 299 survey questionnaires. The respondents were told to select a specific service provider with whom they had a strong, established relationship. Then they were asked to assess the extent to which they received each of the 21 benefits (derived from an analysis of the first study) as a result of their relationship with the specific provider they had identified. Finally, they were asked to assess the importance of these benefits for them. A factor analysis of the results showed that most of the benefits that customers derived from relationships could be grouped into three categories. The first and most important group involved what the researchers labeled confidence benefits, followed by social benefits, and lastly, special treatment.

Confidence benefits included feelings by customers that in an established relationship, there was less risk of something going wrong, greater confidence in correct performance, and the ability to trust the provider. Customers experienced lower anxiety when purchasing because they knew what to expect, and they typically received the firm's highest level of service.

Social benefits embraced mutual recognition between customers and employees, being known by name, having a friendship with the service provider, and enjoyment of certain social aspects of the relationship.

Special treatment benefits included better prices, discounts on special deals that were unavailable to most customers, extra services, higher priority when there was a wait, and faster service than most customers.

Source: Kevin P. Gwinner, Dwayne D. Gremler, and Mary Jo Bitner, "Relational Benefits in Services Industries: The Customer's Perspective," *Journal of the Academy of Marketing Science*, Vol. 26, No. 2, 1998, pp. 101–114.

THE WHEEL OF LOYALTY

Building customer loyalty is difficult. There are very few service firms any customer can count for being loyal to. Most people cannot think of more than perhaps a handful of firms they truly like (i.e., give a high share-of-heart) and to whom they are committed to going back (i.e., give a high share-of-wallet). This shows that although firms put enormous amounts of money and effort into loyalty initiatives, they often are not successful in building true customer loyalty. The Wheel of Loyalty shown in Fig. 12.3 is used as an organizing framework to discuss how to build customer loyalty as discussed in the following sections.

Figure 12.3: The Wheel of Loyalty

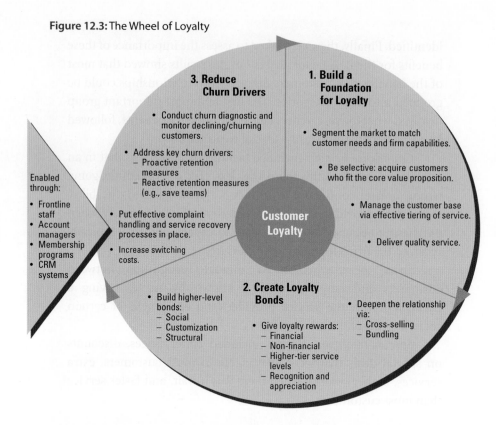

BUILDING A FOUNDATION FOR LOYALTY

Many elements are involved in creating long-term customer relationships and loyalty. In Chap. 3, we discussed segmentation and positioning. In this section, the importance of focusing on serving several desirable customer segments, and then taking the pains to build and maintain their loyalty through carefully thought-out relationship marketing strategies is emphasized.

Target the Right Customers

Loyalty management starts with segmenting the market to match customer needs and firm capabilities. "Who should we be serving?" is a question that every service business needs to ask periodically. Not all customers offer a good fit with the organization's capabilities, delivery technologies, and strategic direction. Companies need to be selective about the segments they target if they want to build successful customer relationships. Managers must think carefully about how customer needs relate to operational elements such as speed and quality, and the physical features and appearance of service facilities. They also need to consider how well their service personnel can meet the expectations of specific types of customers, in terms of both personal style and technical competence.[12]

Leaders are picky about acquiring only the right customers, which are those for whom their firms have been designed to deliver truly special value. Acquiring the right customers often brings long-term revenues and continued growth from referrals. It can also enhance employees' satisfaction, whose daily jobs are improved when they can deal with appreciative customers. Attracting the wrong customers typically results in costly churn, a diminished company reputation, and disillusioned employees.

The result of carefully targeting customers by matching the company capabilities and strengths with customer needs should be a superior service offering in the eyes of those customers who value what the firm has to offer. As Reichheld said, "The result should be a win-win situation, where profits are earned through the success and satisfaction of customers, and not at their expense".[13] Building customer loyalty starts with identifying and targeting the right customers.

Search for Value, Not Just Volume

Too many service firms continue to focus on the *number* of customers they serve without giving sufficient attention to the *value* of each customer.[14] For example, Starwood Hotels & Resorts found that their top 2% of guests generated a whopping 30% of its profits![15] Generally speaking, heavy users who buy more frequently and in larger volumes are more profitable than occasional users. Roger Hallowell makes this point nicely in a banking context:

A bank's population of customers undoubtedly contains individuals who either cannot be satisfied, given the service levels and pricing the bank is capable of offering, or will never be profitable, given their banking activity (their use of resources relative to the revenue they supply). Any bank would be wise to target and serve only those customers whose needs it can meet better than its competitors in a profitable manner. These are the customers who are most likely to remain with that bank for long periods, who will purchase multiple products and services, who will recommend that bank to their friends and relations, and who may be the source of superior returns to the bank's shareholders.[16]

Ironically, it is often the firms that are highly focused and selective in their customer acquisition — rather than those that focus on unbridled acquisition — that are growing fast over long periods. *Service Insights 12.2* shows how Vanguard Group, a leader in the mutual funds industry, designed its products and pricing to attract and retain the right customers for its business model.

Also, relationship customers are by definition not buying commodity services. Service customers who buy strictly based on lowest price (a minority in most markets) are not good target customers for relationship marketing in the first place. They are deal-prone, continuously seeking the lowest price on offer, and switch brands easily.

SERVICE INSIGHTS 12.2
Vanguard Discourages the Acquisition of 'Wrong' Customers[17]

The Vanguard Group is a growth leader in the mutual fund industry that built its $3 trillion in managed assets by 2015 by painstakingly targeting the right customers for its business model. Its share of new sales, which was around 25%, reflected its share of assets or

Take ownership
You own the funds and the funds own Vanguard. That makes you a client-owner and lets us offer you our funds at cost. And that can mean more money in your wallet.

© The Vanguard Group, Inc., used with permission.

market share. However, it had a far lower share of redemptions (customer defections in the fund context), which gave it a market share of net cash flows of 55% (new sales minus redemptions), and this made it the fastest growing mutual fund in its industry.

How did Vanguard achieve such low redemption rates? The secret was in its careful acquisition, and its product and pricing strategies, which encouraged the acquisition of the 'right' customers.

John Bogle, Vanguard's founder, believed in the superiority of index funds and that their lower management fees would lead to higher returns over the long run. He offered Vanguard's clients unparalleled low management fees through a policy of not trading (its index funds hold the market they are designed to track), not having a sales force, and only spending a fraction of what its competitors did on advertising. Another important part of keeping its costs low was its aim to discourage the acquisition of customers who were not long-term index holders.

Bogle attributes the high customer loyalty Vanguard has achieved to a great deal of focus on customer redemptions. "I watched them like a hawk", he explained, and he analyzed them more carefully than new sales to ensure that Vanguard's customer acquisition strategy was on course. Low redemption rates meant that the firm was attracting the right kind of loyal, long-term investors. The inherent stability of its loyal customer base has been key to Vanguard's cost advantage. Bogle's pickiness became legendary. He scrutinized individual redemptions with a fine-tooth comb to see who let the wrong kind of customers on board. When an institutional investor redeemed $25 million from an index fund bought only nine months earlier, he regarded the acquisition of this customer as a failure of the system. He explained, "We don't want short-term investors. They muck up the game at the expense of the long-term investor". At the end of his chairman's letter to the Vanguard Index Trust, Bogle repeated, "We urge them [short-term investors] to look elsewhere for their investment opportunities".

This care and attention to acquiring the right customers is

famous. For example, Vanguard once turned away an institutional investor who wanted to invest $40 million because the firm suspected that the customer would churn the investment within the next few weeks, creating extra costs for existing customers. The potential customer complained to Vanguard's CEO, who in turn not only supported the decision, but also used it as an opportunity to reinforce to his teams why they needed to be selective about the customers they accept.

Furthermore, Vanguard introduced a number of changes to industry practices that discouraged active traders from buying its funds. For example, Vanguard did not allow telephone transfers for index funds, redemption fees were added to some funds, and the standard practice of subsidizing new accounts at the expense of existing customers was rejected because the practice was considered as disloyal to its core investor base. These product and pricing policies in effect turned away heavy traders, but made the fund extremely attractive for long-term investors.

Finally, Vanguard's pricing was set up to reward loyal customers. For many of its funds, investors pay a one-time fee upfront, which goes into the funds themselves (and not to Vanguard) to make up to all current investors for the administrative costs of selling new units. In essence, this fee subsidizes long-term investors, and penalizes short-term investors. Another novel pricing approach was the creation of its Admiral shares for loyal investors, which carried a lower expense fee than ordinary shares (0.15% instead of 0.18% per year).

Different segments offer different value for a service firm. Like investments, some types of customers may be more profitable than others in the short-term, but others may have greater potential for long-term growth. Similarly, the spending patterns of some customers may be stable over time, while others may be more cyclical, e.g., spending heavily in boom times but cutting back sharply in recessions. A wise marketer seeks a mix of segments in order to reduce the risks associated with volatility in demand.[18]

In many cases, David Maister emphasizes, marketing is about getting *better* business, not just *more* business.[19] For instance, the caliber of a professional firm is measured by the type of clients it serves and the nature of tasks on which it works. Volume alone is no measure of excellence, sustainability or profitability. In professional services such as consulting firms or legal partnerships, the mix of attracted business may play an important role in both defining the firm and providing a suitable mix of assignments for staff members at different levels in the organization.

Finally, managers should not assume that the "right customers" are always big spenders. Depending on the service business model, the right customers may come from a large group of people that no other supplier is doing a good job of serving. Many firms have built successful strategies on serving customer segments that had been neglected by established players, which did not see them as being "valuable" enough. Examples include Enterprise Rent-A-Car, which targets customers who need a temporary replacement car. It avoided the more traditional segment of business travelers targeted by its principal competitors. Similarly, Charles Schwab focused on retail stock buyers, and Paychex provides small businesses with payroll and human resource services.[20]

Manage the Customer Base through Effective Tiering of Service

Marketers should adopt a strategic approach to retain, upgrade, and even end relationships with customers. Customer retention involves developing long-term, cost-effective links with customers for the mutual benefit of both parties, but these efforts need not necessarily target all the customers of a firm with the same level of intensity. Research has confirmed that customer profitability and return on sales can be increased by focusing a firm's resources on top-tier customers.[21] Furthermore, different customer tiers often have quite different service expectations and needs. According to Valarie Zeithaml, Roland Rust and Katharine Lemon, it is critical for service firms to understand the needs of customers within different profitability tiers and adjust their service levels accordingly.[22]

Just as service product categories can be tiered to reflect the level of value included (e.g., first, business and economy class in air travel; see Chap. 4), so can groups of customers. In the latter instance, service tiers can be developed around the levels of profit contribution of different

Figure 12.4: The customer pyramid.

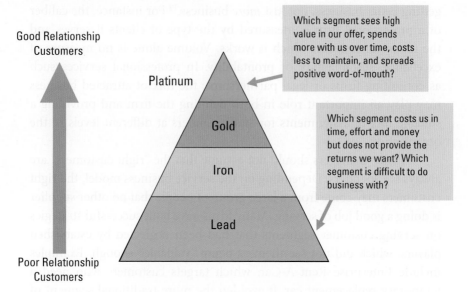

Good Relationship
Customers

Poor Relationship
Customers

Platinum

Gold

Iron

Lead

Which segment sees high value in our offer, spends more with us over time, costs less to maintain, and spreads positive word-of-mouth?

Which segment costs us in time, effort and money but does not provide the returns we want? Which segment is difficult to do business with?

Source: Adapted from Valerie A. Zeithaml, Roland T. Rust, and Katherine N. Lemon (2001), "The Customer Pyramid: Creating and Serving Profitable Customers," *California Management Review*, Vol. 43, No. 4, Summer, Figure 1, pp. 118–142.

groups of customers and their needs (including sensitivities to variables such as price, comfort, and speed), and identifiable personal profiles such as demographics. Zeithaml, Rust and Lemon illustrate this principle through a four-level pyramid (Fig. 12.4).

- *Platinum*. These customers form a very small percentage of a firm's customer base, but are heavy users, and tend to contribute a large share of the profits. This segment is usually less price-sensitive, but expects higher service levels in return, and it is likely to be willing to invest in and try new services.

- *Gold*. The gold tier includes a larger percentage of customers than the platinum, but individual customers contribute less profit than platinum customers. They tend to be slightly more price sensitive and less committed to the firm.

- *Iron*. These customers provide the bulk of the customer base. Their numbers give the firm economies of scale. Hence, they are important so that a firm can build and maintain a certain capacity level and infrastructure, which is often needed for serving gold and platinum customers well. However, iron customers on their own may only be marginally profitable. Their level of business is not enough to justify special treatment.

- *Lead.* Customers in this tier tend to generate low revenues for a firm, but often still require the same level of service as iron customers, which turns them into a loss-making segment from a firm's perspective.

The precise characteristics of customer tiers vary, of course, from one type of business to another, and even from one firm to another. *Service Insights 12.3* provides an illustration from the marketing research industry.

SERVICE INSIGHTS 12.3
Tiering the Customers of a Market Research Agency

Tiering its clients helped a leading US market research agency understand its customers better. The agency defined *platinum clients* as large accounts that were not only willing to plan a certain amount of research work during the year, but were also able to commit to the timing, scope, and nature of their projects, which made capacity management and project planning much easier for the research firm. The acquisition costs for projects sold to these clients were only 2%–5% of project values (as compared to as much as 25% for clients who required extensive proposal work and project-by-project bidding). Platinum accounts were also more willing to try new services, and buy a wider range of services from their preferred provider. These customers were generally very satisfied with the research agency's work and were willing to act as references for potential new clients.

Gold accounts had a similar profile to platinum clients, except that they were more price sensitive, and more inclined to spread their budgets across several firms. Although these accounts had been clients for many years, they were not willing to commit their research work for a year in advance even though the research firm would have been able to offer them better quality and priority in capacity allocation.

Iron accounts spent moderate amounts on research, and commissioned work on a project basis. Selling costs were high, as these firms tended to send out requests-for-proposals (RFPs) to a number of firms for all their projects. They sought the lowest price, and often did not allow sufficient time for the research firm to perform a good quality job.

Lead accounts sought only isolated, low-cost projects which tended to be 'quick and dirty' in nature, with little opportunity for the research firm to add value or apply its skillsets appropriately. Sales costs were high as the client typically invited several firms to quote. Furthermore, as these firms were inexperienced in conducting research and in working with research agencies, selling a project often took several meetings and required multiple revisions to the proposal. Lead accounts also tended to be high maintenance because they did not understand research work well; they often changed project parameters, scope, and deliverables midstream and then expected the research agency to absorb the cost of any rework, thus further reducing the profitability of the engagement.

Source: Adapted Valarie A Zeithaml, Roland T Rust & Katharine N Lemon, "The Customer Pyramid: Creating and serving profitable customers," *California Management Review; Berkeley* 43, no. 4 (Summer 2001), pp. 127–128.

Customer tiers are typically based on profitability and their service needs. Rather than providing the same level of service to all customers, each segment receives a service level that is customized based on its requirements and value to the firm. For example, the platinum tier is provided some exclusive benefits that are not available to other segments. The benefit features for platinum and gold customers should be designed to encourage them to remain loyal because these customers are the very ones competitors would like to steal most.

Marketing efforts can be used to encourage an increased volume of purchases, upgrading the type of service used, or cross-selling additional services to any of the four tiers. However, these efforts have different thrusts for the different tiers, as their needs, usage behaviors, and spending patterns are usually very different. Among the segments for which the firm already has a high share-of-wallet, the focus should be on nurturing, defending, and retaining these customers, possibly by use of loyalty programs.[23]

In contrast, among lead-tier customers at the bottom of the pyramid, the options are either to move them to the iron segment (e.g., through increasing sales, increasing prices and/or cutting servicing costs) or end the relationship with them. Migration can be achieved through a combination of strategies, including upselling, cross-selling, and setting base fees and price increases. For example, imposing a minimum fee that is waived when a certain level of revenue is generated may encourage customers who use several suppliers to consolidate their buying with a single firm instead. Another way to move customers from the lead-tier to the iron-tier is to encourage them to use low-cost service delivery channels. For instance, lead-tier customers may be charged a fee for face-to-face interactions but the fee is waived when such customers use electronic channels. In the cellular telephone industry for example, low-use mobile users can be encouraged to use pre-paid packages that do not require the firm to send out bills and collect payment, which also eliminates the risk of bad debts on such accounts.

Divesting or terminating customers comes as a logical consequence of the realization that not all existing customer relationships are worth keeping.[24] Some relationships may no longer be profitable for the firm because they cost more to maintain than the contributions they generate. Some customers no longer fit the firm's strategy, either because that strategy has changed, or because the customers' behavior and needs have changed.

Occasionally customers are "fired" outright (although the concern for due process is still important). Captial One 360 is the fast-food model of consumer banking — it is about as no-frills as it gets. It only has a handful of basic products, and it lures low-maintenance customers with no minimum balance nor fees, and slightly higher interest rates for its savings accounts and lower interests on its home loans. To offset that generosity, its business model pushes its customers toward online transactions, and the bank routinely fires customers who do not fit its business model. When a customer calls too often (the average customer phone call costs the bank $5.25 to handle), or wants too many exceptions to the rule, the bank's sales associates will say, "Look, this doesn't fit you.

You need to go back to your community bank and get the kind of contact you're comfortable with". As a result, its cost per account are much lower than industry average.[25]

Other examples where customers get fired include students who are caught cheating in examinations, or country club members who consistently abuse the facilities or people. In some instances, termination may be less confrontational. Banks wishing to divest themselves of certain types of accounts that no longer fit their corporate priorities have been known to sell them to other banks (one example is credit card holders who receive a letter in the mail telling them that their account has been transferred to another card issuer).

Just as investors need to dispose of poor investments and banks may have to write off bad loans, each service firm needs to examine its customer portfolio regularly and consider ending unsuccessful relationships. Of course, legal and ethical considerations will determine how to take such actions. For example, a bank may introduce a minimum monthly fee for accounts with a low balance (e.g., below $1,000), but for social responsibility considerations, waive this fee for customers on social security.

Customer Satisfaction and Service Quality are Prerequisites for Loyalty

The foundation for building true loyalty lies in customer satisfaction. Highly satisfied or even delighted customers are more likely to consolidate their buying with one supplier, spread positive word-of-mouth, and become loyal apostles of a firm.[26] In contrast, dissatisfaction drives customers away and is a key factor in switching behavior.

The satisfaction-loyalty relationship can be divided into three main zones: defection, indifference, and affection (Fig. 12.8). The *zone of defection* occurs at low satisfaction levels. Customers will switch unless switching costs are high or there are no viable or convenient alternatives. Extremely dissatisfied customers can turn into 'terrorists' providing an abundance of negative word-of-mouth for the service provider.[27] The *zone of indifference* is found at moderate satisfaction levels. Here, customers are willing to switch if they find a better alternative. Finally, the *zone of affection* is located at very high satisfaction levels, where customers have

Figure 12.8: The customer satisfaction-loyalty relationship.

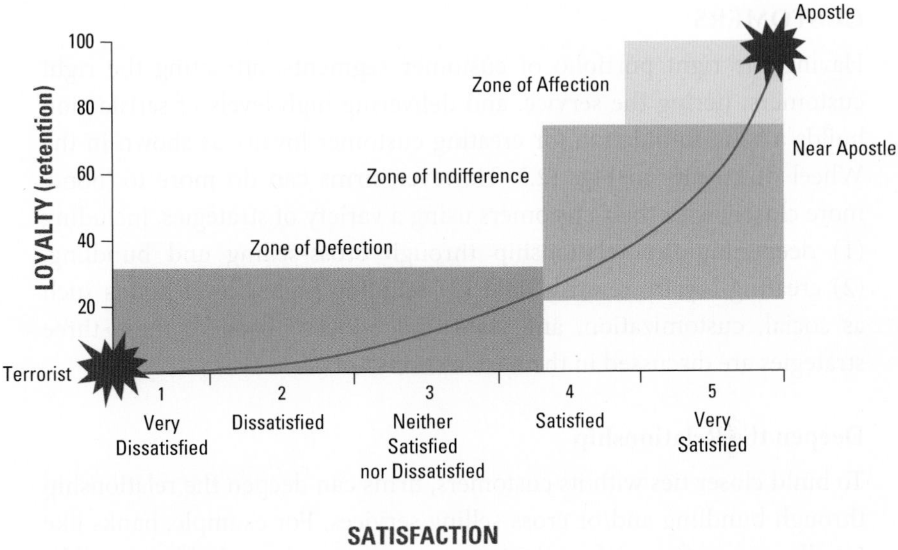

Source: Adapted from Thomas O. Jones and W. Earl Sasser, Jr. (1995), "Why Satisfied Customers Defect," *Harvard Business Review*, November–December, p. 91.

such high attitudinal loyalty that they do not look for alternative service providers. Customers who praise the firm in public and refer others to the firm are described as 'apostles'.

True loyalty is often defined as combining both behavioral and attitudinal loyalty, also referred to as share-of-wallet and share-of-heart. Behavioral loyalty includes behaviors such as buying again, a high share-of-wallet, providing positive word-of-mouth, and attitudinal loyalty refers to a true liking and emotional attachment of the firm, service and brand.

It is important to note though that satisfaction can be seen as a necessary, but not sufficient, driver of true customer loyalty. Satisfaction alone does not explain a large amount of variance in loyalty behaviors, and has to be seen in combination with other factors such as switching costs and customer knowledge (e.g., knowledgeable customers feel more confident in switching and have lower risk perceptions),[28] how the firm compares to competitors (e.g., if a firm is seen as offering the best value proposition compared to that of the next best alternative provider,[29] switching makes little sense and customers keep buying), and the loyalty bonds as discussed in the next section.

STRATEGIES FOR DEVELOPING LOYALTY BONDS WITH CUSTOMERS

Having the right portfolio of customer segments, attracting the right customers, tiering the service, and delivering high levels of satisfaction builds a solid foundation for creating customer loyalty as shown in the Wheel of Loyalty in Fig. 12.3. However, firms can do more to 'bond' more closely with their customers using a variety of strategies, including (1) deepening the relationship through cross-selling and bundling, (2) creating loyalty rewards, and (3) building higher level bonds such as social, customization, and structural bonds.[30] Each of these three strategies are discussed in the next sections.

Deepen the Relationship

To build closer ties with its customers, firms can deepen the relationship through bundling and/or cross-selling services. For example, banks like to sell as many financial products to an account or household as possible. Once a family has a checking, credit card or savings account, safe deposit box, car loan, mortgage, and so on with the same bank, the relationship is so deep that switching becomes a major exercise and is unlikely, unless customers are extremely dissatisfied with the bank.

In addition to raising switching costs, there is often value for the customer when buying all particular services from a single provider. One-stop shopping typically is more convenient than buying individual services from different providers. When having many services with the same firm, the customer may achieve a higher service tier and receive better services, and sometimes service bundles do come with price discounts.

Encourage Loyalty through Financial and Non-financial Rewards

Few customers buy only from a single supplier. This is especially true in situations where service delivery involves separate transactions (such as a car rental) instead of being continuous in nature (as with insurance coverage). In many instances, consumers are loyal to several brands (sometimes described as "polygamous loyalty") but avoid others. In such instances, the marketing goal is to strengthen the customer's preference for one brand over others, and to gain a greater share of the customer's spending in that service category. Once acquired, it tends to be the

Figure 12.5: American Airlines uses its AAdvantage program to promote customer loyalty.

© American Airlines, Inc. 2016.

reward-based bonds (often offered through a loyalty program) that entice customers to spend more money and increase a firm's share-of-wallet.[31] Incentives that offer rewards based on the frequency of purchase, value of purchase, or a combination of both, represent a basic level of customer bonding. These rewards can be financial and non-financial in nature.

Financial Rewards. Financial rewards are customer incentives that have a financial value (also called "hard benefits"). These include discounts on purchases, loyalty program rewards such as frequent flier miles (Fig. 12.5), and the cash-back programs provided by some credit card issuers.

Besides airlines and hotels, an increasing number of service firms ranging from retailers (such as department stores, supermarkets,[32] book shops, and petrol stations), telecommunications providers, café chains, to courier services, and cinema chains have launched similar reward programs in response to the increasing competitiveness of their markets. Although some provide their own rewards — such as free merchandise, vehicle upgrades, or free hotel rooms at vacation resorts — many firms denominate their awards in miles that can be credited to a selected frequent-flyer program. In fact, air miles have become a form of promotional currency in the service sector.[33]

Research in the credit card industry suggests that financial rewards-based loyalty programs strengthen the customers' perception of the value proposition, and lead to increased revenues due to higher usage levels and fewer defections.[34] To assess the potential of a loyalty program to alter normal patterns of behavior, Grahame Dowling and Mark Uncles argue that marketers need to examine three psychological effects[35]:

- *Brand loyalty versus deal loyalty.* To what extent are customers loyal to the core service (or brand) rather than to the loyalty program itself? Marketers should focus on loyalty programs that directly support the value proposition and positioning of the product in question. For example, free upgrades, value-added services, or other core service-related benefits that enhance the overall service experience are directly linked to the core service, but air miles are not.

- *How buyers value rewards.* Several elements determine a loyalty program's value to customers: (1) the cash value of the redemption rewards (if customers had to purchase them); (2) the range of choice among rewards — for instance, a selection of benefits rather than just a single benefit; (3) the aspirational value of the rewards — something exotic that the consumer would not normally purchase may have greater appeal than a cash-back offer; (4) whether the amount of usage required to obtain a reward places it within the realm of possibility for any given consumer; (5) the ease of using the program and making redemptions; and (6) the psychological benefits of belonging to the program and accumulating points.

- *Timing.* How soon can benefits from participating in the rewards program be obtained by customers? Deferred gratification tends to weaken the appeal of a loyalty program. One solution is to send customers periodic statements of their account status, indicating progress toward reaching a particular milestone, and promoting the rewards that might be forthcoming when that point is reached.

Interestingly, if a firm has loyalty program partners, (e.g., an airline may partner credit card companies, hotels, car rental firms, where loyalty program points can also be earned with these companies), satisfaction with the core service can have a positive impact on buying from program partners. In the same way, satisfaction with the service of program partners can have a positive impact on the buying of the core service.[36] It is therefore important for firms to be selective in choosing loyalty program partners.

Even well-designed rewards programs by themselves are not enough to keep a firm's most desirable customers. If the customers are dissatisfied with the quality of service, or believe they can get better value from another provider, they may quickly become disloyal. No service business that has instituted a rewards program for frequent users can ever afford to lose sight of its broader goals of offering high service quality and good value relative to the price and other costs incurred by customers.[37] Sometimes, what the customer wants is just for the firm to deliver the basic service well, meet their needs, and solve their problems quickly and easily, and they will be loyal.[38] One of the risks associated with a focus on strengthening relationships with high-value customers is that a firm may allow service to other customers to deteriorate.

Finally, customers can even get frustrated especially with financial rewards-based programs, so rather than creating loyalty and goodwill, they breed dissatisfaction! This can happen when customers feel they are excluded from a reward program because of low balances or volume of business, if the rewards are seen as having little or no value, if they cannot redeem their loyalty points because of black-out dates during high demand periods, and if redemption processes are too troublesome and time-consuming.[39] And some customers already have so many loyalty cards in their wallet that they are simply not interested in adding to that pile, especially if customers see them as only of marginable value.

Non-financial Rewards. Non-financial rewards (also called "soft benefits") provide benefits that cannot be translated directly into monetary terms. Examples include giving priority to loyalty program members on reservation waitlists and virtual queues in call centers. Some airlines provide benefits such as higher baggage allowances, priority upgrading, access to airport lounges, and the likes, to its frequent flyers even when they are only flying in economy class.

Important intangible rewards include special recognition and appreciation. Customers tend to value the extra attention given to their needs and appreciate the efforts to meet their occasional special requests. High-tier loyalty program members also tend to enjoy an implicit service guarantee. When things go wrong, front-line employees will pay extra attention to their most valuable customers and see that the service is recovered to their satisfaction.

Many loyalty programs also provide important status benefits to customers in the top-tiers who feel part of an elite group (e.g., the Seven Stars card holders with Caesars in our opening vignette) and enjoy their special treatment.[40] Tiered loyalty programs in particular can provide powerful incentives and motivation for customers to achieve the next higher level of membership which often leads to a higher share-of-wallet for the preferred provider.

Non-financial rewards, especially if linked to high-tier service levels, are typically more powerful than financial ones as the former can create tremendous value for customers. Unlike financial rewards, nonfinancial rewards directly relate to the firm's core service and improve customers' experience and value perception. In the context of a hotel, for example, redeeming loyalty points for free gifts does nothing to enhance the guest experience. However, getting priority for reservations, early check-in, late check-out, upgrades, and receiving special attention and appreciation will make your stay more pleasant, leave you with the fuzzy warm feeling that this firm appreciates your business, and makes you want to come back.[41]

Service Insights 12.4 describes how British Airways has designed its Executive Club, effectively combining financial and non-financial loyalty rewards.

Small businesses often do not run formal loyalty programs but can still employ effective bonds. For example, they can use informal loyalty rewards which may take the form of giving regular customers a small treat periodically as a way of thanking them, reserving their favorite table in a restaurant, paying them special attention, and the likes.

SERVICE INSIGHTS 12.4
Rewarding Value of Use, Not Just Frequency, at British Airways

Unlike some frequent-flyer programs, in which customer usage is measured simply in miles, British Airways' (BA) Executive Club members receive both *air miles* toward redemption of air travel rewards and *points* towards silver- or gold-tier status for travel on BA. With the creation of OneWorld alliance with American Airlines, Qantas, Cathay Pacific, and other airlines, Executive Club members have been able to earn miles (and sometimes points) by flying these partner airlines, too.

As shown in Table 12.1, silver and gold cardholders are entitled to special benefits such as priority reservations and a superior level of on-the-ground service. For instance, even if a gold cardholder is only traveling in economy class, he or she will be entitled to first-class standards of treatment at check-in, in the airport lounges and boarding. Miles will not expire as long as the frequent-flyer account has at least one transaction in every 36 months (after which they expire), but tier status is valid for only 12 months beyond the membership year in which it was earned. This means that the right to special privileges must be re-earned each year. The objective of awarding tier status is to encourage passengers who have a choice of airlines to concentrate their travel on BA, rather than to join several frequent-flyer programs and collect mileage awards from all of them. Few passengers travel with such frequency that they will be able to obtain the benefits of gold-tier status (or its equivalent) on more than one airline.

Points given also vary according to the class of service. Longer trips earn more points than shorter ones. However, tickets at deeply discounted prices may earn fewer miles and no points at all. To reward purchase of high-priced tickets, passengers earn points at up to 2.5 times the economy rate if they travel in club (business class), and up to triple the rate in first class.

Although the airline makes no promises about complimentary upgrades, members of BA's Executive Club are more likely to

Table 12.1: Selected Benefits Offered by British Airways to its Most Valued Passengers

Benefit	Bronze-Tier Members	Gold-Tier Members
Reservations		Dedicated gold phone line
Reservation assurance		If flight is full, a guaranteed seat in economy when booking full fare ticket at least 24 hours in advance and checking in at least one hour in advance
Priority waitlist and standby	Higher priority	Highest priority
Check-in desk	According to class of travel	First (regardless of travel class)
Lounge access	According to class of travel	First class departure lounge for passenger and one guest, regardless of travel class; use of arrival lounges; lounge access anytime, allowing use of lounges even when not flying BA intercontinental flights
Special services assistance		Dedicated direct line to customer support staff; problem solving beyond that accorded to other BA travelers
Bonus air miles	+25%	+100%
Upgrade for two		Free upgrade to next cabin for member and companion after earning 2,500 tier points in one year; another upgrade for two after 3,500 points in same year
Partner cards		Upon reaching 5,000 points, the member will receive two Executive Club Silver cards and one Gold Partner so that the benefits can be shared with loved ones
Special privilege		Concorde Room access at Heathrow Terminal 5 and New York JFK Terminal 7 after earning 5,000 points
Lifetime membership		Upon earning 35,000 points, Gold membership status will be awarded for life

receive such invitations than other passengers. Tier status is an important consideration when employees decide whom to upgrade on an overbooked flight. Unlike many airlines, BA tends to limit upgrades to situations in which a lower-class cabin is overbooked. They do not want frequent travelers to believe that they can plan on buying a less expensive ticket and then automatically receive an upgrade.

BA has even created a Household Account that allows for up to six family members who live at the same address to pool their miles and allow them to make full use of the collective balance.

Source: British Airways Executive Club benefits, https://www.britishairways.com/en-gb/executive-club/tiers-and-benefits/compare-the-tiers accessed 1 July, 2016.

Build Higher-Level Bonds

One objective of loyalty rewards is to motivate customers to combine their purchases with one provider, or at least make it the preferred provider. However, reward-based loyalty programs are quite easy for other suppliers to copy, and they rarely provide a sustained competitive advantage. In contrast, high-level bonds tend to offer a more sustained competitive advantage. Next section discusses the three main types of high-level bonds, which are: (1) social, (2) customization, and (3) structural bonds.

Social Bonds. It is interesting to notice how a hairdresser addresses her customer by name who came for a haircut, or how she asks why she has not seen her for a long time, and hopes everything went well when the said customer was away on a long business trip. Social bonds and related personalization of services are usually based on personal relationships between providers and customers. Social bonds are more difficult to build than financial bonds and may take longer to achieve, but they are also harder for other suppliers to replicate for that same customer. A firm that has created social bonds with its customers has a better chance of retaining them for the long term because of the trust the customers place in the staff. [42] When social bonds include shared relationships or experiences between customers, such as in country clubs or educational settings, they can be a major loyalty driver for the organization. [43]

Customization Bonds. These bonds are built when the service provider succeeds in providing customized service to its loyal customers. For example, Starbucks' employees are encouraged to learn their regular customers' preferences and customize their services accordingly. Many large hotel chains capture the preferences of their customers through their loyalty program databases. Firms offering customized service are likely to have more loyalty customers, so that, when customers arrive at their hotel for example, they find their individual needs have already been anticipated, from the preferred room type (e.g., smoking vs. non-smoking) and bed type (e.g., twins or king size), to the kind of pillow they like, and the newspaper they want to read in the morning. Among many other benefits, Fairmont Hotels & Resorts' loyalty program provides its members with jogging shoes and apparel of the right size, and yoga mats and stretch bands waiting in the guests' rooms at their arrival.[44] When a customer becomes used to this special service level, he or she may find it difficult to adjust to another service provider who is not able to customize the service (or at least immediately, as it takes time for the new provider to learn about someone's needs and preferences).[45]

Structural Bonds. Structural bonds are frequently seen in B2B settings. They are created by getting customers to align their way of doing things with the supplier's own processes, thus linking the customer to the firm. This situation makes it more difficult for competitors to draw them away. Examples include joint investments in projects and sharing of information, processes, and equipment.

Structural bonds can be created in a B2C environment too. For instance, some car rental companies offer travelers the opportunity to create a customized account on the firm's website and mobile app, where they can retrieve details of past trips, including pick-up and return locations, types of cars, insurance coverage, billing address, credit card details, and so forth. This simplifies the task of making new bookings. Once customers have integrated their way of doing things with the firm's processes, structural bonds are created, linking the customer to the firm and making it more difficult for the competition to draw them away.

While all these bonds tie a customer closer to the firm, they also deliver the confidence, social, and special treatment benefits that customers desire (refer to *Service Insights 12.1*). In general, bonds will not work well in the long term unless they generate value for the customer!

STRATEGIES FOR REDUCING CUSTOMER DEFECTIONS

A complementary approach is to understand the drivers of customer defections, also called customer churn, and work on eliminating or at least reducing those drivers.

Analyze Customer Defections and Monitor Declining Accounts

A first step is to understand the reasons for customer switching. Susan Keaveney conducted a large-scale study across a range of services and found several key reasons why customers switch to another provider (Fig. 12.6).[46] These were:

- Core service failures (44% of respondents)
- Dissatisfactory service encounters (34%)
- High, deceptive, or unfair pricing (30%)
- Inconvenience in terms of time, location, or delays (21%)
- Poor response to service failure (17%)

Figure 12.6: What drives customers to switch away from a service firm?

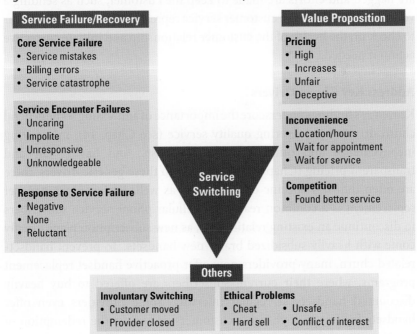

Service Failure/Recovery	Value Proposition
Core Service Failure • Service mistakes • Billing errors • Service catastrophe	**Pricing** • High • Increases • Unfair • Deceptive
Service Encounter Failures • Uncaring • Impolite • Unresponsive • Unknowledgeable	**Inconvenience** • Location/hours • Wait for appointment • Wait for service
Response to Service Failure • Negative • None • Reluctant	**Competition** • Found better service

Service Switching

Others

Involuntary Switching	Ethical Problems	
• Customer moved • Provider closed	• Cheat • Hard sell	• Unsafe • Conflict of interest

Source: Adapted from Susan M. Keaveney (1995), "Customer Switching Behavior in Service Industries: An Exploratory Study," *Journal of Marketing*, Vol. 59, April, pp. 71–82.

Many respondents decided to switch after a series of related incidents, such as a service failure followed by an unsatisfactory service recovery. Other important factors that drive switching include overall dissatisfaction with the current service provider and the perception that it has an inferior performance on important attributes compared to the best alternative provider.[47]

Progressive service firms regularly conduct what is called *churn diagnostics* to gain a better understanding of why customers defect. This includes the analysis of data from churned and declining customers, exit interviews (call-center staff often have a short set of questions they ask when a customer cancels an account), and in-depth interviews of former customers by a third-party research agency, which typically yield a more detailed understanding of churn drivers.[48]

Some firms even try to predict churn of individual accounts. For example, cell phone service providers use churn alert systems, which monitor the activity in individual customer accounts with the objective of predicting impending customer switching. Important accounts at risk are flagged and efforts are made to keep the customer, such as sending a voucher and/or having a customer service representative call the customer to check on the health of the customer relationship and initiate corrective action if needed.

Address Key Churn Drivers

Keaveney's findings underscore the importance of addressing some general churn drivers by delivering quality service (see Chap. 14), minimizing inconvenience and other nonmonetary costs, and having fair and transparent pricing (Chap. 6). In addition to these generic drivers, there are often industry-specific churn drivers as well. For example, handset replacement is a common reason for cellular phone service subscribers to discontinue an existing relationship, as new subscription plans usually come with heavily subsidized brand-new handsets. To prevent handset-related churn, many providers now offer proactive handset replacement programs, where their current subscribers are offered to buy heavily discounted handsets at regular intervals. Some providers even offer handsets for free to high-value customers or against the redemption of loyalty points.

In addition to such proactive retention measures, many firms also use reactive measures. These include specially trained call-center staff called *save teams*, who deal with customers who intend to cancel their accounts. The main job of save team employees is to listen to customer needs and issues, and try to address them with the key focus of retaining the customer. However, you need to be careful on how to reward save teams (see *Service Insights 12.5*).

SERVICE INSIGHTS 12.5
Churn Management Gone Wrong

America Online (AOL) found itself on the wrong end of churn management when about 300 of its subscribers filed complaints with the New York state attorney general's office, saying that AOL had ignored their demands to cancel the service and stop billing them. After an investigation by the State of New York, AOL eventually agreed to pay $1.25 million in penalties and costs, and to change some of its customer service practices to settle the case.

What went wrong? AOL had been rewarding its call-center employees for 'saving' customers who called in to cancel their service. Employees could earn high bonuses if they were able to persuade half or more of such customers to stay with the firm. As claimed by the attorney general's office, this may have led AOL's employees to make it difficult to cancel service. As a response, AOL agreed in a settlement to have service cancellations requests recorded and verified by a third-party monitor, and to provide up to four months' worth of refunds to all New York subscribers who claim that their cancellations had been ignored (AOL did not admit to any wrongdoing in that settlement). The New York's Attorney General at the time said, "This agreement helps to ensure that AOL will strive to keep its customers through quality service, not stealth retention programs".

Source: The Associated Press, "AOL to Pay $1.25 M to Settle Spitzer Probe," *USA Today*, 25.08.2005, p. 5B.

Implement Effective Complaint Handling and Service Recovery Procedures

Effective complaint handling and excellent service recovery are crucial for keeping unhappy customers from switching providers. Well-managed firms make it easy for customers to voice their problems and respond with suitable service-recovery strategies. In that way, customers will remain satisfied, and this will reduce the intention to switch[49] (see Chap. 13 for more details).

Increase Switching Costs

Another way to reduce churn is to increase switching costs.[50] Many services have natural switching barriers. For example, it is a lot of work for customers to change their primary banking account, especially when many direct debits, credits, and other related banking services are tied to that account, plus many customers are reluctant to learn about the products and processes of a new provider.[51] Firms can increase these switching costs further by focusing on providing added value to customers through increased convenience, customization, and priority (collectively called "positive switching costs" or "soft lock-in strategies") to tie a customer closer to the firm and make switching more costly. Such strategies have been shown to be more effective in generating both attitudinal and behavioral loyalty than the "hard lock-in strategies" discussed next.[52]

Hard lock-in strategies refer to switching costs created by having contractual penalties for switching, such as transfer fees payable to some brokerage firms for moving shares and bonds to another financial institution. Cellular phone service providers often impose contractual penalties if a contract is cancelled during a lock-in period. However, firms need to be careful so that they are not seen as holding their customers hostage. A firm with high switching barriers and poor service quality is likely to generate negative attitudes and bad word-of-mouth. At some point, the last straw is reached and a customer will have had enough and continue to switch service providers even with significant switching costs, or at the first opportune moment, for example, when a contract expires.[53]

ENABLERS OF CUSTOMER LOYALTY STRATEGIES

Most strategies discussed in the Wheel of Loyalty require an in-depth understanding of its customers to actively improve their loyalty. Enablers of customer loyalty strategies provide this understanding and include the creation of "membership-type" of relationships such as through loyalty programs and CRM systems, account managers, and frontline employees. Before discussing these enablers, the fundamental difference between strategies intended to produce a single transaction (i.e., transaction marketing) and those designed to create extended relationships with customers (relationship marketing) will be discussed.

Customer Loyalty in a Transactional Marketing Context

A *transaction* is an event during which an exchange of value takes place between two parties. One transaction or even a series of transactions do not necessarily constitute a relationship, which requires mutual recognition and knowledge between the parties. When each transaction between customer and supplier is essentially discrete and anonymous, with no long-term record kept of customer's purchasing history, and little or no mutual recognition between the customer and employees, then no meaningful marketing relationship can be said to exist. This is true for many services, ranging from passenger transport to food service, or visits to a movie theater, in which each purchase and use is a separate event.

Customer loyalty strategies in a transactional marketing context have to focus mostly on the foundation strategies of the Wheel of Loyalty, such as segmenting the market and matching customer needs with firm capabilities, and delivering high service quality. However, most other strategies require a good understanding of a firm's customer behavior. For example, unless a firm knows the consumption behavior of individual customers, it cannot apply tiering of service, loyalty rewards, customization, personalization, churn management and the like. For all those strategies, a firm has to have individual customer data, which is the case in relationship marketing.

Relationship Marketing

The term *relationship marketing* has been widely used to describe the type of marketing activity designed to create extended relationships with customers. Ideally, both the firm and the customer have an interest in a deeper engagement and higher value-added exchange. A firm may have transactions with some customers who have neither the desire nor the need to make future purchases, while working hard to move others up the loyalty ladder.[54] Evert Gummesson identified no fewer than 30 types of relationships. He advocates *total relationship marketing*, describing it as:

> *...marketing based on relationships, networks, and interaction, recognizing that marketing is embedded in the total management of the networks of the selling organization, the market, and society. It is directed to long-term, win-win relationships with individual customers, and value is jointly created between the parties involved.*[55]

Relationship marketing requires a membership-type relationship. The next section shows that some service industries naturally have a membership-type relationship, whereas others have to work hard to create them.

Creating "Membership-type" Relationships as Enablers for Loyalty Strategies

The nature of the current relationship with customers can be analyzed by asking first: does the supplier enter into a formal "membership"

Table 12.2: Relationships with Customers

Nature of Service Delivery	Type of Relationship Between the Service Organization and Its Customers	
	Membership Relationship	No Formal Relationship
Continuous delivery of service	• Insurance • Cable TV subscription • College enrollment • Banking	• Radio station • Police protection • Lighthouse • Public highway
Discrete transactions	• Long-distance calls from subscriber phone • Theater series subscription • Travel on commuter ticket • Repair under warranty • Health treatment for HMO member	• Mail service • Toll highway • Movie theater • Public transportation • Restaurant

relationship with customers, as with telephone subscriptions, banking, and the family doctor? Or is there no defined relationship? Second, is the service delivered on a continuous basis, as in insurance, broadcasting and police protection? Or is each transaction recorded and charged separately? Table 12.2 shows the matrix resulting from this categorization, with examples in each category. A *membership relationship* is a formalized relationship between the firm and an identifiable customer, which often provides special benefits to both parties.

Discrete transactions in which every use involves a payment to the service supplier by an essentially "anonymous" consumer, are typical of services such as transport, restaurants, cinemas and shoe repairs. The problem for marketers of such services is that they tend to be less informed about who their customers are and what use each customer makes of the service than their counterparts in membership-type organizations. Managers in businesses that sell discrete transactions have to work a little harder to establish relationships.

In small businesses such as hair salons, frequent customers are (or should be) welcomed as "regulars" whose needs and preferences are remembered. Keeping formal records of customers' needs, preferences and purchasing behavior is useful even for small firms, as it helps employees to avoid asking the same questions on each service occasion, allowing them to personalize the service given to each customer, and also enables the firm to anticipate future needs. In addition, selling the service in bulk (for instance, a theater series subscription or a commuter ticket on public transport) can also transform discrete transactions into membership relationships, but do not necessarily allow for more customer insight and deployment of more sophisticated loyalty strategies.

In large companies with substantial customer bases, transactions can still be transformed into relationships by offering extra benefits to customers who choose to register with the firm (loyalty programs for hotels, airlines, car rental firms, and mobile apps for café chains fall into this category). Having a loyalty program in place enables a firm to know who its current customers are, to capture their service transactions and preferences. This is valuable information for service delivery, allowing customization and personalization, and for segmentation and tiering of service purposes. For transaction-type businesses, loyalty reward programs, in combination with CRM systems, become a necessary enabler for implementing the strategies discussed in the Wheel of Loyalty.

Novices often equate loyalty points with loyalty programs. However, the most valuable aspect of loyalty programs for both the customer and the firm are often all the other benefits a firm's loyalty strategy brings with it. As discussed in the Wheel of Loyalty, it is often the benefits of the loyalty program that enhance the core service (from priority to customization) and have the highest value. One might ask, why then do firms do away with the points and focus on these other benefits? The answer has to do with consumer psychology; we all need a little incentive to sign up, install an app, provide information and carry a loyalty card. For a firm to gain a system-wide view across outlets (and often, across countries), channels, and services, the only unique identifier that is reliable is typically a loyalty card (or membership card number) or a mobile app connected to a cell phone number. All other unique identifiers such as name, passport numbers, and address have been shown to be problematic, as names and addresses can be misspelled and passport numbers change. Therefore, it is often good to view the points (or air miles) of a loyalty program as a little incentive for customers to sign up and identify themselves at reservations, check-ins, and purchases, through their loyalty program membership number, card, or mobile app. The real customer (and firm) benefits are then delivered through the other bonds as described in the Wheel of Loyalty.

The loyalty program and loyalty strategies undoubtedly have to be delivered, and that typically happens through CRM systems that capture, analyze and deliver the relevant information to front-line employees and account managers (in B2B contexts, or top-tier consumer segments). Front-line employees were discussed in Chap. 11, and the role of CRM systems in delivering loyalty strategies are discussed in the next section.

CRM: CUSTOMER RELATIONSHIP MANAGEMENT

Service marketers have understood for some time the power of customer relationship management, and certain industries have applied it for decades. Examples include the corner grocery store, the neighborhood car repair shop, and providers of banking services to high net-worth clients. Mention CRM and immediately, costly and complex IT systems and infrastructure come to mind. However, CRM actually signifies the whole process by which relations with the customers are built and maintained.[56] It should be seen as an enabler of the successful implementation of the Wheel of Loyalty. The CRM system will be discussed next, before moving on to a more strategic perspective.

Common Objectives of CRM Systems

Many firms have large numbers of customers (sometimes millions), many different touch points (for instance, tellers, call-center staff, self-service machines, apps, and websites), and at multiple geographic locations. At a single large facility, it is unlikely that a customer will be served by the same front-line staff on two consecutive visits. In such situations, managers historically lacked the tools to practice relationship marketing. Today, CRM systems allow customer information to be captured and delivered to the various touch points. From a customer perspective, well-implemented CRM systems can offer a unified customer interface that delivers customization and personalization. This means that at each transaction, the relevant account details, knowledge of customer preferences and past transactions, or history of a service problem are at the fingertips of the person serving the customer. This can result in a vast service improvement and increased customer value.

From a company's perspective, CRM systems allow the company to better understand, segment, and tier its customer base, better target promotions and cross-selling, and even implement churn alert systems that signal if a customer is in danger of defecting.[57] *Service Insights 12.6* highlights some common CRM applications.

SERVICE INSIGHTS 12.6
Common CRM Applications

- *Data collection.* The system captures customer data such as contact details, demographics, purchasing history, service preferences, and the like.
- *Data analysis.* The data captured is analyzed and grouped by the system according to the criteria set by the firm. This is used to tier the customer base and tailor service delivery accordingly.

- *Sales force automation.* Sales leads, cross-sell and upsell opportunities can be effectively identified and processed, and the entire sales cycle from lead generation to the closing of sales, and provision of after-sales services can be tracked and facilitated through the CRM system.

- *Marketing automation.* Mining of customer data allows the firm to target its market. A good CRM system enables the firm to achieve one-to-one marketing and cost savings, often in the context of loyalty and retention programs. This results in increasing the ROI on its marketing expenditure. CRM systems also allow firms to assess the effectiveness of marketing campaigns through the analysis of responses.

- *Call center automation.* Call-center staff have customer information at their fingertips and can improve their service levels to all customers. Caller ID and account numbers also allow call centers to identify the customer tier the caller belongs to, and to tailor the service accordingly. For example, platinum callers get priority in waiting loops.

What does a Comprehensive CRM Strategy Include?[58]

Rather than viewing CRM as a technology, we subscribe to a more strategic view of CRM that focuses on the profitable development and management of customer relationships. Fig. 12.7 provides an integrated framework of five key processes involved in a CRM strategy.

1. *Strategy development* involves the assessment of business strategy, including articulation of the company's vision, industry trends, and competition. The business strategy is typically the responsibility of top management. For customer relationship management to have a positive impact on a firm's performance, the firm's strategy is key.[59] Therefore, business strategy should guide the development of customer strategy, including the choice of target segments, customer-base tiering, design of loyalty bonds, and churn management as discussed in the Wheel of Loyalty.

Figure 12.7: An integrated framework for CRM strategy.

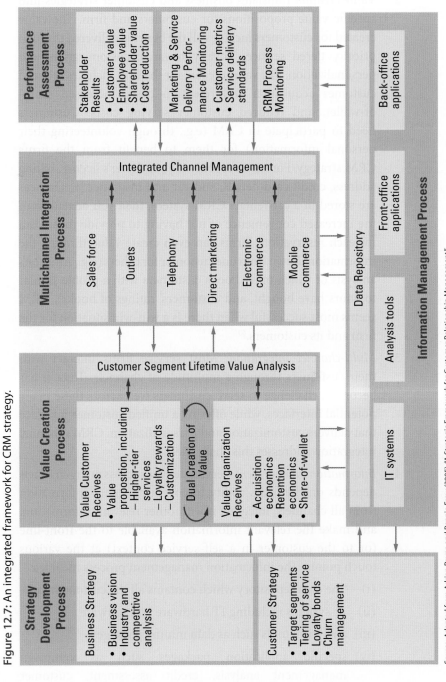

2. *Value creation* translates business and customer strategies into specific value propositions for customers and firm. The value created for customers includes all the benefits delivered through priority tiered services, loyalty rewards, customization, and personalization. The value created for the firm includes reduced customer acquisition and retention costs, increased share-of-wallet, and reduced customer serving costs. Customers need to participate in CRM (e.g., through volunteering their personal information) for them to benefit from the firm's CRM strategy. For instance, only if your driver's license, billing address, credit card details, and car and insurance preferences are stored in a car rental's CRM system, then you benefit from the increased convenience of not having to provide those data for each reservation. Firms can even create value through the information drawn from one customer for others (e.g., Amazon's analysis of which other books customers with a profile similar to yours have bought, and customers' ratings of books). CRM seems most successful when there is a win-win situation for the firm and its customers.[60]

3. *Multi-channel integration.* Most service firms interact with their customers through a multitude of channels. Thus, it has become a challenge to serve customers well across these many potential interfaces, while offering a unified customer interface that delivers customization and personalization. CRM's channel integration addresses this challenge.

4. *Information management.* Service delivery across many channels depends on the firm's ability to collect customer information from all channels, integrate it with other relevant information, and make the relevant information available to the front-line (or to the customer in a self-service context) at the various touch points. The information management process includes:

   (i) The data repository which contains all the customer data

   (ii) IT systems including IT hardware and software

   (iii) analytical tools such as data mining packages

   (iv) specific application packages such as campaign management analysis, credit assessment, customer profiling, churn alert systems, and even customer fraud detection and management

(v) front office applications which support activities that involve direct customer contact, including sales force automation and call center management applications

(vi) back office applications which support internal customer-related processes, including, logistics, procurement, and financial processing

5. *Performance assessment* must address three critical questions:

(i) Is the CRM strategy creating value for its key stakeholders (i.e., customers, employees, and shareholders)?

(ii) Are the marketing objectives (ranging from customer acquisition, share-of-wallet, retention to customer satisfaction) and service delivery performance objectives (e.g., call-center service standards such as call-waiting time, abortion, and first-time resolution rates) being achieved?

(iii) Is the CRM process itself performing up to expectations? Are the relevant strategies being set, is customer and firm value being created, is the information management process working effectively, and is integration across customer service channels being achieved effectively? The performance assessment process should drive the continuous improvement of the CRM strategy itself.

Common Failures in CRM Implementation[61]

Unfortunately, majority of CRM implementations have failed in the past. According to the Gartner Group, the CRM implementation failure rate is 55%, and Accenture claims it to be as high as 60%. A key reason for this high failure rate is that firms often equate installing CRM systems with having a customer relationship strategy. They forget that the system is just a tool to enhance the firm's customer servicing capabilities, and is not the strategy in itself.

Furthermore, CRM cuts across many departments and functions (e.g., from customer contact centers and online services, to branch operations, employee training, and IT departments), programs (ranging from sales and loyalty programs to launching of new services, and cross-selling initiatives), and processes (e.g., from credit-line authorization to complaint handling and service recovery). The wide-ranging scope of CRM implementation and the unfortunate reality that it is often the weakest link that determines the success of an implementation, shows the challenge of getting it right. Common reasons for CRM failures include:

- *Viewing CRM as a technology initiative.* It is easy to let the focus shift towards technology and its features, whereby the IT department takes the lead in devising the CRM strategy rather than top management or marketing. This often results in a lack of strategic direction, understanding of customers and markets during implementation.

- *Lack of customer focus.* Many firms implement CRM without the ultimate goal of enhancing the service value and enabling consistent service delivery for valued customers across all customer service processes and delivery channels.

- *Insufficient appreciation of customer lifetime value (LTV).* The marketing of many firms is not sufficiently structured around the vastly different profitability of different customers. Furthermore, servicing costs for different customer segments are often not well captured (e.g., by using activity-based costing as discussed in Chap. 6).

- *Inadequate support from top management.* Without ownership and active involvement from top management, the CRM strategic intent will not survive the implementation intact.

- *Failing to re-engineer business processes.* It is nearly impossible to implement CRM successfully without redesigning customer service and back-office processes. Many implementations fail because CRM is fitted into existing processes, rather than redesigning the processes to fit a customer-centric CRM implementation. Redesigning also requires change management, employee involvement and support, which are often lacking.

- *Underestimating the challenges in data integration.* Firms frequently fail to integrate customer data that are usually scattered all over the organization. A key to unlocking the full potential of CRM is to make customer knowledge available in real time to all employees who need it.

Finally, firms might put their CRM strategies at substantial risk if customers believe that CRM is used in a way that is harmful to them.[62] Examples include feeling that they are not being treated fairly (for example, not being offered attractive promotions that are offered to new accounts but not to existing customers), and potential privacy concerns. Being aware of and actively avoiding these pitfalls is a first step towards a successful CRM implementation.

How to Get CRM Implementation Right

Despite the many horror stories of millions of dollars sunk into unsuccessful CRM projects, more firms are getting it right. "No longer a black hole, CRM is becoming a basic building block of corporate success", argue Darrell Rigby and Dianne Ledingham.[63] Seasoned McKinsey consultants believe that even CRM systems that have been implemented but have not yet shown results can still be turned around. They recommend taking a step back and focusing on how to build customer loyalty, rather than focusing on the technology itself.[64] Rather than using CRM to transform entire businesses through the wholesale implementation of the CRM model shown in Fig. 12.7, service firms should focus on clearly defined problems within their customer relationship cycle. These narrow CRM strategies often reveal additional opportunities for further improvements which, when taken together, can evolve into broad CRM implementation extending across the entire company.[65] Likewise, Rigby, Reichheld and Schefter recommend focusing on the customer strategy and not the technology, posing the question:

> *If your best customers knew that you planned to invest $130 million to increase their loyalty…, how would they tell you to spend it? Would they want you to create a loyalty card or would they ask you to open more cash registers and keep enough milk in stock. The answer depends on the kind of company you are and the kinds of relationships you and your customers want to have with one another.*[66]

Among the key issues managers should debate when defining their customer relationship strategy for a potential CRM system implementation are:

1. How should our value proposition change to increase customer loyalty?

2. How much customization or one-to-one marketing and service delivery is appropriate and profitable?

3. What is the incremental profit potential of increasing the share-of-wallet with our current customers? How much does this vary by customer tier and/or segment?

4. How much time and resources can we allocate to CRM right now?

5. If we believe in customer relationship management, why have we not taken more steps in that direction in the past? What can we do today to develop customer relationships without spending a lot on technology?[67]

Answering these questions may lead to the conclusion that a CRM system may currently not be the best investment or the highest priority, or that a scaled-down version may suffice to deliver the intended customer strategy. In any case, the system is merely a tool to drive the strategy, and thus must be tailored to deliver that strategy.

CONCLUSION

Many elements are involved in gaining market share, increasing share-of-wallet, and cross-selling other products and services to existing customers, and creating long-term loyalty. The Wheel of Loyalty is used as an organizing framework, which starts with a solid foundation that includes targeting the right portfolio of customer segments, attracting the right customers, tiering the service, and delivering high levels of satisfaction. Second, to truly build loyalty, a firm needs to develop close bonds with its customers that ideally deepen the relationship through cross-selling and bundling, and add value to the customer through loyalty rewards and higher-level bonds including social, customization, and structural bonds. Finally, a firm needs to identify and reduce the factors that result in "churn" — the loss of existing customers and the need to replace them with new ones.

Marketers need to pay special attention to those customers who offer the firm the greatest value, as they purchase its products with the greatest frequency and spend the most on premium services. Customer relationship management is a key enabler for the strategies discussed in the Wheel of Loyalty and is often integrated with loyalty programs. Loyalty programs help to create membership-type relationships with customers even in transaction-type businesses which, together with effective CRM systems, enable marketers to track the behavior of high-value customers in terms of where and when they use the service, what service classes or types of products they buy, and how much they spend. With the relevant knowledge delivered at key service touch points, frontline employees, account managers, and systems (e.g., ATMs, websites, and mobile apps) can deliver the high value-add benefits inherent in many of the loyalty bonds as discussed in this chapter. From a customer perspective, customer relationship management can result in vast service improvements and increased customer value such as through customization and increased convenience.

CHAPTER SUMMARY

Importance of Customer Loyalty to Firm Profitability

- Higher purchases, share-of-wallet, & cross-buying
- Reduced customer service costs
- Positive word-of-mouth and referrals
- Lower price sensitivity
- Amortization of acquisition costs over a longer period

Customer Loyalty

Value Analysis
- Lifetime value computation
- Gap analysis between actual and potential customer value

Loyalty Drivers
- Confidence benefits
- Social benefits
- Special treatment benefits

Customer Loyalty Strategies — The Wheel of Loyalty

Foundation for Loyalty
- Target the right customers, match firm capabilities with customer requirements
- Search for value, not just volume
- Use tiering of the customer base to focus resources and attention on the firm's most valuable customers
- Deliver service quality to win behavioral (share-of-wallet) and attitudinal loyalty (share-of-heart)

Loyalty Bonds
- Deepen the relationship through bundling & cross-selling
- Offer loyalty rewards
  - Financial rewards (hard benefits), e.g., points, frequent flyer miles; free upgrades
  - Non-financial rewards (soft benefits), e.g., priority waitlisting, upgrading, early check-in, etc; special recognition and appreciation; implicit service guarantee
- Higher-level loyalty bonds
  - Social bonds
  - Customization bonds
  - Structural bonds

Reduce Customer Churn
- Churn analysis
- Address key churn drivers
- Effective complaint handling & service recovery
- Increase switching costs
  - Positive switching costs (soft lock-in strategies) through adding value (see loyalty bonds)
  - Contractual & other hard lock-in strategies (e.g., early cancellation fees)

Enablers of Customer Loyalty Strategies

Frontline Employees & Account Managers

Membership-type Relationships
- Achieved through loyalty programs even for transaction-type services
- Loyalty programs provide a unique identifier of the customer that facilitates an integrated view of the customer across all channels, branches, and product lines

CRM Systems
- Strategy development (e.g., customer strategy, target segments, tiering of customers, design of loyalty bonds)
- Value creation for customers and the firm (e.g., customer benefits through tiering, customization and priority service, and higher share-of-wallet for firm)
- Multichannel integration (e.g., provide a unified customer interface)
- Information management (e.g., deliver customer data to all touchpoints)
- Performance assessment of strategy

CHAPTER 13

Complaint Handling and Service Recovery

A complaint is a gift.

Claus Møller
management consultant and author

Customers don't expect you to be perfect. They do expect you to fix things when they go wrong.

Donald Porter
V.P. British Airways

To err is human; to recover, divine.

Christopher Hart, James Heskett, and Earl Sasser
current and former professors at Harvard Business School
(paraphrasing 18th century poet Alexander Pope)

CUSTOMER COMPLAINING BEHAVIOR

The first unspoken law of service quality and productivity is: Do it right the first time. However, the fact that failures continue to occur cannot be ignored, often for reasons outside of the organization's control such.[1] Many "moments of truth" in service encounters are vulnerable to breakdowns. Distinctive service characteristics such as real-time performance, customer involvement, and people as part of the product can greatly increase the chances of service failures. How well a firm handles complaints and resolves problems frequently determines whether it builds customer loyalty or it should just watch its customers take their business elsewhere.

Customer Response Options to Service Failure

Chances are that the customers may not be always satisfied with some of the services they receive. How do they respond to their dissatisfaction with these services? Do they complain informally to an employee, ask to speak to the manager, or file a formal complaint? Or perhaps just mutter darkly to themselves, grumble to friends and family, and choose an alternative supplier the next time they need a similar type of service?

However, there are few customers who do not complain to the firm about poor service. Research around the globe has shown that most people will choose not to complain, especially if they think it will do no good. Fig. 13.1 depicts the courses of action a customer may take in response to a service failure. This model suggests at least three major steps:

(1) Take some form of *public action* (including complaining to the firm or to a third party, such as customer advocacy groups, consumer affairs or regulatory agencies, or even take the matter to the civil or criminal courts).

(2) Take some form of *private action* (including abandoning the supplier).

(3) Take *no action* (Fig. 13.2).

It is important to remember that a customer can take any one or a combination of actions. Managers need to be aware that the impact of a defection can go far beyond the loss of that customer's future revenue stream. Angry customers often tell other people about their problems,[2]

Figure 13.1: Customer response categories to service failures.

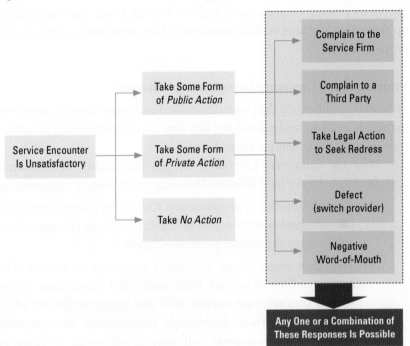

Figure 13.2: Some customers may just be frustrated but do not take any action to complain, as seen here in an interaction with an online service.

and the Internet allows for unhappy customers to reach thousands of people by posting complaints on bulletin boards, blogs, and even setting up their own websites to talk about their bad experiences with specific organizations.

Understanding Customer Complaining Behavior

To be able to effectively deal with dissatisfied and complaining customers, managers need to understand the key aspects of complaining behavior, starting with the questions posed below.

Why Do Customers Complain? In general, studies of consumer complaining behavior have identified four main purposes for complaining:

(1) *Obtain restitution or compensation.* Consumers often complain to recover some economic loss by seeking a refund, compensation, and/or have the service performed again.[3]

(2) *Vent their anger.* Some customers complain to rebuild self-esteem and/or to release their anger and frustration. When service processes are bureaucratic and unreasonable, or when employees are rude, deliberately intimidating, or apparently uncaring, the customers' self-esteem, self-worth or sense of fairness can be negatively affected. They may become angry and emotional.

(3) *Help to improve the service.* When customers are highly involved with a service (e.g., at a college, an alumni association, or their main banking connection), they give feedback to try and contribute towards service improvements.

(4) *For altruistic reasons.* Some customers are motivated by altruistic reasons. They want to spare other customers from experiencing the same shortcomings, and they may feel bad if they fail to draw attention to a problem that will raise difficulties for others if it remains unnoticed and uncorrected.

What Proportion of Unhappy Customers Complain? Research shows that on average, only 5–10% of customers who have been unhappy with a service actually complain.[4] Sometimes the percentage is far lower. A review of the records of a public bus company showed that formal complaints occurred at the rate of about three complaints for every million passenger trips. Assuming two trips a day, a person would need 1, 370 years (roughly 27 lifetimes) to make a million trips. In other words, the rate of complaints was incredibly low, especially when public bus companies are rarely known for service excellence. Although only a minority of dissatisfied customers complain, there is evidence that consumers across the world are becoming better informed, more self-confident, and more assertive about seeking satisfactory outcomes for their complaints.

Why Do Unhappy Customers Not Complain? A number of studies have identified a number of reasons why customers do not complain. Customers may not want to take the time to write a letter, send an e-mail, fill in a form or make a phone call, particularly if they do not see the service as being important enough to be worth the effort. Many customers see the payoff as uncertain and believe that no one would be concerned about their problem or would be willing to deal with it, and that complaining is simply not worth their while. In some situations, people simply do not know where to go or what to do. Also, many people feel that complaining is unpleasant and may be afraid of confrontation, especially if the complaint involves someone whom the customer knows and may have to deal with again.[5]

Finally, complaining behavior can be influenced by role perceptions and social norms. Customers are less likely to voice complaints in service situations in which they perceive they have "low power" (the ability to influence or control the transaction).[6] This is particularly true when the problem involves professional service providers such as doctors, lawyers or architects. Social norms tend to discourage customer criticism of such individuals.

Who Is Most Likely to Complain? Research findings consistently show that people in higher socio-economic levels are more likely to complain than those in the lower levels. They are better educated, have higher income, and are more socially involved, and this gives them the confidence, knowledge and motivation to speak up when they encounter problems.[7] Furthermore, those who complain also tend to be more knowledgeable about the product in question.

Where Do Customers Complain? Studies show that the majority of complaints are made at the place where the service was received. One of the authors of this book completed a consulting project developing and implementing a customer feedback system. He found that an amazing

99% of customer feedback was given face-to-face or over the phone to customer service representatives. Less than 1% of all complaints were submitted via firms' websites, social media pages, email, letters, or feedback cards. A survey of airline passengers found that only 3% of respondents who were unhappy with their meal actually complained about it, and they all complained to the flight attendants. None of them complained to the company's headquarters or to a consumer affairs office.[8] Also, customers tend to use interactive channels such as face-to-face, or the telephone when they want a problem to be fixed, but use non-interactive channels to complain (e.g., email or websites) when they mainly want to vent their anger and frustration.[9]

In practice, even when customers do complain, managers often do not hear about the complaints made to frontline employees. Without a formal customer feedback system, only a tiny proportion of the complaints may reach corporate headquarters.[10] If unhappy customers have already used other channels of complaint but their problem is not solved, they are more likely to turn to online public complaining. This is due to "double deviation". The service performance already caused dissatisfaction in the first instance, and the resolution of the problem also failed.[11]

What do Customers Expect Once They Have Made a Complaint?

Whenever a service failure occurs, people expect to be treated fairly. However, research has shown that many customers feel that they have not been treated fairly nor received adequate compensation. When this happens, their reactions tend to be immediate, emotional and enduring. In contrast, outcomes that are perceived as fair have a positive impact on customer satisfaction.[12]

Stephen Tax and Stephen Brown found that as much as 85% of the variation in the satisfaction with a service recovery was determined by three dimensions of fairness (Fig. 13.3):[13]

- *Procedural justice* refers to the policies and rules that any customer has to go through to seek fairness. Customers expect the firm to take responsibility, which is the key to the start of a fair procedure, followed by a convenient and responsive recovery process. That includes flexibility of the system and consideration of customer inputs into the recovery process.

Figure 13.3: Three dimensions of perceived fairness in service recovery processes.

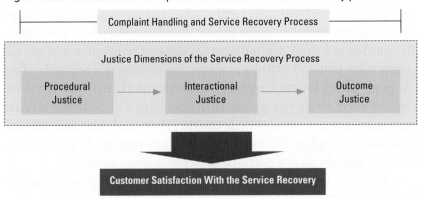

Source: Adapted from Stephen S. Tax and Stephen W. Brown, "Recovering and Learning from Service Failure," *Sloan Management Review* 49, no. 1 (Fall 1998), pp. 75–88.

- *Interactional justice* involves the employees of the firm who provide the service recovery and their behavior toward the customer. It is important to give an explanation for the failure and make an effort to resolve the problem. The recovery effort must also be seen as genuine, honest, and polite.

- *Outcome justice* concerns the restitution or compensation that a customer receives as a result of the losses and inconveniences caused by the service failure. This includes compensation for not only the failure, but also for the time, effort, and energy spent during the process of service recovery.

CUSTOMER RESPONSES TO EFFECTIVE SERVICE RECOVERY

"Thank Heavens for Complainers" was the provocative title of an article about customer complaining behavior, which also featured a successful manager exclaiming, "Thank goodness I've got a dissatisfied customer on the phone! The ones I worry about are the ones I never hear from".[14] Customers who do complain give a firm the chance to correct its problems (including some the firm may not even know of), restore relationships with the complainer, and improve future satisfaction for all.

Service recovery is a term for the systematic efforts of a firm to correct a problem following a service failure and to retain a customer's goodwill. Service-recovery efforts play an important role in achieving (or restoring) customer satisfaction and loyalty.[15] In every organization, things that occur may have a negative impact on relationships with customers. The true test of a firm's commitment to customer satisfaction and service quality is not in the advertising promises, but in the way it responds when things go wrong for the customer. Although complaints tend to have a negative effect on service personnel's commitment to customer service, employees with a positive attitude toward service and their own jobs are more likely to explore additional ways in which they can help customers and view complaints as a potential source of improvement.[16]

Effective service recovery requires thoughtful procedures for resolving problems and handling disgruntled customers. It is critical for firms to have effective recovery strategies, as even a single service problem under the following conditions can destroy a customer's confidence in a firm:

- Failure is totally outrageous (e.g., blatant dishonesty on the part of the supplier).
- Problem fits a pattern of failure rather than being an isolated incident.
- Recovery efforts are weak, serving to compound the original problem rather than correct it.[17]

The risk of defection is high, especially when there are variety of competing alternatives available. One study of customer switching behavior in service industries found that close to 60% of all respondents who reported changing suppliers did so because of a service failure; 25% cited failures in the core service, 19% reported an unsatisfactory encounter with an employee, 10% reported an unsatisfactory response to a prior service failure, and 4% described unethical behavior on the part of the provider.[18]

Impact of Effective Service Recovery on Customer Loyalty

When complaints are resolved satisfactorily, there is a much higher chance that the customers involved will remain loyal. In fact, research has shown that complainants who are satisfied with the service-recovery experience are 15 times more likely to recommend a company than dissatisfied complainants.[19] TARP research found that intentions to repurchase different types of products ranged between 9–37% when customers were dissatisfied but did not complain. For a major complaint, the retention rate increased from 9% when dissatisfied customers did not complain to 19% if the customer complained and the company offered a sympathetic ear but was unable to resolve the complaint to the satisfaction of the customer. If the complaint could be resolved to the satisfaction of the customer, the retention rate jumped to 54%. The highest retention rate of 82% was achieved when problems were fixed quickly, typically on the spot![20]

Complaint handling should be seen as a profit center, not a cost center. When a dissatisfied customer defects, the firm loses more than just the value of the next transaction. It may also lose a long-term stream of profits from that customer and from anyone else who is deterred from patronizing that firm as a result of negative comments from an unhappy friend. However, many organizations have yet to buy into the concept that it pays to invest in service recovery designed to protect those long-term profits.[21]

The Service Recovery Paradox

The *service recovery paradox* describes the phenomenon where customers who experience an excellent service recovery after a failure feel even more satisfied than customers who had no problem in the first place.[22] For example, a passenger may arrive at the check-in counter and find there are no seats for him due to overbooking, even though he has a confirmed seat. To recover the service, the passenger is upgraded to a business class seat, at no additional cost. The customer ends up being more satisfied than before the problem had occurred.

The service-recovery paradox may lead to the thinking that it may be good for customers to experience service failure so they can be delighted as a result of an excellent service recovery. However, this approach would be too expensive for the firm. It is also important to note that the service-recovery paradox does not always apply. In fact, research has shown that the service-recovery paradox is far from universal.[23] For example, a study of repeated service failures in a retail banking context showed that the service-recovery paradox held for the first service failure that was recovered to customers' full satisfaction.[24] However, if a second service failure occurred, the paradox disappeared. It seems that customers may forgive a firm once, but become disillusioned if failures recur. The study also showed that customers' expectations were raised after they experienced a very good recovery; thus, excellent recovery becomes the standard they expect for dealing with future failures.

Whether a customer comes out delighted from a service recovery may also depend on the severity and "recoverability" of the failure — no one can replace spoiled wedding photos, a ruined holiday, or eliminate the consequences of a debilitating injury caused by service equipment. In such situations, it is hard to imagine anyone being truly delighted even when the most professional service recovery is conducted. Compare these examples with a lost hotel reservation for which recovery is an upgrade to a better room, or even a suite. When poor service is recovered by delivery of a superior product, the customer is usually delighted and will probably hope for another lost reservation in the future.

The best strategy is to do it right the first time. As Michael Hargrove puts it, "Service recovery is turning a service failure into an opportunity you wish you never had".[25] Unfortunately, empirical evidence shows that some 40–60% of customers reported dissatisfaction with the service-recovery processes they experienced.[26]

PRINCIPLES OF EFFECTIVE SERVICE-RECOVERY SYSTEMS

Recognizing that current customers are a valuable asset base, managers need to develop effective procedures for service recovery following unsatisfactory experiences. Unfortunately, many service recoveries fail and some of the common causes for failure are shown in *Service Insights 13.1*. The three guiding principles for how to get it right are as follows: (1) make it easy for customers to give feedback, (2) enable effective service recovery, and (3) establish appropriate compensation levels. A fourth principle, learning from customer feedback and driving service improvements, will be discussed in Chap. 14 in the context of customer feedback systems. The components of an effective service-recovery system are shown in Fig. 13.4.[27]

SERVICE INSIGHTS 13.1
Common Service Recovery Mistakes

Here are some typical service recovery mistakes made by many organizations:

- *Managers disregard evidence that shows that service recovery provides a significant financial return.* In recent years, many organizations have focused on cost cutting, paying only lip service to retain their most profitable customers. On top of that, they have also lost sight of the need to respect all their customers.

- *Companies do not invest enough in actions that would prevent service issues.* Ideally, service planners address potential problems before they become customer problems. Although preventive measures do not eliminate the need for good service recovery systems, they greatly reduce the burden on frontline staff and the service recovery system in its entirety.

- *Customer service employees fail to display good attitudes.* The three most important things in service recovery are attitude, attitude and attitude. No matter how well-designed and well-planned the service recovery system is, it would not work well without the friendly and proverbial smile-in-the-voice attitude from frontline staff.

- *Organizations fail to make it easy for customers to complain or give feedback.* Although some improvement can be seen, such as hotels and restaurants offering comment cards and links on their websites and apps, little is done to communicate their simplicity and value to customers. Research shows that a large proportion of customers are unaware of the existence of a proper feedback system that could help them get their problems solved.

Source: Adapted from Rod Stiefbold, "Dissatisfied Customers Requires Service Recovery Plans," *Marketing News* 37, issue 22 (October 27, 2003): 44-45.

Figure 13.4: Components of an effective service recovery system.

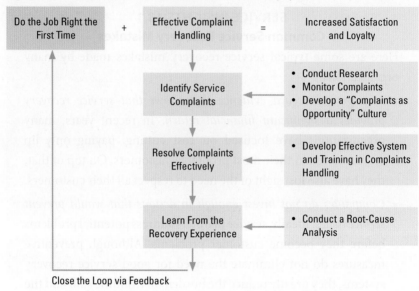

Source: Christopher H. Lovelock, Paul G. Patterson, and Jochen Wirtz, *Services Marketing: An Asia-Pacific and Australian Perspective*, 6th edition (Sydney: Pearson Australia, 2015), p. 419.

Make it Easy for Customers to Give Feedback

How can managers overcome unhappy customers' reluctance to complain about service failures? The best way is to directly address the reasons for their reluctance. Table 13.1 gives an overview of potential measures that can be taken to overcome these reasons identified earlier. Many companies have improved their complaint-collection procedures by adding special toll-free phone lines, links on their websites and social media pages, and clearly-displayed customer comment cards in their branches. In their customer communications, some companies feature service improvements that were the direct result of customer feedback under the motto "You told us, and we responded".

Enable Effective Service Recovery

Recovering from service failures takes more than just pious expressions of determination to resolve any problems that may occur. It requires commitment, planning, and clear guidelines. Specifically, effective service recovery should be: (1) proactive, (2) planned, (3) trained, and (4) empowered.

Table 13.1: Strategies to reduce customer complaint barriers.

Complaint Barriers for Dissatisfied Customers	Strategies to Reduce These Barriers
Inconvenience • Difficult to find the right complaint procedure • Effort, for example, writing and mailing a letter	Make feedback easy and convenient: • Put customer service hotline numbers, email the website and/or postal addresses on all customer communications materials (letters, bills, brochures, website, phone book, yellow pages listings, etc.)
Doubtful payoff • Uncertain whether any or what action will be taken by the firm to address the issue the customer is unhappy with	Reassure customers that their feedback will be taken seriously and will pay off: • Have service recovery procedures in place and communicate this to customers, for example, in customer newsletter and website • Feature service improvements that resulted from customer feedback
Unpleasantness • Fear of being treated rudely • Fear of being hassled • Feeling embarrassed	Make providing feedback a positive experience: • Thank customers for their feedback (can be done publicly and in general by addressing the entire customer base) • Train service employees not to hassle and to make customers feel comfortable • Allow for anonymous feedback

Service Recovery Should Be Proactive. Service recovery is ideally initiated on the spot, preferably before customers have a chance to complain (*Service Insights 13.1*). Service personnel should be sensitive to signs of dissatisfaction, and ask whether customers might be experiencing a problem. For example, the waiter may ask a guest who has only eaten half of his dinner: "Is everything all right, sir?" The guest may say, "Yes, thank you, I am not very hungry", or "The steak is well done but I had asked for medium rare". The second response then gives the waiter a chance to recover the service, rather than have an unhappy diner leave the restaurant and potentially not return.

Recovery Procedures Need to Be Planned. Contingency plans have to be developed for service failures, especially for those that occur regularly and cannot be designed out of the system.[28] For example, revenue management practices in the travel and hospitality industries often result in overbooking, and travelers are denied boarding or hotel guests are "walked" even though they had confirmed seats or reservations. To simplify the task of frontline staff, firms should identify the most common service problems such as overbooking, and then develop solution sets for employees to follow. In contact centers, the customer service representatives have prepared scripts to guide them in a service recovery situation.

Recovery Skills Must Be Taught.[29] As a customer, you may quickly feel insecure at the point of service failure because things are not turning out as expected; so you look to an employee for assistance. However, are they willing and able to help you? Effective training builds confidence and competence among frontline staff, enabling them to turn distress into delight. With effective training of how to handle recovery solution sets for routine service failures (see *Service Insights 13.2*) and for non-routine service failures, frontline staff can turn distress into delight with confidence and skill.

Recovery Requires Empowered Employees. Service recovery efforts should be flexible and employees should be empowered to use their judgment and communication skills to develop solutions that will satisfy complaining customers.[30] This is especially true for out-of-the-ordinary failures for which a firm may not have developed and trained solution sets. Employees need to be able to make decisions and spend money in order to resolve service problems promptly and recover customer goodwill. At the Ritz-Carlton and Sheraton hotels, employees are given the freedom to be proactive, rather than reactive. They take ownership of the situation and help resolve customers' problems to the best of their ability. In this day and age where online public complaining is gaining popularity, employees may even be empowered to respond online; for example, to complaints in the form of tweets, by tweeting back with a solution to resolve the problem.[31]

SERVICE INSIGHTS 13.2
Effective Service Recovery in Action

The lobby is deserted. It is not hard to overhear the conversation between the front desk receptionist at the Marriott Long Wharf Hotel in Boston and the late-arriving guest.

"Yes, Dr. Jones, we've been expecting you. I know you are scheduled to be here for three nights. I'm sorry to tell you, sir, but we are booked solid tonight. A large number of guests we assumed were checking out did not. Where is your meeting tomorrow, sir?"

The doctor told the receptionist where it was.

"That's near the Omni Parker House! That's not very far from here. Let me call them and get you a room for the evening. I'll be right back".

A few minutes later the receptionist returned with the good news.

"They're holding a room for you at the Omni Parker House, sir. And, of course, we'll pick up the tab. I'll forward any phone calls that come here for you. Here's a letter that will explain the situation and expedite your check-in, along with my business card so you can call me directly here at the front desk if you have any problems".

The doctor's mood was moving from exasperation towards calm. However, the receptionist was not finished with the encounter. He reached into the cash drawer. "Here is a $50 bill. That should more than cover your cab fare from here to the Parker House and back again in the morning. We don't have a problem tomorrow night, just tonight. And here's a coupon that will get you complimentary continental breakfast on our concierge level on the fifth floor tomorrow morning… and again, I am so sorry this happened".

As the doctor walks away, the hotel's night manager turns to the receptionist, "Give him about 15 minutes and then call to make sure everything went okay".

A week later when it was still a peak period for hotels in that city, the same guest who had overheard the exchange is in a taxi, *en route* to the same hotel. Along the way, he tells about the great service recovery episode he had witnessed the week before. The two travelers arrive at the hotel and make their way to the front desk, ready to check in.

They are greeted with unexpected news: "I am so sorry gentlemen. I know you were scheduled here for two nights. But we are booked solid tonight. Where is your meeting scheduled tomorrow?"

The would-be guests exchange a rueful glance as they give the receptionist their future plans. "That's near the Méridien. Let me call over there and see if I can get you a room. It won't but take a minute". As the receptionist walks away, the tale teller says, "I'll bet he comes back with a letter and a business card".

Sure enough, the receptionist returns to deliver the solution; it is not a robotic script but all the elements from the previous week's show are on display. What the tale teller thought was pure initiative from front desk receptionist the previous week, he now realizes was a planned, seemingly spontaneous yet predetermined response to a specific category of service problem.

Adapted from: Ron Zemke and Chip R. Bell, *Knock Your Socks Off Service Recovery*. New York: AMACOM, 2000, pp. 59–60.

How Generous Should Compensation be?

Vastly different costs are associated with possible recovery strategies. How much compensation should a firm offer when there has been a service failure, or would an apology be sufficient instead? The following rules of thumb can help managers to answer these questions:

- *What is the positioning of your firm?* If a firm is known for service excellence and charges a premium price for quality, then customers will expect service failures to be rare, so the firm should make a demonstrable effort to recover the few failures that do occur and be prepared to offer something of significant value. However, in a mass market business, customers are likely to accept an apology and rework of the service.

- *How severe was the service failure?* The general guideline is "let the punishment fit the crime". Customers expect little for minor inconveniences (in this case, often a sincere apology will do), but a much more significant compensation if there was major damage in terms of time, effort, annoyance, or anxiety was created by the failure.[32]

- *Who is the affected customer?* Long-term customers and those who spend heavily at a service provider expect more, and it is worth making an effort to save their business. One-time customers tend to be less demanding, and have less economic importance to the firm. Hence, compensation can be less, but should still be fair. There is always the possibility that a first-time user will become a repeat customer if he or she is treated well.

The overall rule of thumb for compensation at service failures should be "well-dosed generosity". Being perceived as stingy adds insult to injury, and the firm will probably be better off apologizing than offering a minimal compensation. Overly-generous compensation is not only expensive, customers may even interpret such a response negatively by raising questions in their minds about the soundness of the business and leading them to become suspicious about the underlying motives. Customers may worry about the implications for the employee as well as for the business. Also, over-generosity does not seem to result in higher repeat purchase rates than simply offering a fair compensation.[33] There is also a risk that a reputation for over-generosity may encourage dishonest customers to actively 'seek' service failures.[34] In fact, what customers really want is often just a satisfactory solution to their service problem rather than bells and whistles![35]

Dealing with Complaining Customers

Both managers and frontline employees must be prepared to deal with distressed customers, including jaycustomers who can become confrontational and behave in unacceptable ways towards service personnel who often are not at fault in any way.

Good interactive skills combined with training and on-the-spot thinking are critical for frontline employees to deal with such situations. *Service Insights 13.3* provides specific guidelines for effective problem resolution, designed to help calm upset customers and to deliver a resolution that they will see as fair and satisfying.[36]

SERVICE INSIGHTS 13.3
Guidelines for the Frontline:
How to Handle Complaining Customers
and Recover from a Service Failure

1. *Act fast.* If the complaint is made during service delivery, then time is of the essence to achieve a full recovery. When complaints are made after the fact, many companies have established policies of responding within 24 hours, or sooner. Even when full resolution is likely to take longer, fast acknowledgment remains very important.

2. *Acknowledge the customer's feelings.* Do this either tacitly or explicitly (for example, "I can understand why you're upset"). This action helps to build rapport, the first step in rebuilding a bruised relationship.

3. *Do not argue with customers.* The goal should be to gather facts to reach a mutually acceptable solution, not to win a debate or prove that the customer is wrong. Arguing gets in the way of listening and seldom diffuses anger.

4. *Show that you understand the problem from each customer's point of view.* Seeing situations through the customers' eyes is the only way to understand what they think has gone wrong and why they are upset. Service personnel should avoid jumping to conclusions with their own interpretations.

5. *Clarify the facts and sort out the cause.* A failure may result from inefficiency of service, misunderstanding by customers, or the misbehavior of a third party. If you have done something wrong, apologize immediately in order to win the understanding and trust of the customer. The more the customer can forgive you, the less he or she will expect to be compensated. Do not be defensive; reacting defensively may suggest that the organization has something to hide or is reluctant to fully look into the situation.

6. *Give customers the benefit of the doubt.* Not all customers are truthful and not all complaints are genuine. However,

customers should be treated as though they have a valid complaint until clear evidence proves that it is not true. If a lot of money is at stake (as in insurance claims or potential lawsuits), careful investigation needs to be carried out. If the amount involved is small, it may not be worth haggling over a refund or other compensation. However, it is still a good idea to check the records to see if there is a past history of dubious complaints by the same customer.

7. *Propose the steps needed to solve the problem.* When instant solutions are not immediately available, tell customers how the firm intends to take action to deal with the problem. This also sets expectations about the time involved, so firms should be careful not to overpromise!

8. *Keep customers informed of progress.* Nobody likes being left in the dark. Uncertainty causes people to be anxious and stressed. People tend to be more accepting if they know what's going on and receive periodic progress reports. Therefore, people should be kept informed about what is going on regularly.

9. *Consider compensation.* When customers do not receive the service outcomes they believe they have paid for or have suffered serious inconvenience and/or loss of time and money because the service failed, either a monetary payment or some other compensation in kind (e.g., an upgrade on a flight or a free dessert in a restaurant) is appropriate. This type of recovery strategy may also reduce the risk of legal action by an angry customer. Service guarantees often lay out in advance what such compensation will be, and the firm should ensure that all guarantees are met.

10. *Persevere to regain customer goodwill.* When customers have been disappointed, one of the hardest things to do is to restore their confidence and keep the relationship going. Perseverance may be required to defuse customers' anger and to convince them that actions are being taken to avoid a recurrence of the problem. Truly exceptional recovery efforts can be extremely effective in building loyalty and referrals.

11. *Self-check the service delivery system and improve it.* After the customer has left, you should check to see whether the service failure was caused by accidental mistakes or system defects. Take advantage of every complaint to perfect the whole service system. Even if the complaint is found to be a result of a misunderstanding by customer, this implies that some part of your communication system is ineffective.

SERVICE GUARANTEES

One way for particularly customer-focused firms to institutionalize professional complaint handling and effective service recovery is through offering service guarantees. In fact, a growing number of companies offer customers a service guarantee, promising that if service delivery fails to meet pre-defined standards, the customer will be entitled one or more forms of compensation, such as an easy-to-claim replacement, refund or credit. A well-designed service guarantee not only facilitates effective service recovery, but also institutionalizes learning from service failures and subsequent system improvements.[37]

The Power of Service Guarantees

Service guarantees are powerful tools for both promoting and achieving service quality for the following reasons:[38]

(1) They force firms to focus on what their customers want and expect in each element of the service.

(2) They set clear standards, telling customers and employees alike what the company stands for. Payouts to compensate customers for poor service cause managers to take guarantees seriously as they highlight the financial costs of quality failures.

(3) They require the development of systems for generating meaningful customer feedback and acting on it.

(4) They force service organizations to understand why they fail and encourage them to identify and overcome potential fail points.

Figure 13.5: Hampton Inn includes its "100% satisfaction guaranteed" in its advertising.

(5) They build "marketing muscle" by reducing the risk of the purchase decision and building long-term loyalty.

From the customer's perspective, the primary function of service guarantees is to lower the perceived risks associated with purchase.[39] The presence of a guarantee may also make it easier for customers to complain and they will more likely do so, because they will anticipate that frontline employees will be prepared to resolve the problem and provide appropriate compensation. Sara Björlin Lidén and Per Skålén found that even when dissatisfied customers were unaware that a service guarantee existed before making their complaint, they were positively impressed to learn that the company has a pre-planned procedure for handling failures and to find that their complaints were taken seriously.[40]

The benefits of service guarantees can be seen clearly in the case of Hampton Inn's "100% Hampton Guarantee" ("If you're not 100% satisfied, you don't pay"; see Fig. 13.5). As a business-building program, Hampton's strategy of offering to refund the cost of the room to a guest who expresses dissatisfaction has attracted new customers and also served as a powerful retention device. People choose to stay at a Hampton Inn because they are confident they will be satisfied. At least as important, the guarantee has become a vital tool to help managers identify new opportunities for quality improvement.

In discussing the impact on staff and managers, the vice president–marketing of Hampton Inn stated, "Designing the guarantee made us understand what made guests satisfied, rather than what *we thought* made them satisfied". It became imperative that everyone from reservationists and frontline employees, to general managers and personnel at corporate headquarters, listen carefully to guests, anticipate their needs to the greatest extent possible, and remedy problems quickly so that guests were satisfied with the solution. Viewing a hotel's function in this customer-centric way had a profound impact on the way the firm conducted business.

The guarantee "turned up the pressure in the hose", as one manager put it, showing where "leaks" existed, and providing the financial incentive to plug them. As a result, the "100% Hampton Guarantee" has had an important impact on product consistency and service delivery across the Hampton Inn chain, and it showed a dramatically positive effect on its financial performance. [41]

How to Design Service Guarantees

Some guarantees are simple and unconditional. Others appear to have been written by lawyers and contain many restrictions. The examples in *Service Insights 13.4* give an idea about which guarantees instill trust and confidence, and would make a customer like to do business with a firm.

SERVICE INSIGHTS 13.4
Examples of Service Guarantees
United States Postal Service Express Mail Guarantee

Service Guarantee: Express Mail international mailings are not covered by this service agreement. Military shipments delayed due to customs inspections are also excluded. If the shipment is mailed at a designated USPS Express Mail facility on or before the specified deposit time for overnight delivery to the addressee, delivery to the addressee or agent will be attempted before the applicable guaranteed time. Signature of the addressee's agent, or delivery employee is required upon delivery. If a delivery attempt is not made by the guaranteed time and the mailer files a claim for a refund, the USPS will refund the postage unless the delay was caused by: proper retention for law enforcement purposes; strike or work stoppage; late deposit of shipment; forwarding, return, incorrect address or incorrect ZIP code; delay or cancellation of flights; governmental action beyond the control of the Postal Service or air carriers; war, insurrection or civil disturbance; breakdowns of a substantial portion of the USPS transportation network resulting from events or factors outside the control of the Postal Service or Acts of God.

Source: Printed on back of Express Mail receipt, January 2006. (Note that USPS has dramatically improved its guarantee since.)

L. L. Bean's Guarantee

100% Guaranteed. Our products are guaranteed to give 100% satisfaction in every way. Return anything purchased from us at any time if it proves otherwise. We do not want you to have anything from LL Bean that is not completely satisfactory.

Our guarantee is based on something as simple as a handshake — the deal that you'll be satisfied with a purchase, and if you are not, we'll make it right. We guarantee that we'll hold up our end of the bargain. It's just how we do business. If your purchase isn't completely satisfactory, we're happy to accept your exchange or return at any time.

Source: Printed in all L. L. Bean catalogs and on the company's website, http://global.llbean.com/guarantee.html, accessed 26 August 2016.

MFA Group Inc. (a Professional Recruitment Agency)

We "put our money where our mouth is", in two ways:

1. *Money back*: We offer an unconditional money back guarantee — if at any point during the search process you are unhappy with progress, simply address the fact with us and if you are still not 100% satisfied after that discussion, we will cheerfully and unconditionally, refund every cent you have paid as a retainer. No quibble, no hassle, guaranteed period.

2. *Twelve-month candidate guarantee*: All candidates placed by us are guaranteed for a full 12 months. If, during this period they leave your firm, for any reason whatsoever, we will conduct an additional search, completely free of charge, until a suitable replacement has been found.

Source: MGA Group's website, *http://www.mfagroup.com/recruiting.htm,* accessed 1 June, 2009.

The Bugs Burger Bug Killer Guarantee (a Pest Control Company)

- You don't owe us a penny until all the pests on your premises have been eradicated.

- If you're ever dissatisfied with the BBBK's service you will receive a refund for as much as 12 months of service — plus fees for another exterminator of your choice for the next year.

- If a guest spots a pest on your premises, the exterminator will pay for the guest's meal or room, send a letter of apology, and pay for a future meal or stay.

- If your premises are closed down because of the presence of roaches or rodents, BBBK will pay any fines, as well as all lost profit, plus $5000.

Source: Reproduced in Christopher W. Hart, "The Power of Unconditional Service Guarantees." *Harvard Business Review* (July-August 1990).

All three service guarantees — from LL Bean, MFA Group and BBBK — are powerful, unconditional, and instill trust. The other guarantee is weakened by the many conditions attached to it. Hart argues that service guarantees should be designed to meet the following criteria:[42]

(1) Whatever is promised in the guarantee must be totally *unconditional* and there should not be any element of surprise for the customer.

(2) *Easy to understand and communicate* to the customer so that he is clearly aware of the benefits that can be gained from the guarantee.

Figure 13.6: To leave a clear stamp of service quality on customers, the guarantee must be unconditional, meaningful, credible, easily understood, invoked and collectable.

(3) *Meaningful to the customer* in that the guarantee is on something important to the customer and the compensation should be more than adequate to cover the service failure.[43]

(4) It should be *easy* for the customer *to invoke* the guarantee.

(5) If a service failure occurs, the customer should *be able to easily collect* on the guarantee without any problems.

(6) The guarantee should be *credible* and believable (Fig. 13.6).

Is Full Satisfaction the Best You Can Guarantee?

Full satisfaction guarantees have generally been considered the best possible design. However, it has been suggested that the ambiguity associated with such guarantees can lead to the discounting of their perceived value. For example, customers may raise questions such as "What does full satisfaction mean?" or "Can I invoke a guarantee when I am dissatisfied, although the fault does not lie with the service firm?"[44] Attribute-specific guarantees (e.g., guaranteed delivery within 24 hours) are highly specific and therefore do not suffer from ambiguity, although their coverage is not comprehensive and limits their appeal. A hybrid version of the full satisfaction and attribute-specific guarantee, referred to as the "combined guarantee", addresses this issue. It combines the wide scope of a full-satisfaction guarantee with the low uncertainty of attribute-specific performance standards. The combined guarantee has been shown to be superior to the pure full-satisfaction or attribute-specific guarantee

Table 13.2: Types of Service Guarantees.

Term	Guarantee Scope	Example
Single attribute-specific guarantee	One key attribute of the service is covered by the guarantee.	"Any of three specified popular pizzas is guaranteed to be served within 10 minutes of ordering on working days between 12 am and 2 pm. If the pizza is late, the customer's next order is free."
Multiattribute-specific guarantee	A few important attributes of the service are covered by the guarantee.	Minneapolis Marriott's guarantee: "Our quality commitment to you is to provide: • a friendly, efficient check-in; • a clean, comfortable room, where everything works; • a friendly efficient check-out. If we, in your opinion, do not deliver on this commitment, we will give you $20 in cash. No questions asked. It is your interpretation."
Full-satisfaction guarantee	All aspects of the service are covered by the guarantee. There are no exceptions.	Lands' End's guarantee: "If you are not completely satisfied with any item you buy from us, at any time during your use of it, return it and we will refund your full purchase price. We mean every word of it. Whatever. Whenever. Always. But to make sure this is perfectly clear, we've decided to simplify it further. GUARANTEED. Period."
Combined guarantee	All aspects of the service are covered by the full-satisfaction promise of the guarantee. Explicit minimum performance standards on important attributes are included in the guarantee to reduce uncertainty	Datapro Information Services guarantees "to deliver the report on time, to high quality standards, and to the contents outlined in this proposal. Should we fail to deliver according to this guarantee, or should you be dissatisfied with any aspect of our work, you can deduct any amount from the final payment which is deemed as fair."

Source: Wirtz, J. and Kum, D (2002). "Designing Service Guarantees — Is Full Satisfaction the Best You Can Guarantee?" *Journal of Services Marketing*, Vol. 15, No. 14, pp. 282–299.

designs.[45] Specific performance standards are guaranteed (e.g., on-time delivery), but should the consumer be dissatisfied with any other element of the service, the full-satisfaction coverage of the combined guarantee applies. Table 13.2 shows examples of various types of guarantees.

Is It Always Beneficial to Introduce a Service Guarantee?

Managers should think carefully about their firm's strengths and weaknesses when deciding whether or not to introduce a service guarantee. There are a number of situations in which a guarantee may not be appropriate:[46]

- Companies that already have a strong reputation for service excellence may not need a guarantee. In fact, it can be incongruent with their image to offer one as it might confuse the market.[47] Rather, best practice service firms will be expected to do what's right without offering a service guarantee.

- In contrast, a firm whose service is currently poor must first work to improve its quality to a level above what is guaranteed. Otherwise, too many customers will invoke the guarantee with serious cost implications.

- Service firms whose quality is truly uncontrollable due to external forces would be foolish to consider a guarantee. For example, when Amtrak realized that it was paying out substantial refunds because it lacked sufficient control over its railroad infrastructure, it was forced to drop a service guarantee that included the reimbursement of fares in the event of unpunctual train service.

- In a market where consumers see little financial, personal, or physiological risk associated with purchasing and using a service, a guarantee adds little value but still costs money to design, implement, and manage.

In markets where there is little perceived difference in service quality among competing firms, the first firm to institute a guarantee may also be able to obtain a first-mover advantage and create value differentiation for its services. If more than one competitor already have guarantees in place, offering one may become a qualifier for the industry, and the only real way to make an impact is to launch a highly distinctive guarantee beyond what is already offered by competitors.[48]

DISCOURAGING ABUSE AND OPPORTUNISTIC CUSTOMER BEHAVIOR

Throughout this chapter, firms are advocated to welcome complaints and invocations of service guarantees and even encourage them. While discussing the importance of professional complaint handling and service recovery, it is acknowledged that not all complaints are honest. When firms have generous service recovery policies or offer guarantees, there is always the fear that some customers may take advantage of them. Also, not all complaining customers are right or reasonable in their behavior, and some may actually be the cause of complaints by other customers.[49] Such people are referred to as *jaycustomers*.

Visitors to North America from other English-speaking countries are often puzzled by the term "jaywalker", a distinctively American word used to describe people who cross streets at unauthorized places or in a dangerous manner. The prefix "jay" comes from a 19th-century slang for "a stupid person". A jaycustomer is defined as someone who acts in a thoughtless or abusive way, causing problems for the firm, its employees and other customers.

Customers who act in uncooperative or abusive ways are a problem for any organization. However, they have even more potential for mischief in service businesses, particularly those in which many other customers are present in the same service environment. As known from personal experience, other people's behavior can affect your enjoyment of a service. If you like classical music and attend symphony concerts, you expect audience members to keep quiet during the performance, and to not spoil the experience for others by talking, coughing loudly or failing to turn off their cell phones. In contrast, a silent audience would be deadly during a rock concert or team sports event, where active audience participation adds to the excitement. However, there is a fine line between spectator enthusiasm and abusive behavior by supporters of rival sports teams. Firms that fail to deal effectively with customer misbehaviors risk damaging their relationships with all the other customers they would like to keep.

However, opinions on this topic seem to polarize around two opposing views. One is denial: "the customer is king and can do no wrong". The other view sees the marketplace of customers as positively overpopulated with nasty people who cannot be trusted to behave in ways that self-respecting service providers should expect and require. The first viewpoint has received wide publicity in gung-ho management books and in motivational presentations to captive groups of employees. The second view often appears to be dominant among cynical managers and frontline employees who have been burned at some point by customer misbehaviors. As with many opposing viewpoints, there are important grains of truth in both perspectives. What is clear, however, is that no self-respecting firm wants an ongoing relationship with an abusive customer.

Every service has its share of jaycustomers. They are undesirable. At best, a firm should avoid attracting them in the first place, and at worst, a firm needs to control or prevent their abusive behavior.

Seven Types of Jaycustomers[50]

Defining a problem is the first step in resolving it. Seven broad categories of jaycustomers have been identified and given generic names, but many customer contact personnel have also come up with their own special terms.

The Cheat. There are many ways in which customers can cheat service firms. Cheating ranges from writing complaint letters with the sole purpose of exploiting service recovery policies and cheating on service guarantees, to inflating or faking insurance claims and "wardrobing" (e.g., using an evening dress or tuxedo for an evening and then returning it back to the retailer).[51] Fake returns have become more common and socially accepted, especially so with online retailers. One company reported that 1% of its customers who bought five or more items sent back 90% or more of their purchases![52] The following quotes describe the thinking of these customers nicely in other contexts:

> *On checking in to a hotel I noticed that they had a '100% satisfaction or your money back' guarantee, I just couldn't resist the opportunity to take advantage of it, so on checking out I told the receptionist that I wanted a refund as the sound of the traffic kept me awake all night.*

> *They gave me a refund, no questions asked. These companies can be so stupid they need to be more alert.*[53]
>
> *I've complained that service was too slow, too quick, too hot, too cold, too bright, too dark, too friendly, too impersonal, too public, too private... it doesn't matter really, as long as you enclose a receipt with your letter, you just get back a standard letter and gift coupon.*[54]

Firms cannot easily check whether a customer is faking dissatisfaction or truly is unhappy. At the end of this section, we will discuss how to deal with this type of consumer fraud.

The Thief. The thief jaycustomer has no intention of paying and sets out to steal goods and services (or to pay less than full price by switching price tickets, or contesting bills on baseless grounds). Shoplifting is a major problem in retail stores. What retailers euphemistically call "shrinkage" is estimated to cost them huge sums of money in annual revenues. Many services lend themselves to clever schemes for avoiding payment. For those with technical skills, it is sometimes possible to bypass electricity meters, access telephone lines free of charge, or bypass normal cable TV feeds. Riding free on public transportation, sneaking into movie theaters, or not paying for restaurant meals are also popular, not forgetting the use of fraudulent forms of payment such as using stolen credit cards or checks drawn on accounts without any funds. Finding out how people steal a service is the first step in preventing theft or catching thieves and, where appropriate, prosecuting them. However, managers should try not to alienate honest customers by degrading their service experiences. Provision must also be made for honest but absent-minded customers who forget to pay.

The Rule Breaker. Just as highways need safety regulations (including "Don't Jaywalk"), many service businesses need to establish rules of behavior for customers to guide them safely through the various steps of the service process. Some of these rules are imposed by government agencies for health and safety reasons. The sign found in many restaurants that states "No shirt, no shoes, no service" demonstrates a health-related regulation. Air travel provides one of the best examples of rules designed to ensure safety; there are few other environments outside prison where healthy, mentally competent, adult customers are quite so constrained (albeit for good reason).

In addition to enforcing government regulations, suppliers often impose their own rules to facilitate smooth operations, avoid unreasonable demands on employees, prevent misuse of products and facilities, protect themselves legally, and discourage individual customers from misbehaving. For instance, ski resorts are strict on careless skiers who pose risks to both themselves and others. Collisions can cause serious injury and even death. As such, ski patrol members must be safety-oriented and sometimes take on a policing role. Just as dangerous drivers can lose their licenses, dangerous skiers can lose their lift tickets. For example, at Vail and Beaver Creek in Colorado, ski patrollers once revoked nearly 400 lift tickets in just a single weekend. At Winter Park near Denver, skiers who lose their passes for dangerous behavior may have to attend a 45-minute safety class before they can get their passes back. Ski patrollers at Vermont's Okemo Mountain may issue warnings to reckless skiers by attaching a bright orange sticker to their lift tickets. If pulled over again for inappropriate behavior, such skiers may be escorted off the mountain and banned for a day or more. "We're not trying to be Gestapos on the slopes", says the resort's marketing director, "just trying to educate people".

How should a firm deal with rule breakers? Much depends on which rules have been broken. In the case of legally enforceable ones — theft, bad debts, or trying to take guns on an aircraft — the courses of action need to be laid down explicitly to protect employees and to punish or discourage wrongdoing by customers.

Company rules are a little more ambiguous. Are they really necessary in the first place? If not, the firm should get rid of them. Do they deal with health and safety? If so, educating customers about the rules should reduce the need for taking corrective action. The same is true for rules designed to protect the comfort and enjoyment of all customers. There are also unwritten social norms such as "thou shalt not cut in line", although this is a much stronger cultural expectation in the US or Canada than in many countries, as any visitor to Paris or Hong Kong Disneyland can attest! Other customers can often be relied upon to help service personnel enforce rules that affect everybody else; they may even take the initiative in doing so.

There are risks attached to making lots of rules. The firm may become too inflexible and make it appear bureaucratic and overbearing. Instead of being customer-oriented, employees become like police officers, making sure that customers follow all the rules. However, the fewer the rules, the clearer the important ones can be.

The Belligerent. A type of customer probably seen in a store, at the airport, in a hotel or restaurant — red in the face and shouting angrily, or perhaps icily calm and mouthing insults, threats and obscenities. Things do not always work as they should: machines break down, service is clumsy, customers are ignored, a flight is delayed, an order is delivered incorrectly, staff are unhelpful, or a promise is broken. Perhaps the customer in question is expressing resentment at being told to abide by the rules. Service personnel are often abused, even when they are not to blame. If an employee lacks the power to resolve the problem, the belligerent may become still angrier, even to the point of physical attack. Unfortunately, when angry customers rant at service personnel, the latter sometimes respond in kind, thus escalating the confrontation and reducing the likelihood of resolution.

Drunkenness and drug abuse add extra layers of complication. Organizations that care about their employees go to great efforts to develop skills in dealing with these difficult situations. Training exercises that involve role-playing help employees develop the self-confidence and assertiveness needed to deal with upset, belligerent customers (sometimes referred to as "irates"). Employees also need to learn how to defuse anger, calm anxiety, and comfort distress (particularly when there is good reason for the customer to be upset with the organization's performance).

"We seem to live in an age of rage", declared Stephen Grove, Raymond Fisk, and Joby John, noting a general decline in civility.[55] They suggest that rage behaviors are learned via socialization as appropriate responses to certain situations. Anger and dissatisfaction are qualitatively different emotions. Whereas dissatisfied customers had a feeling of non-fulfillment or "missing out" and wanted to find out who or what was responsible for the event, angry customers were thinking how unfair the situation was, sought to get back at the organization, and wanted to hurt someone.[56] The problem of "Air Rage" has attracted particular attention in recent years due to the risks it poses to innocent people (*Service Insights 13.5*).[57]

SERVICE INSIGHTS 13.5
Air Rage: Unruly Passengers Pose a Continuing Problem

Joining the term "road rage" — coined in 1988 to describe angry, aggressive drivers who threaten other road users — is "air rage", describing the behavior of violent, unruly passengers who endanger flight attendants, pilots and other passengers. Incidents of air rage are perpetrated by only a tiny fraction of all airline passengers — reportedly about 5,000 times a year — but each incident in the air may affect the comfort and safety of hundreds of other people.

Although terrorism is an ongoing concern, out-of-control passengers pose a serious threat to safety too. On a flight from Orlando, Florida to London, a drunken passenger smashed a video screen and began ramming a window, telling fellow passengers they were about to "get sucked out and die". The crew strapped him down and the aircraft made an unscheduled landing in Bangor, Maine, where US marshals arrested him. Another unscheduled stop in Bangor involved a drug smuggler flying from Jamaica to the Netherlands. When a balloon filled with cocaine ruptured in his stomach, he went berserk, pounding a bathroom door to pieces and grabbing a female passenger by the throat.

On a flight from London to Spain, a passenger who was already drunk at the time of boarding became angry when a flight attendant told him not to smoke in the lavatory and then refused to serve him another drink. Later, he smashed her over the head with a duty-free vodka bottle before being restrained by other passengers (she required 18 stitches to close the wound). Other dangerous incidents have included throwing hot coffee at flight attendants, head-butting a co-pilot, trying to break into the cockpit, throwing a flight attendant across three rows of seats, and attempting to open an emergency door in flight. On a US domestic flight with a tragic outcome, a violent passenger was restrained and ultimately suffocated by other passengers after he kicked through the cockpit door of an airliner 20 minutes before it was scheduled to land in Salt Lake City.

A growing number of carriers are taking air rage perpetrators to court. Northwest Airlines permanently blacklisted three violent travelers from flying on its aircraft. British Airways gives out "warning cards" to any passenger getting dangerously out of control. Celebrities are not immune to air rage. Rock star Courtney Love blamed her "potty mouth" after being arrested on arrival in London for disruptive behavior on board a flight from Los Angeles. Some airlines carry physical restraints to subdue out-of-control passengers until they can be handed over to airport authorities.

In April 2000, the US Congress increased the civil penalty for air rage from $1,100 to $25,000 in an attempt to discourage passengers from misbehaving. Criminal penalties — a $10,000 fine and up to 20 years in jail — can also be imposed for the most serious incidents. Some airlines have been reluctant to publicize this information for fear of appearing confrontational or intimidating. However, the visible implementation of anti-terrorist security precautions have made it more acceptable to tighten enforcement of procedures designed to control and punish air rage.

What causes air rage? Psychological feelings of a loss of control, or problems with authority figures may be causal factors for angry behavior in many service settings. Researchers suggest that air travel, in particular, has become increasingly stressful as a result of crowding and longer flights; the airlines themselves may have contributed to the problem by squeezing rows of seats more tightly together and failing to explain delays. Findings suggest that risk factors for air travel stress include anxiety and an anger-prone personality; they also show that traveling on unfamiliar routes is more stressful than traveling on a familiar one. Another factor may be restrictions on smoking. However, alcohol abuse underlies a majority of incidents!

Airlines are training their employees to handle violent individuals and to spot problem passengers before they start causing serious problems. Some carriers offer travelers specific suggestions on how to relax during long flights. Some airlines have also considered offering nicotine patches to passengers who are desperate for a smoke but are not allowed to light up. Increased security in the air may be curtailing rage behavior on board flights, but concern continues to grow about passenger rage on the ground. An Australian survey of airport employees found that 96% of airport staff had experienced air rage at work: 31% of agents experienced some form of air rage daily, and 15% of agents reported that they had been physically touched or assaulted by a passenger.

Based on information from multiple sources, including: Daniel Eisenberg, "Acting Up in the Air," *Time,* 21 December 1998; "Air Rage Capital: Bangor Becomes Nation's Flight Problem Drop Point," *The Baltimore Sun,* syndicated article, September, 1999; Melanie Trottman and Chip Cummins, "Passenger's Death Prompts Calls for Improved 'Air Rage' Procedures," *The Wall Street Journal,* 26 September 2000; Blair J. Berkley and Mohammad Ala, "Identifying and Controlling Threatening Airline Passengers, *Cornell Hotel and Restaurant Administration Quarterly* 42 (August-September) 2001: 6-24; www.airsafe.com/issues/rage.htm , accessed 26 August 2016.

What should an employee do when an aggressive customer brushes off attempts to defuse the situation? In a public environment, one priority should be to move the person away from other customers. Sometimes supervisors may have to settle disagreements between customers and staff members; at other times, they need to support the employee's actions. If a customer has physically attacked an employee, then it may be necessary to summon security officers or the police. Some firms try to conceal such events, fearing bad publicity. Others however, feel obliged to make a public stand on behalf of their employees, such as the Body Shop manager who ordered an ill-tempered customer out of the store, telling her: "I won't stand for your rudeness to my staff".

Telephone rudeness poses a different challenge. Service personnel have been known to hang up on angry customers, but that action does not resolve the problem. For instance, bank customers tend to get upset upon learning that checks have been returned because the account is overdrawn (which means they have broken the rules), or that a request for a loan has been denied. One approach for handling customers who continue to shout at a telephone-based employee is for the latter to say firmly: "This conversation isn't getting us anywhere. Why don't I call you back in a few minutes when you've had time to digest the information?" In many cases, taking a break to think (and cool down) is exactly what's needed.

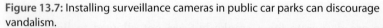

Figure 13.7: Installing surveillance cameras in public car parks can discourage vandalism.

The Family Feuders. People who get into arguments with members of their own family — or worse, with other customers — make up a subcategory of belligerents we call "family feuders". Employee intervention may calm the situation or actually make it worse. Some situations require detailed analysis and a carefully thought out response. Others, such as customers starting a food fight in an upscale restaurant, require an almost immediate response. Service managers in these situations need to be prepared to think on their feet and act fast.

The Vandal. Soft drinks are poured into bank cash machines; graffiti are scrawled on both interior and exterior surfaces; burn holes from cigarettes scar carpets, tablecloths, and bedcovers; bus seats are slashed and hotel furniture broken; customers' cars are vandalized; glass is smashed and fabrics are torn — the list is endless. Customers do not cause all of the damage, of course. Bored or drunk young people are the source of much exterior vandalism. Disgruntled employees have been known to commit sabotage. Much of the problem does originate with paying customers who choose to misbehave. Alcohol and drugs are sometimes the cause, at other times psychological problems may contribute, and carelessness can play a role. There are also occasions when unhappy customers, feeling mistreated by the service firm, try to take revenge in some way.

The best cure for vandalism is prevention. Improved security discourages some vandals (Fig. 13.7). Good lighting helps, as well as open design of public areas. Companies can choose vandal-resistant surfaces and protective coverings for equipment, and rugged furnishings. Educating customers to use equipment properly (rather than fighting with it) and providing warnings about fragile objects can reduce the likelihood of abuse or careless handling. Finally, there are economic sanctions: security deposits or signed agreements in which customers agree to pay for any damage that they cause.

What should managers do if prevention fails and damage is done? If the perpetrator is caught, they should first clarify whether there are any extenuating circumstances (because accidents do happen). Sanctions for deliberate damage can range from a warning to prosecution. As far as the physical damage itself is concerned, it is best to fix it fast (within any constraints imposed by legal or insurance considerations). The general manager of a bus company had the right idea when he said: "If one of our buses is vandalized, whether it's a broken window, a slashed seat, or graffiti on the ceiling, we take it out of service immediately so nobody sees it. Otherwise you just give the same idea to five other characters who were too dumb to think of it in the first place"!

The Deadbeat. Leaving aside those individuals who never intended to pay in the first place (our term for them is "the thief"), there are many reasons why customers fail to pay for services they have received. They are the ones who delay payment. Once again, preventive action is better than a cure. A growing number of firms insist on pre-payment. Any form of ticket sale is a good example of this. Direct marketing organizations ask for your credit card number as they take your order, as do most hotels when you make a reservation. The next best thing is to present the customer with a bill immediately on completion of service. If the bill is to be sent by mail, the firm should send it fast, while the service is still fresh in the customer's mind.

Not every apparent delinquent is a hopeless deadbeat. Perhaps there is a good reason for the delay and acceptable payment arrangements can be worked out. A key question is whether such a personalized approach can be cost justified, relative to the results obtained by purchasing the services of a collection agency. There may be other considerations too. If the client's problems are only temporary, what is the long-term value of maintaining the relationship? Will it create positive goodwill and word-of-mouth to help the customer work things out? These decisions are judgment calls, but if creating and maintaining long-term relationships is the firm's ultimate goal, they are worth exploring.

Consequences of Dysfunctional Customer Behavior

Dysfunctional customer behavior has consequences for frontline staff, other customers, and the organization itself.[58] Employees who are abused may not only find their mood or temper negatively affected in the short run, but may eventually suffer long-term psychological damage. Their own behavior too may take on negative dimensions, such as taking revenge on abusive customers. Staff morale can be hurt, with implications for both productivity and quality.[59]

The consequences for customers can take both positive and negative forms. Other customers may rally to the support of an employee whom they perceive as having been abused; however, bad behavior can also be contagious, leading a bad situation to escalate as others join in. More broadly, being exposed to negative incidents can spoil the consumption experience for many customers. Companies suffer financially when demotivated employees no longer work as efficiently and effectively as before, or when employees are forced to take medical leave. There may also be direct financial losses from restoring stolen or damaged property, legal costs and paying fraudulent claims.

As suggested in the earlier discussion of air rage, the nature of jaycustomer behavior is likely to be shaped by the characteristics of the service industry in which it occurs. *Service Insights 13.6* reports on a study of jaycustomers in the hospitality industry.

SERVICE INSIGHTS 13.6

Categorizing Jaycustomers in Hotels, Restaurants, and Bars

To learn more about dysfunctional customer behavior in the hospitality industry, Lloyd Harris and Kate Reynolds developed a research project to identify and categorize different types of misconduct. Open-ended interviews, typically lasting one hour (but sometimes longer) were conducted with 31 managers, 46 frontline employees, and 29 customers. These interviews took place in 19 hotels (all of which had restaurants and bars), 13 restaurants, and 16 bars. A purposive sampling plan was employed, with the goal of selecting informants with extensive participation in and insights of service encounters. All informants had encountered — or had perpetrated — what could be considered as jaycustomer behavior and were invited to give details of specific incidents. In total, the 106 respondents generated 417 critical incidents.

Based on analysis of these incidents, Harris and Reynolds codified eight types of behavior:

1. *Compensation letter writers* who deliberately and fraudulently wrote to centralized customer service departments with largely unjustified complaints in anticipation of receiving a check or gift voucher.

2. *Undesirable customers* whose behavior fell into three subgroups: (a) irritating behavior by "jaykids" and "jayfamilies"; (b) criminal behavior, typically involving drug sales or prostitution; and (c) homeless individuals who used an organization's facilities and stole other customers' refreshments.

3. *Property abusers* who vandalized facilities and stole items, often to keep as souvenirs.

Table 13.3: Percentage of Respondents Reporting Incidents by Category.

Category	Employees (%)	Customers (%)
Compensation letter writers	30	20
Undesirable customers	39	47
Property abusers	51	20
[Off-duty] service workers	11	11
Vindictive customers	30	22
Oral abusers	92	70
Physical abusers	49	20
Sexual predators	38	0

Source: Lloyd C. Harris and Kate L. Reynolds (2004), "Jaycustomer Behavior: An Exploration of Types and Motives in the Hospitality Industry," *Journal of Services Marketing*, Vol. 18, No. 5, pp. 339–357.

4. *(Off-duty) service workers* who know how to work the system to their own advantage as customers and deliberately disrupt service encounters, either for financial gain or simply to cause problems for frontline staff.

5. *Vindictive customers* who are violent towards people or property, possibly because of some perceived injustice.

6. *Oral abusers* include professional complainers seeking compensation, and "ego hunters" who take pleasure in offending frontline staff and other customers.

7. *Physical abusers* who physically harm frontline staff.

8. *Sexual predators* — often acting in groups — engage in sexual harassment of frontline personnel either verbally or behaviorally.

Some of these behaviors, such as letter writing and property abuse, are covert in nature (that is, not evident to others at the time they are committed). Certain underlying causes assert themselves across multiple categories; they include desire for personal gain, drunkenness, personal psychological problems, and negative group dynamics.

Table 13.3 shows the percentage of employees and customers reporting incidents within each category. Rather remarkably, with the exception of the "undesirable customers" category, the incidents in the customer column are all self-reports of the respondents' own misbehavior.

The verbatim reports of jaycustomer behavior recorded in this study make for somber, even scary reading. In particular, they demonstrate especially the challenges posed to management and staff by manipulative customers seeking personal financial gain, and by the abusive behavior of individuals, sometimes acting in groups and fueled by alcohol, who appear unconstrained by traditional societal norms.

Source: Lloyd C. Harris and Kate L. Reynolds, "Jaycustomer Behavior: An Exploration of Types and Motives in the Hospitality Industry," *Journal of Services Marketing* 18, No. 5, 2004, 339-357.

Dealing with Customer Fraud

Dishonest customers can take advantage of generous service recovery strategies, service guarantees, or simply a strong customer orientation in a number of ways. For example, they may steal from the firm, refuse to pay for the service, fake dissatisfaction, purposefully cause service failures to occur, or overstate losses at the time of genuine service failures. What steps can a firm take to protect itself against opportunistic customer behaviors?

Treating customers with suspicion is likely to alienate them, especially in situations of service failure. The president of TARP notes:

> *Our research has found that premeditated rip-offs represent 1–2% of the customer base in most organizations. However, most organizations defend themselves against unscrupulous customers by… treating the 98% of honest customers like crooks to catch the 2% who are crooks.*[60]

Using this knowledge, the working assumptions should be, "If in doubt, believe the customer". However, as *Service Insights 13.7* shows, it's crucial to keep track of customers who repeatedly "experience service failures", and ask for compensation or invoke the firm's service guarantee. For example, one Asian airline found that the same customer lost his suitcase on three consecutive flights. The chances of this truly happening are probably lower than winning in the national lottery, so frontline staff were made aware of this individual. The next time he checked in his suitcase, the check-in staff followed the video image of the suitcase almost from check-in to pick up at the baggage claim carrousel at the traveler's destination. It turned out that a companion collected the suitcase and took it away while the traveler again made his way to the lost baggage counter to report his missing suitcase. This time, the police were waiting for him and his friend.

In another example, Continental Airlines consolidated some 45 separate customer databases into a single data warehouse to improve service and to also detect customer fraud. The airline found one customer who received 20 bereavement fares in 12 months off the same dead grandfather!

To be able to effectively detect consumer fraud, maintaining a central database of all compensation payments, service recoveries, returned goods, and any other benefits given to customers based on special circumstances are needed (i.e., such transactions cannot be retained only at the local or branch level, but must be captured in a centralized system), and it is important to merge customer data across departments and channels for detecting unusual transactions and the systems that allow them.[61]

Research has shown that customers who think they were treated unfairly in any way (refer to our earlier discussion regarding distributive, procedural and interactive fairness) are much more likely to take advantage of a firm's service recovery effort. In addition, consumers tend to take advantage of large firms more often than small ones — customers think that large firms can easily afford the recovery costs. Also, one-time customers are much more likely to cheat than loyal customers, and customers who do not have a personal relationship with service employees are more likely to take advantage of service recovery policies.

Service guarantees are often used as payouts in service recovery, and it has been shown that the amount of a guarantee payout (e.g., whether it is a 10% or 100% money-back guarantee) had no effect on consumer cheating. It seems that customers who cheat for a 100% refund also cheat for 10%, and that customer who does not cheat for 10% also would not do so for 100%. However, repeat purchase intention significantly reduced cheating intent. A further finding was that customers were also reluctant to cheat if the service quality provided was truly high compared to when it was just satisfactory.[62]

These findings suggest a number of important managerial implications:

(1) Firms should ensure that their service recovery procedures are fair.

(2) Large firms should recognize that consumers are more likely to cheat on them and have robust fraud detection systems in place.

(3) Firms can implement and thus reap the bigger marketing benefits of 100% money-back guarantees without worrying that the large payouts would increase cheating by much.

(4) Guarantees can be offered to regular customers or as part of a membership program, because repeat customers are unlikely to cheat on service guarantees.

(5) Truly excellent services firms have less to worry about cheating than the average service provider.

SERVICE INSIGHTS 13.7
Tracking Down Guests Who Cheat

As part of its guarantee tracking system, Hampton Inn has developed ways to identify guests who appeared to be cheating, using aliases or various dissatisfaction problems to invoke the guarantee repeatedly in order to get the cost of their room refunded. Guests showing high invocation trends receive personalized attention and follow-up from the company's Guest Assistance Team. Wherever possible, senior managers telephone these guests to ask about their recent stays. The conversation might go as follows: "Hello, Mr. Jones. I'm the director of guest assistance at Hampton Inn, and I see that you've had some difficulty with the last four properties you've visited. Since we take our guarantee very seriously, I thought I'd give you a call and find out what the problems were".

The typical response is dead silence! Sometimes the silence is followed by questions of how headquarters could possibly know about their problems. These calls have their humorous moments as well. One individual, who had invoked the guarantee 17 times in what appeared to be a trip that took him across the US and back was asked, "Where do you like to stay when you travel?" "Hampton Inn", came the enthusiastic response. "But", said the executive making the call, "Our records show that the last seventeen times you have stayed at a Hampton Inn, you have invoked the 100% Satisfaction Guarantee". "That's why I like them!" proclaimed the guest (who turned out to be a long-distance truck driver on a per diem for his accommodation expenses).

Source: Christopher W. Hart and Elizabeth Long, *Extraordinary Guarantees* (New York: AMACOM, 1997).

CONCLUSION

Encouraging customer feedback provides an important means of increasing customer satisfaction and retention. It is an opportunity to get into the hearts and minds of the customer. In all but the worst instances, complaining customers are indicating that they want to continue their relationship with the firm, but also that all is not well and they expect the company to make things right. Here, service firms need to develop effective strategies to recover from service failures so that they can maintain customer goodwill. That is vital for the long-term success of the company.

Having professional and generous service recovery systems does not mean "the customer is always right" and that the firm is open to customer abuse. Rather, it is important for the benefit of all (i.e., other customers, service employees, and the service firm) to effectively deal with jaycustomers.

CHAPTER SUMMARY

Customer Responses to Service Failure

- Take public action (complain to the firm, to a third party, take legal action)
- Take private action (switch provider, spread negative word-of-mouth)
- Take no action

Customer Expectations Once a Complaint Is Made

Customers expect fair treatment along three dimensions:
- Procedural justice: Customers expect a convenient, responsive, and flexible service recovery process
- Interactional justice: The recovery effort must be seen as genuine, honest, and polite
- Outcome justice: The restitution has to reflect the customer loss and inconveniences suffered

Customer Complaining

Why do customers complain?
- Obtain restitution or compensation
- Vent anger
- Help to improve the service
- For altruistic reasons

What proportion of unhappy customers complains?
- 5%–10% complain

Why do unhappy customers not complain?
- It takes time and effort
- The payoff is uncertain
- Complaining can be unpleasant

Who is most likely to complain?
- Higher socioeconomic class customers
- Customers with more product knowledge

Where do customers complain?
- Vast majority of complaints are made at the point of service provision (face-to-face or over the phone)
- Only a small proportion of complaints is sent via email, social media, websites, or letters

Customer Responses to an Effective Service Recovery

- Avoids switching, restores confidence in the firm
- The Service Recovery Paradox: an excellent recovery can even result in higher satisfaction and loyalty than if a service was delivered as promised

Principles of Effective Service Recovery Systems

- Make it easy for customers to provide feedback and reduce customer complaint barriers
- Enable effective service recovery: Make it (1) proactive, (2) planned, (3) trained, and (4) empowered
- Establish appropriate compensation levels: Set based on the (1) positioning of the firm, (2) severity of the service failure, and the (3) importance of the customer. Target for "well-dosed generosity"

Dealing with Complaining Customers:
- Act fast
- Acknowledge customer's feelings
- Do not argue
- Show understanding
- Clarify the facts
- Give customer the benefit of the doubt
- Propose steps to solve the problem
- Keep the customer informed
- Consider compensation
- Persevere to regain customer goodwill
- Improve the service system

Service Guarantees

- Institutionalize professional complaint handling & service recovery
- Drive improvement of processes
- Design: (1) unconditional, (2) easy to understand, (3) meaningful, (4) easy to invoke, (5) easy to collect on, and (6) credible
- Unsuitable for firms with (1) a reputation for excellence, (2) poor quality service, and (3) uncontrollable quality due to external factors (e.g., weather)

Jaycustomers

There are 7 types of jaycustomers:
- The Cheat
- The Thief
- The Rule Breaker
- The Belligerent
- The Family Feuders
- The Vandal
- The Deadbeat

- Jaycustomers cause problems for firms and can spoil the service experience of other customers.
- Firms need to keep track and manage their behavior, including, as a last resort, blacklisting them from using the firm's facilities.

Part V

Striving for Service Excellence

CHAPTER 14

Improving Service Quality and Productivity

Not everything that counts can be counted, and not everything that can be counted, counts

Albert Einstein
Theoretical physicist and Nobel Price winner

Improve quality and you automatically improve productivity. You capture the market with lower price and better quality. You stay in business and you provide jobs. It's so simple.

W. Edwards Deming
Engineer, statistician, professor, and management consultant
Father of the Total Quality Management movement

Our mission remains inviolable: Offer the customer the best service we can provide; cut our costs to the bones; and generate a surplus to continue the unending process of renewal.

Joseph Pillay
Former Chairman, Singapore Airlines

INTEGRATING SERVICE QUALITY AND PRODUCTIVITY STRATEGIES

This chapter describes that the quality and productivity are twin paths in creating value for both customers and organizations. The relationships between service quality, productivity and profitability will also be examined in detail.

Service Quality, Productivity, and Profitability[1]

The individual relationships between service productivity, customer satisfaction (i.e., excellence) and profitability are shown in Fig. 14.1. When examining the individual links, one can see that, everything being equal, higher customer satisfaction should improve the bottom line through higher repeat purchases, share-of-wallet, and referrals. Likewise, everything being equal, higher productivity should lead to higher profitability as costs are reduced.

The relationship between productivity and customer satisfaction is more complex. There is the general notion of a service productivity–customer satisfaction trade-off. However, although the relationships between productivity, service quality and profitability can conflict, there are examples where productivity gains and customer satisfaction are aligned. For example, if a service firm redesigns customer service processes to be leaner, faster, and more convenient by eliminating non-value-adding

Figure 14.1: The service quality–productivity–profit triangle

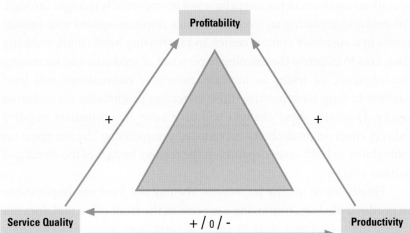

work steps, then both productivity and customer satisfaction should improve, and both should have a direct and indirect positive effect on profitability. An example would be serve-it-yourself yogurt stores, which substitute relatively inexpensive and easy-to-use self-serve machines for multiple human contact people. In this case, there is a positive impact on profitability through increased productivity and increased customer satisfaction, resulting in higher customer loyalty.

In contrast, if productivity improvements result in changes in the service experience that customers do not like, customer satisfaction will drop. For example, getting service employees to work faster may make customers feel rushed and unwanted. Likewise, replacing a human agent in a customer contact center with an interactive voice response system to reduce headcount, doubling class sizes to increase the productivity of university professors, and reducing the frequency of trains to increase load factors can all have negative implications for the customer experience. In these cases, there is a trade-off to be expected, whereby in the short term, productivity enhancements have an immediate and direct positive effect on profitability. However, these productivity enhancements lead to lower customer satisfaction which, over the medium to long term, are likely to lead to lower customer loyalty and referrals. This means that these productivity improvements not only have a positive direct effect, but also a negative indirect effect (via customer satisfaction) on profitability.

Likewise, marketing strategies designed to improve customer satisfaction can prove costly and disruptive if the implications for operations and human resources have not been carefully thought through. For example, replacing an interactive voice response system with human agents in a customer contact center and increasing head count, reducing class sizes to improve the learning experience of students, and increasing the frequency of trains to increase passenger convenience will have medium to long-term positive direct effects on profitability via customer loyalty. However, these changes will also have an immediate negative indirect effect on profitability via reduced productivity. The net result on profitability in both cases depends on the relative impact of the direct and indirect effects.

Finally, some quality improvements may not have any implications on productivity (e.g., improving a process in the front office that does not change the cost of providing it) and vice versa (e.g., improving efficiency of back office operations that do not have implications for customer touch points). In these cases, there is only a single positive effect of productivity improvements on profitability, or of customer satisfaction improvements on profitability.

One can see that the relationship between productivity and customer satisfaction can be positive, neutral, or negative. In broad terms, quality focuses on the benefits created for the customer's side of the equation, and productivity addresses the financial costs incurred by the firm, and if not properly integrated, these two foci can be in conflict. The bottom line is that service quality and productivity-improvement strategies must be considered jointly, not in isolation. Next, the ways to improve service quality will be examined.

WHAT IS SERVICE QUALITY?

Quality can mean different things to people depending on the context.[2] Common perspectives on quality include the manufacturing-based approach. It is primarily concerned with engineering and manufacturing practices and typically means delivery against measurable standards within certain tolerance levels (e.g., tolerance levels for weld seams in car manufacturing). In services, we would say that quality is operations-driven.

Figure 14.2: Service quality can be difficult to manage for the fussy diner.

It focuses on the conformance to internally developed specifications, and they tend to be tightly aligned with productivity and cost-containment goals.

Service researchers argue that the nature of services require a distinctive approach in defining and measuring service quality. The intangible, multifaceted nature of many services makes it harder to evaluate the quality of a service compared to a good. As customers are often involved in service production, a distinction needs to be drawn between the *process* of service delivery (what Christian Grönroos calls functional quality) and the actual *output* (or outcome) of the service (what he calls technical quality).[3] Grönroos and others also suggest that the perceived quality of a service is the result of an evaluation process in which customers compare their perceptions of service delivery and its outcome to what they expect. Therefore, service quality from the user's perspective is defined as a high standard of performance that consistently meets or exceeds customer expectations (see Chap. 2 for more details).

IDENTIFYING AND CORRECTING SERVICE-QUALITY PROBLEMS

Next, a model that helps to identify and correct service-quality problems at the overall firm level will be explored.

The Gaps Model in Service Design and Delivery

Valarie Zeithaml, A. Parasuraman, and Leonard Berry identified four potential gaps within the service organization that may lead to the fifth and most serious final gap — the difference between what customers expected and what they perceived was delivered.[4] Fig. 14.2 extends and refines their framework to identify a total of six types of gaps that can occur at different points during the design and delivery of a service performance:

- **Gap 1:** The *knowledge gap* is the difference between what senior management believes customers expect and what customers actually need and expect.
- **Gap 2:** The *policy gap* is the difference between management's understanding of customers' expectations and the service standards

Figure 14.3: The Gaps Model

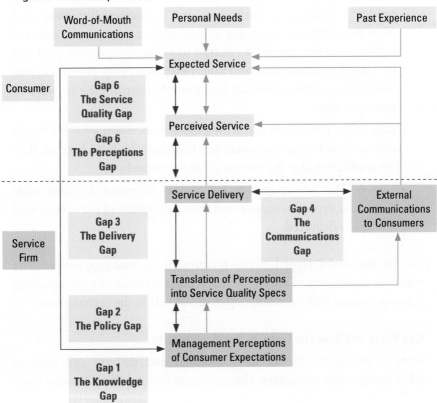

Source: Adapted from the original five-gaps model developed by Parasuraman, A., Zeithaml, V. A., & Berry, L. L. "A conceptual model of service quality and its implications for future research". *Journal of Marketing* 49, Fall 1985 41–50; Zeithaml, V. A., Bitner, M. J., & Gremler, D. *Services Marketing: Integrating Customer Focus Across the Firm* (p. 46.). NY: McGraw Hill/Irwin, 2006. A further gap (Gap 5) was added by Christoper Lovelock (1994), *Product Plus* (p. 112). NY: McGraw Hill.

they set for service delivery. We call it the policy gap because the management has made a policy decision not to deliver what they think customers expect. Reasons for setting standards below customer expectations are typically cost and feasibility considerations.

- **Gap 3:** The *delivery gap* is the difference between specified service standards and service delivery teams' actual performance on these standards.

- **Gap 4:** The *communications gap* is the difference between what the company communicates, and what the customer understands and subsequently experiences. This gap is caused by two sub-gaps.[5] First, the *internal* communication gap is the difference between what the company's advertising and sales personnel think are the product's features, performance, and service-quality level, and what the company is actually able to deliver. Second, the *external* communications gap (also referred to as the overpromise gap) can be caused by advertising and sales personnel being assessed by the sales they generate. This can lead them to overpromise in order to generate sales.

- **Gap 5:** The *perceptions gap* is the difference between what is actually delivered and what customers feel they have received because they are unable to judge the service quality accurately.

- **Gap 6:** The *service quality gap* is the difference between what customers expect to receive and their perception of the service that is actually delivered.

In this model, Gaps 1, 5, and 6 represent external gaps between the customer and the organization. Gaps 2, 3, and 4 are internal gaps occurring between various functions and departments within the organization.

Key Ways to Close the Gaps in Service Quality

Gaps at any point in the service design and delivery can damage relationships with customers. The service quality gap (Gap 6) is the most critical. Hence, the ultimate goal in improving service quality is to close or narrow this gap as much as possible. To achieve this, service organizations usually need to first work on closing the other five gaps depicted in Fig. 14.2. Improving service quality requires identifying the specific causes of each gap, and then developing strategies to close them.

The strength of the gaps model is that it offers generic insights and solutions that can be applied across industries. Table 14.1 summarizes the series of generic prescriptions for closing the six quality gaps. These prescriptions are a good starting point to think about how to close specific gaps in an organization, and the details of how to do this at the micro or process level will be discussed later in this chapter.

MEASURING SERVICE QUALITY

It is commonly said that "what is not measured is not managed". Without measurement, managers cannot be sure whether service-quality gaps

Table 14.1: Suggestions for closing service-quality gaps.

Gap 1: The Knowledge Gap

Suggestion: Educate Management About What Customers Expect

- Implement an effective customer feedback system that includes satisfaction research, complaint and compliment content analysis, customer panels, and online monitoring.
- Sharpen market research procedures including questionnaire and interview design, sampling, and field implementation, and periodically repeat research studies.
- Increase interactions between customers and senior management (e.g., programs such as "a day in the field" and senior management taking calls in customer contact centers).
- Improve upward communications, and facilitate and encourage communication between frontline employees and management.

Gap 2: The Policy Gap

Suggestion: Establish the Right Service Products, Processes and Standards That Are Based on Customer Needs and Expectations

- Get the products and customer service processes right:
  - Use a rigorous, systematic, and customer-centric process for designing and redesigning service products and customer service processes.
  - Standardize repetitive work tasks to ensure consistency and reliability by substituting hard technology for human contact and improving work methods (soft technology).
- Set, communicate, and reinforce measurable customer-oriented service standards for all work units:
  - Establish a set of clear service quality goals for each step in the service delivery that are challenging, realistic, and explicitly designed to meet customer expectations.
  - Ensure that employees understand and accept these goals, standards, and priorities.
- Develop tiered service products that meet customer expectations:
  - Consider premium, standard, and economy-level products to allow customers to self-segment according to their needs, or
  - Offer customers different levels of service at different prices.

Gap 3: The Delivery Gap

Suggestion: Ensure That Performance Meets Standards

- Ensure that customer service teams are motivated and are able to meet service standards:
  - Improve recruitment with a focus on employee–job fit; select employees for the abilities and skills needed to perform their job well.
  - Train employees on the technical and soft skills needed to perform their assigned tasks effectively, including interpersonal skills, especially for dealing with customers under stressful conditions.
  - Clarify employee roles and ensure that employees understand how their jobs contribute to customer satisfaction; teach them about customer expectations, perceptions, and problems.
  - Build cross-functional service teams that can offer customer-centric service delivery and problem resolution, including effective service recovery.
  - Empower managers and employees in the field by pushing decision-making power down the organization.
  - Measure performance, provide regular feedback, and reward customer service team performance as well as individual employees and managers for attaining quality goals.

- Install the right technology, equipment, support processes, and capacity:
  - Select the most appropriate technologies and equipment for enhanced performance.
  - Ensure that employees working on internal support jobs provide good service to their own internal customer, the frontline personnel.
  - Balance demand against productive capacity.
- Manage customers for service quality:
  - Educate customers to perform their roles and responsibilities in a service delivery effectively.
- Effectively align intermediaries and third parties involved in service delivery:
  - Align objectives, performance, costs and rewards with intermediaries (e.g., as in outsourced service delivery in customer contact centers or airline check in counters).
  - Monitor and incentivize service quality.

Gap 4: The Communications Gap

Suggestion: Close the Internal and External Communications Gaps by Ensuring That Communication Promises Are Realistic and Correctly Understood by Customers

- Ensure that communications content sets realistic customer expectations, and educate managers responsible for sales and marketing communications about operational capabilities:
  - Seek inputs from frontline employees and operations personnel when new communications programs are developed.
  - Let service providers preview advertisements and other communications before customers are exposed to them.
  - Get sales staff to involve operations staff in face-to-face meetings with customers.
  - Develop internal educational and motivational campaigns to strengthen understanding and integration among the marketing, operations, and human resource functions, and to standardize service delivery across different locations.
- Align incentives for sales teams with those of service delivery teams. This will avoid the problem where the sale teams focus exclusively on generating sales (e.g., through overpromising) and neglect customer satisfaction (e.g., through disappointed expectations).
- Be specific with promises and manage customers' understanding of communication content:
  - Pre-test all advertising, brochures, telephone scripts, and website content to see if target audience interprets them as the firm intends (if not, revise and retest). Make sure the advertising content reflects service characteristics most important to customers. Let them know what is and is not possible, and why.
  - Identify and explain, in real time, the reasons for shortcomings in service performance, highlighting those that cannot be controlled by the firm.
  - Document beforehand what tasks and performance guarantees are included in an agreement or contract.

Gap 5: The Perception Gap

Suggestion: Tangibilize and Communicate the Service Quality Delivered

- Make service quality tangible and communicate the service quality delivered:
  - Develop service environments and physical evidence cues that are consistent with the level of service provided.
  - For complex and credence services, keep customers informed during service delivery on

what is being done, and give debriefings after the delivery so customers can appreciate the quality of service received.
- After completion of the work, explain what work was performed in relation to a specific billing statement.
- Provide physical evidence (e.g., for repairs, show customers the damaged components that were removed).

Gap 6: The Service Gap

Suggestion: Close Gaps 1 to 5 to Consistently Meet Customer Expectations

- Gap 6 is the accumulated outcome of all the preceding gaps. It will be closed when Gaps 1 to 5 have been addressed.

Source: Adapted and extended from Valarie A. Zeithaml, A. Parasuraman, and Leonard L. Berry, *Delivering Service Quality: Balancing Customer Perceptions and Expectations*. New York: The Free Press, 1990, Chapters 4–7; and Valarie A. Zeithaml, Mary Jo Bitner, and Dwayne D. Gremler (2013), *Services Marketing: Integrating Customer Focus Across the Firm*. 5th ed., New York: McGraw-Hill, Chapter 2. The remaining prescriptions were developed by the authors.

exist, let alone what types of gaps, where they exist, and what potential corrective actions should be taken. Certainly, measurement determines whether goals for improvement are met after changes have been implemented. The next section will discuss how to use measurements to guide our service-quality improvement efforts.

SOFT AND HARD SERVICE QUALITY MEASURES

Customer-defined standards and measures of service quality can be grouped into two broad categories: "soft" and "hard". Soft standards and their measures are those that cannot be easily observed and are typically gathered by talking to customers. Soft standards provide direction, guidance and feedback to employees on how to achieve customer satisfaction, and they can be quantified by measuring customer perceptions and beliefs.[6] SERVQUAL (as seen in Chap. 2) is an example of a sophisticated soft measurement system. A variety of other customer feedback tools are discussed later in this chapter.

Hard standards and measures, in contrast, are typically process activities and outcomes that can be counted, timed or measured. Such measures may include how many orders were filled correctly, the time required to complete a specific task, how many minutes customers had to wait in line at a particular stage in the service delivery, how many trains arrived late, how many bags were lost, the temperature of a particular food

Figure 14.4: Social media such as Facebook and Twitter have been deployed by organizations to gather valuable feedback from customers.

item, how many telephone calls were dropped while customers were on hold, or how many patients made a complete recovery following a specific type of surgery. Standards are often set with reference to the percentage of occasions on which a particular measure is achieved. The challenge for service marketers is to ensure that operational measures of service quality reflect customer needs and wants.

Organizations known for service excellence make use of both soft and hard measures. These organizations are good at listening to both their customers and their customer–contact employees. The larger the organization, the more important it is to create formalized feedback systems using a variety of professionally-designed and implemented customer feedback and research procedures. The next section provides an overview of soft measures on customer feedback, followed by hard measures.

LEARNING FROM CUSTOMER FEEDBACK[7]

How can companies measure their performance against soft standards of service quality? According to Leonard Berry and A. Parasuraman:

> [C]ompanies need to establish ongoing listening systems using multiple methods among different customer groups. A single service quality study is a snapshot taken at a point in time and from a particular angle. Deeper insight and more informed decision-making come from a continuing series of snapshots taken from various angles

and through different lenses, which form the essence of systematic listening.[8]

This section discusses how customer feedback can be systematically collected, analyzed and disseminated to relevant departments via an institutionalized customer feedback system to achieve customer-driven learning and service improvements.[9]

Key Objectives of Effective Customer Feedback Systems

"It is not the strongest species that survive, nor the most intelligent, but the ones most responsive to change", stated Charles Darwin. Similarly, many strategists have concluded that in increasingly competitive markets, the best competitive advantage for a firm is to learn and change faster than its competition.[10] This notion is echoed by Jack Welch, former CEO of General Electric, who said when he outlined his strategy for the 21st century, "We have only two sources of competitive advantage: first, the ability to learn more about our customers faster than the competition, and second, the ability to turn that learning into action faster than the competition".

Customer feedback is a key input for becoming and remaining a customer-driven learning organization, and effective customer feedback systems facilitate fast learning. Their objectives typically fall into the following three main categories:

(1) *Assessment and Benchmarking of Service Quality and Performance.* The objective is to answer the question "How satisfied are our customers?" This objective includes learning about how well a firm performed in comparison to its main competitor(s), in comparison to the previous year (or quarter, or month), whether investments in certain service aspects have paid off in terms of customer satisfaction, and where the firm wants to be the following year. Often, a key objective of comparison against other units (branches, teams, service products, and competitors) is to motivate managers and service staff to improve performance, especially when the results are linked to compensation.

Benchmarking does not only have to be with companies from the same industry. For example, Southwest Airlines benchmarked Formula One pit-stops for speedy turnaround of aircraft; Pizza Hut benchmarked FedEx for on-time package delivery; and Ikea examined the military for excellence in coordination and logistics management.

(2) *Customer-Driven Learning and Improvements.* Here, the objective is to answer the questions, "What makes our customers happy or unhappy?" and "What are our strengths we want to cement, and what are our weaknesses we need to improve on?" For this, more specific or detailed information on processes and products is required to guide a firm's service improvement efforts, and to pinpoint which areas have possible high returns for quality investment.

(3) *Creating a Customer-Oriented Service Culture.* This objective is concerned with bringing the "voice of the customer" into the organization, focusing the organization on customer needs and customer satisfaction, and rallying the entire organization towards a service-quality culture. It also includes fostering a culture of continuous improvement and change.

Of the three objectives just discussed, firms seem to do well on the first point, but often miss great opportunities in the other two. Neil Morgan, Eugene Anderson, and Vikas Mittal concluded in their research on customer satisfaction information usage (CSIU) the following:

> *Many of the firms in our sample do not appear to gain significant customer-focused learning benefits from their CS [customer satisfaction] systems, because they are designed to act primarily as a control mechanism [i.e., for assessment and benchmarking]. ... [Firms] may be well served to re-evaluate how they deploy their existing CSIU resources. The majority of CSIU resources...are consumed in CS data collection. This often leads to too few resources being allocated to the analysis, dissemination, and utilization of this information to fully realize the potential payback from the investment in data collection.*[11]

Use a Mix of Customer Feedback Collection Tools

Renee Fleming, soprano and America's beautiful voice, once said: "We

Table 14.2: Strengths and weaknesses of key customer feedback collection tools.

Collection Tools	Level of Measurement			Actionable	Representative, reliable	Potential for Service Recovery	First-hand Learning	Cost-Effectiveness
	Firm	Process	Transaction Specific					
Total market survey (including competitors)	●	○	○	○	●	○	○	○
Annual survey on overall satisfaction	●	◐	○	○	●	○	○	○
Transactional survey	●	●	◐	◐	●	○	○	○
Service feedback cards and messages	◐	●	●	◐	◐	●	◐	●
Mystery shopping	○	●	●	●	○	○	◐	○
Unsolicited feedback (e.g., Complaints)	○	◐	●	●	○	●	●	●
Focus group discussions	○	◐	●	●	○	◐	●	◐
Service reviews	○	◐	●	●	○	●	●	○
Online reviews and discussions (e.g., Reviews and social media postings)	○	◐	●	●	○	●	●	●

Legend: ● Meets requirements fully; ◐ moderately; ○ hardly at all

Adapted from Jochen Wirtz and Monica Tomlin (2000), "Institutionalizing Customer-driven Learning through Fully Integrated Customer Feedback Systems," *Managing Service Quality*, Vol. 10, No. 4, p. 210.

singers are unfortunately not able to hear ourselves sing. You sound entirely different to yourself. We need the ears of others — from outside." Likewise, firms need to listen to the voice of the customer. Table 14.2 gives an overview of typically used feedback tools and their ability to meet various requirements. Recognizing that different tools have different strengths and weaknesses, service marketers should select a mix of customer feedback collection tools that jointly deliver the needed information. As Leonard Berry and A. Parasuraman observed, "Combining approaches enables a firm to tap the strengths of each and compensate for weaknesses".[12]

Total Market, Annual, and Transactional Surveys. Total market and annual surveys typically measure satisfaction with all major customer service processes and products.[13] The level of measurement is usually high, with the objective of obtaining a global index or indicator of overall service satisfaction for the entire firm. This could be based on indexed (e.g., using various attribute ratings) and/or weighted data (e.g., weighted by core segments and/or products).

Overall indices such as these tell us how satisfied customers are, but not why they are happy or unhappy. There are limits to the number of questions that can be asked about each individual process or product. For example, a typical retail bank may have 30 to 50 key customer service processes (e.g., from car loan applications and cash deposits at the teller to online banking). Due to the sheer number of processes, many surveys have room for only one or two questions per process (e.g., how satisfied are you with our ATM services?) and cannot address issues in greater detail.

In contrast, transactional surveys, also called intercept surveys, are typically conducted after customers have completed a specific transaction (Fig. 14.3). At this point, if time permits, they may be queried about the process in some depth. In the case of the bank, all key attributes and aspects of ATM services could be included in the survey, including some open-ended questions, such as "liked best", "liked least", and "suggested improvements". Such feedback is more actionable, can tell the firm why customers are happy or unhappy with the service, and usually yields specific insights on how customer satisfaction can be improved.

Many market research agencies offer cost-effective email, SMS, electronic terminals, and app-based transactional survey tools. For example, hotel guests receive an automated email or message with a link

Figure 14.5: Transactional surveys are typically conducted following service delivery.

Photo Credit: Changi Airport Group

to an online survey after checking out. Monthly online reports are then automatically generated for the hotel group at the overall level, for each of the individual hotels in a chain, and even for individual units within each hotel (e.g., front desk, rooms, room service, restaurants, spa, and gym). Such solutions are fully automated and can therefore be provided at lower cost of as little as $100 per hotel per month in a large chain.

Similarly, point-of-transaction surveys on touchscreen terminals allow the measurement of customer satisfaction on key attributes immediately after a transaction has taken place. Again, the collection, analysis and reporting are fully automated and cost-effective, and the analysis can even be broken down to the individual service employee as they sign out of their service terminals.

All three survey types are representative and reliable when designed properly. Representativeness and reliability are required for:

(1) Accurate assessments of where the company, a process, branch, team, or individual stands relative to quality goals; it is important to have a representative and reliable sample, to ensure that observed changes in quality scores are not the result of sample biases and/or random errors;

(2) Evaluations of individual service employees, service-delivery teams, branches, and/or processes, especially when incentive schemes are linked to such measures; the methodology has to be water-tight if staff are to trust and buy into the results, especially when surveys deliver bad news.

The potential for service recovery is important and should, if possible, be designed into feedback collection tools. However, many surveys promise anonymity, making it impossible to identify and respond to dissatisfied respondents. In personal encounters or telephone surveys, interviewers can be instructed to ask customers whether they would like the firm to get back to them on dissatisfying issues.

Service Feedback Cards, Online, and Mobile Messages. These powerful and inexpensive tools involve providing customers the opportunity to use feedback cards, online forms, e-mail, text messaging or apps[14] to provide feedback, typically to a central customer feedback unit. For example, a feedback card can be attached to each housing loan approval letter or to each hospital invoice. These cards are a good indicator of process quality and yield specific feedback on what works well and what doesn't. However, customers who are delighted or very dissatisfied are likely to be overrepresented among the respondents, which affects the reliability and representativeness of this tool.

Mystery Shopping. Service businesses often use "mystery shoppers" to determine whether frontline staff display desired behaviors (*Service Insights 14.1*). Banks, retailers, car rental firms and hotels are among the industries actively using mystery shoppers. For example, the central reservation offices of a global hotel chain may appoint a research agency to conduct a large-scale monthly mystery caller survey to assess the skills of individual associates in relation to the phone sales process. Actions such as the correct positioning of the various products, upselling and cross-selling, and closing the deal are measured. The survey also examines the quality of the phone conversation on criteria such as "a warm and friendly greeting" and "establishing rapport with the caller". Mystery shopping provides highly actionable and in-depth insights for coaching, training, and performance evaluation.

As the number of mystery calls or visits is typically small, no individual survey is reliable or representative. However, if a particular staff member performs well (or poorly) month after month, managers can infer with reasonable confidence that this person's performance is good (or poor).

SERVICE INSIGHTS 14.1
Customers as Quality Control Inspectors?

Mystery shopping is a good method for checking whether frontline employees display the desired and trained behaviors and follow the specified service procedures, but don't use customer surveys for this. Ron Kaufman, founder of Up Your Service! College, describes a service experience:

"We had a wonderful ride in the hotel car from the airport. The driver was so friendly. He gave us a cold towel and a cool drink. He offered a choice of music, talked about the weather, and made sure we were comfortable with the air conditioning. His smile and good feelings washed over us, and I liked it!"

"At the hotel, I signed the guest registration and gave my credit card. Then the counter staff asked me to complete another form". It read:

LIMOUSINE SURVEY

To consistently ensure the proper application of our quality standards, we value your feedback on our limousine service:

1. Were you greeted by our airport representative?	YES/NO
2. Were you offered a cold towel?	YES/NO
3. Were you offered cold water?	YES/NO
4. Was a selection of music available?	YES/NO
5. Did the driver ask you about the air conditioning?	YES/NO
6. Was the driver driving at a safe speed?	YES/NO

Room Number: _____

Limo Number: _____ Date: _____

Kaufman continued: "As I read the form, all the good feelings fell away. The driver's enthusiasm suddenly seemed a charade. His concern for our well-being became just a checklist of actions to follow. His good mood was merely an act to meet the standard, not a connection with his guests. I felt like the hotel's quality control inspector, and I did not like it. If the hotel wants my opinion, make me an advisor, not an inspector. Ask me: What did you enjoy most about your ride from the airport? (I had told them about their wonderful driver). What else could we do to make your ride even more enjoyable? (I'd have recommended offering the use of a cell phone)."

Unsolicited Customer Feedback. Customer complaints, compliments, and suggestions can be transformed into a stream of information that can be used to help monitor quality, and highlight improvements needed to the service design and delivery. Complaints and compliments are rich sources of detailed feedback on what makes customers unhappy and what delights them.

Like feedback cards, unsolicited feedback is not a reliable measure of overall customer satisfaction, but it is a good source of ideas for improvement. If the objective of collecting feedback is mainly to get ideas on what to improve (rather than for benchmarking and/or assessing staff), reliability and representativeness are not needed, and more qualitative tools such as complaints/compliments or focus groups generally suffice.

Detailed customer complaint and compliment letters, recorded telephone conversations, and direct feedback from employees can also serve as an excellent tool for communicating internally what customers want, and allowing employees and managers at all levels to "listen" to customers first hand. Such learning is much more powerful for shaping the thinking and customer orientation of service staff than using "clinical" statistics and reports. For example, Singapore Airlines prints excerpts from complaint and compliment letters in its monthly employee magazine. Southwest Airlines shows video footage of customers providing feedback to service staff in their training sessions. Seeing actual customers giving comments about their service (positive and negative) leaves a much deeper and lasting impression on staff than any statistical analysis, and encourages them to further improve.

For complaints, suggestions, and inquiries to be useful as research input, they have to be funneled into a central collection point, logged, categorized, and analyzed.[15] That requires a system for capturing customer feedback where it is made, and then reporting it to a central unit. Some firms use a simple Intranet site to record all feedback received by any staff member. Coordinating such activities is not a simple matter, due to many entry points, including the firm's own frontline employees who may be in contact with customers face-to-face, by telephone, or via mail or email, intermediary organizations acting on behalf of the original supplier, and managers who normally work backstage, but who are contacted by a customer seeking higher authority.

Focus Group Discussions and Service Reviews. Both tools give specific insights on potential service improvements and ideas. Typically, focus groups are organized by key customer segments or user groups to drill down on the needs of these users. Service reviews are in-depth, one-on-one interviews that are usually conducted once a year with a firm's most valuable customers. Typically, a senior executive of the firm visits the customer and discusses issues, such as how well the firm performed the previous year and what should be maintained or changed. The senior executive then goes back to the organization and discusses the feedback with his or her account managers, and then both write a letter back to the client detailing how the firm will respond to that customer's service needs and how the account will be managed the following year.

Apart from providing an excellent learning opportunity (especially when the reviews across all customers are compiled and analyzed), service reviews focus on the retention of the most valuable customers and get high marks for service recovery potential.

Online Reviews and Discussions. User-generated content and data can increasingly provide rich insights into quality perceptions of a firm and its competitors, and how these comparisons vary over time at an increasingly granular attribute and temporal level.[16] Sentiment analysis of postings and automated text processing often allows real time insights into changes in consumer perceptions.[17] As one study showed, monitoring online sentiments has been shown to be a leading indicator of offline brand tracking surveys and even stock market prices.[18] Online monitoring tools combined with big data analytics allow real-time sensing of information, location-based and user-generated content will be analyzed increasingly using techniques such as text mining, image processing and classification, social geotagging, human annotations, and geo-mapping.[19]

However, such analyses should be seen as augmenting more traditional tools such as surveys and focus groups. Consider the following example. A high quality, high-priced grab-and-go-food business showed high growth (i.e., their customers must have loved what they offer), but online reviews were critical (e.g., "If you have money to spare, you could do worse", and "The prices are seriously whacked"), and its rating on an important review website was only three out of five stars.

One of the co-owners then attended a meeting with the elite reviewers of this site and, to his surprise, found these reviewers looked nothing like their customers, who tended to be professionals in their 30s and older. These reviewers were mostly in their 20s, had ample spare time to write free reviews, and seemed much less affluent than the firm's customers. The co-owner learned from his conversations with these reviewers that they were highly price sensitive and were not willing to pay premium prices for premium food, which were factors that undoubtedly colored their reviews. In fact, they liked the food, but they downgraded the business as they felt the price was too high. The management of this firm responded to these findings with increasing investment in traditional focus groups to ensure that they respond to the needs of their core market.[20] Not relying too much on online user-generated content seems especially important if a firm's core target segments are expected to differ from the people who post their comments online.

Analysis, Reporting, and Dissemination of Customer Feedback

Choosing the relevant feedback tools and collecting customer feedback is meaningless if the company is unable to disseminate the information to the relevant parties to take action. Hence, to drive continuous improvement and learning, a reporting system needs to deliver feedback and its analysis to frontline staff, process owners, branch or department managers, and top management. Fig. 14.4 provides an overview of which information should go to different key stakeholders in the organization. It also illustrates nicely how different tools complement each other: the top-level tools provide the

Figure 14.6: Mapping reporting of tools to levels of management.

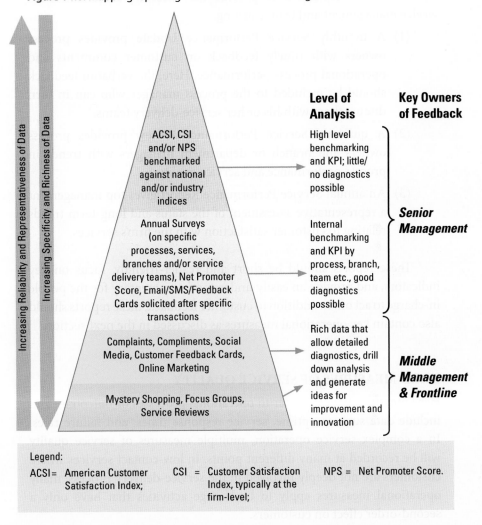

benchmarking over time and against competition, and the lower-level tool allows us to identify what ratings go up or down, and generate insights and ideas on how the service can be improved.

The feedback loop to the frontline should be immediate for complaints and compliments, as is practiced in a number of service businesses where complaints, compliments, and suggestions are discussed with staff during a daily morning brief. In addition, three types of service-performance reports are recommended to provide the necessary information for service management and team learning:

(1) A monthly Service Performance Update provides process owners with timely feedback on customer comments and operational process performance. Here, the verbatim feedback should be included to the process manager who can in turn discuss them with his or her service-delivery teams.

(2) A quarterly Service Performance Review provides process owners and branch or department managers with trends in process performance and service quality.

(3) An annual Service Performance Report gives top management a representative assessment of the status and long-term trends relating to customer satisfaction with the firm's services.

These reports should be short and reader-friendly, focus on key indicators, and provide an easily understood commentary for the people in-charge to act on. In addition to customer feedback, these reports should also contain key operational measures as discussed in the next section.

HARD MEASURES OF SERVICE QUALITY

Hard measures typically refer to operational processes or outcomes, and include data such as uptime, service response times, and failure rates. In a complex service operation, multiple measures of service quality will be recorded at many different points. In low-contact services where customers are not deeply involved in the service-delivery process, many operational measures apply to back-stage activities that have only a second-order effect on customers.

FedEx was one of the first service companies to understand the need for a firm-wide index of service quality that embraced all the key activities that affect customers. By publishing a single, composite index on a frequent basis, senior managers hoped that all FedEx employees would work toward improving quality. The firm recognized the danger of using percentages as targets, because they might lead to complacency. In an organization as large as FedEx, which ships millions of packages a day, even delivering 99.9% of packages on time (which would mean one in

1,000 packages is delivered late), or having 99.999% of flights arrive safely would lead to horrendous problems. Instead, the company decided to approach quality measurement from the baseline of zero failures (*Service Insights 14.2*). As noted by a senior executive:

It's only when you examine the types of failures, the number that occur of each type, and the reasons why, that you begin to improve the quality of your service. For us the trick was to express quality failures in absolute numbers. That led us to develop the Service Quality Index or SQI [pronounced "sky"], which takes each of 12 different events that occur every day, takes the numbers of those events and multiplies them by a weight...based on the amount of aggravation caused to customers — as evidenced by their tendency to write to FedEx and complain about them.[21]

SERVICE INSIGHTS 14.2
FedEx's Approach to Listening to the Voice of the Customer

"We believe that service quality must be mathematically measured", declared Frederick W. Smith, Chairman, President, and CEO of FedEx Corporation. The company has a commitment to clear quality goals, and follows them up with continuous measurement of progress against those goals. This practice forms the foundation for its approach to quality.

FedEx initially set two ambitious quality goals: 100% customer satisfaction for every interaction and transaction, and 100% service performance on every package handled. Customer satisfaction was measured by the percentage of on-time deliveries, which referred to the number of packages delivered on time as a percentage of total package volume. However, as things turned out, the percentage of on-time delivery was an internal standard that was not synonymous with customer satisfaction.

As FedEx had systematically cataloged customer complaints, it was able to develop what CEO Smith calls the "Hierarchy of Horrors", which referred to the eight most common complaints by customers: (1) wrong day delivery, (2) right day, late delivery,

(3) pick-up not made (4) lost package, (5) customer misinformed, (6) billing and paperwork mistakes, (7) employee performance failures, and (8) damaged packages. In other words, the design of this "hard" index reflected the findings of extensive "soft" customer research. The "Hierarchy of Horrors" was the foundation on which FedEx built its customer feedback system.

FedEx refined the list of "horrors" and developed its service quality index (SQI), a 12-item measure of satisfaction and service quality from the customers' viewpoint. The raw numbers of each event are multiplied by a weight that highlights the seriousness of that event for customers (Table 14.3). The result is a point score for each item. The points are then added up to generate that day's index. Like a golf score, the lower the index, the better the performance. However, unlike golf, the SQI involves substantial numbers — typically six figures — reflecting the huge numbers of packages shipped daily. The total SQI and all its 12 items are tracked daily, so that a continuous index can be computed.

An annual goal is set for the average daily SQI, based on reducing the occurrence of failures over the previous year's total. To ensure a continuing focus on each separate component of the SQI, FedEx established 12 Quality Action Teams, one for each component. The teams were charged with understanding and correcting the root causes underlying the observed problems.

In addition to the SQI, which has been modified over time to reflect changes in procedures, services, and customer priorities, FedEx uses a variety of other ways to capture feedback.

Customer Satisfaction Survey. This telephone survey is conducted on a quarterly basis with several thousand randomly selected customers, stratified by its key segments. The results are relayed to senior management on a quarterly basis.

Targeted Customer Satisfaction Survey. This covers specific customer service processes and is conducted on a semiannual basis with clients who have experienced one of the specific FedEx processes within the last three months.

FedEx Center Comment Cards. Comment cards are collected

Table 14.3: Composition of FedEx's Service Quality Index (SQI)

Failure Type	Weighting Factor x No. of Incidents = Daily Points
Late delivery—right day	1
Late delivery—wrong day	5
Tracing requests unanswered	1
Complaints reopened	5
Missing proofs of delivery	1
Invoice adjustments	1
Missed pickups	10
Lost packages	10
Damaged packages	10
Aircraft delays (minutes)	5
Overgoods (packages missing labels)	5
Abandoned calls	1
Total failure points (SQI)	225

from each FedEx storefront business center. The results are tabulated twice a year and relayed to managers in charge of the centers.

Online Customer Feedback Surveys. FedEx has commissioned regular studies to get feedback for its online services, such as package tracking, as well as ad hoc studies on new products.

The information from these various customer feedback measures has helped FedEx to maintain a leadership role in its industry, and played an important role in enabling it to receive the prestigious Malcolm-Baldrige National Quality Award.

Sources: "Blueprints for Service Quality: The Federal Express Approach", *AMA Management Briefing*, New York: American Management Association, 1991, 51–64; Linda Rosencrance, "BetaSphere Delivers FedEx Some Customer Feedback", *Computerworld*, 14, No. 14, 2000, 36; Madan Birla, *Fedex Delivers: How the World's Leading Shipping Company Keeps Innovating and Outperforming the Competition*, John Wiley, 2005, pp. 91–92; Madan Birla (2013), *FedEx Delivers: How the World's Leading Shipping Company Keeps Innovating and Outperforming the Competition*. Wiley, ISBN-13: 978-0471715795

How is performance on hard measures shown? For this, *control charts* are a simple method of displaying performance over time against specific quality standards. The charts can be used to monitor and communicate individual variables or an overall index. Since they are visual, trends are easily identified. Fig. 14.5 shows an airline's performance on the important hard standard of on-time departures. The trends displayed suggest that this issue needs to be addressed by management, as its performance is erratic and not satisfactory. Of course, control charts are only as good as the data on which they are based.

TOOLS TO ANALYZE AND ADDRESS SERVICE-QUALITY PROBLEMS

When a problem is caused by controllable, internal forces, there is no excuse for allowing it to recur. After all, maintaining customers' goodwill after a service failure depends on keeping promises made to the effect of "we're taking steps to ensure that it doesn't happen again!" With prevention as a goal, the next section will touch on some tools for determining the root causes of specific service quality problems.

Figure 14.8: Control chart for departure delays showing percentage of flights departing within 15 minutes of schedule.

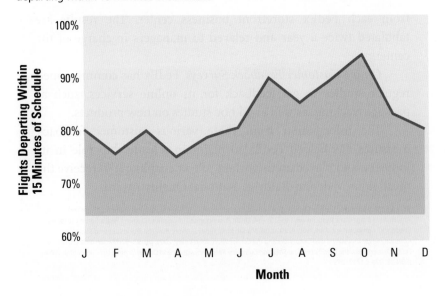

Root Cause Analysis: The Fishbone Diagram

The cause-and-effect analysis uses a technique first developed by Japanese quality expert, Kaoru Ishikawa. Groups of managers and staff brainstorm all the possible reasons that might cause a specific problem. The reasons are then grouped into one of five groupings — Equipment, Manpower (or People), Material, Procedures, and Other — on a cause-and-effect chart, popularly known as a fishbone diagram due to its shape. This technique has been used initially in manufacturing but is now widely used for services.

To apply this tool better to service organizations, an extended framework that has eight instead of five groupings is used.[22] "People" has been further broken down into "Front-Stage Personnel" and "Backstage Personnel". This highlights the fact that front-stage service problems are often experienced directly by customers, whereas backstage failures tend to show up more obliquely through a ripple effect.

In addition, "Information" has been separated from "Procedures", recognizing the fact that many service problems result from information failures. For example, these failures are often because front-stage personnel do not readily have the required information or do not tell customers what to do and when to do it.

"Customers" were added as a further source of root causes. In manufacturing, customers do not really affect the day-to-day operations. However, in a high-contact service, they are involved in front-stage operations. If they do not play their own role correctly, they may reduce service productivity and cause quality problems for themselves and other customers. For instance, an aircraft can be delayed if a passenger tries to board at the last minute with an oversized suitcase, which then has to be loaded into the cargo hold. An example of the extended fishbone is shown in Fig. 14.6, displaying 27 possible reasons for late departures of passenger aircraft.[23]

Once all the main potential causes for flight delays have been identified, it is necessary to assess how much impact each cause has on actual delays. This can be established using frequency counts in combination with Pareto analysis, which is discussed next.

Pareto Analysis

Pareto analysis (so named after the Italian economist who first developed it)

Figure 14.9: Cause-and-effect chart for flight departure delays.

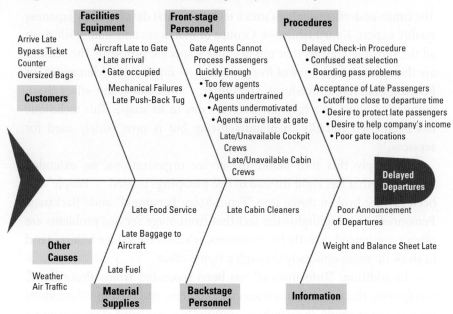

identifies the main causes of observed outcomes. It separates the important from the trivial and helps a service firm to focus its improvement efforts on the most important problem areas. This type of analysis underlies the so-called 80/20 rule, because it often reveals that around 80% of the value of one variable (in this instance, the number of service failures) is caused by only 20% of the causal variables (i.e., the number of possible causes as identified by the fishbone diagram). By combining the fishbone diagram and Pareto analysis, we can identify the main causes of service failure.

In the airline example, findings showed that 88% of the company's late departing flights from the airports it served were caused by only four (15%) of all the possible factors (Fig. 14.7). In fact, more than half of the delays were caused by a single factor: acceptance of late passengers (i.e., situations when the staff held a flight for one more passenger who was checking in after the official cutoff time).

On such occasions, the airline made a friend of the passenger who was late — possibly encouraging a repeat of this undesirable behavior on future occasions — but risked alienating all the other passengers who were already onboard, waiting for the aircraft to depart. Other major delays included waiting for pushback (a vehicle must arrive to pull the aircraft away from the gate), waiting for fueling, and delays in signing the weight and balance sheet (a safety requirement relating to the distribution of the aircraft's load that the captain must follow on each flight).

However, further analysis showed significant variations in the reasons from one airport to another (Fig. 14.8). This finding suggests that the individual airport teams should set slightly different priorities for improvements.

Blueprinting — A Powerful Tool for Identifying Fail Points

Fishbone diagrams and Pareto analyses tell us the causes and importance of quality problems. Blueprints allow us to drill down further to identify where exactly in a service process the problem was caused. As described in Chap. 8, a well-constructed blueprint enables us to visualize the process of service delivery by showing the sequence of front-stage interactions that customers experience as they encounter service providers, facilities,

Figure 14.10: Pareto analysis of causes of flight departure delays.

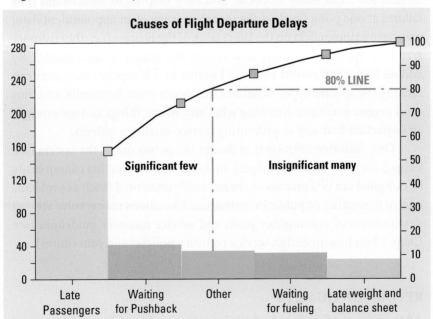

Figure 14.11: Analysis of causes of flight departure delays by station.

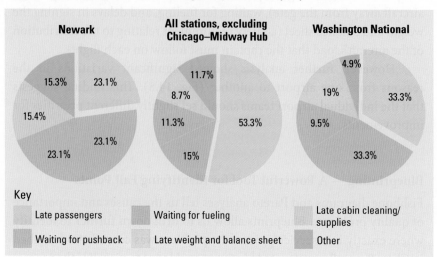

Key:
Late passengers

Waiting for pushback

Waiting for fueling

Late weight and balance sheet

Late cabin cleaning/supplies

Other

and equipment, together with supporting backstage activities, which are hidden from the customers and are not part of their service experience.

Blueprints can be used to identify the potential fail points where failures are most likely to occur, and they help us to understand how failures at one point (such as the incorrect entry of an appointment date) may have a ripple effect on the later stages of the process (i.e., the customer arrives at the doctor's office and is told the doctor is unavailable). By adding frequency counts to the fail points in a blueprint, managers can identify the specific types of failures that occur most frequently, and thus need urgent attention. Knowing what and where things can go wrong is an important first step in preventing service-quality problems.

One desirable solution is to design fail points out of the system (see Chap. 8 for *poka-yokes* technique). In the case of failures that cannot easily be designed out of a process or are not easily prevented (such as problems related to weather or public infrastructure), solutions may revolve around development of contingency plans and service recovery guidelines (see Chap. 13 on how to design service recovery policies and procedures).

RETURN ON QUALITY

After understanding how to drill down to specific quality problems, and using what is learnt from Chap. 8 on how to design and redesign improved service processes, the picture is still incomplete without understanding the financial implications related to quality improvements. Many firms pay a lot of attention on improving service quality; however, quite a few of them have been disappointed by the results. Even firms recognized for service quality efforts have sometimes run into financial difficulties. This is partly because they spent too lavishly on quality improvements that customers do not value or even recognize. In other instances, such results show poor or incomplete execution of the quality program itself.

Assess Costs and Benefits of Quality Initiatives

A return on quality (ROQ) approach assesses the costs and benefits of quality initiatives. This is based on the assumptions that (1) quality is an investment, (2) quality efforts must make sense financially, (3) it is possible to spend too much on quality, and (4) not all quality expenditures are equally justified.[24] Hence, expenditures on quality improvement must be related to anticipated increases in profitability. An important implication of the ROQ perspective is that quality improvement efforts may benefit from being coordinated with productivity improvement programs.

To determine the feasibility of new quality improvement efforts, they must be carefully costed in advance and then related to anticipated customer response. Will the program enable the firm to attract more customers (e.g., through word-of-mouth of current customers), increase share-of-wallet and reduce defections? If so, how much additional net income will be generated?

With good documentation, it is sometimes possible for a firm that operates in a number of locations to examine past experience and judge the strength of a relationship between specific service-quality improvements and revenues (*Service Insights 14.3*). Methods that can help to identify the improvements with the greatest impact on customer satisfaction and purchase behaviors include the importance-performance matrix (see Fig. 14.9), multiple regression analyses that establish the attributes with the highest impact on overall satisfaction, and a new method called Marginal Utility Analysis (MUA) which uses direct questioning of customers on their improvement priorities (e.g., "if you could make an improvement... which four would be your top priorities").[25]

Figure 14.12: The importance-performance matrix compares a firm's service performance against competition and customer needs.

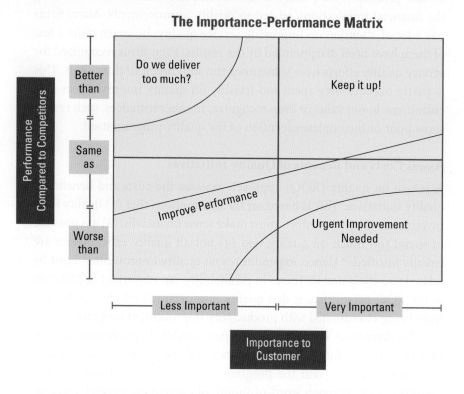

The Importance-Performance Matrix

Performance Compared to Competitors

Better than | Do we deliver too much? | Keep it up!

Same as | Improve Performance

Worse than | | Urgent Improvement Needed

Less Important ——— Very Important

Importance to Customer

SERVICE INSIGHTS 14.3

Quality of Facilities and Room Revenues at Holiday Inn

To find out the relationship between product quality and financial performance in a hotel context, Sheryl Kimes analyzed three years of quality and operational performance data from 1,135 franchised Holiday Inn hotels in the US and Canada.

Indicators of product quality came from the franchisor's quality assurance reports. These reports were based on unannounced, semi-annual inspections by trained quality auditors who were rotated among different regions, and inspected and rated different quality dimensions of each hotel. Sheryl Kimes used 12 of these quality dimensions in her study: two relating to the guest rooms (bedroom and bathroom) and 10 relating to commercial areas (e.g., exterior, lobby, public restrooms, dining facilities, lounge facilities, corridors, meeting area, recreation area, kitchen, and back of house). Each quality dimension usually included 10 to 12 individual items that could be passed or failed. The inspector noted the number of defects for each dimension and the total number for the entire hotel.

Holiday Inn Worldwide also provided data on the revenue per available room (RevPAR) at each hotel. To adjust for differences in local conditions, Kimes analyzed sales and revenue statistics obtained from thousands of US and Canadian hotels, and reported in the monthly Smith Travel Accommodation Reports (a widely used service in the travel industry). This data enabled Kimes to calculate the RevPAR for the immediate midscale competitors of each Holiday Inn hotel. The results were then used to make the RevPARs comparable across all Holiday Inns in the sample.

For the purpose of the research, if a hotel had failed at least one item in an area, it was considered "defective" in that area. The findings showed that as the number of defects in a hotel increased, the RevPAR decreased. Quality dimensions that showed quite a strong impact on RevPAR were the exterior, the guest room, and the guest bathroom. Even a single defect resulted in a statistically significant reduction in RevPAR. However, the combination of defects in all three areas showed an even larger effect on RevPAR over time. Kimes calculated that the average annual revenue impact on a defective hotel was a revenue loss of $204,400 compared to a non-defective hotel.

Using a Return on Quality (ROQ) perspective, the results showed that the main focus of increased expenditures on housekeeping and preventive maintenance should be the hotel exterior, the guest rooms, and bathrooms.

Source: Sheryl E. Kimes, "The Relationship between Product Quality and Revenue per Available Room at Holiday Inn", *Journal of Service Research*, 2, November 1999, pp. 138–144.

Determine the Optimal Level of Reliability

How far should we go in improving service reliability? A company with poor service quality can often achieve big jumps in reliability with relatively modest investments in improvements. As illustrated in Fig. 14.10, initial investments in reducing service failure often bring dramatic results. At some point however, diminishing returns set in as further improvements require increasing the initial levels of investment, and can even become prohibitively expensive. What level of reliability should be targeted then?

Typically, the cost of service recovery is lower than the cost of an unhappy customer. This suggests that service firms should increase reliability up to the point that the incremental improvement equals the cost of service recovery (which is the actual cost of failure). Although this strategy results in a service that is less than 100% failure-free, the firm can still aim to satisfy 100% of its target customers by ensuring that either they receive the service as planned or, if a failure occurs, they obtain a satisfying service recovery.

Figure 14.13: When does improving service reliability become uneconomical?

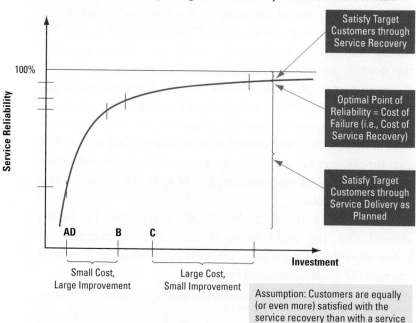

DEFINING AND MEASURING PRODUCTIVITY

Historically, services have lagged behind manufacturing in productivity growth, but research by the McKinsey Global Institute shows that five of the seven largest contributors to labor productivity growth in the US since 2000 have been service industries, including retail and wholesale trade, finance and insurance, administrative support, and scientific and technical services.[26] Clearly, advances in technology enable dramatic improvements in productivity. The introduction of this chapter highlighted the importance of looking at quality and productivity improvement strategies together rather than in isolation. A firm needs to ensure that it can deliver quality experiences more efficiently to improve its long-term profitability. The next section discusses what productivity is and how it can be measured.

Defining Productivity in a Service Context

Simply defined, productivity measures the amount of output produced relative to the amount of input used. Hence, improvements in productivity are reflected by an increase in the ratio of outputs to inputs. An improvement in this ratio might be achieved by cutting the resources required to create a given volume of output, and/or by increasing the output obtained from a given level of inputs.

What is meant by "input" in a service context? Input varies according to the nature of the business. It may include labor, materials, energy, and capital (consisting of land, buildings, equipment, information systems, and financial assets). The intangible nature of service performances makes it more difficult to measure the productivity of service industries than that of manufacturing. The problem is especially acute for information-based services.

Measuring Productivity

Measuring productivity is difficult in services when the output is frequently difficult to define. In a people-processing service such as a hospital, we can look at the number of patients treated in the course of a year, and the hospital's "census" or average bed occupancy. However, how do we take into account the different types of medical activities performed, such as the removal of cancerous tumors, treatment of diabetes, or setting of broken bones? What about the differences between patients? How do we judge the inevitable difference in outcomes? Some patients get better, some develop complications, and sadly, some even die. Relatively few standardized medical procedures offer highly predictable outcomes.

The measurement task is perhaps simpler in possession-processing services, since many quasi-manufacturing are performing routine tasks with easily measurable inputs and outputs. Examples include garages that change a car's oil and rotate its tires, or fast food restaurants that offer limited and simple menus. However, the task gets more complicated when the garage mechanic has to find and repair a water leak, or when we are dealing with a French restaurant known for its varied and exceptional cuisine. What about information-based services? How should we define the output of an investment bank or a consulting firm?

Independent of these more detailed considerations, i.e., labor productivity (e.g., revenue per employee, value-added per employee, and number of customers served per employee) and asset productivity (e.g., return on assets) are the frequently used measures to capture productivity at a high level.

Service Productivity, Efficiency, and Effectiveness

When looking at the issue of productivity, there is a need to distinguish among productivity, efficiency and effectiveness.[27] Productivity refers to the output one can get from a certain amount of inputs (e.g., labor and asset productivity). Efficiency involves comparison to a standard which is usually time-based. It is a measure of how well you do things. For example, how long does it take for an employee to perform a particular task compared to industry average or some other standard? The faster the task can be completed, the higher the efficiency. Effectiveness can be defined as the degree to which an organization meets its goals and desired outcomes, which would typically include customer satisfaction. Peter Drucker expressed it succinctly: "Efficiency is doing the thing right. Effectiveness is doing the right thing".

Classical techniques of productivity and efficiency measurement focus on outputs and benchmarking, rather than outcomes. This means that productivity and efficiency are stressed, but effectiveness is neglected. In freight transport for instance, a ton-mile of output for freight that is delivered late is treated the same for productivity purposes as a similar

Figure 14.14: Productivity for the firm may result in customer frustration when they cannot easily talk to service personnel.

Copyright 2003 by Randy Glasbergen.
www.glasbergen.com

GLASBERGEN

"If you're losing patience with our endless automated system and need to run outside and scream, press 44. If you're feeling better now and wish to continue, press 45..."

shipment delivered on time. Similarly, suppose a hairdresser usually serves three customers per hour. However, she can increase her output to one every 15 minutes by reducing conversation with the customer and by rushing her customers. Even if the haircut itself is just as good, the delivery process may be perceived as functionally inferior, leading customers to rate the overall service experience less positively (Fig. 14.11). In this example, productivity and efficiency have been achieved, but not effectiveness.

In the long run, organizations that are more effective in consistently delivering outcomes desired by customers should be able to command higher prices for their output, and build a loyal and profitable customer base. Therefore, there is a need to place emphasis on effectiveness and outcomes (including quality and value generated for customers) in addition to productivity and efficiency.[28]

IMPROVING SERVICE PRODUCTIVITY

Intense competition in many service sectors pushes firms to continually seek ways to improve their productivity.[29] This section discusses various sources of and possible approaches to productivity gains.

Generic Productivity Improvement Strategies

Traditionally, operations managers have been in charge of improving service productivity and their focus can be summed up as achieving the same output "better, faster and cheaper". This approach typically centers on actions such as:

- Careful cost control at every step in the process. Many senior managers subscribe to the saying, "Costs are like fingernails: You have to cut them constantly".

- Reduce the waste of materials and labor.

- Train and motivate employees to do things faster, better, and more efficiently. As a result, employees should work more productively (note that faster is not necessarily better if it leads to mistakes or unsatisfactory work that has to be redone).

- Broaden the variety of tasks that a service worker can perform (which may require revised labor agreements) so as to eliminate bottlenecks and wasteful downtime, by allowing managers to deploy workers wherever they are needed most.

- Improve capacity utilization through better matching of supply and demand, and/or match productive capacity to average levels of demand rather than at peak levels, so that workers and equipment are not underemployed for extended periods.

- Use machines, equipment, technology, and data that enable employees to work faster and/or to a higher level of quality.

- Install expert systems that allow paraprofessionals to take on work previously performed by more experienced individuals earning higher salaries.

- Redesign customer service processes to be more productive and effective (e.g., through Lean Six Sigma).

- Replace service employees with automated machines and customer-operated self-service technologies (SSTs).

- Tier service levels to allocate resources better to more important customers.

- Outsource non-core activities that can be provided more cost-effectively by third parties.

Although improving productivity can be approached incrementally, major gains often require redesigning customer service processes. For example, it is time for service process redesign when customers face unbearably long waits, as often experienced in healthcare. Service process redesign is discussed in depth in Chap. 8.

Customer-Driven Approaches to Improve Productivity

In situations where customers are deeply involved in the service production process, operations managers should also examine how customer inputs can be made more productive. Marketing managers should be thinking about what marketing strategies should be used to influence customers to behave in more productive ways. Some of these strategies include:

- *Change the timing of customer demand.* By encouraging customers to use a service outside of peak periods and offering them incentives to do so, managers can make better use of their productive assets and provide better service. The issues related to managing demand in capacity-constrained service businesses are discussed in detail in Chap. 9; revenue management strategies are explored in Chap. 6.

- *Encourage use of lower cost service-delivery channels and self-service.* Shifting transactions to more cost-effective service-delivery channels such as the Internet, through apps or self-service machines, improves productivity. It also helps in demand management by reducing the pressure on employees and certain types of physical facilities at peak hours. Many technological innovations are designed to get customers to perform tasks previously undertaken by service employees (Fig. 14.12). The issues related to customers playing a more active role as co-producers of the service are discussed in detail in the context of service-process design in Chap. 8.

- *Ask customers to use third parties.* In some instances, managers may be able to improve service productivity by delegating one or more service support functions to third parties. Specialist intermediaries may enjoy economies of scale, allowing them to perform the task more cheaply than the core service provider. This allows the service provider to focus on quality and productivity in its own area of expertise. An example of an intermediary is a travel agency. The use of intermediaries is discussed in detail in Chap. 5 in the context of distribution.

Figure 14.12: Self-service pumps with credit card readers have increased gas station productivity.

How Productivity Improvements Impact Quality and Value

Managers would do well to examine productivity enhancements from the broader perspective of the business processes used to transform resource inputs into the outcomes desired by customers — especially for processes that are not only cross-departmental and sometimes geographic boundaries, but also link the backstage and front-stage areas of the service operation. Hence, as firms make productivity improvements, they need to examine the impact on the customer experience. See also the discussion on the service quality-productivity-profitability triangle at the beginning of this chapter.

Front-Stage Efforts to Improve Productivity. In high-contact services, many productivity improvements are quite visible. Some changes simply require acceptance by customers, while others require customers to adopt new patterns of behavior in their dealings with the organization. If substantial changes are proposed, then it makes sense to conduct market research first to determine how customers may respond. Failure to consider the effects on customers may result in a loss of business and cancel out anticipated productivity gains. Refer to Chap. 8 on how to manage and overcome customers' reluctance to change in service processes.

How Backstage Changes May Impact Customers. The marketing implications of backstage changes depend on whether they affect or are noticed by customers. If airline mechanics develop a procedure for servicing jet engines more quickly without incurring increased wage rates or material costs, the airline has obtained a productivity improvement that has no impact on the customer's service experience.

Other backstage changes however, may have ripple effects that extend to the front-stage and affect customers. Marketers should be aware of proposed backstage changes, not only to identify such ripples but also to pre-empt customers. For instance, at the bank, the decision to install new computers and printer peripherals may be due to plans to improve internal quality controls and reduce the cost of preparing monthly statements. However, this new equipment may change the appearance of bank statements and the time of the month when they are posted. If customers are likely to notice such changes, an explanation may be warranted. If the new statements are easier to read and understand, the change may be worth promoting as a service improvement.

A Caution on Cost Reduction Strategies. In the absence of new technology, most attempts to improve service productivity tend to center on efforts to eliminate waste and reduce labor costs. Cutbacks in front-stage staffing can mean that the remaining employees have to work harder and faster, or that there are insufficient personnel to serve customers promptly at busy times. Although employees may be able to work faster for a brief period of time, few can maintain a rapid pace for extended periods. They become exhausted, make mistakes, and treat customers in a cursory manner. Workers who are trying to do two or three things at once — for example, serving a customer face-to-face while simultaneously answering the telephone and sorting papers — may do a poor job of each task. Excessive pressure breeds discontent and frustration, especially among customer contact personnel who are caught in between trying to meet customer needs and attempting to achieve management's productivity goals.

A better way is to search for service process redesign opportunities that lead to drastic improvements in productivity and at the same time increase service quality. Biometrics is set to become a new technology that may allow for both (*Service Insights 14.4*).

SERVICE INSIGHTS 14.4
Biometrics — The Next Frontier in Driving Productivity and Service Quality?

Intense competitive pressures and razor-thin margins in many service industries do not allow firms the luxury of increasing costs to improve quality. Rather, the trick is to constantly seek ways to simultaneously achieve great improvements in service quality and efficiency at the same time. In the past, Internet and service apps have allowed many firms to do just that, and redefined industries including financial services, music distribution, and travel agencies. Biometrics may be the next major technology driving further service and productivity improvements in the service sector.

Biometrics is the authentication or identification of individuals based on a physical characteristic or trait. Physical characteristics include fingerprints, facial recognition, hand geometry, and the structure of the iris, and traits include signature formation, keystroke patterns, and voice recognition. Biometrics, as something you are, is more convenient and more secure than something you know (passwords or pieces of personal information) or something you have (card keys, smart cards or tokens). There is no risk of forgetting, losing, copying, loaning, or getting your biometrics stolen (Fig. 14.13).

Applications of biometrics range from controlling access to service facilities (used by Disney World to provide access to season pass holders), voice recognition at call centers (used by the Home Shopping Network and Charles Schwab to enable fast and hassle-free client authentication), self-service access to safe-deposit vaults at banks (used by the Bank of Hawaii and First Tennessee Bank), cashing in checks at supermarkets (used by Kroger, Food 4 Less, and BI-LO), and even in schools (for library book issue and for debiting of catering accounts based on the child's finger-scan). The use of biometrics will become more prevalent.

Biometrics clearly have exciting applications. They are generally more secure, but if handled wrongly, the potential damage could also be far more serious. Even biometrics can be cloned. For example, fingerprints can be replicated (or "spoofed") from something a person has touched. Resetting a compromised password is merely a hassle, but what will happen if someone stole the digital version of your fingerprint or your retina? Perhaps, biometrics will be supplemented by additional safety features for the highest risk applications. Future service innovation will show where biometrics can add the highest value to service organizations and their customers.

Figure 14.13: Customers cannot forget or lose their biometrics!

Sources: Jochen Wirtz and Loizos Heracleous, "Biometrics Meets Services", *Harvard Business Review*, February 2005, 48–49; Loizos Heracleous and Jochen Wirtz, "Biometrics — The Next Frontier in Service Excellence, Productivity and Security in the Service Sector", *Managing Service Quality*, 16, No. 1, 2006; *The Economist*, "Internet Security: Kill or Cure", September 7, 2013, p. 52.

Integration and Systematic Approaches to Improving Service Quality and Productivity

A number of tools and concepts on how to improve service quality and productivity have been discussed in depth. Table 14.4 integrated the key tools discussed into a generic nine-step framework to use to structure your approach to improve the quality and productivity of a single customer service process. Such projects are typically conducted by experienced in-house teams or external consultants. However, the continual improvement of a process (as described in step 9) should typically be the responsibility of the process owner.

There are also systematic approaches that help service firms to achieve an organization-wide culture of becoming customer, service quality and productivity focused. In fact, much of the thinking, tools and concepts introduced in this chapter originate from these approaches, which include the Total Quality Management (TQM), ISO 9000, Six Sigma, and the Malcolm-Baldrige and European Foundation for Quality Management (EFQM) approaches. The following sections will briefly

Table14.4: An Integrated Nine-Step Approach to Customer Service Process Improvement

Step	Objectives	Potential Tools to Apply
1	Determine priority processes for improvement and redesign	• Frequency count of process occurrence and number of complaints per process to identify priority processes • Use prioritization matrix (ease of implementation vs. potential business impact) to identify "low hanging fruits" with which to start a service improvement initiative
2	For the shortlisted processes, set targets for (1) customer satisfaction, (2) defects, (3) cycle-time, and (4) productivity improvements	• Benchmarking internally, against competition, best in class and world-class to determine targets for all four priorities • Decide the target level of performance (e.g., do you aim to be the best in your industry, or just catch up with industry average on those four priorities?) • Use a project charter to formalize the objectives of this customer service process redesign project
3	Identify key elements of quality in priority service processes and determine customer needs and expectations	• Use blueprinting to identify all touchpoints of a customer journey and the line of visibility to understand the customer view of a process • For each touch point, determine what quality means in the customer's eyes (e.g., use the five dimensions of service quality (see Chap. 2) to cover all important dimensions, review customer feedback, content analysis of compliments and complaints to understand drivers of customer delight and disgust, conduct focus groups)
4	Assess process performance	• Review hard, operational process measures (e.g., cycle times, customer waiting times, one-time resolution, etc.) • Measure customer perceptions of process performance (e.g., process-specific customer satisfaction surveys) • Interview frontline employees to obtain their view of what works and what does not, and what needs urgent improvement
5	Identify performance shortfalls and quality gaps	• Map customer needs and wants of the process against process performance measures to determine important performance and quality gaps. • Identify the main performance gaps, e.g., map frequency counts of service failures (and/or complaints) on service blueprints to understand where exactly service processes fail

Step	Objectives	Potential Tools to Apply
6	Identify root causes of quality gaps	• Use the Gaps Model to capture all possible sources of gaps in customer's service quality perceptions • Use TQM tools to drill down on specific gaps, e.g., use Pareto charts to understand which fail points to focus on, use Fishbone diagrams to identify the exact causes of key fail points, and again use Pareto charts to identify the main root causes to be designed out of the processes
7	Improve process performance	• Use prescriptions from the Gaps Model to close each of the six gaps (see Table 14.1) • Use customer service design and redesign tools (see Chap. 8, including design fail points of the system through use of poka-yokes) • Plan service recovery for fail points that cannot be designed out of the system (i.e., make it proactive, preplanned, trained and empowered, see Chap. 13)
8	Control and continuously fine-tune and further improve the process	• After redesign, monitor the performance of the redesigned process using operational measures and customer feedback • Make it a routine process at the new, high level of performance • Ask the process owner to fine-tune the process through incremental improvements (e.g., use Kaizen or other tools to get the process team to monitor and continually improve the process it is responsible for)
9	Start over, the journey is the destination…	• Create a culture of customer-centricity, process improvement, and change by continuously working and redesigning customer service processes; become a customer-driven learning organization

discuss each of these approaches and relate them to the service quality and productivity context.

Total Quality Management

Total Quality Management (TQM) was originally developed in Japan. It is probably the most widely known approach to continuous improvement in manufacturing, and more recently, in service firms. TQM can help organizations to attain service excellence, increase productivity, and be a continued source of value creation through innovative process improvements.[30]

Some concepts and tools of TQM can be applied directly to services. As discussed in this chapter, TQM tools such as control charts, Pareto analysis, blueprints, and fishbone diagrams are used by service firms with great results for monitoring service quality and determining the root causes of specific problems.

Twelve critical dimensions for successful implementation of TQM in a service context have been identified: (1) top management commitment and visionary leadership; (2) human resource management; (3) technical system, including service process design and process management; (4) information and analysis system; (5) benchmarking; (6) continuous improvement; (7) customer focus; (8) employee satisfaction; (9) union intervention and employee relations; (10) social responsibility; (11) servicescapes; and (12) service culture.[31]

ISO 9000 Certification[32]

There are 162 countries that are members of ISO (the International Organization for Standardization based in Geneva, Switzerland), which promote standardization and quality to facilitate international trade. ISO 9000 is all about quality management and it comprises requirements, definitions, guidelines, and related standards to provide an independent assessment and certification of a firm's quality management system. The official ISO 9000 definition of quality is: "The totality of features and characteristics of a product or service that bear on its ability to satisfy a stated or implied need. Simply stated, quality is about meeting or exceeding your customer's needs and requirements".

The ISO 9000 comprises a family of sub-standards family addressing various aspects of quality management. These standards provide guidance and tools for organizations who want to ensure their products and services consistently meet customers' requirements, and that quality is consistently improved.

To ensure quality, ISO 9000 uses many TQM tools and internalizes their use in participating firms and makes use of W. Edwards Deming's PDCA Cycle (i.e., Plan-Do-Act-Check Cycle).

Service firms generally adopted ISO 9000 standards later than manufacturing firms. Major service sectors that have adopted ISO 9000 certification include wholesale and retail firms, IT service providers, healthcare providers, consultancy firms, and educational institutions. By adopting the ISO 9000 standards, service firms can ensure that their services conform to customer expectations and achieve improvements in productivity.

Six Sigma

The Six Sigma approach was originally developed by Motorola to improve product quality and reduce warranty claims, and was soon adopted by other manufacturing firms to reduce defects in a variety of areas.

Subsequently, service firms embraced various Six Sigma strategies to reduce defects, reduce cycle times, and improve productivity.[33] As early as 1990, GE Capital applied Six Sigma methodology to reduce the backroom costs of selling consumer loans, credit card insurance, and payment protection. Its former president and COO Denis Nayden said:

Although Six Sigma was originally designed for manufacturing, it can be applied to transactional services. One obvious example is in making sure the millions of credit card and other bills GE sends to customers are correct, which drives down our costs of making adjustments. One of our biggest costs in the financial business is winning new customers. If we treat them well, they will stay with us, reducing our customer-origination costs.[34]

Statistically, Six Sigma means achieving a quality level of only 3.4 defects per million opportunities (DPMO). To understand how stringent this target is, consider mail deliveries. If a mail service delivers with 99% accuracy, it misses 3,000 items out of 300,000 deliveries. However, if it achieves a Six Sigma performance level, only one item out of this total will go astray.

Over time, Six Sigma has evolved from a defect reduction approach to an overall business improvement approach. As defined by Pande, Neuman and Cavanagh:

Six Sigma is a comprehensive and flexible system for achieving, sustaining and maximizing business success. Six Sigma is uniquely driven by close understanding of customer needs, disciplined use of facts, data and statistical analysis, and diligent attention to managing, improving, and reinventing business processes.[35]

Process improvement and process design/redesign are two strategies that form the cornerstone of the Six Sigma approach. Process improvement strategies aim to identify and eliminate the root causes of service-delivery problems, thereby improving service quality. Process design/redesign strategies act as a supplementary strategy to improvement strategy. If a root cause cannot be identified or effectively eliminated within the existing processes, either new processes are *designed* or existing process are *redesigned* to fully or partially address the problem.

The most popular Six Sigma improvement tool for analyzing and improving business processes is the DMAIC model, shown in Table 14.5. DMAIC stands for:

- *D*efine the opportunities (including the problem, scope, and goals).
- *M*easure the current performance along key steps/inputs.
- *A*nalyze to identify root causes.
- *I*mprove the process and its performance.
- *C*ontrol the process to sustain a higher level of performance.

Malcolm-Baldrige and EFQM Approaches

The Malcolm-Baldrige National Quality Award (MBNQA) was developed by the National Institute of Standards and Technology (NIST) with the goal of promoting best practices in quality management, and recognizing and publicizing quality achievements among US firms. Countries other than the US have similar quality awards, of which the most widely used is probably the European Foundation for Quality Management (EFQM) approach.[36]

While the framework is generic and does not distinguish between manufacturing and service organizations, the award has a specific service category, and the model can be used to create a culture of ongoing service improvements. Major services firms that have won the award include PricewaterhouseCoopers, Ritz-Carlton, FedEx, University of Wisconsin, Xerox Business Services, Boeing Aerospace Support, Caterpillar Financial Services Corp, and AT&T. Research has confirmed that employing this framework can improve organizational performance.[37]

Table 14.5: Applying the DMAIC Model to Process Improvement and Redesign

	Process Improvement	Process Design/Redesign
Define	• Identify the problem • Define requirements • Set goals	• Identify specific or broad problems • Define goal/change vision • Clarify scope and customer requirements
Measure	• Validate problem/process • Refine problem/goal • Measure key steps/inputs	• Measure performance to requirements • Gather process efficiency data
Analyze	• Develop causal hypothesis • Identify root causes • Validate hypothesis	• Identify best practices • Assess process design • Refine requirements
Improve	• Develop ideas to measure root causes • Test solutions • Measure results	• Design new process • Implements new process, structures, and systems
Control	• Establish measures to maintain performance • Correct problems as needed	• Establish measures and reviews to maintain performance • Correct problems as needed

Source: Republished with permission of McGraw-Hill Companies from *The Six SIGMA Way: How GE, Motorola, and Other Top Companies Are Honing Their Performance* by Peter S. Pande, Roland R. Cavanagh, Robert P. Neuman, Copyright 2000; permission conveyed through Copyright Clearance Center, Inc.

The Malcolm-Baldrige Model assesses firms on seven areas:

(1) Leadership commitment to a service-quality culture.

(2) Planning priorities for improvements, including service standards, performance targets, and measurement of customer satisfaction, defects, cycle-time, and productivity.

(3) Information and analysis that will aid the organization to collect, measure, analyze, and report strategic and operational indicators.

(4) Human resources management that enables the firm to deliver service excellence, ranging from hiring the right people to development, involvement, empowerment, and motivation.

(5) Process management, including monitoring, continuous improvement, and process redesign.

(6) Customer and market focus that allows the firm to determine customer requirements and expectations.

(7) Business results.[38]

Which Approach Should a Firm Adopt?

As there are various approaches to systematically improving a service firm's service quality and productivity, the question of which approach should be adopted arises — TQM, ISO 9000, the Malcolm-Baldrige Model, or Six Sigma? It is better to see these approaches as complementary and building on another, and not as mutually exclusive. TQM can be applied at differing levels of complexity, and basic tools such as flowcharting, frequency charts, and fishbone diagrams probably should be adopted by any type of service firm. Six Sigma and ISO 9000 seem to suit the next level of commitment and complexity, and focus on process improvements and compliance to performance standards, followed by the Malcolm-Baldrige Model or the European Foundation for Quality Management (EFQM) approaches that offer comprehensive frameworks for organizational excellence. The complementarity of approaches can be seen in a study on educational institutions in *Service Insights 14.5*.

SERVICE INSIGHTS 14.5
TQM and ISO-Certification in Educational Institutions

Higher educational institutions are increasingly competing for talented students and have started to accept that they have to be more customer-centric in their approach to increase student satisfaction. What is the meaning of service quality in a higher educational institution? A TQM model has been proposed with the following five variables that measure different dimensions of service quality in an institution of higher learning, and they suggest that these variables will increase student satisfaction:

- *Commitment of Top Management*: Top management has to "walk the talk" and make sure that what is preached in terms of educational excellence and service quality is really being practiced.

- *Course Delivery*: While institutions of higher learning hire people with expert knowledge, there is a need for such expert knowledge to be transmitted expertly, with passion.

- *Campus Facilities*: Attention needs to be focused on having excellent infrastructure and facilities for student learning as well as for their extracurricular activities. These facilities also have to be properly maintained.

- *Courtesy*: This is a positive attitude toward students that will create a friendly learning environment.

- *Customer Feedback and Improvement*: Continuous feedback from students can lead to improvements.

The researchers studied TQM in a mix of ISO-certified and non-ISO certified institutions, and found that ISO 9001:2000 certified institutions were adopting TQM faster and offered a better quality education than non-ISO certified institutions.

Their findings showed that while all five variables together did predict student satisfaction, two variables in particular were more important in affecting student satisfaction. The variables were top management commitment and campus facilities. Top management needs to be committed to quality assurance in making sure the other variables are in place to improve the student experience.

Source: P. B. Sakthivel, G. Rajendran, and R. Raju, "TQM Implementation and Students' Satisfaction of Academic Performance", *The TQM Magazine*, 17, No. 6, 2005, pp. 573–589.

Figure 14.14: Higher learning increasingly focus on service quality.

Any one of the approaches can be a useful framework for understanding customer needs, analyzing processes, and improving service quality and productivity. Firms can choose a particular program, depending on their own needs and desired level of sophistication. Each program has its own strengths, and firms can use more than one program to add on to the other. For example, the ISO 9000 program can be used for standardizing the procedures and process documentation, and the Six Sigma and Malcolm-Baldrige programs can then be used to improve processes and focus on performance improvement across the organization.

A key success factor of any of these programs depends on how well the particular quality improvement program is part of the overall business strategy. Service champions make best practices in service-quality management a core part of their organizational culture.[39] The National Institute of Standards and Technology (NIST), which organizes the Malcolm-Baldrige Award program has an index called the "Baldrige Index" of Malcolm-Baldrige Award winners. It was observed that winners always outperformed the S&P 500 index![40]

Ironically however, the two-time winner of the award and Six Sigma pioneer, Motorola, had suffered financially and lost market share, partly due to the firm's failure to keep up with new technology. Also, firms which implement one of these programs due to peer pressure or just as a marketing tool are less likely to succeed than firms which view these programs as important development tools.[41] Clearly, success cannot be taken for granted. Commitment, implementation and constant improvement that follow changing markets, technologies, and environments are keys for sustained success.

CONCLUSION

Enhancing service quality and improving service productivity are often two sides of the same coin, offering powerful potential to improve value for both customers and the firm. It is a key challenge for any service business to deliver service quality and satisfaction to its customers in ways that are cost-effective for the firm. Strategies to improve service quality and productivity should reinforce rather than counteract each other. In a world of continuous innovation and competitive markets, only few businesses can afford to spend more money (i.e., allow lower productivity) for better quality. Therefore, the game is to seek improvements that offer a quantum leap in service quality and productivity at the same time.

CHAPTER SUMMARY

Integrating Service Quality & Productivity
- Quality and productivity are twin paths to creating value for customers and firms
- Service quality and productivity improvements can reinforce, be independent or even counter each others' impact on profitability

What Is Service Quality?
- Customer defined
- Consistently meeting or exceeding customer expectations

The Gaps Model
The Gaps Model helps to identify the causes of quality problems at the macro level through a gap analysis:
Gap 1: The Knowledge Gap
Gap 2: The Policy Gap
Gap 3: The Delivery Gap
Gap 4: The Communications Gap
Gap 5: The Perceptions Gap
Gap 6: The Service Quality Gap

Each of the gaps has distinct causes. Prescriptions are provided on how to address the causes of each gap.

Measuring Service Quality

Customer Feedback
- Referred to as "soft measures"

Objectives:
- Assess and benchmark performance
- Improve performance by cementing strengths and improving weaknesses
- Create a customer-oriented service culture and a culture for change

Use a mix of tools to obtain reliable, and actionable feedback, such as:
- Surveys, feedback cards, & online/mobile messages, complaints & compliments
- Mystery shopping
- Focus groups and service reviews
- Online reviews and discussions

Operational Measures
- Process & outcome measures
- Referred to as "hard measures"
- Relate to process activities and outcomes that can be counted, timed or measured (e.g., system uptime, on-time departure, service response time, and failure rates)

Analysis, Reporting, & Dissemination of Customer Feedback & Operational Measures
- Daily morning briefings to the frontline
- Monthly service performance updates to process owners & service teams
- Quarterly service performance reviews to middle management & process owners
- Annual service performance reports to top management & entire firm

Analyzing Service Quality Problems

Analytical tools:
- Fishbone diagram to conduct root cause analysis
- Pareto charts to identify key fail points & root causes
- Blueprinting

Return on quality:
- Assess costs and benefits of quality initiatives
- Importance-performance matrix
- Optimal level of reliability depends on cost of service recovery

Systematic Approaches to Improving Service Quality & Productivity

Nine-step approach to service process improvement:
- Determine priority processes for improvement
- Set targets for (a) customer satisfaction, (b) defects, (c) cycle-time, and (d) productivity improvements
- Identify key elements of quality
- Assess process performance
- Identify quality gaps
- Identify root causes of gaps
- Improve process performance
- Control and fine-tune
- Start again, the journey is the destination…

Widely-used organization-wide systematic approaches:
- Total quality management (TQM)
- ISO 9000 Certification
- Six Sigma (i.e., DMAIC)
- Malcolm-Baldrige and EFQM Approaches

Measuring & Improving Service Productivity

Defining and measuring productivity:
- Productivity: output/input
- Efficiency: compared to a standard (i.e., "do things right")
- Effectiveness: compared to a goal (i.e., "do the right things")
- All three have to be balanced

Productivity improvement strategies:
- Generic productivity strategies (i.e., "doing the same things better, faster, cheaper")
- Customer-driven approaches (e.g., shifting time of demand, using lower cost service delivery channels, and self-service)
- Outsourcing to third parties
- Monitor potential customer implications of productivity enhancement

CHAPTER 15

Building a World-Class Service Organization

Marketing is so basic that it cannot be considered a separate function... It is the whole business seen from the point of view of its final result, that is, from the customer's point of view. Concern and responsibility for marketing must, therefore, permeate all areas of the enterprise.

Peter Drucker,
Management consultant, educator, and author
Described as a founder of modern management

[T]he more short-term a company's focus becomes, the more likely the firm will be to engage in behavior that actually destroys value.

Don Peppers and Martha Rogers
Founding partners of Peppers & Rogers Group
A customer-centric management consulting firm

"Why is it so hard for so many to realize that winners are usually the ones who work harder, work longer, and as a result, perform better?" and "Big things are accomplished only through the perfection of minor details".

John Wooden
Legendary former UCLA Basketball Team Coach

INTRODUCTION

This final chapter provides a summary of how a world-class service organization looks like, which can be used as an assessment tool. Financial impact of being a service leader is also discussed and the chapter concludes with a call to action on the readers' part!

CREATING A WORD CLASS SERVICE ORGANIZATION

How would one describe a breakthrough service organization? Based on our observations having worked in the field of services marketing for decades, we observed that a number of characteristics are necessary (but may not be sufficient) for becoming and remaining a breakthrough service organization. Next, we will analyze more comprehensively how firms can be categorized into four performance levels, and how they can then move up the performance ladder.

From Losers to Leaders: Four Levels of Service Performance

Service leadership is not based on outstanding performance within a single dimension. Rather, it reflects excellence across multiple dimensions. In an effort to capture this performance spectrum, we need to evaluate the organization within each of the three functional areas described earlier — marketing, operations, and human resources. Table 15.1 categorizes service performers into four levels: *loser, non-entity, professional,* and *leader.*[2] At each level, there is a brief description of a typical organization across 12 dimensions.

Under the marketing function, we look at the role of marketing, competitive appeal, customer profile and service quality. Under the operations function, we consider the role of operations, service delivery (front-stage), backstage operations, productivity, and introduction of new technologies. Finally, under the human resources function, we examine the role of HRM, the workforce, and frontline management. Obviously, there are overlaps between these dimensions and across functions. There may also be differences in the relative importance of some dimensions in different industries and across different delivery systems. For instance, human resource management tends to play a more prominent strategic role in high-contact services. The goal of this overall service performance framework is to generate insights into how service leaders perform so well and what needs to be changed in organizations that are not performing as well as they might.

Table 15.1 is a useful tool to perform an in-depth appraisal of a company in a specific industry, as a point of departure, modifying some of the elements to create a customized assessment tool.

Service Losers. These firms are at the bottom of the barrel from customer, employee, and managerial perspectives, and get failing grades in marketing, operations, and HRM. Customers patronize them for reasons other than performance, typically because there is no viable alternative, which is one reason why service losers continue to survive. Managers of such organizations may even see service delivery as a necessary evil. New technology is introduced only under duress, and the uncaring workforce is a negative constraint on performance.

Service Non-entities. Although their performance still leaves much to be desired, service nonentities have eliminated the worst features of losers. Non-entities are dominated by a traditional operations mindset, typically based on achieving cost savings through standardization. Their marketing strategies are unsophisticated, and the roles of human resources and operations might be summed up respectively by the philosophies "adequate is good enough" and "if it ain't broke, don't fix it". Managers may talk about improving quality and other goals, but are unable to set clear priorities to have a clear direction, nor gain the respect and commitment of their employees (Fig. 15.1). Several such firms are often found competing in a lackluster fashion within a given marketplace, and you might have difficulty distinguishing one from the others. Periodic price discounts tend to be the primary means of trying to attract new customers.

Service Professionals. Service professionals are in a different league from non-entities and have a clear market positioning strategy. Customers within the target segments seek out these firms based on their sustained reputation for consistently meeting expectations. Marketing is sophisticated, using targeted communications and pricing based on value to the customer. Research is used to measure customer satisfaction and obtain ideas for service enhancement. Operations and marketing work together to introduce new delivery systems, and recognize the trade-off between productivity and customer-defined quality. There are explicit

Table 15.1: Four Levels of Service Performance Assessment Tool.

Marketing Function			
Level	**1. Loser**	**2. Nonentity**	
Role of Marketing	• Tactical role only • Advertising and promotions lack focus • No involvement in product or pricing decision	• Uses mix of selling and mass communication, using simple segmentation strategy • Makes selective use of price discounts and promotions; conducts and tabulates basic satisfaction surveys	
Competitive Appeal	• Customers patronize a firm for reasons other than performance	• Customers neither seek nor avoid the firm	
Customer profile	• Unspecified • A mass market to be served at a minimum cost	• One or more segments whose basic needs are understood	
Service Quality	• Highly variable, usually unsatisfactory. • Subservient to operations priorities	• Meets some customer expectations • Consistent on one or two key dimensions, but not all	

Legend: Score each area from '1' to '4' depending on the performance level of the organization that is being assessed. Average the scores for each function, and then average the functions to obtain the total assessment score.

Marketing Function		
3. Professional	**4. Leader**	**Assessment Score**
• Has clear positioning strategy against competition • Uses focused communications with distinctive appeals to clarify promises and educate customers • Pricing is based on value • Monitors customer usage and operates loyalty programs • Uses a variety of research techniques to measure customer satisfaction and obtain ideas for service enhancements • Works with operations to introduce new delivery systems	• Innovative leader in chosen segments, known for marketing skills • Brands at product/process level • Conducts sophisticated analysis of relational databases as inputs to one-to-one marketing and proactive account management • Uses state-of-the-art research techniques • Uses concept testing, observation, and lead customers as inputs to new-product development • Close to operations/HR	....
• Customers seek out the firm based on its sustained reputation for meeting customer expectations	• Company's name is synonymous with service excellence • Its ability to delight customers raises expectations to levels that competitors cannot meet	....
• Groups of individuals whose variation in needs and value to the firm are clearly understood	• Individuals are selected and retained based on their future value to the firm, including their potential for new service opportunities and their ability to stimulate innovation	....
• Consistently meets or exceeds customer expectations across multiple dimensions	• Raises customer expectations to new levels • Improves continuously	....
	Subtotal	

A score of "3.5 and above" indicates excellent performance; a score from "2.5. to 3.4" indicates good performance, a score from "1.5 to 2.4" indicates average to poor performance, and a score of "1.4 and lower" indicates very poor performance.

Operations Function			
Level	**1. Loser**	**2. Nonentity**	
Role of Operations	• Reactive • Cost-oriented	• The principal line management function creates and delivers product • Focuses on standardization as key to productivity • Defines quality from internal perspective	
Service Delivery (front-stage)	• A necessary evil • Locations and schedules are unrelated to preferences of customers who are routinely ignored	• Sticklers for tradition; "If it ain't broke, don't fix it" • Tight rules for customers • Each step in delivery runs independently	
Back-stage Operations	• Divorced from front-stage operations • Cogs in a machine	• Contributes to individual front-stage delivery steps but organized separately • Unfamiliar with customers	
Productivity	• Undefined • Managers are punished for failing to stick within budget	• Based on standardization • Rewarded for keeping costs below budget	
Introduction of New Technology	• Late adopter, under duress, when necessary for survival	• Follows the crowd when justified by cost savings	

Legend: Score each area from '1' to '4' depending on the performance level of the organization that is being assessed. Average the scores for each function, and then average the functions to obtain the total assessment score.

Operations Function		
3. Professional	**4. Leader**	**Assessment Score**
• Plays a strategic role in competitive strategy • Recognizes a trade-off between productivity and customer-defined quality • Willing to outsource • Monitors competing operations for ideas, threats	• Recognized for innovation, focus, and excellence; an equal partner with marketing and HR management • Has in-house research capability and academic contacts • Continually experimenting	....
• Driven by customer satisfaction, not tradition • Willing to customize, embrace new approaches • Emphasis on speed, convenience, and comfort	• Delivery is a seamless process organized around the customer • Employees know whom they are serving • Focuses on continuous improvement	....
• Process is explicitly linked to front-stage activities • Sees role as serving "internal customers" who, in turn, serve external customers	• Closely integrated with front-stage delivery, even when geographically far apart • Understands how own role relates to the overall process of serving external customers • Continuing dialog	....
• Focuses on re-engineering backstage processes • Avoids productivity improvements that will degrade customers' service experience • Continually refining processes for efficiency	• Understands the concept of return on quality • Actively seeks customer involvement in productivity improvement • Ongoing testing of new processes and technologies	....
• An early adopter when IT promises to enhance service for customers and provide a competitive edge	• Works with technology leaders to develop new applications that create first-mover advantage • Seeks to perform at levels competitors cannot match	....
	Subtotal	

A score of "3.5 and above" indicates excellent performance; a score from "2.5. to 3.4" indicates good performance, a score from "1.5 to 2.4" indicates average to poor performance, and a score of "1.4 and lower" indicates very poor performance.

Human Resources Function			
Level	**1. Loser**	**2. Nonentity**	
Role of Human Resources	• Supplies low-cost employees who meet minimum skill requirements for the job	• Recruits and trains employees who can perform competently	
Workforce	• Negative constraints: poor performers, do not care, disloyal	• Adequate resources, follows procedures but uninspired • Turnover often high	
Frontline Management	• Controls workers	• Controls the process	

Legend: Score each area from '1' to '4' depending on the performance level of the organization that is being assessed. Average the scores for each function, and then average the functions to obtain the total assessment score.

Human Resources Function		
3. Professional	**4. Leader**	**Assessment Score**
• Invests in selective recruiting, ongoing training • Keeps close to employees, promotes upward mobility • Strives to enhance the quality of working life	• Sees the quality of employees as a strategic advantage • The firm is recognized as outstanding place to work • HR helps top management to nurture culture	
• Motivated, hardworking • Allowed some discretion in choice of procedures • Offers suggestions	• Innovative and empowered • Very loyal, committed to the firm's values and goals • Creates procedures	
• Listens to customers • Coaches and facilitates workers	• Source of new ideas for top management • Mentors, workers to enhance career growth, value to firm	
	Subtotal	
	Overall Total	

A score of "3.5 and above" indicates excellent performance; a score from "2.5. to 3.4" indicates good performance, a score from "1.5 to 2.4" indicates average to poor performance, and a score of "1.4 and lower" indicates very poor performance.

Note: This framework was inspired by, and expands upon, work in service operations management by Richard Chase and Robert Hayes.

Figure 15.1: Dilbert's boss loses focus — and his audience.

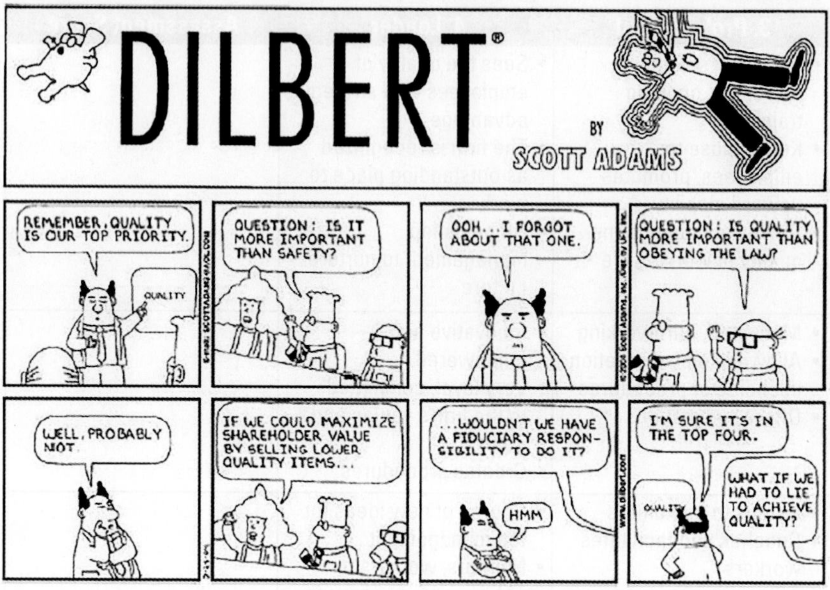

links between backstage and front-stage activities, and the firm has a much more proactive, investment-oriented approach to HRM than is found among nonentities.

Service Leaders. These organizations are breakthrough service organizations, world-class service leaders, and are the *crème de la crème* of their respective industries. Where service professionals are good, service leaders are outstanding. When we think of service leaders, we think of Amazon, McKinsey, Ritz Carlton, Southwest Airlines, Starbucks, and Zappos. Their company names are synonymous with service excellence and the ability to delight customers. Service leaders are recognized for their innovation in each functional area of management as well as for their superior internal communications and coordination among these three functions, often the result of a relatively flat organizational structure and the extensive use of teams. As a result, service delivery is a seamless process organized around the customer.

Marketing efforts by service leaders make extensive use of customer relationship management (CRM) systems that offer strategic insights about customers, who are often addressed on a one-to-one basis. Concept

Figure 15.2: Creating an outstanding work environment attracts and retains the best people.

testing, observation, and contacts with lead customers are employed in the development of new, breakthrough services that respond to previously unrecognized needs. Operations specialists work with technology leaders around the world to develop new applications that will create a first mover advantage, and enable the firm to perform at levels that competitors cannot hope to reach for a long time to come. Senior executives see quality of employees as a strategic advantage. HRM works on building and maintaining a service-oriented culture and creating an outstanding working environment that simplifies the task of attracting and retaining the best people (Fig. 15.2).[3] The employees themselves are committed to the firm's values and goals. Because they are engaged, empowered, and quick to embrace change, they are an ongoing source of new ideas and they continuously drive improvement.

Moving to a Higher Level of Performance

Almost all companies want to be service leaders. We want to win our customers' loyalty and we want our customers to say good things about us. If we can achieve these objectives, we will increase our market share, our shareholder value, and our share of community goodwill. These are powerful reasons for moving to a higher performance level.[4] This view is becoming widely accepted, and in most markets we can find companies moving up the performance ladder through conscious efforts to improve and coordinate their marketing, operations, and HRM functions, in a bid to establish more favorable competitive positions and better satisfy their customers.

It requires human leaders at all levels of an organization to take a service firm in the right direction, set the right strategic priorities, and ensure the relevant strategies are implemented throughout the organization. And the various chapters throughout this book discuss exactly how it can be done through various tools, concepts, and theories.

CUSTOMER SATISFACTION AND CORPORATE PERFORMANCE

The philosophy of this book has been all about customer centricity and creating value for customers as a long-term core strategy. This perspective permeates many of the key concepts and models you have learned in this book, including the Service-Profit Chain, Cycle of Success, Service Talent Cycle, Wheel of Loyalty, and the Gaps Model. We therefore feel it is fitting to end this book with a final piece of evidence that long-term perspective and customer centricity will pay off financially.

There is convincing evidence of strategic links between the level of customer satisfaction with a firm's service offerings and overall firm performance. Researchers from the University of Michigan found that on average, every 1% increase in customer satisfaction is associated with a 2.4% increase in a firm's return on investment (ROI).[5] Analysis of companies' scores on the American Customer Satisfaction Index (ACSI) shows that, on average, among publicly traded firms, a 5% change in the ACSI score is associated with a 19% change in the market value of common equity.[6] In other words, by creating more value for the customer, as measured by increased satisfaction, the firm creates more value for its owners (*Service Insights 15.1*).

SERVICE INSIGHTS 15.1
Customer Satisfaction and Wall Street:
High Returns and Low Risk!

Does a firm's customer satisfaction levels have anything to do with its stock price? This was the research question Claes Fornell and his colleagues wanted to answer. More specifically, they examined whether investments in customer satisfaction led to excess stock returns (Fig. 15.3), and if so, whether these returns were associated with higher risks as would be predicted by finance theory.

The researchers built two stock portfolios, one hypothetical back-dated portfolio and a real-world portfolio that tracked stock market performance in real time over several years. Both portfolios only consisted firms that did well in terms of their customer satisfaction ratings, as measured by the American Customer Satisfaction Index (ACSI).

The ACSI-based portfolios were rebalanced once a year on the day when the annual ACSI results were announced. Only firms in the top 20% in terms of customer satisfaction ratings were included (firms were either retained if they already were in the top 20% last year, or firms that improved their satisfaction ranking into the top 20% were added to the portfolio). Firms that fell below the 20% cut-off were sold. The return and risk of both portfolios were measured and their risk-adjusted returns were then compared to broad market indices such as the S&P 500 and NASDAQ.

Their findings are striking for managers and investors alike! Fornell and his colleagues discovered that the ACSI-based portfolios generated significantly higher risk-adjusted returns than their market benchmark indices and outperformed the market. Changes in the ACSI ratings of individual firms were significantly related to their future stock price movement, and as another study showed, even CEO compensation.[7]

However, simply publishing the latest data on the ACSI index did not immediately move share prices as efficient market theory would have predicted. Instead, share prices seemed to adjust slowly over time as firms published other results (perhaps earnings data or other 'hard' facts which may lag behind changes in customer satisfaction). A recent study in a retail context confirmed this time lag, whereby increases in customer satisfaction were shown to lag operational improvements, and profits lagged increases in customer satisfaction. Therefore, becoming a service champion requires a longer term perspective.[8]

The conclusion is that acting faster than the market to

Figure 15.3: Can customer satisfaction data help to outperform the market?

changes in the ACSI index generated excess stock returns. This finding represents a stock market imperfection, but it is consistent with research in marketing, which holds that satisfied customers improve the level and the stability of cash flow.

In a later study, Lerzan Aksoy and her colleagues built on these findings and also confirmed that a portfolio based on ACSI data outperformed the S&P 500 index over a 10-year period and delivered risk-adjusted abnormal returns.

For marketing managers, the findings of both studies confirm that investments (or "expenses") into managing customer relationships and the cash flows they produce are fundamental to the firm's, and therefore shareholders' value creation.

Although the results are convincing, care must be taken while exploiting this apparent market inefficiency and investing in firms that show high increases in customer satisfaction in future ACSI releases as the efficient markets learn fast. It is evident from the movement of stock prices as a response of future ACSI releases. For more details about ACSI, visit www.theacsi.org.

Sources: Claes Fornell, Sunil Mithas, Forrest V. Morgeson III, and M.S. Krishnan, "Customer Satisfaction and Stock Prices: High Returns, Low Risk," *Journal of Marketing*, Vol. 70, January 2006, pp. 3–14. Lerzan Aksoy, Bruce Cooil, Christopher Groening, Timothy L. Keiningham, and Atakan Yalçin, "The Long-Term Stock Market Valuation of Customer Satisfaction," *Journal of Marketing*, Vol. 72, no. 4 (2008): 105–122.

CONCLUSION

Transforming an organization and maintaining service leadership is no easy task for even the most gifted leader. I hope that having worked through this book will help you to become a more effective marketer and leader in any service organization. I also hope we not only managed to equip you with the necessary knowledge, understanding and insights, but also with the beliefs and attitudes about what propels a firm to service leadership. If this book has motivated and excited you to become a service champion yourself, I as author have achieved my objectives.

For further readings, see the Appendix, where some of my favorite books and resources on services marketing and management are listed. If you have feedback and suggestions on how to further improve this book, do contact me via www.JochenWirtz.com or sg.linkedin.com/in/jochenwirtz. I would love to hear from you!

I started each chapter with inspirational quotes, and like to end the book with a final quote by Tony Robins: "*It's not knowing what to do, it's doing what you know*". On this note, I wish you enjoyment, fulfillment and success in applying what you have learned.

APPENDIX: FURTHER RESOURCES ON SERVICES MARKETING AND MANAGEMENT

Below is a list of useful books, websites, and resources which is not exhaustive, but provides a starting point for anyone who is interested in delving deeper into this exciting topic. I also list some earlier books as they are classics and are still highly relevant. I apologize should we have missed important sources and, if so, let me know and I will update the list in the next edition.

Books

- Janelle Barlow and Claus Moller (2008), *A Complaint is a Gift*, 2nd Ed. Berrett-Koehler Publishers.

- Jonah Berger (2013), *Contagious: Why Things Catch On*. Simon & Schuster.

- Leonard L. Berry and Kent D. Seltman (2008), *Management Lessons from Mayo Clinic: Inside One of the Most Admired Service Organizations*. McGraw-Hill.

- Sriram Dasu and Richard B. Chase (2013), *The Customer Service Solution: Managing Emotions, Trust, and Control to Win Your Customer's Business*. McGraw Hill.

- Thomas J. DeLong, John J. Gabarro and Robert J. Lees (2007), *When Professionals Have to Lead: A New Model for High Performance*. Harvard Business School Press.

- James A. Fitzsimmons and Mona J. Fitzsimmons (2013), *Service Management: Operations, Strategy, Information Technology*, 8th Ed. McGraw–Hill.

- Frances Frei and Anne Morriss (2012), *Uncommon Service: How to Win by Putting Customers at the Core of Your Business*. Harvard Business Review Press.

- James L. Heskett, W. Earl Sasser, Jr. and Joe Wheeler (2008), *The Ownership Quotient*. Harvard Business School Press.

- Tony Hsieh (2013), *Delivering Happiness: A Path to Profits, Passion, and Purpose*. Grand Central Publishing.

- Robert Johnston, Graham Clark, and Michael Shulver (2012), *Service Operations Management: Improving Service Delivery*, 4th Ed. Prentice Hall.

- Robert F. Lusch and Stephen L. Vargo (2014), *Service-Dominant Logic: Premises, Perspectives, Possibilities*. Cambridge University Press.

- Richard L. Oliver (2010), *Satisfaction: A Behavioral Perspective on the Consumer*, 2nd Ed. M.E. Sharpe.

- Roland T. Rust, Katherine N. Lemon and Das Narayandas (2005), *Customer Equity Management*. Pearson Prentice Hall.

- Valarie A. Zeithaml, Mary Jo Bitner and Dwayne D. Gremler (2012), *Services Marketing: Integrating Customer Focus Across the Firm*, 6th Ed. McGraw–Hill.

- Laurie Young (2005), *Marketing the Professional Service Firm*. John Wiley & Sons.

Leading Service Research Centers and Their Websites

- The Cambridge Service Alliance at the University of Cambridge in England (http://cambridgeservicealliance.eng.cam.ac.uk).

- The Center for Excellence in Service of Robert H. Smith School of Business at University of Maryland (www.rhsmith.umd.edu/ces).

- The Center for Services Leadership at the W. P. Carey School of Business at Arizona State University (http://wpcarey.asu.edu/csl).

- The Institute of Service Excellence at the Singapore Management University (http://ises.smu.edu.sg).

- The Service Research Center at Karlstad University in Sweden (www.ctf.kau.se).

Listing of Other Resources

There are a number of websites and blogs of firms with in-depth service expertise and leading service providers, but blogs and their contents and focus change fast. I therefore list a few companies you can follow on LinkedIn or search for their websites and blogs;

- Firms: Accenture, Disney Institute, Forrester, McKinsey & Company, Salesforce.com, UP! Your Service College.[9]

- For a listing of leading service-related blogs see: *50 Customer Experience Blogs You Should Be Reading*, available at http://www.ngdata.com/50-customer-experience-blogs-you-should-be-reading.

- Service design and innovation uses many different tools and methods originating from various disciplines. Several websites provide further resources, e.g. ServiceDesignTools.org and ServiceDesignThinking.com.

ENDNOTES

Chapter 1

1   Organization for Economic Co-operation and Development, *The Service Economy*. Paris: OECD, 2000.

2   Michael Peneder, Serguei Kaniovsky, and Bernhard Dachs, "What Follows Tertiarisation? Structural Change and the Rise of Knowledge-Based Industries," *The Service Industries Journal*, 23, March 2003, pp. 47–66; Jochen Wirtz, Sven Tuzovic and Michael Ehret (2015), "Global Business Services: Increasing Specialization and Integration of the World Economy as Drivers of Economic Growth," *Journal of Service Management*.

3   Roland Rust and Ming-Hui Huang, "The Service Revolution and the Transformation of Marketing Science," *Marketing Science*, 33 (2), 2014: 206–221.

4   Marion Weissenberger-Eibl and Daniel Jeffrey Koch, "Importance of Industrial Services and Service Innovations," *Journal of Management and Organization*, No. 13 (2007): 88–101; Jochen Wirtz and Michael Ehret, "Creative Restruction — How Business Services Drive Economic Evolution," *European Business Review*, Vol. 21, No. 4 (2009), pp. 380–394.

5   Roland Rust and Ming-Hui Huang, "The Service Revolution and the Transformation of Marketing Science," *Marketing Science*, 33 (2), 2014: 206–221.

6   This section is based on: Michael Ehret and Jochen Wirtz (2010), "Division of Labor between Firms: Business Services, Non-ownership-value and the Rise of the Service Economy," *Service Science*, Vol. 2, No. 3, pp. 136–145; and Jochen Wirtz and Michael Ehret (2013), "Service-based Business Models: Transforming Businesses, Industries and Economies," in: *Serving Customers: Global Services Marketing Perspectives*, by Raymond P. Fisk, Rebekah Russell-Bennett, and Lloyd C. Harris (eds.), Tilde University Press, Melbourne, Australia, pp. 28–46.

7   McKinsey & Company, *Manufacturing the Future: The Next Era of Global Growth and Innovation*. McKinsey Global Institute, November 2012.

8   This section was adapted from Jochen Wirtz, Sven Tuzovic and Michael Ehret (2015), "Global Business Services: Increasing Specialization and Integration of the World Economy as Drivers of Economic Growth," *Journal of Service Management*.

9   This section is based on: Gereffi, G. and Fernandez-Stark, K. (2010), The Offshore Services Global Value Chain, Center on Globalization, Governance & Competitiveness, Duke University, March; Massini, S. and Miozzo, M. (2010), Outsourcing and Offshoring of Business Services: Challenges to Theory, Management and Geography of Innovation, Manchester Business School Working Paper, No. 604, Manchester; Sako, M. (2005), "Outsourcing and Offshoring: Key Trends and Issues," Emerging Markets Forum, November, Oxford, UK, http://brie.berkeley.edu/conf/Sako.pdf, accessed on 22 January 2016.

10   Diana Farrell, Martha A. Laboissière, and Jaeson Rosenfeld, "Sizing the Emerging Global Labor Market," *The McKinsey Quarterly*, No. 3, 2005, pp. 93–103.

11   Thomas H. Davenport and Bala Iyer, "Should You Outsource Your Brain?" *Harvard Business Review*, February 2009, p. 38; Paul Sergius Koku (2013), "A View from the Street: An Exploratory Study of Consumer Attitudes Toward Offshoring of Professional Services in the United States", *Journal of Services Marketing*, Vol. 29, No. 2, pp. 150–159.

12   Smith, Adam (1776), *The Wealth of Nations, Books I–III*, with an Introduction by Alan B. Krueger. London: Bantam Classics, 2003.

13   Say, Jean Baptiste (1803), *A Treatise on Political Economy: or. The Production Distribution and Consumption of Wealth. Translated by and with notes from C.R. Prinsep. M.A,* Scholarly Publishing Office, University of Michigan Library, 2005.

14   Lesley Brown (ed.), *Shorter Oxford English Dictionary,* 5ᵗʰ ed., 2002.

15   Rathmell, John M. (1966), "What is Meant by Services?" *Journal of Marketing,* 30 (October), pp. 32–36.

16   Evert Gummesson, (citing an unknown source) "Lip Service: A Neglected Area in Services Marketing," *Journal of Consumer Services,* No. 1, Summer 1987, pp. 19–22.

17   Christopher H. Lovelock and Evert Gummesson, "Whither Services Marketing? In Search of a New Paradigm and Fresh Perspectives," *Journal of Service Research,* 7, August 2004, pp. 20–41.

18   Adapted from a definition by Christopher Lovelock (identified anonymously as Expert 6, Table II, 112) in Bo Edvardsson, Anders Gustafsson, and Inger Roos, "Service Portraits in Service Research: A Critical Review," *International Journal of Service Industry Management,* 16, No. 1, 2005, pp. 107–121.

19   For recommendations for manufacturing firms to successfully offer services see: Werner Reinartz and Wolfgang Ulaga, "How to Sell Services Profitably," *Harvard Business Review,* May 2008: 90–96; Wolfgang Ulaga and Werner Reinartz, "Hybrid Offerings: How Manufacturing Firms Combine Goods and Services Successfully," *Journal of Marketing,* Vol. 75 (November 2011): 5–23; Andreas Eggert, Jens Hogreve, Wolfgang Ulaga and Eva Muenkhoff, "Revenue and Profit Implications of Industrial Service Strategies," *Journal of Service Research,* Vol. 17, No. 1, 2014: 23–39.

20   Theodore Levitt, *Marketing for Business Growth,* (New York, McGraw-Hill, 1974), p. 5.

21   Roland Rust and Ming-Hui Huang, "The Service Revolution and the Transformation of Marketing Science," *Marketing Science,* 33(2), 2014: 206–221.

22   Stephen L. Vargo and Robert R. Lusch, "Evolving to a New Dominant Logic for Marketing," *Journal of Marketing,* 9(2), 2004, 1–21; Stephen L. Vargo and Robert R. Lusch, "Service-dominant Logic: Continuing the Evolution," *Journal of the Academy of Marketing Science,* 36(1), 2008, pp. 1–10. For a recent review of the S-D logic, see Stephen L. Vargo, Robert R. Lusch and Cristina Mele, "Service for Service Exchange and Value Co-Creation," in: *Serving Customers: Global Services Marketing Perspectives,* by Raymond P. Fisk, Rebekah Russell-Bennett, and Lloyd C. Harris (eds.), Tilde University Press, Melbourne, Australia, pp. 208–228; Ingo O. Karpen, Liliana L. Bove, and Bryan A. Lukas, "Linking Service-Dominant Logic and Strategy Business Practice: A Conceptual Model of a Service-Dominant Orientation," *Journal of Service Research,* Vol. 15, No. 1, 2012: 21–38.

23   These classifications are derived from Christopher H. Lovelock, "Classifying Services to Gain Strategic Marketing Insights," *Journal of Marketing,* 47 (Summer 1983): 9–20.

24   Valarie A. Zeithaml, A. Parasuraman, Leonard L. Berry, "Problems and Strategies in Services Marketing." *Journal of Marketing,* 49, Spring 1985, pp. 33–46.

25   Christopher H. Lovelock and Evert Gummesson, "Whither Services Marketing? In Search of a New Paradigm and Fresh Perspectives," *Journal of Service Research,* 7, August 2004, pp. 20–41.

26   G. Lynn Shostack, "Breaking Free from Product Marketing," *Journal of Marketing,* 41 (April 1977): 73–80.

27   The 4 'P's classification of marketing decision variables was created by E. Jerome McCarthy, *Basic Marketing: A Managerial Approach,* (Homewood, IL: Richard D. Irwin, Inc., 1960.) It

was a refinement of the long list of ingredients included in the marketing mix concept, created by Professor Neil Borden at Harvard in the 1950s. Borden got the idea from a colleague who described the marketing manager's job as being a "mixer of ingredients."

28   An expanded 7 'P's marketing mix was first proposed by Bernard H. Booms and Mary J. Bitner, "Marketing Strategies and Organization Structures for Service Firms," in J. H. Donnelly and W.R. George, *Marketing of Services,* (Chicago: American Marketing Association, 1981, pp. 47–51).

29   The term "part-time marketer" was coined by Evert Gummesson, "The New Marketing: Developing Long-Term Interactive Relationships," *Long Range Planning,* Vol. 4, 1987. See also, Christian Grönroos, *Service Management and Marketing, 3rd ed.* Hoboken, NY: John Wiley & Sons, Ltd., 2007; and Evert Gummesson, *Total Relationship Marketing, 3rd* ed., Routledge, 2008.

30   James L. Heskett, Thomas O. Jones, Gary W. Loveman, W. Earl Sasser Jr., and Leonard A. Schlesinger, "Putting the Service Profit Chain to Work," *Harvard Business Review,* 72, March/April 1994; James L. Heskett, W. Earl Sasser, Jr., and Leonard A. Schlesinger, *The Service Profit Chain.* New York: The Free Press, 1997.

Chapter 2

1   Valarie A. Zeithaml, "How Consumer Evaluation Processes Differ Between Goods and Services," in J.A. Donnelly and W.R. George, eds. *Marketing of Services,* Chicago: American Marketing Association, 1981, pp. 186–190.

2   Interestingly, when buying credence services, consumers do not necessarily undertake a more comprehensive information search. Rather, they rely more on word-of-mouth from friends and family, credible publications such as consumer reports, and the recommendations by sales people; see: Kathleen Mortimer and Andrew Pressey (2013), "Consumer Information Search and Credence Services: Implications for Service Providers", *Journal of Services Marketing,* Vol. 27, No. 1, pp. 49–58.

3   Leonard L. Berry and Neeli Bendapudi, "Clueing in Customers," *Harvard Business Review,* 81, February 2003, pp. 100–107.

4   Valarie A. Zeithaml, Leonard L. Berry, and A. Parasuraman, "The Behavioral Consequences of Service Quality," *Journal of Marketing,* Vol. 60, April 1996, pp. 31–46; R. Kenneth Teas and Thomas E. DeCarlo, "An Examination and Extension of the Zone-of-Tolerance Model: A Comparison to Performance-Based Models on Perceived Quality," *Journal of Service Research,* 6, No. 3, 2004: 272–286.

5   Robert Johnston, "The Zone of Tolerance: Exploring the Relationship between Service Transactions and Satisfaction with the Overall Service," *International Journal of Service Industry Management,* 6, No. 5, 1995, 46–61; Michael Stodnick and Kathryn A. Marley, "A Longitudinal Study of the Zone of Tolerance," *Managing Service Quality,* 23(1), 2013, pp. 25–42.

6   Jan Carlzon, *Moments of Truth,* Cambridge, MA: Ballinger Publishing Co., 1987, p. 3.

7   Pierre Eiglier and Eric Langeard, "Services as Systems: Marketing Implications," in Pierre Eiglier, Eric Langeard, Christopher H. Lovelock, John E. G. Bateson, and Robert F. Young, eds. *Marketing Consumer Services: New Insights.* Cambridge, MA: Marketing Science Institute, Report #77-115, November 1977, pp. 83–103; Eric Langeard, John E. Bateson, Christopher H. Lovelock, and Pierre Eiglier, *Services Marketing: New Insights from Consumers and Managers,* Marketing Science Institute, Report #81-104, August 1981.

8   Richard B. Chase, "Where Does the Customer Fit in a Service Organization?" *Harvard Business Review,* 56, November–December 1978, pp. 137–142. Stephen J. Grove, Raymond P. Fisk, and Joby John, "Services as Theater: Guidelines and Implications," in Teresa A. Schwartz and Dawn Iacobucci, eds. *Handbook of Services Marketing and Management,* Thousand Oaks, CA: Sage, 2000, pp. 21–36.

9   Stephen J. Grove, Raymond P. Fisk and Joby John, "Services as Theater", *(op. cit.)* Kim Harris, and Steve Baron, "Theatrical Service Experiences: Dramatic Script Development with Employees," *International Journal of Service Industry Management,* 14, No. 2, 2003, pp. 184–199.

10   Stephen J. Grove and Raymond P. Fisk, "The Dramaturgy of Services Exchange: An Analytical Framework for Services Marketing," in L. L. Berry, G. L. Shostack, and G. D. Upah, eds. *Emerging Perspectives on Services Marketing,* Chicago, IL: The American Marketing Association, 1983, pp. 45–49.

11   Parts of this section were adapted from K. Douglas Hoffman and John E.G. Bateson, *Services Marketing: Concepts, Strategies, & Cases.* 4th ed., South-Western Cengage Learning, OH: Mason, USA, 2011, pp. 100–101.

12   The research in consumer behavior was based on earlier work in psychology, see Averill, J.R. (1973), 'Personal control over aversive stimuli and its relationship to stress', *Psychological Bulletin,* 80(4), pp. 286–303; and Langer, E.J. (1983), The Psychology of Control. Beverly Hills, CA: Sage. The following studies applied perceived control to service encounters: Michael K. Hui and John E.G. Bateson (1991), "Perceived Control and the Effects of Crowding and Consumer Choice on the Service Experience," *Journal of Consumer Research,* Vol. 18, No. 2, pp. 174–184. Michael K. Hui, and Roy Toffoli, "Perceived Control and Consumer Attribution for the Service Encounter", *Journal of Applied Psychology,* Vol 32, No. 9, 2006, pp. 1,825–1,844.

13   Richard B. Chase and Sriram Dasu, "Experience Psychology – A Proposed New Subfield of Service Management," *Journal of Service Management,* 25(5), 2014, pp. 574–577.

14   For an excellent and comprehensive review of the extant literature on customer satisfaction and its outcomes see: Richard L. Oliver, *Satisfaction: A Behavioral Perspective on the Consumer.* 2nd ed., NY: Armonk, M.E. Sharpe, 2010.

15   Richard L. Oliver, "A Cognitive Model of the Antecedents and Consequences of Satisfaction Decisions," *Journal of Marketing Research,* Vol. 17 (November 1980), pp. 460–469; Eugene W. Anderson, and Mary W. Sullivan (1993), "The Antecedents and Consequences of Customer Satisfaction for Firms," *Marketing Science,* 12 (Spring), pp. 125–143.

16   Ray W. Coye, "Managing Customer Expectations in the Service Encounter," *International Journal of Service Industry Management,* 15, No. 4, 2004: 54–71

17   Richard L. Oliver, *Satisfaction: A Behavioral Perspective on the Consumer.* 2nd ed., NY: Armonk, M.E. Sharpe, 2010.

18   Jochen Wirtz and Patricia Chew, "The Effects of Incentives, Deal Proneness, Satisfaction and Tie Strength on Word-of-Mouth Behavior," *International Journal of Service Industry Management,* 13, 2, 2002, pp. 141–162; V. Kumar, Ilaria Dalla Pozza, Jaishankar Ganesh, "Revisiting the Satisfaction-Loyalty Relationship: Empirical Generalizations and Directions for Further Research," *Journal of Retailing,* Vol. 89, No. 3, 2013, pp. 246–262. Timothy L. Keiningham, Larzan Aksoy, Edward C. Malthouse, Bart Lariviere, and Alexander Buoye, "The Cumulative Effect of Satisfaction with Discrete Transactions on Share of Wallet," *Journal of Service Management,* Vol. 25, No. 3, 2014, pp. 310–333.

19 Jaishankar Ganesh, Mark J. Arnold, and Kristy E. Reynolds, "Understanding the Customer Base of Service Providers: An Examination of the Differences Between Switchers and Stayers," *Journal of Marketing*, 64, No. 3, 2000, pp. 65–87; Jochen Wirtz, Ping Xiao, Jeongwen Chiang and Naresh Malhotra (2014), "Contrasting Switching Intent and Switching Behavior in Contractual Service Settings", *Journal of Retailing*, Vol. 90, No. 4, pp. 463–480.

20 Mittal, V., W.T. Ross and P.M. Baldasare (1998),'The asymmetric impact of negative and positive attribute-level performance on overall satisfaction and repurchase intentions', *Journal of Marketing*, 62 (1), pp. 33–47; Mittal, V., P. Kumar and M. Tsiros (1999),'Attribute-level performance, satisfaction, and behavioral intentions over time: a consumption-system approach', *Journal of Marketing*, 63(2), 88–101; Thomas Falk, Maik Hammerschmidt, Joeron J.L. Schepers, "The Service Quality-Satisfaction Link Revisited: Exploring Asymmetries and Dynamics," *Journal of the Academy of Marketing Science*, Vol. 38, No. 3, 2010, pp. 288–301.

21 Christian Grönroos, *Service Management and Marketing. 3rd ed.* Chichester, NY: Wiley, 2007.

22 For a detailed discussion on the difference between customer satisfaction and service quality at the encounter (or individual transaction level) and the global overall constructs see: Richard L. Oliver, *Satisfaction: A Behavioral Perspective on the Consumer.* 2nd ed., NY: Armonk, M.E. Sharpe, 2010, pp. 173–185.

23 Boulding, W., A. Kalia, R. Staelin, and V.A. Zeithaml (1993), 'A dynamic process model of service quality: from expectations to behavioral intentions', *Journal of Marketing Research*, 30 (1), pp. 7–27; Palmer, A. and M. O'Neill (2003), 'The effects of perceptual processes on the measurement of service quality', *Journal of Services Marketing*, 17(3), pp. 254–274.

24 Valarie A. Zeithaml, A. Parasuraman, and Leonard L. Berry, *Delivering Quality Service* (New York: The Free Press, 1990). See also Valarie A. Zeithaml, Mary Jo Bitner, and Dwayne D. Gremler, Services Marketing: Integrating Customer Focus Across the Firm. McGraw-Hill, NY: New York, 2013, pp. 49–105.

25 A. Parasuraman, Valarie A. Zeithaml, and Leonard Berry, "SERVQUAL: A Multiple Item Scale for Measuring Consumer Perceptions of Service Quality," *Journal of Retailing*, 64 (1988): 12–40.

26 See, for instance, Anne M. Smith, "Measuring Service Quality: Is SERVQUAL Now Redundant?" *Journal of Marketing Management,* 11 (Jan/Feb/April 1995): 257–276; Francis Buttle, "SERVQUAL: Review, Critique, Research Agenda," *European Journal of Marketing*, 30, No. 1, (1996): 8–32; Simon S.K. Lam and Ka Shing Woo, "Measuring Service Quality: A Test-Retest Reliability Investigation of SERVQUAL," *Journal of the Market Research Society,* 39 (April 1997): 381–393; Terrence H. Witkowski, and Mary F. Wolfinbarger, "Comparative Service Quality: German and American Ratings Across Service Settings," *Journal of Business Research,* 55 (2002): 875–881; Lisa J. Morrison Coulthard, "Measuring Service Quality: A Review and Critique of Research Using SERVQUAL," *International Journal of Market Research,* 46 (Quarter 4, 2004): 479–497.

27 Gerhard Mels, Christo Boshoff, and Denon Nel, "The Dimensions of Service Quality: The Original European Perspective Revisited," *The Service Industries Journal,* 17 (January 1997): 173–189; see also: Christian Grönroos, *Service Management and Marketing, 3rd ed.,* Chichester, NY: Wiley, 2007), pp. 84–86.

Chapter 3

1 Roland Rust and Ming-Hui Huang, "The Service Revolution and the Transformation of Marketing Science," *Marketing Science, 33(2), 2014: 206–221.

2   Daniel Yankelovich and David Meer, "Rediscovering Marketing Segmentation," *Harvard Business Review*, 84, No. 2, 2006, pp. 122-131. A best practice example in a B2B context is discussed in: Ernest Waaser, Marshall Dahneke, Michael Pekkarinen, and Michael Weissel, "How You Slice It: Smarter Segmentation for Your Sales Force," *Harvard Business Review*, 82, No. 3, 2004, pp. 105−111.

3   Frances X. Frei, "The Four Things a Service Business Must Get Right," *Harvard Business Review*, April 2008, pp. 70−80.

4   Robert Johnston, "Achieving Focus in Service Organizations," *The Service Industries Journal*, 16, January 1996, pp. 10−20.

5   For a detailed approach to exploring synergies in marketing or production, see Michael E. Porter, *Competitive Strategy*, Chapter 3, "A Framework for Competitor Analysis" (New York: The Free Press, 1980), pp. 47–74.

6   Frances Frei and Anne Morriss (2012), *Uncommon Service: How to Win by Putting Customers at the Core of Your Business*. MA: Boston, Harvard Business Review Press.

7   George S. Day, *Market Driven Strategy*. New York: The Free Press, 1990, p. 164.

8   Jack Trout, *The New Positioning: The Latest on the World's #1 Business Strategy*. New York: McGraw-Hill, 1997.

9   Kevin Lane Keller, Brian Sternthal, and Alice Tybout, "Three Questions You Need to Ask about Your Brand," *Harvard Business Review*, 80, September 2002, p. 84.

10   Roger Brown, "How We Built a Strong Company in a Weak Industry," *Harvard Business Review*, 79, February 2001, pp. 51−57.

11   W. Chan Kim and Renée Mauborgne, "Charting Your Company's Future," *Harvard Business Review*, 80, June 2002, pp. 77–83.

12   Robert Simons (2014), "Choosing the Right Customer: The First Step in a Winning Strategy," *Harvard Business Review*, Vol. 92, No. 3, pp. 49–55. https://www.linkedin.com/company/linkedin, accessed 2 February 2016.

13   http://www.brandeo.com/positioning%20statement, accessed 2 February 2016.

Chapter 4

1   If you want to build a nest egg, do have a look at ETFs as they tend to be an excellent financial product for this purpose for retail investors. According to Salim Ramji, a consultant at McKinsey: "If you were inventing the mutual fund industry today, it would look like this [ETFs]". Exchange-traded Funds: From Vanilla to Rocky Road", The Economist, 25 February 2012; https://investor.vanguard.com and http://en.wikipedia.org/wiki/Exchange-traded_fund; accessed on 16 February 2016.

       For an excellent overview for retail investors, see: Burton G. Malkiel (2015), *A Random Walk Down Wall Street: The Time-Tested Strategy for Successful Investing*. 11th ed., W. W. Norton & Company.

2   Jochen Wirtz and May O. Lwin (2009), "Regulatory Focus Theory, Trust and Privacy Concern," *Journal of Service Research*, Vol. 12, No. 2, pp. 190–207; May O. Lwin, Jochen Wirtz and Jerome D. Williams (2007), "Consumer Online Privacy Concerns and Responses: A Power-Responsibility Equilibrium Perspective," *Journal of the Academy of Marketing Science*, 35(4), pp. 572–585.

3   James C. Anderson and James A. Narus, "Capturing the Value of Supplementary Services," *Harvard Business Review*, Vol. 73, January–February 1995, pp. 75–83.

4   Leonard L. Berry, "Cultivating Service Brand Equity," *Journal of the Academy of Marketing Science*, 28, No. 1, 2000, pp. 128–137.

5   James Devlin, "Brand Architecture in Services: The Example of Retail Financial Services, *Journal of Marketing Management*, 19, 2003, pp. 1,043–1,065.

6   David Aaker and Erich Joachimsthaler, "The Brand Relationship Spectrum: The Key to the Brand Challenge," *California Management Review*, 42, No. 4, 2000, pp. 8–23.

7   www.fedex.com, http://en.wikipedia.org/wiki/FedEx_Office, accessed 17 February 2016.

8   www.ihgplc.com, accessed 17 February 2016.

9   www.avis.com, accessed 17 February 2016.

10   www.britishairways.com, accessed on 17 February 2016

11   http://www.sun.com/service/serviceplans/sunspectrum/index.jsp accessed 7 May 2009.

12   Don E. Shultz, "Getting to the Heart of the Brand," *Marketing Management*, September–October 2001, pp. 8–9.

13   For an excellent and detailed introduction to the development of customer experience strategies, see:
     Phillip Klaus (2014), *Measuring Customer Experience: How to Develop and Execute the Most Profitable Customer Experience Strategies*. Palgrave MacMillan.
     For a review of experience marketing in general, see Bernd Schmitt (2010), "Experience Marketing: Concepts, Frameworks and Consumer Insights," *Foundations and Trends in Marketing*, Vol. 5, No. 2, pp. 55–112.

14   Sharon Morrison and Frederick G. Crane, "Building the Service Brand by Creating and Managing an Emotional Brand Experience," *Brand Management*, 14(5), 2007, pp. 410–421.

15   For an overview of service innovation research, see: Per Carlborg, Daniel Kindström and Christian Kowalkowski (2014), "The Evolution of Service Innovation Research: A Critical Review and Synthesis," *The Service Industries Journal*, Vol. 34, No. 5, pp. 373–398.
     For recent research on the impact of Internet- and people-enabled innovation on customer satisfaction and firm value, see: Thomas Dotzel, Venkatesh Shankar, and Leonard L. Berry (2013), "Service Innovativeness and Firm Value", *Journal of Marketing Research*, Vol. 50 (April), pp. 259–276.
     For research that integrated service innovation networks, organization- and customer co-creation, see: Luis Rubalcaba, Stefan Michel, Jon Sundbo, Stephen W. Brown, and Javier Reynoso (2012), "Shaping, Organizing, and Rethinking Service Innovation: A Multidimensional Framework," *Journal of Service Management*, Vol. 23, No. 5, pp. 696–715;
     For research examining the integration of planning and innovation, see: Jaakko Siltaloppi and Marja Toivonen (2015), "Integration of Planning and Execution in Service Innovation," *The Service Industries Journal*, Vol. 35, No. 2, pp. 197–216.
     For research on the elements of service innovation that classified those along the three core innovation types of new service concepts, new service processes, and new service business models, see: Jung-Kuei Hsieh, Hung-Chang Chiu, Chih-Ping Wei, HsiuJu Rebecca Yen, and Yu-Chun Cheng (2013), "A Practical Perspective on the Classification of Service Innovations", *Journal of Services Marketing*, Vol. 27, No. 5, pp. 371–384.

16   Talk by Rory Sutherland: Sweat the Small Stuff, http://www.ted.com/talks/lang/eng/rory_sutherland_sweat_the_small_stuff.html, accessed 17 February 2016.

17   *Harvard Business Review,* "Life's Work, Salman Khan", 2014, Vol. 92. No. 1/2, p. 124.

18   *The Economist,* "Learning New Lessons: Online Courses are Transforming Higher Education, Creating New Opportunities for the Best and Huge Problems for the Rest," 22 December 2012, pp. 95–96.

19   http://en.wikipedia.org/wiki/Space_tourism and http://www.spaceadventures.com/, accessed 17 February 2016.

20   Clayton M. Christenson, Scott Cook, and Taddy Hall, "Marketing Malpractice: The Cause and the Cure," *Harvard Business Review,* December 2005, pp. 4–12.

21   H. G. Parsa, John T. Self, David Njite, and Tiffany King, "Why Restaurants Fail," *Cornell Hotel and Restaurant Administration Quarterly,* 46, August 2005, pp. 304–322.

22   Scott Edgett and Steven Parkinson, "The Development of New Financial Services: Identifying Determinants of Success and Failure," *International Journal of Service Industry Management,* 5, No. 4, 1994, pp. 24–38; Christopher D. Storey and Christopher J. Easingwood, "The Impact of the New Product Development Project on the Success of Financial Services," *Service Industries Journal,* 13, No. 3, July 1993, pp. 40–54; Michael Ottenbacher, Juergen Gnoth, and Peter Jones, "Identifying Determinants of Success in Development of New High-Contact Services," *International Journal of Service Industry Management,* 17, No. 4, 2006, pp. 344–363.

23   Bo Edvardsson, Lars Haglund, and Jan Mattsson, "Analysis, Planning, Improvisation and Control in the Development of New Services," *International Journal of Service Industry Management,* Vol. 6, No. 2, 1995, pp. 24–35 (at page 34).
      See also Bo Edvardsson and Jan Olsson, "Key Concepts for New Service Development," *The Service Industries Journal,* Vol. 16 (April 1996), pp. 14–164.

24   Peter R. Magnusson, Jonas Matthing, and Per Kristensson, "Managing User Involvement in Service Innovation: Experiments with Innovating End Users," *Journal of Service Research,* 6, November 2003, pp. 111–124; Jonas Matthing, Bodil Sandén, and Bo Edvardsson, "New Service Development: Learning from and with Customers," *International Journal of Service Industry Management,* 15, No. 5, 2004, pp. 479–498.

25   Kevin J. Boudreau and Karim R. Lakhani (2013), "Using the Crowd as an Innovation Partner," *Harvard Business Review,* Vol. 91, No. 4, pp. 61–69.

Chapter 5

1   Jochen Wirtz and Jeannette P. T. Ho, "Westin in Asia: Distributing Hotel Rooms Globally," in Jochen Wirtz and Christopher H. Lovelock, eds. *Services Marketing in Asia — A Case Book.* Singapore: Prentice Hall, 2005, pp. 253–259. www.starwoodhotels.com, accessed 21 February 2016.

2   Research on the adoption of self-service technologies includes: Matthew L. Meuter, Mary Jo Bitner, Amy L. Ostrom, and Stephen W. Brown, "Choosing Among Alternative Service Delivery Modes: An Investigation of Customer Trial of Self-Service Technologies," *Journal of Marketing,* 69, April 2005, pp. 61–83; James M. Curran and Matthew L. Meuter, "Self-Service Technology Adoption: Comparing Three Technologies," *Journal of Services Marketing,* 19, No. 2, 2005, pp. 103–113.

3   The section was based on the following research: Nancy Jo Black, Andy Lockett, Christine Ennew, Heidi Winklhofer, and Sally McKechnie, "Modelling Consumer Choice of Distribution Channels: An Illustration from Financial Services," *International Journal of Bank Marketing,* 20, No. 4, 2002, pp. 161–173; Jinkook Lee, "A Key to Marketing Financial Services: The Right Mix of Products, Services, Channels and Customers," *Journal of Services Marketing,* 16, No. 3, 2002,

pp. 238–258; Leonard L Berry, Kathleen Seiders, and Dhruv Grewal, "Understanding Service Convenience," *Journal of Marketing*, 66, No. 3, July 2002, pp. 1–17; Jiun-Sheng C. Lin and Pei-ling Hsieh, "The Role of Technology Readiness in Customers' Perception and Adoption of Self-Service Technologies," *International Journal of Service Industry Management*, 17, No. 5, 2006, pp. 497–517.

4   Madhumita Banerjee (2014), "Misalignment and Its Influence on Integration Quality in Multichannel Services", *Journal of Service Research*, Vol. 17, No. 4, pp. 460–474.

     Regarding optimizing the integration of physical and electronic channels in retailing, see: Stephen Mahar, P. Daniel Wright, Kurt M. Bretthauser, and Ronald Paul Hill (2014), "Optimizing Marketer Costs and Consumer Benefits Across 'Clicks' and 'Bricks'," *Journal of the Academy of Marketing Science*, Vol. 42, No. 6, pp. 619–641.

5   Paul F. Nunes and Frank V. Cespedes, "The Customer has Escaped," *Harvard Business Review*, 81, No. 11, 2003, pp. 96–105.

6   Locating a service outlet is in many ways akin to locating a retail facility. A detailed discussion on location in a retail context is provided in Barry Berman and Joel R. Evans (2013), *Retail Management: A Strategic Approach,* 12th ed., Upper Saddle River, New Jersey: Prentice Hall. Of particular interest are Chap. 9 "Trading-Area Analysis" and Chap. 12 "Site Selection". Parts of this section were adapted from these two chapters.

7   Michael A. Jones, David L. Mothersbaugh, and Sharon E. Beatty, "The Effects of Locational Convenience on Customer Repurchase Intentions across Service Types," *Journal of Services Marketing*, 17, No. 7 (2004): 701–712.

8   Erin Harris, "Inside Starbucks' GIS Strategy," www.retailsolutionsonline.com, published 22 April 2011, accessed on 24 February 2016.

9   *The Economist*, "Health Care in America: Medicine at the Mall", 6 April 2013, p. 66.

10   www.swissotel.com, and http://www.eyefortravel.com/node/9187, accessed 25 February 2016.

11   http://www.easyjet.com/en/cheap-flights, https://www.southwest.com/flight, accessed 24 February 2016.

12   For a special issues on franchising in services that features the latest academic thinking on this topic, see: *The Service Industries Journal*, Special Double Issue: Franchising in Services, editors: Domingo Ribeiro and Gary Akehurst, 2014, Vol. 34, No. 9–10; and *Journal of Retailing*, Special Issue: Franchising and Retailing, eds. Rajiv P. Dant, Marko Grünhagen and Josef Windsperger, 2011, Vol. 87, No. 3.

13   www.franchise.org, accessed 18 February 2016.

     If you are interested in potentially starting your own business as a franchisee, you should carefully research the franchise industry, the franchise model and the pros and cons of owning any particular franchise. The International Franchise Association has developed a resource full of tips and information to help you get started. Have a look at their website and at the posted franchising opportunities at http://www.franchise.org/franchise-opportunities.

14   James Cross and Bruce J. Walker, "Addressing Service Marketing Challenges Through Franchising," in Teresa A. Swartz and Dawn Iacobucci, eds. *Handbook of Services Marketing & Management*. Thousand Oaks, CA: Sage Publications, 2000, pp. 473–484; Lavent Altinay, "Implementing International Franchising: The Role of Intrapreuneurship," *International Journal of Service Industry Management*, 15, No. 5, 2004, pp. 426–443.

15   Quick Franchise Facts, Franchising Industry Statistics, http://www.azfranchises.com/franchisefacts.htm, accessed 25 February 2016.

16   Melih Madanoglu, Kyuho Lee, and Gary J. Castrogiovanni (2011), "Franchising and Firm Financial Performance among U.S. Restaurants", *Journal of Retailing*, Vol. 87, No. 3, pp. 406–417.

17   Scott Shane and Chester Spell, "Factors for New Franchise Success," *Sloan Management Review*, 39, Spring 1998, pp. 43–50.

18   Firdaus Abdullah and Mohd Rashidee Alwi, "Measuring and Managing Franchisee Satisfaction: A Study of Academic Franchising," *Journal of Modelling in Management*, 3, 2008, pp. 182–199.
        For more research on factors that affect the success of franchises, see Scott Weaven and Debra Grace "Franchisee Personality: An Examination in the Context of Franchise Unit Density and Service Classification," *European Journal of Marketing*, 43, No. 1/2, 2009, pp. 90–109; Markus Blut, Christof Backhaus, Tobias Heussler, David M. Woisetschläger, Heiner Evanschintzky, and Dieter Ahlert (2011), "What to Expect After the Honeymoon: Testing a Lifecycle Theory of Franchise Relationships", *Journal of Retailing*, Vol. 87, No. 3, pp. 306–319; Levent Altinay, Maureen Brookes, Ruth Yeung, and Gurhan Aktas (2014), "Franchisees' Perceptions of Relationship Development in Franchise Partnerships", *Journal of Service Research*, Vol. 28, No. 6, pp. 509–519.
        For a conceptual discussion and review on the critical role of knowledge management in franchising, see: Scott Weaven, Debra Grace, Rajiv Dant, and James R. Brown (2014), "Value Creation through Knowledge Management in Franchising: A Multi-level Conceptual Framework", *Journal of Services Marketing*, Vol. 28, No. 2, pp. 97–104.

19   For a discussion on what to watch for when parts of the service are outsourced, see Lauren Keller Johnson, "Outsourcing Postsale Service: Is Your Brand Protected? Before You Spin Off Repairs, or Parts Distribution, or Customer Call Centers, Consider the Cons as well as the Pros," *Supply Chain Strategy*, 1, No. 5, July 2005, pp. 3-5.

20   A recent study ranked the attractiveness of international markets for US-based franchise firms. The study concluded that key factors that determine a market's attractiveness were size of the market, country risks, and cultural and geographic distance. This made large European countries, and Canada, Japan and Australia the most attractive markets, while the small and unstable African counties were the least attractive. China and the other BRIC countries (i.e., Brazil, Russia, and India) were not so highly ranked in spite of their size because of their significant risks and large cultural and geographic distances.
        E. Hachemi Aliouche and Udo A. Schlentich (2011), "Towards a Strategic Model of Global Franchise Expansion", *Journal of Retailing*, Vol. 87, No. 3, pp. 345–365.

21   For more information on foreign market entry modes, read Shawn M. Carraher and Dianne H. B. Welsh, *Global Entrepreneurship*, Kendall Hunt Publishing Inc., 2009.

22   J. J. Boddewyn, Marsha Baldwin Halbrich and A. C. Perry, "Service Multinationals: Conceptualization, Measurement and Theory," *Journal of International Business Studies*, Fall 1986, pp. 41-58; Sandra Vandermerwe and Michael Chadwick, "The Internationalization of Services," *The Services Industries Journal*, 9, No. 1, January 1989, pp. 79–93.

Chapter 6

1   Joan Magretta, "Why Business Models Matter." *Harvard Business Review*, 80 (May 2002): pp. 86–92.

2   This section is based on: Robin Cooper and Robert S. Kaplan, "Profit Priorities from Activity-Based Costing," *Harvard Business Review* 69, No. 3, May–June 1991: 130–135; Craig A. Latshaw and Teresa M. Cortese-Daniele, "Activity-Based Costing: Usage and Pitfalls," *Review of Business*, Winter 2002, pp. 30–32; Robert S. Kaplan and Steven R. Anderson, "Time-Driven Activity Based Costing," *Harvard Business Review*, November, 2004; Daniel J. Goebel, Greg

W. Marshall, and William B. Locander, "Activity Based Costing: Accounting for a Marketing Orientation," *Industrial Marketing Management*, 27, No. 6, 1998, pp. 497–510; Thomas H. Stevenson and David W.E. Cabell, "Integrating Transfer Pricing Policy and Activity-Based Costing," *Journal of International Marketing*, 10, No. 4, 2002, pp.77–88.

3   Gerald E. Smith and Thomas T. Nagle, "How Much Are Customers Willing to Pay?" *Marketing Research*, Winter 2002, pp. 20–25.

4   Parts of this section are based on Leonard L. Berry and Manjit S. Yadav, "Capture and Communicate Value in the Pricing of Services," *Sloan Management Review*, 37, Summer 1996, pp. 41–51.

5   Anna S. Mattila and Jochen Wirtz, "The Impact of Knowledge Types on the Consumer Search Process — An Investigation in the Context of Credence Services," *International Journal of Service Industry Management*, 13, No. 3, 2002, pp. 214–230.

6   It has even be shown that music piracy can be reduced by making purchase and use of music more convenient. Ironically, the use of digital rights management (DRM), which has the aim to reduce unauthorized copying and piracy, actually increases piracy not because of consumers' unwillingness to pay but because of the inconvenience entailed in using DRM protected files. See Rajiv K. Sinha, Fernando S. Machado, and Collin Sellman (2010), "Don't Think Twice, It's All Right: Music Piracy and Pricing in a DRM-Free Environment," *Journal of Marketing*, Vol. 74, No. 2, pp. 40–54.

7   Leonard L. Berry, Kathleen Seiders, and Dhruv Grewal, "Understanding Service Convenience," *Journal of Marketing*, 66, July 2002, pp. 1–17. For study examining the tradeoff between price and effort (i.e., self-service), see Lan Xia and Rajneesh Suri (2014), "Trading Effort for Money: Consumers' Cocreation Motivation and the Price of Service Options", *Journal of Service Research*, Vol. 17, No. 2, pp. 229–242.

8   Laurie Garrow, "Online Travel Data: A Goldmine of New Opportunities," *Journal of Revenue and Pricing Management*, 8, No. 2/3, 2009, pp. 247–254.

9   Jochen Wirtz, Ping Xiao, Jeongwen Chiang and Naresh Malhotra (2014), "Contrasting Switching Intent and Switching Behavior in Contractual Service Settings", *Journal of Retailing*, Vol. 90, No. 4, pp. 463–480.

10   Kristina Heinonen, "Reconceptualizing Customer Perceived Value: The Value of Time and Place," *Managing Service Quality*, 14, No. 3, 2004, pp. 205–215.

11   For a review of the extant revenue management literature see: Sheryl E. Kimes and Jochen Wirtz (2015), "Revenue Management: Advanced Strategies and Tools to Enhance Firm Profitability", *Foundations and Trends in Marketing*, Vol. 8, No. 1, pp. 1–68.

12   For airline and hotel revenue management, see Yoon Sook Song, Seong Tae Hong, Myung Sun Hwang and Moon Gil Yoon, "MILP Model for Network Revenue Management in Airlines," *Journal of Business & Economics Research*, 6, No. 2, 2010, pp. 55–62; and demand for different fare classes: see Guillermo Gallego, Lin Li and Richard Ratliff, "Choice-based EMSR Methods for Single-leg Revenue Management with Demand Dependencies," *Journal of Revenue and Pricing Management*, 8, 2/3, 2009, pp. 207–240; Sunmee Choi and Anna S. Mattila, "Hotel Revenue Management and Its Impact on Customers' Perception of Fairness," *Journal of Revenue and Pricing Management*, 2, No. 4, 2004, pp. 303–314.

     For application of yield management to industries beyond the traditional airline, hotel and car rental contexts, see: Frédéric Jallat and Fabio Ancarani, "Yield Management, Dynamic Pricing and CRM in Telecommunications," *Journal of Services Marketing*, 22, No. 6, 2008, pp. 465–478; Sheryl E. Kimes and Jochen Wirtz, "Perceived Fairness of Revenue Management in the US Golf Industry," *Journal of Revenue and Pricing Management*, 1, No. 4, 2003, pp. 332–344; Sheryl E. Kimes and Jochen Wirtz, "Has Revenue Management Become Acceptable? Findings from an International Study and the Perceived Fairness of Rate Fences," *Journal of Service Research*, 6, November 2003, pp. 125–135; Richard Metters and Vicente Vargas, "Yield Management for the Nonprofit Sector," *Journal of Service Research*, 1, February 1999, pp. 215–226; Alex M. Susskind, Dennis Reynolds, and Eriko Tsuchiya, "An Evaluation of Guests' Preferred Incentives to Shift Time-Variable Demand in Restaurants," *Cornell Hotel and Restaurant Administration Quarterly*, 44, No. 1, 2004, pp. 68–84; Parijat Dube, Yezekael Hayel, and Laura Wynter, "Yield Management for IT Resources on Demand: Analysis and Validation of a New Paradigm for Managing Computing Centres," *Journal of Revenue and Pricing Management*, 4, No. 1, 2005, pp. 24-38; and Sheryl E. Kimes and Sonee Singh, "Spa Revenue Management," *Cornell Hospitality Quarterly*, 40, No. 1, 2009, pp. 82–95. Ting Li, Eric van Heck, Peter Vervest, "Information Capability and Value Creation Strategy: Advancing Revenue Management through Mobile Ticketing Technologies," *European Journal of Information Systems*, 18, 2009, pp. 38–51.

13   Hermann Simon and Robert J. Dolan, "Price Customization," *Marketing Management*, 7, Fall 1998, pp. 11–17.

14   Lisa E. Bolton, Luk Warlop, and Joseph W. Alba, "Consumer Perceptions of Price (Un)Fairness," *Journal of Consumer Research*, 29, No. 4, 2003, pp. 474–491; Lan Xia, Kent B. Monroe, and Jennifer L. Cox, "The Price is Unfair! A Conceptual Framework of Price Fairness Perceptions," *Journal of Marketing*, 68, October 2004, pp. 1–15. Christian Homburg, Wayne D. Hoyer, and Nicole Koschate, "Customer's Reactions to Price Increases: Do Customer Satisfaction and Perceived Motive Fairness Matter?" *Journal of the Academy of Marketing Science*, 33, No. 1, 2005, pp. 36–49.

15   Jim Guest, "Cell Hell" (p. 3) and "Complete Cell-Phone Guide," *Consumer Reports*, February 2003, pp. 11–27; Ken Belson, "A Monthly Mystery," New York Times, 27 August, 2005.

16   Scott Adams, *The Dilbert™ Future — Thriving on Business Stupidities in the 21ˢᵗ Century*. New York: Harper Business, 1997, p. 160.

17   Ian Ayres and Barry Nalebuff, "In Praise of Honest Pricing," *Sloan Management Review*, 45, Fall 2003, pp. 24–28.

18   Dean Foust, "Protection Racket? As Overdraft and Other Fees Become Huge Profit Sources for Banks, Critics See Abuses," *Business Week*, 5, February 2005, pp. 68–89.

19   Consumer Financial Protection Bureau (2014), *Data Point: Cecking Account Overdraft*, http://files.consumerfinance.gov/f/201407_cfpb_report_data-point_overdrafts.pdf, accessed 2 March 2016.

20   The banking examples and data in this section were from Dean Foust, "Protection Racket? As Overdraft and Other Fees Become Huge Profit Sources for Banks, Critics See Abuses," *Business Week*, 5, February 2005, pp. 68–89.

21   For the effect of charging or waiving penalties on loyalty and word-of-mouth behaviors, see Lan Xia and Monika Kukar-Kinney (2013), "Examining the Penalty Resolution Process: Building Loyalty Through Gratitude and Fairness", *Journal of Service Research*, Vol. 16, No. 4, pp. 518–532.

22   Parts of this section are based on Jochen Wirtz, Sheryl E. Kimes, Jeannette P. T. Ho, and Paul Patterson, "Revenue Management: Resolving Potential Customer Conflicts," *Journal of Revenue and Pricing Management*, 2, No. 3, 2003, pp. 216–228.

23   Jochen Wirtz and Sheryl E. Kimes, "The Moderating Role of Familiarity in Fairness Perceptions of Revenue Management Pricing," *Journal of Service Research*, 9, No. 3, 2007, pp. 229–240.

24   Judy Harris and Edward A. Blair, "Consumer Preference for Product Bundles: The Role of Reduced Search Costs," *Journal of the Academy of Marketing Science*, 34, No. 4, 2006, pp. 506–513.

25   Rafi Mohammed, "A Better Way to Make Deals on Meals," *Harvard Business Review*, January–February (2011): 25.

26   Florian v. Wangenheim and Tomas Bayon, "Behavioral Consequences of Overbooking Service Capacity," *Journal of Marketing*, 71, No. 4, October 2007, pp. 36–47.

27   Peter J. Danaher, "Optimal Pricing of New Subscription Services: An Analysis of a Market Experiment," *Marketing Science*, 21. Spring 2002, pp. 119–129; Gilia E. Fruchter and Ram C. Rao, "Optimal Membership Fee and Usage Price Over Time for a Network Service," *Journal of Services Research*, 4, No. 1, 2001, pp. 3–14.

28   Fabian Uhrich, Jan H. Schumann, and Florian von Wangenheim (2012), "The Impact of Consumption Goals on Flat-Rate Choice: Can "Hedonizing" a Service Increase Customers' Propensity to Choose a Flat Rate?" *Journal of Service Research*, Vol. 16, No. 2, pp. 216–230.

29   Irene C.L. Ng, David Xing Ding and Nick Yip (2013), Outcome-based Contracts as New Business Model: The Role of Partnership and Value-driven Relational Assets", *Industrial Marketing Management*, Vol. 42, No. 5, pp. 730–743; Irene C.L. Ng, Roger Maull and Nick Yip (2009), Outcome-based Contracts as a Driver for Systems Thinking and Service-Dominant Logic in Service Science: Evidence from the Defence Industry," *European Management Journal*, Vol. 27, No. 6, pp, 377–387.

30   Avery Johnson, "Northwest to Charge Passengers in Coach for Meals," *Wall Street Journal*, 16 February 2005.

31   Eoghan Macguire (2012), "'Hidden' Airline Charges: Dirty Tricks or Customer Choice?" for CNN, http://edition.cnn.com/2012/07/10/travel/airline-charges/index.html, accessed 27 February 2016.

32   Vineet Kumar (2014), "Making 'Freemium' Work", *Harvard Business Review*, Vol. 92, No. 5, pp. 27–29.

33   John Gourville and Dilip Soman, "Pricing and the Psychology of Consumption," *Harvard Business Review*, 9, September 2002, pp. 90-96.

34   Dilip Soman, "The Effect of Payment Transparency on Consumption: Quasi-Experiments from the Field," *Marketing Letters*, 14, No. 3, 2003, pp. 173–183.

35   See, for example, Anita Sharpe, "The Operation Was a Success; The Bill Was Quite a Mess," *Wall Street Journal*, (17 September 1997): 1; Gary Stoller, "Hotel Bill Mistakes Mean Many Pay Too Much," *USA Today*, 12 July 2005.

Chapter 7

1   Note that this chapter was not written to provide the reader with an in-depth understanding of marketing communications in general. Rather, the focus is on service-specific issues, while covering the basics of marketing communications.

For a detailed coverage of marketing communications in general, refer to William F. Arens, Michael F. Weigold, and Christian Arens (2013), *Contemporary Advertising & Integrated Marketing Communications*. 14th ed., NY: New York, McGraw-Hill; and George E. Belch and Michael A. Belch (2015), *Advertising and Promotion: An Integrated Marketing Communications Perspective*. 10th ed., NY: New York, McGraw-Hill.

2   Daniel Wentzel, Sven Henkel and Torsten Tomczak (2010), "Can I Live Up to That Ad? Impact of Implicit Theories of Ability on Service Employees' Responses to Advertising", *Journal of Service Research*, Vol. 13, No. 2, pp. 137–152; Mary Wolfinbarger Celsi and Mary C. Gilly (2010), "Employees as Internal Audience: How Advertising Affects Employees' Customer Focus", *Journal of the Academy of Marketing Science*, Vol. 38, No. 4, pp. 520–529.

3   JD Power's Consumer Center website includes ratings of service providers in finance and insurance, health care, telecommunications, and travel, plus useful information and advice, see http://www.jdpower.com/, accessed 22 March 2016.

4   Edward K. Strong (1925), "Theories of Selling", *Journal of Applied Psychology*, Vol. 9, No. 1, pp. 75–86.

5   Robert .J. Lavidge and Gary A. Steiner (1961), "A Model for Predictive Measurement of Advertising Effectiveness", *Journal of Marketing*, Vol. 25 (October), pp. 59–62.

6   Starbucks story on how coffee beans are grown and harvested, see vidoes on YouTube such as: https://www.youtube.com/watch?v=bNcx_E1x3D0, https://www.youtube.com/watch?v=lOjL4izOZNQ, and http://news.starbucks.com/news/starbucks-coffee-journey-the-first-10-feet-the-last-10-feet., accessed 21 March 2016.

7   For a good overview of message strategy, execution and styles, see Philip Kotler and Gary Armstrong (2014), *Chapter 14: Communicating Customer Value: Integrated Marketing Communications Strategy;* and *Chapter 15: Advertising and Public Relations,* in Principles of Marketing, 15th edition, NJ: New Jersey: Upper Saddle River, Person Education. See also: William F. Arens, Michael F. Weigold, and Christian Arens (2013), *Contemporary Advertising & Integrated Marketing Communications.* 14th ed., NY: New York, McGraw-Hill; and George E. Belch and Michael A. Belch (2015), *Advertising and Promotion: An Integrated Marketing Communications Perspective.* 10th ed., NY: New York, McGraw-Hill.

8   For a review, see Kathleen Mortimer and Brian P. Mathews, "The Advertising of Services: Consumer Views v. Normative Dimensions," *The Service Industries Journal,* Vol. 18, July 1998, pp. 14–19. See also James F. Devlin and Sarwar Azhar, "Life Would be a Lot Easier if We Were a Kit Kat: Practitioners' Views on the Challenges of Branding Financial Services Successfully," *Brand Management*, Vol. 12, No. 1, 2004, pp. 12–30.

9   Banwari Mittal, "The Advertising of Services: Meeting the Challenge of Intangibility," *Journal of Service Research,* 2, August 1999, pp. 98–116.

10   Banwari Mittal and Julie Baker, "Advertising Strategies for Hospitality Services," *Cornell Hotel and Restaurant Administration Quarterly*, 43, April 2002, pp. 51–63.

11   Donna Legg and Julie Baker, "Advertising Strategies for Service Firms," in C. Surprenant (ed.), *Add Value to Your Service.* Chicago: American Marketing Association, 1987, pp. 163–168. See also Donna J. Hill, Jeff Blodgett, Robert Baer and Kirk Wakefield, "An Investigation of Visualization and Documentation Strategies in Service Advertising," *Journal of Service Research,* Vol. 7, November 2004, pp. 155–166; Debra Grace and Aron O'Cass, "Service Branding: Consumer Verdicts on Service Brands," *Journal of Retailing and Consumer Services,* Vol. 12, 2005, pp. 125–139.

12   Banwari Mittal, "The Advertising of Services: Meeting the Challenge of Intangibility," *Journal of Service Research*, 2, August 1999, pp. 98–116.

13   See how a nonprofit organization optimized its marketing mix by shifting online spent to TV: "Boosting Demand in the "Experience Economy", *Harvard Business Review*, 2015, Vol. 93, No. 1/2, pp. 24–26.

14   Adrian Palmer (2011), *Principles of Services Marketing*. London: McGraw-Hill, 6th ed., p. 450.

15   Stephen J. Grove, Gregory M. Pickett, and David N. Laband, "An Empirical Examination of Factual Information Content among Service Advertisements," *The Service Industries Journal*, Vol. 15, April 1995, pp. 216–233.

16   "The Future of Advertising — The Harder Hard Sell," *The Economist*, 24 June, 2004.

17   *Ibid.*

18   Penelope J. Prenshaw, Stacy E. Kovar, and Kimberly Gladden Burke, "The Impact of Involvement on Satisfaction for New, Nontraditional, Credence-based Service Offerings," *Journal of Services Marketing*, 20, No. 7, 2006, pp. 439–452.

19   "Got Game: Inserting Advertisements into Video Games Holds Much Promise," *The Economist*, 9 June 2007, p. 69.

20   Experian, www.experian.co.uk, accessed 14 January 2009.

21   Seth Godin and Don Peppers, *Permission Marketing: Turning Strangers into Friends and Friends into Customers*. New York: Simon & Schuster, 1999; Ray Kent and Hege Brandal, "Improving Email Response in a Permission Marketing Context," *International Journal of Market Research*, 45, (Quarter 4, 2003, pp. 489–503; for recent work exploring customer opt-in and opt-out behaviors see: V. Kumar, Xi (Alan) Zhang, and Anita Luo (2014), "Modeling Customer Opt-In and Opt-Out in a Permission-Based Marketing Context", *Journal of Marketing Research*, Vol. 51, No. 4, pp. 403–419.

22   Gila E. Fruchter and Z. John Zhang, "Dynamic Targeted Promotions: A Customer Retention and Acquisition Perspective," *Journal of Service Research*, Vol. 7, August 2004, pp. 3–19.

23   Ken Peattie and Sue Peattie, "Sales Promotion — A Missed Opportunity for Service Marketers," *International Journal of Service Industry Management*, 5, No. 1, 1995, pp. 6–21.

24   Michael Lewis (2006), "Customer Acquisition Promotions and Customer Asset Value," *Journal of Marketing Research*, Vol. 43, No. 2, pp. 195–203.
      For research on how to optimize promotion campaign based on customer lifetime value, see: Yeliz Ekinci, Füsun Ulengin, and Nimet Uray (2014), "Using Customer Lifetime Value to Plan Optimal Promotions", *The Service Industries Journal*, Vol. 34, No. 2, pp. 103–122.

25   For instructions on how to register, refer to https://www.donotcall.gov/register/registerinstructions.aspx, accessed on 21 March 2016.

26   For more detailed chapters on marketing on the Internet and in social media, see: William F. Arens, Michael F. Weigold, and Christian Arens (2013), Chapter 17: Introducing Social Media, in *Contemporary Advertising & Integrated Marketing Communications*. 14th ed., NY: New York, McGraw-Hill, pp. 526–541; and George E. Belch and Michael A. Belch (2015), Chapter 15: The Internet: Digital and Social Media, in: *Advertising and Promotion: An Integrated Marketing Communications Perspective*. 10th ed., NY: New York, McGraw-Hill, pp. 497–524.

27   Stefan Lagrosen, "Effects of the Internet on the Marketing Communication of Service Companies," *Journal of Services Marketing*, 19, No. 2, 2005, pp. 63–69; Thorsten Hennig-Thurau, Edward C. Malthouse, Christian Friege, Sonja Gensler, Lara Lobschat, Arvind Rangaswamy and Bernd Skiera (2010), "The Impact of New Media on Customer Relationships," *Journal of Service Research*, Vol. 13, No. 3, pp. 311–330; Koen Pauwels, Peter S.H. Leeflang, Marije L. Teerling, and K.R. Eelko Huizingh (2011), "Does Online Information Drive Offline Revenues? Only for Specific Products and Consumer Segments", *Journal of Retailing*, Vol. 87, No. 1, pp. 1–17;

For an overview of direct digital marketing see: Alan Tapp, Ian Whitten, and Matthew Housden (2014), *Principles of Direct, Database and Digital Marketing.* 5th ed., Pearson Education, Harlow, United Kingdom.

28   Paul Smith and Dave Chaffey, *eMarketing Excellence.* Oxford, UK: Elsevier Butterworth-Heinemann, 2005, p. 173.

29   "The Future of Advertising — The Harder Hard Sell," *The Economist,* 24 June 2004.

30   Nadia Abou Nabout, Markus Lilienthal, and Bernd Skiera (2014), "Empirical Generalizations in Search Engine Advertising", *Journal of Retailing,* Vol. 90, No. 2, pp. 206–216.

31   Initial research also seems to suggest that customers acquired through search advertising have a higher lifetime value than customers acquired through traditional media, see: Tat Y. Chan, Chunhua Wu, and Ying Xie (2011), "Measuring the Lifetime Value of Customers Acquired from Google Search Advertising", *Marketing Science,* Vol. 30, No. 5, pp. 837–850.

32   Amin Sayedi, Kinshuk Jerath, and Kannan Srinivasan (2014), "Competitive Poaching in Sponsored Search Advertising and Its Strategic Impact on Traditional Advertising", *Marketing Science,* Vol. 33, No. 4, pp. 586–608.

33   Ron Berman and Zsolt Katona (2013), "The Role of Search Engine Optimization in Search Marketing", *Marketing Science,* Vol. 32, No. 4, pp. 644–651.

      It has even been shown that click through for common search terms is heavily concentrated on the organic list rather than sponsored links. This makes SEO critical; see Kinshuk Jerath, Liye Ma, and Young-Hoon Park (2014), "Consumer Click Behavior at a Search Engine: The Role of Keyword Popularity", *Journal of Marketing Research,* Vol. 51 (August), pp. 480–486.

34   Roland Rust and Ming-Hui Huang, "The Service Revolution and the Transformation of Marketing Science", *Marketing Science,* 33, (2), 2014: 206–221.

35   Yakov Bart, Andrew T. Stephen, and Miklos Sarvary (2014), "Which Products are Best Suited to Mobile Advertising? A Field Study of Mobile Display Advertising Effects on Consumer Attitudes and Behaviors", *Journal of Marketing Research,* Vol. 51 (June), pp. 270–285.

      For a detailed discussion on mobile marketing, see: Daniel Rowles (2014), *Mobile Marketing: How Mobile Technology is Revolutionizing Marketing, Communications, and Advertising.* London, United Kingdom: Kogan Page.

36   Stephanie Rosenbloom (2015), "Apps to Help Navigate Cruise Lines", *The New York Times,* p. TR2.

37   V. Kumar and Rohan Mirchandani (2012), "Increasing the ROI of Social Media Marketing", *Sloan Management Review,* Vol. 54. No. 1, pp. 55–61; Roxane Divol, David Edelman, and Hugo Sarrazin (2012), "Demystifying Social Media", *McKinsey Quarterly,* April.

38   Kathleen Seiders, Andrea Godfrey Flynn, Leonard L. Berry, and Kelly L. Haws (2015), "Motivating Customers to Adhere to Expert Advice in Professional Services: A Medical Service Context", *Journal of Service Research,* Vol. 18, No. 1, pp. 39–58.

39   Harvir S. Bansal and Peter A. Voyer, "Word-of-Mouth Processes Within a Services Purchase Decision Context," *Journal of Service Research,* 3, No. 2, November 2000, pp. 166–177.

40   Anna S. Mattila and Jochen Wirtz, "The Impact of Knowledge Types on the Consumer Search Process — An Investigation in the Context of Credence Services," *International Journal of Research in Service Industry Management* 13, No. 3, 2002, pp. 214–230.

41   Kim Harris and Steve Baron, "Consumer-to-Consumer Conversations in Service Settings," *Journal of Service Research*, 6, No. 3 (2004): 287–303.

42   Frederick F. Reichheld, "The One Number You Need to Grow," *Harvard Business Review*, 81, No. 12, 2003, pp. 46–55.

43   See Jacques Bughin, Jonathan Doogan and Ole Jorgen Vetvik, "A New Way to Measure Word-of-Mouth Marketing," *McKinsey Quarterly*, April (2010): 1–9.
      For online WOM, see: Shyam Gopinath, Jacquelyn S. Thomas, Lakshman Krishnamurthi (2015), "Investigating the Relationship Between the Content of Online Word of Mouth, Advertising and Brand Performance", *Marketing Science*, Vol. 33, No. 2, pp. 241–258.

44   Eugene W. Anderson, "Customer Satisfaction and Word of Mouth," *Journal of Service Research*, Vol. 1, August 1998, pp. 5–17; Magnus Söderlund, "Customer Satisfaction and Its Consequences on Customer Behavior Revisited: The Impact of Different Levels of Satisfaction on Word of Mouth, Feedback to the Supplier, and Loyalty, *International Journal of Service Industry Management*, Vol. 9, No. 2, 1998, pp. 169–188. Srini S. Srinivasan, Rolph Anderson and Kishore Ponnavolu, "Customer Loyalty in e-Commerce: An Exploration of its Antecedents and Consequences," *Journal of Retailing*, 78, No. 1 (2002): 41–50; Chatura Ranaweera and Kalyani Menon (2013), "For Better or Worse? Adverse Effects of Relationship Age and Continuance Commitment on Positive and Negative Word of Mouth", *European Journal of Marketing*, Vol. 47, No. 10, pp. 1,598–1,621.
      For a meta-analysis of research on word of mouth, see: Celso Augusto de Matos and Carlos Alberto Vargas Rossi, "Word-of-Mouth Communications in Marketing: A Meta-Analytic Review of the Antecedents and Moderators," *Journal of the Academy of Marketing Science*, Vol. 36, No. 4 (2008): 578–596.

45   Jeffrey G. Blodgett, Kirk L. Wakefield, and James H. Barnes, "The Effects of Customer Service on Consumers Complaining Behavior," *Journal of Services Marketing*, Vol. 9, No. 4 (1995): 31–42; Jeffrey G. Blodgett, and Ronald D. Anderson, "A Bayesian Network Model of the Consumer Complaint Process," *Journal of Service Research* 2, No. 4 (May 2000): 321–338; Stefan Michel, "Analyzing Service Failures and Recoveries: A Process Approach," *International Journal of Service Industry Management*, 12, No. 1 (2001): 20–33. James G Maxham III and Richard G Netemeyer, "A Longitudinal Study of Complaining Customers' Evaluations of Multiple Service Failures and Recovery Efforts," *Journal of Marketing*, 66, No. 4 (2002): 57–72.

46   http://en.wikiquote.org/wiki/Ron_Kaufman, accessed 21 March 2016.

47   Jochen Wirtz and Patricia Chew, "The Effects of Incentives, Deal Proneness, Satisfaction and Tie Strength on Word-of-Mouth Behaviour," *International Journal of Service Industry Management*, 13, No. 2, 2002, pp. 141–162; Tom J. Brown, Thomas E. Barry, Peter A. Dacin, and Richard F. Gunst, "Spreading the Word: Investigating Antecedents of Consumers' Positive Word-of-Mouth Intentions and Behaviors in a Retailing Context," *Journal of the Academy of Marketing Science*, 33, No. 2, 2005, pp. 123–138; John E. Hogan, Katherine N. Lemon, and Barak Libai, "Quantifying the Ripple: Word-of-Mouth and Advertising Effectiveness," *Journal of Advertising Research*, September 2004, pp. 271–280; Jonah Berger and Raghuram Iyengar (2013), "Communication Channels and Word of Mouth: How the Medium Shapes the Message", *Journal of Consumer Research*, Vol. 40 (October), pp. 567–579.
      To understand how different types of epidemics, including word-of-mouth epidemics, develop, see: Malcom Gladwell, *The Tipping Point*, Little, NY: Brown and Company, 2000, p. 32.
      For an award-winning book on how you can get people to share your message, read also: Jonah Berger (2013), *Contagious: Why Things Catch On*. Simon & Schuster; and view an interview with Berger at: http://knowledge.wharton.upenn.edu/article/contagious-jonah-berger-on-why-things-catch-on/.

For a study that identifies brand characteristics that stimulate WOM, see Mitchell J. Lovett, Renana Peres, and Ron Shachar (2013), "On Brands and Word of Mouth", *Journal of Marketing Research*, Vol. 50 (August), pp. 427–444.

For an excellent review on the interplay between WOM and advertising, see: Guillermo Armelini and Julian Villanueva (2010), "Marketing Expenditures and Word-of-Mouth Communications: Complements or Substitues?" *Foundations and Trends in Marketing*, Vol. 5, No. 1, pp. 1–53.

48   Phillipp Schmitt, Bernd Skiera, and Christophe Van den Bulte (2011), "Referral Programs and Customer Value", *Journal of Marketing*, Vol. 75, No. 1, pp. 46–59; V. Kumar, J. Andrew Petersen, and Robert P. Leone (2010), "Driving Profitability by Encouraging Customer Referrals: Who, When, and How", *Journal of Marketing*, Vol. 74, No. 5, pp. 1–17.

      It has even been shown that customers who make referrals via reward programs show increased loyalty. That is, recommenders' defection rates fell and average monthly spent increases, see: Ina Garnefeld, Andreas Eggert, Sabrina V. Helm, and Stephen S. Tax (2013), "Growing Existing Customers' Revenue Streams through Customer Referral Programs", *Journal of Marketing*, Vol. 77, No. 4, pp. 17–32.

49   Ping Xiao, Christopher S. Tang and Jochen Wirtz (2011), "Optimizing Referral Reward Programs Under Impression Management Considerations," *European Journal of Operational Research*, Vol. 215, No. 3, pp. 730–739; Jochen Wirtz, Chiara Orsingher, Patricia Chew and Siok Tambyah (2013), "The Role of Metaperception on the Effectiveness of Referral Reward Programs," *Journal of Service Research*, Vol. 16, No. 1, pp. 82–98; Peeter W.J. Verlegh, Gangseok Ryu, Mirjam A. Tuk, and Lawrence Feick (2013), "Receiver Responses to Rewarded Referrals: The Motive Inferences Framework", *Journal of the Academy of Marketing Science*, Vol. 41, No. 6, pp. 669–682.

50   Inès Blal and Michael C. Sturman (2014), "The Differential Effects of the Quality and Quantity of Online Reviews on Hotel Room Sales", *Cornell Hospitality Quarterly*, Vol. 55, No. 4, pp. 365–375.

51   For research on online reviews, see: Kristopher Floyd, Ryan Freling, Saad Alhoqail, Hyun Young Cho, and Traci Freling (2014), "How Online Product Reviews Affect Retail Sales: A Meta-Analysis", *Journal of Retailing*, Vol. 90, No. 2, pp. 217–232; Nga N. Ho-Dac, Stephen J. Carson, and William L. Moore (2013), "The Effects of Positive and Negative Online Customer Reviews: Do Brand Strength and Category Maturity Matter?", *Journal of Marketing*, Vol. 77, No. 6, pp. 37–53; Eric T. Anderson and Duncan I. Simester (2014), "Reviews Without a Purchase: Low Ratings, Loyal Customers, and Deception", *Journal of Marketing Research*, Vol. 51 (June), pp. 249–269; Andreas Munzel and Werner H. Kunz (2014), "Creators, Multipliers, and Lurkers: Who Contributes and who Benefits at Online Review Sites", *Journal of Service Management*, Vol. 25, No. 1, pp. 49–74.

52   Jochen Wirtz, Anouk den Ambtman, Josee Bloemer, Csilla Horváth, B. Ramaseshan, Joris Van De Klundert, Zeynep Gurhan Canli and Jay Kandampully (2013), "Managing Brands and Customer Engagement in Online Brand Communities," *Journal of Service Management*, Vol. 24, No. 3, pp. 223–244; Richard L. Gruner, Christian Homburg, and Bryan A. Lukas (2014), "Firm-Hosted Online Brand Communities and New Product Success", *Journal of the Academy of Marketing Science*, Vol. 42, No. 1, pp. 29–48.

53   Renee Dye, "The Buzz on Buzz," *Harvard Business Review*, (November–December 2000): 139–146. Sandeep Krishnarmurthy, "Viral Marketing: What Is It and Why Should Every Service Marketer Care?" *Journal of Services Marketing*, 15 (2001); Joseph E. Phelps, Regina Lewis, Lynne Mobilio, David Perry, and Niranjan Raman, "Viral Marketing or Electronic

Word-of-Mouth Advertising: Examining Consumer Responses and Motivations to Pass Along Emails," *Journal of Advertising Research*, December 2004, pp. 333–348; Robert V. Kozinets, Kristine de Valck, Andrea C. Wojnicki, and Sarah J.S. Wilner (2010), "Networked Narratives: Understanding Word-of-Mouth Marketing in Online Communities", *Journal of Marketing*, Vol. 74, No. 2, pp. 71–89; Jonah Berger and Katherine L. Milkman (2012), "What Makes Online Content Viral?", *Journal of Marketing Research*, Vol. 49 (April), pp. 192–205.

For a review of generation Y and their social media use, see: Ruth N. Bolton, A. Parasuraman, Ankie Hoefnagels, Nanne Migchels, Sertan Kabadayi, Thorsten Gruber, Yuliya Komarova Loureiro, and David Solnet (2013), "Understanding Generation Y and Their Use of Social Media: A Review and Research Agenda," *Journal of Service Management*, Vol. 24, No. 3, pp. 245–267.

54   Steve Jurvetson (2000), "What exactly is viral marketing?" *Red Herring*, Vol. 78, pp. 110–112.

55   "Selling Becomes Sociable," *The Economist*, 11 September 2010.

56   See also Barak Libai, Eitan Muller, and Renana Peres (2013), "Decomposing the Value of Word-of-Mouth Seeding Programs: Acceleration Versus Expansion", *Journal of Marketing Research*, Vol. 50 (April), pp. 161–176.

57   http://en.wikipedia.org/wiki/Twitter, accessed 21 March 2016.

58   This section draws on Philip Kotler and Gary Armstrong (2014), *Chapter 14: Communicating Customer Value: Integrated Marketing Communications Strategy,* in Principles of Marketing, 15th ed., NJ: New Jersey: Upper Saddle River, Person Education, pp. 426–453; and William F. Arens, Michael F. Weigold, and Christian Arens (2013), "Marketing and IMC Planning", in *Contemporary Advertising & Integrated Marketing Communications.* 14th ed., NY: New York, McGraw-Hill, pp. 263–267.

59   https://www.donotcall.gov/default.aspx, accessed 21 March 2016.

60   https://www.dmachoice.org, accessed 21 March 2016.

Chapter 8

1   To analyze, improve and design end-to-end customer journey using bottom-up (data driven) and top down judgment driven approaches, see: Alex Rawson, Ewan Duncan, and Conor Jones (2013), "The Truth About Customer Experience: Touchpoints Matter, But It's the Full Journey that Really Counts", *Harvard Business Review*, Vol. 91, No. 9, pp. 90–98.

2   G. Lynn Shostack (1984), "Designing Services That Deliver", *Harvard Business Review*, January–February, pp. 133–139; Jane Kingman-Brundage (1989), "The ABCs of Service System Blueprinting," in M.J. Bitner and L.A. Crosby (eds.), *Designing a Winning Service Strategy.* Chicago: American Marketing Association; Lia Patrício, Raymond P. Fisk, and João Falcãe Cunha (2008), "Designing Multi-Interface Service Experiences: The Service Experience Blueprint," *Journal of Service Research*, Vol. 10, No. 4, pp. 318–334.

For an excellent approach to designing and mapping complex service systems, see: Lia Patrício, Raymond P. Fisk, João Falcão e Cunha, and Larry Constantine (2011), "Multilevel Service Design: From Customer Value Constellation to Service Experience Blueprinting", *Journal of Service Research*, Vol. 14, No. 2, pp. 180–200.

An additional tool that helps to visualize service operations, processes and interactions involving networks of entities is the Process-Chain-Network (PCN) analysis, see: Scott E. Sampson (2012), "Visualizing Service Operations", *Journal of Service Research*, Vol. 15, No. 2, pp. 182–198.

3   Laurette Dube, Bernd H. Schmitt, and France Leclerc (1991), "Consumers' Affective Responses to Delays at Different Phases of a Service Delivery", *Journal of Applied Social Psychology*, Vol. 21 No. 10, pp. 810–820.

4   David Maister, now President of Maister Associates, coined the term "Opportunities to Screw Up" (OTSU) while teaching at Harvard Business School.

5   For descriptions of how poka-yokes can be used to improve business operations see: Sameer Kumar, Brett Hudson and Josie Lowry (2010), "Consumer Purchase Process Improvements in E-tailing Operations," *International Journal of Productivity and Performance Management*, Vol. 59, No. 4, pp. 388–403; Sameer Kumar, Angelena Phillips and Julia Rupp (2009), "Using Six Sigma DMAIC to Design a High-quality Summer Lodge Operation," *Journal of Retail & Leisure Property*, Vol. 8, No. 3, pp. 173–191.

6   This section is based in part on Richard B. Chase and Douglas M. Stewart, "Make Your Service Fail-Safe," *Sloan Management Review*, 35, Spring 1994, pp. 35–44.

7   This section was adapted from Jochen Wirtz and Monica Tomlin, "Institutionalizing Customer-driven Learning through Fully Integrated Customer Feedback Systems," Managing *Service Quality*, Vol. 10, No. 4 (2000): 205–215.

8   Parts of this section were based on: Sriram Dasu and Richard B. Chase (2013), *The Customer Service Solution: Managing Emotions, Trust, and Control to Win Your Customer's Business*. New York: McGraw-Hill. This book provides an excellent overview of designing service processes with emotional intelligence.

9   Adapted from: Sriram Dasu and Richard B. Chase (2013), *The Customer Service Solution: Managing Emotions, Trust, and Control to Win Your Customer's Business*. New York: McGraw-Hill, pp. 134–135.
        We added the item "start strong" based on the following research: Eric J. Arnould and Linda L. Price, "River Magic: Extraordinary Experience and the Extended Service Encounter," *Journal of Consumer Research*, Vol. 20, June 1993, pp. 24–25; Richard B. Chase and Sriram Dasu (2014), "Experience Psychology — A Proposed New Subfield of Service Management", *Journal of Service Management*, Vol. 25, No. 5, pp. 574–577.

10   David E. Hansen and Peter J. Danaher, "Inconsistent Performance during the Service Encounter: What's a Good Start Worth?" *Journal of Service Research*, Vol. 1 (February 1999), pp. 227–235; Richard B. Chase and Sriram Dasu OP. COIT., 2001. Richard B. Chase and Sriram Dasu, "Want to Perfect Your Company's Service? Use Behavioral Science." *Harvard Business Review*, 79, June 2001, pp. 79–84.
        A recent study also showed that a service failure at the end of an extended service encounter has a stronger impact on overall satisfaction than a failure earlier in the process; see: Ina Garnefeld and Lena Steinhoff (2013), "Primary versus Recency Effects in Extended Service Encounters", *Journal of Service Management*, Vol. 24, No. 1, pp. 64–81.

11   Sriram Dasu and Richard B. Chase (2010), "Designing the Soft Side of Customer Service," *MIT Sloan Management Review*, Vol. 52, No. 1, pp. 33–39.

12   Mitchell T. Rabkin, MD, cited in Christopher H. Lovelock, *Product Plus*. New York: McGraw-Hill, 1994, pp. 354–355.

13   Source: Christopher Lovelock (1994), *Product Plus*. New York: McGraw-Hill, p. 355.

14   See, for example, Michael Hammer and James Champy, *Reengineering the Corporation: A Manifesto for Business Revolution*, (New York: Harper Business, revised edition, 2006).

For a nice documentation of a service process redesign cum introducing cross-functional teams, see: Agneta Larsson, Mats Johansson, Fredrik Bååthe, and Sanna Neselius (2012), "Reducing Throughput Time in a Service Organization by Introducing Cross-Functional Teams", *Production Planning & Control*, Vol. 23, No. 7, pp. 571–580.

15   www.patientvisitredesign.com, accessed 30 April 2016.

16   This section is partially based on Leonard L. Berry and Sandra K. Lampo, "Teaching an Old Service New Tricks — The Promise of Service Redesign," *Journal of Service Research*, 2, no. 3 (2000): 265–275. Berry and Lampo identified the five service redesign concepts: self-service, direct service, pre-service, bundled service, and physical service. We expanded some of these concepts in this section to embrace more of the productivity enhancing aspects of process redesign.

17   Parts of this section were adapted from: Robert Johnston, Graham Clark, and Michael Shulver (2012), *Service Operations Management: Improving Service Delivery.* 4ᵗʰ ed., Essex, United Kingdom: Pearson Education.

18   Leonard L. Berry and Sandra K. Lampo, "Teaching an Old Service New Tricks — The Promise of Service Redesign," *Journal of Service Research,* 2, No. 3 (February 2000): 265–275.

19   Victoria Ho, "Businesses Swallow the Tablet and Smile," *The Business Times*, 14 March 2011.

20   Atsuko Fukase (2015), "Robots to Greet Customers at Japanese Bank", The Wall Street Journal, 13 January 2015. http://blogs.wsj.com/japanrealtime/2015/01/13/robots-to-greet-customers-at-japanese-bank, accessed on 3 May 2016.

21   Amy Risch Rodie and Susan Schultz Klein, "Customer Participation in Services Production and Delivery," in T. A. Schwartz and D. Iacobucci, eds. *Handbook of Service Marketing and Management.* Thousand Oaks, CA: Sage Publications, 2000, pp. 111–125.

22   Mary Jo Bitner, William T. Faranda, Amy R. Hubbert, and Valarie A. Zeithaml, "Customer Contributions and Roles in Service Delivery," *International Journal of Service Industry Management*, 8, No. 3, 1997, pp. 193–205.

23   There is a large body of literature dealing with customer co-creation of value. Key articles include: Atefeh Yazdanparast, Ila Manuj and Stephen M. Swartz, "Co-creating Logistics Value: A Service-Dominant Logic Perspective," *The International Journal of Logistics Management*, 21, No. 3, 2010: 375–403; Evert Gummesson, Robert F. Lusch and Stephen L. Vargo, "Transitioning from Service Management to Service-Dominant Logic," *International Journal of Quality and Service Sciences*, 2, No. 1, 2010: 8–22; Kristina Heinonen, Tore Strandvik and Karl-Jacob Mickelsson, "A Customer-Dominant Logic of Service," *Journal of Service Management*, 21, No. 4, 2010: 531–548; Robert F. Lusch, Stephen L. Vargo and Matthew O'Brien, "Competing Through Service: Insights from Service Dominant Logic," *Journal of Retailing*, 83, No. 1, 2007: 5–18; Stephen L. Vargo and Robert F. Lusch, "Service-Dominant Logic: Continuing the Evolution," *Journal of the Academy of Marketing Science*, 36, No. 1, 2008: 1–10. Loic Ple and Ruben Chumpitaz Caceres, "Not Always Co-Creation: Introducing Interactional Co-Destruction of Value in Service-Dominant Logic" *Journal of Services Marketing*, 24, No. 6, 2010: 430–437.

Additional important research on customer participation in service processes is published in: Kimmy Wa Chan, Chi Kin (Bennett) Yim, and Simon S.K. Lam (2010), "Is Customer Participation in Value Creation a Double-Edged Sword? Evidence from Professional Financial Services Across Cultures", *Journal of Marketing*, Vol. 74, No. 3, pp. 48–64; Andrew S. Gallan, Cheryl Burke Jarvis, Stephen W. Brown, and Mary Jo Bitner (2013), "Customer Positivity and Participation in Services: An Empirical Test in a Health Care Context", *Journal of the Academy of Marketing Science*, Vol. 41, No. 3, pp. 338–356; Thomas Eichentopf, Michael Kleinaltenkamp, and Janine van Stiphout (2011), "Modelling Customer Process Activities in Interactive Value Creation", *Journal of Service Management*, Vol. 22, No. 5, pp. 650–663; Beibei Dong, K. Sivakumar, Kenneth R. Evans, and Shaoming Zou (2015), "Effect of Customer Participation on Service Outcomes: The Moderating Role of Participation Readiness", *Journal of Service Research*, Vol. 18, No. 2, pp. 160–176.

24   Stephen S. Tax, Mark Colgate, and David E. Bowen, "How to Prevent Customers from Failing," *MIT Sloan Management Review*, 47, Spring 2006, pp. 30–38.

25   Matthew L. Meuter, Amy L. Ostrom, Robert I. Roundtree, and Mary Jo Bitner, "Self-Service Technologies: Understanding Customer Satisfaction with Technology-Based Service Encounters," *Journal of Marketing*, 64, July 2000, pp. 50–64.

26   Gerard Haübl and Kyle B. Murray, "Preference Construction and Persistence in Digital Marketplaces: The Role of Electronic Recommendation Agents," *Journal of Consumer Psychology*, 13, No. 1, 2003, pp. 75–91; Lerzan Aksoy, Paul N. Bloom, Nicholas H. Lurie, and Bruce Cooil, "Should Recommendation Agents Think Like People?" *Journal of Service Research*, 8, May 2006, pp. 297–315.

27   Sterling A. Bone, Paul W. Fombelle, Kristal R. Ray, and Katherine N. Lemon (2015), "How Customer Participation in B2B Peer-to-Peer Problem-Solving Communities Influences the Need for Traditional Customer Service", *Journal of Service Research*, Vol. 18, No. 1, pp. 23–38.

28   Matthew L. Meuter, Mary Jo Bitner, Amy L. Ostrom, and Stephen W. Brown, "Choosing Among Alternative Service Delivery Modes: An Investigation of Customer Trial of Self-Service Technologies," *Journal of Marketing*, 69, April 2005, pp. 61–83.

29   A large number of studies examined the attitudes and perceptions that drive adoption of SST. Important studies include: James M. Curran, Matthew L. Meuter, and Carol G. Surprenant, "Intentions to Use Self-Service Technologies: A Confluence of Multiple Attitudes," *Journal of Service Research*, 5, February 2003, pp. 209–224; Joel E. Collier and Daniel L. Sherrell (2010), "Examining the Influence of Control and Convenience in a Self-Service Setting", *Journal of the Academy of Marketing Science*, Vol. 38, No. 4, pp. 490–509; Jeffrey S. Smith, Mark R. Gleim, Stacey G. Robinson, William J. Kettinger, and Sung-Hee 'Sunny' Park (2014), "Using an Old Dog for New Tricks: A Regulatory Focus Perspective on Consumer Acceptance of RFID Applications", *Journal of Service Research*, Vol. 17, No. 1, pp. 85–101; Katja Gelbrich and Britta Sattler (2014), "Anxiety, Crowding, and Time Pressure in Public Self-Service Technology Acceptance", *Journal of Service Marketing*, Vol. 28, No. 1, pp. 82–94; Toni Hilton, Tim Hughes, Ed Little and Ebi Marandi (2013), "Adopting Self-Service Technology to Do More with Less", *Journal of Service Marketing*, Vol. 27, No. 1, pp. 3–12; Joel E. Collier and Sheryl E. Kimes, "Only if it is Convenient: Understanding How Convenience Influences Self-Service Technology Evaluation", *Journal of Service Research*, Vol. 16, No. 1, pp. 39–51.

30   Pratibha A. Dabholkar, "Consumer Evaluations of New Technology-Based Self-Service Options: An Investigation of Alternative Models of Service Quality," International *Journal of Research in Marketing*, 13, 1996, pp. 29–51; David G. Mick and Susan Fournier, "Paradoxes of Technology: Consumer Cognizance, Emotions, and Coping Strategies," *Journal of Consumer Research*, 25, September 1998, pp. 123–143; Mary Jo. Bitner, Stephen W. Brown, and Matthew L. Meuter, "Technology Infusion in Service Encounters," *Journal of the Academy of Marketing Science*, 28, No. 1, 2000, pp. 138–149; Dabholkar *et al.*, 2003 op. cit. Maria Åkesson, Bo Edvardsson, and Bård Tronvoll (2014), "Customer Experience from a Self-Service System Perspective", *Journal of Service Management*, Vol. 25, No. 5, pp. 677–698; Meuter *et al.*, 2000; Mary Jo Bitner, "Self-Service Technologies: What Do Customers Expect?" *Marketing Management*, Spring 2001, pp. 10–11.

31   Jeffrey F. Rayport and Bernard J. Jaworski, "Best Face Forward," *Harvard Business Review*, 82, December 2004,

32   Kortney Stringer, "Have a Pleasant Trip: Eliminate All Human Contact," *Wall Street Journal*, 31 October 2002.

33   Cheng Wang, Jennifer Harris, and Paul Patterson (2013), "The Roles of Habit, Self-Efficacy, and Satisfaction in Driving Continued Use of Self-Service Technologies: A Longitudinal Study", *Journal of Service Research*, Vol. 16, No. 3, pp. 400–414.
       If a SST is perceived as delivering service quality, it has a positive impact on the intention to return to a retail store; see Hyun-Joo Lee, Ann E. Fairhurst and Min-Young Lee, "The Importance of Self-Service Kiosks in Developing Consumers' Retail Patronage Intentions," *Managing Service Quality*, 19, No. 6, 2009: 687–701.

34   Neeli Bendapudi and Robert P. Leone, "Psychological Implications of Customer Participation in Co-Production," *Journal of Marketing*, 67, January 2003, pp. 14–28.

35   Zhen Zhu, Cheryl Nakata, K. Sivakumar, and Dhruv Grewal (2013), "Fix It or Leave It? Customer Recovery from Self-Service Technology Failures", *Journal of Retailing*, Vol. 89, No. 1, pp. 15–29.

36   Bitner, 2001, op. cit.

37   Brad Stone (2013), *The Everything Store: Jeff Bezos and the Age of Amazon*. Little, Brown and Company.

38   Machiel J. Reinders, Pratibha A. Dabholkar, and Ruud T. Frambach, "Consequences of Forcing Consumers to Use Technology-Based Self-Service," *Journal of Service Research*, 11, No. 2, 2008, pp. 107–123.

Chapter 9

1   Kenneth J. Klassen and Thomas R. Rohleder, "Combining Operations and Marketing to Manage Capacity and Demand in Services," *The Service Industries Journal*, 21, April 2001, pp. 1–30.

2   Breffni M. Noone, Sheryl E. Kimes, Anna S. Mattila, and Jochen Wirtz, "The Effect of Meal Pace on Customer Satisfaction," *Cornell Hospitality Quarterly*, 48, No. 3, 2007, pp. 231–245; 14. Breffni M. Noone, Jochen Wirtz and Sheryl E. Kimes (2012), "The Effect of Perceived Control on Consumer Responses to Service Encounter Pace: A Revenue Management Perspective," *Cornell Hospitality Quarterly*, Vol. 53, No. 4, pp. 295–307.

3   Based on material in James A. Fitzsimmons and M.J. Fitzsimmons, *Service Management: Operations, Strategy, and Information Technology*, 6th ed. New York: Irwin McGraw-Hill, 2008; W. Earl Sasser, Jr., "Match Supply and Demand in Service Industries," *Harvard Business Review*, 54, November–December 1976, pp. 133–140

4   See also the discussion on bottlenecks in service processes and how to balance the capacity in each of the steps in a customer service process (Chapter 8, Designing Service Processes) to maximize overall process capacity.

5   Kenneth J. Klassen and Thomas R. Rohleder, "Using Customer Motivations to Reduce Peak Demand: Does It Work?" *The Service Industries Journal*, 24, September 2004, pp. 53–70.

6   http://en.wikipedia.org/wiki/Queueing_theory, accessed on 25 March 2016.

7   The Case Bank's survey were reported in: "Contactless Payments in a 'blink'", http://www.cr80news.com/news-item/contactless-payments-in-a-blink/, accessed on 25 March 2016.

8   Kelly A. McGuire and Sheryl E. Kimes, "The Perceived Fairness of Waitlist-Management Techniques for Restaurants," *Cornell Hotel and Restaurant Administration Quarterly*, 47, May 2006, pp. 121–134.

9   Anat Rafaeli, G. Barron, and K. Haber, "The Effects of Queue Structure on Attitudes," *Journal of Service Research*, 5, November 2002, pp. 125–139.

10   Duncan Dickson, Robert C. Ford, and Bruce Laval, "Managing Real and Virtual Waits in Hospitality and Service Organizations," *Cornell Hotel and Restaurant Administration Quarterly*, 46, February 2005, pp. 52–68.

11   Ana B. Casado Diaz and Francisco J. Más Ruiz, "The Consumer's Reaction to Delays in Service," *International Journal of Service Industry Management*, 13, No. 2, 2002, pp. 118–140.

12   Frederic Bielen and Nathalie Demoulin, "Waiting Time Influence on the Satisfaction-Loyalty Relationship in Services," *Managing Service Quality*, 17, No. 2, 2007: 174–193.

13   Jay R. Chernow, "Measuring the Values of Travel Time Savings, *Journal of Consumer Research*, Vol. 7, March 1981, pp. 360–371. Note: this entire issue of Journal of Consumer Research was devoted to the consumption of time.

14   This section is based on David H. Maister, "The Psychology of Waiting Lines," in J. A. Czepiel, M.R. Solomon, and C. F. Surprenant, eds. *The Service Encounter*. Lexington, MA: Lexington Books/D.C. Heath, 1986, pp. 113–123. Peter Jones and Emma Peppiat, "Managing Perceptions of Waiting Times in Service Queues," *International Journal of Service Industry Management*, 7, No. 5, 1996, pp. 47–61. Clay M. Voorhees, Julie Baker, Brian L. Bourdeau, E. Deanne Brocato, and J. Joseph Cronin, Jr. "Moderating the Relationships Among Perceived Waiting Time, Anger and Regret," *Journal of Service Research*, 12, No. 2, (November 2009): 138–155. Kelly A. McGuire, Sheryl E. Kimes, Michael Lynn, Madeline E. Pullman and Russell C. Lloyd, "A Framework for Evaluating the Customer Wait Experience," *Journal of Service Management*, 21, No. 3, (2010): 269–290.

     See also the findings for wait situations in stressful service encounters such as dental appointments by Elizabeth Gelfand Miller, Barbarah E. Kahn, and Mary Frances Luce, "Consumer Wait Management Strategies for Negative Service Events: A Coping Approach," *Journal of Consumer Research*, 34, No. 5, 2008, pp. 635–648.

     For customer abandoning of waits for service: Narayan Janakiraman, Robert J. Meyer, and Stephen J. Hoch (2011), "The Psychology of Decisions to Abandon Waits for Service", *Journal of Marketing Research*, Vol. 48 (December), pp. 970–984.

15   Irene C.L. Ng, Jochen Wirtz, and Khai Sheng Lee (1999), "The Strategic Role of Unused Service Capacity," *International Journal of Service Industry Management*, Vol. 10, No. 2, pp. 211–238.

Chapter 10

1   See also Hooper and Coughlan (2013) who show that the quality of a service environment should be modeled as a separate construct which precedes overall service quality perceptions; Daire Hooper and Joseph Coughlan (2013), The Servicescape as an Antecedent to Service Quality and Behavioral Intentions", *Journal of Services Marketing*, Vol. 27, No. 4, pp. 271–280.

2   The term *servicescape* was coined by Mary Jo Bitner in her paper "Servicescapes: The Impact of Physical Surroundings on Customers and Employees," *Journal of Marketing*, 56, 1992: 57–71.

3   Madeleine E. Pullman and Michael A. Gross, "Ability of Experience Design Elements to Elicit Emotions and Loyalty Behaviors," *Decision Sciences*, Vol. 35, No. 1, (2004): 551–578.

A recent study in a retail context has shown that retail shops were remodeled, sales increased and continued to outperform shops there were not remodeled. Interestingly, customers acquired in the remodeled shops had a higher spent than customers acquired before the remodeling, and had overall more positive attitudes towards the retailer. See: Tracy S. Dagger and Peter J. Danaher (2014), "Comparing the Effect of Store Remodeling on New and Existing Customers", *Journal of Marketing*, Vol. 78, No. 3, pp. 62–80.

4   Anja Reimer and Richard Kuehn, "The Impact of Servicescape on Quality Perception," *European Journal of Marketing*, 39, 7/8, 2005: 785–808.

5   Julie Baker, Dhruv Grewal, and A. Parasuraman, "The Influence of Store Environment on Quality Inferences and Store Image," *Journal of the Academy of Marketing Science*, Vol. 22, No. 4 (1994): 328–339.

6   Barbara Thau, "Apple And The Other Most Successful Retailers By Sales Per Square Foot", *Forbes*, 20 May 2014, http://www.forbes.com/sites/barbarathau/2014/05/20/apple-and-the-other-most-successful-retail-stores-by-sales-per-square-foot/accessed on 25 April 2016; Yukari Iwatani Kane and Ian Sherr, "Secrets from Apple's Genius Bar: Full Loyalty, No Negativity", The Wall Street Journal, 12 June 2011, http://www.wsj.com/articles/SB10001424 052702304563104576364071955678908, accessed on 25 April 2016; http://en.wikipedia.org/wiki/Apple_Store, accessed on 25 April 2016.

7   Ulrich, R., Quan, X., Zimring, C., Joseph, A., & Choudhary, R. (2004). *The role of the physical environment in the hospital of the 21ˢᵗ century: A once-in-a-lifetime opportunity*. Report to the center for health design for the Designing the 21ˢᵗ Century Hospital Project, funded by the Robert Wood Johnson Foundation. (September).

       For a review of the literature on hospital design effects on patients, see: Karin Dijkstra, Marcel Pieterse, and Ad Pruyn, "Physical Environmental Stimuli That Turn Healthcare Facilities into Healing Environments Through Psychologically Mediated Effects: Systematic Review," *Journal of Advanced Nursing*, Vol. 56, No. 2 (2006): 166–181. See also the painstaking effort the Mayo Clinic extends to lowering noise levels in their hospitals: Leonard L. Berry and Kent D. Seltman, *Management Lessons from Mayo Clinic: Inside One of the World's Most Admired Service Organization*. McGraw-Hill (2008): 171–172. For a study on the effects of servicescape design in a hospital setting on service workers' job stress and job satisfaction, and subsequently, their commitment to the firm, see: Janet Turner Parish, Leonard L. Berry, and Shun Yin Lam, "The Effect of the Servicescape on Service Workers," *Journal of Service Research*, Vol. 10, No. 3 (2008): 220–238.

8   Robert J. Donovan and John R. Rossiter, "Store Atmosphere: An Environmental Psychology Approach," *Journal of Retailing*, 58, No. 1, 1982: 34–57.

9   James A. Russell, "A Circumplex Model of Affect," *Journal of Personality and Social Psychology*, 39, No. 6, 1980: 1161–1178.

10   Jochen Wirtz and John E.G. Bateson, "Consumer Satisfaction with Services: Integrating the Environmental Perspective in Services Marketing into the Traditional Disconfirmation Paradigm," *Journal of Business Research*, 44, No. 1, (1999): 55–66.

11   Jochen Wirtz, Anna S. Mattila, and Rachel L.P. Tan, "The Moderating Role of Target-Arousal on the Impact of Affect on Satisfaction — An Examination in the Context of Service Experiences," *Journal of Retailing*, 76, No. 3 (2000): 347–365; Jochen Wirtz, Anna S. Mattila and Rachel L. P. Tan, "The Role of Desired Arousal in Influencing Consumers' Satisfaction Evaluations and In-

Store Behaviours," *International Journal of Service Industry Management*, Vol. 18, No. 2, (2007): 6–24.

12   Mary Jo Bitner, "Servicescapes: The Impact of Physical Surroundings on Customers and Employees," *Journal of Marketing*, 56, (April 1992): 57–71.

13   When servicescapes are designed or redesigned, it is important to use cross-functional teams as there are significant perception gaps between managers and fontline employees, and the latter's perspective is important for servicescapes to facilitate productive and effective service delivery, see: Herman Kok, Mark Moback and Onno Omta (2015), "Facility Design Consequences of Different Employees' Quality Perceptions", *The Service Industries Journal*, Vol. 35, No. 3, pp. 152–178.

14   For a comprehensive review of experimental studies on the atmospheric effects refer to: L.W. Turley and Ronald E. Milliman, "Atmospheric Effects on Shopping Behavior: A Review of the Experimental Literature," *Journal of Business Research*, 49, 2000: 193–211.

15   Patrick M. Dunne, Robert F. Lusch and David A. Griffith, *Retailing*, 8th ed., Orlando, FL: Hartcourt, 2013.

16   Steve Oakes, "The Influence of the Musicscape Within Service Environments," *Journal of Services Marketing*, 14, No. 7, 2000: 539–556.

17   Morris B. Holbrook and Punam Anand, "Effects of Tempo and Situational Arousal on the Listener's Perceptual and Affective Responses to Music," *Psychology of Music*, 18, 1990: 150–162; and S.J. Rohner and R. Miller, "Degrees of Familiar and Affective Music and Their Effects on State Anxiety", *Journal of Music Therapy*, 17, No. 1 (1980): 2–15.

18   Laurette Dubé and Sylvie Morin, "Background Music Pleasure and Store Evaluation Intensity Effects and Psychological Mechanisms," *Journal of Business Research*, 54 (2001): 107–113.

19   Clare Caldwell and Sally A. Hibbert, "The Influence of Music Tempo and Musical Preference on Restaurant Patrons' Behavior," *Psychology and Marketing*, 19, No. 11 (2002): 895–917.

20   For a review of the effects of music on various aspects of consumer responses and evaluations, see: Steve Oakes and Adrian C. North, "Reviewing Congruity Effects in the Service Environment Musicscape," *International Journal of Service Industry Management*, Vol. 19, No. 1 (2008): 63–82.

21   See www.moodmedia.com for in-store music solutions provided by Mood Media, and *The Economist*, "Christmas Music: Dreaming of a Hip-Hop Christmas", 14 December 2013, p. 36.

22   *The Economist*, "Classical Music and Social Control: Twilight of the Yobs," 8 January 2005, p. 48.

23   *Ibid.*

24   Eric R. Spangenberg, Ayn E. Crowley, and Pamela W. Henderson, "Improving the Store Environment: Do Olfactory Cues Affect Evaluations and Behaviors?" *Journal of Marketing*, 60, April 1996: 67–80; Paula Fitzerald Bone and Pam Scholder Ellen, "Scents in the Marketplace: Explaining a Fraction of Olfaction," *Journal of Retailing*, 75, No. 2, 1999: 243–262; Jeremy Caplan, "Sense and Sensibility," *Time*, 168, No. 16 (2006): 66, 67.

25   Alan R. Hirsch, "Dr. Hirsch's Guide to Scentsational Weight Loss," UK: Harper Collins, January 1997, pp. 12–15. http://www.smellandtaste.org/, accessed on 25 April 2016.

26   Alan R. Hirsch, "Effects of Ambient Odors on Slot Machine Usage in a Las Vegas Casino," *Psychology and Marketing*, 12, No. 7, 1995: 585–594.

27   Alan R. Hirsch and S.E. Gay, "Effect on Ambient Olfactory Stimuli on the Evaluation of a Common Consumer Product," *Chemical Senses*, 16, 1991: 535.

28   See Ambius' website for details of its scent marketing, ambient scenting and sensory branding services at: http://www.ambius.com/ambius-catalogs/scent/index.html; accessed at 24 April 2016.

29   *The Economist*, "Christmas Music: Dreaming of a Hip-Hop Christmas", 14 December 2013, p. 36.

30   Andreas Herrmann, Manja Zidansek, David E. Sprott, and Eric R. Spangenberg (2013), "The Power of Simplicity: Processing Fluency and the Effects of Olfactory Cues on Retail Sales", *Journal of Retailing*, Vol. 89, No. 1, pp. 30–43.

31   Ayn E. Crowley, "The Two-Dimensional Impact of Color on Shopping," *Marketing Letters*, 4, No. 1, 1993: 59–69; Gerald J. Gorn, Amitava Chattopadhyay, Jaideep Sengupta, and Shashank Tripathi, "Waiting for the Web: How Screen Color Affects Time Perception," *Journal of Marketing Research*, XLI, May 2004: 215–225; Iris Vilnai-Yavetz and Anat Rafaeli (2006), "Aesthetics and Professionalism of Virtual Servicescapes," *Journal of Service Research*, Vol. 8, No. 3, pp. 245–259.

32   Linda Holtzschuhe, *Understanding Color — An Introduction for Designers*, New Jersey: John Wiley, 3rd ed., 2006, p. 51.

33   Albert Henry Munsell, *A Munsell Color Product*. New York: Kollmorgen Corporation, 1996.

34   Linda Holtzschuhe, *Understanding Color — An Introduction for Designers*, New Jersey: John Wiley, 3rd ed., 2006.

35   Heinrich Zollinger, *Color: A Multidisciplinary Approach*. Zurich: Verlag Helvetica Chimica Acta (VHCA) Weinheim, Wiley-VCH, 1999, pp. 71–79.

36   Joseph A. Bellizzi, Ayn E. Crowley, and Ronald W. Hasty, "The Effects of Color in Store Design," *Journal of Retailing*, 59, No. 1. 1983: 21–45.

37   Sara O. Marberry and Laurie Zagon, *The Power of Color — Creating Healthy Interior Spaces*. New York: John Wiley & Sons, 1995, p. 38.

38   Justin Bachman (2015): "Airlines Add Mood Lighting to Chill Passengers Out: New Boeing and Airbus Models Offer Cabin Designers Splashy Ways to Engage Passengers with Light", Bloomberg Business, http://www.bloomberg.com/news/articles/2015-04-22/airlines-add-mood-lighting-to-chill-passengers-out, accessed 24 April 2016.

39   Anat Rafaeli and Iris Vilnai-Yavetz, "Discerning organizational boundaries through physical artifacts," in *Managing boundaries in organizations: Multiple perspectives*, eds. N. Paulsen and T. Hernes, UK: Basingstoke, Hampshire, Macmillan, 2003; Anat Rafaeli and Iris Vilnai-Yavetz, "Emotion as a Connection of Physical Artifacts and Organizations," *Organization*

Science, Vol. 15, No. 6 (2004): 671–686; and Anat Rafaeli and Iris Vilnai-Yavetz, "Managing Organizational Artifacts to Avoid Artifact Myopia," in A. Rafaeli and M. Pratt (Eds.), *Artifacts and Organization: Beyond Mere Symbolism*, (Mahwah, NJ: Lawrence Erlbaum Associates Inc., 2005, pp. 9–21.

40   For an excellent review of the quality of signage management, see: Angelo Bonfani (2013), "Towards an Approach to Signage Management Quality (SMQ)", *Journal of Services Marketing*, Vol. 27, No. 4, pp. 312–321.

41   Lewis P. Carbone and Stephen H. Haeckel, "Engineering Customer Experiences," *Marketing Management*, 3, No. 3, Winter 1994: 9–18; Lewis P. Carbone, Stephen H. Haeckel and Leonard L. Berry, "How to Lead the Customer Experience," *Marketing Management*, 12, No. 1, Jan/Feb 2003:18; Leonard L. Berry and Lewis P. Carbone, "Build Loyalty Through Experience Management," *Quality Progress*, 40, No. 9 (September 2007): 26–32.

42   Roscoe Hightower, Jr. and Mohammad Shariat (2009), "Servicescape's Hierarchical Factor Structure Model", *Global Review of Business and Economic Research*, Vol. 5, No. 2, pp. 375–398; Roscoe Hightower, Jr. (2010), "Commentary on Conceptualizing the Servicescape Construct in 'A Study of the Service Encounter in Eight Countries'", *Marketing Management Journal*, (Spring), Vol. 20, No. 1, pp. 75–86.

43   Dennis Nickson, Chris Warhurst, and Eli Dutton, "The Importance of Attitude and Appearance in the Service Encounter in Retail and Hospitality," *Managing Service Quality*, 2, 2005, pp. 195–208.

44   Christine M. Piotrowski, *Designing Commercial Interiors* (New York: John Wiley & Sons, Inc., 2007); Martin M. Pegler, *Cafes & Bistros.* (New York: Retail Reporting Corporation, 1998); Paco Asensio, *Bars & Restaurants.* (New York: HarperCollins International, 2002); Bethan Ryder, *Bar and Club Design*, (London: Laurence King Publishing, 2002).

45   Ron Kaufman, "Service Power: Who Were They Designing it For?" Newsletter, May 2001, http://Ron Kaufman.com.

46   Alan d'Astous, "Irritating Aspects of the Shopping Environment," *Journal of Business Research*, 49, (2000): 149–156. See also: K. Douglas Hoffman, Scott W. Kelly and Beth C. Chung, "A CIT Investigation of Servicscape Failures and Associated Recovery Strategies," *Journal of Services Marketing*, Vol. 17, No. 4, (2003): 322–40.

47   Jörg Pareigis, Per Echeverri and Bo Edvardsson (2012), "Exploring Internal Mechanisms Forming Customer Servicescape Experiences", *Journal of Service Management*, Vol. 23, No. 5, pp. 677–695.

48   Interestingly, visual complexity in environments hinders shoppers' information processing and thereby reduces their satisfaction. This finding is especially applicable in utilitarian service contexts and also suggest that it is better for service organizations to reduce complexity in servicescape design and make it easy for customers to sense and process a servicescape. This finding is well-aligned with the study by Jörg Pareigis, Per Echeverri and Bo Edvardsson (2012); see: Ulrich R. Orth, Frauke Heinrich and Keven Malkewitz (2012), "Servicescape Interior Design and Consumer Personality Impressions", *Journal of Services Marketing*, Vol. 26, No. 3, pp. 194–203; Ulrich R. Orth and Jochen Wirtz (2014), "Consumer Processing of Interior Service Environments", *Journal of Service Research*, Vol. 17, No. 3, pp. 296–309.

49   Audit tools and checklists can be used to determine environmental dimensions that are important to customers; for example, see the auditing tool provided in: Mark S. Rosenbaum and Corolyn Massiah (2013), "The Challenge of Managing a Service Context", in: *Serving Customers: Global Services Marketing Perspectives*, by Raymond P. Fisk, Rebekah Russell-Bennett, and Lloyd C. Harris (eds.), Tilde University Press, Melbourne, Australia, pp. 287–310.

50   Madeleine E. Pullman and Stephani K.A. Robson, "Visual Methods: Using Photographs to Capture Customers' Experience with Design," *Cornell Hotel and Restaurant Administration Quarterly*, 48, No. 2, (2007): 121–144.

Chapter 11

1   Adapted from Leonard L. Berry, *Discovering the Soul of Service — The Nine Drivers of Sustainable Business Success*. New York: Free Press, 1999, pp. 156–159.

2   Recent research focuses on how strategically aligning front line employees and their behaviors with a firm's brand positioning strengthens brand equity, see: Nancy J. Sirianni, Mary Jo Bitner, Stephen W. Brown, and Naomi Mandel (2013), "Branded Service Encounters: Strategically Aligning Employee Behavior with the Brand Positioning", *Journal of Marketing*, Vol. 77, No. 6, pp. 108–123.

3   Liliana L. Bove, and Lester W. Johnson, "Customer Relationships with Service Personnel: Do We Measure Closeness, Quality or Strength?" *Journal of Business Research*, 54 (2001): 189–197; Magnus Söderlund and Sara Rosengren, "Revisiting the Smiling Service Worker and Customer Satisfaction," *International Journal of Service Industry Management*, Vol. 19, No. 5 (2008): 552–574; Anat Rafaeli, Lital Ziklik, and Lorna Doucet, "The Impact of Call Center Employees' Customer Orientation Behaviors and Service Quality," *Journal of Service Research*, Vol. 10, No. 3 (2008): 239–255.

4   The following study established the link between extra-role effort and customer satisfaction; e.g., Carmen Barroso Castro, Enrique Martín Armario, and David Martín Ruiz, "The Influence of Employee Organizational Citizenship Behavior on Customer Loyalty," *International Journal of Service Industry Management*, 15, No. 1, (2004): 27–53.
      There is a large body of research that documented how and why employees have such a strong impact on customers' satisfaction and future behaviors. Recent studies include: Alicia A. Grandey, Lori S. Goldberg, and S. Douglas Pugh (2011), "Why and When do Stores With Satisfied Employees Have Satisfied Customers", *Journal of Service Research*, Vol. 14, No. 4, pp. 397–409; Heiner Evanschitzky, Christopher Groening, Vikas Mittal, and Maren Wunderlich (2011), "How Employer and Employee Satisfaction Affect Customer Satisfaction: An Application to Franchise Services," *Journal of Service Research*, Vol. 14, No. 2, pp. 136–148; Gabriel Gazzoli, Murat Hancer, and Beom Cheol (Peter) Kim (2013), "Explaining Why Employee-Customer Orientation Influences Customers' Percpetions of the Service Encounter", *Journal of Service Management*, Vol. 24, No. 4, pp. 382–400; Cécile Delcourt, Dwayne D. Gremmler, Allard C.R. van Riel, and Marcel van Birgelen (2013), "Effects of Perceived Employee Emotional Competence on Customer Satisfaction and Loyalty: The Mediating Role of Rapport", *Journal of Service Management*, Vol. 24, No. 1, pp. 5–24; Kumar Rakesh Ranjan, Praveen Sugathan, and Alexander Rossmann (2014), "A Narrative Review and Meta-Analysis of Service Interaction Quality: New Research Directions and Implications" *Journal of Services Marketing*, Vol. 29, No. 1, pp. 3–14.

5   James L. Heskett, Thomas O. Jones, Gary W. Loveman, W. Earl Sasser, Jr., and Leonard A. Schlesinger, " Putting the Service Profit Chain to Work," *Harvard Business Review*, 72 (March–April 1994), pp. 164–174.

6   Benjamin Schneider and David E. Bowen, "The Service Organization: Human Resources Management is Crucial," *Organizational Dynamics*, 21, No. 4 (Spring 1993): 39–52.

7   http://www.fiveguysproductions.com/2010/08/just-little-excitement-on-my-flight.html, "Just a Little Excitement on my Flight Today," posted on 9 August 2010; accessed 11 May 2016.

8   David E. Bowen and Benjamin Schneider, "Boundary-Spanning Role Employees and the Service Encounter: Some Guidelines for Management and Research." In J.A. Czepiel, M. R. Solomon, and C.F. Surprenant, eds., *The Service Encounter*. Lexington, MA: Lexington Books, 1985, pp. 127–148.

    For a recent study on the effects of stress on employee performance and how this effect can be mitigated, see: Kimmy Wa Chan and Echo Wen Wan (2012), "How Can Stressed Employees Deliver Better Customer Service: The Underlying Self-Regulation Depletion Mechanism", *Journal of Marketing*, Vol. 76, No. 1, pp. 119–137.

9   Conflicting goals (e.g., short average call duration and customer satisfaction) set by the organization are also a key cause of burnout, see: Michael Rod and Nicholas J. Ashill (2013), "The Impact of Call Centre Stressors on Inbound and Outbound Call-Center Agent Burnout", *Managing Service Quality*, Vol. 23, No. 3, pp. 245–264; Benjamin Piers William Ellway (2014), "Is The Quality-Quantity Trade-Off in Call Centres a False Dichotomy?", *Managing Service Quality*, Vol. 24, No. 3, pp. 230–251.

    For a recent study on selling in a call center service context, see: Claudia Jasmand, Vera Blazevic, and Ko de Ruyter (2012), "Generating Sales While Providing Service: A Study of Customer Service Representatives' Ambidextrous Behavior", *Journal of Marketing*, Vol. 76, No. 1, pp. 20–37.

10 Vaikakalathur Shankar Mashesh and Anand Kasturi, "Improving Call Centre Agent Performance: A UK–India Study Based on the Agents' Point of View." *International Journal of Service Industry Management,* Vol. 17, No. 2 (2006): 136–157.

    On potentially conflicting goals, see also: Detelina Marinova, Jun Ye and Jagdip Singh, "Do Frontline Mechanisms Matter? Impact of Quality and Productivity Orientations on Unit Revenue, Efficiency, and Customer Satisfaction," *Journal of Marketing*, Vol. 72, No. 2 (2008): 28–25.

11 Arlie R. Hochschild, *The Managed Heart: Commercialization of Human Feeling*, (Berkeley: University of California Press, 1983).

12 Won-Moo Hur, Tae-Won Moon, and Yeon Sung Jung (2015), "Customer Response to Employee Emotional Labor: The Structural Relationship Between Emotional Labor, Job Satisfaction, and Customer Satisfaction", *Journal of Services Marketing*, Vol. 29, No. 1, pp. 71–80.

13 Panikkos Constanti and Paul Gibbs, "Emotional labor and Surplus Value: The Case of Holiday 'Reps,'" *The Service Industries Journal,* 25, January 2005, pp. 103–116.

14 Arlie Hochschild, "Emotional Labor in the Friendly Skies," *Psychology Today,* (June 1982): 13–15.

15 Michel Rod and Nicholas J. Ashill, "Symptoms of Burnout and Service Recovery Performance," *Managing Service Quality*, Vol. 19, No. 1 (2009): 60–84; Jody L. Crosno, Shannon B. Rinaldo, Hulda G. Black and Scott W. Kelley, "Half Full or Half Empty: The Role of Optimism in Boundary-Spanning Positions," *Journal of Service Research*, Vol. 11, No. 3 (2009): 295–309.

    Recent research has linked emotional exhaustion to turnover intentions, see: Tobias Kraemer and Matthias H.J. Gouthier (2014), "How Organizational Pride and Emotional Exhaustion Explain Turnover Intentions in Call Centers", *Journal of Service Management*, Vol. 25, No. 1, pp. 125–148.

Note that there is emotional contagion for both positive and negative emotions from service employees to customers; therefore how frontline employees deal with stress is important for the customer experience. See: Jiangang Du, Xiucheng Fan, and Tianjun Feng (2011), "Multiple Emotional Contagions in Service Encounters", *Journal of the Academy of Marketing Science*, Vol. 39, No. 3, pp. 449–466.

Emotional support seems particularly important when employees have to deal with unreasonable and dysfunctional customers; see: Taeshik Gong, Youjae Yi, and Jin Nam Choi (2014), "Helping Employees Deal with Dysfunctional Customers: The Underlying Employee Perceived Justice Mechanism", *Journal of Service Research*, Vol. 17, No. 1, pp. 102–116.

For how frontline staff resist emotional labor, see: Jocelyn A. Hollander and Rachel L. Einwohner, "Conceptualizing Resistance," *Sociological Forum*, 19, No. 4, (2004): 533–554; Diane Seymour, "Emotional Labour: A Comparison Between Fast Food and Traditional Service Work," *International Journal of Hospitality Management*, 19, No. 2, (2000): 159–171; Peter John Sandiford and Diane Seymour, "Reacting to the Demands of Service Work: Emotional Resistance in the Coach Inn Company," *The Service Industries Journal*, 31, Nos. 7–8, May (2011): 1195–1217.

16   Jochen Wirtz and Robert Johnston, "Singapore Airlines: What It Takes to Sustain Service Excellence — A Senior Management Perspective," *Managing Service Quality*, 13, No.1 (2003): 10–19; and Loizos Heracleous, Jochen Wirtz, and Nitin Pangarkar, *Flying High in a Competitive Industry: Secrets of the World's Leading Airline.* (Singapore: McGraw-Hill, 2009).

17   Dan Moshavi and James R. Terbord, "The Job Satisfaction and Performance of Contingent and Regular Customer Service Representatives — A Human Capital Perspective," *International Journal of Service Industry Management,* 13, No. 4 (2002): 333–347.

18   Vaikalathur Shankar Mahesh and Anand Kasturi, "Improving Call Centre Agent Performance," *International Journal of Service Industry Management*, Vol. 17, No. 2 (2006): 136–157.

19   The terms "cycle of failure" and "cycle of success" were coined by Leonard L. Schlesinger and James L. Heskett, "Breaking the Cycle of Failure in Services," *Sloan Management Review,* (Spring 1991): 17–28. The term "cycle of mediocrity" comes from Christopher H. Lovelock, "Managing Services: The Human Factor," in *Understanding Services Management,* eds. W.J. Glynn and J.G. Barnes (Chichester, UK: John Wiley & Sons, 1995), p. 228.

20   Leonard Schlesinger and James L. Heskett, "Breaking the Cycle of Failure," *Sloan Management Review,* (Spring 1991): pp. 17–28.

21   Reg Price and Roderick J. Brodie, "Transforming a Public Service Organization from Inside out to Outside in," *Journal of Service Research,* 4, No. 1 (2001): 50–59.

22   Mahn Hee Yoon, "The Effect of Work Climate on Critical Employee and Customer Outcomes," *International Journal of Service Industry Management,* 12, No. 5 (2001): 500–521.

23   Tor W. Andreassen and Even J. Lanseng (2010), "Service Differentiation: A Self-Image Congruency Perspective on Brand Building in the Labor Market", *Journal of Service Management*, Vol. 21, No. 2, pp. 212–236.

24   Kathleen A. Keeling, Peter J. McGoldrick and Henna Sadhu (2013), "Staff Word-of-Mouth (SWOM) and Retail Employee Recruitment" *Journal of Retailing*, Vol. 89, No. 1, pp. 88–104.

25   www.glassdoor.com and http://en.wikipedia.org/wiki/Glassdoor; accessed on 7 May 2016.

26   Charles A. O'Reilly III and Jeffrey Pfeffer, *Hidden Value — How Great Companies Achieve Extraordinary Results with Ordinary People,* (Boston, Massachusetts: Harvard Business School Press, 2000), p. 1.

27   Being seen as a good company and engaging in corporate social responsibility is increasingly seen as important in both labor and consumer markets. See also: Daniel Korschun, C.B. Bhattavharya, and Scott D. Swain (2014), "Corporate Social Responsibility, Customer Orientation, and the Job Performance of Frontline Employees", *Journal of Marketing*, Vol. 78, No. 3, pp. 20–37.

28   Patty McCord (2014), "How Netflix Reinvented HR", *Harvard Business Review*, Vol. 92, No 1/2, pp. 70–76.

29   Nancy J. Sirianni, Mary Jo Bitner, Stephen W. Brown, and Naomi Mandel (2013), "Branded Service Encounters: Strategically Aligning Employee Behavior with the Brand Positioning", *Journal of Marketing*, Vol. 77, No. 6, pp. 108–123; Birgit Löndorf and Adamantios Diamantopoulos (2014), "Internal Branding: Social Identify and Social Exchange Perspectives on Turning Employees into Brand Champions", *Journal of Service Research*, Vol. 17, No. 3, pp. 310–325.
      It also has shown that frontline employees have mental models of the meaning of customer service, ranging from satisfying the customers' needs efficiently, filling sales quota to forming a mutually beneficial relationship. The mental model of employees therefore should fit the firm's marketing strategy and positioning. See: Rita Di Mascio (2010), "The Service Models of Frontline Employees", *Journal of Marketing*, Vol. 74, No. 4, pp. 63–80.

30   Scott A. Hurrell and Dora Scholarios (2014), "'The People Make the Brand': Reducing Social Skills Gaps Through Person–Brand Fit and Human Resource Management Practices", *Journal of Service Research*, Vol. 17, No. 1, pp. 54–67. This study has also shown that a firm that recruits based on person-brand fit leads to their employees having better identification with the brand and smaller skills gaps.

31   Bill Fromm and Len Schlesinger, *The Real Heroes of Business* (New York: Currency Doubleday, 1994), pp. 315–316.

32   Jim Collins, "Turning Goals into Results: The Power of Catalytic Mechanisms," *Harvard Business Review*, (July–August 1999): 77.

33   Thomas H. Davenport, Jeanne Harris and Jeremy Shapiro, "Competing on Talent Analytics" *Harvard Business Review*, October (2010): 52–58.

34   This section was adapted from: Benjamin Schneider and David E. Bowen, *Winning the Service Game,* (Boston: Harvard Business School Press, 1995), pp. 115–126.

35   John Wooden, *A Lifetime of Observations and Reflections On and Off the Court,* (Chicago: Lincolnwood, 1997), p. 66.

36   For a review of this literature see Benjamin Schneider, "Service Quality and Profits: Can You Have Your Cake and Eat It, Too? *Human Resource Planning,* 14, No. 2 (1991): 151–157.

37   There is a large literature on the effects and how to select employees based on personality. Important and recent research includes: Tom J. Brown, John C. Mowen, D. Todd Donovan and Jane W. Licata, "The Customer Orientation of Service Workers: Personality Trait Effects on Self- and Supervisor Performance Ratings," *Journal of Marketing Research*, 39, No. 1, (2002): 110–119; Salih Kusluvan, Zeynep Kusluvan, Ibrahim Ilhan and Lutfi Buyruk, "The Human Dimension: A Review of Human Resources Management Issues in the Tourism and Hospitality Industry," *Cornell Hospitality Quarterly*, 51, No. 2, May (2010): 171–214; Hui Liao and Aichia Chuang, "A Multilevel Investigation of Factors Influencing Employee Service Performance and Outcomes," *Academy of Management Journal*, 47, No. 1, (2004): 41–58; Androniki Papadopoulou-Bayliss, Elizabeth M. Ineson and Derek

Wilkie, "Control and Role Conflict in Food Service Providers," *International Journal of Hospitality Management*, 20, No. 2, (2001): 187–199; Michael J. Tews, Kathryn Stafford and J. Bruce Tracey, "What Matters Most? The Perceived Importance of Ability and Personality for Hiring Decisions," Cornell Hospitality Quarterly, 52, No. 2, (2011): 94–101; John E.G. Bateson, Jochen Wirtz, Eugene F. Burke and Carly J. Vaughan (2014), "Sifting to Efficiently Select the Right Service Employees", *Organizational Dynamics*, Vol. 43, pp. 312–320.

If you want to understand assessment tests better as a candidate who has to go through such tests, see: Tomas Chamorro-Premuzic (2015), "Managing Yourself: Ace the Assessment", *Harvard Business Review*, Vol. 93, No. 7/8, pp. 118–121.

38   Serene Goh, "All the Right Staff," and Arlina Arshad, "Putting Your Personality to the Test," *The Straits Times,* Singapore, 5 September 2001, p. H1.

39   This section was adapted from Leonard L. Berry, *On Great Service — A Framework for Action* (New York: The Free Press, 1995), pp. 181–182.

40   Leonard Schlesinger and James L. Heskett, "Breaking the Cycle of Failure," *Sloan Management Review,* (Spring 1991): 17–28.

41   Donald W. Jackson Jr. and Nancy J. Sirianni, "Building the Bottomline by Developing the Frontline: Career Development for Service Employees," *Business Horizons*, 52 (2009): 279–287; Timothy R. Hinkin and J. Bruce Tracey, "What Makes it So Great? An Analysis of Human Resources Practices among Fortune's Best Companies to Work For," *Cornell Hospitality Quarterly*, 51, No. 2, May (2010): 158–170; Rick Garlick, "Do Happy Employees Really Mean Happy Customers? Or Is There More to the Equation? *Cornell Hospitality Quarterly*, 51, No. 3, August (2010): 304–307.

42   Yukari Iwatani Kane and Ian Sherr, "Secrets From Apple's Genius Bar: Full Loyalty, No Negativity," *The Wall Street Journal*, 15 June 2011, http://www.wsj.com/articles/SB1000142405 2702304563104576364071955678908, accessed 11 May 2016.

43   Benjamin Schneider and David E. Bowen, *Winning the Service Game* (Boston, MA: Harvard Business School Press, 1995), p. 131.

44   Leonard L. Berry, *Discovering the Soul of Service — The Nine Drivers of Sustainable Business Success* (New York: The Free Press, 1999), 161; Pep Simo, Mihaela Enache, Jose M. Sallan, and Vicenc Fernandez (2014), "Relations Between Organizational Commitment and Focal and Discretionary Behaviors", *The Service Industries Journal*, Vol. 34, No. 5, pp. 422–438.

45   Disney Institute, *Be Our Guest: Perfecting the Art of Customer Service.* Disney Enterprises (2011), updated edition.

46   David A. Tansik, "Managing Human Resource Issues for High Contact Service Personnel," in *Service Management Effectiveness*, eds. D.E. Bowen, R. B. Chase, T.G. Cummings, and Associates (San Francisco: Jossey-Bass, 1990), pp. 152–176; Kelly M. Wilder, Joel E. Collier and Donald C. Barnes (2014), "Tailoring to Customers' Needs: Understanding How to Promote an Adaptive Service Experience With Frontline Employees", *Journal of Service Research*, Vol. 17, No. 4, pp. 446–459.

Recent research has even focused on how obese frontline employees can counter a negative stereotype (e.g., perceived lack of energy) with lower customer evaluations of frontline transactions. The research found that through outwards expression of joviality (e.g., displaying an attitude of being "jolly" and "fun") can attenuate negative effects of obesity. Likewise, sending strong signals of quality of the encounter (e.g., extra attention to facility cleanliness, merchandize neatness, and displaying employee accomplishments) reduced the negative effects of obesity on customer perceptions. Training can help employees to to use these tactics. See: Kelly O. Cowart and Michael K. Brady (2014), "Pleasantly Plum: Offsetting

Negative Obesity Stereotypes for Frontline Employees", *Journal of Service Research*, Vol. 90, No. 3, pp. 365–378.

47 Joseph A. Mitchelli, *The New Gold Standard: 5 Leadership Principles for Creating a Legendary Customer Experience Courtesy of The Ritz-Carton Hotel Company*. McGraw-Hill, 2008: 61–66, and 191–197.

48 Paul Hemp, "My Week as a Room-Service Waiter at the Ritz," *Harvard Business Review*, 80, June 2002: 8–11.

49 Parts of this section are based on David E. Bowen, and Edward E. Lawler, III, "The Empowerment of Service Workers: What, Why, How and When," *Sloan Management Review*, (Spring 1992): 32–39.

50 For important recent research on discretionary employee behavior in the frontline, see: Steffen Raub and Hui Liao (2012), "Doing the Right Thing Without Being Told: Joint Effects of Initiative Climate and General Self-Efficacy on Employee Proactive Customer Service Performance", *Journal of Applied Psychology*, Vol. 97, No. 3, pp. 651–667; Jeroen Schepers, Tomas Falk, Ko de Ruyter, Ad de Jong, and Maik Hammerschmidt (2012), "Principles and Principals: Do Customer Stewardship and Agency Control Compete or Complement When Shaping Frontline Employee Behavior?" *Journal of Marketing*, Vol. 76, No. 6, pp. 1–20.

51 Michael K. Brady, Clay M. Voorhees, and Michael J. Brusco (2012), "Service Sweethearting: Its Antecedents and Customer Consequences", *Journal of Marketing*, Vol. 76, No. 2, pp. 81–98.

52 Dana Yagil, "The Relationship of Customer Satisfaction and Service Workers' Perceived Control — Examination of Three Models," *International Journal of Service Industry Management*, 13, No. 4 (2002): 382–398.

53 Graham L. Bradley and Beverley A. Sparks, "Customer Reactions to Staff Empowerment: Mediators and Moderators," *Journal of Applied Social Psychology*, 30, No. 5 (2000): 991–1012.

54 David E. Bowen, and Edward E. Lawler, III, "The Empowerment of Service Workers: What, Why, How and When," *Sloan Management Review*, (Spring 1992): 32–39.

55 Benjamin Schneider and David E. Bowen, *Winning the Service Game*, (Boston, MA: Harvard Business School Press, 1995), p. 250.

56 The system is described in: Serguei Netessine and Valery Yakubovich (2012), "The Darwinian Workplace", *Harvard Business Review*, Vol. 90 (May), pp. 25–28. Karan Girotra and Serguei Netessine (2014), "Four Paths to Business Model Innovation: The Secret to Success Lies in Who Makes the Decisions When and Why", *Harvard Business Review*, Vol. 92, No. 7/8, pp. 96–103.

57 Jun Ye, Detelina Marionova, and Jagdip Singh (2012), "Bottom-Up Learning in Marketing Frontlines: Conceptualization, Processes, and Consequences", *Journal of the Academy of Marketing Science*, Vol. 40, No. 6, pp. 821–844.

58 Susan Cadwallader, Cheryl Burke Jarvis, Mary Jo Bitner, and Amy L. Ostrom (2010), "Frontline Employee Motivation to Participate in Service Innovation Implementation", *Journal of the Academy of Marketing Science*, Vol. 38, No. 2, pp. 219–239.

59 This paragraph is based on Kevin Freiberg and Jackie Freiberg, *Nuts! Southwest Airlines' Crazy Recipe for Business and Personal Success*, (New York: Broadway Books, 1997), pp. 87–88.

60 Jon R. Katzenbach and Douglas K. Smith, "The Discipline of Teams," *Harvard Business Review*, (March–April, 1993): 112.

61   Andrew Sergeant and Stephen Frenkel, "When Do Customer Contact Employees Satisfy Customers?" *Journal of Service Research,* 3, No. 1 (August 2000): 18–34.

62   Ad de Jong, Ko de Ruyter, and Jos Lemmink, "Antecedents and Consequences of the Service Climate in Boundary-Spanning Self-Managing Service Teams," *Journal of Marketing,* 68 (April 2004): 18–35.

63   For the effects and drivers of alignment between leaders and their service delivery teams see: Alexander Benlian (2014), "Are We Aligned … Enough? The Effects of Perceptual Congruence Between Service Teams and Their Leaders on Team Performance", *Journal of Service Research,* Vol. 17, No. 2, pp. 212–228.

64   Leonard L. Berry, *On Great Service — A Framework for Action,* p. 131.

65   Charles A. O'Reilly III and Jeffrey Pfeffer, *Hidden Value — How Great Companies Achieve Extraordinary Results with Ordinary People,* (Boston, Massachusetts: Harvard Business School Press, 2000), p. 9.

66   Leonard L. Berry, *Discovering the Soul of Service — The Nine Drivers of Sustainable Business Success,* p. 189.

67   Schneider and Bowen, *Winning the Service Game,* 141; Leonard L. Berry, *On Great Service — A Framework for Action,* p. 225.

68   Mike Osheroff, "Teamwork in the Global Economy," *Strategic Finance,* 88, No. 8 (Feb 2007): 25, 61.

69   Robert J. Kwortnik Jr. and Gary M. Thompson, "Unifying Service Marketing and Operations With Service Experience Management," *Journal of Service Research,* 11, No. 4, 2009, pp. 389–406.

70   Adapted from Kevin and Jackie Freiberg, *Nuts! Southwest Airlines' Crazy Recipe for Business and Personal Success,* (New York: Broadway Books, 1997), pp. 165–168.

71   This section is based on Schneider and Bowen, *Winning the Service Game,* pp. 145–173.

72   Linda Nasr, Jamie Burton, Thorsten Gruber, and Jan Kitshoff (2014), "Exploring the Impact of Customer Feedback on the Well-Being of Service Entities: a TSR Perspective", *Journal of Service Management,* Vol. 25, No. 4, pp. 531–555; Regina-Viola Frey, Tomás Bayón, and Dirk Totzek (2013), "How Customer Satisfaction Affects Employee Satisfaction and Retention in a Professional Service Context", *Journal of Service Research,* Vol. 16, No. 4, pp. 503–517.

73   Adam M. Grant, "How Customers Can Rally Your Troops," *Harvard Business Review,* June (2011): 96–103.

74   A good summary of goal setting and motivation at work can be found in Edwin A. Locke and Gary Latham, *A Theory of Goal Setting and Task Performance,* (New Jersey: Englewood Cliffs, Prentice Hall, 1990).

75   Charles A. O'Reilly III and Jeffrey Pfeffer, *Hidden Value — How Great Companies Achieve Extraordinary Results with Ordinary People,* (Boston, Massachusetts: Harvard Business School Press, 2000), p. 232.

76   Jeffrey Pfeffer, *Competitive Advantage Through People,* (Boston: Harvard Business School Press, 1994), pp. 160–163.

77   Jody Hoffer Gittell, Andrew von Nordenflycht, and Thomas A. Kochan, "Mutual Gains for

Zero Sum? Labor Relations and Firm Performance in the Airline Industry," *Industrial and Labor Relations Review,* 57, No. 2 (2004): pp. 163–180.

78   This section is based, in part, on Benjamin Schneider and David E. Bowen, *Winning the Service Game.* Boston: Harvard Business School Press, 1995; David E. Bowen and Benjamin Schneider (2014), "A Service Climate Synthesis and Future Research Agenda", *Journal of Service Research,* Vol. 17, No. 1, pp. 5–22.

79   The authors of the following paper emphasize the role of alignment between tradition, culture and strategy that together form the basis for the firms HR practices: Benjamin Schneider, Seth C Hayes, Beng-Chong Lim, Jana L. Raver, Ellen G. Godfrey, Mina Huang, Lisa H. Nishii, and Jonathan C. Ziegert, "The Human Side of Strategy: Employee Experiences of a Strategic Alignment in a Service Organization," *Organizational Dynamics,* 32, No. 2 (2003): 122–141.
      A study exploring the fit of company culture with the national context the firm operates in found that a good fit improves firm performance. For example, cultural values of stability, people orientation, and detail orientation and outcomes are significantly more important to Japanese retailers compared to their US counterparts. The study showed that if a firm operated in other countries with different cultural values show lower performance. See: Cynthia Webster and Allyn White (2010), "Exploring the National and Organizational Culture Mix in Service Firms", *Journal of the Academy of Marketing Science,* Vol. 38, No. 6, pp. 691–703.

80   Leonard L. Berry, *On Great Service — A Framework for Action,* pp. 236–237; Leonard L. Berry and Kent D. Seltman, *Management Lessons from Mayo Clinic: Inside One of the World's Most Admired Service Organization.* McGraw-Hill (2008).
      The following study emphasized the importance of the perceived ethical climate in driving service commitment of service employees: Charles H. Schwepker Jr. and Michael D. Hartline, "Managing the Ethical Climate of Customer-Contact Service Employees," *Journal of Service Research,* 7, No. 4 (2005): 377–397.

81   For an excellent review of the extant service climate literature and related constructs, see: David E. Bowen and Benjamin Schneider (2014), "A Service Climate Synthesis and Future Research Agenda", *Journal of Service Research,* Vol. 17, No. 1, pp. 5–22.

82   For example, two recent studies linked service climate to service innovation and to customer loyalty, respectively. See: Ping-Jen Kao, Peiyu Pai, Tingling Lin and Jun-Yu Zhong (2015), "How Transformational Leadership Fuels Employee' Service Innovation Behavior", *The Service Industries Journal,* Vol. 35, No. 7–8, pp. 448–466; Mei-Ling Wang (2015), "Linking Service Climate to Customer Loyalty", *The Service Industries Journal,* Vol. 35, No. 7–8, pp. 403–414.

83   Hans Kasper, "Culture and Leadership in Market-oriented Service Organisations," *European Journal of Marketing,* 36, No. 9/10, 2002, pp. 1047–1057; Ronald A. Clark, Michael D. Hartline, and Keith C. Jones, "The Effects of Leadership Style on Hotel Employees' Commitment to Service Quality," *Cornell Hospitality Quarterly,* Vol. 50, No. 2 (2009): 209–231.

84   James L. Heskett, W. Earl Sasser, Jr., and Leonard A. Schlesinger, *The Service Profit Chain,* p. 236.

85   Leonard L. Berry, *Discovering the Soul of Service* (New York,: The Free Press, 1999), pp. 44, 47. See also D. Micheal Abrashoff, "Retention Through Redemption," *Harvard Business Review,* February 2001, pp. 136–141, which provides a fascinating example on successful leadership in the US Navy.

86   Hamm, J. (2006). The five messages leaders must manage. *Harvard Business Review,* (May), pp. 115–123.

87   Blagg, D., & Young, S. (2001). What makes a leader? *Harvard Business School Bulletin*, (February), pp. 31–36.

88   Rakesh Karma, "The Curse of the Superstar CEO," *Harvard Business Review*, 80 (September 2002): 60–66.

89   Jim Collins, "Level 5 Leadership: The Triumph of Humility and Fierce Resolve," *Harvard Business Review*, January 2001, pp. 66–76.

90   Sandra Vandermerwe (1993), *From Tin Soldiers to Russian Dolls*, Butterworth-Heinemann; Reprint edition, p. 129.

91   This section was adapted from: David E. Bowen and Benjamin Schneider (2014), "A Service Climate Synthesis and Future Research Agenda", *Journal of Service Research*, Vol. 17, No. 1, pp. 5–22. This article provides a detailed review of the research that underlies this section.

92   James L. Heskett, Thomas O. Jones, Gary W. Loveman, W. Earl Sasser, Jr., and Leonard A. Schlesinger, " Putting the Service Profit Chain to Work," *Harvard Business Review*, 72 (March–April 1994), p. 164.

93   Thomas J. Peters and Robert H. Waterman, *In Search of Excellence*. New York: Harper & Row, 1982, p. 122.

94   Tony Simons, "The High Cost of Lost Trust," *Harvard Business Review*, (September 2002): 2–3.

95   Rik Kirkland (2013), "Leading in the 21st Century: An Interview with Hertz CEO Mark Frissora," *McKinsey Quarterly*, November.

96   Catherine DeVrye, *Good Service is Good Business*, (Upper Saddle River, NJ: Prentice Hall, 2000), p. 11.

97   Tony Hsieh (2010), *Delivering Happiness: A Path to Profits, Passion and Purpose*. NY: New York, Business Plus, p. 153; On how to create committable core values for a service organization, see: http://www.deliveringhappiness.com/core-values; accessed 27 October 2016.

Chapter 12

1   Frederick F. Reichheld and Thomas Teal (1996), *The Loyalty Effect*. Boston: Harvard Business School Press.

2   The first four factors were proposed by Frederick F. Reichheld and W. Earl Sasser, Jr., "Zero Defections: Quality Comes to Services," *Harvard Business Review*, (October 1990): 105–111. The fifth factor was added by the authors of this book.

3   Christian Homburg, Nicole Koschate, and Wayne D. Hoyer, "Do Satisfied Customers Really Pay More? A Study of the Relationship Between Customer Satisfaction and Willingness to Pay," *Journal of Marketing*, 69 (April 2005): 84–96.

4   Frederick F. Reichheld and W. Earl Sasser, Jr., "Zero Defections: Quality Comes to Services," *Harvard Business Review*, (October 1990): 105–111.

5   For a discussion on how to evaluate the customer base of a firm, see Sunil Gupta, Donald R. Lehmann, and Jennifer Ames Stuart, "Valuing Customers," *Journal of Marketing Research*, 41, No.1 (2004): 7–18.

     An excellent overview of the metric of CLV and related concept such as RFM (i.e., recency, frequency, and monetary spent), PCV (i.e., past customer value, also called customer profitability analysis or CPA), and share-of-wallet is provided in: V. Kumar (2007), "Customer Lifetime Value — The Path to Profitability", *Foundations and Trends in Marketing*, Vol. 2, No. 1, pp. 1–96.

A review of when to use and how to measure CLV (a prospective perspective on customer life time value which attempts to predict future customer behaviors and discounts derived future cash flows) and customer profitability analysis (CPA, with deploys a retrospective profitability analysis that measures the costs and revenues per customer in the past) is provided in: Morten Holm, V. Kumar, and Carsten Rohde (2012), "Measuring Customer Profitability in Complex Environments: An Interdisciplinary Contingency Framework", *Journal of the Academy of Marketing Science*, Vol. 30, No. 3, pp. 387–401.

6 John E. Hogan, Katherine N. Lemon, and Barak Libai, "What is the True Cost of a Lost Customer?" *Journal of Services Research*, 5, No. 3 (2003): 196–208.

7 Grahame R. Dowling and Mark Uncles, "Do Customer Loyalty Programs Really Work?' *Sloan Management Review*, (Summer 1997): 71–81; Werner Reinartz and V. Kumar, "The Mismanagement of Customer Loyalty," *Harvard Business Review*, (July 2002): 86–94.

8 Werner J. Reinartz and V. Kumar, "On the Profitability of Long-Life Customers in a Non-contractual Setting: An Empirical Investigation and Implications for Marketing," *Journal of Marketing*, 64 (October 2000): 17–35.

9 Jochen Wirtz, Indranil Sen, and Sanjay Singh, "Customer Asset Management at DHL in Asia," in: *Services Marketing in Asia — A Case Book*, by Jochen Wirtz and Christopher Lovelock (Singapore: Prentice Hall, 2005), pp. 379–396.

10 Alan W. H. Grant and Leonard H. Schlesinger, "Realize Your Customer's Full Profit Potential," *Harvard Business Review*, 73 (September–October, 1995): 59–75. See also Nicolas Glady and Christophe Croux, "Predicting Customer Wallet Without Survey Data," *Journal of Service Research*, Vol. 11, No. 3 (2009): 219–231.

11 Ruth Bolton, Katherine N. Lemon, and Peter C. Verhoef, "The Theoretical Underpinnings of Customer Asset Management: A Framework and Propositions for Future Research," *Journal of the Academy of Marketing Science*, 32, No. 3 (2004): 271–292.

12 It has even been suggested to let "chronically dissatisfied customer go to allow front-line staff focus on satisfying the 'right' customers," see Ka-shing Woo and Henry K.Y. Fock, "Retaining and Divesting Customers: An Exploratory Study of Right Customers, "At-Risk" Right Customers, and Wrong Customers," *Journal of Services Marketing*, 18, No. 3 (2004): 187–197.

13 Frederick F. Reichheld, *Loyalty Rules — How Today's Leaders Build Lasting Relationships*, (Boston: MA, Harvard Business School Press, 2001), p. 45.

14 Yuping Liu, "The Long-Term Impact of Loyalty Programs on Consumer Purchase Behavior and Loyalty," *Journal of Marketing*, 71, No. 4 (October 2007): 19–35.

15 Mark R. Vondrasek (2015), "Redefining Service Innovation at Starwood", *McKinsey Quarterly*, (February).

16 Roger Hallowell, "The Relationships of Customer Satisfaction, Customer Loyalty, and Profitability: An Empirical Study," *International Journal of Service Industry Management*, 7, No. 4 (1996): 27–42.

17 This feature was adapted from Frederick F. Reichheld, *Loyalty Rules! How Today's Leaders Build Lasting Relationships*. Boston: MA, Harvard Business School Press, 2001, pp. 24–29, 84–87, 144–145; John C. Bogle (2011), *Don't Count On it! Reflections on Investment Illusions, Capitalism, 'Mutual' Funds, Indexing, Entrepreneurship, Idealism, and Heroes*. NJ: John Wiley & Sons; https://en.wikipedia.org/wiki/The_Vanguard_Group, accessed on 20 June 2016.

18 Ravi Dhar and Rashi Glazer, "Hedging Customers," *Harvard Business Review*, 81 (May 2003): 86–92.

19   David H. Maister, *True Professionalism* (New York: The Free Press, 1997). (See especially Chapter 20).

20   David Rosenblum, Doug Tomlinson and Larry Scott, "Bottom-Feeding for Blockbuster Business," *Harvard Business Review*, (March 2003): 52–59.

21   Christian Homburg, Mathias Droll and Dirk Totzek, "Customer Prioritization: Does it Pay Off, and How Should It Be Implemented?" *Journal of Marketing*, Vol. 72, No. 5 (2008): 110–130.

22   Valarie A. Zeithaml, Roland T. Rust and Katharine N. Lemon, "The Customer Pyramid: Creating and Serving Profitable Customers," *California Management Review*, 43, No. 4 (Summer 2001): 118–142.

23   Werner J. Reinartz and V. Kumar (2003), "The Impact of Customer Relationship Characteristics on Profitable Lifetime Duration," *Journal of Marketing*, Vol. 67, No. 1, pp. 77–99.

24   Vikras Mittal, Matthew Sarkees, and Feisal Murshed, "The Right Way to Manage Unprofitable Customers," *Harvard Business Review*, April (2008): 95–102.

25   Elizabeth Esfahani, "How to Get Tough with Bad Customers," *ING Direct*, October 2004, and https://home.ingdirect.com/index.html, accessed on 5 August 2011.
      Capital One Financial Corporation purchased ING Direct in 2012 and rebranded it as Capital One 360 in 2013. The positioning of the firm remained unchanged and focuses on saving customers time and money by offering simple products at low costs; see https://home.capitalone360.com; accessed on 30 June 2016.

26   Not only is there a positive relationship between satisfaction and share-of-wallet, but the greatest positive impact is seen at the upper extreme levels of satisfaction. For details, refer to Timothy L. Keiningham, Tiffany Perkins-Munn, and Heather Evans, "The Impact of Customer Satisfaction on Share-of-wallet in a Business-to-Business Environment," *Journal of Service Research*, 6, No. 1 (2003): 37–50;
      See also: Neil A. Morgan, and Lopo Leotte Rego, "The Value of Different Customer Satisfaction and Loyalty Metrics in Predicting Business Performance," *Marketing Science*, 25, No. 5 (September–October 2006): 426–439; Beth Davis-Sramek, Cornelia Droge, John T. Mentzer and Matthew B. Myers, "Creating Commitment and Loyalty Behavior Among Retailers" What Are the Roles of Service Quality and Satisfaction?" *Journal of the Academy of Marketing Science*, 37, No. 4 (2009): 440–454.; Ina Garnefeld, Sabrina Helm and Andreas Eggert, "Walk Your Talk: An Experimental Investigation of the Relationship Between Word of Mouth and Communicators' Loyalty," *Journal of Service Research*, 14, No. 1 (2011): 93–107.

27   Florian v. Wangenheim, "Postswitching Negative Word of Mouth," *Journal of Service Research*, 8, No. 1 (2005): 67–78.

28   For a review of the satisfaction-loyalty link see: V. Kumar, Ilaria Dalla Pozza, and Jaishankar Ganesh (2013), "Revisiting the Satisfaction-Loyalty Relationship: Empirical Generalizations and Directions for Further Research", *Journal of Retailing*, Vol. 89, No. 3, pp. 246–262.
      For a review of the quantiative impact of customer satisfaction on various loyalty behaviors see: Mittal, Vikas and Carly Frennea (2010) "Customer Satisfaction: A Strategic Review and Guidelines for Managers," *MSI Fast Forward Series*, Marketing Science Institute, Cambridge, MA.

29   Absolute satisfaction scores are less important in determining loyalty behaviors compared to being seen as the best or preferred provider, see: Timothy L. Keiningham, Lerzan Aksoy, Alexander Buoye, and Bruce Cooil (2011), "Customer Loyalty Isn't Enough. Grow Your Share-of-wallet", *Harvard Business Review*, Vol. 89, No. 10, pp. 29–31; Timothy L. Keiningham, Lerzan

Aksoy, Luke Williams, and Alexander Buoye (2015), *The Wallet Allocation Rule: Winning the Battle for Share*. Wiley, Hoboken, NJ.

30   Leonard L. Berry and A. Parasuraman, "Three Levels of Relationship Marketing," in *Marketing Services — Competing through Quality* (New York: N.Y.: The Free Press, 1991), pp. 136–142; and Valarie A. Zeithaml, Mary J. Bitner, and Dwayne D. Gremler, *Services Marketing*. 6th ed., (New York: N.Y.: McGraw-Hill, 2012), Chap. 7.

31   Heiner Evanschitzky, B. Ramaseshan, David M. Woisetschlager, Verena Richelsen, Markus Blut and Christof Backhaus (2012), "Consequences of Customer Loyalty to the Loyalty Program and to the Company," *Journal of the Academy of Marketing Science*, Vol. 40, No. 5, pp. 625–638; Michael Lewis, "The Influence of Loyalty Programs and Short-Term Promotions on Customer Retention", *Journal of Marketing Research*, 41 (August 2004): 281–292; Jochen Wirtz, Anna S. Mattila, and May O. Lwin, "How Effective are Loyalty Reward Programs in Driving Share-of-wallet?" *Journal of Service Research*, Vol. 9, No. 4 (2007): 327–334.
        For an excellent review of the academic literature and effectiveness of loyalty programs see: Tammo H. A. Bijmolt, Matilda Dorotic, and Peter C. Verhoef (2010), "Loyalty Programs: Generalizations on Their Adoption, Effectiveness and Design", *Foundations and Trends in Marketing*, Vol. 5, No. 5, pp. 197–258.

32   Richard Ho, Leo Huang, Stanley Huang, Tina Lee, Alexander Rosten and Christopher S. Tang, "An Approach to Develop Effective Customer Loyalty Programs: The VIP Program at T&T Supermarkets Inc," *Managing Service Quality*, 19, No. 6 (2009): 702–720.

33   Katherine N. Lemon and Florian v. Wangenheim, "The Reinforcing Effects of Loyalty Program Partnerships and Core Service Usage," *Journal of Service Research*, Vol. 11, No. 4 (2009): 357–370; Frederick DeKay, Rex S. Toh and Peter Raven, "Loyalty Programs: Airlines Outdo Hotels," *Cornell Hospitality Quarterly*, 50, No. 3 (2009): 371–382.

34   Ruth N. Bolton, P.K. Kannan and Matthew D. Bramlett, "Implications of Loyalty Program Membership and Service Experience for Customer Retention and Value," *Journal of the Academy of Marketing Science*, 28, No. 1 (2000): 95–108; Michael Lewis, "The Influence of Loyalty Programs and Short-Term Promotions on Customer Retention," *Journal of Marketing Research*, 41, No. 3 (2004): 281–292.

35   Dowling and Uncles (1997), "Do Customer Loyalty Programs Really Work?" *Sloan Management Review*, Vol. 38, No. 4, pp. 71–82.

36   Katherine N. Lemon and Florian v. Wangenheim, "The Reinforcing Effects of Loyalty Program Partnerships and Core Service Usage," *Journal of Service Research*, 11, No. 4 (2009): 357–370.

37   See for example: Iselin Skogland and Judy Siguaw, "Are Your Satisfied Customers Loyal?" *Cornell Hotel and Restaurant Administration Quarterly*, 45, No. 3 (2004): 221–234.

38   Matthew Dixon, Karen Freeman and Nicholas Toman, "Stop Trying to Delight Your Customers," *Harvard Business Review*, July–August (2010): 116–122.

39   Bernd Stauss, Maxie Schmidt, and Andreas Schoeler, "Customer Frustration in Loyalty Programs," *International Journal of Service Industry Management*, 16, No. 3 (2005): 229–252.

40   On the perception of design of loyalty tiers see: Xavier Drèze and Joseph C. Nunes, "Feeling Superior: The Impact of Loyalty Program Structure on Consumers' Perceptions of Status," *Journal of Consumer Research*, Vol. 35, No. 6 (2009): 890–905.

41   Concrete benefits related to the core service (e.g., priority early check-in and priority waitlisting) are more effective in driving customer gratitude and sales growth than status elevation without concrete benefits (i.e., the status is mostly symbolic). The latter can have a negative effect on

profitability as they are more likely to increase customer entitlement perceptions which in turn result in higher service costs; see: Hauke A. Wetzel, Maik Hammerschmidt, and Alex R. Zablah (2014), "Gratitude Versus Entitlement: A Dual Process Model of the Profitability Implications of Customer Prioritization", *Journal of Marketing*, Vol. 78, No. 2, pp. 1–19.

Furthermore, preferences for soft and hard benefits differ between customer segments, see: Praveen K. Kopalle, Yacheng Sun, Scott A. Neslin, Baohong Sun, and Vanitha Swaminathan (2012), "The Joint Sales Impact of Frequency Reward and Customer Tier Components of Loyalty Programs", *Marketing Science*, Vol. 31, No. 2, pp. 216–235. This study also found that customers experience "points pressure" which induces them to increase their spending with the firm as customer get closer to a reward or a higher service tier level. Finally, it found that both the loyalty points and service tiering have synergy and generate incremental sales.

42   Paolo Guenzi, Michael D. Johnson and Sandro Castaldo, "A Comprehensive Model of Customer Trust in Two Retail Store," *Journal of Service Management*, 20, No. 3 (2009): 290–316; Dwayne Ball, Pedro S. Coelho and Manuel J. Vilares, "Service Personalization and Loyalty," *Journal of Services Marketing*, 20, No. 6 (2006): 391–403; Alessandro Arbore, Paolo Guenzi and Andrea Ordanini, "Loyalty Building, Relational Trade-offs and Key Service Employees: The Case of Radio DJs," *Journal of Service Management*, 20, No. 3 (2009): 317–341.

43   Mark S. Rosenbaum, Amy L. Ostrom, and Ronald Kuntze, "Loyalty Programs and a Sense of Community," *Journal of Services Marketing*, 19, No. 4 (2005): 222–233; Isabelle Szmigin, Louise Canning, and Alexander E. Reppel, "Online Community: Enhancing the Relationship Marketing Concept Through Customer Bonding," *International Journal of Service Industry Management*, 16, No. 5 (2005): 480–496; Inger Roos, Anders Gustafsson and Bo Edvardsson, "The Role of Customer Clubs in Recent Telecom Relationships," *International Journal of Service Industry Management,* 16, No. 5 (2005): 436–454; Dennis Pitta, Frank Franzak, Danielle Fowler, "A Strategic Approach to Building Online Customer Loyalty: Integrating Customer Profitability Tiers," *Journal of Consumer Marketing*, 23, No. 7 (2006): 421–429; Nelson Oly Ndubisi, "Relationship Marketing and Customer Loyalty," *Marketing Intelligence & Planning*, 25, No. 1 (2007): 98–106.

44   https://www.fairmont.com/fpc/benefits; accessed 20 July 2016.

45   Rick Ferguson and Kelly Hlavinka, "The Long Tail of Loyalty: How Personalized Dialogue and Customized Rewards Will Change Marketing Forever," *Journal of Consumer Marketing*, 23, No. 6 (2006): 357–361.

46   Susan M. Keaveney, "Customer Switching Behavior in Service Industries: An Exploratory Study," *Journal of Marketing,* 59 (April 1995): 71–82.

47   Jochen Wirtz, Ping Xiao, Jeongwen Chiang and Naresh Malhotra (2014), "Contrasting Switching Intent and Switching Behavior in Contractual Service Settings", *Journal of Retailing*, Vol. 90, No. 4, pp. 463–480.

48   For a more detailed discussion of situation-specific switching behavior, refer to Inger Roos, Bo Edvardsson, and Anders Gustafsson, "Customer Switching Patterns in Competitive and Noncompetitive Service Industries," *Journal of Service Research*, 6, No. 3, (2004): 256–271.

49   Gianfranco Walsh, Keith Dinnie, and Klaus-Peter Wiedmann, "How do Corporate Reputation and Customer Satisfaction Impact Customer Defection? A Study of Private Energy Customers in Germany," *Journal of Services Marketing*, 20, No. 6, (2006): 412–420.

50   Jonathan Lee, Janghyuk Lee, and Lawrence Feick, "The Impact of Switching Costs on the Consumer Satisfaction-Loyalty Link: Mobile Phone Service in France," *Journal of Services Marketing,* 15, No. 1, (2001): 35–48; Shun Yin Lam, Venkatesh Shankar, M. Krishna Erramilli,

and Bvsan Murthy, "Customer Value, Satisfaction, Loyalty, and Switching Costs: An Illustration from a Business-to-Business Service Context," *Journal of the Academy of Marketing Science,* 32, No. 3, (2004): 293–311; Michael A. Jones, Kristy E. Reynolds, David L. Mothersbaugh and Sharon Beatty, "The Positive and Negative Effects of Switching Costs on Relational Outcomes," *Journal of Service Research,* Vol. 9, No. 4 (2007): 335–355.

For an excellent review and meta-analysis of customer perception of switching costs, see: Doreén Pick and Martin Eisend (2014), "Buyers' Perceived Switching Costs and Switching: A Meta-Analytic Assessment of Their Antecedents", *Journal of the Academy of Marketing Science,* Vol. 42, No. 2, pp. 186–204.

51 Simon J. Bell, Seigyoung Auh, and Karen Smalley, "Customer Relationship Dynamics: Service Quality and Customer Loyalty in the Context of Varying Levels of Customer Expertise and Switching Costs," *Journal of the Academy of Marketing Science,* 33, No. 2 (2005): 169–183; Markus Blut, Sharon E. Beatty, Heiner Evanschitzky, and Christian Brock (2014), "The Impact of Service Characteristics on the Switching Cost-Customer Loyalty Link", *Journal of Retailing,* Vol. 90, No. 2, pp. 275–290.

52 Arvind Malhotra and Claudia Kubowicz Malhotra (2013), "Exploring Mobile Switching Behavior of US Mobile Service Customers", *Journal of Services Marketing,* Vol. 27, No. 1, pp. 13–24; Liane Nagengast, Heiner Evanschitzky, Markus Blut and Thomas Rudolph (2014), "New Insights in the Moderating Effect of Switching Costs on the Satisfaction-Repurchase Behavior Link", *Journal of Retailing,* Vol. 90, No. 3, pp. 408–427.

53 Lesley White and Venkat Yanamandram, "Why Customers Stay: Reasons and Consequences of Inertia in Financial Services," *International Journal of Service Industry Management,* 14, No. 3 (2004): 183–194.

54 Johnson and Selnes proposed a typology of exchange relationships that included 'strangers,' 'acquaintances,' 'friends,' and 'partners' and derived implications for customer portfolio management. For details, see: Michael D. Johnson and Fred Selnes (2002), "Customer Portfolio Management: Towards a Dynamic Theory of Exchange Relationships," *Journal of Marketing,* Vol. 68, No. 2, pp. 1–17.

55 Evert Gummesson (1999), *Total Relationship Marketing.* Oxford: Butterworth-Heinemann, p. 24.

56 For an overview on CRM, see: V. Kumar and Werner J. Reinartz, *Customer Relationship Management: A Database Approach.* Hoboken, NJ: John Wiley & Sons, 2006; B. Ramaseshan, David Bejou, Subhash C. Jain, Charlotte Mason and Joseph Pancras, "Issues and Perspective in Global Customer Relationship Management," *Journal of Service Research,* 9, No. 2 (2006): 195–207; V. Kumar, Sarang Sunder and B. Ramaseshan, "Analyzing the Diffusion of Global Customer Relationship Management: A Cross-Regional Modeling Framework," *Journal of International Marketing,* 19, No. 1 (2011): 23–39.

57 Kevin N. Quiring and Nancy K. Mullen, "More Than Data Warehousing: An Integrated View of the Customer," in: *The Ultimate CRM Handbook — Strategies & Concepts for Building Enduring Customer Loyalty & Profitability,* John G. Freeland, ed., (New York: McGraw-Hill, 2002), pp. 102–108.

58 This section is adapted from: Adrian Payne and Pennie Frow, "A Strategic Framework for Customer Relationship Management," *Journal of Marketing,* 69 (October 2005): 167–176.

59 Martin Reimann, Oliver Schilke and Jacquelyn S. Thomas, "Customer Relationship Management and Firm Performance: The Mediating Role of Business Strategy," *Journal of the Academy of Marketing Science,* 38, No. 3 (2010): 326–346. The authors found that the effect

of CRM is fully mediated by the two basic strategic postures of firms: differentiation versus cost leadership. Furthermore, their study found that the effects of CRM on differentiation are stronger in highly commoditized industries compared to highly differentiated industries.

60   William Boulding, Richard Staelin, Michael Ehret and Wesley J. Johnston, "A Customer Relationship Management Roadmap: What is Known, Potential Pitfalls, and Where to Go," *Journal of Marketing,* 69, No. 4 (2005): 155–166.

61   This section is based on: Sudhir H. Kale, "CRM Failure and the Seven Deadly Sins," *Marketing Management,* (September/October 2004): 42–46.

62   William Boulding, Richard Staelin, Michael Ehret and Wesley J. Johnston, "A Customer Relationship Management Roadmap: What is Known, Potential Pitfalls, and Where to Go," *Journal of Marketing,* 69, No. 4 (2005): 155–166.

63   Darrell K. Rigby and Dianne Ledingham, "CRM Done Right," *Harvard Business Review,* (November 2004): 118–129.

64   Manuel Ebner, Arthur Hu, Daniel Levitt, and Jim McCrory, "How to Rescue CRM?" *The McKinsey Quarterly,* 4, (Technology, 2002).

65   Darrell K. Rigby and Dianne Ledingham, "CRM Done Right," *Harvard Business Review,* (November 2004): 118–129.

66   Darrell K. Rigby, Frederick F. Reichheld, and Phil Schefter, "Avoid the Four Perils of CRM," *Harvard Business Review,* (February 2002): 108.

67   Darrell K. Rigby, Frederick F. Reichheld, and Phil Schefter, "Avoid the Four Perils of CRM," *Harvard Business Review,* (February 2002): 108.

        Interestingly, research has shown that firms that implement CRM mostly because of competitive pressure reap less benefits from their CRM systems than firms that use CRM to proactively pursue their own strategic objectives; see: Bas Hillebrand, Jurriaan J. Nijholt, and Edwin J. Nijssen (2011), "Exploring CRM Effectiveness: An Institutional Theory Perspective", *Journal of the Academy of Marketing Science,* Vol. 39, No. 4, pp. 592–608.

Chapter 13

1   Even failures by other customers also have an impact on how a firm's customers feel about the firm, see Wen-Hsien Huang (2010), "Other-Customer Failure: Effects of Perceived Employee Effort and Compensation on Complainer and Non-Complainer Service Evaluations," *Journal of Service Management,* Vol. 21, No. 2, pp. 191–211.

2   Roger Bougie, Rik Pieters, and Marcel Zeelenberg, "Angry Customers Don't Come Back, They Get Back: The Experience and Behavioral Implications of Anger and Dissatisfaction in Service," *Journal of the Academy of Marketing Science,* 31, No. 4 (2003): 377–393; Florian v. Wangenheim, "Postswitching Negative Word of Mouth," *Journal of* Service *Research,* 8, No. 1 (2005): 67–78.

3   For research on cognitive and affective drivers of complaining behavior see: Jean-Charles Chebat, Moshe Davidow, and Isabelle Codjovi, "Silent Voices: Why Some Dissatisfied Consumers Fail to Complain," *Journal of Service Research,* 7, No. 4 (2005): 328–342.

4   Stephen S. Tax and Stephen W. Brown "Recovering and Learning from Service Failure", *Sloan Management Review,* 49, No. 1 (Fall 1998): 75–88.

5   A large body of literature has examined consumer complaining behavior. Important studies

include: Jean-Charles Chebat, Moshe Davidow and Isabelle Codjovi, "Silent Voices: Why Some Dissatisfied Consumers Fail to Complain," *Journal of Service Research*, 7, No. 4 (2005): 328–342; Nancy Stephens and Kevin P. Gwinner, "Why Don't Some People Complain? A Cognitive-Emotive Process Model of Consumer Complaining Behavior," *Journal of the Academy of Marketing Science*, 26, No. 3 (1998): 172–189; Kelli Bodey and Debra Grace, "Segmenting Service "Complainers" and "Non-Complainers" on the Basis of Consumer Characters," *Journal of Services Marketing*, 20, No. 3 (2006): 178–187.

6   Cathy Goodwin and B.J. Verhage, "Role Perceptions of Services: A Cross-Cultural Comparison with Behavioral Implications," *Journal of Economic Psychology*, 10 (1990): 543–558.

7   Nancy Stephens, "Complaining," in *Handbook of Services Marketing and Management*, Teresa A. Swartz & Dawn Iacobucci (eds.), (California: Thousand Oaks, Sage Publications, 2000), 291; Alex M. Susskind (2015), "Communication Richness: Why some Guest Complaints Go Right to the Top — and Others Don't", *Cornell Hospitality Quarterly*, Vol. 56, No. 3, pp. 320–331.

8   John Goodman, "Basic Facts on Customer Complaint Behavior and the Impact of Service on the Bottom Line," *Competitive Advantage*, June 1999, pp. 1–5.

9   Anna Mattila and Jochen Wirtz, "Consumer Complaining to Firms: The Determinants of Channel Choice," *Journal of Services Marketing*, 18, No. 2 (2004): 147–155; Kaisa Snellman and Tiina Vihtkari, "Customer Complaining Behavior in Technology-based Service Encounters," *International Journal of Service Industry Management*, 14, No. 2 (2003): 217–231; Terri Shapiro and Jennifer Nieman-Gonder, "Effect of Communication Mode in Justice-Based Service Recovery." *Managing Service Quality*, 16, No. 2 (2006): 124–144.

10   Technical Assistance Research Programs Institute (TARP), *Consumer Complaint Handling in America; An Update Study, Part II* (Washington DC: TARP and US Office of Consumer Affairs, April 1986).

11   Thomas M. Tripp and Yany Gregoire, "When Unhappy Customers Strike Back on the Internet," *MIT Sloan Management Review*, 52, No. 3 (Spring 2011): 37–44; Sven Tuzovic, "Frequent (Flier) Frustration and the Dark Side of Word-of-Web: Exploring Online Dysfunctional Behavior in Online Feedback Forums," *Journal of Services Marketing*, 24, No. 6 (2010): 446–457.

12   Kathleen Seiders and Leonard L. Berry, "Service Fairness: What it is and Why it Matters," *Academy of Management Executive*, 12, No. 2 (1990): 8–20.

       For review on complaint handling and customer satisfaction, see Katja Gelbrich and Holger Roschk, "A Meta-Analysis of Organizational Complaint Handling and Customer Responses," *Journal of Service Research*, 14, No. 1 (2011): 24–43.

       See also Klaus Schoefer and Adamantios Diamantopoulos (2008), "The Role of Emotions in Transaction Perceptions of (In)Justice into Postcomplaint Behavioral Responses," *Journal of Service Research*, Vol. 11, No. 1, pp. 91–103; Yany Grégoire and Robert J. Fisher (2008), "Customer Betrayal and Retaliation: When Your Best Customers Become Your Worst Enemies," *Journal of the Academy of Marketing Science*, Vol. 36, No. 2, pp. 247–261; Zheng Fang, Xueming Luo, and Minghua Jiang (2012), "Quantifying the Dynamic Effects of Service Recovery on Customer Satisfaction: Evidence from Chinese Mobile Phone Markets", *Journal of Service Research*, Vol. 16, No. 3, pp. 341–355; Ana Belén del Río-Lanza, Rodolfo Vázquez-Casielles, Ana María Díaz-Martín (2009), "Satisfaction with Service Recovery: Perceived Justice and Emotional Responses", *Journal of Business Research*, Vol. 62, Vol. 8, pp. 775–781.

13   Stephen S. Tax and Stephen W. Brown "Recovering and Learning from Service Failure", *Sloan Management Review*, 49, No. 1 (Fall 1998): 75–88;

       See also Tor Wallin Andreassen, "Antecedents of Service Recovery," *European Journal of Marketing*, 34, No. 1 and 2 (2000): 156–175; Ko de Ruyter and Martin Wetzel, "Customer

Equity Considerations in Service Recovery," *International Journal of Service Industry Management*, 13, No. 1 (2002): 91–108; Janet R. McColl-Kennedy and Beverley A. Sparks, "Application of Fairness Theory to Service Failures and Service Recovery," *Journal of Service Research*, 5, No. 3 (2003): 251–266; Jochen Wirtz and Anna Mattila, "Consumer Responses to Compensation, Speed of Recovery and Apology After a Service Failure," *International Journal of Service Industry Management*, 15, No. 2 (2004): 150–166.

For a meta-analysis of the effects of fairness on consumer responses, see: Chiara Orsingher, Sara Valentini, and Matteo de Angelis (2010), "A Meta-Analysis of Satisfaction with Complaint Handling in Services", *Journal of the Academy of Marketing Science*, Vol. 38, No. 2, pp. 169–186.

14   Oren Harari, "Thank Heavens for Complainers," *Management Review*, (March 1997): 25–29.

15   Tom DeWitt, Doan T. Nguyen, and Roger Marshall, "Exploring Customer Loyalty Following Service Recovery," *Journal of Service Research*, Vol. 10, No. 3 (2008): 269–281.

16   Simon J. Bell and James A. Luddington, "Coping with Customer Complaints." *Journal of Service Research*, 8, No. 3 (February 2006): 221–233.

17   Leonard L. Berry, *On Great Service: A Framework for Action* (New York: The Free Press, 1995), p. 94.

For a meta-analysis on the customer attribution process and how to effectively manage customer attributions of service failures see: Yves Van Vaerenbergh, Chiara Orsingher, Iris Vermeir, and Bart Larivière (2014), "A Meta-Analysis of Relationships Linking Service Failure Attributions to Customer Outcomes", *Journal of Service Research*, Vol. 17, No. 4, pp. 381–398.

18   Susan M. Keaveney, "Customer Switching Behavior in Service Industries: An Exploratory Study," *Journal of Marketing*, 59 (April 1995): 71–82.

19   Customer Care Measurement & Consulting (CCMC), *2007 National Customer Rage Study*, Customer Care Alliance, 2007.

20   Technical Assistance Research Programs Institute (TARP), *Consumer Complaint Handling in America; An Update Study, Part II* (Washington DC: TARP and US Office of Consumer Affairs, April 1986). Since this study, CCMC and W. P. Carey School of Business, Arizona State University (ASU) have conducted six follow-on studies, known as the "Customer Rage Studies", to explore important, emerging trends in the customer experience related to complaining behavior and service recovery. For highlights of the latest study, "The 2013 Customer Rage Study", see http://www.customercaremc.com/wp/wp-content/uploads/2014/01/KeyFindingsFrom2013NationalCustomerRageSurvey.pdf.

Not addressing a service failure or dissatisfaction with a service recovery effort has been shown to result in various negative customer responses, including revenge, rage, and opportunistic behaviors; Yany Grègoire, Daniel Laufer and Thomas M. Tripp (2010), "A Comprehensive Model of Customer Direct and Indirect Revenge: Understanding the Effects of Perceived Greed and Customer Power", *Journal of the Academy of Marketing Science*, Vol. 38, No. 6, pp. 738–758.

21   For a discussion on how to quantify complaint management profitability, see: Bernd Stauss and Andreas Schoeler, "Complaint Management Profitability: What do Complaint Managers Know?" *Managing Service Quality*, 14, No. 2/3 (2004): 147–156.

For a comprehensive treatment of all aspects of effective complaint management see Bernd Stauss and Wolfgang Seidel, *Complaint Management: The Heart of CRM* (Mason, Ohio: Thomson, 2004); and Janelle Barlow and Claus Møller, *A Complaint is a Gift*. 2nd ed., San Francisco, CA: Berrett-Koehler Publishers, 2008.

22   Celso Augusto de Matos, Jorge Luiz Henrique, and Carlos Alberto Vargas Rossi, "Service

Recovery Paradox: A Meta-Analysis," *Journal of Service Research,* Vol. 10, No. 1 (2007): 60–77; Randi Priluck and Vishal Lala, "The Impact of the Recovery Paradox on Retailer-Customer Relationships," *Managing Service Quality,* Vol. 19, No. 1 (2009): 42–59.

23   Stefan Michel and Matthew L. Meuter, "The Service Recovery Paradox: True but Overrated?" *International Journal of Service Industry Management,* Vol. 19, No. 4 (2008): 441–457.

Other studies also confirmed that the service recovery paradox does not hold universally; Tor Wallin Andreassen, "From Disgust to Delight: Do Customers Hold a Grudge?" *Journal of Service Research,* 4, No. 1 (2001): 39–49; Michael A. McCollough, Leonard L. Berry and Manjit S. Yadav, "An Empirical Investigation of Customer Satisfaction after Service Failure and Recovery," *Journal of Service Research,* 3, No. 2 (2000): 121–137; James G. Maxhamm III, "Service Recovery's Influence on Consumer Satisfaction, Positive Word-of-Mouth, and Purchase Intentions," *Journal of Business Research,* 54 (2001): 11–24; Chihyung Ok, Ki-Joon Back and Carol W. Shankin, "Mixed Findings on the Service Recovery Paradox," *The Service Industries Journal,* Vol. 27, No. 5 (2007): 671–686.

24   James G. Maxham III and Richard G. Netemeyer, "A Longitudinal Study of Complaining Customers' Evaluations of Multiple Service Failures and Recovery Efforts," *Journal of Marketing,* 66, No. 4 (2002): 57–72.

25   Michael Hargrove, cited in Ron Kaufman, UP! Your Service (Singapore: Ron Kaufman Plc. Ltd., 2005): 225.

26   Steven S. Tax and Steven W. Brown (1998), "Recovering and Learning from Service Failure", Sloan Management Review, Vol. 40, No. 1, pp. 75–88; Stephen S. Tax, Stephen W. Brown, and Murali Chandrashekaran, "Customer Evaluation of Service Complaint Experiences: Implications for Relationship Marketing," *Journal of Marketing,* 62, No. 2 (Spring 1998): 60–76.

For a study in the online environment, see: Betsy B. Holloway and Sharon E. Beatty, "Service Failure in Online Retailing: A Recovery Opportunity," *Journal of Service Research,* 6, No. 1 (2003): 92–105.

27   For a discussion on how to quantify complaint management profitability see: Bernd Stauss and Andreas Schoeler, "Complaint Management Profitability: What do Complaint Managers Know?" *Managing Service Quality,* 14, No. 2/3 (2004): 147–156).

For a comprehensive treatment of all aspects of effective complaint management, see Bernd Stauss and Wolfgang Seidel, *Complaint Management: The Heart of CRM* (Mason, Ohio: Thomson, 2004); and Janelle Barlow and Claus Móller, *A Complaint is a Gift.* 2nd ed., San Francisco, CA: Berrett-Koehler Publishers, 2008.

28   Christian Homburg and Andreas Fürst, "How Organizational Complaint Handling Drives Customer Loyalty: An Analysis of the Mechanistic and the Organic Approach," *Journal of Marketing,* 69, (July 2005): 95–114.

29   Ron Zemke and Chip R. Bell, *Knock Your Socks Off Service Recovery,* (New York: AMACOM, 2000), p. 60.

30   Barbara R. Lewis, "Customer Care in Services," in *Understanding Services Management,* eds. W.J. Glynn and J.G. Barnes (UK: Chichester, Wiley 1995), pp. 57–89.

Prior rapport between employees and customers has also been shown to improve service recovery satisfaction, see: Tom DeWitt and Michael K. Brady, "Rethinking Service Recovery Strategies: The Effect of Rapport on Customer Responses to Service Failure," *Journal of Service Research,* 6, No. 2 (2003): 193–207.

31   Josh Bernoff and Ted Schadler, "Empowered," *Harvard Business Review,* July–August (2010): 95–101.

32   The incremental impact of increasing compensation depends on whether customer accept the value proposition of the service delivered (i.e., the service provided value-in-use to the customer). If not, high levels of compensation are required to achieve post-complaint satisfaction; see: Katja Gelbrich, Jana Gäthke and Yany Grégoire (2015), "How Much Compensation Should a Firm Offer for a Flawed Service? An Examination of the Nonlinear Effects of Compensation on Satisfaction", *Journal of Service Research*, Vol. 18, No. 1, pp. 107–123.

33   Rhonda Mack, Rene Mueller, John Crotts, and Amanda Broderick, "Perceptions, Corrections and Defections: Implications for Service Recovery in the Restaurant Industry," *Managing Service Quality*, 10, No. 6 (2000): 339–46.

34   Jochen Wirtz and Janet R. McColl-Kennedy, "Opportunistic Customer Claiming During Service Recovery," *Journal of the Academy of Marketing Science*, 38, No. 5 (2010): 654–675.

35   Matthew Dixon, Karen Freeman and Nicholas Toman (2010), "Stop Trying to Delight Your Customers: To Really Win their Loyalty, forget the bells and whistles and just solve their problems", *Harvard Business Review*, Vol. 88, No. 7/8, pp. 116–122.

36   A comprehensive assessment tool of service recovery performance comprises of the following nine dimensions: (1) Apology, (2) Compensation, (3) Explanation, (4) Follow-up, (5) Facilitation, (6) Speed of Response, (7) Courtesy, (8) Effort, and (9) Problem-solving. The tool is called CURE scale (CUstomer REcovery scale), which organizations can use to identify the impact of these service recovery actions on customer responses; see: Rania Mostafa, Cristiana R. Lages, and Maria Sääksjärvi (2014), "The CURE Scale: A Multidimensional Measure of Service Recovery Strategy", *Journal of Services Marketing*, Vol. 28, No. 4, pp. 300–310.

37   For an excellent review of extant academic literature on service guarantees see: Jens Hogreve and Dwayne D. Gremler, "Twenty Years of Service Guarantee Research," *Journal of Service Research*, Vol. 11, No. 4 (2009): 322–343.

38   Christopher W. L Hart, "The Power of Unconditional Service Guarantees," *Harvard Business Review*, (July–August 1988), pp. 54–62.

39   L.A. Tucci and J. Talaga, "Service guarantees and consumers' evaluation of services." *Journal of Services Marketing*, 11, No. 1 (1997), 10–18; Amy Ostrom and Dawn Iacobucci, "The Effect of Guarantees on Consumers' Evaluation of Services," *Journal of Services Marketing*, 12, No. 5 (1998), pp. 362–78.

40   Sara Björlin Lidén and Per Skålén, "The Effect of Service Guarantees on Service Recovery," *International Journal of Service Industry Management*, 14, No. 1, (2003), pp. 36–58.

41   Christopher W. Hart and Elizabeth Long, *Extraordinary Guarantees*, (New York: AMACOM, 1997).

42   Christopher W. Hart, "The Power of Unconditional Service Guarantees."

43   For a scientific discussion on the optimal guarantee payout amount, see: Tim Baker and David A. Collier, "The Economic Payout Model for Service Guarantees," *Decision Sciences*, 36, No. 2 (2005): 197–220).

44   McDougall, Gordon H., Terence Levesque and Peter VanderPlaat, "Designing the Service Guarantee: Unconditional or Specific?" *Journal of Services Marketing*, 12, No. 4 (1998): 278–293; Jochen Wirtz, "Development of a Service Guarantee Model," *Asia Pacific Journal of Management*, 15, No. 1 (1998): 51–75.

45   Jochen Wirtz and Doreen Kum, "Designing Service Guarantees — Is Full Satisfaction the Best You can Guarantee?" *Journal of Services Marketing*, 15, No. 4 (2001): 282–299.

46　Amy L. Ostrom and Christopher Hart, "Service Guarantee: Research and Practice," in *Handbook of Services Marketing and Management*, ed. T. Schwartz and D. Iacobucci (California: Thousand Oaks, Sage Publications, 2000), pp. 299–316.

47　Jochen Wirtz, Doreen Kum and Khai Sheang Lee (2000), "Should a Firm with a Reputation for Outstanding Service Quality Offer a Service Guarantee?" *Journal of Services Marketing*, Vol. 14, No. 6, pp. 502–512.
　　For the impact of implicit service guarantees on business performance see: Hyunju Shin and Alexander E. Ellinger (2013), "The Effect of Implicit Service Guarantees on Business Performance", *Journal of Services Marketing*, Vol. 27, No. 6, pp. 431–442.

48　For a decision support model and whether to have a service guarantee, and if yes, on how to design and implement it, see: Louis Fabien, "Design and Implementation of a Service Guarantee," *Journal of Services Marketing*, 19, No. 1 (2005): 33–38.

49　A large body of literature has examined the behavior of jaycustomers. Important studies include: Ray Fisk, Stephen Grove, Lloyd C. Harris, Kate L. Daunt, Dominique Keeffe, Rebekah Russell-Bennett and Jochen Wirtz, "Customers Behaving Badly: A State of the Art Review, Research Agenda and Implications for Practitioners", *Journal of Services Marketing*, 24, No. 6 (2010): 417–429; Lloyd C. Harris and Kate L. Reynolds, "Jaycustomer Behavior: An Exploration of Types and Motives in the Hospitality Industry," *Journal of Services Marketing*, 18, No. 5 (2004): 339–357; Kate L. Reynolds and Lloyd C. Harris, "Dysfunctional Customer Behavior Severity: An Empirical Examination," *Journal of Retailing*, 85, No. 3 (2009): 321–335; Kate L. Daunt and Harris C. Lloyd, "Customers Acting Badly: Evidence from the Hospitality Industry," *Journal of Business Research*, 64, No. 10 (2011): 1034–1042.

50　This section is adapted and updated from Christopher Lovelock, *Product Plus*. New York: McGraw-Hill, 1994, Chap. 15. For an additional discussion of jaycustomers, see Leonard L. Berry and Kathleen Seiders (2008), "Serving Unfair Customers", *Business Horizons*, Vol. 51, No. 1, pp. 29–37.

51　There is a large literature on opportunistic customer behavior. Important studies include: Harris, Lloyd C. and Kate L. Reynolds (2003), "The Consequences of Dysfunctional Customer Behavior", *Journal of Service Research*, 6(2), 144–161; Jochen Wirtz and Janet R. McColl-Kennedy (2010), "Opportunistic Customer Claiming During Service Recovery," *Journal of the Academy of Marketing Science*, Vol. 38, No. 5, 654–675; Chu Wujin, Eitan Gerstner and James D. Hess (1998), "Managing Dissatisfaction: How to Decrease Customer Opportunism by Partial Refunds," *Journal of Service Research*, Vol. 1, No. 2, pp. 140–155.
　　Important research exploring opportunism in the B2B context includes: Steven H. Seggie, David A. Griffith, and Sandy D. Jap (2013), "Passive and Active Opportunism in Interorganizational Exchange", *Journal of Marketing*, Vol. 77, No. 6, pp. 73–90; Qiong Wang, Julie Juan Li, William T. Ross Jr., Christopher W. Craighead (2013), "The Interplay of Drivers and Deterrents of Opportunism in Buyer-Supplier Relationships", *Journal of the Academy of Marketing Science*, Vol. 41, No. 1, pp. 111–131. Lloyd C. Harris, "Fraudulent Return Proclivity: An Empirical Analysis," *Journal of Retailing*, 84, No. 4, (2008): 461–476. Some customers are out to take full advantage of return policies.

52　*The Economist* (2013), "Online Retailing, Return to Santa: E-commerce Firms have a Hard Core of Costly, Impossible-to-please Customers", 21 December 2013, p. 103.

53　Kate L. Reynolds and Lloyd C. Harris (2005), "When Service Failure is Not Service Failure: An Exploration of the Forms and Motives of "Illegitimate" Customer Complaining," *Journal of Services Marketing*, Vol. 19, No. 5, p. 326.

54   Harris, Lloyd C. and Kate L. Reynolds (2004), "Jaycustomer Behavior: An Exploration of Types and Motives in the Hospitality Industry", *Journal of Services Marketing*, Vol. 18, No. 5, p. 339.

55   Stephen J. Grove, Raymond P. Fisk, and Joby John, "Surviving in the Age of Rage," *Marketing Management*, March/April 2004, pp. 41–46.

56   Roger Bougie, Rik Pieters, and Marcel Zeelenberg, Angry Customers Don't Come Back, They Get Back: The Experience and Behavioral Implications of Anger and Dissatisfaction in Services," *Journal of the Academy of Marketing Science*, 31, No. 4, 2003: 377–393.
        Further important studies on customer rage include: Jiraporn Surachartkumtonkun, Paul G. Patternson, and Janet R. McColl-Kennedy (2013), "Customer Rage Back-Story: Linking Needs-Based Cognitive Appraisal to Service Failure Type", *Journal of Retailing*, Vol. 89, No. 1, pp. 72–87; Thomas M. Tripp and Yany Grégoire (2011), "When Unhappy Customers Strike Back on the Internet", *Sloan Management Review*, Vol. 52, No. 3, pp. 1–10; Stephen J. Grove, Gregory M. Pickett, Scott A. Jones, and Michael J. Dorsch (2012), "Spectator Rage as the Dark Side of Engaging Sport Fans: Implications for Service Marketers", *Journal of Service Research*, Vol. 15, No. 1, pp. 3–20.

57   Blair J. Berkley and Mohammad Ala, "Identifying and Controlling Threatening Airline Passengers, *Cornell Hotel and Restaurant Administration Quarterly*, 42, August–September 2001: 6–24.

58   Lloyd C. Harris and Kate L. Reynolds, "The Consequences of Dysfunctional Customer Behavior," *Journal of Service Research*, 6, November 2003: 144–161; Lloyd C. Harris and Kate L. Reynolds, "Jaycustomer Behavior: An Exploration of Types and Motives in the Hospitality Industry," *Journal of Services Marketing*, 18, No. 5, 2004: 339–357.

59   Recent research has explored how firms can help their frontline employees to deal with the job stress related to illegitimate and unreasonable dysfunctional customer behavior: Taeshik Gong, Youjae Yi, and Jin Nam Choi (2014), "Helping Employees Deal with Dysfunctional Customers: Employee Perceived Justice Mechanism", *Journal of Service Research*, Vol. 17, No. 1, pp. 102–116.

60   John Goodman, quoted in "Improving Service Doesn't Always Require Big Investment," *The Service Edge*, (July–August, 1990): 3.

61   Jill Griffin, "What Your Worst Customers Teach You About Loyalty," 24 January 2006, http://www.marketingprofs.com/6/griffin5.asp; accessed on 22 August 2016.

62   Jochen Wirtz and Doreen Kum, "Consumer Cheating on Service Guarantees," *Journal of the Academy of Marketing Science*; 32, No. 2. (2004): 159–175; Jochen Wirtz and Janet R. McColl-Kennedy, "Opportunistic Customer Claiming During Service Recovery," *Journal of the Academy of Marketing Science*, 38, No. 5, (2010): 654–675; Heejung Ro and June Wong (2012), "Customer Opportunistic Complaints Management: A Critical Incident Approach," *International Journal of Hospitality Management*, Vol. 31, No. 2, pp. 419–427.
        For additional research on how to manage opportunistic customers and jaycustomers, see: Lloyd C. Harris and Kate Daunt (2013), "Managing Customer Misbehavior: Challenges and Strategies", *Journal of Services Marketing*, Vol. 27, No. 4, pp. 281–293.

Chapter 14

1   This section was adapted from Jochen Wirtz and Valarie Zeithaml (2015), "Cost-Effective Service Excellence: Developing a Conceptual Framework", in: *Always Ahead in Marketing: Offensiv, Digital, Strategisch*, by Bartsch, Silke and Blümelhuber, Christian (eds.), Wiesbaden: Gabler Verlag, Germany, pp. 547–557.

2   For an integrative framework of quality that captures how firms and customers produce quality, see: Peter N. Golder, Debanjan Mitra, and Christine Moorman (2012), "What is Quality? An Integrative Framework of Processes and States", *Journal of Marketing*, Vol. 76, No. 4, pp. 1–12.

3   Christian Grönroos, *Service Management and Marketing. 3rd ed.*, (Chichester, NY: Wiley, 2007).

4   A. Parasuraman, Valarie A. Zeithaml, and Leonard L. Berry, "A Conceptual Model of Service Quality and Its Implications for Future Research," *Journal of Marketing*, 49, Fall 1985, pp. 41–50; Valarie A. Zeithaml, Leonard L. Berry, and A. Parasuraman, "Communication and Control Processes in the Delivery of Services," *Journal of Marketing*, 52, April 1988, pp. 36–58.

5   The sub-gaps in this model are based on the 7-gaps model by Christopher Lovelock (1994), *Product Plus: How Product + Service = Competitive Advantage*. New York: McGraw-Hill, p. 112.

6   Valarie A. Zeithaml, Mary Jo Bitner, and Dwayne D. Gremler (2013), *Services Marketing: Integrating Customer Focus Across the Firm. 5th ed.*, New York: McGraw-Hill, p. 261.

7   This section is based partially on Jochen Wirtz and Monica Tomlin, "Institutionalizing Customer-driven Learning Through Fully Integrated Customer Feedback Systems," *Managing Service Quality*, 10, No. 4, (2000): 205–215.

        Additional reading on service quality measurement can be found in Ching-Chow Yang, "Establishment and Applications of the Integrated Model of Service Quality Measurement," *Managing Service Quality*, 13, No. 4, (2003): 310–324.

8   Leonard L. Berry and A. Parasuraman, "Listening to the Customer — The Concept of a Service Quality Information System," *Sloan Management Review*, 38, Spring 1997, pp. 65–76.

9   Customer listening practices have been shown to affect service performance, growth and profitability, see: William J. Glynn, Sean de Búrca, Teresa Brannick, Brian Fynes, and Sean Ennis, "Listening Practices and Performance in Service Organizations," *International Journal of Service Industry Management*, 14, (No. 3, 2003), pp. 310–330.

10   Baker W. E., and Sinkula J. M., "The Synergistic Effect of Market Orientation and Learning Orientation on Organizational Performance", *Journal of the Academy of Marketing Science*, 27, No. 4 (1999): 411–427.

11   Neil A. Morgan, Eugene W. Anderson, and Vikas Mittal, "Understanding Firms' Customer Satisfaction information Usage," *Journal of Marketing*, 69, July 2005, pp. 131–151.

12   Leonard L. Berry and A. Parasuraman provide an excellent overview of all key research approaches discussed in this section plus a number of other tools in their paper, "Listening to the Customer — The Concept of a Service Quality Information System," *Sloan Management Review*, 38, Spring 1997: 65–76.

13   For a discussion on suitable satisfaction measures, see Jochen Wirtz and Lee Meng Chung, "An Examination of the Quality and Context-Specific Applicability of Commonly Used Customer Satisfaction Measures," *Journal of Service Research*, 5, May 2003: 345–355.

14   Mobile apps have been developed that can track customers' experiences in real time, supply instant information and are highly cost-effective, see: Emma K. Macdonald, Hugh N. Wilson, and Umut Konuş (2012), *Harvard Business Review*, Vol. 90, No. 9, pp. 90, pp. 102–108.

15   Robert Johnston and Sandy Mehra, "Best-Practice Complaint Management," *Academy of Management Executive*, 16, No. 4 (2002): 145–154.

16   Seshadri Tirunillai and Gerard J. Tellis (2014), "Mining Marketing Meaning from Online

Chatter: Strategic Brand Analysis of Big Data Using Latent Dirichlet Allocation", *Journal of Marketing Science*, Vol. 51, No. 4, pp. 463–479.

17   Advanced analytical tools allow analysis and visualization of online posted reviews; see Thomas Y. Lee and Eric T. Bradlow (2011), "Automated Marketing Research Using Online Customer Reviews", *Journal of Marketing Research*, Vol. 48, No. 5, pp. 881–894.

The technology for analyzing unstructured textual data (provided to the firm as customer feedback, or if posted online) is advancing rapidly. For a recent study exploring the use for customer feedback mapping on service blue prints, see: Francisco Villarroel Ordenes, Babis Theodoulidis, Jamie Burton, Thorsten Gruber, and Mohamed Zaki (2014), "Analyzing Customer Experience Feedback Using Text Mining: A Linguistics-Based Approach", *Journal of Service Research*, Vol. 17, No. 3, pp. 278–295.

18   Note, however, that there are differences across online media. For example, sentiments expressed in blogs tend to be more positive than those posted in other media such as forums, see: David A. Schweidel and Wendy W. Moe (2014), "Listening In on Social Media: A Joint Model of Sentiment and Venue Format Choice", *Journal of Marketing Research*, Vol. 51, No. 4, pp. 387–402.

19   Roland T. Rust and Ming-Hui Huang (2014), "The Service Revolution and the Transformation of Marketing Science", *Marketing Science*, Vol. 33, No. 2, pp. 206–221; Anindya Ghose, Panagiotis G. Ipeirotis P.G., and Beibei Li (2012), "Designing Marketing Ranking Systems for Hotels on Travel Search Engines by Mining User-Generated and Crowdsourced Content", *Marketing Science*, Vol. 31, No. 3, pp. 493–520.

20   Duncan Simester (2011), "When You Shouldn't Listen to Your Critics", *Harvard Business Review*, Vol. 89, No. 6, p. 42.

21   Comments by Thomas R. Oliver, then senior vice president, sales and customer service, Federal Express; reported in Christopher H. Lovelock, *Federal Express: Quality Improvement Program, Lausanne: International Institute for Management Development*, (1990).

22   Christopher Lovelock, *Product Plus: How Product + Service = Competitive Advantage* (New York: McGraw-Hill, 1994), p. 218.

23   These categories and the research data that follow have been adapted from information in D. Daryl Wyckoff, "New Tools for Achieving Service Quality", *Cornell Hotel and Restaurant Administration Quarterly*, (August–September 2001), pp. 25–38.

24   Roland T. Rust, Anthony J. Zahonik, and Timothy L. Keiningham, "Return on Quality (ROQ): Making Service Quality Financially Accountable", *Journal of Marketing*, 59 (April 1995): 58–70; and Roland T. Rust, Christine Moorman, and Peter R. Dickson, "Getting Return on Quality: Revenue Expansion, Cost Reduction, or Both?" *Journal of Marketing*, 66 (October 2002), pp. 7–24.

25   Marginal utility analysis was found to outperform analyses based on importance-performance and regression analyses, see: Donald R. Bacon (2012), "Understanding Priorities for Service Attribute Improvement", *Journal of Service Research*, Vol. 15, No. 2, pp. 199–214.

26   Martin Neil Baily, Diana Farrell, and Jaana Remes (2006), "Where US Productivity is Growing." *The McKinsey Quarterly*, No. 2, pp. 10–12.

For EU data, see: Kristian Uppenberg and Hubert Strauss (2010), *Innovation and Productivity Growth in the EU Services Sector*. European Investment Bank, the publication is available at: http://www.eib.org/attachments/efs/efs_innovation_and_productivity_en.pdf.

27   Kenneth J. Klassen, Randolph M. Russell, and James J. Chrisman, "Efficiency and Productivity Measures for High Contact Services," *The Service Industries Journal*, 18 (October 1998): 1–18; James L. Heskett, *Managing in the Service Economy*, (New York: The Free Press, 1986).
      For a review and discussion on service productivity, see: Christian Grönroos and Katri Ojasalo (2004), "Service Productivity: Towards a Conceptualization of the Transformation of Inputs into Economic Results in Services," *Journal of Business Research*, Vol. 57, No. 4, pp. 414–423.

28   Rust and Huang examined the trade-off between using labor to provide service (which generally increases service quality and effectiveness) and using automation and technology (which increases productivity). Depending on the competitive positioning of a firm, different levels of optimal productivity emerge, see: Roland T. Rust and Ming-Hui Huang (2012), "Optimizing Service Productivity," *Journal of Marketing*, Vol. 76, No. 2, pp. 47–66.

29   For a more in-depth discussion on service productivity, refer to Cynthia Karen Swank, "The Lean Service Machine," *Harvard Business Review*, 81, No. 10, 2003, pp. 123–129.

30   C. Mele and M. Colurcio, "The Evolving Path of TQM: Towards Business Excellence and Stakeholder Value," *International Journal of Quality and Reliability Management*, 23, No. 5, 2006, pp. 464–489; C. Mele, "The Synergic Relationship Between TQM and Marketing in Creating Customer Value," *Managing Service Quality*, 17, No. 3, 2007, pp. 240–258.

31   G. S. Sureshchandar, Chandrasekharan Rajendran, and R. N. Anantharaman, "A Holistic Model for Total Service Quality," *International Journal of Service Industry Management*, 12, No. 4, 2001, pp. 378–412.

32   See the official website of (International Organization for Standardization (ISO) for detailed information on ISO: http://www.iso.org.
      The ISO 9000 family of standards is described at: http://www.iso.org/iso/home/standards/management-standards/iso_9000.htm and an introduction is provided in the publication: ISO Central Secretariat (2009), *Selection and Use of the ISO 9000 Family of Standards*. ISO, ISBN: 978-92-67-10494-2; (this book can be downloaded for free from the ISO 9000 website).

33   Jim Biolos, "Six Sigma Meets the Service Economy," *Harvard Business Review*, 80, November 2002, pp. 3–5.

34   Mikel Harry and Richard Schroeder, *Six Sigma — The Breakthrough Management Strategy Revolutionizing the World's Top Corporations*, New York: Currency, 2000, p. 232.

35   Peter S. Pande, Robert P. Neuman, and Ronald R. Cavanagh, *The Six Sigma Way: How GE, Motorola, and Other Top Companies Are Honing their Performance*, New York: McGraw-Hill, 2000.

36   The official website for the Malcolm Baldrige Award is http://www.nist.gov/baldrige.
      The official website for the European Foundation for Quality Management (EFQM) it is http://www.efqm.org, and an overview of the EFQM model is provided at http://www.efqm.org/sites/default/files/overview_efqm_2013_v1.1.pdf.

37   Susan Meyer Goldstein and Sharon B. Schweikhart, "Empirical Support for the Baldrige Award Framework in U.S. Hospitals," *Health Care Management Review*, 27, No. 1, 2002, pp. 62–75.

38   Allan Shirks, William B. Weeks, and Annie Stein, "Baldrige-Based Quality Awards: Veterans Health Administration's 3-Year Experience," *Quality Management in Health Care*, 10, No. 3, 2002, pp. 47–54; National Institute of Standards and Technology, "Baldrige FAQs," http://www.nist.gov/baldrige/about/baldrige_faqs.cfm, accessed 1 September 2015.

39   Cathy A. Enz and Judy A. Siguaw, "Best Practices in Service Quality," *Cornell Hotel and Restaurant Administration Quarterly,* (October 2000): 20–29.

40   Eight NIST Stock Investment Study, (USA: Gaithersburg, National Institute of Standards and Technology, March 2002).

41   Gavin Dick, Kevin Gallimore and Jane C. Brown, "ISO 9000 and Quality Emphasis: An Empirical study of Front-Room and Back Room Dominated Service Industries," *International Journal of Service Industry Management,* 12, No. 2 (2001): 114–136; and Adrian Hughes and David N. Halsall, "Comparison of the 14 Deadly Diseases and the Business Excellence Model," *Total Quality Management,* 13, No. 2 (2002): 255–263.

Chapter 15

1   Peter Drucker did not regard himself as a marketer, yet his writing has had profound impact on the marketing field and discipline. The opening quote is discussed further in: Frederick E. Webster Jr., "Marketing IS management: The wisdom of Peter Drucker," *Journal of the Academy of Marketing Science,* Vol. 37, No. 1 (2009): 20–27.

2   The operations perspective was originally developed by: Richard B. Chase and Robert H. Hayes, "Beefing Up Operations in Service Firms," *Sloan Management Review,* Fall 1991, pp. 15–26. The framework shown in this chapter has been significantly extended to incorporate the marketing and HR functions, and has been updated.

3   Claudia H. Deutsch, "Management: Companies Scramble to Fill Shoes at the Top," *nytimes. com,* 1 November 2000.

4   This book provides you with the tools and knowledge to develop a winning services marketing strategy and with key tools to shape HR, operations and IT towards service excellence. In addition, there are a number of audit tools and checklists you can consult to assess a service organization. They include:
      James L. Heskett, W. Earl Sasser, and Leonard A. Schlesinger (2003), *The Value Profit Chain: Treat Employees Like Customers and Customers Like Employees.* Free Press, NY: New York, Appendix B: The Value Profit Chain Audit, pp. 318–337.
      James L. Heskett, W. Earl Sasser, and Joe Wheeler (2008), *The Ownership Quotient: Putting the Service Profit Chain to Work for Unbeatable Competitive Advantage.* Boston, Massachusetts: Harvard Business Press, Appendix B: Audition Ownership, pp. 193–203.
      The European Foundation for Quality Management (EFQM) has detailed assessment sheets for all dimensions of the EFQM Model. They can be downloaded free-of-charge from http://www.efqm.org/efqm-model/efqm-model-in-action-0.

5   Eugene W. Anderson and Vikas Mittal, "Strengthening the Satisfaction-Profit Chain," *Journal of Service Research,* 3, November 2000, pp. 107–120.

6   Claes Fornell, Sunil Mithas, Forrest V. Morgeson III, and M.S. Krishnan, "Customer Satisfaction and Stock Prices: High Returns, Low Risk," *Journal of Marketing,* Vol. 70, January 2006, pp. 3–14.

7   A large-scale empirical study based on the ACSI showed that CEOs benefit if their firms outperform their peer group in terms of customer satisfaction in form of higher annual bonuses over and above what was explained by typical financial performance metrics and key control variables; see: Vincent O'Connel and Don O'Sullivan (2011), "The Impact of Customer Satisfaction on CEO Bonuses," *Journal of the Academy of Marketing Science,* Vol. 39, No. 6, pp. 828–845.

8   The authors estimated that a 20% increase in operational investments to improve service resulted in an immediate drop in operating profits, which only in the next year resulted in an increase in profit of twice the drop experienced in the year of investment, see: Heiner Evanschitzky, Florian v. Wangenheim and Nancy V. Wünderlich (2012), "Perils of Managing the Service Profit Chain: The Role of Time Lags and Feedback Loops", *Journal of Retailing*, Vol. 88, No. 3, pp. 356–366.

9   Disclosure: Jochen Wirtz has a small equity stake in UP! Your Service College and was involved in early development and positioning of the college.

INDEX

Note: Page numbers followed by f and t indicates figures and tables respectively.

About the Author

Jochen Wirtz is Professor of Marketing at the National University of Singapore (NUS), the founding director of the dual degree UCLA–NUS Executive MBA Program (ranked globally #6 in the Financial Times 2016 EMBA rankings), an international fellow of the Service Research Center at Karlstad University, Sweden, and Academic Scholar at the Cornell Institute for Healthy Futures (CIHF) at Cornell University, US. Professor Wirtz holds a PhD in services marketing from the London Business School and has worked in the field of services for more than 25 years.

Previously, Professor Wirtz was an Associate Fellow at the Saïd Business School, University of Oxford from 2008 to 2013, and a founding member of the NUS Teaching Academy (the NUS think-tank on education matters) from 2009 to 2015.

Professor Wirtz's research focuses on service marketing and has been published in over 200 academic articles, book chapters and industry reports. He is an author or co-author of more than 10 books, including *Services Marketing — People, Technology, Strategy* (8th edition) (World Scientific, 2016), co-authored with Professor Lovelock, which has become one of the world's leading services marketing text book that has been translated and adapted for more than 26 countries and regions, and with sales of some 800,000 copies. His other books include *Flying High in a Competitive Industry: Secrets of the World's Leading Airline* (McGraw Hill, 2009), *Essentials of Services Marketing* (Prentice Hall, 3rd edition, 2017), and *Winning In Service Markets: Success Through People, Technology, and Strategy* (World Scientific, 2017).

In recognition of his excellence in teaching and research, Professor Wirtz has received more than 40 awards, including the prestigious Academy of Marketing Science (AMS) 2012 Outstanding Marketing Teacher Award (the highest recognition of teaching excellence of AMS globally), and the top university-level Outstanding Educator Award at NUS. He was also the winner of the inaugural Outstanding Service Researcher Award 2010, and the Best Practical Implications Award 2009, both by Emerald Group Publications. He serves on the editorial review boards of more than 10 academic journals, including the *Journal of Service Management, Journal of Service Research, Journal of Service Science* and *Cornell Hospitality Quarterly*, and is also an *ad hoc* reviewer for the *Journal of Consumer Research* and *Journal of Marketing*. Professor Wirtz chaired the American Marketing Association's biennial Service Research Conference in 2005 when it was held for the first time in Asia.

Professor Wirtz was a banker and took the banking exam at Chamber of Commerce and Industry in Munich. He has since been an active management consultant, working with international consulting firms including Accenture, Arthur D. Little and KPMG, and major service firms in the areas of strategy, business development and customer feedback systems. He has also been involved in a number of start-ups including in Accellion (www.accellion.com), Angeloop (https://angeloop.co), TranscribeMe (www.transcribeme.com), and UP! Your Service Pte. Ltd. (www.upyourservice.com).

Originally from Germany, Professor Wirtz spent seven years in London before moving to Asia. Today, he shuttles between Asia, the US and Europe. For further information, see www.JochenWirtz.com.

Acknowledgments

First, I would like to thank my mentor, friend and co-author Professor Christopher Lovelock. Since first meeting in 1992, he has become a dear friend who has had significant influence on my thinking and development. We have worked together on a variety of projects, including cases, articles, conference papers, and a number of books. *Winning in Service Markets* is, in fact, derived from our best-selling textbook, *Services Marketing: People, Technology, Strategy*, 8th edition. I am eternally grateful to Christopher for his friendship and support.

Although it's impossible to mention everyone who has contributed in some way to this book through their research, their contributions and discussions at the many academic conferences where we have met, as collaborators on various research projects, and as friends who have always been ready to discuss, criticize, and provide feedback and suggestions. I particularly want to express my appreciation to the following: Tor Andreassen, Norwegian School of Management; Steve Baron of University of Liverpool; John Bateson of Cass Business School; Leonard Berry of Texas A&M University; Mary Jo Bitner and Stephen Brown of Arizona State University; Ruth Bolton of Arizona State University; David Bowen of Thunderbird Graduate School of Management; Richard Chase of the University of Southern California; Jayanta Chatterjee of Indian Institute of Technology at Kanpur, India; John Deighton, Theodore Levitt, James Heskett, Earl Sasser and Leonard Schlesinger, all currently or formerly of

Harvard Business School; Bo Edvardsson of University of Karlstad; Pierre Eiglier of Université d'Aix-Marseille III; Michael Ehret of Nottingham Trent University; Xiucheng Fan of Fudan University, China; Raymond Fisk of the Texas State University; Dominik Georgi of Lucerne School of Business; Christian Grönroos of the Swedish School of Economics in Finland; Stephen Grove of Clemson University; Evert Gummesson of Stockholm University; Loizos Heracleous of University of Warwick; Miguel Angelo Hemzo, Universidade de São Paulo, Brazil; Irene Ng of University of Warwick; Jay Kandampully of Ohio State University; Ron Kaufman of UP! Your Service College; Sheryl Kimes of Cornell University; Tim Keiningham of Rockbridge Associate; Jean-Claude Larréché of INSEAD; Jos Lemmink of Maastricht University; Kay Lemon of Boston College; Xiongwen Lu of Fudan University, China; Paul Maglio of University of California, Merced, USA; David Maister of Maister Associates; Anna Mattila of Pennsylvania State University; Ulrich Orth of Kiel University; Chiara Orsingher of University of Bologna; A. "Parsu" Parasuraman of University of Miami; Paul Patterson of the University of New South Wales, Australia; Anat Rafaeli of Technion-Israeli Institute of Technology, Ram Ramaseshan of Curtin University; Frederick Reichheld of Bain & Co; Roland Rust of the University of Maryland; Benjamin Schneider formerly of the University of Maryland; Jim Spohrer of IBM; Javier Reynoso of Tec de Monterrey, Mexico; Christopher Tang of UCLA; Rodoula Tsiotsou of University of Macedonia; Charles Weinberg of the University of British Columbia; Lauren Wright of California State University, Chico; George Yip of London Business School; Ping Xiao of the National University of Singapore; and Valarie Zeithaml of the University of North Carolina.

It takes more than an author to create a book. Warm thanks are due to the editing and production team who worked hard to transform this manuscript into a beautiful book. They include Chua Hong Koon, Acquisitions Editor; Karimah Samsudin, Desk Editor, and Loo Chuan Ming, Graphic Designer.

Finally, I'd like to thank you, the reader of this book, for your interest in this exciting and fast-evolving field of services management and marketing. If you have any feedback, please contact me via www.JochenWirtz.com. I'd love to hear from you!

Jochen Wirtz

Services Marketing is available for various audiences:

Essentials of Services Marketing	Services Marketing: People, Technology, Strategy	Winning in Service Markets: Success Through People, Technology Strategy
Published by Pearson Education		

Essentials of Services Marketing

Suitable for:
- Polytechnic Students
- Undergraduate Students

Available in the following formats:
- Paperback
- E-book

Services Marketing: People, Technology, Strategy

Suitable for:
- Advanced Undergraduate Students
- Master's-Level/MBA Students

Available in the following formats:
- Hardcover
- Paperback
- E-book
- Bundle of Paperback & E-book
- Rental 6 months

Winning in Service Markets: Success Through People, Technology Strategy

Suitable for:
- Executive Program/EMBA Participants
- Practitioners/Senior Management

Available in the following formats:
- Hardcover
- Paperback
- E-book
- Bundle of Paperback & E-book

Services Marketing Series

- The content in terms of core theory, models and frameworks is largely the same across these publications. However, they are presented and designed to fit their particular target audiences.
- Services Marketing is available in some 26 languages and adaptations for key markets around the world.

Winning in Service Markets Series

Key chapters of Winning in Service Markets are available as stand-alone publications in e-book and paperback:
- Vol. 1: Understanding Service Consumers
- Vol. 2: Positioning Services in Competitive Markets
- Vol. 3: Developing Service Products & Brands
- Vol. 4: Service Pricing and Revenue Management
- Vol. 5: Service Marketing Communications
- Vol. 6: Designing Service Processes
- Vol. 7: Balancing Demand and Capacity
- Vol. 8: Crafting the Service Environment
- Vol. 9: Managing People for Service Advantage
- Vol. 10: Managing Relationships and Building Loyalty
- Vol. 11: Complaint Handling and Service Recovery
- Vol. 12: Improving Service Quality and Productivity
- Vol. 13: Building a World Class Service Organization

Contact
- For orders of individual copies, course adoptions, bulk purchases: sales@wspc.com
- For orders for individual chapters, customized course packs: sales@wspc.com
- For adaptions or translation rights, permissions to reprint: rights@wspc.com
- For further information see: www.JochenWirtz.com
- For questions regarding contents: Jochen Wirtz, jochen@nus.edu.sg.